D1499642

West's Law School Advisory Board

JESSE H. CHOPER
Professor of Law,
University of California, Berkeley

DAVID P. CURRIE
Professor of Law, University of Chicago

YALE KAMISAR
Professor of Law, University of Michigan
Professor of Law, University of San Diego

MARY KAY KANE
Chancellor, Dean and Distinguished Professor of Law,
University of California,
Hastings College of the Law

WAYNE R. LaFAVE
Professor of Law, University of Illinois

ARTHUR R. MILLER
Professor of Law, Harvard University

GRANT S. NELSON
Professor of Law,
University of California, Los Angeles

JAMES J. WHITE
Professor of Law, University of Michigan

CASES AND MATERIALS ON
TORTS
Third Edition

By

David W. Robertson
W. Page Keeton Chair in Tort Law
University Distinguished Teaching Professor
The University of Texas School of Law

William Powers, Jr.
Dean
Hines H. Baker & Thelma Kelley Baker Chair in Law
John Jeffers Research Chair in Law
University Distinguished Teaching Professor
The University of Texas School of Law

David A. Anderson
Fred and Emily Marshall Wulff Centennial Chair in Law
The University of Texas School of Law

Olin Guy Wellborn III
William C. Liedtke, Sr. Professor of Law
The University of Texas School of Law

AMERICAN CASEBOOK SERIES®

Mat #40144613

West, a Thomson business, has created this publication to provide you with accurate and authoritative information concerning the subject matter covered. However, this publication was not necessarily prepared by persons licensed to practice law in a particular jurisdiction. West is not engaged in rendering legal or other professional advice, and this publication is not a substitute for the advice of an attorney. If you require legal or other expert advice, you should seek the services of a competent attorney or other professional.

American Casebook Series and West Group are trademarks registered in the U.S. Patent and Trademark Office.

COPYRIGHT © 1989 WEST PUBLISHING CO.
COPYRIGHT © 1998 WEST GROUP
© 2004 West, a Thomson business
      610 Opperman Drive
      P.O. Box 64526
      St. Paul, MN 55164–0526
      1–800–328–9352

Printed in the United States of America

ISBN 0–314–14615–6

 *TEXT IS PRINTED ON 10% POST CONSUMER RECYCLED PAPER*

Preface

The wonderfully rich field of tort law is never at rest. In the second half of the twentieth century tort liability expanded dramatically. Since this casebook was first published in 1989 the trend has been mostly in the other direction. The first and second editions observed the successes of the "tort reform" movement in state legislatures and the shift of judicial attitudes that has occurred on many courts. This third edition reflects a broader and deeper transformation of tort law. The effects of "tort reform" are no longer confined to discrete matters such as caps on damages, but now permeate the entire fabric of tort liability, including such basics as proof of causation, apportionment of harm, and calculation of damages. The widespread adoption of comparative fault has had unforeseen consequences throughout tort law. The most important sections of the Third Restatement of Torts, covering liability for physical harm, apportionment of liability, and products liability, are now complete and in many respects reflect different views of tort law than their predecessors.

There are many intellectual prisms through which tort law can usefully be observed and evaluated, but we continue to believe that the best one for the purpose of learning tort law is the litigation perspective. We take note of the most prominent theoretical strands of tort jurisprudence in this book, but our emphasis is on the law as it appears today to the tort lawyer and judge, with all of its controversies, uncertainties, and complex dynamics. For one thing, litigators can access academic theory more readily and proficiently than pure theoreticians can access the realities of litigation. More importantly, we know that most of our students aspire to be great lawyers, and we feel obliged and honored to help them toward that goal by providing enough of a grounding in procedure, evidence, and litigation practices for the beginning student to make a start on understanding tort law in action. Put differently, no one can become a great tort lawyer without a deep appreciation of the ways in which the substantive law of torts is influenced by the realities of litigation, such as difficulties of proof and division of responsibility between judge and jury.

Of the 109 principal cases included, a few are landmarks that should be part of every lawyer's vocabulary, such as *Palsgraf* and *Rylands v. Fletcher*. But we have generally used modern cases to demonstrate the key features of tort law as it exists at the moment. We believe the controversies of tort law are best presented through the cases in which the issues are fought out.

Like all tort lawyers, the editors have strong views about many of these issues. We have tried to keep our political and ideological predilections out of the book. As we said in the first edition, our objective is to present tort law as it exists, not as we wish it were.

The organizational scheme reflects our determination to present tort law as it appears to the litigator. The opening chapter is designed to give the beginning law student a primer on the procedural and tactical framework within which tort matters are resolved. After a concise survey of the distinctive world of intentional torts, negligence law is presented in the way lawyers approach it: elements of the prima facie case, defenses, and immunities. We then branch out to other bases of liability, such as strict liability and nuisance.

The principal cases have been tightly edited in recognition of the fact that introductory tort courses, which used to be allocated five or six semester hours, now rarely receive more than three or four. Omission of text is indicated by * * *. Footnotes and citations in text are generally omitted without indication. The beginning student should be forewarned that this gives the edited opinions quite a different flavor from the originals. An edited opinion may appear to be little more than a judicial essay reflecting the judge's unconstrained view of the law, but a reading of the full opinion usually will show that it is carefully crafted from the holdings of previous cases and that statements that appear to be the judge's inventions are in fact drawn from many other sources. Consulting the full opinions from time to time will be a useful reminder of the conventions within which judges operate.

Numbered footnotes are the courts' and retain their original numbering, although some have been relocated to accommodate our editing of the text. Our own footnotes generally are indicated with an asterisk and are signed "Ed."

We wish to thank other users of the previous editions, especially our colleagues Sarah Buel and Mark Gergen, for their helpful comments and advice. We are also grateful for the research assistance of Shaun Rogers.

Summary of Contents

*

Table of Contents

*

Table of Cases

The principal cases are in bold type. Cases cited or discussed in the text are roman type. References are to pages.

*

CASES AND MATERIALS ON
TORTS
Third Edition

*

Chapter I

TRIAL COURT PROCEDURE
IN TORTS CASES

Almost all of the cases in this book were decided by appellate courts. It is necessary to study appellate decisions: The opinion of an appeals court is usually the earliest available written record of a tortious occurrence and its treatment by the legal system. But the appellate focus has its drawbacks. Reading the decision of an appellate court to determine what happened at the trial of a torts case—or trying to look even further back in time at what went wrong between the parties to cause them to become adversaries in the first place—is something like looking through the wrong end of a telescope: One can see, but mastering the relevant details demands a certain amount of determination and skill.

The proper starting point in studying an appellate decision is always to ask what the appellate court is telling the trial judge about the handling of this particular case. It is obvious that a torts case comes to an appellate court because at least one of the parties is dissatisfied with the way things turned out in the trial court. What may not be so obvious is that the appellant (the party who initially brings the case to the appellate court) must be complaining of some mistake that the trial *judge* has made. It is not enough to tell the appellate court that the result was unjust or that the jury got the wrong answer. The appellant must pinpoint an error of law committed by the trial judge; otherwise the appeal has no chance.

So when reading an appellate decision, the first thing to look for is, *what does the appellant claim the trial judge did wrong?* You should be able to find the answer to that question for all the lead cases in this book. But you need a rudimentary understanding of trial court procedure to do it. The following material outlines the principal stages at which a trial judge is likely to commit an appealable error while handling a torts case. It is loosely based on the model of a trial judge sitting with a jury and operating under the Federal Rules of Civil Procedure. Nowadays most state procedural systems are patterned closely enough after the federal rules that the model is reasonably instructive.

1

Note that the following discussion proceeds through the torts lawsuit in roughly chronological order, beginning with the filing of the plaintiff's complaint. You should bear in mind that most torts cases are settled (compromised) by agreement of the parties, either before the complaint is filed or at some stage thereafter. Settlements can occur at any stage of the litigation, including the appeal process.

A.

The plaintiff initiates the lawsuit by filing a complaint and causing it to be served on the defendant. The complaint sets forth the facts that plaintiff contends should mean the defendant is obliged to pay damages to the plaintiff.

The defendant's first response can be a motion to dismiss the complaint for failure to state a legally valid claim. What this response says, in effect, is this: Let us assume for purposes of argument that every fact alleged in the plaintiff's complaint is true; even so, it is clear that the law affords no relief, so that the complaint must simply be dismissed, without further ado. For example, suppose that my complaint against you alleges that, as I was jogging past your house, you caused me great emotional anguish by calling out, "You're too old to go out for track, Grandpa." Your motion to dismiss does not admit or deny the accuracy of my complaint, but contends that, even if it is true, it does not describe tortious conduct on your part; ordinary everyday insults are not torts. A trial judge who failed to grant your motion would be making a mistake about tort law.

B.

The defendant's motion for summary judgment is similar in content and intended effect to the motion to dismiss. The significant difference is that the motion to dismiss is directed solely at what the plaintiff has claimed in the complaint, whereas with the motion for summary judgment the defendant brings additional facts to the court's attention. For example, suppose that my complaint alleges that you deprived me of my liberty by keeping me locked for a period of three months in a room in premises owned and occupied by you. Suppose that your response is a summary judgment motion, accompanied by affidavits attesting that you are a duly accredited psychiatrist and the director of a sanitarium properly licensed by the state, and by a certified copy of the court order whereby I was judicially committed to your institution for three months of psychiatric care and observation. Unless I have further facts, your motion for summary judgment should be granted. (A motion to dismiss the complaint would not by itself have killed this lawsuit, because the key facts did not appear from the complaint I filed.)

Summary judgment is an important tool, and present–day courts use it much more frequently than in the past. When reviewing a trial judge's grant or denial of summary judgment, appellate courts usually begin their opinions by reciting a standard test for when summary judgment is appropriate. (We have edited these out of the cases in this book.) A typical rendition is the following:

> Summary judgment is appropriate if the pleadings, depositions, answers to interrogatories, and admissions on file, together with the affidavits, if any, show there is no genuine issue as to any material fact and the moving party is entitled to judgment as a matter of law. The movant has the burden of establishing that there are no genuine issues of material fact, which may be accomplished by demonstrating that the non–moving party lacks evidence to support an essential element of its case. In response, the non–moving party must present significant probative evidence to show that there is more than some metaphysical doubt as to the material facts. Summary judgment will not lie if the dispute is about a material fact that is genuine, that is, if the evidence is such that a reasonable jury could return a verdict for the non–moving party.
>
> In evaluating a motion for summary judgment, the evidence must be viewed in the light most favorable to the non–moving party. The non–moving party, however, may not rest upon its mere allegations but must set forth specific facts showing that there is a genuine issue for trial. The existence of a scintilla of evidence in support of the non–moving party's position will not be sufficient; there must be evidence on which the jury could reasonably find for the non–moving party.[1]

C.

If the case is not dismissed at a preliminary stage, the defendant must file an answer to the plaintiff's complaint. The answer is a fact pleading in which the defendant typically denies the plaintiff's version of the facts and sets forth the defendant's version. (If the case gets that far, eventually a jury will decide which version, if either, is accurate.) The complaint and answer are the only essential pleadings, and once they are on file the case is formally in a posture to be tried. The parties will doubtless spend a great deal of time investigating and negotiating, and they may generate disputes about discovery[2] that need sorting out by the trial judge, but (unless a summary judgment motion is filed after the defendant has answered, which frequently happens) the next major involvement of the trial judge will come when the trial begins.

D.

When the trial date arrives, the lawyers and the judge must first select a jury. If the judge permits it, the lawyers will begin trying to influence the potential jurors at this earliest opportunity, and occasionally an appellant in a torts case will urge that the trial judge erred by

1. Hunley v. DuPont Automotive, 341 F.3d 491, 495–96 (6th Cir. 2003) (citations and internal quotation marks omitted).

2. Discovery is the process of investigating a case that follows the initiation of a lawsuit. It includes written interrogatories, depositions, and other formalized evidence–gathering procedures.

permitting improper and prejudicial remarks to be made during the jury selection process.

E.

When the jury selection process is finished, the lawyers for the parties may then make opening statements, each outlining a theory of the case and alerting the jury to what the evidence will show. A trial judge may commit reversible error at this stage by permitting counsel to make improper remarks (or by forbidding proper remarks) during opening statement. But again, this is relatively rare.

F.

Once the opening statements have been completed, the plaintiff's lawyer puts on the case in chief on behalf of the plaintiff. This involves questioning witnesses under oath and, often, introducing documents into evidence. During this phase of the case the lawyer for the defendant will have the opportunity to cross–examine each witness and to object to the admissibility of documents and other evidence offered by the plaintiff. The trial judge must rule on these objections, and may commit reversible error by allowing the introduction of evidence that should have been kept out or by excluding evidence that should have been let in. For example, the defendant/appellant in South v. National R.R. Passenger Corp., 290 N.W.2d 819 (N.D.1980), urged that the jurors, who found the defendant railroad guilty of negligence in causing a grade crossing accident, had been prejudiced by being allowed to hear irrelevant testimony that the train's engineer refused to put his jacket over an injured man after the wreck because he did not want to soil it. The appellate court reasoned that such testimony would not be irrelevant if the engineer had a tort–law duty to render aid, and concluded that he did.

G.

Eventually the plaintiff's lawyer will complete the presentation of the case in chief on behalf of the plaintiff. At this point the defendant may file a motion for a directed verdict.[3] This motion says, in effect: Now that we've heard all of the evidence the plaintiff has to offer, it is plain that the plaintiff has not shown a sufficient basis for holding defendant responsible under the law. (The plaintiff cannot file a motion for directed verdict at this point, because defendant has not yet put on its factual case.)

For example: My complaint alleges that you ran over me at the corner of 5th and Congress in Austin, Texas, on November 11, 2003. But all I can show at trial is that I was hit by a late–model green Ford sedan and that you own such a car. Your motion for directed verdict should

---

3. Rule 50 of the Federal Rules of Civil Procedure has been changed relatively recently to rename the motion for directed verdict and the motion for judgment notwithstanding the verdict. Both are now called "motions for judgment as a matter of law" (JAML). For this book's purposes, the older terminology, which is still in use in many states, is preferable.

succeed; I have not produced facts from which a reasonable juror could conclude that, more probably than not, you were a cause of my injuries. (In most modern procedural systems, when a judge grants a directed verdict, there is nothing for the jury to do; the judge simply enters judgment for the prevailing party.)

H.

If the trial judge denies the defendant's motion for directed verdict at the conclusion of plaintiff's case in chief, the defendant will then put on its case in chief, with plaintiff's lawyer having the opportunity to cross–examine witnesses and object to the introduction of evidence. (Here again the trial judge may commit reversible error by letting in evidence that should be kept out or keeping out evidence that should be let in.)

When defendant's lawyer announces that the case in chief for defendant has been concluded, plaintiff may have the opportunity to offer certain rebuttal evidence. Once that is done, the trial judge (and jury) have heard all the evidence that the parties will present. At this stage either party may move for a directed verdict. If the trial judge believes that there is only one reasonable outcome, he will grant one of these motions.

For example: My complaint alleges that you ran over me at the corner of 5th and Congress in Austin on November 11, 2003. Suppose my trial evidence shows that I was struck and injured on that date by a recklessly driven yellow Bentley with Texas license plates; that in 2003 you owned a yellow Bentley with Texas plates; and that in 2003 there was only one Bentley automobile registered in the state of Texas. Probably your motion for a directed verdict at the close of my case in chief will fail, because the evidence produced at the trial creates a permissible inference that I have correctly identified the tortfeasor. So you put on your case in chief, proving that your Bentley was stolen from you on November 10, and also proving that you were in New York all day on November 11. Your motion for directed verdict should now succeed; clearly, on all the evidence in the case, I have not met my fundamental burden of proving that you caused me an injury.

Defendants' motions for directed verdict are granted with some frequency, and the legal standard for when a directed verdict is appropriate is well established:

> In ruling on the motion, the court must take the strongest legitimate view of the evidence in favor of the non–moving party. In other words, the court must remove any conflict in the evidence by construing it in the light most favorable to the non–movant and discarding all countervailing evidence. The court may grant the motion only if, after assessing the evidence according to the foregoing standards, it determines that reasonable minds could not differ as to the conclusions to be drawn from the evidence.[4]

---

   4.   Eaton v. McLain, 891 S.W.2d 587, 590 (Tenn. 1994).

I.

Even if inclined to believe that there is only one reasonable outcome, the trial judge may well deny a directed verdict motion made at the conclusion of all the evidence. (For one thing, as will be seen in a moment, the judge will have another chance to rule for the party who should prevail.) If the trial judge does not grant a motion for directed verdict at the close of the evidence, the lawyers will then make their closing arguments.[5] The judge may commit reversible error by permitting improper closing argument or, conceivably, by forbidding appropriate closing argument.

J.

After the lawyers' closing arguments, the trial judge instructs (or "charges") the jury on the law they are to apply. Here is perhaps the most fertile source of claims of trial court error. The jury may be told something that is inaccurate or misleading; they may be told too much; they may be told too little. Probably no one fully believes that human beings actually conform their actions and decisions to refined and prolix verbal formulations of the sort often used in jury instructions. Nevertheless, the system's traditions tend to insist on great precision and conformity. See, e.g., Bengston v. Estes, 260 Wis. 595, 51 N.W.2d 539 (1952), reversing because the instructions said "clear preponderance of the evidence" instead of "fair preponderance of the evidence."

K.

When closing arguments and instructions are done, the jury retires, deliberates, and returns with a verdict. At this point the winner moves for judgment on the verdict, and the disappointed litigant (there is guaranteed to be at least one) can move for judgment notwithstanding the verdict or for a new trial.[6]

The motion for judgment notwithstanding the verdict (often called judgment non obstante veredicto and abbreviated JNOV) has exactly the same theory and content as the motion for directed verdict at the conclusion of the evidence. So why would a trial judge ever deny a directed verdict motion and then turn around and grant JNOV? It is a purely pragmatic move. If the directed verdict motion is granted and the

---

5. In most systems, closing arguments by the lawyers precede the judge's instructions to the jury. A few states do it backward.

6. Other possible post–verdict motions include motions for remittitur or additur. The defendant's remittitur motion asserts that the damages awarded by the jury are unreasonably high. If the trial judge grants the motion, the plaintiff is forced to choose between accepting a specified reduction or submitting to a new trial. The additur motion is just the opposite; the plaintiff claims that the jury's damage award is so low as to defy reason, and seeks to have the defendant forced to choose between agreeing to a specified addition or undergoing a new trial. The federal procedural system does not have the additur device, but most states do.

appellate court eventually disagrees, the case will have to be retried, because the jury never got to rule on it. But if the appellate court disagrees with JNOV, the jury verdict can simply be reinstated.

The motion for JNOV, like the directed verdict motions, asserts that there is only one reasonable and correct outcome and thus seeks a dispositive judgment in the movant's favor. The assertion of a motion for a new trial—whereby the movant seeks not a dispositive judgment in its favor but rather a second chance—is somewhat weaker; it claims in effect that the jury's verdict looks very peculiar and that errors of sufficient importance occurred during the trial to suggest rather strongly that the jurors were prejudiced or misled.

L.

In summary, here are the major stages at which trial judges make tort–law mistakes:

1.   Granting or denying motions to dismiss the complaint.

2.   Granting or denying motions for summary judgment.

3.   Permitting improper statements by counsel (or squelching proper ones) during jury selection, opening statement, or closing argument.

4.   Excluding relevant evidence or admitting improper evidence.

5.   Granting or denying motions for directed verdict.

6.   Erroneous jury instructions.

7.   Granting or denying motions for judgment notwithstanding the verdict.

8.   Granting or denying motions for new trial, additurs, or remittiturs.

Chapter II

INTENTIONAL HARMS
TO PERSONS AND
PROPERTY

A. INTRODUCTION

The cases in this chapter deal with several torts that share a similar analytical structure. They are battery, assault, false imprisonment, intentional infliction of emotional distress, trespass to land, trespass to chattels, and conversion. Each is an intentional tort, meaning that the plaintiff can recover only if the defendant intentionally invaded the specific interest that is protected by the tort. The torts differ from each other in that they protect different interests of the plaintiff.

For each tort, the plaintiff must prove the "elements" of the tort in order to recover. (Some courts call these elements the plaintiff's "prima facie case.") The plaintiff has the burden of introducing evidence tending to prove every element in order to avoid suffering a directed verdict, that is, in order to have the case submitted to the jury. If the plaintiff does produce evidence on every element and the case is submitted to the jury, the plaintiff has the burden of persuading the jury that every element has been met. Even if the plaintiff proves every element of a tort, the defendant can nevertheless escape liability by establishing a defense. The defendant has the burden of producing evidence and persuading the jury on these defenses.

The material is organized to address the elements of each of the several torts and then to address defenses. Although the defenses applicable to each tort are not identical, considerable overlap exists among the available defenses. As you study the elements of each tort, keep in mind that proof of these elements does not guarantee recovery by the plaintiff. A defense, especially consent, may be available to the defendant.

Causation is an element of each of the torts covered in this chapter. Indeed, causation is an element of all tort actions. Issues concerning causation can be difficult. They are addressed in detail in Chapter IV.

Causation is not specifically addressed in this chapter, but you should nevertheless be aware that causation is an element of these torts, and the plaintiff must prove it.

B. BATTERY

GHASSEMIEH v. SCHAFER

Court of Special Appeals of Maryland, 1982.
52 Md.App. 31, 447 A.2d 84.

MOORE, JUDGE.

In this case, a 13–year–old girl in eighth grade pulled a chair away from her teacher who fell to the floor, hurting her back. Approximately one month less than three years later, the teacher filed a negligence action against her former pupil in the Circuit Court for Baltimore County (Sfekas, J.). From a judgment for the defendant, this appeal is taken. For the reasons stated herein, we shall affirm.

* * *

The appellant, Karen B. Ghassemieh, age 29 on February 24, 1977, was a teacher of art with the Baltimore County Schools, assigned to Old Court Junior High. On that date, she was teaching an 8th grade class of "above average" students, including the appellee, Elaine Schafer, then 13. While the teacher was about to sit down to assist another student, Elaine pulled the chair away. At trial the teacher described what happened:

> I got to Terri's seat and because I am very tall it is my practice either to kneel down next to the children or to sit down. Terri got up very quickly and I went to sit in her seat. As I went to sit down, I tucked the chair underneath me as I usually do. As I relaxed to sit down, the chair was gone. It was pulled out and I fell to the floor hurting my back.

Elaine Schafer testified that she pulled the chair away "as a joke." She further testified on direct examination:

> Q. When you pulled the chair, was there any doubt in your mind that she would miss the chair and fall to the floor?
>
> A. I knew she was going to fall to the floor.
>
> Q. Was that your intent?
>
> A. Yes.

On cross–examination she repeated that, "I did it as a joke." She also said that she did not intend any injury. Thus:

> Q. You mean you did not intend to have any harm done to her, is that right?
>
> A. I intended for her to fall to the floor, not for her to be injured.

The declaration was not filed until January 24, 1980, although in answers to interrogatories, Mrs. Ghassemieh said she was treated for back problems throughout 1977 and 1978.[2]

* * * At the close of the evidence, each side moved for a directed verdict. * * * The appellee's (defendant's) motion was predicated on a claim that the evidence established a battery, an intentional tort, and not negligence, as alleged.

Both motions were denied. With respect to the defendant's motion, the court ruled:

> As to the motion of the defendant, the Court will deny that motion, but I will include in the instructions the definition of a battery and let the jury make the determination whether this in fact was, if it was a negligent act on the part of the defendant or if in fact it was a battery, which would certainly not be encompassed in the action brought by the plaintiff in this case, but I would allow that to go to the jury by way of instruction.

Before the judge instructed the jury, the following exchange occurred:

> MR. CASKEY (counsel for defendant/appellee): I would move that the Court present the question to the jury as a question as to the battery versus negligence issue. I would request that the jury be given the instructions as to what constitutes negligence and as to what constitutes battery and to have them answer the question—do you find that it was negligence, battery, or neither?

> MR. HUESMAN (counsel for plaintiff/appellant): Well, I think, Your Honor, before I respond to that, I guess a lot would depend on exactly the way the questions are phrased.

In the instructions which immediately followed, the court began by saying: "The case before you is an action based on a claim of negligence." * * * The court then instructed on battery, as follows:

> The Court has indicated that this is an action in negligence. *A battery is an intentional touching which is harmful or offensive.* Touching includes the intentional putting into motion of anything which touches another person or the intentional putting into motion of anything which touches something that is connected with or in contact with another person. A touching is harmful if it causes physical pain, injury or illness. A touching is offensive if it offends a person's reasonable sense of personal dignity.

> *If you find that the defendant acted with the intent to cause a harmful or offensive touching of the plaintiff and that that offensive*

---

2. This action was brought almost three years after the incident. However, appellant began experiencing back pain in March 1977, a month or so later; she had a myelogram then and again in early 1978. In September 1978, she had a spinal fusion. We observe that appellee did not plead the one-year statute of limitations, Md.Cts. & Jud. Proc.Code Ann., § 5–105 (1980 Repl.Vol.), governing battery, but she had no occasion to do so in light of the allegations in the declaration.

touching directly or indirectly resulted, then this constitutes a battery and your verdict must be for the defendant, as this suit has been brought in negligence and is not an action in battery. (Emphasis added.)

At the conclusion of the instructions, trial counsel for the plaintiffs (appellants) excepted as follows:

Also, we except to the portion of the charge with regard to the definition of battery. * * * We believe that it is necessary to show that the defendant *actually intended to harm the plaintiff* and we believe on the basis of the defendant's own testimony that she did this as a joke, that she had no intention to commit bodily harm. (Emphasis added.)

The trial court overruled all objections. With respect to the battery objection, the court did not address the definitional point raised, but said:

The battery instruction, the Court felt was appropriate in view of the fact that this is an action in negligence, and if the jury would find from hearing the testimony in the case that in fact there was a battery and not negligence, it may very well have the opportunity to make a determination in favor of the defendant.

Approximately 25 minutes after the jury retired, the court received a request that the definition of battery be given again. Counsel for the teacher objected. The court stated that, in the absence of agreement of counsel, it would decline to repeat the instruction. One–half hour later, the jury returned a verdict for the defendant.

* * *

The gravamen of the plaintiffs' appeal is that the trial court erred in giving the following portion of the instruction on battery quoted above:

If you find that the defendant acted with the intent to cause a harmful or offensive touching of the plaintiff and that that offensive touching directly or indirectly resulted, then this constitutes a battery and your verdict must be for the defendant, as this suit has been brought in negligence and is not an action in battery.

In support of this principal contention, appellants maintain that:

(1) The mere fact that the evidence adduced may have established that the defendant acted intentionally in pulling the chair out from under the appellant, Karen B. Ghassemieh, does not preclude recovery of damages for a cause of action in negligence.

* * *

(3) To permit the defendant to escape liability for her tortious conduct merely because she acted intentionally, rather than negligently, would be fundamentally unjust and contrary to public policy.

We are confronted with a threshold consideration not raised by the appellee and, therefore, neither briefed nor argued but essentially jurisdictional: Was the appellants' objection to the battery instruction, quoted above, a sufficient predicate for their position on appeal? They now argue:

> The instruction given by the trial judge was improper because if the jury had found that the defendant acted intentionally in pulling the chair out from under the appellant, Karen B. Ghassemieh, it could nevertheless have awarded damages for negligence.

And further:

> Thus, a finding of gross negligence or of willful and wanton misconduct may impute a finding of intentional conduct. Consequently, a finding that the appellee had acted intentionally would have been fully consistent with the allegations of the declaration charging negligence. The trial court, therefore, erred in instructing the jury to the contrary. While it is clear that [appellee] intended to pull the chair out from under Mrs. Ghassemieh, it is equally clear that she did not intend to injure Mrs. Ghassemieh.

Our problem arises from Maryland Rule 554 (Instructions to the Jury) (1982 ed.), particularly subsections (d) and (e) concerning, respectively, "objection" and "appeal." Subsection (d) provides in part:

> If a party has an objection to any portion of any instruction given, or to any omission therefrom, or the failure to give any instruction, *he shall before the jury retires to consider its verdict make such objection stating distinctly the portion, or omission, or failure to instruct to which he objects and the ground of his objection.* (Emphasis added.)

And subsection (e) provides in its entirety:

> Upon appeal a party in assigning error in the instructions, *shall be restricted* to (1) the particular portion of the instructions given or the particular omission therefrom or the particular failure to instruct *distinctly objected to before the jury retired* and (2) *the grounds of objection distinctly stated at the time,* and *no other errors or assignments of error in the instructions shall be considered by the appellate court.* (Emphasis added.)

Trial counsel for the plaintiffs did not object, as appellate counsel now objects, to *any* instruction on battery, but only to "that portion of the charge with regard to the *definition* of battery." (Emphasis added.) Trial counsel was objecting to the court's definition of battery as an "intentional touching which is harmful or offensive" * * *.

Trial counsel never stated as a basis for his objection that no instruction on battery should be given because this was an action in negligence. The objection at trial was simply that the definition of battery lacked an essential element, i.e., the defendant actually intended to harm the plaintiff. However, intent to do harm is not essential to a battery. The gist of the action is not hostile intent on the part of the defendant, but the absence of consent to the contact on the plaintiff's part. Thus, horseplay, pranks, or jokes can be a battery regardless of whether the intent was to harm. Garratt v. Dailey, 46 Wash.2d 197, 279 P.2d 1091 (1955), aff'd, 49 Wash.2d 499, 304 P.2d 681 (1956).

Trial counsel never argued to the trial court that, as contended at oral argument before us, negligence and battery are not mutually exclusive, or that a single intentional act can be the basis for both battery and negligence, or that the jury could award damages for negligence even if a battery had also been proved. Only on appeal do appellants make clear their challenge to the instruction that "this suit has been brought in negligence and is not an action in battery" and if battery were found, "your verdict must be for the defendant." The trial judge was not given to understand that the plaintiff really objected to any instruction on battery. The judge reiterated his negligence versus battery instruction in explaining why he felt the battery instruction was appropriate, and the plaintiff did not object.

Thus, the objection below did not reach the broader issue raised on appeal, and under Rule 554(e) it "may not be considered by the appellate court."

* * *

[T]he presence of an intent to do an act does not preclude negligence. The concepts of negligence and battery are not mutually exclusive.

* * *

The plaintiffs in this case could properly have sought a negligence instruction * * *.

We see no reason why an intentional act that produces unintended consequences cannot be a foundation for a negligence action. Here, an intentional act—the pulling away of the chair—had two possible consequences: the intended one of embarrassment and the unintended one of injury. The battery—an indirect offensive touching, a technical invasion of the plaintiff's personal integrity—was proved. However, a specific instruction on negligence—namely, that the defendant had a duty to refrain from conduct exposing the plaintiff to unreasonable risk of injury and breached that duty, resulting in her injury—was not requested. Nor was any exception made to the general negligence instruction that was given. Nor did the plaintiff at trial take the unequivocal position that she was proceeding on a theory of negligence, notwithstanding the co-existence of an intentional act, *i.e.*, a battery. In sum, appellants are asserting now the arguments they should have made at trial. Such hindsight can avail them nothing.

Judgment affirmed; appellants to pay the costs.

Note

Generally, a party can raise an issue on appeal only if counsel has "preserved" the issue by a timely and specific objection or request in the trial court. As you read appellate opinions, you should look for the effect trial court procedure has on the posture of the case on appeal.

GARRATT v. DAILEY

Supreme Court of Washington, 1955.
46 Wash.2d 197, 279 P.2d 1091.

HILL, JUSTICE.

The liability of an infant for an alleged battery is presented to this court for the first time. Brian Dailey (age five years, nine months) was visiting with Naomi Garratt, an adult and a sister of the plaintiff, Ruth Garratt, likewise an adult, in the back yard of the plaintiff's home, on July 16, 1951. It is plaintiff's contention that she came out into the back yard to talk with Naomi and that, as she started to sit down in a wood and canvas lawn chair, Brian deliberately pulled it out from under her. The only one of the three persons present so testifying was Naomi Garratt. (Ruth Garratt, the plaintiff, did not testify as to how or why she fell.) The trial [judge, sitting without a jury], unwilling to accept this testimony, adopted instead Brian Dailey's version of what happened, and made the following findings:

III. * * * that while Naomi Garratt and Brian Dailey were in the back yard the plaintiff, Ruth Garratt, came out of her house into the back yard. Some time subsequent thereto defendant, Brian Dailey, picked up a lightly built wood and canvas lawn chair which was then and there located in the back yard of the above described premises, moved it sideways a few feet and seated himself therein, at which time he discovered the plaintiff, Ruth Garratt, about to sit down at the place where the lawn chair had formerly been, at which time he hurriedly got up from the chair and attempted to move it toward Ruth Garratt to aid her in sitting down in the chair; that due to the defendant's small size and lack of dexterity he was unable to get the lawn chair under the plaintiff in time to prevent her from falling to the ground. That plaintiff fell to the ground and sustained a fracture of her hip, and other injuries and damages as hereinafter set forth.

IV. That the preponderance of the evidence in this case establishes that when the defendant, Brian Dailey, moved the chair in question *he did not have any wilful or unlawful purpose* in doing so; that *he did not have any intent to injure the plaintiff, or any intent to bring about any unauthorized or offensive contact with her person* or any objects appurtenant thereto; that the circumstances which immediately preceded the fall of the plaintiff established that the defendant, *Brian Dailey, did not have purpose, intent or design to perform a prank or to effect an assault and battery upon the person of the plaintiff.*

(Italics ours, for a purpose hereinafter indicated.)

It is conceded that Ruth Garratt's fall resulted in a fractured hip and other painful and serious injuries. To obviate the necessity of a retrial in the event this court determines that she was entitled to a judgment against Brian Dailey, the amount of her damage was found to be $11,000. Plaintiff appeals from a judgment dismissing the action and asks for the entry of a judgment in that amount or a new trial.

* * *

It is urged that Brian's action in moving the chair constituted a battery. A definition (not all–inclusive but sufficient for our purpose) of a battery is the intentional infliction of a harmful bodily contact upon another. * * *

* * *

* * * In the comment [to section 13 of the Restatement of Torts] the Restatement says:

> *Character of actor's intention.* In order that an act may be done with the intention of bringing about a harmful or offensive contact * * * to a particular person, * * * the act must be done for the purpose of causing the contact * * * or with knowledge on the part of the actor that such contact * * * is substantially certain to be produced.

We have here the conceded volitional act of Brian, i.e., the moving of a chair. Had the plaintiff proved to the satisfaction of the trial court that Brian moved the chair while she was in the act of sitting down, Brian's action would patently have been for the purpose or with the intent of causing the plaintiff's bodily contact with the ground, and she would be entitled to a judgment against him for the resulting damages.

The plaintiff based her case on that theory, and the trial court held that she failed in her proof and accepted Brian's version of the facts rather than that given by the eyewitness who testified for the plaintiff. After the trial court determined that the plaintiff had not established her theory of a battery (i.e., that Brian had pulled the chair out from under the plaintiff while she was in the act of sitting down), it then became concerned with whether a battery was established under the facts as it found them to be.

In this connection, we quote another portion of the comment [to section 13 of the Restatement of Torts]:

> It is not enough that the act itself is intentionally done and this, even though the actor realizes or should realize that it contains a very grave risk of bringing about the contact * * *. Such realization may make the actor's conduct negligent or even reckless but unless he realizes that to a substantial certainty, the contact * * * will result, the actor has not that intention which is necessary to make him liable under the rule stated in this section.

A battery would be established if, in addition to plaintiff's fall, it was proved that, when Brian moved the chair, he knew with substantial certainty that the plaintiff would attempt to sit down where the chair had been. If Brian had any of the intents which the trial court found, in the italicized portions of the findings of fact quoted above, that he did not have, he would of course have had the knowledge to which we have referred. The mere absence of any intent to injure the plaintiff or to play a prank on her or to embarrass her, or to commit an assault and battery on her would not absolve him from liability if in fact he had such knowledge. Without such knowledge, there would be nothing wrongful about Brian's act in moving the chair and, there being no wrongful act, there would be no liability.

While a finding that Brian had no such knowledge can be inferred from the findings made, we believe that before the plaintiff's action in such a case should be dismissed there should be no question but that the trial court had passed upon that issue; hence, the case should be remanded for clarification of the findings to specifically cover the question of Brian's knowledge, because intent could be inferred therefrom. If the court finds that he had such knowledge the necessary intent will be established and the plaintiff will be entitled to recover, even though there was no purpose to injure or embarrass the plaintiff. If Brian did not have such knowledge, there was no wrongful act by him and the basic premise of liability on the theory of a battery was not established.

It will be noted that the law of battery as we have discussed it is the law applicable to adults, and no significance has been attached to the fact that Brian was a child less than six years of age when the alleged battery occurred. The only circumstance where Brian's age is of any consequence is in determining what he knew, and there his experience, capacity, and understanding are of course material.

* * *

The cause is remanded for clarification, with instructions to make definite findings on the issue of whether Brian Dailey knew with substantial certainty that the plaintiff would attempt to sit down where the chair which he moved had been, and to change the judgment if the findings warrant it.

* * *

Remanded for clarification.

Notes

1. One of the issues in *Garratt* was whether a battery plaintiff is required to prove that the defendant intended injury. This is a legal issue that was also addressed by the court in *Ghassemieh*. Are the two cases in agreement?

2. You should distinguish the foregoing legal issue from the specific fact issue in *Garratt,* whether the defendant even intended that the plaintiff hit the ground.

On remand, the *Garratt* trial judge re-evaluated the facts in light of the Supreme Court's clarification of the law. He stated that in order to determine Brian's knowledge, "it was necessary for him to consider carefully the time sequence, as he had not done before; and this resulted in his finding that the arthritic woman had begun the slow process of being seated when the defendant quickly removed the chair and seated himself upon it, and that he knew, with substantial certainty, at that time that she would attempt to sit in the place where the chair had been." He accordingly entered judgment in favor of the plaintiff, and on a second appeal the Supreme Court affirmed. 49 Wash.2d 499, 304 P.2d 681 (1956).

3. ***Torts of young children.*** Not all courts would impose battery liability upon a child of Brian Dailey's age on facts like those of *Garratt*. The Supreme Court of Ohio, for example, held that a child under the age of seven cannot be held liable for an intentional tort, reasoning that "[o]ur laws and our moral concepts assume actors capable of legal and moral choices, of which a young child is incapable." DeLuca v. Bowden, 42 Ohio St.2d 392, 329 N.E.2d 109, 111 (1975). Accord, Queen Ins. Co. v. Hammond, 374 Mich. 655, 132 N.W.2d 792 (1965). In a case involving defendants who were three and four years of age, the Supreme Court of Colorado rejected *Garratt*'s holding "that infants are liable for their intentional torts irrespective of intent to cause harm." The infant need not intend or foresee the particular harm that resulted, but "must appreciate the fact that the contact may be harmful." Horton v. Reaves, 186 Colo. 149, 526 P.2d 304, 307–08 (Colo. 1974).

The liability of a young child for negligence is considered in Chapter III.

4. ***Intent to touch vs. intent to injure or offend.*** Cases involving adult defendants can present similar problems and similar judicial disagreements. In White v. University of Idaho, 118 Idaho 400, 797 P.2d 108 (1990), a music professor approached the seated plaintiff, a longtime acquaintance, from behind "and touched her back with both of his hands in a movement later described as one a pianist would make in striking and lifting the fingers from a keyboard. The resulting contact generated unexpectedly harmful injuries * * *." The professor denied any intent to harm or offend. The Idaho Supreme Court affirmed a partial summary judgment that the act constituted a battery; "under Idaho law the intent required for the commission of a battery is simply the intent to cause an unpermitted contact not an intent that the contact be harmful or offensive." 118 Idaho at 401, 797 P.2d at 109. In White v. Muniz, 999 P.2d 814 (Colo.2000), an 83–year–old Alzheimer's patient struck the jaw of a caregiver who was attempting to change her diaper. In the ensuing battery action, the trial court, relying upon Horton v. Reaves, note 3, supra, instructed the jury that in order to possess the necessary intent, the patient must have appreciated the offensiveness of her conduct. The jury found against the plaintiff. The Supreme Court of Colorado affirmed, rejecting plaintiff's argument that *Horton* was limited to children and rejecting the reasoning of the Idaho court in White v. University of Idaho.

5. ***The Restatement.*** The Restatement of Torts, which the *Garratt* court quoted, is a summary of the law of torts that was prepared by Professor Francis Bohlen and was published by the American Law Institute. A newer version, called the Restatement (Second) of Torts, was prepared by Professors William Prosser and John Wade and was also published by the ALI. The ALI, which is composed of lawyers, judges, and law professors, is

currently in the process of producing the Restatement (Third) of Torts. The ALI has published the Restatement (Third) of Torts: Products Liability and the Restatement (Third) of Torts: Apportionment of Liability. It is moving toward completion of the Restatement (Third) of Torts: Liability for Physical Harm (Basic Principles).[1] The Restatement is not authoritative in the sense that precedent in the relevant jurisdiction would be authoritative. Nevertheless, courts often cite the Restatement and are influenced by it. See, e.g., Webber v. Sobba, 322 F.3d 1032, 1037 (8th Cir. 2003) (using the Second Restatement to fill a hiatus in Arkansas law only after ascertaining that "[t]he Arkansas Supreme Court frequently looks to the Restatement to answer unsettled questions of tort law").

The Restatement (Third) of Torts: Liability for Physical Harm (Basic Principles) § 1 (Tent. Draft No. 1, March 2001), defines intent as follows:

> A person acts with the intent to produce a consequence if: (a) the person has the purpose of producing that consequence, or (b) the person knows to a substantial certainty that the consequence will ensue from the person's conduct.

6. ***Transferred intent.*** Sometimes actual contact occurs, but the defendant intended only apprehension of contact or confinement. Intentionally causing apprehension of imminent harmful or offensive contact constitutes an assault. See section C, infra. Intentionally causing confinement constitutes false imprisonment. See section D, infra. In a case in which contact occurs but the defendant intends only apprehension or confinement, the defendant is still liable for battery, as though the defendant had intended the contact. Similarly, if the defendant intends actual contact but causes only apprehension or confinement, the defendant is liable for assault or false imprisonment respectively, as though the defendant had intended the apprehension or confinement. See Restatement (Second) of Torts §§ 18, 21 (1965).

A similar principle governs cases in which the defendant intends contact, apprehension, or confinement to one person but unintentionally causes contact, apprehension, or confinement to another person. The person who actually suffers the invasion can recover for battery, assault, or false imprisonment, respectively, on the theory that the defendant's intent toward the first person "transfers" to the plaintiff. See Restatement (Second) of Torts §§ 18, 20, 21, 32 (1965).[2] This principle is often called "transferred intent."

FISHER v. CARROUSEL MOTOR HOTEL, INC.

Supreme Court of Texas, 1967.
424 S.W.2d 627.

GREENHILL, JUSTICE.

This is a suit for actual and exemplary damages growing out of an alleged assault and battery. The plaintiff Fisher was a mathematician

---

1. The Third Restatement is a work in progress. At this writing it replaces some sections of the Second Restatement but not all. In our own text and notes we generally refer to the Second Restatement only when the Third has not addressed the subject. In principal cases we have left references to the earlier Restatements unchanged.

2. The Restatement (Third) of Torts: Liability for Physical Harm (Basic Principles) § 5, cmt. *c* (Tent. Draft No. 1, March 2001) says "the Restatement Second remains largely authoritative in explaining the details of intentional-tort law."

with the Data Processing Division of the Manned Spacecraft Center, an agency of the National Aeronautics and Space Agency, commonly called NASA, near Houston. The defendants were the Carrousel Motor Hotel, Inc., located in Houston, the Brass Ring Club, which is located in the Carrousel, and Robert W. Flynn, who as an employee of the Carrousel was the manager of the Brass Ring Club. Flynn died before the trial, and the suit proceeded as to the Carrousel and the Brass Ring. Trial was to a jury which found for the plaintiff Fisher. The trial court rendered judgment for the defendants notwithstanding the verdict. The Court of Civil Appeals affirmed. The question before this Court [is] whether there was evidence that an actionable battery was committed * * *.

The plaintiff Fisher had been invited by Ampex Corporation and Defense Electronics to a one day's meeting regarding telemetry equipment at the Carrousel. The invitation included a luncheon. The guests were asked to reply by telephone whether they could attend the luncheon, and Fisher called in his acceptance. After the morning session, the group of 25 or 30 guests adjourned to the Brass Ring Club for lunch. The luncheon was buffet style, and Fisher stood in line with others and just ahead of a graduate student of Rice University who testified at the trial. As Fisher was about to be served, he was approached by Flynn, who snatched the plate from Fisher's hand and shouted that he, a Negro, could not be served in the club. Fisher testified that he was not actually touched, and did not testify that he suffered fear or apprehension of physical injury; but he did testify that he was highly embarrassed and hurt by Flynn's conduct in the presence of his associates.

The jury found that Flynn "forceably dispossessed plaintiff of his dinner plate" and "shouted in a loud and offensive manner" that Fisher could not be served there, thus subjecting Fisher to humiliation and indignity. It was stipulated that Flynn was an employee of the Carrousel Hotel and, as such, managed the Brass Ring Club. The jury also found that Flynn acted maliciously and awarded Fisher $400 actual damages for his humiliation and indignity and $500 exemplary damages for Flynn's malicious conduct.

The Court of Civil Appeals held that there was no assault because there was no physical contact and no evidence of fear or apprehension of physical contact. However, it has long been settled that there can be a battery without an assault, and that actual physical contact is not necessary to constitute a battery, so long as there is contact with clothing or an object closely identified with the body.

Under the facts of this case, we have no difficulty in holding that the intentional grabbing of plaintiff's plate constituted a battery. The intentional snatching of an object from one's hand is as clearly an offensive invasion of his person as would be an actual contact with the body. "To constitute an assault and battery, it is not necessary to touch the plaintiff's body or even his clothing; knocking or snatching anything from plaintiff's hand or touching anything connected with his person, when done in an offensive manner, is sufficient." Morgan v. Loyacomo, 190 Miss. 656, 1 So.2d 510 (1941).

Such holding is not unique to the jurisprudence of this State. In S.H. Kress & Co. v. Brashier, 50 S.W.2d 922 (Tex.Civ.App.1932, no writ), the defendant was held to have committed "an assault or trespass upon the person" by snatching a book from the plaintiff's hand. The jury findings in that case were that the defendant "dispossessed plaintiff of the book" and caused her to suffer "humiliation and indignity."

* * *

We hold, therefore, that the forceful dispossession of plaintiff Fisher's plate in an offensive manner was sufficient to constitute a battery, and the trial court erred in granting judgment notwithstanding the verdict * * *.

* * * Damages for mental suffering are recoverable without the necessity for showing actual physical injury in a case of willful battery because the basis of that action is the unpermitted and intentional invasion of the plaintiff's person and not the actual harm done to the plaintiff's body. Personal indignity is the essence of an action for battery; and consequently the defendant is liable not only for contacts which do actual physical harm, but also for those which are offensive and insulting. We hold, therefore, that plaintiff was entitled to actual damages for mental suffering due to the willful battery, even in the absence of any physical injury.

* * *

The judgments of the courts below are reversed, and judgment is here rendered for the plaintiff $900 with interest from the date of the trial court's judgment, and for costs of this suit.

Notes

1. The court at some points describes the plaintiff's suit as one for "assault." Some courts, especially in older opinions, use the term "assault" to describe conduct that today would normally be called "battery."

2. Is it a battery to blow cigar smoke in the face of an anti–smoking activist during a radio talk show? Yes, according to Leichtman v. WLW Jacor Communications, Inc., 92 Ohio App.3d 232, 634 N.E.2d 697 (1994).

3. Whether contact is offensive is judged by an "objective" standard, not a "subjective" standard. This means that a community norm defines offensiveness, not the idiosyncratic views of either the plaintiff or the defendant. Would you distinguish a defendant who actually knows that the plaintiff has an idiosyncratic objection to a touching that most people would consider to be innocuous? What arguments could a plaintiff make that a touching under such circumstances would be "objectively" offensive?

4. Note that the Carrousel Motor Hotel was liable on the basis of conduct of one of its employees. This is called "vicarious liability." General-

ly, an employer is liable for torts committed by employees within the scope of employment. Vicarious liability is addressed in Chapter VII.

C. ASSAULT

VETTER v. MORGAN

Court of Appeals of Kansas, 1995.
22 Kan.App.2d 1, 913 P.2d 1200.

BRISCOE, CHIEF JUDGE.

Laura Vetter appeals the summary judgment dismissal of her * * * assault * * * claim against Chad Morgan for injuries sustained in an automobile accident. * * *

Vetter was injured when her van ran off the road after an encounter with a car owned by Morgan's father and driven by Dana Gaither. Morgan and Jerrod Faulkner were passengers in the car. Vetter was alone at 1:30 or 1:45 a.m. when she stopped her van in the right–hand westbound lane of an intersection at a stoplight. Morgan and Gaither drove up beside Vetter. Morgan began screaming vile and threatening obscenities at Vetter, shaking his fist, and making obscene gestures in a violent manner. According to Vetter, Gaither revved the engine of the car and moved the car back and forth while Morgan was threatening Vetter. Vetter testified that Morgan threatened to remove her from her van and spat on her van door when the traffic light turned green. Vetter stated she was very frightened and thought Morgan was under the influence of drugs or alcohol. She was able to write down the license tag number of the car. Morgan stated he did not intend to scare, upset, or harm Vetter, but "didn't really care" how she felt. He was trying to amuse his friends, who were laughing at his antics.

When the traffic light changed to green, both vehicles drove forward. According to Vetter, after they had driven approximately 10 feet, the car driven by Gaither veered suddenly into her lane, and she reacted by steering her van sharply to the right. Vetter's van struck the curb, causing her head to hit the steering wheel and snap back against the seat, after which she fell to the floor of the van. Morgan and Gaither denied that the car veered into Vetter's lane, stating they drove straight away from the intersection and did not see Vetter's collision with the curb.

* * *

Vetter argues the trial court erred in dismissing her assault claim against Morgan. Assault is defined as "an intentional threat or attempt, coupled with apparent ability, to do bodily harm to another, resulting in immediate apprehension of bodily harm. No bodily contact is necessary." Taiwo [v. Vu], 249 Kan. [585,] 596, 822 P.2d 1024 [(1991)] (quoting PIK Civ.2d 14.01).

The trial court concluded there was no evidence that Morgan threatened or attempted to harm Vetter, that he had no apparent ability to harm her because her van was locked and the windows were rolled up, and there was no claim of immediate apprehension of bodily harm. Vetter contends all of these conclusions involved questions of fact that should have been resolved by a jury.

There was evidence of a threat. Vetter testified in her deposition that Morgan verbally threatened to take her from her van. Ordinarily, words alone cannot be an assault. However, words can constitute assault if "together with other acts or circumstances they put the other in reasonable apprehension of imminent harmful or offensive contact with his person." Restatement (Second) of Torts § 31 (1964).

The record is sufficient to support an inference that Morgan's threat and the acts and circumstances surrounding it could reasonably put someone in Vetter's position in apprehension of imminent or immediate bodily harm. Morgan's behavior was so extreme that Vetter could reasonably have believed he would immediately try to carry out his threat. It is not necessary that the victim be placed in apprehension of instantaneous harm. It is sufficient if it appears there will be no significant delay. See Restatement (Second) of Torts § 29(1), comment b (1964).

The record also supports an inference that Morgan had the apparent ability to harm Vetter. Although Vetter's van was locked and the windows rolled up, the windows could be broken. The two vehicles were only six feet apart, and Morgan was accompanied by two other males. It was late at night, so witnesses and potential rescuers were unlikely. Although Vetter may have had the ability to flee by turning right, backing up, or running the red light, her ability to prevent the threatened harm by flight or self-defense does not preclude an assault. It is enough that Vetter believed that Morgan was capable of immediately inflicting the contact unless prevented by self-defense, flight, or intervention by others. See Restatement (Second) of Torts § 24, comment b (1964).

The trial court erred in concluding there was no evidence that Vetter was placed in apprehension of bodily harm. Whether Morgan's actions constituted an assault was a question of fact for the jury.

* * *

Notes

1. Even though Gaither, not Morgan, was driving, Morgan could be found liable for Gaither's acts because the trier could find that they acted in concert. See 913 P.2d at 1205–06.

2. "Finally, we disagree with Geary Huntsberger's claim that the evidence was insufficient to prove that he assaulted Mr. Cleland. An assault occurs when an actor intends to cause an imminent apprehension of a harmful or offensive bodily contact. Restatement (Second), of Torts, § 21.

When a person approaches another with two associates wielding chainsaws, screams 'Bring on the chainsaws!,' to which the sawyers respond by dismembering the tree in which the person sits, a factfinder could reasonably conclude that an assault has occurred. Frankly, we are at a loss to understand how a factfinder could arrive at any other conclusion." Sides v. Cleland, 436 Pa.Super. 618, 626, 648 A.2d 793, 796–97 (1994), appeal denied, 540 Pa. 613, 656 A.2d 119 (1995).

3.   Like battery, assault is an intentional tort. The plaintiff must prove that the defendant intended to cause apprehension of imminent harmful or offensive bodily contact, intended to cause actual harmful or offensive bodily contact, or intended to cause a confinement.

D.   FALSE IMPRISONMENT

HERBST v. WUENNENBERG

Supreme Court of Wisconsin, 1978.
83 Wis.2d 768, 266 N.W.2d 391.

ABRAHAMSON, JUSTICE.

Carol Wuennenberg appeals from a judgment entered by the trial court on a jury's special verdict finding that she falsely imprisoned Jason A. Herbst, Ronald B. Nadel, and Robert A. Ritholz ("plaintiffs"). Because there is no credible evidence to sustain a finding of false imprisonment, we reverse the judgment and order the cause remanded so that plaintiffs' complaint can be dismissed and judgment entered in favor of Wuennenberg.

* * *

* * * Plaintiffs' cause of action for false imprisonment arose from an incident which took place on September 19, 1974 in the vestibule of a three–unit apartment building owned and lived in by Wuennenberg and located within the district which Wuennenberg represented as alderperson in the city of Madison. * * *

[T]he plaintiffs were comparing the voter registration list for the city of Madison with names on the mailboxes in multi–unit residential dwellings in Wuennenberg's aldermanic district. Plaintiffs' ultimate purpose was to "purge the voter lists" by challenging the registrations of people whose names were not on mailboxes at the addresses from which they were registered to vote.

The plaintiffs and Wuennenberg gave somewhat differing accounts of the incident which gave rise to the action for false imprisonment, but the dispositive facts are not in dispute.

According to Ritholz, whose version of the incident was corroborated by Herbst and Nadel, when the plaintiffs reached Wuennenberg's house at approximately 4:30 p.m. they entered unannounced through the outer door into a vestibule area which lies between the inner and outer doors to Wuennenberg's building. The plaintiffs stood in the vestibule near the mailboxes, which were on a wall in the vestibule approximately two feet inside the front door to the building. Neither he nor the other plaintiffs touched the mailboxes, stated Ritholz; he simply read the names listed for Wuennenberg's address from a computer printout of the registered voters in Wuennenberg's district, and the others checked to see if those names appeared on the mailboxes.

When they were half way through checking, testified Ritholz, Wuennenberg entered the vestibule from an inner door and asked plaintiffs what they were doing. Ritholz replied that they were working for the Republican party, purging voter lists. According to Ritholz, Wuennenberg became very agitated and told the plaintiffs that she did not want them in her district. "At first she told us to leave," testified Ritholz, "and we agreed to leave, but she very quickly changed her mind and wanted to know who we were. Since we already agreed to leave, we didn't think this was necessary."

After the plaintiffs had refused to identify themselves to her, Wuennenberg asked them whether they would be willing to identify themselves to the police. Ritholz replied that they would be willing to do so. Nonetheless, testified Ritholz, he would have preferred to leave, and several times he offered to leave. Both Nadel and Herbst, who agreed that Ritholz was acting as spokesman for the group, testified to Ritholz's statement to Wuennenberg that the plaintiffs were willing to identify themselves to the police.

Subsequently, Wuennenberg's husband came to the vestibule to see what was going on, and Wuennenberg asked him to call the police. About this time Wuennenberg moved from the inner door to a position in front of the outer door. According to Nadel, Wuennenberg blocked the outer door by "standing there with her arms on the pillars to the door to block our exit." The plaintiffs agreed that Wuennenberg had not threatened or intimidated them and that they neither asked her permission to leave nor made any attempt to get her to move away from the doorway. When asked why he had not attempted to leave the vestibule, each of the plaintiffs answered, in effect, that he assumed he would have had to push Wuennenberg out of the way in order to do so.

The plaintiffs waited in the vestibule, stated Ritholz, until the police came some five minutes later. They gave their names and explained their errand to a police officer who told them that they were not doing anything wrong and that they could continue checking the mailboxes in the district.

* * *

After her husband left to call the police, testified Wuennenberg, she positioned herself in front of the outer doorway because she could watch for the arrival of the police from that vantage and because "I didn't want someone trying to run away at that point." She stated she did not brace her arms against the door frame. She would not have made any effort to stop the plaintiffs had they attempted to leave, stated Wuennenberg, because "I'm not physically capable of stopping anybody."

Plaintiffs' cause of action for false imprisonment [was] tried before a jury. At the close of the evidence, the trial court * * * denied Wuennenberg's motion for a directed verdict * * *.

The jury returned a special verdict finding that Wuennenberg had falsely imprisoned the plaintiffs and awarded Herbst, Nadel and Ritholz a total of $1,500 in actual damages. * * *

* * *

We reiterate the rule which this court must follow in reviewing the record to determine if the jury verdict is supported by the evidence: A jury verdict will not be upset if there is any credible evidence which under any reasonable view fairly admits of an inference supporting the findings. The evidence is to be viewed in the light most favorable to the verdict. A jury cannot base its findings on conjecture and speculation. We hold that the evidence adduced in the case before us does not support a finding that the plaintiffs were falsely imprisoned, and accordingly we reverse the judgment of the trial court.

The action for the tort of false imprisonment protects the personal interest in freedom from restraint of movement. The essence of false imprisonment is the intentional, unlawful, and unconsented restraint by one person of the physical liberty of another. There is no cause of action unless the confinement is contrary to the will of the "prisoner." It is a contradiction to say that the captor imprisoned the "prisoner" with the "prisoner's" consent.

* * *

After review of the record we conclude that the evidence is not sufficient to support the conclusion that Wuennenberg's acts "directly or indirectly result[ed] in * * * a confinement of the [plaintiffs]," a required element of the cause of action.

The Restatement [(Second) of Torts] lists the ways in which an actor may bring about a "confinement": "by actual or apparent physical barriers" [Sec. 38, Comment a]; "by overpowering physical force, or by submission to physical force" [Sec. 39]; "by submission to a threat to apply physical force to the other's person immediately upon the other's going or attempting to go beyond the area in which the actor intends to confine him" [Sec. 40]; "by submission to duress other than threats of physical force, where such duress is sufficient to make the consent given ineffective to bar the action" (as by a threat to inflict harm upon a member of the other's immediate family, or his property) [Sec. 40A]; "by taking a person into custody under an asserted legal authority" [Sec. 41].

The plaintiffs do not contend that confinement was brought about by an actual or apparent physical barrier, or by overpowering physical force, or by submission to duress, or by taking a person into custody under an asserted legal authority. The parties agree that the central issue is whether there was confinement by threat of physical force and thus argue only as to the applicability of section 40 of the Restatement * * *.

* * *

The comments to section 40 provide that a person has not been confined by "threats of physical force" unless by words or other acts the actor "threatens to apply" *and* "has the apparent intention and ability to apply" force to his person. It is not a sufficient basis for an action for false imprisonment that the "prisoner" remained within the limits set by the actor. Remaining within such limits is not a submission to the threat unless the "prisoner" believed that the actor had the ability to carry his threat into effect.

* * *

As plaintiffs state in their brief, the question before this court is whether there is any credible evidence which supports a conclusion that the plaintiffs did not consent to the confinement and that they remained in the vestibule only because Wuennenberg indicated by standing in the doorway that she had "the apparent intention and ability to apply" force to their persons should they attempt to leave. We have reviewed the record, and we find that it does not support this conclusion. Ritholz testified that Wuennenberg had not verbally threatened the plaintiffs, and since none of the plaintiffs asked Wuennenberg to step aside, it could be no more than speculation to conclude that Wuennenberg would not only have refused this request but also would have physically resisted had the plaintiffs attempted to leave. At best, the evidence supports an inference that plaintiffs remained in the vestibule because they *assumed* they would have to push Wuennenberg out of the way in order to leave. This assumption is not sufficient to support a claim for false imprisonment.

We do not intend to suggest that false imprisonment will not lie unless a "prisoner" attempts to assault his captor or unless he fails to make such attempt only because he fears harm. The plaintiffs in the case at bar were not required to obtain their freedom by taking steps dangerous to themselves or offensive to their reasonable sense of decency or personal dignity. At a minimum, however, plaintiffs should have attempted to ascertain whether there was any basis to their assumption that their freedom of movement had been curtailed. False imprisonment may not be predicated upon a person's unfounded belief that he was restrained.

Dupler v. Seubert, [69 Wis.2d 373, 230 N.W.2d 626 (1975)] relied on by plaintiffs, does not support plaintiffs' contention that the trial court properly submitted to the jury the question whether the plaintiffs submitted to "an implied threat of actual physical restraint." We concluded in *Dupler* that the record contained sufficient evidence from which a jury could have concluded that plaintiff had been falsely imprisoned "by an implied threat of actual physical restraint":

> [Plaintiff] testified that defendant Peterson ordered her in a loud voice to remain seated several times, after she expressed the desire to leave. She reported being 'berated, screamed and hollered at,' and said the reason she did not just walk out of the room was that 'Mrs. Seubert had blocked the door, and tempers had been raised with all the shouting and screaming, I was just plain scared to make an effort. There were two against one.'

As Wuennenberg notes in her brief, the only similarity between *Dupler* and the case at bar is that Wuennenberg stood in the doorway. Plaintiffs were not "berated, screamed, and hollered at"; they outnumbered Wuennenberg three–to–one; and they gave no testimony to the effect that they were frightened of Wuennenberg or that they feared she would harm them.

Viewed in the light most favorable to plaintiffs, the evidence shows that the plaintiffs were willing to identify themselves to the police, but that they would have preferred to leave Wuennenberg's premises. It is not a sufficient basis for an action for false imprisonment that the plaintiffs remained on the premises although they would have preferred not to do so. Because plaintiffs did not submit to an apprehension of force, they were not imprisoned.

Judgment reversed, and cause remanded with directions to the trial court to enter judgment in favor of Wuennenberg dismissing plaintiffs' complaint.

Notes

1. Confinement must be within a boundary. Excluding someone from a building does not constitute a confinement.

2. A reasonable and reasonably discoverable alternative means of escape negates a confinement. In Geddes v. Daughters of Charity of St. Vincent De Paul, Inc., 348 F.2d 144 (5th Cir.1965), the plaintiff alleged that she was falsely imprisoned by a mental hospital. The defendant argued that she had a reasonable means of escape when she was permitted to take escorted trips into town. The court refused to overturn a jury verdict for the plaintiff. Evidence that she was escorted on her trips downtown, that she was old, in ill health and weak, and that she was never given more than ten dollars supported a finding that the alleged means of escape was not reasonable.

3. An often cited case on false imprisonment is Whittaker v. Sandford, 110 Me. 77, 85 A. 399 (1912). The defendant lured the plaintiff onto a yacht for a trip from Jaffa, Syria, to Maine, implicitly agreeing that the plaintiff would be permitted to go ashore in Maine. When the yacht was anchored in a harbor in Maine, the defendant refused to provide a boat to take the plaintiff ashore. The court held that because the defendant had implicitly promised to take the plaintiff ashore, his failure to provide a boat constituted a false imprisonment. This does not mean, however, that, absent an (implic-

it) agreement, individuals have an affirmative duty to extricate others from a confinement.

Note that it might have been possible for the plaintiff to swim ashore. But this was not considered a "reasonable" means of escape.

4. To recover for false imprisonment, a plaintiff must prove that he or she was aware of the imprisonment at the time *or* that the confinement caused actual harm. In Parvi v. City of Kingston, 41 N.Y.2d 553, 394 N.Y.S.2d 161, 362 N.E.2d 960 (1977), the plaintiff was intoxicated during the imprisonment and could not remember it at the time of trial. The court held that the trial court improperly dismissed the complaint, reasoning that the trial court had "failed to distinguish between a later recollection of consciousness and the existence of that consciousness at the time when the imprisonment itself took place."

5. A person may be liable for false imprisonment for wrongfully directing the police to arrest another person. The cases distinguish between "directing" the police to arrest someone and providing the police with information upon which the police exercise judgment. See King v. Crossland Savings Bank, 111 F.3d 251, 256–57 (2d Cir.1997). Knowingly providing the police with incorrect information is the equivalent of "directing" an arrest, but innocently providing incorrect information is not. See Godines v. First Guaranty Savings & Loan Ass'n, 525 So.2d 1321 (Miss.1988).

6. In addition to proving a confinement, the plaintiff must also prove that the defendant intended a confinement, an assault, or a battery of the plaintiff or a third person. See Restatement (Second) of Torts, § 35 (1965).

E. INTENTIONAL INFLICTION OF EMOTIONAL DISTRESS

ECKENRODE v. LIFE OF AMERICA INSURANCE COMPANY

United States Court of Appeals, Seventh Circuit, 1972.
470 F.2d 1.

KILEY, CIRCUIT JUDGE.

Plaintiff, a resident of Pennsylvania, filed this * * * diversity complaint to recover damages for severe emotional injury suffered as a result of the deliberate refusal of Life of America Insurance Company (Insurer), of Chicago, to pay her the proceeds of Insurer's policy covering the life of her husband. The district court dismissed the suit. Plaintiff has appealed. We reverse.

* * *

Taking the allegations, properly pleaded in Counts II and III, as true, the following facts are stated: Defendant's life insurance policy covering plaintiff's husband issued September 22, 1967. Under the policy Insurer agreed to pay plaintiff $5,000 immediately upon due proof of death from "accidental causes." On December 17, 1967, insured was an accidental victim of a homicide. Plaintiff met all conditions of the policy and repeatedly demanded payment, but Insurer refused to pay. Decedent left plaintiff with several children, but no property of value. She had no money, none even for the funeral expenses. Denied payment by Insurer, she was required to borrow money to support her family, while her financial condition worsened. The family was required to live with, and accept charity from, relatives.

Further: Insurer knew or should have known of the death of decedent from accidental causes and of plaintiff's dire need of the policy proceeds. Yet Insurer repeatedly and deliberately refused her demands for payment, and as a proximate result she was caused to suffer "severe distress and disturbance of [her] mental tranquility." Instead of paying her the proceeds of the policy, and being fully aware of the accidental cause of decedent's death and of plaintiff's financial distress, Insurer breached the policy promise to pay immediately upon proof of death. Insurer, knowing full well that plaintiff needed the proceeds of the policy to provide necessaries for her children, applied "economic coercion" in refusing to make payment on the policy, and in "inviting" plaintiff to "compromise" her claim by implying it (Insurer) had a valid defense to the claim.[2]

* * *

The issue before us * * * is whether plaintiff—beneficiary of her husband's life insurance policy—may on the foregoing "facts" recover damages for severe mental distress allegedly suffered as a result of Insurer's conduct. Illinois law controls our decision, and, in anticipation that the Illinois Supreme Court would hold as we do, we decide the issue in favor of plaintiff.

We have no doubt, in view of Knierim v. Izzo, 22 Ill.2d 73, 174 N.E.2d 157 (1961), that the Illinois Supreme Court would sustain plaintiff's complaint against Insurer's motion to dismiss.

In *Knierim,* plaintiff filed a wrongful death action alleging, inter alia, that defendant Izzo threatened her with the murder of her husband, carried out the threat, and thereby proximately caused her severe emotional distress. The trial court dismissed her complaint, but the Illinois Supreme Court reversed and held that plaintiff had stated a cause of action for an intentional causing of severe emotional distress by Izzo's "outrageous conduct."

The court recognized the "new tort" of intentional infliction of severe emotional distress, following similar recognition by an "increasing number of courts," and cited several state decisions. The court rejected reasons given by other courts not recognizing the "new tort." As to the reason that mental disturbance is incapable of financial measurement, the court pointed out that "pain and suffering" and "mental suffering"

---

2. Attached to the complaint is a copy of Insurer's letter of January 12, 1968. The letter suggests that in view of a police investigation not likely to be completed until the "very distant future," plaintiff might like to suggest an offer to "settle" rather than wait for the police report.

are elements of damage, respectively, in personal injury and malicious prosecution cases. As to the reason that mental consequences are too evanescent for the law to deal with, the court noted that psychosomatic medicine had learned much in the past "thirty years" about the bodily effects of man's emotions, and that symptoms produced by "stronger emotions" are now visible to the professional eye. As to the reason that recognizing the "new tort" would lead to frivolous claims, the court observed that triers of fact from their own experiences would be able to draw a line between "slight hurts" and "outrageous conduct." And finally, as to the reason that mental consequences vary greatly with the individual so as to pose difficulties too great for the law, the court adopted an objective standard against which emotional distress could be measured. The court thought that the standard of "severe emotional distress to a person of ordinary sensibilities, in the absence of special knowledge or notice" would be a sufficient limit for excluding "mere vulgarities * * * as meaningless abusive expressions." The court noted that the "reasonable man" is well known to triers of fact who are also well acquainted with "the man of ordinary sensibilities."

The court added a cautionary note, expressing confidence that Illinois trial judges would not permit litigation to introduce "trivialities and mere bad manners" under the cloak of the "new tort." * * *

In *Knierim* the court, inter alia, relied upon State Rubbish Collectors Association v. Siliznoff, 38 Cal.2d 330, 240 P.2d 282 (1952), and Restatement, Torts § 46 (1948 Supp.). In *Siliznoff* the California Supreme Court, in an opinion by Justice Roger Traynor, recognized the "new tort" for the first time and held that Siliznoff could recover from the cross-defendant Rubbish Collectors Association for mental distress caused by the Association's severe threats to beat him up, destroy his truck and put him out of business unless Siliznoff offered to pay over certain proceeds to the Association. Later, the California Supreme Court *en banc* affirmed a trial court judgment against an insurance company, including $25,000 for mental suffering caused by the insurance company's earlier unreasonable refusal to accept a settlement within the limits of the liability policy. Crisci v. Security Ins. Co. of New Haven, 66 Cal.2d 425, 58 Cal.Rptr. 13, 426 P.2d 173 (1967). There Mrs. Crisci's mental distress claim was in addition to her loss of property caused by the insurance company's failure to settle. The court thought that where there were substantial damages apart from the mental distress, the danger of fictitious claims was reduced. Subsequently in Fletcher v. Western National Life Ins. Co., 10 Cal.App.3d 376, 89 Cal.Rptr. 78 (1970), an appellate court relying upon *Siliznoff* and *Crisci,* held that the defendant insurance company's threatened and actual bad faith refusals to make payments under the disability policy were essentially tortious in nature and could legally be the basis for an action against the company for intentional infliction of emotional distress. The decision rested on the finding that the refusals were maliciously employed by the company in concert with false and threatening communications directed to the badly injured plaintiff-insured for the purpose of causing him to surrender his policy or disadvantageously settle a nonexistent dispute. The court found sufficient evidence showing emotional distress of the "requisite severity" (i.e., outrageousness), and thus affirmed the trial court's denial of judgment N.O.V.

We think that the California court in *Fletcher*, supra, set out correctly the elements of a prima facie case for the tort of "intentional infliction of severe emotional distress":

(1) Outrageous conduct by the defendant;

(2) The defendant's intention of causing, or reckless disregard of the probability of causing emotional distress;

(3) The plaintiff's suffering severe or extreme emotional distress; and

(4) Actual and proximate causation of the emotional distress by the defendant's outrageous conduct.

It is our view that were this case before the Illinois Supreme Court, that court would find the foregoing elements substantially correct; and that plaintiff here has sufficiently pleaded the elements.

It is recognized that the outrageous character of a person's conduct may arise from an abuse by that person of a position which gives him power to affect the interests of another; and that in this sense extreme "bullying tactics" and other "high pressure" methods of insurance adjusters seeking to force compromises or settlements may constitute outrageous conduct. It is also recognized that the extreme character of a persons' conduct may arise from that person's knowledge that the other is peculiarly susceptible to emotional distress by reason of some physical or mental condition or peculiarity.

Here Insurer's alleged bad faith refusal to make payment on the policy, coupled with its deliberate use of "economic coercion" (i.e., by delaying and refusing payment it increased plaintiff's financial distress thereby coercing her to compromise and settle) to force a settlement, clearly rises to the level of "outrageous conduct" to a person of "ordinary sensibilities."

Furthermore, it is common knowledge that one of the most frequent considerations in procuring life insurance is to ensure the continued economic and mental welfare of the beneficiaries upon the death of the insured. The very risks insured against presuppose that upon the death of the insured the beneficiary might be in difficult circumstances and thus particularly susceptible and vulnerable to high pressure tactics by an economically powerful entity. In the case before us Insurer's alleged high pressure methods (economic coercion) were aimed at the very thing insured against, and we think that the insurance company was on notice that plaintiff would be particularly vulnerable to mental distress by reason of her financial plight.

* * *

It is true that settlement tactics may be privileged under circumstances where an insurer has done no more than insist upon his legal rights in a permissible way. But we do not think that a refusal to make payments based on a bad faith insistence on a non–existent defense is privileged conduct against the complaint here.

* * *

For the reasons given, the judgment of the district court dismissing Counts II and III of plaintiff's complaint is hereby reversed.

CHUY v. PHILADELPHIA EAGLES FOOTBALL CLUB

United States Court of Appeals, Third Circuit, 1979.
595 F.2d 1265.

ROSENN, CIRCUIT JUDGE.

This appeal presents several interesting questions growing out of the employment by the Philadelphia Eagles Football Club ("the Eagles") of a former professional player, Don Chuy ("Chuy"). * * *

* * *

Chuy joined the Eagles in 1969, having been traded from the Los Angeles Rams, another professional football club with which he had played for a half dozen years. On June 16, 1969, he met with the Eagles general manager, Palmer "Pete" Retzlaff, in Philadelphia, Pennsylvania, to negotiate a contract with the Eagles for the 1969, 1970, and 1971 football seasons. The parties concluded their negotiations by executing three National Football League (NFL) standard form player contracts on June 16, 1969, covering the 1969, 1970, and 1971 football seasons respectively at a salary of $30,000 for each season, with a $15,000 advance for the 1969 season.

The contracts each contained a standard NFL injury–benefit provision entitling a player injured in the performance of his service to his salary "for the term of his contract." Chuy sustained a serious injury to his shoulder during his first season in a game between the Eagles and the New York Giants in November, 1969. Sidelined for the remainder of the season, Chuy had to be hospitalized for most of December, 1969. During the hospitalization, his diagnosis revealed a pulmonary embolism, a blood clot in his lung, which marked the end of his professional athletic career. Following the advice of his physician, Chuy decided to retire from professional football and notified the Eagles of his intention. At the same time, Chuy requested that the Eagles pay him for the remaining two years of what he asserted was a three–year contract.

The Eagles requested that Chuy submit to a physical examination which Dr. Dick D. Harrell conducted in March, 1970. After extensive tests, Dr. Harrell concluded that Chuy suffered from an abnormal cell condition, presumably stress polycythemia, which may have predisposed him to the formation of dangerous blood clots. He therefore recommended to the Eagles that Chuy should "not be allowed to participate further in contact sports." Shortly after receiving Dr. Harrell's recommendation, General Manager Retzlaff informed Hugh Brown, a sports columnist for the Philadelphia Bulletin, that Chuy had been advised to quit football because of his blood clot condition. Brown thereupon telephoned Dr. James Nixon, the Eagles' team physician, for further information on Chuy's medical status.

On April 9, 1970, Hugh Brown's by–lined column in the Philadelphia Bulletin carried an account of Chuy's premature retirement. The column opened with the following:

> It's a jaw–breaker * * * Polycythemia Vera * * * and the question before the house is how Don Chuy, the Eagles' squatty guard, got hit with the jaw–breaker.

> "One of the consequences of Polycythemia Vera," said Dr. James Nixon, the Eagles' physician, "is that the blood cells get in each other's way. It's a definite threat to form embolisms, or emboli."

The remainder of the column quoted Retzlaff, Dr. Nixon, and Chuy's attorney concerning Chuy's medical condition and his effort to obtain compensation for the additional two years of his putative three–year contract. The Associated Press wire service picked up the story and articles appeared the next day in newspapers throughout the country, including the Los Angeles Times. The articles reported that Chuy had been "advised to give up football and professional wrestling because of a blood condition" and that, according to Dr. James Nixon, the Eagles' physician, "Chuy is suffering from polycythemia vera. Nixon said it is considered a threat to form blood clots."

After reading the Los Angeles Times article, Chuy testified that he panicked and immediately called his personal physician, Dr. John W. Perry. Dr. Perry informed Chuy that polycythemia vera was a fatal disease but that, from his records, Chuy did not have that disease. Dr. Perry added that he would run a series of tests to confirm his diagnosis. Chuy testified that he became apprehensive, despite Dr. Perry's assurances, broke down emotionally, and, frightened by the prospect of imminent death, refused to submit to any tests. Chuy stated that for the next several months, he could not cope with daily routines and he avoided people. He returned to Dr. Perry, who gave him numerous tests which disproved the presence of polycythemia vera. Nonetheless, Chuy testified that he continued to be apprehensive about death and that marital difficulties also developed.

Chuy eventually brought suit against the Eagles and the National Football League, alleging [among other causes of action] breach of contract and intentional infliction of emotional distress. * * * The court submitted [these] claims to the jury by special interrogatories, and the jury returned a verdict for the plaintiff. On the basis of the jury's findings, the district court molded a damages award for breach of contract in the amount of $45,000, which reflected $60,000 salary due for the 1970 and 1971 seasons, less a $15,000 debt Chuy owed the Eagles.

The jury also awarded Chuy $10,000 compensatory damages for the intentional infliction of emotional distress claim and punitive damages in the sum of $60,590.96. * * *

[Before the case was submitted to the jury, the Eagles moved for a directed verdict, and they objected to the court's instruction on the issue of intent.] After the entry of judgment against the Eagles[, the Eagles moved for judgment notwithstanding the verdict or, alternatively, for a new trial. The district court denied the motions, and the Eagles appealed.] We affirm.

* * *

Plaintiff's recovery of damages for emotional distress, stemming from having read Dr. Nixon's statement that Chuy was suffering from polycythemia vera, was predicated upon the principle enunciated in section 46 of the Restatement (Second) of Torts (1965). That section provides:

> One who by extreme and outrageous conduct intentionally or recklessly causes severe emotional distress to another is subject to liability for such emotional distress, and if bodily harm to the other results from it, for such bodily harm.

Thus, there are four elements to the action under § 46: (1) the conduct must be extreme and outrageous; (2) the conduct must be intentional or reckless; (3) it must cause emotional distress; and (4) the distress must be severe. Although the Pennsylvania Supreme Court has not as yet specifically adopted in its entirety the Restatement's formulation and comments, Pennsylvania courts have signalled their acceptance of this evolving tort. In light of the extant case law, we believe that the black letter rule of § 46 of the Restatement, along with the interpretive comments, may be applied as the basis in Pennsylvania law for the tort of intentional infliction of emotional distress.

The Eagles argue that the district court should not have submitted to the jury the question whether Dr. Nixon's statements constituted "extreme and outrageous conduct"; that the court gave improper instructions concerning the intent necessary for the tort and that there was insufficient evidence for the jury to find the requisite intent; [and] that Chuy's allegedly exaggerated and unreasonable reaction to Dr. Nixon's remarks precludes the Eagles' liability * * *.

The Eagles contend first that the trial judge erred in submitting to the jury the issue whether Dr. Nixon's statements constituted "extreme and outrageous conduct." * * * Comment h to § 46 * * * divides the functions of the court and jury in a conventional manner. The court must determine, as a matter of law, whether there is sufficient evidence for reasonable persons to find extreme or outrageous conduct. If the plaintiff has satisfied this threshold evidentiary requirement, the jury must find the facts and make its own characterization. The district court followed precisely the Restatement's procedure.

In applying the legal standard for sufficiency of the evidence to support a finding of extreme and outrageous conduct, the district court correctly ruled that if Dr. Nixon advised sportswriter Brown that Chuy suffered from polycythemia vera, knowing that Chuy did not have the disease,[10] such conduct could reasonably be regarded as extreme and outrageous. According to comment d of the Restatement, it has not been sufficient for a finding of liability that "the defendant has acted with an intent which is tortious or even criminal, or that he has intended to inflict emotional distress, or even that his conduct has been characterized by 'malice.' "

> Liability has been found only where the conduct has been so outrageous in character, and so extreme in degree, as to go beyond all possible bounds of decency, and to be regarded as atrocious, and utterly intolerable in a civilized community.

Restatement (Second) of Torts, § 46, comment d.

Accepting as we must at this stage Chuy's version of the events, we have a statement to the press by a physician assumed to know the facts that a person is suffering from a potentially fatal disease, even though the physician was aware that the person was not stricken with that condition. This, of course, constituted intolerable professional conduct. Disseminating the falsehood through the national press compounded the harm. Surely Dr. Nixon's statements, as understood by the jury, went beyond the "mere insults, indignities * * * or annoyances" which people are prepared to withstand.

The Eagles next contend that the district court erred in charging the jury on intent and recklessness. Section 46 does not recognize liability for mere negligent infliction of emotional distress. However, reckless conduct causing emotional distress renders an actor as liable as if he had acted intentionally. See comment i to § 46.[12] To facilitate the jury's answer to the interrogatories, the trial judge gave instructions on the elements of the tort of infliction of emotional distress. With respect to requisite intent, he stated that the plaintiff could prevail only if the jury found (a) that Dr. Nixon's statement was intentional and (b) that the natural and probable consequences of making the statement were that it would become known to Chuy and that such awareness would cause him emotional distress.[13]

---

10. We recognize that Dr. Nixon testified that he never told Brown of a positive diagnosis of polycythemia vera and that he only suggested that Chuy may have suffered from *a* polycythemia, a non-fatal blood condition. The jury, however, believed Brown's recollection of the phone conversation with Dr. Nixon. We are bound to accept the jury's finding.

12. Comment i reads: "*Intention and recklessness.*" The rule stated in this Section applies where the actor desires to inflict severe emotional distress, and also

where he knows that such distress is certain, or substantially certain, to result from his conduct. It applies also where he acts recklessly ... in deliberate disregard of a high degree of probability that the emotional distress will follow."

13. The district court explained the tort in these precise words:

So if you intentionally make a statement the natural and probable consequences of which it will be known to the person and cause him or her emotional distress and if the making of that statement is shocking

As we understand the Eagles' argument, unless Dr. Nixon was aware that his comments were substantially certain to cause Chuy severe emotional distress, his remarks cannot be found to be "reckless." We are persuaded, however, that if Dr. Nixon's statements were intentional, he need not have been *aware* of the natural and probable consequences of his words. It is enough that Chuy's distress was substantially certain to follow Dr. Nixon's rash statements. Intentionally to propagate a falsehood, the natural and probable consequences of which will be to cause the plaintiff emotional distress, is equivalent, in the language of the Restatement's comment i, to the "deliberate disregard of a high degree of probability that the emotional distress will follow." Thus, the district court's instruction comported with the Restatement's requirements for recklessness.

Having been properly charged, the jury reasonably could have found that the requirements of section 46 as to intent had been met. The testimony given by Brown sufficiently supported a finding that Dr. Nixon's remarks were reckless.

Beyond the characterization of Dr. Nixon's statement as reckless and outrageous, the Eagles assert that Chuy's reaction to the statement was exaggerated and unreasonable. The Eagles point to evidence that Chuy, after reading the statement attributed to Dr. Nixon in the local newspaper, refused to undergo tests which he had been advised would disprove the presence of polycythemia vera. Nor did Chuy attempt to communicate with Dr. Nixon or Dr. Harrell to verify the newspaper account of his illness. Instead, Chuy became depressed and despondent, delaying tests for a period of six months. The Eagles assert that Chuy's failure to secure prompt medical verification of his putative illness was unjustified, precluding liability for the infliction of emotional distress.

Comment j to § 46 requires that a plaintiff prove that he suffered severe distress that is not unreasonable, exaggerated, or unjustified. The same comment further notes that severe distress may encompass mental anguish, fright, horror, grief, worry, and other emotional disturbances. The extent of the severity is to be measured by whether any "reasonable man could be expected to endure it." Restatement (Second) of Torts, § 46, comment j. The jury in this case was asked to determine whether the "natural and probable" impact of Dr. Nixon's statements rendered the statements beyond the bounds of decency and it responded affirmatively. Thus, implicit in the jury's affirmative answer is its determination that a person of ordinary sensibility could not have withstood the distress without severe mental anguish and that Chuy did not feign his mental anxiety.

* * *

and outrageous and exceeds the bounds of decency with respect to its natural and probable impact, then a case of intention-al infliction of emotional distress is made out.

The judgment of the district court will be affirmed. The parties to bear their own costs.

Notes

1. Do you agree that "the district court's instruction comported with the Restatement's requirements for recklessness"? If not, consider whether the particular shortcomings of the instruction could have affected the verdict, given that the jury had to have resolved the central fact dispute described in footnote 10 in favor of Brown's version, and that Dr. Nixon testified that he knew that Chuy did not have polycythemia vera.

2. In Vetter v. Morgan, section C, supra p. 21, in addition to assault, the plaintiff claimed intentional infliction of emotional distress. As to the latter claim, the court of appeals affirmed summary judgment for the defendant on the following ground:

> There was no evidence that Vetter suffered extreme emotional distress sufficient to support her claim. Her testimony that she was "very, very frightened" during the incident does not establish the kind of extreme emotional distress required for liability. Although Vetter testified that she later became very depressed and was given a prescription for Prozac for a short time, this testimony was given when she was describing her physical injuries and medical treatment for them rather than her emotional reaction to Morgan's actions.

How did Chuy show that he suffered the requisite severe distress?

3. In Fisher v. Carrousel Motor Hotel, Inc., section B, supra p. 18, the plaintiff alleged a cause of action for intentional infliction of emotional distress. The court declined to hold for the plaintiff on that ground because other grounds were available, and Texas courts had not fully embraced the principles set forth in Restatement (Second) section 46.* How should the case be decided under section 46?

F.   TRESPASS TO LAND

AMPHITHEATERS, INC. v. PORTLAND MEADOWS

Supreme Court of Oregon, 1948.
184 Or. 336, 198 P.2d 847.

BRAND, JUSTICE.

[Plaintiff owned an outdoor, drive–in movie theater. Defendant owned a horse race track on adjacent property. The race track was equipped with lights for night racing. The plaintiff sued for trespass to land and nuisance, claiming that the lights from the race track interfered with the movie screen. The trial court directed a verdict for the defendant.]

In installing outdoor moving picture theaters, it is necessary to protect the premises from outside light interference. For that purpose

---

* The Texas Supreme Court explicitly recognized the tort of intentional infliction of emotional distress in Twyman v. Twyman, 855 S.W.2d 619 (Tex. 1993).

the plaintiff constructed wing fences for a considerable distance on each side of the screen and along the westerly line of Union Avenue for the purpose of shutting off the light from the cars traveling on that arterial highway. It was also necessary to construct a shadow box extending on both sides and above the screen for the purpose of excluding the light from the moon and stars. The testimony indicates that the construction of the shadow box was necessary if a good picture was to be presented on the screen. The extreme delicacy of plaintiff's operation and the susceptibility of outdoor moving pictures to light in any form was conclusively established by the evidence.

In order to illuminate the defendant's track for night horse racing, approximately 350 1500–watt lights are mounted in clusters on 80–foot poles placed at intervals of approximately 250 feet around the track. The flood lights are in general, directed at the track, but there is substantial evidence to the effect that reflected light "spills" over onto the plaintiff's premises and has a serious effect on the quality of pictures shown on the screen. The nearest cluster of lights on the defendant's track is 832 feet distance from the plaintiff's screen. The light from the defendant's track not only impairs the quality of the pictures exhibited by the plaintiff, but there is also substantial evidence that plaintiffs have suffered financial loss as the result of the illumination of which they complain. On one occasion at least, plaintiffs felt themselves required to refund admission fees to their patrons on account of the poor quality of the picture exhibited. The evidence discloses that the light from the defendant's race track when measured at plaintiff's screen is approximately that of full moonlight.

Upon the opening of the racing season in September, 1946, the plaintiff immediately complained to the defendant concerning the detrimental effect of defendant's lights, and shortly thereafter suit was filed. In the fall of 1946 the defendant, while denying liability, nevertheless made substantial efforts to protect the plaintiff from the effect of defendant's lights. One hundred hoods were installed on the lights, and particular attention was given to those nearest to the plaintiff's property. In 1947, and prior to the spring racing season, which was to last 25 days, thirty louvers were also installed for the purpose of further confining the light to the defendant's property. These efforts materially reduced, but did not eliminate the conditions of which plaintiff complains.

Plaintiff contends that the defendant, by casting light equivalent to that of a full moon upon plaintiff's screen has committed a trespass upon real property and error is assigned by reason of the failure of the court to submit to the jury the question of trespass. While the dividing line between trespass and nuisance is not always a sharp one, we think it clear that the case at bar is governed by the law of nuisance and not by the law of trespass. Under our decisions every unauthorized entry upon land of another, although without damage, constitutes actionable trespass. The mere suggestion that the casting of light upon the premises of a plaintiff would render a defendant liable without proof of any actual damage, carries its own refutation. Actions for damages on account of smoke, noxious odors and the like have been universally classified as falling within the law of nuisance. In fact, cases of this type are described in the Restatement of the Law as "non trespassory" invasions. Restatement of The Law of Torts, Vol. 4, Ch. 40, p. 214, et seq.

Many of the cases on which plaintiff relies in support of its theory of trespass involve the flight of airplanes at low level over plaintiffs' land. The modern law with reference to trespass by airplanes has developed under the influence of ancient rules concerning the nature of property. Ownership of lands, it has been said, "includes, not only the face of the earth, but everything under it or over it, and has in its legal signification an indefinite extent upward and downward * * *." * * *

In support of its theory of trespass, the plaintiff cites Swetland v. Curtiss Airports Corporation, 6 Cir., 55 F.2d 201, 83 A.L.R. 319; United States v. Causby, 328 U.S. 256, 66 S.Ct. 1062, 90 L.Ed. 1206; and Guith v. Consumers Power Co., D.C., 36 F.Supp. 21. They are all cases which involve the flight of airplanes and which reflect the influence of the ancient rules of ownership ad coelum as modified by the rules of privilege set forth in the Restatement. The historical background of these cases distinguishes them from the non trespassory cases which are controlled by the law of nuisance. Portsmouth Harbor Land & Hotel Co. v. United States, 260 U.S. 327, 43 S.Ct. 135, 67 L.Ed. 287, was similar in principle to the *Causby* case, supra. The case involved a taking by the United States by means of the continuous firing of artillery over the petitioners' land. We need not argue the distinction between a cannon ball and a ray of light. Upon this issue plaintiff also cites National Refining Co. v. Batte, 135 Miss. 819, 100 So. 388, 35 A.L.R. 91, and The Shelburne, Inc. v. Crossan Corporation, 95 N.J.Eq. 188, 122 A. 749, both of which cases involve the shedding of light upon defendant's property, but both were decided upon the theory of nuisance and not of trespass. * * *

[The court then held that the defendant's conduct did not constitute a nuisance. See Chapter XVI, infra.]

The trial court did not err in directing a verdict. The judgment is affirmed.

Notes

1. *Trespass vs. nuisance.* To recover for trespass to land (or for battery, assault, or false imprisonment), a plaintiff need not prove that the invasion was unreasonable or that it caused actual damage. Thus, a plaintiff has certain advantages if he can prove an "entry" and fit his case under trespass to land rather than nuisance.

The law of nuisance is addressed in Chapter XVI. Basically, the plaintiff must prove that the defendant caused a *substantial, unreasonable* interference with the plaintiff's quiet use and enjoyment of real property. Unlike under trespass to land, a plaintiff need not prove a physical entry. The interference can be caused by a physical, trespassory entry, but it can also be caused by other means, such as odor or noise. On the other hand, under nuisance the plaintiff normally must prove that the interference was unreasonable and that it caused actual damage.

2. *Title disputes.* A plaintiff's ability to make out a case for trespass to land without proving damages has at least one important consequence. If two parties dispute ownership, they can resolve their dispute in an action for trespass to land, even though neither party can show actual damage. Moreover, the law of property provides that a trespasser can sometimes acquire legal rights in land if he is in "adverse possession" for a sufficient length of time. An action for trespass to land gives the actual owner the ability to cut off the trespasser's potential rights, even though the owner is not otherwise harmed by the trespass.

3. *Airplane overflights.* The court in *Amphitheaters* stated that reasonable overflight by aircraft constitutes a privileged entry. The court cited sections 158 and 159 of the First Restatement of Torts. Under the approach of the First Restatement, an overflight that was not reasonable was not privileged and, therefore, was an actionable trespass.

Section 159 of the Restatement (Second) of Torts provides that overflights into "the immediate reaches" above land constitute an entry. Under the approach of the Second Restatement, higher overflights do not constitute an entry and, therefore, do not require a privilege.

4. *The intent requirement.* Trespass to land is an intentional tort in the same sense that battery, assault, and false imprisonment are intentional torts. The plaintiff must prove that the defendant intended (i.e., desired or knew with a substantial certainty) that physical facts constituting an entry would be a result of the defendant's actions. A few older cases suggest that the defendant must merely intend an act that leads to an entry, but the overwhelming modern view is that the defendant must intend facts that constitute an entry. The defendant need not, however, know that the entry is wrongful, or even that it is an "entry." Thus, a defendant who intentionally enters land he mistakenly assumes he owns is liable for trespass to land.

MARTIN v. REYNOLDS METALS COMPANY

Supreme Court of Oregon, 1959.
221 Or. 86, 342 P.2d 790.

O'CONNELL, JUSTICE.

This is an action of trespass. The plaintiffs allege that during the period from August 22, 1951 to January 1, 1956 the defendant, in the operation of its aluminum reduction plant near Troutdale, Oregon caused certain fluoride compounds in the form of gases and particulates to become airborne and settle upon the plaintiffs' land rendering it unfit for raising livestock during that period. * * *

* * *

Through appropriate pleadings the defendant set up the two–year statute of limitations applicable to nontrespassory injuries to land (ORS 12.110). If the defendant's conduct created a nuisance and not a trespass the defendant would be liable only for such damage as resulted from its conduct during a period of two years immediately preceding the date upon which plaintiffs' action was instituted. On the other hand, if the defendant's conduct resulted in a trespass upon plaintiffs' land the six-year statute of limitations provided for in ORS 12.080 would be applicable and plaintiffs would be entitled to recover damages resulting from the trespasses by defendant during the period from August 22, 1951 to January 1, 1956. [The trial court allowed damages for the full period.]

The gist of the defendant's argument is as follows: a trespass arises only when there has been a "breaking and entering upon real property," constituting a direct, as distinguished from a consequential, invasion of the possessor's interest in land; and the settling upon the land of fluoride compounds consisting of gases, fumes and particulates is not sufficient to satisfy these requirements.

Before appraising the argument we shall first describe more particularly the physical and chemical nature of the substance which was deposited upon plaintiffs' land. In reducing alumina (the oxide of aluminum) to aluminum the alumina is subjected to an electrolytic process which causes the emanation of fluoridic compounds consisting principally of hydrogen fluoride, calcium fluoride, iron fluoride and silicon tetrafluoride. The individual particulates which form these chemical compounds are not visible to the naked eye. A part of them were captured by a fume collection system which was installed in November, 1950; the remainder became airborne and a part of the uncaptured particles eventually were deposited upon plaintiffs' land.

There is evidence to prove that during the period from August, 1951, to January, 1956 the emanation of fluorides from defendant's plant averaged approximately 800 pounds daily. Some of this discharge was deposited upon the plaintiffs' land. There is sufficient evidence to support the trial court's finding that the quantity of fluorides deposited upon the plaintiffs' land was great enough to cause $91,500 damage to the plaintiffs in the use of their land for grazing purposes and in the deterioration of their land as alleged.

* * *

Trespass and private nuisance are separate fields of tort liability relating to actionable interference with the possession of land. They may be distinguished by comparing the interest invaded; an actionable invasion of a possessor's interest in the exclusive possession of land is a trespass; an actionable invasion of a possessor's interest in the use and enjoyment of his land is a nuisance.

The same conduct on the part of a defendant may and often does result in the actionable invasion of both of these interests * * *. * * *

However, there are cases which have held that the defendant's interference with plaintiff's possession resulting from the settling upon his land of effluents emanating from defendant's operations is exclusively nontrespassory. Although in such cases the separate particles which collectively cause the invasion are minute, the deposit of each of the particles constitutes a physical intrusion and, but for the size of the particle, would clearly give rise to an action of trespass. The defendant asks us to take account of the difference in size of the physical agency through which the intrusion occurs and relegate entirely to the field of nuisance law certain invasions which do not meet the dimensional test, whatever that is. In pressing this argument upon us the defendant must admit that there are cases which have held that a trespass results from the movement or deposit of rather small objects over or upon the surface of the possessor's land.

Thus it has been held that causing shot from a gun to fall upon the possessor's land is a trespass.

The dropping of particles of molten lead upon the plaintiff's land has been held to be a trespass. And the defendant was held liable in trespass where spray from a cooling tower on the roof of its theater fell upon the plaintiff's land.

The deposit of soot and carbon from defendant's mill upon plaintiff's land was held to be a trespass * * *.

And liability on the theory of trespass has been recognized where the harm was produced by the vibration of the soil or by the concussion of the air which, of course, is nothing more than the movement of molecules one against the other. * * *

The view recognizing a trespassory invasion where there is no "thing" which can be seen with the naked eye undoubtedly runs counter to the definition of trespass expressed in some quarters. It is quite possible that in an earlier day when science had not yet peered into the molecular and atomic world of small particles, the courts could not fit an invasion through unseen physical instrumentalities into the requirement that a trespass can result only from a *direct* invasion. But in this atomic age even the uneducated know the great and awful force contained in the atom and what it can do to a man's property if it is released. In fact, the now famous equation $E = mc^2$ has taught us that mass and energy are equivalents and that our concept of "things" must be reframed. If these observations on science in relation to the law of trespass should appear theoretical and unreal in the abstract, they become very practical and real to the possessor of land when the unseen force cracks the foundation of his house. The force is just as real if it is chemical in nature and must be awakened by the intervention of another agency before it does harm.

If, then, we must look to the character of the instrumentality which is used in making an intrusion upon another's land we prefer to emphasize the object's energy or force rather than its size. Viewed in this way we may define trespass as any intrusion which invades the possessor's protected interest in exclusive possession, whether that intrusion is by visible or invisible pieces of matter or by energy which can be measured only by the mathematical language of the physicist.

We are of the opinion, therefore, that the intrusion of the fluoride particulates in the present case constituted a trespass.

The defendant argues that our decision in Amphitheaters, Inc. v. Portland Meadows requires a contrary conclusion. In discussing the distinction between trespass and nuisance the court referred to a difference between "a cannon ball and a ray of light" indicating that the former but not the latter could produce a trespassory invasion. The court also said "The mere suggestion that the casting of light upon the premises of a plaintiff would render a defendant liable without proof of any actual damage, carries its own refutation." We do not regard this statement as a pronouncement that a trespass can *never* be caused by the intrusion of light rays or other intangible forces; more properly the case may be interpreted as stating that the conduct of the defendant in a particular case may not be actionable if it does not violate a legally protected interest of the plaintiff. The court states that the defendant is not liable *without proof of actual damage*. In that case the plaintiff contended that he had suffered damage in the form of a less efficient cinema screen due to the defendant's lights. In denying recovery the court found that there was no damage, apparently because whatever harm the plaintiff suffered was damnum absque injuria.

* * *

The *Amphitheaters* case may also be viewed as a pronouncement that a possessor's interest is not invaded by an intrusion which is so trifling that it cannot be recognized by the law. Inasmuch as it is not necessary to prove actual damage in trespass the magnitude of the intrusion ordinarily would not be of any consequence. But there is a point where the entry is so lacking in substance that the law will refuse to recognize it, applying the maxim de minimis non curat lex. Thus it would seem clear that ordinarily the casting of a grain of sand upon another's land would not be a trespass. And so too the casting of diffused light rays upon another's land would not ordinarily constitute a trespass. Conceivably such rays could be so concentrated that their entry upon the possessor's land would result in a trespassory invasion. * * *

* * *

We think that a possessor's interest in land as defined by the considerations recited above may, under the appropriate circumstances, be violated by a ray of light, by an atomic particle, or by a particulate of fluoride and, contrariwise, if such interest circumscribed by these considerations is not violated or endangered, the defendant's conduct, even though it may result in a physical intrusion, will not render him liable in an action of trespass. Amphitheaters, Inc. v. Portland Meadows, supra.

We hold that the defendant's conduct in causing chemical substances to be deposited upon the plaintiffs' land fulfilled all of the requirements under the law of trespass.

The defendant [also] contends that trespass will not lie in this case because the injury was indirect and consequential and that the requirement that the injury must be direct and immediate to constitute a trespass was not met. We have held that the deposit of the particulates upon the plaintiff's land was an intrusion within the definition of trespass. That intrusion was direct. * * * The distinction between direct and indirect invasions where there has been a physical intrusion upon the plaintiff's land has been abandoned by some courts. Since the invasion in the instant case was direct it is not necessary for us to decide whether the distinction is recognized in this state.

* * *

The judgment of the lower court is affirmed.

McALLISTER, CHIEF JUSTICE (specially concurring):

I concur in the result of the above opinion but dissent from that portion thereof that attempts to reconcile the holding in this case with the holding in the case of Amphitheaters, Inc. v. Portland Meadows, 184 Or. 336, 198 P.2d 847.

Notes

1. *Direct vs. indirect entry.* As the court's opinion in *Martin* indicates, some older opinions held that an action for trespass to land could lie only if the defendant directly caused an entry. An indirect entry would not suffice. The prevailing modern view is that the plaintiff need not show a direct entry, as long as the defendant intended the entry.

An example of a case abandoning the directness requirement is Rushing v. Hooper–McDonald, Inc., 293 Ala. 56, 300 So.2d 94 (1974). The defendant dumped asphalt uphill and away from the plaintiff's land, knowing that some of the asphalt would seep downhill and pollute the plaintiff's pond. The court recognized that under the old rule in Alabama, the plaintiff could not recover for trespass to land because the defendant had not directly caused the asphalt to enter the plaintiff's land. The court also recognized, however, that the modern view is to abandon the distinction between direct and indirect entries, as long as the defendant intended the entry. The court held that the trial court erred in directing a verdict for the defendant.

2. *The writs of trespass quare clausem fregit and trespass on the case.* The direct–indirect issue arose from the system of writs or forms of action of the early common law. The early writ of trespass *quare clausem fregit* ("wherefore he broke the close") lay for invasions of real property. It originally required neither intent nor negligence nor harm, but it did require that the invasion be "direct." The later writ of trespass on the case covered indirect invasions, but it required intent or negligence plus harm. The modern tort of trespass to land differs from both: it requires an intended entry, which need not be harmful and which may be direct or indirect.

G. TRESPASS TO CHATTELS AND CONVERSION

PEARSON v. DODD

United States Court of Appeals, District of Columbia, 1969.
410 F.2d 701.

WRIGHT, CIRCUIT JUDGE.

This case arises out of the exposure of the alleged misdeeds of Senator Thomas Dodd of Connecticut by newspaper columnists Drew Pearson and Jack Anderson. The District Court has granted partial summary judgment to Senator Dodd, appellee here, finding liability on a theory of conversion. * * *

The undisputed facts in the case were stated by the District Court as follows:

> * * * [O]n several occasions in June and July, 1965, two former employees of the plaintiff, at times with the assistance of two members of the plaintiff's staff, entered the plaintiff's office without authority and unbeknownst to him, removed numerous documents from his files, made copies of them, replaced the originals, and turned over the copies to the defendant Anderson, who was aware of the manner in which the copies had been obtained. The defendants Pearson and Anderson thereafter published articles containing information gleaned from these documents.

* * *

The District Court ruled that appellants' receipt and subsequent use of photocopies of documents which appellants knew had been removed from appellee's files without authorization established appellants' liability for conversion. We conclude that appellants are not guilty of conversion on the facts shown.

* * *

Conversion is the substantive tort theory which underlay [or grew out of] the ancient common law form of action for trover. A plaintiff in trover alleged that he had lost a chattel which he rightfully possessed,[23] and that the defendant had found it and converted it to his own use. With time, the allegations of losing and finding became fictional, leaving the question of whether the defendant had "converted" the property the only operative one.

---

23. A threshold question, not briefed by either party and hence not decided by us, is the nature of the property right held by appellee in the contents of the files in his Senate office. Those files, themselves paid for by the United States, are maintained in an office owned by the United States, by employees of the United States. They are meant to contribute to the work of appellee as an officer of the United States. The question thus is not entirely free from doubt whether appellee has title to the contents of the files or has a right of exclusive possession of those contents, or is a bailee, or even a mere custodian of those contents.

The most distinctive feature of conversion is its measure of damages, which is the value of the goods converted. The theory is that the "converting" defendant has in some way treated the goods as if they were his own, so that the plaintiff can properly ask the court to decree a forced sale of the property from the rightful possessor to the converter. Because of this stringent measure of damages, it has long been recognized that not every wrongful interference with the personal property of another is a conversion. Where the intermeddling falls short of the complete or very substantial deprivation of possessory rights in the property, the tort committed is not conversion, but the lesser wrong of trespass to chattels.

* * *

The difference is more than a semantic one. The measure of damages in trespass is not the whole value of the property interfered with, but rather the actual diminution in its value caused by the interference. More important for this case, a judgment for conversion can be obtained with only nominal damages, whereas liability for trespass to chattels exists only on a showing of actual damage to the property interfered with.[32] Here the District Court granted partial summary judgment on the issue of liability alone, while conceding that possibly no more than nominal damages might be awarded on subsequent trial. Partial summary judgment for liability could not have been granted on a theory of trespass to chattels without an undisputed showing of actual damages to the property in question.

It is clear that on the agreed facts appellants committed no conversion of the physical documents taken from appellee's files. Those documents were removed from the files at night, photocopied, and returned to the files undamaged before office operations resumed in the morning. Insofar as the documents' value to appellee resided in their usefulness as records of the business of his office, appellee was clearly not substantially deprived of his use of them.

This of course is not an end of the matter. It has long been recognized that documents often have value above and beyond that springing from their physical possession. They may embody information or ideas whose economic value depends in part or in whole upon being kept secret. The question then arises whether the information taken by means of copying appellee's office files is of the type which the law of conversion protects. The general rule has been that ideas or information are not subject to legal protection, but the law has developed exceptions

---

32. "To support an action of trespass to a chattel where the invasion of interests does not result in its destruction or in a dispossession thereof, it was early held there must be some physical harm to the chattel or to its possessor. Unlike the action of trespass quare clausum fregit in the case of land, no action could be maintained for a mere harmless intermeddling with goods. The possessor's proprietary interest in the inviolability of his personal property did not receive that protection which the similar interest in the possession of land or the dignitary interest in the inviolability of the person receives. * * *" 1 F. Harper & F. James, supra Note 25, § 2.3. (Footnotes omitted.)

to this rule. Where information is gathered and arranged at some cost and sold as a commodity on the market, it is properly protected as property. Where ideas are formulated with labor and inventive genius, as in the case of literary works or scientific researches, they are protected. Where they constitute instruments of fair and effective commercial competition, those who develop them may gather their fruits under the protection of the law.

The question here is not whether appellee had a right to keep his files from prying eyes, but whether the information taken from those files falls under the protection of the law of property, enforceable by a suit for conversion. In our view, it does not. The information included the contents of letters to appellee from supplicants, and office records of other kinds, the nature of which is not fully revealed by the record. Insofar as we can tell, none of it amounts to literary property, to scientific invention, or to secret plans formulated by appellee for the conduct of commerce. Nor does it appear to be information held in any way for sale by appellee, analogous to the fresh news copy produced by a wire service.

Appellee complains, not of the misappropriation of property bought or created by him, but of the exposure of information either (1) injurious to his reputation or (2) revelatory of matters which he believes he has a right to keep to himself. Injuries of this type are redressed at law by suit for libel and invasion of privacy respectively, where defendants' liability for those torts can be established under the limitations created by common law and by the Constitution.

Because no conversion of the physical contents of appellee's files took place, and because the information copied from the documents in those files has not been shown to be property subject to protection by suit for conversion, the District Court's ruling that appellants are guilty of conversion must be reversed.

So ordered.

TAMM, CIRCUIT JUDGE, concurring.

Some legal scholars will see in the majority opinion—as distinguished from its actual holding—an ironic aspect. Conduct for which a law enforcement officer would be soundly castigated is, by the phraseology of the majority opinion, found tolerable; conduct which, if engaged in by government agents would lead to the suppression of evidence obtained by these means, is approved when used for the profit of the press. There is an anomaly lurking in this situation: the news media regard themselves as quasi–public institutions yet they demand immunity from the restraints which they vigorously demand be placed on government. That which is regarded as a mortal taint on information secured by any illegal conduct of government would appear from the majority opinion to be permissible as a technique or modus operandi for the journalist. Some will find this confusing, but I am not free to act on my own views under the doctrine of stare decisis which I consider binding upon me.

* * *

Notes

1. Dodd also sued for invasion of privacy, a tort that is not addressed in this book. His argument had two prongs. First, he argued that the publication of private information invaded his privacy. This theory is usually called "publication of private facts." The court held that the information published "was of obvious public interest," which constitutes a privilege.

Second, Dodd argued that the defendants had physically "intruded" into his private space. The court held that whereas the two former employees might have been liable for intrusion, Pearson and Anderson were not. They merely received the fruits of the intrusion after the fact. Similarly, Dodd might have argued that the defendants were liable for trespass to land. Presumably, the court would have concluded that whereas the two former employees might have been trespassers, Pearson and Anderson were not.

2. With respect to the conversion claim, the court apparently assumes that had a conversion occurred, Anderson and Pearson could be liable, despite their lack of personal participation in the removal of information from Dodd's files. Section 229 of the Restatement (Second) of Torts states the rule that one who receives converted property from another may also be liable for conversion:

> One who receives possession of a chattel from another with the intent to acquire for himself or a third person a proprietary interest in the chattel which the other has not the power to transfer is subject to liability for conversion to a third person then entitled to immediate possession of the chattel.

According to this well–established doctrine, if A steals a bicycle from B and C innocently buys it at A's garage sale, C is subject to liability to B for conversion. Of course, C may seek indemnity from A on A's implied warranty of title. But if A is insolvent or has vanished, C nevertheless owes B return or full value of the bicycle.

3. *Conversion vs. trespass to chattels*. The difference between trespass to chattels and conversion is one of degree. Trespass to chattels involves a less substantial interference. Conversion involves a more substantial interference, such as outright destruction or long term interference with use. The remedy for trespass to chattels is damages for repairs, loss of use, and incidental damages. The remedy for conversion is fair market value of the chattel, plus incidental damages. The dividing line between the two torts often depends on the court's evaluation of whether one remedy or the other is more appropriate. For example, if a plaintiff whose car is stolen "covers"—that is, buys a new car—returning the car and paying damages for loss of use is not a very effective remedy.

4. For both trespass to chattels and conversion, the plaintiff must prove that the defendant intended the interference with the chattel.

H. DEFENSES

If the plaintiff makes out a prima facie case for battery, assault, false imprisonment, trespass to land, trespass to chattels, or conversion, the defendant can still escape liability by establishing one of several defenses. Normally, the defendant has the burden of proof on these defenses.*

Most of the defenses addressed in this section are applicable to each of the six torts listed above, that is, they negate liability for conduct that would otherwise have constituted one of the six torts. (An exception, discussed in more detail below, is the privilege of necessity.) Nevertheless, most of the best treatments of the defenses happen to be battery cases. As you go through the material, you should realize that the defense under consideration would usually also be a defense to the other intentional torts.

1. CONSENT

O'BRIEN v. CUNARD S.S. CO.

Supreme Judicial Court of Massachusetts, 1891.
154 Mass. 272, 28 N.E. 266.

KNOWLTON, JUSTICE.

[The plaintiff sued the defendant for battery and negligence for injuries arising out of a vaccination she received on one of the defendant's ships. The trial court directed a verdict for the defendant. The plaintiff appealed.]

This case presents two questions: First, whether there was any evidence to warrant the jury in finding that the defendant, by any of its servants or agents, committed an assault on the plaintiff; secondly, whether there was evidence on which the jury could have found that the defendant was guilty of negligence towards the plaintiff. To sustain [her action for "assault"], the plaintiff relied on the fact that the surgeon who was employed by the defendant vaccinated her on shipboard, while she was on her passage from Queenstown to Boston. On this branch of the case the question is whether there was any evidence that the surgeon used force upon the plaintiff against her will. In determining whether the act was lawful or unlawful, the surgeon's conduct must be considered in connection with the surrounding circumstances. If the plaintiff's behavior was such as to indicate consent on her part, he was justified in his act, whatever her unexpressed feelings may have been. In determining whether she consented, he could be guided only by her overt acts and

---

* "Students are sometimes confused on one point. To say that the defendant has the burden of proving an affirmative defense * * * is not to say that the evidence on that topic must originate with the defendant. The plaintiff's own evidence or admissions may suffice * * *. To say that the defendant has the burden is to say that the defendant will be the party to suffer if the evidence is not forthcoming, so that the defendant must be sure that, from whatever source, evidence on the issue does in fact appear." Dobbs, The Law of Torts § 198, p. 493 (2000).

the manifestations of her feelings. It is undisputed that at Boston there are strict quarantine regulations in regard to the examination of [immigrants] to see that they are protected from small–pox by vaccination, and that only those persons who hold a certificate from the medical officer of the steam–ship, stating that they are so protected, are permitted to land without detention in quarantine, or vaccination by the port physician. It appears that the defendant is accustomed to have its surgeons vaccinate all [immigrants] who desire it, and who are not protected by previous vaccination, and give them a certificate which is accepted at quarantine as evidence of their protection. Notices of the regulations at quarantine, and of the willingness of the ship's medical officer to vaccinate such as needed vaccination, were posted about the ship in various languages, and on the day when the operation was performed the surgeon had a right to presume that she and the other women who were vaccinated understood the importance and purpose of vaccination for those who bore no marks to show that they were protected. By the plaintiff's testimony, which, in this particular, is undisputed, it appears that about 200 women passengers were assembled below, and she understood from conversation with them that they were to be vaccinated; that she stood about 15 feet from the surgeon, and saw them form in a line, and pass in turn before him; that he "examined their arms, and, passing some of them by, proceeded to vaccinate those that had no mark;" that she did not hear him say anything to any of them; that upon being passed by they each received a card, and went on deck; that when her turn came she showed him her arm; he looked at it, and said there was no mark, and that she should be vaccinated; that she told him she had been vaccinated before, and it left no mark; "that he then said nothing; that he should vaccinate her again;" that she held up her arm to be vaccinated; that no one touched her; that she did not tell him she did not want to be vaccinated; and that she took the ticket which he gave her, certifying that he had vaccinated her, and used it at quarantine. She was one of a large number of women who were vaccinated on that occasion, without, so far as appears, a word of objection from any of them. They all indicated by their conduct that they desired to avail themselves of the provisions made for their benefit. There was nothing in the conduct of the plaintiff to indicate to the surgeon that she did not wish to obtain a card which would save her from detention at quarantine, and to be vaccinated, if necessary, for that purpose. Viewing his conduct in the light of the surrounding circumstances, it was lawful; and there was no evidence tending to show that it was not. The ruling of the court on this part of the case was correct. * * *

[The court further held that the defendant was not liable for negligence.]

Exceptions overruled.

Notes

1. In addition to being a defense, consent has a considerable effect on the prima facie case. For example, consent can negate the offensiveness of a touching, and it can negate a confinement.

2. Most courts consider consent to be a "defense" that the defendant must plead and prove. A few courts, however, define the prima facie case for some intentional torts as an *unconsented* invasion of the particular interest.

OVERALL v. KADELLA

Court of Appeals of Michigan, 1984.
138 Mich.App. 351, 361 N.W.2d 352.

PER CURIAM.

On April 17, 1975, two amateur hockey teams, the Waterford Lakers and the Clarkston Flyers, played each other in a hockey game. After the game had ended, a fight broke out between defendant, who played for the Flyers, and a member of the opposing team. This fight soon became general, with players leaving the benches to join the melee. During the fight, defendant struck plaintiff, knocking him unconscious and fracturing the bones around plaintiff's right eye.

At trial, defendant stated that he had gone to shake hands with the opposing team after the game when he was struck from behind. Both benches cleared and a scuffle ensued, during which defendant stated he saw a hockey stick coming toward his head. Defendant testified that he was hit several times before he turned around and hit the person swinging the stick. He did not know plaintiff had been injured by the blow and, in fact, did not know whom he had struck until much later. Three witnesses testifying on behalf of defendant stated that plaintiff remained on the bench during the fight, but poked or hit defendant with a hockey stick during the fight. They all saw defendant retaliate by turning and throwing one punch.

Plaintiff's testimony and that of two spectators at the game differed from this testimony in significant respects. According to these witnesses, plaintiff remained on the bench even after all other players had joined the fray. The bench was well removed from the fighting and plaintiff did not poke or hit anyone with a hockey stick. Defendant skated over to the bench and struck plaintiff who had done nothing to provoke the attack. Defendant then skated away.

The hockey referees at the game testified that defendant had engaged in at least three separate fights after the game was over. He was given three game misconducts because fighting is against the rules of the Michigan Amateur Hockey Association. These rules are designed to stop violence. The bench is considered part of the playing field. One of the referees saw plaintiff poke defendant with a hockey stick to get defendant's attention and then saw defendant attack plaintiff by striking him.

At the conclusion of the bench trial, the district court found that "without provocation the Defendant in the heat of his battles swung his hockey stick at the Plaintiff who was off the field of play and not engaged in the fight and struck him on the right side resulting in the injuries of which he complained." The court also found that plaintiff had suffered damages of $21,000 for out–of–pocket expenses, pain and suffering, and permanent injury, and awarded an additional $25,000 as exemplary damages because defendant's act had been "intentional and malicious."

* * *

Defendant's last objection is to the court's finding that defendant struck plaintiff with a hockey stick. We find, and plaintiff concedes, that this statement is clearly erroneous as there was no evidence that defendant used anything but his fist in striking plaintiff. However, this erroneous finding is harmless as it is clear that the court properly found that a battery was committed.

Defendant's next contention is that plaintiff may not sue for an injury incurred while plaintiff was voluntarily participating in a hockey game. This argument is expressed in the phrase, "*volenti non fit injuria*," or "he who consents cannot receive an injury."

Participation in a game involves a manifestation of consent to those bodily contacts which are permitted by the rules of the game. However, there is general agreement that an intentional act causing injury, which goes beyond what is ordinarily permissible, is an assault and battery for which recovery may be had.

In Nabozny v. Barnhill, 31 Ill.App.3d 212, 334 N.E.2d 258 (1975), a player in an amateur soccer match kicked the opposing goalkeeper in the head while the goalkeeper was in possession of the ball in the penalty area. This act directly violated the safety rules of the game. In deciding whether or not the goalkeeper could bring a tort action against the soccer player, the *Nabozny* Court held that a player is charged with a legal duty to every other player to refrain from conduct proscribed by a safety rule. The Court then rejected the defendant's contention that there should be tort immunity for any injury to another player that occurs during the course of a game:

> This court believes that the law should not place unreasonable burdens on the free and vigorous participation in sports by our youth. However, we also believe that organized, athletic competition does not exist in a vacuum. Rather, some of the restraints of civilization must accompany every athlete onto the playing field.
> * * *

* * *

It is our opinion that a player is liable for injury in a tort action if his conduct is such that it is either deliberate, wilful or with a reckless disregard for the safety of the other player so as to cause injury to that player, the same being a question of fact to be decided by a jury.

Other cases have also held that the violation of safety rules during a game gives rise to tort liability. In Griggas v. Clauson, 6 Ill.App.2d 412, 128 N.E.2d 363 (1955), a player who intentionally struck an opposing player during a basketball game was found liable, and, in Bourque v.

Duplechin, 331 So.2d 40 (La.App.1976), liability was found where a baserunner in a softball game dove into the second baseman five feet from the base and struck him with his forearm in order to break up a double play. We agree with these Courts that liability may be found on such facts. In this case, defendant's own witness testified that the rule against fighting in hockey is designed to stop violence. Defendant's intentional battery certainly violated this rule. In addition, under the facts found by the trial court, it is arguable that the battery did not even occur during the hockey game. It is therefore doubtful whether consent to a battery during a game would constitute consent to a battery after the game.

Defendant also argues that he was merely exercising his right of self–defense by striking back at the person who was hitting him with a hockey stick. The trial court rejected this contention after concluding that plaintiff had not had a hockey stick and that, even if he had had one, the area of the fight was beyond plaintiff's reach. We do not find this conclusion to be clearly erroneous.

Affirmed.

Notes

1. Many sports involve contacts that may be injurious. By entering the field of play, a player obviously manifests consent to many contacts, but just as obviously does not manifest consent to all imaginable contacts. If the contact in question was accidental, it is governed by the law of negligence, which generally absolves the defendant by holding that the plaintiff is not owed a duty of reasonable care in the play but only a duty to refrain from "willful" misconduct. If the contact was intentional, the issue is whether it was outside the boundaries of the implied consent. As the *Overall* opinion indicates, an intentional contact that violates a rule of the game designed to protect the players' safety will generally be beyond the consent. A violation of a non–safety rule is generally considered irrelevant. Hence, in football, a personal foul or an intentional roughing of a kicker may be an actionable battery; a normal block by a player who was off sides will not.

2. Analyzing a battery claim arising from a fight requires, first, distinguishing three situations: fighting for sport, e.g., a boxing match; consensual fighting in anger ("Let's settle this outside."); and unconsented attack met with self–defense. The first situation is governed by the usual principles of sports cases. The third is governed by the self–defense privilege, considered in Subsection 2, infra. In the second situation, American courts are divided. Some courts, often said to be the majority, reason rather formalistically that the consent is legally void, since such a fight is a breach of the peace that constitutes a crime (misdemeanor) on the part of each participant. Under this view, therefore, either combatant can recover in battery despite the consent. Other courts uphold the consent defense. The latter view is endorsed by section 60 of the Restatement (Second) of Torts.

HOGAN v. TAVZEL

District Court of Appeal of Florida, Fifth District, 1995.
660 So.2d 350, review denied, 666 So.2d 901 (Fla.1996).

SHARP, JUDGE.

* * *

Hogan and Tavzel were married for fifteen years but encountered marital problems which caused them to separate. During a period of attempted reconciliation between October of 1989 and January 1990, Tavzel infected Hogan with genital warts. He knew of his condition but failed to warn Hogan or take any precaution against infecting her. The parties were divorced on May 8, 1990. Hogan brought this suit in 1993.
* * *

Tavzel moved to dismiss. The trial court * * * dismissed the battery count because he found that consensual sexual intercourse fails as a matter of law to establish the element of unconsented to touching which is required to sustain the tort of battery. * * *

* * *

We next turn our attention to dismissal of the battery count. Since this is a case of first impression in Florida, it is appropriate to look to other jurisdictions for guidance. A case similar to the one presented here is Kathleen K. v. Robert B., 150 Cal.App.3d 992, 198 Cal.Rptr. 273 (Cal.2d Dist.1984). There, a cause of action in battery was approved when one partner contracted genital herpes from the other partner. The facts indicated that the infecting partner had represented he was free from any sexually infectious disease, and the infected partner would not have engaged in sexual relations if she had been aware of the risk of infection. The court held that one party's consent to sexual intercourse is vitiated by the partner's fraudulent concealment of the risk of infection with venereal disease (whether or not the partners are married to each other). This is not a new theory. *See,* De Vall v. Strunk, 96 S.W.2d 245 (Tx.App.1936); Crowell v. Crowell, 180 N.C. 516, 105 S.E. 206 (1920).

The *Kathleen K.* court recognized that

> [a] certain amount of trust and confidence exists in any intimate relationship, at least to the extent that one sexual partner represents to the other that he or she is free from venereal or other dangerous contagious disease.

Kathleen K. at 150 Cal.App.3d 996, 198 Cal.Rptr. 273. See also S.S. v. State Farm & Casualty Co., 808 S.W.2d 668, 671 (Tx.App.1991), affirmed, 858 S.W.2d 374 (Tx.1993) (no disagreement with theory in *Kathleen K.* that cause of action for intentional tort exists where person fails to disclose a herpes infection before engaging in sexual intercourse).[3] See generally Braun v. Flynt, 726 F.2d 245, 255 (5th Cir.1984) (fraudulently induced consent is the equivalent of no consent).

The Restatement of Torts Second (1977) also takes the view that consent to sexual intercourse is not the equivalent of consent to be infected with a venereal disease. Specifically, it provides the following example:

> A consents to sexual intercourse with B, who knows that A is ignorant of the fact that B has a venereal disease. B is subject to liability to A for battery.

Illus. 5 § 892B. Other authorities also conclude that a cause of action in battery will lie, and consent will be ineffective, if the consenting person was mistaken about the nature and quality of the invasion intended. See, Prosser and Keeton, n. 105, § 18 at 119–20; 1986 U.Il.L.Rev. 779 Paul Murray & Brenda J. Winslett, "The Constitutional Right to Privacy and Emerging Tort Liability for Deceit in Interpersonal Relationships."

We see no reason, should the facts support it, that a tortfeasor could not be held liable for battery for infecting another with a sexually transmissible disease in Florida. In so holding, we align ourselves with the well established, majority view which permits lawsuits for sexually transmitted diseases. Hogan's consent, if without the knowledge that Tavzel was infected with a sexually transmitted disease, was the equivalent of no consent, and would not be a defense to the battery charge if successfully proven.

Reversed and remanded.

NEAL v. NEAL

Court of Appeals of Idaho, 1993.
125 Idaho 627, 873 P.2d 881, reversed, 125 Idaho 617, 873 P.2d 871 (1994).

WALTERS, CHIEF JUDGE.

This is an appeal from an order dismissing a wife's action for damages allegedly suffered as a result of the adulterous relationship between her husband and his mistress. * * *

For purposes of this review, we deem the following facts to be true. Thomas and Mary Neal were married in 1984. They had one child. In 1988, the couple moved to Boise where Thomas, a licensed physician, took a residency at a local medical clinic. His work also took him to Spokane, Washington, the home of Jill LaGasse. In November of 1988,

---

3. The issue of consent was discussed in depth in 1986 U.Il.L.Rev. 779 Paul Murray & Brenda J. Winslett, "The Constitutional Right to Privacy and Emerging Tort Liability for Deceit in Interpersonal Relationships." One must give *knowing* consent for it to be an effective legal defense; consent is vitiated if it is procured by fraud or concealment. Id. at 793. As noted:

One may also commit a battery in the case of consensual sexual [intercourse] as to the nature of the contact. An action for battery lies in the herpes transmission cases, for example, since *consent to sexual intercourse cannot be equated with consent to infection with a 'vile and loathsome' disease.* (id. at 809; emphasis supplied.)

Thomas and LaGasse began an extra–marital affair which they kept secret from Mary for approximately five months. During this time Thomas engaged in sexual intercourse with Mary and also with LaGasse. Mary did not discover the affair until the spring of 1989, when she confronted Thomas with her suspicions. Thomas admitted the relationship and advised he wanted a divorce.

In 1990, Thomas filed an action for divorce * * *. [Among Mary's responses were counterclaims on various tort theories, including battery. The husband was awarded summary judgment on the tort claims.]

* * *

* * * A civil battery consists of any intentional, unpermitted contact upon the person of another, which is either unlawful, harmful, or offensive. See White v. University of Idaho, 118 Idaho 400, 797 P.2d 108 (1990); W. Prosser and W. Keeton, The Law of Torts § 9 at 41 (5th ed. 1984). Lack of consent to the particular contact is an essential element of battery. Prosser & Keeton, supra, § 9, at 41 and § 18, at 112. The critical inquiry here is whether Mary has alleged facts sufficient to show that there was an absence of effective consent by her to engage in sexual intercourse with Thomas. Mary asserts that although she consented to sexual intercourse with her husband, Thomas, at the time, she would not have done so had she known he was sexually involved with another woman. Therefore, she argues, Thomas' failure to disclose the fact of his extra–marital affair rendered her consent ineffective, and subjected him to liability for battery. We disagree.

Where a person's consent to physical contact is given based upon a substantial mistake, known to or induced by the actor, concerning the nature of the contact itself or the extent of the harm to be expected therefrom, the consent is deemed to be ineffective, and the actor may be held liable as if no consent had been given. See Restatement (Second) of Torts § 57 (1965); Restatement (Second) of Torts § 892B(2) (1979). For this rule to apply, however, the mistake must extend to the essential character of the act itself, rather than to some collateral matter which merely operates as an inducement. See Prosser and Keeton, supra, § 18, at 120. "This is true, in general, whenever the other has given his consent with full understanding of the conduct, the invasion of his interests and the harm expected to follow, but has done so because of a mistake concerning some other reason for consenting." Restatement, supra, § 892B(2) comment g.

In this case, we conclude that Thomas' failure to disclose his relationship with Jill LaGasse did not invalidate Mary's consent to engage in sexual intercourse with him. Although Thomas deceived Mary as to the exclusivity of their relationship—a factor arguably[14] bearing upon her consent to sexual intercourse with him—it did not directly or substantially relate to the essential nature of the physical contact she

14. The record reveals that after Mary discovered Thomas' extra-marital affair, she consented to sexual intercourse with him on at least one occasion.

consented to. Thus, Mary's misapprehension concerning Thomas' sexual fidelity did not operate to invalidate her consent to engage in sexual intercourse with him. Accordingly, we hold that Mary's allegations are insufficient to establish lack of consent. Her claim for battery, therefore, was properly dismissed.

* * *

Notes

1. *The "essential" versus "collateral" distinction.* Freedman v. Superior Court, 214 Cal.App.3d 734, 263 Cal.Rptr. 1 (1989), held that a physician attending a woman during a difficult childbirth did not commit an actionable battery when he persuaded her to accept the administration of Pitocin, a labor-inducing drug, by misrepresenting that the drug would not induce labor but only prevent infection. The court provided the following summary of the controlling law:

> [A] distinction [is] made in legal texts as to the varying kinds of misrepresentations which can give rise to mistaken consent. To vitiate consent the mistake must extend to the essential character of the act itself, which is to say that which makes it harmful or offensive, rather than to some collateral matter which merely operates as an inducement. The illuminating example given in the texts is that of the seduction of the voice pupil by the choirmaster upon the representation that it would improve her voice; as compared to the seduction of a woman by the false promise of marriage. In the first instance the physical contact is a battery because the essential character of the act has been misrepresented—it is not an exercise for voice improvement but for the personal gratification of the seducer. In the second case both parties know the essential character of the act, and the inducement which gains the consent relates to a collateral matter: marriage. (263 Cal.Rptr. at 3; citations and internal quotation marks omitted.)

The choirmaster example is based on The King v. Williams, [1923] 1 K.B. 340 (English Court of Criminal Appeal 1922), which upheld the choirmaster's rape conviction. One of the authorities cited in *Freedman* was Rains v. Superior Court, 150 Cal.App.3d 933, 198 Cal.Rptr. 249 (1984), which held that psychiatrists committed actionable batteries when they induced their patients to accept beatings by misrepresenting that it was a beneficial form of "sluggo therapy."

2. The Supreme Court of Idaho granted review in Neal v. Neal and reversed the dismissal of the battery count, holding that "Mary Neal's affidavit [stating that had she known about her husband's affair with LaGasse she would not have consented to intercourse with him and to do so would have been offensive] at least raises a genuine issue of material fact as to whether there was indeed consent to the alleged act of battery," because "Mary Neal may have engaged in a sexual act based upon a substantial mistake concerning the nature of the contact or the harm to be expected from it." Neal v. Neal, 125 Idaho 617, 873 P.2d 871, 877 (1994).

Which Idaho court was right?

3. Consent may also be rendered ineffective if it was coerced or if the party was incapacitated on account of infancy, mental incompetency, or intoxication.

2. SELF–DEFENSE AND DEFENSE OF OTHERS

TATMAN v. CORDINGLY

Supreme Court of Wyoming, 1983.
672 P.2d 1286.

BROWN, JUSTICE.

E. Ben Tatman, appellant, sued Gary L. Cordingly, appellee, for assault and battery after the two had an altercation. Judgment was entered pursuant to a jury verdict finding that Cordingly acted out of self–defense. Tatman appeals the judgment on the grounds of faulty jury instructions and lack of sufficient evidence to support the verdict.

* * *

There was a dispute between Tatman and Cordingly. This dispute precipitated a confrontation on June 1, 1982, in Albany County near the Old Fort Fetterman Road, miles from the nearest town. Tatman was 66 years old at the time of the incident, Cordingly in his early 20's. As a result of the fight that occurred Tatman was hospitalized for eight days and incurred substantial medical expenses. There were no witnesses to the scuffle other than the parties themselves, and they disagree as to the details. Both parties contend that the other was the aggressor.

* * *

In this case, judgment was entered on a jury verdict finding that Tatman committed a battery and Cordingly exercised reasonable self–defense. The jury was certainly entitled to believe Cordingly's testimony and find in his favor. There was evidence that Tatman had a bad temper, that he carried a gun and used it often, that he ran over Cordingly's motorcycle with his pickup truck, that Tatman struck Cordingly first, that Tatman was repeatedly trying to get to his rifle and that Cordingly feared for his life. From our review of the record, we find sufficient evidence for the jury to decide as they did.

* * *

The appellant contends that the trial court erred in refusing * * * [the] portion of plaintiff's proposed Instruction 3 [that] reads:

> * * * Thus, even acting in self–defense, a person may be liable for injury inflicted upon the aggressor. That is the case when the defender is not justified in his belief that he was in danger, or when the defender uses excessive force, or when the defender continues to exert force after the aggressor is rendered disarmed or helpless.

This instruction is an accurate statement of Wyoming law on self–defense and its limits. The trial judge did, however, properly instruct the jury on these matters. The court gave jury Instructions 7, 8, and 9 which read:

INSTRUCTION NO. 7

When it is apparent to a person that he is threatened with a battery, he has the right to determine from appearances and the circumstances then existing the necessity of resorting to force to repel any such apparent, threatened battery, and he has the right to do what seems reasonably necessary to protect himself against any such apparent, threatened attack, whether it is real or not, provided he believes it to be real.

INSTRUCTION NO. 8

The defendant however is not liable to the plaintiff on his claim of battery if the affirmative defense of self–defense of a person is established. This defense is established if you find both of the following:

1. The defendant honestly and reasonably believed (although perhaps mistakenly) that under the circumstances it was necessary for him to use force to protect himself against an actual or apparent threatened harmful contact; and

2. The defendant used no more force than a reasonably prudent person would have used under the same or similar circumstances to protect himself against the actual or apparent threatened contact.

INSTRUCTION NO. 9

A person who is battered by another has the privilege of self–defense, but that privilege ends when the aggressor is disarmed or helpless, or when all the danger has clearly passed.

Instructions 8 and 9 adequately cover the issue of self–defense and where the privilege of self–defense ends. It was not necessary for the court to duplicate these instructions by giving plaintiff's proposed Instruction 3 in full.

Instruction 7, however, does not fully state the law in regard to the apparent necessity for acting in self–defense. According to Prosser [§ 19, p. 109 (4th Ed. 1971)]:

The privilege to act in self–defense arises, not only where there is real danger, but also where there is a reasonable belief that it exists. * * *

The belief must, however, be one which a reasonable man would have entertained under the circumstances. * * * [I]t is not enough that he really believes that he is about to be attacked, unless he has some reasonable ground for the belief. * * *

* * *

Therefore, the standard to be applied in determining if there is the apparent necessity to act in self-defense is both subjective and objective. Not only must a person believe that a real danger exists, but that belief must also be reasonable. In the court's Instruction 7, a subjective standard is set out but the objective, "reasonable," standard is missing. * * *

This incomplete instruction is not reversible error. When the instructions given by the court are viewed in their entirety, a true and accurate representation of the law is given. Instruction 8 requires that the jury find both a subjective and an objective belief by the defendant that it was necessary for him to protect himself. Appellant has not established any prejudice as a result of this incomplete instruction or that a different result would have occurred had another instruction been given. We find that the error was harmless.

* * *

There was sufficient evidence in the record to support the verdict reached by the jury. The instructions given by the court adequately represented the law of self-defense and its limits. * * *

We affirm.

Notes

1. *Self defense vs. retaliation.* Self-defense can be asserted only to prevent or resist an attack, not to retaliate. In Coleman v. Moore, 426 So.2d 652 (La.App.1982), the defendant shot the plaintiff in the buttocks as the plaintiff was leaving the fray. The court held that the defendant could not successfully claim self-defense, even though the plaintiff had been the original aggressor.

2. A person exercising the privilege of self-defense can use only that amount of force that he reasonably believes is necessary to prevent the attack. If he uses excessive force he is liable for the excess but does not lose the privilege altogether.

3. *Deadly force.* A person can use deadly force only if he reasonably believes that doing so is necessary to resist an attack of deadly force. Even if the attack is one of deadly force, however, the person being attacked cannot use more force than he reasonably believes is necessary to prevent the attack.

4. *Retreat, or stand and fight?* Most courts permit a defender to stand and fight, as long as the defender is using non-deadly force. Deadly force may not be used if a completely safe retreat is available, but one defending himself against deadly force may stand and kill if he has any reasonable doubt as to the safety of retreat. Even when a safe retreat is available, a defender threatened with deadly force need not flee from his home or place of business prior to using deadly force.

5. *The breadth of the self-defense privilege.* Self-defense can be asserted as a privilege for conduct that would otherwise be an actionable battery, assault, false imprisonment, intentional infliction of emotional distress, trespass to land, trespass to chattels, or conversion.

6. *What can the self-defender defend against?* The privilege can be used to prevent a battery, assault, false imprisonment, negligently caused bodily injury, or even bodily injury innocently caused or threatened by the person against whom the privilege is asserted.

7. *Defense of others.* At early common law, courts were reluctant to recognize a privilege to use force to defend others, possibly on the ground that people should not meddle in other people's affairs. An early relaxation of this position permitted individuals to use force to defend members of their family. Now, all American jurisdictions recognize a privilege to use force to protect others from attack, without limiting the privilege to family members.

Some courts still suggest that, unlike self-defense, the privilege of defense of others cannot be based on an erroneous but reasonable belief that force is necessary. Under this view, the person exercising the privilege must be correct. Most courts, however, require only that the person exercising the privilege act on a reasonable belief that force is necessary.

3. DEFENSE OF PROPERTY

KATKO v. BRINEY

Supreme Court of Iowa, 1971.
183 N.W.2d 657.

MOORE, CHIEF JUSTICE.

The primary issue presented here is whether an owner may protect personal property in an unoccupied boarded-up farm house against trespassers and thieves by a spring gun capable of inflicting death or serious injury.

We are not here concerned with a man's right to protect his home and members of his family. Defendants' home was several miles from the scene of the incident to which we refer infra.

Plaintiff's action is for damages resulting from serious injury caused by a shot from a 20-gauge spring shotgun set by defendants in a bedroom of an old farm house which had been uninhabited for several years. Plaintiff and his companion, Marvin McDonough, had broken and entered the house to find and steal old bottles and dated fruit jars which they considered antiques.

At defendants' request plaintiff's action was tried to a jury consisting of residents of the community where defendants' property was located. The jury returned a verdict for plaintiff and against defendants for $20,000 actual and $10,000 punitive damages.

After careful consideration of defendants' motions for judgment notwithstanding the verdict and for new trial, the experienced and capable trial judge overruled them and entered judgment on the verdict. Thus we have this appeal by defendants.

* * *

* * * Most of the facts are not disputed. In 1957 defendant Bertha L. Briney inherited her parents' farm land in Mahaska and Monroe Counties. Included was an 80–acre tract in southwest Mahaska County where her grandparents and parents had lived. No one occupied the house thereafter. Her husband, Edward, attempted to care for the land. He kept no farm machinery thereon. The outbuildings became dilapidated.

For about 10 years, 1957 to 1967, there occurred a series of trespassing and housebreaking events with loss of some household items, the breaking of windows and "messing up of the property in general." The latest occurred June 8, 1967, prior to the event on July 16, 1967 herein involved.

Defendants through the years boarded up the windows and doors in an attempt to stop the intrusions. They had posted "no trespass" signs on the land several years before 1967. The nearest one was 35 feet from the house. On June 11, 1967 defendants set "a shotgun trap" in the north bedroom. After Mr. Briney cleaned and oiled his 20–gauge shotgun, the power of which he was well aware, defendants took it to the old house where they secured it to an iron bed with the barrel pointed at the bedroom door. It was rigged with wire from the doorknob to the gun's trigger so it would fire when the door was opened. Briney first pointed the gun so an intruder would be hit in the stomach but at Mrs. Briney's suggestion it was lowered to hit the legs. He admitted he did so "because I was mad and tired of being tormented" but "he did not intend to injure anyone." He gave no explanation of why he used a loaded shell and set it to hit a person already in the house. Tin was nailed over the bedroom window. The spring gun could not be seen from the outside. No warning of its presence was posted.

Plaintiff lived with his wife and worked regularly as a gasoline station attendant in Eddyville, seven miles from the old house. He had observed it for several years while hunting in the area and considered it as being abandoned. He knew it had long been uninhabited. In 1967 the area around the house was covered with high weeds. Prior to July 16, 1967 plaintiff and McDonough had been to the premises and found several old bottles and fruit jars which they took and added to their collection of antiques. On the latter date about 9:30 p.m. they made a second trip to the Briney property. They entered the old house by removing a board from a porch window which was without glass. While McDonough was looking around the kitchen area plaintiff went to another part of the house. As he started to open the north bedroom door the shotgun went off striking him in the right leg above the ankle bone. Much of his leg, including part of the tibia, was blown away. Only by McDonough's assistance was plaintiff able to get out of the house and after crawling some distance was put in his vehicle and rushed to a doctor and then to a hospital. He remained in the hospital 40 days.

* * *

* * * Plaintiff testified he knew he had no right to break and enter the house with intent to steal bottles and fruit jars therefrom. He further testified he had entered a plea of guilty to larceny in the nighttime of property of less than $20 value from a private building. He stated he had been fined $50 and costs and paroled during good behavior from a 60–day jail sentence. * * *

* * * The main thrust of defendants' defense in the trial court and on this appeal is that "the law permits use of a spring gun in a dwelling or warehouse for the purpose of preventing the unlawful entry of a burglar or thief." They repeated this contention in their exceptions to the trial court's instructions 2, 5 and 6. They took no exception to the trial court's statement of the issues or to other instructions.

In the statement of issues the trial court stated plaintiff and his companion committed a felony when they broke and entered defendants' house. In instruction 2 the court referred to the early case history of the use of spring guns and stated under the law their use was prohibited except to prevent the commission of felonies of violence and where human life is in danger. The instruction included a statement breaking and entering is not a felony of violence.

Instruction 5 stated: "You are hereby instructed that one may use reasonable force in the protection of his property, but such right is subject to the qualification that one may not use such means of force as will take human life or inflict great bodily injury. Such is the rule even though the injured party is a trespasser and is in violation of the law himself."

Instruction 6 stated: "An owner of premises is prohibited from willfully or intentionally injuring a trespasser by means of force that either takes life or inflicts great bodily injury; and therefore a person owning a premise is prohibited from setting out 'spring guns' and like dangerous devices which will likely take life or inflict great bodily injury, for the purpose of harming trespassers. The fact that the trespasser may be acting in violation of the law does not change the rule. The only time when such conduct of setting a 'spring gun' or a like dangerous device is justified would be when the trespasser was committing a felony of violence or a felony punishable by death, or where the trespasser was endangering human life by his act."

* * *

The overwhelming weight of authority, both textbook and case law, supports the trial court's statement of the applicable principles of law.

Prosser on Torts, Third Edition, pages 116–118, states:

* * * the law has always placed a higher value upon human safety than upon mere rights in property, it is the accepted rule that there is no privilege to use any force calculated to cause death or serious bodily injury to repel the threat to land or chattels, unless there is also such a threat to the defendant's personal safety as to justify a self–defense. * * * spring guns and other mankilling de-

vices are not justifiable against a mere trespasser, or even a petty thief. They are privileged only against those upon whom the land-owner, if he were present in person would be free to inflict injury of the same kind.

* * *

In Hooker v. Miller, 37 Iowa 613, we held defendant vineyard owner liable for damages resulting from a spring gun shot although plaintiff was a trespasser and there to steal grapes. * * *

* * *

In United Zinc & Chemical Co. v. Britt, 258 U.S. 268, 275, 42 S.Ct. 299, the court states: "The liability for spring guns and mantraps arises from the fact that the defendant has * * * expected the trespasser and prepared an injury that is no more justified than if he had held the gun and fired it."

In addition to civil liability many jurisdictions hold a land owner criminally liable for serious injuries or homicide caused by spring guns or other set devices.

In Wisconsin, Oregon and England the use of spring guns and similar devices is specifically made unlawful by statute.

The legal principles stated by the trial court in instructions 2, 5 and 6 are well established and supported by the authorities * * *. There is no merit in defendants' objections and exceptions thereto. Defendants' various motions based on the same reasons stated in exceptions to instructions were properly overruled.

* * *

Affirmed.

Larson, Justice, dissenting.

I respectfully dissent, first, because the majority wrongfully assumes that by installing a spring gun in the bedroom of their unoccupied house the defendants intended to shoot any intruder who attempted to enter the room. Under the record presented here, that was a fact question. Unless it is held that these property owners are liable for any injury to an intruder from such a device regardless of the intent with which it is installed, liability under these pleadings must rest upon two definite issues of fact, i.e., did the defendants intend to shoot the invader, and if so, did they employ unnecessary and unreasonable force against him?

* * *

Although the court told the jury the plaintiff had the burden to prove "That the force used by defendants was in excess of that force reasonably necessary and which persons are entitled to use in the protection of their property," it utterly failed to tell the jury it could find the installation was not made with the intent or purpose of striking or injuring the plaintiff. There was considerable evidence to that effect. As I shall point out, both defendants stated the installation was made for the purpose of scaring or frightening away any intruder, not to seriously injure him. It may be that the evidence would support a finding of an intent to injure the intruder, but obviously that important issue was never adequately or clearly submitted to the jury.

Unless, then, we hold for the first time that liability for death or injury in such cases is absolute, the matter should be remanded for a jury determination of defendant's intent in installing the device under instructions usually given to a jury on the issue of intent.

* * *

Note

Most states have statutes dealing specifically with the use of force to protect property. Some of these statutes broaden the common law privilege by giving individuals the right to use deadly force to protect property under certain circumstances. Even those jurisdictions, however, often specifically prohibit the use of lethal devices such as the one employed in *Katko.*

TEEL v. MAY DEPARTMENT STORES CO.

Supreme Court of Missouri, 1941.
348 Mo. 696, 155 S.W.2d 74.

HYDE, COMMISSIONER.

This is an action for $20,000 actual and $20,000 punitive damages for false arrest and imprisonment. The jury returned a verdict for $500 actual and $500 punitive damages, a total of $1,000 for which judgment was entered. Plaintiff appealed and raises only the issue of inadequate damages. Defendant also appealed and assigns error in the refusal of a peremptory instruction [directed verdict] and in Instruction No. 1 on which the case was submitted. * * *

The facts hereinafter stated were shown by plaintiff's evidence (mainly testimony of plaintiff and A.F. Foster) considered most favorably to plaintiff's contentions. (We use the term defendant to refer to the corporate defendant.) Plaintiff's sister–in–law Leona Teel, who was separated from plaintiff's brother and had a divorce suit pending against him, lived with plaintiff in St. Louis during October and November of 1939. She went by the name of Leona Nesslein, the name of her former husband to whom she was married before she married plaintiff's brother. Leona had met Mr. A.F. Foster of Wood River, Illinois, that spring and he frequently came to see her. [Foster told Leona that she could charge on his account and that when she did so, she should say she was Mrs. Foster.] * * *

On November 29th Leona asked plaintiff to accompany her to defendant's store. Leona purchased items there amounting to a total of $93.39. She told each of defendant's clerks from whom she purchased goods that she was Mrs. A.F. Foster. Plaintiff said that of course she knew Leona was not Mrs. Foster. Leona had left her car in a parking lot nearby and she and plaintiff carried some of the packages there and put them in her automobile, making at least two trips with packages to the car. The largest amount of the purchases were in the bedding department where she bought blankets and linens amounting to $53.26. When they went back to the bedding department to get these purchases defendant's detective Mr. Zytowski came over to plaintiff and asked her if she was charging on the Foster account and she motioned to Leona. Plaintiff testified as to what occurred thereafter as follows:

> He stepped over and asked her if she was charging on the Foster account, and she said that she was, and he said, 'Are you Mrs. Foster?' and she said, 'Yes;' and he said then to the girl at the wrapping desk, 'Well, you can hand each one a package,' and the girl did so, and then Mr. Zytowski said, 'Now, you will have to come along with me.' * * * I was afraid if we didn't go, we would be forced to go, so I didn't want a scene, so I went with him. * * * He took us up to the eighth floor, credit department. * * * Two lady detectives were seated directly behind us, and there were a couple of girls right in front of us at typewriters that looked at us. * * * Mr. Jackson, (the credit manager, who had already called the Foster home, talked to Mrs. Foster, and had been advised by her that no one was authorized to buy on their account) asked Leona then if she was Mrs. Foster, and she said again that she was, and he said, 'You know you are not telling the truth and might as well admit that you are not Mrs. Foster, because I know Mrs. Foster.' * * *

* * *

* * * [T]he owner of property has the right to take action (by force or confinement reasonable under the circumstances) in defense of his property. In such cases, probable cause may be an important element of the defense of justification. Therefore, it has been recognized that an owner of a store or other premises has the right to detain a person therein, for a reasonable time for a reasonable investigation, whom he has reasonable grounds to believe has not paid for what he has received or is attempting to take goods without payment. * * *

* * *

[W]e will separately consider whether the evidence in this case, viewed most favorably to plaintiff, would show any unlawful conduct on the part of defendant, prior to the time of the return of the goods from the automobile in the parking lot to defendant's store, or any conduct so unreasonable that it would be actionable. * * * Plaintiff helped to carry some of the goods to the car, so knew where they were, when, at the credit department, Leona continued to insist that she was Mrs. Foster, and she (plaintiff) was refusing to answer when first asked there who Leona was. Finally, when Zytowski took her to one side, she did tell him the truth about her identity, and explained about her understanding of Leona's relation with Foster. Even then, in view of the fact that defendant had no notice from Foster of any such authority to buy on his credit, and had found the real Mrs. Foster at the Foster home, defendant's agents were undoubtedly justified in not accepting this explanation as the complete truth, and at least demanding the return of the goods. * * * Under all these circumstances * * *, we cannot say that defendant should have inferred lack of criminal intent. On the contrary, our conclusion is that defendant's agents were within their rights in demanding and thus obtaining the return of the merchandise obtained from defendant by means of such false personation. We would not be willing to hold that the evidence shows unreasonable or unlawful detention of plaintiff and Leona by defendant's agents up to the time of obtaining the return of the goods.

However, we do not think we can say that there could be no jury case of false imprisonment after the goods were returned. Defendant's agents, if they did not believe the explanation made by plaintiff and Leona (and there was evidence of reasonable grounds after investigation for not believing it), might have been within their rights if they had called the authorities to take them into custody and preferred charges against them under the statutes above cited. Instead of doing this (accepting plaintiff's evidence as true) Zytowski undertook to do something that not even the public authorities had any right to do, namely: to compel them to sign confessions under threat of not permitting them to leave his office until they did so. Plaintiff said that after she got back with the merchandise from the car, Zytowski was writing a confession for Leona, and that it was "about twenty–five minutes" after she got back, "before he got it finished," then "he gave it to Leona and wanted her to sign it," but "she said she didn't want to sign it." Plaintiff further testified: "He told us before we would have to sign those statements, or we would not be permitted to leave." * * *

It is well settled that unreasonable delay in releasing a person, who is entitled to be released, or such delay in calling, taking him before or turning him over to proper authorities, or in wrongfully denying opportunity to give bond would thereafter amount to false imprisonment. Although defendant was within its rights in doing what it did to obtain the return of the goods, nevertheless, as said in Restatement, p. 317, Zytowski was "not privileged to use the power, which his custody of another [here held for the purpose of obtaining return of its goods] gives him over the other, to force the other to comply with any demand which has no relation to accomplishing the purpose for which the custody is privileged." Certainly, neither the privilege to restrain plaintiff for the purpose of obtaining return of the goods or in order to turn her over to the proper authorities charged with a felony under the above–cited statutes would give defendant any authority to hold plaintiff to compel her to give a confession * * *. Of course, defendant had evidence to show that this statement and the stay in Zytowski's office for its preparation was wholly voluntary but that issue was for the jury. While it would not be improper to request a written statement, defendant had no right to compel it by coercion. We also approve of the rule adopted by the Restatement that defendant's "misconduct [if found] makes it liable to [plaintiff] only for such harm as is caused thereby and does not make [it] liable for the arrest or for the keeping [of plaintiff] in custody prior to the misconduct." We must, however, hold that the court correctly denied defendant's request for a peremptory instruction.

The court recognized that defendant's conduct was not wholly wrongful, and refused the instructions of plaintiff submitting the case on such theory as well as refusing defendant's theory that defendant had the right to do everything that was shown. The court, of its own motion, gave an instruction which stated that "if you further find and believe from the evidence that such imprisonment, if you find there was such imprisonment, was to a greater extent than was reasonably necessary to enable defendants to recover or retake from plaintiff and her companion Leona Teel the merchandise * * * then such imprisonment, if any, constitutes false imprisonment and plaintiff is entitled to recover."* This was erroneous because it authorized the jury to make imprisonment shown prior to the return of the merchandise (or some part thereof) a basis for recovery, instead of only what occurred thereafter.

The judgment is reversed and the cause remanded.

Note

The privilege to protect property against dispossession or destruction, illustrated by *Katko*, does not extend to recapturing property once it has been taken. A different, limited privilege is recognized for recapture after dispossession. It permits necessary nondeadly force to effect recapture in "fresh pursuit," subject to certain limitations. This is the privilege that applied in *Teel* up to the point of recovery of the goods.

After the goods were secured, however, the defendant could no longer invoke any protection–of–property privilege. Its only possibility was some form of arrest privilege. The common law recognized arrest privileges for both law officers and citizens in specific circumstances. Today these common–law doctrines are superseded by statutes in every jurisdiction. Missouri, at the time of *Teel*, typically allowed a shopkeeper a privilege to detain a suspected shoplifter to summon law enforcement. But as the court held, the statutory privilege did not authorize the defendant's conduct in the case.

4. NECESSITY

PLOOF v. PUTNAM

Supreme Court of Vermont, 1908.
81 Vt. 471, 71 A. 188.

MUNSON, JUSTICE.

It is alleged as the ground of recovery that on the 13th of November, 1904, the defendant was the owner of a certain island in Lake Champlain, and of a certain dock attached thereto, which island and dock were

---

* This is apparently the instruction that the court, in the first paragraph of its opin- ion, called "instruction No. 1." [Ed.]

then in charge of the defendant's servant; that the plaintiff was then possessed of and sailing upon said lake a certain loaded sloop, on which were the plaintiff and his wife and two minor children; that there then arose a sudden and violent tempest, whereby the sloop and the property and persons therein were placed in great danger of destruction; that, to save these from destruction or injury, the plaintiff was compelled to, and did, moor the sloop to defendant's dock; that the defendant, by his servant, unmoored the sloop, whereupon it was driven upon the shore by the tempest, without the plaintiff's fault; and that the sloop and its contents were thereby destroyed, and the plaintiff and his wife and children cast into the lake and upon the shore, receiving injuries. This claim is set forth in two counts—one in trespass, charging that the defendant by his servant with force and arms willfully and designedly unmoored the sloop; the other in case, alleging that it was the duty of the defendant by his servant to permit the plaintiff to moor his sloop to the dock, and to permit it to remain so moored during the continuance of the tempest, but that the defendant by his servant, in disregard of this duty, negligently, carelessly, and wrongfully unmoored the sloop. Both counts are demurred to generally.

There are many cases in the books which hold that necessity, and an inability to control movements inaugurated in the proper exercise of a strict right, will justify entries upon land and interferences with personal property that would otherwise have been trespasses. A reference to a few of these will be sufficient to illustrate the doctrine. In Miller v. Fandrye, Poph. 161, trespass was brought for chasing sheep, and the defendant pleaded that the sheep were trespassing upon his land, and that he with a little dog chased them out, and that, as soon as the sheep were off his land, he called in the dog. It was argued that, although the defendant might lawfully drive the sheep from his own ground with a dog, he had no right to pursue them into the next ground; but the court considered that the defendant might drive the sheep from his land with a dog, and that the nature of a dog is such that he cannot be withdrawn in an instant, and that, as the defendant had done his best to recall the dog, trespass would not lie. * * * If one have a way over the land of another for his beasts to pass, and the beasts, being properly driven, feed the grass by morsels in passing, or run out of the way and are promptly pursued and brought back, trespass will not lie. A traveler on a highway who finds it obstructed from a sudden and temporary cause may pass upon the adjoining land without becoming a trespasser because of the necessity. An entry upon land to save goods which are in danger of being lost or destroyed by water or fire is not a trespass. In Proctor v. Adams, 113 Mass. 376, 18 Am.Rep. 500, the defendant went upon the plaintiff's beach for the purpose of saving and restoring to the lawful owner a boat which had been driven ashore, and was in danger of being carried off by the sea; and it was held no trespass.

This doctrine of necessity applies with special force to the preservation of human life. One assaulted and in peril of his life may run through the close of another to escape from his assailant. One may sacrifice the personal property of another to save his life or the lives of his fellows. In Mouse's Case, 12 Co. 63, the defendant was sued for taking and carrying away the plaintiff's casket and its contents. It appeared that the ferryman of Gravesend took 47 passengers into his barge to pass to London, among whom were the plaintiff and defendant; and the barge being upon the water a great tempest happened, and a strong wind, so that the barge and all the passengers were in danger of being lost if certain ponderous things were not cast out, and the defendant thereupon cast out the plaintiff's casket. It was resolved that in case of necessity, to save the lives of the passengers, it was lawful for the defendant, being a passenger, to cast the plaintiff's casket out of the barge * * *.

It is clear that an entry upon the land of another may be justified by necessity, and that the declaration before us discloses a necessity for mooring the sloop. But the defendant questions the sufficiency of the counts because they do not negative the existence of natural objects to which the plaintiff could have moored with equal safety. The allegations are, in substance, that the stress of a sudden and violent tempest compelled the plaintiff to moor to defendant's dock to save his sloop and the people in it. The averment of necessity is complete, for it covers not only the necessity of mooring, but the necessity of mooring to the dock; and the details of the situation which created this necessity, whatever the legal requirements regarding them, are matters of proof, and need not be alleged. It is certain that the rule suggested cannot be held applicable irrespective of circumstance, and the question must be left for adjudication upon proceedings had with reference to the evidence or the charge.

* * *

Judgment affirmed and cause remanded.

VINCENT v. LAKE ERIE TRANSP. CO.

Supreme Court of Minnesota, 1910.
109 Minn. 456, 124 N.W. 221.

O'BRIEN, JUSTICE.

[Plaintiff sued for damage to his dock caused by defendant's ship, which was tied to the dock during a storm. After the jury rendered a verdict awarding the plaintiff $500, the defendant moved for a new trial. The trial court denied the motion, and the defendant appealed.]

The steamship Reynolds, owned by the defendant, was for the purpose of discharging her cargo on November 27, 1905, moored to plaintiff's dock in Duluth. While the unloading of the boat was taking place a storm from the northeast developed, which at about 10 o'clock p.m., when the unloading was completed, had so grown in violence that the wind was then moving at 50 miles per hour and continued to increase during the night. There is some evidence that one, and perhaps two, boats were able to enter the harbor that night, but it is plain that navigation was practically suspended from the hour mentioned until the morning of the 29th, when the storm abated, and during that time no master would have been justified in attempting to navigate his vessel, if he could avoid doing so. After the discharge of the cargo the Reynolds signaled for a tug to tow her from the dock, but none could be obtained because of the severity of the storm. If the lines holding the ship to the dock had been cast off, she would doubtless have drifted away; but, instead, the lines were kept fast, and as soon as one parted or chafed it was replaced, sometimes with a larger one. The vessel lay upon the outside of the dock, her bow to the east, the wind and waves striking her starboard quarter with such force that she was constantly being lifted and thrown against the dock, resulting in its damage, as found by the jury, to the amount of $500.

We are satisfied that the character of the storm was such that it would have been highly imprudent for the master of the Reynolds to have attempted to leave the dock or to have permitted his vessel to drift away from it. * * * [T]he record in this case fully sustains the contention of the appellant that, in holding the vessel fast to the dock, those in charge of her exercised good judgment and prudent seamanship.

* * *

The appellant contends by ample assignments of error that, because its conduct during the storm was rendered necessary by prudence and good seamanship under conditions over which it had no control, it cannot be held liable for any injury resulting to the property of others, and claims that the jury should have been so instructed. An analysis of the charge given by the trial court is not necessary, as in our opinion the only question for the jury was the amount of damages which the plaintiffs were entitled to recover, and no complaint is made upon that score.

The situation was one in which the ordinary rules regulating property rights were suspended by forces beyond human control, and if, without the direct intervention of some act by the one sought to be held liable, the property of another was injured, such injury must be attributed to the act of God, and not to the wrongful act of the person sought to be charged. If during the storm the Reynolds had entered the harbor, and while there had become disabled and been thrown against the plaintiffs' dock, the plaintiffs could not have recovered. Again, if while attempting to hold fast to the dock the lines had parted, without any negligence, and the vessel carried against some other boat or dock in the harbor, there would be no liability upon her owner. But here those in charge of the vessel deliberately and by their direct efforts held her in such a position that the damage to the dock resulted, and, having thus preserved the ship at the expense of the dock, it seems to us that her owners are responsible to the dock owners to the extent of the injury inflicted.

In Depue v. Flateau, 100 Minn. 299, 111 N.W. 1, 8 L.R.A. (N.S.) 485, this court held that where the plaintiff, while lawfully in the defendants' house, became so ill that he was incapable of traveling with safety, the defendants were responsible to him in damages for compelling him to leave the premises. If, however, the owner of the premises had furnished the traveler with proper accommodations and medical attendance, would he have been able to defeat an action brought against him for their reasonable worth?

In Ploof v. Putnam, [supra p. 68], the Supreme Court of Vermont held that where, under stress of weather, a vessel was without permission moored to a private dock at an island in Lake Champlain owned by the defendant, the plaintiff was not guilty of trespass, and that the defendant was responsible in damages because his representative upon the island unmoored the vessel, permitting it to drift upon the shore, with resultant injuries to it. If, in that case, the vessel had been permitted to remain, and the dock had suffered an injury, we believe the shipowner would have been held liable for the injury done.

Theologians hold that a starving man may, without moral guilt, take what is necessary to sustain life; but it could hardly be said that the obligation would not be upon such person to pay the value of the property so taken when he became able to do so. And so public necessity, in times of war or peace, may require the taking of private property for public purposes; but under our system of jurisprudence compensation must be made.

Let us imagine in this case that for the better mooring of the vessel those in charge of her had appropriated a valuable cable lying upon the dock. No matter how justifiable such appropriation might have been, it would not be claimed that, because of the overwhelming necessity of the situation, the owner of the cable could not recover its value.

This is not the case where life or property was menaced by any object or thing belonging to the plaintiff, the destruction of which became necessary to prevent the threatened disaster. Nor is it a case where, because of the act of God, or unavoidable accident, the infliction of the injury was beyond the control of the defendant, but is one where the defendant prudently and advisedly availed itself of the plaintiffs' property for the purpose of preserving its own more valuable property, and the plaintiffs are entitled to compensation for the injury done.

Order affirmed.

Chapter III

NEGLIGENCE—INTRODUCTION AND STANDARD OF CARE

A. INTRODUCTION

American and English courts developed negligence as a separate cause of action in the early and middle part of the nineteenth century. Prior to that time, these courts used the term "negligence" to refer to any failure to perform a legal obligation; "negligence" did not itself define a legal obligation. The actual standard of liability before the advent of negligence seems to have been very close to strict liability: if an active defendant injured a passive victim, the defendant was liable without much reference to his state of mind or to the reasonableness of his conduct. For example, in The Case of the Thorns, Y.B. 6 Ed. 4, 7a, pl. 18 (1466), the defendant cut a hedge of thorns, some of which fell on the plaintiff's land. The court held for the plaintiff and stated that

> for though a man doth a lawful thing, yet if any damage do thereby befall another, he shall answer for it, if he could have avoided it. As if a man lop a tree, and the boughs fall upon another ipso invito [of their own weight], yet an action lies. If a man shoots at butts [targets] and hurt another unawares, an action lies. If I have land through which a river runs to your mill, and I lop the sallows [willows] growing upon the riverside, which accidentally stop the water, so as your mill is injured, an action lies. If I am building my own house, and a piece of timber falls on my neighbor's house and breaks part of it, an action lies. If a man assault me, and I lift up my staff to defend myself, and in lifting it up hit another, an action lies by that person, and yet I did a lawful thing. And the reason of all these cases is, because he that is damaged ought to be recompensed.

After negligence was established as a separate cause of action in the nineteenth century, a defendant was liable, by and large, only if he was at "fault." This meant that the plaintiff was required to prove that the defendant either injured the plaintiff intentionally or injured the plaintiff negligently by failing to exercise reasonable care.

The exact standard of liability before the nineteenth century has not been free from doubt. One source of uncertainty is that the structure of tort law has changed dramatically during the last two centuries. We now organize tort law according to separate causes of action ("torts") based primarily on the nature of the plaintiff's injury and the defendant's state of mind. As we saw in Chapter 2, battery differs from assault in that battery law compensates a plaintiff who suffers actual harmful or offensive bodily contact, whereas assault law compensates a plaintiff who suffers apprehension of such contact. Battery and assault, in turn, differ from negligence in that the plaintiff in a case of battery or assault must prove that the defendant intended the invasion, whereas a plaintiff in a negligence case need show only that the defendant failed to exercise reasonable care. Before the development of modern tort law in the nineteenth and twentieth centuries, however, the common law principles governing recovery for personal injury and property damage were organized according to the "forms of action" under the English writ system. To bring a case before a royal court, a plaintiff was required to obtain a writ from the chancellor that directed the defendant to appear. The defendant could complain that the case did not fall within the specific writ or form of action, meaning that it was not the type of case over which the royal court had jurisdiction. Much of early English law dealt with the scope of the various writs.

An early writ was the writ of trespass. It covered cases in which the defendant caused *direct* injury to the plaintiff. Direct injuries were more likely to lead to breaches of the peace and were, therefore, within the king's scope of concern. One form of the writ—trespass *vi et armis* (with force of arms)—covered injuries that today would be batteries, assaults, or false imprisonments, though apparently the plaintiff was not required to prove intent. Another form of the writ—trespass *quare clausem fregit* (breaking the "close" or real property)—covered what today we would call trespass to land, though again the plaintiff was not required to prove intent. Later, the chancellor began to issue the writ of trespass on the case. This writ expanded the jurisdiction of the royal courts because it covered indirect injuries (though unlike in cases brought under the writ of trespass, the plaintiff was required to prove actual damages.)

A common question in early English cases was whether the plaintiff had obtained the correct writ. If the injury was direct, the plaintiff had to sue under one of the writs of trespass; if the injury was indirect, the plaintiff had to sue under the writ of trespass on the case. Some people analyzing these early English cases have relied on this feature of the writ system to argue that English tort law has always been based on "fault," that is, that the plaintiff was always required to prove something like intent or negligence. Seemingly contrary statements in early English cases, these people have argued, did not actually address the question of whether a defendant's conduct could, under the correct writ, serve as a basis for liability. Instead, these statements addressed the question of whether the case was brought under the correct writ. For example, in Brown v. Kendall, 60 Mass. (6 Cush.) 292, 295 (1850), Chief Justice Lemuel Shaw said:

In these discussions, it is frequently stated by judges, that when one receives injury from the direct act of another, trespass will lie. But we think this is said in reference to the question, whether trespass and not case will lie, assuming that the facts are such, that some action will lie. These dicta are no authority, we think, for holding, that damage received by a direct act of force from another will be sufficient to maintain an action of trespass, whether the act was lawful or unlawful, and neither willful, intentional, or careless.

Oliver Wendell Holmes made a similar argument in his famous book, *The Common Law* (1881).

Notwithstanding these arguments, current scholarship gives substantial support to the conclusion that the law governing personal injury and property damage changed dramatically during the early and middle parts of the nineteenth century. Before that time English and American courts did not require proof of anything like our current notions of intent or negligence. By the middle of the nineteenth century, however, they had begun to do so.

Chief Justice Shaw's opinion in Brown v. Kendall was a landmark event in the development of negligence law in the nineteenth century. Kendall accidentally struck Brown with a stick that Kendall was using to separate two fighting dogs. Brown sued Kendall to recover for his injuries. Writing for the Supreme Judicial Court of Massachusetts, Chief Justice Shaw wrote that no liability existed in the absence of a showing either that Kendall struck Brown intentionally or that Kendall failed to use "ordinary care." Whether or not Shaw misread history in the previously quoted passage, Brown v. Kendall makes clear that, by the middle of the nineteenth century, an injured plaintiff was required to prove that the defendant acted either intentionally or negligently.

Scholars have strenuously debated the reasons negligence law arose as a separate cause of action in the early and middle parts of the nineteenth century. Some scholars have explained the shift from strict liability (that is, liability without proof of fault) to negligence as a "subsidy" to burgeoning industry during the industrial revolution. Others have attributed it to courts' inability to apply strict liability to cases in which both parties were active, such as cases in which two carriages collided. Still others have attributed it to the difference between the old writs of trespass and trespass on the case. Whatever the cause—and it is likely that the development of negligence law had multiple causes—negligence as a separate theory of liability was firmly established by the late nineteenth century. See generally, Morton Horowitz, The Transformation of American Law: 1770–1860, 85–99 (1977).

* * *

Courts today use the term "negligence" in two distinct ways. Sometimes they use the term to refer to a conclusion that the defendant failed to exercise reasonable care, that is, that the defendant acted "negligently." But the defendant's failure to exercise reasonable care is only one element of the liability theory or cause of action known as "negligence." Thus, the term negligence denotes both the overall cause of action and one of its elements.

Under the formal theory of the negligence cause of action, the plaintiff ordinarily has the burden of establishing five elements in order to recover. These five elements are said to constitute the prima facie case in negligence, meaning that the plaintiff will lose if he fails to establish any one of them. (For a similar description with respect to intentional torts, see the Introduction to Chapter II.)

First, the plaintiff must establish that the defendant had a duty to conform its conduct to a specific standard. This matter is addressed in Chapter VI. Usually this standard requires the defendant to exercise "ordinary" or "reasonable" care. In some situations, however, a stricter or more lenient standard is imposed on the defendant.

Second, the plaintiff must prove that the defendant's conduct failed to conform to the appropriate standard. Courts often refer to such failure as a breach of the defendant's duty, or as substandard conduct on the part of the defendant, or (when the standard requires the defendant to exercise reasonable care) as negligence. This element is the subject of this chapter.

Third, the plaintiff must prove that the defendant's substandard conduct was a factual cause or cause in fact of the plaintiff's injuries. This element is treated in Chapter IV.

Fourth, the plaintiff must prove that the defendant's substandard conduct was a legal cause of the plaintiff's injuries. This element is addressed in Chapter V.

And fifth, the plaintiff must prove actual damages. Unlike some intentional torts, the cause of action for negligence has actual damage as an element of the plaintiff's prima facie case. This element is addressed in Chapter VIII.

The first issue is normally for the judge to determine, with little or no role for the jury. The other issues are normally for the jury to determine, unless reasonable minds could not differ.

If the plaintiff establishes all five elements, he has made out a prima facie case in negligence. The defendant can still escape liability (or reduce its liability) by establishing one of several affirmative defenses, the most important of which is the plaintiff's own negligence. The affirmative defenses are treated in Chapter IX.

The remainder of this chapter is devoted to the second element of the plaintiff's prima facie case: the determination of whether the defendant exercised reasonable or ordinary care. As you go through the material, you should keep in mind that in order to win, the plaintiff must also establish the other four elements of the cause of action in negligence. The defendant may also have one or more affirmative defenses.

B. SUBSTANDARD CARE

GRACE & CO. v. CITY OF LOS ANGELES

United States District Court, Southern District of California, 1958.
168 F.Supp. 344, affirmed, 278 F.2d 771 (9th Cir. 1960).

WESTOVER, DISTRICT JUDGE.

Defendant, City of Los Angeles, was and now is the owner of Berth 59, Los Angeles Harbor, and together with defendant, Outer Harbor Dock and Wharf Co., operated a certain steel and concrete shed at Berth 59 in that portion of Los Angeles County known as San Pedro.

Plaintiff was the owner of approximately 1,960 bags of coffee, which had been stored in the shed at Berth 59 after having been discharged by various vessels and was awaiting delivery to plaintiff.

Defendants maintained in the public street adjacent to the shed at Berth 59 a certain 8–inch cast–iron water pipe–line. A lateral line leading into the shed from the 8–inch pipe burst, allowing a great quantity of water to escape from the pipe–line under high pressure, which water flooded the floor of the shed at Berth 59 and damaged plaintiff's coffee.

Plaintiff alleges the defendants permitted the pipe to remain beneath the shed, although defendants knew or in the exercise of due care should have known that the pipe was in an ancient, weak, corroded and decaying condition, so that the pipe could not have reasonably been expected to contain water under high pressure.

At the time the pipe was installed it was the best pipe available. Plaintiff makes no contention that the pipe–line or the lateral where the break occurred was negligently installed. At the time of installation defendants did not know of the corrosive nature of the soil, but subsequent to the installation the City, or some of its departments, became cognizant that the soil in the harbor area was highly corrosive. Based upon economic consideration, defendants established a policy of doing nothing about maintaining, repairing or replacing such water pipe–lines until a leak occurred and water was discovered on the surface of the ground.

Plaintiff contends defendants knew or should have known that the pipe was located in highly corrosive soil and, over the period of years involved, defendants should have conducted some sort of inspection to ascertain if the pipe had corroded in order to determine whether there was likelihood of the pipe bursting. Plaintiffs contend that failure to make an inspection for forty years was negligence.

At the trial experts testified the pipe in question failed because of graphitic corrosion. Graphitic corrosion occurs when iron in pipe is leached out and replaced by graphite. The leaching of the iron from the pipe and the replacement thereof by graphite occurs over a long period of time and does not change the pipe shape or contour. The only effect upon the pipe is that it loses strength so that under pressure the pipe in those particular spots where graphitic corrosion occurs gives way.

Plaintiffs contend defendants had knowledge that a break was imminent, for some months prior thereto there appeared to be a leakage in the system of more than 130.00 cubic feet of water per day. However, experts testified at the trial that in a graphitic corrosion break there is no gradual leakage, but that the surface of the pipe gives way all at once and thus allows water to spurt from the pipe.

After defendants received notice of the break in the pipe, the line was repaired by cutting out an eight or ten–foot length of pipe and inserting therein a new piece of cast–iron pipe. Defendants' employees found in the pipe removed an opening, caused by graphitic corrosion, approximately the size of a human hand. They also discovered that within a short distance on either side of the opening the pipe was in sound condition, so that it could be continued in use.

* * *

If, in the case at bar, the court is to find for plaintiff, it will be necessary to find defendants have been negligent either in the installation, maintenance or inspection of the pipe in question. As stated before, there is no contention by plaintiff that the pipe was negligently installed; hence, the negligence, if any, would have to be found in the City's failure to inspect the pipe. Plaintiff's entire case rests upon the theory that defendants were negligent in failing to make inspection of the pipe–line during a period of forty years to determine its condition. * * * Plaintiff admits, however, there was no reasonable manner in which the line could be adequately inspected, other than to excavate the soil along the pipe–line and make physical inspection thereof.

The pipe–line was some ten feet beneath the surface of the ground. The break occurred in a lateral leading into the shed under a cement platform adjacent to Berth 59. To make an inspection, it would have been necessary for the City to excavate the line in its entirety, including the line under the cement platform, which would mean the breaking of the cement platform to get to the pipe below.

According to the testimony of experts, graphitic corrosion occurs sporadically. Graphitic corrosion may occur on the top of the pipe and not on the bottom, or on one side and not the other. Graphitic corrosion may occur in one spot and then may not occur for many feet along the line. It would be necessary to excavate around the entire pipe to locate a corroded area. An examination of the upper half of the pipe would not be sufficient because graphitic corrosion could manifest itself on the lower portion of the pipe and not on the top or sides. To make complete inspection it would be necessary to remove the earth from beneath the line. The removal of earth from beneath the pipe would remove its support, putting a strain upon the pipe itself, and might cause a sinking or bending of the pipe, occasioning damage more extensive than the corrosion itself.

Testimony at the trial indicated the City of Los Angeles has adopted a "do nothing" policy regarding inspection of its water lines. It places water lines in the earth and then neither makes inspection nor replacement until leaks occur. When leaks develop they are repaired. When they become too numerous the pipe–line is replaced.

Defendants contend that when the line was installed it was the best pipe available and that such cast–iron pipe will ordinarily last for many, many years. In fact, evidence indicated that in Pennsylvania similar cast–iron pipe has been in use for more than 150 years in a non–corrosive soil.

If any policy has been adopted by municipalities in California, the policy is the same as that followed by the City of Los Angeles; that is, that after cast–iron water pipe is installed the line is used without inspection or replacement until there are sufficient breaks to indicate the pipe has corroded or has become undependable. Defendants contend there was nothing to indicate the break in question was imminent or the line undependable. In fact, the line was repaired and returned to use, and so far as this court is informed is in use today.

Negligence is a question of fact to be determined from all the surrounding circumstances. Although it might have been desirable to make an inspection of the water lines every two or three years, such inspection would be prohibitively expensive and economically unfeasible. The City, like individuals, is required to take only reasonable precautions.

Although there is some evidence that in other parts of the harbor area there had been pipe failure because of graphitic corrosion, nevertheless, we are of the opinion that considering all the evidence in this case the City was not negligent in failing to inspect the pipe.

Judgment will be for defendants. Counsel for defendants shall prepare findings of fact, conclusions of law and judgment in accordance with the rule.

Notes

1. A determination of whether certain conduct constitutes reasonable care is usually a question of fact, to be decided by the jury. *Grace & Co.* was a bench trial, that is, a case tried to the court without the aid of a jury. Thus, the trial judge sat as the fact finder.

2. A determination that a defendant failed to exercise reasonable care has two components. First, the fact finder—usually a jury—must determine what the defendant actually did. For example, in a case involving an automobile accident, a dispute may exist as to whether the defendant actually crossed the center line before the collision. In *Grace & Co.,* a similar issue might have arisen as to whether the city had in fact inspected the pipes. Apparently no such dispute did arise. The parties seemed to agree, by and large, about what actually happened.

Second, the fact finder must evaluate the defendant's behavior to determine whether it was "reasonable" under the circumstances. This evaluation is not about a "fact" in the ordinary sense of the term; it is a judgment about how people ought to behave. Thus, it is sometimes called a "mixed question" of fact and law. Nevertheless, it too is normally a "question of fact" for the jury.

As with any fact issue, a trial or appellate court can take the issue of reasonable care away from the jury only if no evidence supports a finding of substandard care or if reasonable minds could not differ on the issue. A court can do this at various stages of the proceedings: by giving the defendant judgment on the pleadings, by giving the defendant summary judgment, by directing a verdict in favor of the defendant, or by giving the defendant judgment notwithstanding the verdict. (These procedural devices are discussed in Chapter I. They are also part of the subject matter in courses on Civil Procedure.) In such cases, the court may say that the defendant was not negligent as a matter of law. Courts occasionally hold that certain conduct is negligent as a matter of law, but this is rare because the plaintiff has the burden of proof on this issue.

For the purpose of ascertaining the respective roles of the judge and jury, the question of determining what the defendant did is like any other fact. The question of determining whether the defendant's conduct was reasonable is less "factual," and some courts seem to be more willing to substitute their own judgment for that of the jury on such an issue than they would be on a "pure" issue of fact. Most courts, however, *proclaim* that evaluating the defendant's conduct is an issue of fact for the jury, just like any other issue of fact. In *Grace & Co.,* the plaintiff appealed the trial court's decision. The court of appeals affirmed, saying:

> The appellant [plaintiff] had the burden of establishing the negligence of the appellee [defendant]. The District Court found against the claims of the appellant and found that appellee was not negligent. There was ample evidence to support this finding. (278 F.2d 771, 774 (9th Cir. 1960).)

3. Negligence uses a foresight standard, not a hindsight standard. Thus, reasonable care requires only that a person take reasonable precautions with respect to risks that a reasonable person would foresee. In *Grace & Co.,* both parties seemed to agree that a reasonable party in the City's position could foresee that *some* pipes would break *some* time. The City just argued that digging up all the pipes for inspection would have been too burdensome. What if the City could reasonably have foreseen which pipe would break and when? In this regard, consider the following portion of the court of appeals' decision, which expanded on a point made by the trial court.

> The meters showed that for some months prior to the failure in question there had been a considerable flow of water into the system. The rate of flow was variable, but averaged about 140 cubic feet a day. As this was a "dead-end" system and its sole purpose was to provide water for fighting fires, appellant claims the City should have made a thorough investigation, in the interest of safety, to determine the cause of the flow or loss of water.

> However, the meter readings do not indicate that any water was escaping from the pipe at the point where it burst. The evidence of the

experts indicates that if there was a failure by reason of graphitic corrosion that there would have been a flood of water, such as occurred, rather than gradual leakage, which does not necessarily indicate a corrosion failure. Further, in the absence of water coming to the surface the source of the leak could not be found without digging up the pipe.

The evidence indicates a number of possible explanations for the flow. The fire line involved was approximately 5,000 to 6,000 feet long, containing a leaded joint every ten feet. Water could be lost through leaks in these joints or through various valves in the line.

278 F.2d at 774–75.

4. *Learned Hand's famous "formula."* In United States v. Carroll Towing Co., 159 F.2d 169 (2d Cir.1947), the plaintiff's barge broke loose from its moorings. One issue was whether the custodian of the barge was negligent for leaving the barge unattended. In a famous analysis of the negligence issue, Judge Learned Hand stated:

Since there are occasions when every vessel will break from her moorings, and since, if she does, she becomes a menace to those about her; the owner's duty, as in other similar situations, to provide against resulting injuries is a function of three variables: (1) The probability that she will break away; (2) the gravity of the resulting injury, if she does; (3) the burden of adequate precautions. Possibly it serves to bring this notion into relief to state it in algebraic terms: if the probability be called P; the injury, L; and the burden, B; liability depends upon whether B is less than L multiplied by P: i.e., whether $B < PL$. Applied to the situation at bar, the likelihood that a barge will break from her fasts and the damage she will do, vary with the place and time; for example, if a storm threatens, the danger is greater; so it is if she is in a crowded harbor where moored barges are constantly being shifted about. On the other hand, the barge must not be the bargee's prison, even though he lives aboard; he must go ashore at times.*

* In Brotherhood Shipping Co. v. St. Paul Fire & Marine Ins. Co., 985 F.2d 323 (7th Cir. 1993), Judge Posner offered the following formulation of the *Carroll Towing* standard:

Under that standard, a defendant is negligent if the burden (cost) of the precautions that he could have taken to avoid the accident (B in Hand's formula) is less than the loss that the accident could reasonably be anticipated to cause (L), discounted (i.e., multiplied) by the probability that the accident would occur unless the precautions were taken. So: $B < PL$. The cost–justified level of precaution (B)—the level that the defendant must come up to on penalty of being found to have violated his duty of due care if he does not—is thus higher, the likelier the accident that the precaution would have prevented was to occur (P) and the greater the loss that the accident was likely to inflict if it did occur (L). Looked at from a different direction, the formula shows

that the cheaper it is to prevent the accident (low B), the more likely prevention is to be cost–justified and the failure to prevent therefore negligent. Negligence is especially likely to be found if B is low and both P and L (and therefore PL, the expected accident cost) are high.

The Restatement (Third) of Torts: Liability for Physical Harm (Basic Principles) § 3 (Tent. Draft No. 1, March 2001) expresses the same general idea as follows:

A person acts with negligence if the person does not exercise reasonable care under all the circumstances. Primary factors to consider in ascertaining whether the person's conduct lacks reasonable care are the foreseeable likelihood that it will result in harm, the foreseeable severity of the harm that may ensue, and the burden that would be borne by the person and others if the person takes precautions that eliminate or reduce the possibility of harm.

5. *Some B<PL exercises.* In light of *Grace, Carroll Towing,* and the requirement of foreseeability addressed in note 3, consider the following cases:

A. In Beatty v. Central Iowa Ry., 58 Iowa 242, 12 N.W. 332 (1882), the plaintiff's decedent was killed when the "unmanageable" horse he was riding collided with the defendant's train at a crossing. The crossing was at an acute angle, so that the rider was required to ride close to the track for a long time. The plaintiff's estate argued that the railroad was negligent for not regrading the crossing so that the road and track had more separation and then crossed at right angles, affording less opportunity for trains to scare horses. The court held that the railroad was not negligent.

"Such increase of danger is necessarily incident to and attendant upon this improved mode of transportation. All persons must accept the advantages of this mode of intercommunication with the dangers and inconveniences which necessarily attend it. The price of progress cannot be withheld."

B. In Kimbar v. Estis, 1 N.Y.2d 399, 153 N.Y.S.2d 197, 135 N.E.2d 708 (1956), the plaintiff broke his nose at a summer camp when he stepped off a path at night and hit a tree. He alleged that the operators of the summer camp were negligent for not illuminating the path. The court held that the summer camp was not negligent for failing to illuminate the path.

C. In Allien v. Louisiana Power & Light Co., 202 So.2d 704 (La.App. 1967), the plaintiff's decedent was electrocuted when a drilling rig he was using touched a power line. The defendant had installed the line thinking it went to a working well but later learned that the well was located elsewhere. The defendant installed a new line but did not deactivate the old line. The plaintiff argued that the defendant should have foreseen the risk of electrocution and showed that the defendant could have prevented the accident by deactivating the wire at a cost of $48.00. The court held that the defendant was negligent for failing to deactivate the wire.

6. *Jury instructions.* No one, including Judge Hand, thinks reasonable care can be measured with mathematical precision. His "formula" in *Carroll Towing* merely suggests the kind of evidence that is relevant on the issue of reasonable care and the kinds of jury arguments the lawyers for each side might make. In fact, in most jurisdictions the jury is not told very much about reasonable care. The pattern jury instruction in Texas is typical:

PJC 2.01 Ordinary Care and Negligence

"ORDINARY CARE" means that degree of care which would be used by a person of ordinary prudence under the same or similar circumstances.

"NEGLIGENCE" means failure to use ordinary care; that is to say, failure to do that which a person of ordinary prudence would have done under the same or similar circumstances, or doing that which a person of ordinary prudence would not have done under the same or similar circumstances.

1 State Bar of Texas, Texas Pattern Jury Charges 45 (1969).

7. The wording of the jury instructions (or "charge") can have a psychological effect by focusing jurors' attention on particular aspects of the case. One issue that has been the focus of much attention is the effect that a sudden "emergency" has on evaluating the reasonableness of an actor's behavior. For example, what if a motorist swerves into another lane to avoid an object that suddenly falls on the road from a truck? All courts agree that the motorist's lawyer can argue that the jury should take the sudden emergency into account. But should the court instruct the jury on this aspect of the case? The traditional rule, which most American courts still follow, is that a party is entitled to such an instruction if the evidence supports a conclusion that the party was acting during a sudden emergency not of his own making. One court has held that failure to give "sudden emergency" instruction is wrong but not *reversible* error. Martin v. City of New Orleans, 678 F.2d 1321 (5th Cir.1982). Another court has held that it is reversible error to give such an instruction. Knapp v. Stanford, 392 So.2d 196 (Miss. 1980) (en banc). See also, Lyons v. Midnight Sun Transp. Services, Inc., 928 P.2d 1202 (Alaska 1996) (per curiam) (emergency instruction should not be given except in special circumstances).

8. *Industry custom.* In *Grace* the court of appeals relied in part on the fact that "[n]o expert testified that it was the practice in any municipality to dig up underground pipe to ascertain its condition, no matter when it was installed." The court then said, "Observance of a custom or practice is evidence of due care, although of course it does not conclusively establish the legal standard." 278 F.2d at 774. In that light, consider the following famous case.

T.J. HOOPER

United States Court of Appeals, Second Circuit, 1932.
60 F.2d 737.

L. HAND, CIRCUIT JUDGE.

The barges No. 17 and No. 30, belonging to the Northern Barge Company, had lifted cargoes of coal at Norfolk, Virginia, for New York in March, 1928. They were towed by two tugs of the petitioner, the "Montrose" and the "Hooper," and were lost off the Jersey Coast on March tenth, in an easterly gale. The cargo owners sued the barges under the contracts of carriage; the owner of the barges sued the tugs under the towing contract, both for its own loss and as bailee of the cargoes; the owner of the tug filed a petition to limit its liability. All the suits were joined and heard together, and the judge found that all the vessels were unseaworthy; the tugs, because they did not carry radio receiving sets by which they could have seasonably got warnings of a change in the weather which should have caused them to seek shelter in the Delaware Breakwater en route. He therefore entered an interlocutory decree holding each tug and barge jointly liable to each cargo owner, and each tug for half damages for the loss of its barge. The petitioner appealed, and the barge owner appealed and filed assignments of error.

* * *

A more difficult issue is as to the tugs. We agree with the judge that once conceding the propriety of passing the Breakwater on the night of the eighth, the navigation was good enough. * * * [T]he case as to them turns upon whether they should have put in at the Breakwater.

* * *

[T]he "Montrose" and the "Hooper" would have had the benefit of the evening report from Arlington had they had proper receiving sets. This predicted worse weather; it read: "Increasing east and southeast winds, becoming fresh to strong, Friday night and increasing cloudiness followed by rain Friday." The bare "increase" of the morning had become "fresh to strong." To be sure this scarcely foretold a gale of from forty to fifty miles for five hours or more, rising at one time to fifty–six; but if the four tows thought the first report enough, the second ought to have laid any doubts. The master of the "Montrose" himself, when asked what he would have done had he received a substantially similar report, said that he would certainly have put in. The master of the "Hooper" was also asked for his opinion, and said that he would have turned back also, but this admission is somewhat vitiated by the incorporation in the question of the statement that it was a "storm warning," which the witness seized upon in his answer. All this seems to us to support the conclusion of the judge that prudent masters, who had received the second warning, would have found the risk more than the exigency warranted; they would have been amply vindicated by what followed. To be sure the barges would, as we have said, probably have withstood the gale, had they been well found; but a master is not justified in putting his tow to every test which she will survive, if she be fit. There is a zone in which proper caution will avoid putting her capacity to the proof; a coefficient of prudence that he should not disregard. Taking the situation as a whole, it seems to us that these masters would have taken undue chances, had they got the broadcasts [and not put in].

They did not, because their private radio receiving sets, which were on board, were not in working order. These belonged to them personally, and were partly a toy, partly a part of the equipment, but neither furnished by the owner, nor supervised by it. It is not fair to say that there was a general custom among coastwise carriers so to equip their tugs. One line alone did it; as for the rest, they relied upon their crews, so far as they can be said to have relied at all. An adequate receiving set suitable for a coastwise tug can now be got at small cost and is reasonably reliable if kept up; obviously it is a source of great protection to their tows. Twice every day they can receive these predictions, based upon the widest possible information, available to every vessel within two or three hundred miles and more. Such a set is the ears of the tug to catch the spoken word, just as the master's binoculars are her eyes to see a storm signal ashore. Whatever may be said as to other vessels, tugs towing heavy coal laden barges, strung out for half a mile, have little power to manoeuvre, and do not, as this case proves, expose themselves to weather which would not turn back stauncher craft. They can have at hand protection against dangers of which they can learn in no other way.

Is it then a final answer that the business had not yet generally adopted receiving sets? There are, no doubt, cases where courts seem to make the general practice of the calling the standard of proper diligence; we have indeed given some currency to the notion ourselves. [ ] Indeed in most cases reasonable prudence is in fact common prudence; but strictly it is never its measure; a whole calling may have unduly lagged in the adoption of new and available devices. It never may set its own tests, however persuasive be its usages. Courts must in the end say what is required; there are precautions so imperative that even their universal disregard will not excuse their omission. [ ] But here there was no custom at all as to receiving sets; some had them, some did not; the most that can be urged is that they had not yet become general. Certainly in such a case we need not pause; when some have thought a device necessary, at least we may say that they were right, and the others too slack. The statute (46 USCA § 484) does not bear on this situation at all. It prescribes not a receiving, but a transmitting set, and for a very different purpose; to call for help, not to get news. We hold the tugs therefore because had they been properly equipped, they would have got the Arlington reports. The injury was a direct consequence of this unseaworthiness.

Decree affirmed.

Notes

1. The question in *T.J. Hooper* was whether the tugs were "unseaworthy." This is a concept from maritime law; technically, it does not involve negligence. The standard, however, is whether the tugs were *"reasonably fit,"* so it is a close cousin of negligence. In any event, courts routinely apply the *T.J. Hooper* rule about industry custom to negligence.

2. *Departure* from industry custom or common usage is evidence of negligence, but it is not conclusive.

3. In *T.J. Hooper* a decision to equip the tugs with receiving radios, in departure from industry custom, would not have created countervailing risks of its own. It would just have increased safety. The only question was whether not equipping the tugs with receiving radios was safe enough. Sometimes, however, competing practices create countervailing sets of safety concerns. For example, equipping forklifts with doors might prevent some types of injury, but it might also trap operators inside in other situations of danger. A few courts have expressed concern that individual juries in specific cases could reach contradictory conclusions about which practice is reasonable and that a defendant should be protected if it follows a well–considered industry practice in such a case. See Duran v. General Motors Corp., 101 N.M. 742, 688 P.2d 779 (App.1983).

C. THE "REASONABLE PERSON"

VAUGHAN v. MENLOVE

Common Pleas, 1837.
3 Bing., N.C., 468.

[The plaintiff owned two cottages near the defendant's land. The defendant had a stack or "rick" of hay on his own land. The hay ignited due to spontaneous combustion caused by heat generated by the hay fermenting. The fire spread and the plaintiff's cottages were burned.]

At the trial it appeared that the rick in question had been made by the defendant near the boundary of his own premises; that the hay was in such a state when put together, as to give rise to discussions on the probability of fire; that though there were conflicting opinions on the subject, yet during a period of five weeks the defendant was repeatedly warned of his peril; that this stock was insured; and that upon one occasion, being advised to take the rick down to avoid all danger, he said "he would chance it." He made an aperture or chimney through the rick; but in spite, or perhaps in consequence of this precaution, the rick at length burst into flames from the spontaneous heating of its materials; the flames communicated to the defendant's barn and stables, and thence to the plaintiff's cottages, which were entirely destroyed.

PATTESON, J., before whom the cause was tried, told the jury that the question for them to consider was, whether the fire had been occasioned by gross negligence on the part of the defendant, adding, that he was bound to proceed with such reasonable caution as a prudent man would have exercised under such circumstances.

A verdict having been found for the plaintiff, a rule nisi for a new trial was obtained, on the ground that the jury should have been directed to consider, not whether the defendant had been guilty of a gross negligence with reference to the standard of ordinary prudence, a standard too uncertain to afford any criterion, but whether he had acted bonâ fide to the best of his judgment; if he had, he ought not to be responsible for the misfortune of not possessing the highest order of intelligence. * * *

TINDAL, C.J. I agree that this is a case primae impressionis; but I feel no difficulty in applying to it the principles of law as laid down in other cases of a similar kind. Undoubtedly this is not a case of contract, such as a bailment or the like, where the bailee is responsible in consequence of the remuneration he is to receive; but there is a rule of law which says you must so enjoy your own property as not to injure that of another; and according to that rule the defendant is liable for the consequence of his own neglect; and though the defendant did not himself light the fire, yet mediately he is as much the cause of it as if he had himself put a candle to the rick; for it is well known that hay will ferment and take fire if it be not carefully stacked. It has been decided that if an occupier burns weeds so near the boundary of his own land that damage ensues to the property of his neighbor, he is liable to an action for the amount of injury done, unless the accident were occasioned by a sudden blast which he could not foresee. Turberville v. Stamp, 1 Salk, 13. But put the case of a chemist making experiments with ingredients, singly innocent, but when combined liable to ignite; if he leaves them together, and injury is thereby occasioned to the property of his neighbor, can any one doubt that an action on the case would lie?

It is contended, however, that the learned judge was wrong in leaving this to the jury as a case of gross negligence, and that the question of negligence was so mixed up with reference to what would be the conduct of a man of ordinary prudence that the jury might have thought the latter the rule by which they were to decide; that such a rule would be too uncertain to act upon; and that the question ought to have been whether the defendant had acted honestly and bonâ fide to the best of his own judgment. That, however, would leave so vague a line as to afford no rule at all, the degree of judgment belonging to each individual being infinitely various; and though it has been urged that the care which a prudent man would take, is not an intelligible proposition as a rule of law, yet such has always been the rule adopted in cases of bailment, as laid down in Coggs v. Bernard, 2 Ld.Raym. 909. * * *

The care taken by a prudent man has always been the rule laid down; and as to the supposed difficulty of applying it, a jury has always been able to say, whether, taking that rule as their guide, there has been negligence on the occasion in question.

Instead, therefore, of saying that the liability for negligence should be coextensive with the judgment of each individual, which would be as variable as the length of the foot of each individual, we ought rather to adhere to the rule, which requires in all cases a regard to caution such as a man of ordinary prudence would observe. That was in substance the criterion presented to the jury in this case, and therefore the present rule must be discharged.

[Concurring opinions were delivered by PARK and VAUGHAN, JJ. GASE-LEE, J., concurred in the result.]

Rule discharged.

Notes

1. A "rule nisi" is a term used in England to signify an application for an appeal to an appellate court. When the "rule" is "discharged," the appeal fails. When the "rule" is "made absolute," the appeal is successful.

2. *Inferior abilities.* Courts uniformly apply an "objective" standard of negligence—that is, they do not take into account the actor's idiosyncrasies—when the defendant claims mere clumsiness, stupidity, or low mental ability.

3. *Insanity.* Most courts do not take even insanity into account when evaluating a defendant's conduct in a civil, as opposed to a criminal, case. See Jolley v. Powell, 299 So.2d 647 (Fla.App.1974). A few courts take

insanity into account when it causes the defendant to have a break with reality or precludes the defendant from conforming his conduct to the appropriate standard. Even so, however, a defendant who has reason to (and is able to) foresee such episodes might be negligent for putting himself in a position to do harm, such as by driving an automobile. See Breunig v. American Family Insurance Co., 45 Wis.2d 536, 173 N.W.2d 619 (1970).

4. *Superior abilities*. What if the actor possesses knowledge or skill that is not inferior, but superior to that of the average person? Courts have consistently held that such an actor is not held to a higher standard of care—the standard is still that of the ordinarily prudent person in the circumstances—but that the actor's special skills or experience are to be treated as among the circumstances to be considered when the conduct is judged. See, e.g., LaVine v. Clear Creek Skiing Corp., 557 F.2d 730, 734–35 (10th Cir.1977) (expert skier); Cervelli v. Graves, 661 P.2d 1032, 1034–35 (Wyo.1983) (professional truck driver).

5. *Intoxication*. Several courts have said that self–imposed intoxication does not forgive a defendant of conduct that would be negligent if committed by a sober person. See, e.g., Hamilton v. Kinsey, 337 So.2d 344 (Ala.1976).

ROBERTS v. STATE OF LOUISIANA

Louisiana Court of Appeal, 1981.
396 So.2d 566, aff'd on other grounds, 404 So.2d 1221 (La.1981).

LABORDE, JUDGE.

In this tort suit, William C. Roberts sued to recover damages for injuries he sustained in an accident in the lobby of the U.S. Post Office Building in Alexandria, Louisiana. Roberts fell after being bumped into by Mike Burson, the blind operator of the concession stand located in the building.

Plaintiff sued the State of Louisiana, through the Louisiana Health and Human Resources Administration, advancing two theories of liability: respondeat superior and negligent failure by the State to properly supervise and oversee the safe operation of the concession stand. The stand's blind operator, Mike Burson, is not a party to this suit although he is charged with negligence.

The trial court ordered plaintiff's suit dismissed holding that there is no respondeat superior liability without an employer–employee relationship and that there is no negligence liability without a cause in fact showing.

We affirm the trial court's decision for the reasons which follow.

On September 1, 1977, at about 12:45 in the afternoon, operator Mike Burson left his concession stand to go to the men's bathroom located in the building. As he was walking down the hall, he bumped into plaintiff who fell to the floor and injured his hip. Plaintiff was 75 years old, stood 5' 6" and weighed approximately 100 pounds. Burson, on the other hand, was 25 to 26 years old, stood approximately 6' and weighed 165 pounds.

At the time of the incident, Burson was not using a cane nor was he utilizing the technique of walking with his arm or hand in front of him.

Even though Burson was not joined as a defendant, his negligence or lack thereof is crucial to a determination of the State's liability. Because of its importance, we begin with it.

Plaintiff contends that operator Mike Burson traversed the area from his concession stand to the men's bathroom in a negligent manner. To be more specific, he focuses on the operator's failure to use his cane even though he had it with him in his concession stand.

In determining an actor's negligence, various courts have imposed differing standards of care to which handicapped persons are expected to perform. Professor William L. Prosser expresses one generally recognized modern standard of care as follows:

> As to his physical characteristics, the reasonable man may be said to be identical with the actor. The man who is blind * * * is entitled to live in the world and to have allowance made by others for his disability, and he cannot be required to do the impossible by conforming to physical standards which he cannot meet * * *. At the same time, the conduct of the handicapped individual must be reasonable in the light of his knowledge of his infirmity, which is treated merely as one of the circumstances under which he acts * * *. It is sometimes said that a blind man must use a greater degree of care than one who can see; but it is now generally agreed that as a fixed rule this is inaccurate, and that the correct statement is merely that he must take the precautions, be they more or less, which the ordinary reasonable man would take if he were blind. (W. Prosser, The Law of Torts § 32, pp.151–52 (4th ed. 1971)).

A careful review of the record in this instance reveals that Burson was acting as a reasonably prudent blind person would under these particular circumstances.

* * *

On the date of the incident in question, Mike Burson testified that he left his concession stand and was on his way to the men's bathroom when he bumped into plaintiff. He, without hesitancy, admitted that at the time he was not using his cane, explaining that he relies on his facial sense which he feels is an adequate technique for short trips inside the familiar building. Burson testified that he does use a cane to get to and from work.

Plaintiff makes much of Burson's failure to use a cane when traversing the halls of the post office building. Yet, our review of the testimony received at trial indicates that it is not uncommon for blind people to rely on other techniques when moving around in a familiar setting. For example George Marzloff, the director of the Division of Blind Services, testified that he can recommend to the blind operators that they should use a cane but he knows that when they are in a setting in which they are comfortable, he would say that nine out of ten will not use a cane and in his personal opinion, if the operator is in a relatively busy area, the cane can be more of a hazard than an asset. Mr. Marzloff further testified that he felt a reasonably functioning blind person would learn his way around his work setting as he does around his home so that he could get around without a cane. Mr. Marzloff added that he has several blind people working in his office, none of whom use a cane inside that facility.

* * *

The only testimony in the record that suggests that Burson traversed the halls in a negligent manner was that elicited from plaintiff's expert witness, William Henry Jacobson. Jacobson is an instructor in peripathology, which he explained as the science of movement within the surroundings by visually impaired individuals. Jacobson, admitting that he conducted no study or examination of Mike Burson's mobility skills and that he was unfamiliar with the State's vending program, nonetheless testified that he would require a blind person to use a cane in traversing the areas outside the concession stand. He added that a totally blind individual probably should use a cane * * * in an unfamiliar environment or where a familiar environment involves a change, whether it be people moving through that environment or strangers moving through that environment or just heavy traffic within that environment.

When cross examined however, Jacobson testified:

Q. Now, do you, in instructing blind people on their mobility skills, do you tell them to use their own judgment in which type of mobility assistance technique they're to employ?

A. Yes I do.

Q. Do you think that three (3) years is a long enough period for a person to become acquainted with an environment that he might be working with?

A. Yes I do.

Q. So you think that after a period of three (3) years an individual would probably, if he is normal * * * has normal mobility skills for a blind person, would have enough adjustment time to be * * * to call that environment familiar?

A. Yes.

Q. That's not including the fact that there may be people in and out of the building?

A. Right.

Q. Now is it possible that if he's familiar with the sounds of the people inside a building that he may even at some point in time become so familiar with the people in an area, regular customers or what not that you could say that the environment was familiar, including the fact that there are people there, is that possible?

A. Uh * * * I would hesitate to say that, in a public facility where we could not * * * uh * * * control strangers coming in.

Q. Well, let's say that a business has a particular group of clients that are always there, perhaps on a daily or weekly basis. Now you've stated that a blind person sharpens his auditory skills in order to help him articulate in an area?

A. With instruction, yes.

Q. Right. Isn't it possible that if he can rely on a fixed travel of a fixed type and number of persons that it's possible that that is a familiar environment even though there are people there?

A. Only if they were the same people all the time and they know him, yes.

Upon our review of the record, we feel that plaintiff has failed to show that Burson was negligent. Burson testified that he was very familiar with his surroundings, having worked there for three and a half years. He had special mobility training and his reports introduced into evidence indicate good mobility skills. He explained his decision to rely on his facial sense instead of his cane for these short trips in a manner which convinces us that it was a reasoned decision. Not only was Burson's explanation adequate, there was additional testimony from other persons indicating that such a decision is not an unreasonable one. Also important is the total lack of any evidence in the record showing that at the time of the incident, Burson engaged in any acts which may be characterized as negligence on his part. For example, there is nothing showing that Burson was walking too fast, not paying attention, et cetera. Under all of these circumstances, we conclude that Mike Burson was not negligent.

Our determination that Mike Burson was not negligent disposes of our need to discuss liability on the part of the State.

* * *

Note

The relevance of Burson's blindness to the question of negligence was clearly a question of law for the court. The subsequent question of the reasonableness of Burson's conduct, taking into account the fact that he was blind, would in most states be one for the jury, unless reasonable minds could not differ. But Louisiana has a practice of appellate review whereby appellate courts review the facts and can actually decide the question of negligence. In a normal jurisdiction that submits the issue of reasonable care to the jury unless reasonable minds could not differ, should the issue have been submitted to the jury on the evidence in *Roberts*?

STRAIT v. CRARY

Court of Appeals of Wisconsin, 1992.
173 Wis.2d 377, 496 N.W.2d 634, review denied, 501 N.W.2d 457 (Wis.1993).

EICH, CHIEF JUDGE.

David Strait, a minor at the time of the events leading up to this action, appeals from a judgment dismissing his personal injury claims against Terry Crary after the jury found him sixty–one percent negligent with respect to the incident upon which the action was based. While Strait raises several issues on the appeal, we consider one to be dispositive: whether the trial court erred in refusing to instruct the jury on the "special" standard of care applicable to children. We agree with Strait that the court's refusal to give the instructions was reversible error. We therefore reverse the judgment and remand for a new trial of the liability issues.

The events leading up to Strait's injury are largely undisputed. In May 1987, when Strait was 16 years old, he and several other teen–agers went riding in Crary's pickup truck. Crary [age 21] purchased beer and other intoxicants for the young people, and they soon became quite intoxicated. Crary, who was not drinking himself and remained sober throughout the evening, continued to drive the group through the countryside as they continued their drinking.

At some point in the evening, while Crary was driving down a country road (within the speed limit), Strait, who was sitting in the front seat, attempted to climb out of the passenger window and join the others in the box of the truck. He fell in the attempt and the truck ran over his leg, breaking it. Crary stopped the truck and, rather than call the police or an ambulance, decided to pick Strait up, place him back in the truck and drive him to the hospital—which he did, causing Strait additional pain and discomfort.

Strait and his parents sued Crary, claiming that he was negligent in the manner in which he operated his truck under the circumstances of the case.

At the trial's conclusion, Strait requested several jury instructions, among them Wis J I–Civil 1010, which sets a separate standard of care for children,[2] and its companion, Wis J I–Civil 1582, which instructs the jury that it must consider that special standard in comparing the parties' negligence.

2. Wisconsin J I–Civil 1010 provides:
1010 NEGLIGENCE OF CHILDREN
As a child, (___) was required to use the degree of care which is ordinarily exercised by a child of the same age, intelligence, discretion, knowledge, and experience under the same or similar circumstances.

In determining whether (___) exercised this degree of care, you should consider the child's instincts and impulses with respect to dangerous acts, since a child may not have the prudence, discretion, or thoughtfulness of an adult.

The trial court denied the requests, concluding that under the rather unusual facts of the case—particularly the drinking and the nature of the acts in which Strait was engaged when he fell from the truck—Strait, although a minor, should be held to the standard of care applicable to adults. The court explained its reasoning at the hearing on Strait's postverdict motions:

> If this had been a year–old child or a six–year–old child and the door was unlocked or the window was open or some such thing as that, then, yes, you have to give that instruction * * * as to children, the driver needs to take special precautions, that's obvious, but when you try to tell me that * * * a 21–year–old driver has got to take extra precautions when there is a 16–year–old passenger * * * crawling out the window to get [into] the back end of the truck, that is preposterous * * *.

As indicated, the jury found both Strait and Crary causally negligent and apportioned the negligence sixty–one percent to Strait and thirty–nine percent to Crary. The trial court denied Strait's postverdict motions and dismissed the action.*

* * *

Here the central issue at trial was the comparative negligence of Strait and Crary. At the time of the accident Strait was a child and Crary was an adult. Thus the proper standard of care to be applied to the litigants was plainly raised by the evidence. Indeed, it was essential to the case. Nonetheless, the trial court declined to give the instructions that would have informed the jury of the law: that "different standards of ordinary care apply to [children and adults]." Brice v. Milwaukee Automobile Ins. Co., 272 Wis. 520, 525, 76 N.W.2d 337, 340 (1956).

Crary argues that we should not find error in the court's refusal. He maintains that the case fits an "exception" to the adult/child rule which holds a child to the adult standard when he or she is "engaged in an activity which is typically engaged in only by adults * * *." See Wis J I–Civil 1010, Comment; Restatement, Law of Torts (Second) cmt c (1965). Prosser explains the rule as follows:

> [W]henever a child, whether as plaintiff or as defendant, engages in an activity which is normally one for adults only, such as driving an automobile or flying an airplane, the public interest and the public safety require that any consequences due to his [or her] own incapacity shall fall upon him [or her] rather than the innocent victim, and that he [or she] must be held to the adult standard, without any allowance for * * * age. (Prosser, Law of Torts § 32, at 156–57 (4th ed. 1971).)

Two things are apparent. First, the exception applies only in cases where the child is engaged in an "adults–only" or "licensed" activity,

---

* Under Wisconsin's system of "modified" comparative negligence, a plaintiff found more negligent than the defendant recovers nothing. [Ed.]

such as driving a car or flying an airplane.[5] Second, the rule is grounded on public policy considerations: that when a child is engaged in such adult activities, public policy requires that the child himself or herself, rather than any "innocent victim[s]" of the child's conduct, should suffer the consequences of that conduct.

Here, while it might be said that drinking to the point of intoxication is—generally, but certainly not exclusively—an adult–type activity, climbing around the outside of a moving vehicle may well not be. Even so, however, the policy underlying the rule—the result it was fashioned to avoid—is not implicated in this case, for there is no "innocent victim" of Strait's conduct. We conclude, therefore, that the exception to the rule holding minors to a different standard of care than adults is inapplicable to the facts of this case. As a result, the trial court erred when it implicitly adopted and applied that exception in rejecting Strait's proffered instructions.

* * *

Here the legal error was plain. The instructions as given told the jury to hold Strait to the same standard of care as Crary, an adult, and to compare that negligence without considering Strait's age. As we have indicated above, the law states otherwise. And we believe the error goes to the heart of the case, which was, as we also have indicated, the assessment and comparison of Strait's and Crary's negligence. We are satisfied that it is probable that the jury was misled by such an instruction and that the result of the jurors' assessment and comparison of the parties' negligence might have been different if they had been properly instructed. We therefore reverse and remand for a new trial on those issues.

Judgment reversed and cause remanded with directions for further proceedings consistent with this opinion.

Notes

1. *The old "multiples of seven" approach; minimum age for child negligence.* A few courts created presumptions about children in different age groups: children below age seven were conclusively presumed to be incapable of negligence, children between ages seven and fourteen were presumed to be incapable of negligence, but the presumption could be rebutted by the other party, and children over the age of fourteen were presumed to be capable of negligence, but the presumption could be rebutted by the child. See Dunn v. Teti, 280 Pa.Super. 399, 421 A.2d 782 (1980). Most courts have abolished these presumptions. These courts simply instruct the jury to determine whether the defendant exercised the care of a reasonable child of like age, intelligence and experience. See, e.g., Williamson v. Garland, 402 S.W.2d 80 (Ky.1966) (contributory negligence).

5. The comment to Wis J I–Civil 1010 describes the exception as limited to situations where the child is engaged in an adult activity "for which adult qualification or a license is required."

The Restatement (Third) of Torts § 10(b) (2001) provides that a child under the age of five is incapable of negligence. Most jurisdictions have agreed that some minimum age is appropriate, and while the cases have varied somewhat as to the specific number, the Restatement reporters found that five appeared to have the most support both in judicial authorities and in contemporary social behavior.

2. *The "age, intelligence, and experience" standard.* Note that more than age is taken into account. Unlike adults, children are permitted to excuse their conduct by a showing of low mental ability or lack of experience. In Sherry v. Asing, 56 Haw. 135, 531 P.2d 648 (1975), an issue was whether a seventeen–year–old "mentally slow" plaintiff was contributorily negligent. The plaintiff requested the following jury instruction:

> A minor is not held to the same standard as an adult. A child is only required to use care appropriate to his age and experience and mental capacity.

The trial court gave this instruction, but only after omitting the words "and mental capacity." The defendant requested the following instruction:

> Under the rule of ordinary care which I have just stated, no exception is made for a person who is mentally retarded. A person who is mentally retarded is bound to follow the same standard of care as any person acting under the same circumstances.

The trial court gave this instruction in its entirety. The Hawaii Supreme Court held that because the plaintiff was a child, the trial court erred by deleting the last three words of the plaintiff's proposed instruction and by giving the defendant's proposed instruction.

3. *The adult activity exception.* The leading case on the "adult activity" exception to the special standard for children is Dellwo v. Pearson, 259 Minn. 452, 107 N.W.2d 859 (1961). The defendant, a twelve–year–old boy, drove his motorboat across the plaintiff's fishing line. This caused the reel of the plaintiff's fishing rod to fly off, hit her glasses, and injure her eye. The court said:

> A more important point involves the instruction that defendant was to be judged by the standard of care of a child of similar age rather than of a reasonable man. There is no doubt that the instruction given substantially reflects the language of numerous decisions in this and other courts. However, the great majority of these cases involve the issue of contributory negligence and the standard of care that may properly be required of a child in protecting himself against some hazard. The standard of care stated is proper and appropriate for such situations.
>
> However, this court has previously recognized that there may be a difference between the standard of care that is required of a child in protecting himself against hazards and the standard that may be applicable when his activities expose others to hazards. Certainly in the circumstances of modern life, where vehicles moved by powerful motors are readily available and frequently operated by immature individuals, we should be skeptical of a rule that would allow motor vehicles to be

operated to the hazard of the public with less than the normal minimum degree of care and competence.

* * * While minors are entitled to be judged by standards commensurate with age, experience, and wisdom when engaged in activities appropriate to their age, experience, and wisdom, it would be unfair to the public to permit a minor in the operation of a motor vehicle to observe any other standards of care and conduct than those expected of all others. A person observing children at play with toys, throwing balls, operating tricycles or velocipedes, or engaged in other childhood activities may anticipate conduct that does not reach an adult standard of care of prudence. However, one cannot know whether the operator of an approaching automobile, airplane, or powerboat is a minor or an adult, and usually cannot protect himself against youthful imprudence even if warned. Accordingly, we hold that in the operation of an automobile, airplane, or powerboat, a minor is to be held to the same standard of care as an adult.

107 N.W.2d at 862–63 (citations and footnotes omitted). As indicated by the principal case, the adult activity exception has generally been confined to motor vehicle cases. For example, the majority of cases involving firearms have applied the child rather than the adult standard. See, e.g., Purtle v. Shelton, 251 Ark. 519, 474 S.W.2d 123 (1971) (17–year–old with deer rifle) ("If we should declare that a minor hunting deer with a high–powered rifle must in all instances be held to an adult standard of care, we must be prepared to explain why the same rule should not apply to a minor hunting deer with a shotgun, to a minor hunting rabbits with a high–powered rifle, to a twelve–year–old shooting crows with a .22, and so on down to the six–year–old shooting at tin cans with an air rifle."). Contra, e.g., Huebner by Lane v. Koelfgren, 519 N.W.2d 488 (Minn.App.1994) (14–year–old with BB gun) ("We agree with the trial court that the adult standard of care should be imposed on and expected by a teenager handling a gun; the public generally has a right to expect a single, adult standard of care from individuals who handle guns.").

D. VIOLATION OF STATUTE

MARTIN v. HERZOG

Court of Appeals of New York, 1920.
228 N.Y. 164, 126 N.E. 814.

CARDOZO, JUDGE.

The action is one to recover damages for injuries resulting in death. Plaintiff and her husband, while driving toward Tarrytown in a buggy on the night of August 21, 1915, were struck by the defendant's automobile coming in the opposite direction. They were thrown to the ground, and the man was killed. At the point of the collision the highway makes a curve. The car was rounding the curve, when suddenly it came upon the buggy, emerging, the defendant tells us, from the gloom. Negligence is charged against the defendant, the driver of the car, in that he did not keep to the right of the center of the highway. Highway

Law, § 286, subd. 3, and section 332 (Consol.Laws, c. 25). Negligence is charged against the plaintiff's intestate, the driver of the wagon, in that he was traveling without lights. Highway Law, § 329a, as amended by Laws 1915, c. 367. There is no evidence that the defendant was moving at an excessive speed. There is none of any defect in the equipment of his car. The beam of light from his lamps pointed to the right as the wheels of his car turned along the curve toward the left; and, looking in the direction of the plaintiff's approach, he was peering into the shadow. The case against him must stand, therefore, if at all, upon the divergence of his course from the center of the highway. The jury found him delinquent and his victim blameless. The Appellate Division reversed, and ordered a new trial.

We agree with the Appellate Division that the charge to the jury was erroneous and misleading. The case was tried on the assumption that the hour had arrived when lights were due. It was argued on the same assumption in this court. In such circumstances, it is not important whether the hour might have been made a question for the jury. A controversy put out of the case by the parties is not to be put into it by us. We say this by way of preface to our review of the contested rulings. In the body of the charge the trial judge said that the jury could consider the absence of light "in determining whether the plaintiff's intestate was guilty of contributory negligence in failing to have a light upon the buggy as provided by law. I do not mean to say that the absence of light necessarily makes him negligent, but it is a fact for your consideration." The defendant requested a ruling that the absence of a light on the plaintiff's vehicle was "prima facie evidence of contributory negligence." This request was refused, and the jury were again instructed that they might consider the absence of lights as some evidence of negligence, but that it was not conclusive evidence. The plaintiff then requested a charge that "the fact that the plaintiff's intestate was driving without a light is not negligence in itself," and to this the court acceded. The defendant saved his rights by appropriate exceptions.

We think the unexcused omission of the statutory signals is more than some evidence of negligence. It is negligence in itself. Lights are intended for the guidance and protection of other travelers on the highway. By the very terms of the hypothesis, to omit, willfully or heedlessly, the safeguards prescribed by law for the benefit of another that he may be preserved in life or limb, is to fall short of the standard of diligence to which those who live in organized society are under a duty to conform. That, we think, is now the established rule in this state. Whether the omission of an absolute duty, not willfully or heedlessly, but through unavoidable accident, is also to be characterized as negligence, is a question of nomenclature into which we need not enter, for it does not touch the case before us. There may be times, when, if jural niceties are to be preserved, the two wrongs, negligence and breach of statutory duty, must be kept distinct in speech and thought.

In the conditions here present they come together and coalesce. A rule less rigid has been applied where the one who complains of the omission is not a member of the class for whose protection the safeguard is designed. Some relaxation there has also been where the safeguard is prescribed by local ordinance, and not by statute. Courts have been reluctant to hold that the police regulations of boards and councils and other subordinate officials create rights of action beyond the specific penalties imposed. This has led them to say that the violation of a statute is negligence, and the violation of a like ordinance is only evidence of negligence. An ordinance, however, like a statute, is a law within its sphere of operation, and so the distinction has not escaped criticism. Whether it has become too deeply rooted to be abandoned, even if it be thought illogical, is a question not now before us. * * *

In the case at hand, we have an instance of the admitted violation of a statute intended for the protection of travelers on the highway, of whom the defendant at the time was one. Yet the jurors were instructed in effect that they were at liberty in their discretion to treat the omission of lights either as innocent or as culpable. They were allowed to "consider the default as lightly or gravely" as they would (Thomas, J., in the court below). They might as well have been told that they could use a like discretion in holding a master at fault for the omission of a safety appliance prescribed by positive law for the protection of a workman. Jurors have no dispensing power, by which they may relax the duty that one traveler on the highway owes under the statute to another. It is error to tell them that they have. The omission of these lights was a wrong, and, being wholly unexcused, was also a negligent wrong. No license should have been conceded to the triers of the facts to find it anything else.

We must be on our guard, however, against confusing the question of negligence with that of the causal connection between the negligence and the injury. A defendant who travels without lights is not to pay damages for his fault, unless the absence of lights is the cause of the disaster. A plaintiff who travels without them is not to forfeit the right to damages, unless the absence of lights is at least a contributing cause of the disaster. To say that conduct is negligence is not to say that it is always contributory negligence. "Proof of negligence in the air, so to speak, will not do." Pollock Torts (10th Ed.) p. 472.

We think, however, that evidence of a collision occurring more than an hour after sundown between a car and an unseen buggy, proceeding without lights, is evidence from which a causal connection may be inferred between the collision and the lack of signals. If nothing else is shown to break the connection, we have a case, prima facie sufficient, of negligence contributing to the result.

* * *

Here, on the undisputed facts, lack of vision, whether excusable or not, was the cause of the disaster. The defendant may have been negligent in swerving from the center of the road; but he did not run into the buggy purposely, nor was he driving while intoxicated, nor was he going at such a reckless speed that warning would of necessity have been futile. Nothing of the kind is shown. The collision was due to his failure to see at a time when sight should have been aroused and guided by the statutory warnings. Some explanation of the effect to be given to the absence of those warnings, if the plaintiff failed to prove that other lights on the car or the highway took their place as equivalents, should have been put before the jury. The explanation was asked for and refused.

We are persuaded that the tendency of the charge, and of all the rulings, following it, was to minimize unduly, in the minds of the triers of the facts, the gravity of the decedent's fault. Errors may not be ignored as unsubstantial, when they tend to such an outcome. A statute designed for the protection of human life is not to be brushed aside as a form of words, its commands reduced to the level of cautions, and the duty to obey attenuated into an option to conform.

The order of the Appellate Division should be affirmed * * *.

Hogan, J., dissenting.

* * *

Notes

1. When giving effect to a statute, courts do not distinguish between cases involving the plaintiff's negligence and cases involving the defendant's negligence.

Several courts have held, contrary to *Martin*, that violation of statute is merely evidence of negligence, which the jury can consider.

2. The statute in *Martin* did not address its effect on tort liability. Like most traffic statutes, it merely imposed a nominal fine for violation. It is highly unlikely that the legislature ever thought about the issue of tort liability. Thus, the question for courts is the effect of such statutes in the absence of clear legislative intent. In a few situations, however, the legislature might actually address the effect of the statute on tort liability, or the court might be able to ascertain the legislative intent from the circumstances. In that event, the legislature's decision about the effect of the statute controls.

3. Even in states that follow *Martin* and hold that unexcused violation of statute normally is conclusive on the issue of breach, violation of statute does not conclusively establish liability. The other elements of tort liability are still open for dispute. Thus, in *Martin,* Justice Cardozo still required proof that the plaintiff's failure to have lights was a cause of the accident. Similarly, in a case in which a defendant violates a statute, the defendant can still claim that the plaintiff was contributorily negligent (unless, of course, the statute expressly or impliedly provides a contrary rule).

4. Compliance with a statutory provision is usually just evidence of reasonable care, not conclusive on the issue of reasonable care. See, e.g., Christou v. Arlington Park–Washington Park Race Tracks Corp., 104 Ill. App.3d 257, 60 Ill.Dec. 21, 432 N.E.2d 920 (1982).

TEDLA v. ELLMAN

Court of Appeals of New York, 1939.
280 N.Y. 124, 19 N.E.2d 987.

LEHMAN, JUDGE.

While walking along a highway, Anna Tedla and her brother, John Bachek, were struck by a passing automobile, operated by the defendant Ellman. She was injured and Bachek was killed. Bachek was a deaf-mute. His occupation was collecting and selling junk. His sister, Mrs. Tedla, was engaged in the same occupation. They often picked up junk at the incinerator of the village of Islip. At the time of the accident they were walking along "Sunrise Highway" and wheeling baby carriages containing junk and wood which they had picked up at the incinerator. It was about six o'clock, or a little earlier, on a Sunday evening in December. Darkness had already set in. Bachek was carrying a lighted lantern, or, at least, there is testimony to that effect. The jury found that the accident was due solely to the negligence of the operator of the automobile. The defendants do not, upon this appeal, challenge the finding of negligence on the part of the operator. They maintain, however, that Mrs. Tedla and her brother were guilty of contributory negligence as matter of law.

Sunrise Highway, at the place of the accident, consists of two roadways, separated by a grass plot. There are no footpaths along the highway and the center grass plot was soft. It is not unlawful for a pedestrian, wheeling a baby carriage, to use the roadway under such circumstances, but a pedestrian using the roadway is bound to exercise such care for his safety as a reasonably prudent person would use. The Vehicle and Traffic Law (Consol.Laws, c. 71) provides that "Pedestrians walking or remaining on the paved portion, or traveled part of a roadway shall be subject to, and comply with, the rules governing vehicles, with respect to meeting and turning out, except that such pedestrians shall keep to the left of the center line thereof, and turn to their left instead of right side thereof, so as to permit all vehicles passing them in either direction to pass on their right. Such pedestrians shall not be subject to the rules governing vehicles as to giving signals." Section 85, subd. 6. Mrs. Tedla and her brother did not observe the statutory rule, and at the time of the accident were proceeding in easterly direction on the east bound or right-hand roadway. The defendants moved to dismiss the complaint on the ground, among others, that violation of the statutory rule constitutes contributory negligence as matter of law. They did not, in the courts below, urge that any negligence in other respect of Mrs. Tedla or her brother bars a recovery. The trial judge left to the jury the question whether failure to observe the statutory rule was a proximate cause of the accident; he left to the jury no question of other fault or negligence on the part of Mrs. Tedla or her brother, and the defendants did not request that any other question be submitted. Upon this appeal, the only question presented is whether, as matter of law, disregard of the statutory rule that pedestrians shall keep to the left of the center line of a highway constitutes contributory negligence which bars any recovery by the plaintiff.

Vehicular traffic can proceed safely and without recurrent traffic tangles only if vehicles observe accepted rules of the road. Such rules, and especially the rule that all vehicles proceeding in one direction must keep to a designated part or side of the road—in this country the right–hand side—have been dictated by necessity and formulated by custom. The general use of automobiles has increased in unprecedented degree the number and speed of vehicles. Control of traffic becomes an increasingly difficult problem. Rules of the road, regulating the rights and duties of those who use highways, have, in consequence, become increasingly important. The Legislature no longer leaves to custom the formulation of such rules. Statutes now codify, define, supplement, and, where changing conditions suggest change in rule, even change rules of the road which formerly rested on custom. Custom and common sense have always dictated that vehicles should have the right of way over pedestrians and that pedestrians should walk along the edge of a highway so that they might step aside for passing vehicles with least danger to themselves and least obstruction to vehicular traffic. Otherwise, perhaps, no customary rule of the road was observed by pedestrians with the same uniformity as by vehicles; though, in general, they probably followed, until recently, the same rules as vehicles.

Pedestrians are seldom a source of danger or serious obstruction to vehicles and when horse–drawn vehicles were common they seldom injured pedestrians using a highway with reasonable care, unless the horse became unmanageable or the driver was grossly negligent or guilty of willful wrong. Swift–moving motor vehicles, it was soon recognized, do endanger the safety of pedestrians crossing highways, and it is imperative that there the relative rights and duties of pedestrians and of vehicles should be understood and observed. The Legislature in the first five subdivisions of section 85 of the Vehicle and Traffic Law has provided regulations to govern the conduct of pedestrians and of drivers of vehicles when a pedestrian is crossing a road. Until by chapter 114 of the Laws of 1933, it adopted subdivision 6 of section 85, quoted above, there was no special statutory rule for pedestrians walking along a highway. Then for the first time it reversed, for pedestrians, the rule established for vehicles by immemorial custom, and provided that pedestrians shall keep to the left of the center line of a highway.

The plaintiffs showed by the testimony of a State policeman that "there were very few cars going east" at the time of the accident, but that going west there was "very heavy Sunday night traffic." Until the recent adoption of the new statutory rule for pedestrians, ordinary prudence would have dictated that pedestrians should not expose themselves to the danger of walking along the roadway upon which the "very heavy Sunday night traffic" was proceeding when they could walk in comparative safety along a roadway used by very few cars. It is said that now, by force of the statutory rule, pedestrians are guilty of contributory negligence as matter of law when they use the safer roadway, unless that roadway is left of the center of the road. Disregard of the statutory rule of the road and observance of a rule based on immemorial custom, it is said, is negligence which as matter of law is a proximate cause of the accident, though observance of the statutory rule might, under the circumstances of the particular case, expose a pedestrian to serious danger from which he would be free if he followed the rule that had been established by custom. If that be true, then the Legislature has decreed that pedestrians must observe the general rule of conduct which it has prescribed for their safety even under circumstances where observance would subject them to unusual risk; that pedestrians are to be charged with negligence as matter of law for acting as prudence dictates. It is unreasonable to ascribe to the Legislature an intention that the statute should have so extraordinary a result, and the courts may not give to a statute an effect not intended by the Legislature.

The Legislature, when it enacted the statute, presumably knew that this court and the courts of other jurisdictions had established the general principle that omission by a plaintiff of a safeguard, prescribed by statute, against a recognized danger, constitutes negligence as matter of law which bars recovery for damages caused by incidence of the danger for which the safeguard was prescribed. The principle has been formulated in the Restatement of the Law of Torts: "A plaintiff who has violated a legislative enactment designed to prevent a certain type of dangerous situation is barred from recovery for a harm caused by a violation of the statute if, but only if, the harm was sustained by reason of a situation of that type." § 469. So where a plaintiff failed to place lights upon a vehicle, as required by statute, this court has said: "we think the unexcused omission of the statutory signals is more than some evidence of negligence. It is negligence in itself. Lights are intended for the guidance and protection of other travelers on the highway. Highway Law (Consol.Laws, c. 25) § 329–a. By the very terms of the hypothesis, to omit, willfully or heedlessly, the safeguards prescribed by law for the benefit of another that he may be preserved in life or limb, is to fall short of the standard of diligence to which those who live in organized society are under a duty to conform. That, we think, is now the established rule in this State." Martin v. Herzog, 228 N.Y. 164, 168, 126 N.E. 814, 815, per Cardozo, J. The appellants lean heavily upon that and kindred cases and the principle established by them.

The analogy is, however, incomplete. The "established rule" should not be weakened either by subtle distinctions or by extension beyond its letter or spirit into a field where "by the very terms of the hypothesis" it can have no proper application. At times the indefinite and flexible standard of care of the traditional reasonably prudent man may be, in the opinion of the Legislature, an insufficient measure of the care which should be exercised to guard against a recognized danger; at times, the duty, imposed by custom, that no man shall use what is his to the harm of others provides insufficient safeguard for the preservation of the life or limb or property of others. Then the Legislature may by statute prescribe additional safeguards and may define duty and standard of care in rigid terms; and when the Legislature has spoken, the standard of the care required is no longer what the reasonably prudent man would do under the circumstances but what the Legislature has commanded. That is the rule established by the courts and "by the very terms of the hypothesis" the rule applies where the Legislature has prescribed safeguards "for the benefit of another that he may be preserved in life or limb." In that field debate as to whether the safeguards so prescribed are reasonably necessary is ended by the legislative fiat. Obedience to that fiat cannot add to the danger, even assuming that the prescribed safeguards are not reasonably necessary and where the legislative anticipation of dangers is realized and harm results through heedless or willful omission of the prescribed safeguard, injury flows from wrong and the wrongdoer is properly held responsible for the consequent damages.

The statute upon which the defendants rely is of different character. It does not prescribe additional safeguards which pedestrians must provide for the preservation of the life or limb or property of others, or even of themselves, nor does it impose upon pedestrians a higher standard of care. What the statute does provide is rules of the road to be observed by pedestrians and by vehicles, so that all those who use the road may know how they and others should proceed, at least under usual circumstances. A general rule of conduct—and, specifically, a rule of the road—may accomplish its intended purpose under usual conditions, but, when the unusual occurs, strict observance may defeat the purpose of the rule and produce catastrophic results.

Negligence is failure to exercise the care required by law. Where a statute defines the standard of care and the safeguards required to meet a recognized danger, then, as we have said, no other measure may be applied in determining whether a person has carried out the duty of care imposed by law. Failure to observe the standard imposed by statute is negligence, as matter of law. On the other hand, where a statutory general rule of conduct fixes no definite standard of care which would under all circumstances tend to protect life, limb or property but merely codifies or supplements a common–law rule, which has always been subject to limitations and exceptions; or where the statutory rule of conduct regulates conflicting rights and obligations in manner calculated to promote public convenience and safety, then the statute, in the absence of clear language to the contrary, should not be construed as intended to wipe out the limitations and exceptions which judicial decisions have attached to the common–law duty; nor should it be construed as an inflexible command that the general rule of conduct intended to prevent accidents must be followed even under conditions when observance might cause accidents. We may assume reasonably that the Legislature directed pedestrians to keep to the left of the center of the road because that would cause them to face traffic approaching in that lane and would enable them to care for their own safety better than if the traffic approached them from the rear. We cannot assume reasonably that the Legislature intended that a statute enacted for the preservation of the life and limb of pedestrians must be observed when observance would subject them to more imminent danger.

* * *

Judgment affirmed.

O'Brien and Finch, JJ., dissent on the authority of Martin v. Herzog * * *.

Notes

1. In Krebs v. Rubsam, 91 N.J.L. 426, 104 A. 83 (1918), plaintiff's decedent fell in an unlighted stairway in defendant's building. A state statute required a light. The defendant argued that it was impossible for him to comply because, unknown to him, a third person extinguished the light immediately before the decedent's fall, and the defendant had no opportunity to relight the hallway. The court held that the violation was excused.

2. In Freund v. DeBuse, 264 Or. 447, 506 P.2d 491 (1973), the Oregon Supreme Court went further, holding that the defendant's *reasonable efforts* to comply with the statute excused his violation. The statute required motorists to have "adequate" brakes. The defendant's brakes failed suddenly, and he struck the rear of the plaintiff's car. The defendant successfully argued that he used reasonable care in maintaining his brakes.

3. Some safety statutes expressly or impliedly provide for liability regardless of the defendant's efforts to comply. For example, in O'Donnell v. Elgin, Joliet & Eastern Ry. Co., 338 U.S. 384, 70 S.Ct. 200, 94 L.Ed. 187, reh. den. 338 U.S. 945, 70 S.Ct. 427, 94 L.Ed. 583 (1950), the Court held that the Federal Safety Appliance Act, which requires railroads to maintain their cars with automatic couplers, creates absolute liability for injury caused by a coupler that fails, regardless of the railroad's efforts to maintain the couplers.

4. In Morby v. Rogers, 122 Utah 540, 252 P.2d 231 (1953), a thirteen–year–old child was killed when he was riding his bicycle and was struck by the defendant's car. The boy was turning without signaling, in violation of statute. In a suit by the boy's estate, the defendant argued that the boy's violation of statute established contributory negligence. The court disagreed, holding that the statute was not intended to displace the more forgiving standard of care usually applied to children. The court recognized authority in other jurisdictions to the contrary but described its holding as being in accordance with the majority view.

GORRIS v. SCOTT
Court of Exchequer, 1874.
9 Ex. 125.

Kelly, C.B.

This is an action to recover damages for the loss of a number of sheep which the defendant, a shipowner, had contracted to carry, and which were washed overboard and lost by reason (as we must take it to be truly alleged) of the neglect to comply with a certain order made by the Privy Council, in pursuance of the Contagious Diseases (Animals) Act, 1869. The Act was passed merely for sanitary purposes, in order to prevent animals in a state of infectious disease from communicating it to other animals with which they might come in contact. Under the authority of that Act, certain orders were made; amongst others, an order by which any ship bringing sheep or cattle from any foreign port to ports in Great Britain is to have the place occupied by such animals divided into pens of certain dimensions, and the floor of such pens furnished with battens or foot–holds. The object of this order is to prevent animals from being overcrowded, and so brought into a condition in which the disease guarded against would be likely to be developed. This regulation has been neglected, and the question is, whether the loss, which we must assume to have been caused by that neglect, entitles the plaintiffs to maintain an action.

The argument of the defendant is, that the Act has imposed penalties to secure the observance of its provisions, and that, according to the general rule, the remedy prescribed by the statute must be pursued; that although, when penalties are imposed for the violation of a statutory duty, a person aggrieved by its violation may sometimes maintain an action for the damage so caused, that must be in cases where the object of the statute is to confer a benefit on individuals, and to protect them against the evil consequences which the statute was designed to prevent, and which have in fact ensued; but that if the object is not to protect individuals against the consequences which have in fact ensued, it is otherwise; that if, therefore, by reason of the precautions in question not having been taken, the plaintiffs had sustained that damage against which it was intended to secure them, an action would lie, but that when the damage is of such a nature as was not contemplated at all by the statute, and as to which it was not intended to confer any benefit on the plaintiffs, they cannot maintain an action founded on the neglect. The principle may be well illustrated by the case put in argument of a breach by a railway company of its duty to erect a gate on a level crossing, and to keep the gate closed except when the crossing is being actually and properly used. The object of the precaution is to prevent injury from being sustained through animals or vehicles being upon the line at unseasonable times; and if by reason of such a breach of duty, either in not erecting the gate, or in not keeping it closed, a person attempts to cross with a carriage at an improper time, and injury ensues to a passenger, no doubt an action would lie against the railway company, because the intention of the legislature was that, by the erection of the gates and by their being kept closed individuals should be protected against accidents of their description. And if we could see that it was the object, or among the objects of this Act, that the owners of sheep and cattle coming from a foreign port should be protected by the means described against the danger of their property being washed overboard, or lost by the perils of the sea, the present action would be within the principle.

But, looking at the Act, it is perfectly clear that its provisions were all enacted with a totally different view: there was no purpose, direct or indirect, to protect against such damage; but, as is recited in the preamble, the Act is directed against the possibility of sheep or cattle being exposed to disease on their way to this country. The preamble recites that "it is expedient to confer on Her Majesty's most honorable Privy Council power to take such measures as may appear from time to time necessary to prevent the introduction into Great Britain of contagious or infectious diseases among cattle, sheep, or other animals, by prohibiting or regulating the importation of foreign animals," and also to provide against the "spreading" of such diseases in Great Britain. * * * That being so, if by reason of the default in question the plaintiffs' sheep had been overcrowded, or had been caused unnecessary suffering, and so had arrived in this country in a state of disease[,] I do not say that they might not have maintained this action. But the damage complained of here is something totally apart from the object of the Act of Parliament, and it is in accordance with all the authorities to say that the action is not maintainable.

POTTS v. FIDELITY FRUIT & PRODUCE CO.

Court of Appeals of Georgia, 1983.
165 Ga.App. 546, 301 S.E.2d 903.

BANKE, JUDGE.

The appellant sued to recover for personal injuries which he allegedly sustained when he was bitten by a spider while unloading bananas from a truck. The incident occurred during the course of his employment with Colonial Stores. The defendants are the local distributor of the bananas, Fidelity Fruit and Produce Co., Inc., and the transporter, Refrigerated Transport Co., Inc. Liability was originally predicated both on ordinary negligence and negligence per se under the Georgia Food Act, OCGA §§ 26–2–20 et seq. However, the appellant has since conceded that the evidence would not sustain a finding of ordinary negligence. This appeal is from a grant of summary judgment in favor of Fidelity Fruit and Produce Co., Inc., as to the negligence per se claim, based on a determination that the appellant is not among the class of persons whom the Georgia Food Act was designed to protect. *Held:*

> In determining whether the violation of a statute or ordinance is negligence per se as to a particular person, it is necessary to examine the purposes of the legislation and decide (1) whether the injured person falls within the class of persons it was intended to protect and (2) whether the harm complained of was the harm it was intended to guard against. [ ] Having examined the provisions of the Georgia Food Act, we agree fully with the following analysis made by the trial court: "Clearly, the Act is a consumer protection act, designed not to render the workplace a safe environment, but to prevent the sale and distribution of adulterated or misbranded foods to consumers. While safety in the workplace, and compensation for

injuries arising out of work activities, are indeed matters of contemporary concern, they are the subject of other legislative enactments on both the state and federal level." Because the appellant's alleged injuries did not arise incident to his consumption of the bananas, we hold that the trial court was correct in concluding that the Act affords him no basis for recovery.

Judgment affirmed.

ZERBY v. WARREN

Supreme Court of Minnesota, 1973.
297 Minn. 134, 210 N.W.2d 58.

KELLY, JUSTICE.

* * *

[On August 31, 1969, Steven Zerby, a 14–year–old minor, and Randy Rieken, age 13, went together to the Coast–to–Coast Store in Austin, Minnesota. The store was owned by Chester Warren, who employed Robert Dieke as a clerk in the store.] Rieken purchased two pint containers of Weldwood Contact Cement at the store from Deike, who sold it within the course and scope of his employment as a clerk in the store. The glue contained toluene and was not a part of a packaged kit for construction of a model automobile, airplane, or similar item. At the time of the sale, neither defendant Warren nor Deike were aware that the sale was in violation of Minn. St. 145.38, which had become effective on July 1, 1969.

After Rieken had purchased the glue, he and [Zerby] left the shopping center and within a few hours [intentionally] inhaled the fumes from the glue. [Zerby died as a result of sniffing the glue. The fumes] had an injurious effect on his central nervous system, causing him to fall into a creek and drown. * * *

[Zerby's family brought a wrongful death action against Warren and Deike. Warren and Deike then filed a third–party action against Reiken, seeking contribution, and a third party action against U.S. Plywood Corp., the manufacturer of the glue from whom Warren had acquired it, seeking indemnity under a contractual provision that the manufacturer-seller would indemnify the buyer against all liability resulting from the sale of the glue. Plaintiffs then amended their complaint to assert claims against Reiken and U.S. Plywood. All defendants pleaded the affirmative defenses of contributory negligence and assumption of risk by Zerby.

[The trial judge made a pre–trial ruling that Minn. Stat. 145.38 imposed absolute liability on Warren and Deike and that neither contributory negligence nor assumption of risk would be available as defenses. As a result of those rulings, the parties waived a jury trial and submitted the matter on stipulated facts. The trial judge ordered judgment against Warren and Deike and disallowed both third–party claims. Warren and

Deike have appealed from the denial of their motion for JNOV or a new trial.]

* * *

In 1969, the Minnesota Legislature recognized the potential harm which could result to minors from the sniffing of glue and enacted provisions to control its sale and use. Minn. St. 145.38 provides:

(1) No person shall sell to a person under 19 years of age any glue or cement containing toluene, benzene, zylene, or other aromatic hydrocarbon solvents, or any similar substance which the state board of health has * * * declared to have potential for abuse and toxic effects on the central nervous system. This section does not apply if the glue or cement is contained in a packaged kit for the construction of a model automobile, airplane, or similar item.

(2) No person shall openly display for sale any item prohibited in subdivision 1.

Minn. St. 145.39 reads:

(1) No person under 19 years of age shall use or possess any glue, cement or any other substance containing toluene, benzene, zylene, or other aromatic hydrocarbon solvents, or any similar substance which the state board of health has * * * declared to have potential for abuse and toxic effects on the central nervous system with the intent of inducing intoxication, excitement or stupefaction of the central nervous system, except under the direction and supervision of a medical doctor.

(2). No person shall intentionally aid another in violation of subdivision 1.

A violation of these statutory provisions is a misdemeanor. Minn. St. 145.40.

I.

The threshold question on this appeal is the nature of tort liability which results from a violation of Minn. St. 145.38. The nature of tort liability created by a statutory violation was considered in the leading case of Dart v. Pure Oil Co., 223 Minn. 526, 27 N.W.2d 555 (1947). That case involved an action for wrongful death resulting from the explosion of a mixture of gasoline and kerosene sold in violation of a statute. After examining many cases, we stated (223 Minn. 534, 27 N.W.2d 559):

* * * [I]t has been the long–standing rule of this court, *with certain exceptions,* that the violation of a statutory standard of conduct does not differ from ordinary negligence. (Italics supplied.)

The only difference between a statutorily imposed duty of care and a duty of care under common law is that the duty imposed by statute is fixed, so its breach ordinarily constitutes conclusive evidence of negligence, or negligence per se, while the measure of legal duty in the absence of statute is determined under common–law principles. After thus establishing the general rule, the court considered whether the *Dart* case fell within an exception (223 Minn. 535, 27 N.W.2d 560):

> * * * This brings up the question whether this statute was intended for the protection of the public as a whole or for the protection of a limited class of persons from their inability to protect themselves. There are exceptional statutes which do not permit the defense of contributory negligence. * * *

* * *

The principle of these so–called exceptional statutes is to impose strict or *absolute* liability upon the defendant, which is greater than ordinary negligence liability, by placing upon him the entire responsibility for any injury which may result from their violation. (Italics supplied.)

In order to create absolute liability, it must be found that the legislative purpose of such a statute is to protect a limited class of persons from their own inexperience, lack of judgment, inability to protect themselves or to resist pressure, or tendency toward negligence. In instances such as the present case, this legislative intent can be deduced from the character of the statute and the background of the social problem and the particular hazard at which the statute is directed.

Types of statutes which would be exceptions to the general rule include (1) child labor statutes; (2) statutes for the protection of intoxicated persons; and (3) statutes prohibiting sale of dangerous articles to minors. Obviously, the most direct analogy to the present case is the last–named type of statute. The obvious legislative purpose of § 145.38 is to protect minors unable to exercise self–protective care from harm resulting from sniffing the fumes of glue. This legislative policy inherent in the statute makes one who violates its provisions entirely responsible for damages or deaths which are the direct result of the illegal sale. It is one of the types of statutes referred to by the *Dart* decision as "exceptional statutes" and therefore violation of its provisions creates absolute liability for resulting harm.

II.

Having thus concluded that Minn. St. 145.38 is one of these exceptional statutes which impose absolute liability or liability per se upon one who violates its provisions, we hold that it was proper for the trial court not to allow the defenses of comparative contributory negligence and assumption of risk. If these defenses were permitted, the evident purpose of such statutes would be defeated. Consequently, the legislature must have intended that no defense would displace the responsibility imposed by the statute.

* * *

Defendants [argue] that the enactment of a comparative negligence statute in Minnesota requires the negligence of the parties to be compared in the present case. They argue that the former need to carve exceptions to the general rules of contributory negligence to avoid harsh results is not presently needed under the more equitable comparative negligence statute. However, the adoption of a comparative negligence statute did not create liability where none existed before. Because there can be no contributory negligence as a matter of law when the statute is designed to protect persons from their inability to protect themselves, the adoption of comparative negligence did not alter the exclusion of defenses.

Defendants also argue that decedent's contemporaneous violation of Minn.St. 145.39, which prohibits possession of glue by a minor with the intent to sniff it, should bar his recovery. They cite no cases which support this contention and we must reject it for the same reasons other defenses to the violation of these statutes are barred.

III.

While defendants do not question that the sale of the glue was a direct cause of decedent's death, they argue that the conduct of Randy Rieken in furnishing the glue to him and participating with him in sniffing its fumes in violation of § 145.39, subd. 2, quoted above, was a concurrent cause of the death. For this reason, it is contended that the trial court erred in disallowing defendants' contribution claim against Rieken.

* * *

In the present case, the conduct of Rieken in furnishing the glue to decedent and participating with him in inhaling its fumes was not independent of the original wrongful sale of the glue by defendants. Rather, the sale of the glue set the stage for the subsequent conduct of the minors. While every accident results from a sequence of occurrences or causes, the law disregards all but the substantial. We therefore conclude that the contribution claim against Rieken was properly disallowed because his conduct was merely a reaction to the original wrongful act of defendants and therefore not a proximate cause. * * *

It should not be forgotten that the sale of the glue to Rieken was in violation of Minn. St. 145.38 and that Rieken as a minor was also a member of a limited class of persons that the legislature intended to protect from their inexperience, lack of judgment, and tendency toward negligence. To permit contribution would defeat this legislative purpose.

IV.

Defendants' final contention is that the trial court erred in disallowing their claim for indemnity against United States Plywood Corporation, the manufacturer of the glue. The contact cement was originally purchased through a Coast–to–Coast supply house pursuant to their order form which contained the following language:

* * * Seller agrees to protect, defend, hold harmless and indemnify Buyer and its customers from and against any, and all liability, cost and expense arising from death or injuries to any persons or person or damage to property alleged to have resulted from the handling, display, sale, and use, consumption or distribution of Seller's product(s) or parts * * *.

If an indemnity agreement does not violate public policy, it is generally held that a party may contract to [be indemnified] against his own negligent acts. The leading case in this jurisdiction concerning this point is N.P. Ry. Co. v. Thornton Bros. Co., 206 Minn. 193, 288 N.W. 226 (1939). That case involved an indemnity agreement whereby a construction firm agreed to indemnify the railroad against any and all claims which arose in any manner from the laying of a sewer line underneath the railroad's tracks. In the course of the work, damage occurred to a subcontractor as the result of the railroad's negligence. We held that since the agreement did not relieve the railroad of any absolute duty which it owed to the public, the indemnity provision was as legitimate as insurance. We pointed out, however, that if the contract relieves a person from negligence in the discharge of an absolute duty imposed by law for the protection of others, it is void.

In the present case, a duty is imposed by law not to sell glue to minors. By enactment of Minn. St. 145.38, the legislature has indicated that, in the interest of public welfare, minors should not be sold possibly harmful glue. Any agreement which relieves the defendants of the consequences of the violation of the public duty imposed by § 145.38 is against public policy. For this reason, we hold that the trial court properly disallowed defendants' claim for indemnity based on the contract provision.

Affirmed.

E.   RES IPSA LOQUITUR

COLMENARES VIVAS v. SUN ALLIANCE INSURANCE CO.

United States Court of Appeals, First Circuit, 1986.
807 F.2d 1102.

BOWNES, CIRCUIT JUDGE.

Appellants are plaintiffs in a diversity action to recover damages for injuries they suffered in an accident while riding an escalator. After the parties had presented their evidence, the defendants moved for and were granted a directed verdict. The court held that there was no evidence of negligence and that the doctrine of res ipsa loquitur, which would raise a presumption of negligence, did not apply. We reverse the directed verdict and remand the case to the district court because we hold that res ipsa loquitur does apply.

* * *

The relevant facts are not in dispute. On February 12, 1984, Jose Domingo Colmenares Vivas and his wife, Dilia Arreaza de Colmenares, arrived at the Luis Munoz Marin International Airport in Puerto Rico. They took an escalator on their way to the Immigration and Customs checkpoint on the second level. Mrs. Colmenares was riding the escalator on the right–hand side, holding the moving handrail, one step ahead of her husband. When the couple was about halfway up the escalator, the handrail stopped moving, but the steps continued the ascent, causing Mrs. Colmenares to lose her balance. Her husband grabbed her from behind with both hands and prevented her from falling, but in doing so, he lost his balance and tumbled down the stairs. Mr. and Mrs. Colmenares filed a direct action against the Sun Alliance Insurance Company (Sun Alliance), who is the liability insurance carrier for the airport's owner and operator, the Puerto Rico Ports Authority (Ports Authority). Sun Alliance brought a third–party contractual action against Westinghouse Electric Corporation (Westinghouse) based on a maintenance contract that required Westinghouse to inspect, maintain, adjust, repair, and replace parts as needed for the escalator and handrails, and to keep the escalator in a safe operating condition.

* * *

Sun Alliance moved for a directed verdict [at the close of the plaintiff's evidence]. Appellants argued in opposition that the evidence presented was sufficient to show negligence and, in the alternative, that res ipsa loquitur should be applied to raise an inference that the Ports Authority had been negligent. At this point the court decided to allow the trial to continue. Sun Alliance and Westinghouse submitted their case on the basis of the testimony already presented and Sun Alliance renewed its motion for a directed verdict. After hearing the parties' arguments, the court ruled that there was no evidence that the Ports Authority had been negligent, and that the case could not go to the jury based on res ipsa loquitur because at least one of the requirements for its application—that the injury–causing instrumentality was within the exclusive control of the defendant—was not met.

* * *

Under Puerto Rico law, three requirements must be met for res ipsa loquitur ("the thing speaks for itself") to apply: "(1) the accident must be of a kind which ordinarily does not occur in the absence of someone's negligence; (2) it must be caused by an agency or instrumentality within the exclusive control of defendant; [and] (3) it must not be due to any voluntary action on the part of plaintiff." If all three requirements are met, the jury may infer that the defendant was negligent even though there is no direct evidence to that effect.

A. *The First Requirement: Inference of Negligence*

The first requirement that must be met for res ipsa loquitur to apply is that "the accident must be such that in the light of ordinary experience it gives rise to an inference that someone has been negligent." It is not clear to us whether the district court decided that this requirement was met, although the court did suggest that it was giving the benefit of the doubt on this question to the appellants. We hold that this requirement was met because an escalator handrail probably would not stop suddenly while the escalator continues moving unless someone had been negligent.

This requirement would not be met if appellants had shown nothing more than that they had been injured on the escalator, because based on this fact alone it would not be likely that someone other than the appellants had been negligent. Here, it was not disputed that the handrail malfunctioned and stopped suddenly, an event that foreseeably could cause riders to lose their balance and get injured. Thus, the evidence gave rise to an inference that someone probably had been negligent in operating or maintaining the escalator, and the first requirement for the application of res ipsa loquitur was met.

B. The Second Requirement: Exclusive Control

The second requirement for res ipsa loquitur to apply is that the injury–causing instrumentality—in this case, the escalator—must have been within the exclusive control of the defendant. The district court found that this requisite was not met, despite the parties' stipulation that "[t]he escalator in question is property of and is under the control of the Puerto Rico Ports Authority." We agree that this stipulation was not by itself enough to satisfy the res ipsa loquitur requirement. It did not exclude the possibility that someone else also had control over the escalator; indeed, the stipulation said that Westinghouse maintained the escalator. We hold, however, that the Ports Authority effectively had exclusive control over the escalator because the authority in control of a public area has a nondelegable duty to maintain its facilities in a safe condition.

Few courts have required that control literally be "exclusive." The Supreme Court, reviewing a case in which this court applied the exclusive control requirement literally, said that the question "really is not whether the application of the rule relied on fits squarely into some judicial definition, rigidly construed," because such an approach unduly restricts "the jury's power to draw inferences from facts." The exclusive control requirement, then, should not be so narrowly construed as to take from the jury the ability to infer that a defendant was negligent when the defendant was responsible for the injury–causing instrumentality, even if someone else might also have been responsible. The purpose of the requirement is not to restrict the application of the res ipsa loquitur inference to cases in which there is only one actor who dealt with the instrumentality, but rather "to eliminate the possibility that the accident was caused by a *third party*." It is not necessary, therefore, for the defendant to have had actual physical control; it is enough that the defendant, and not a third party, was ultimately responsible for the instrumentality. Thus, res ipsa loquitur applies even if the defendant shares responsibility with another, or if the defendant is responsible for the instrumentality even though someone else had physical control over it. It follows that a defendant charged with a nondelegable duty of care to maintain an instrumentality in a safe condition effectively has exclusive control over it for the purposes of applying res ipsa loquitur. Unless the duty is delegable, the res ipsa loquitur inference is not defeated if the defendant had shifted physical control to an agent or contracted with another to carry out its responsibilities.

We hold that the Ports Authority could not delegate its duty to maintain safe escalators. There are no set criteria for determining whether a duty is nondelegable; the critical question is whether the responsibility is so important to the community that it should not be transferred to another. The Ports Authority was charged with such a responsibility. * * *

* * * We hold, therefore, that the district court erred in ruling that the exclusive control requirement was not met.

C. The Third Requirement: The Plaintiffs' Actions

The third requirement that must be met for res ipsa loquitur to apply is that the accident must not have been due to the plaintiff's voluntary actions. The district court found, and we agree, that there was no evidence that Mr. and Mrs. Colmenares caused the accident. Indeed, there is no indication that they did anything other than attempt to ride the escalator in the ordinary manner. Therefore, we hold that all three requirements were met and that the jury should have been allowed to consider whether the Ports Authority was liable based on the permissible inference of negligence raised by the application of res ipsa loquitur.

* * *

Reversed in part, affirmed in part.* Remanded.

TORRUELLA, CIRCUIT JUDGE, dissenting.

* * * Although the majority correctly states the Puerto Rican law as to res ipsa loquitur, it overlooks well–established jurisprudence in applying that law to the circumstances of this case.

The majority concludes that the first requirement of res ipsa loquitur, i.e., inference of negligence arising from the occurrence of the accident, "was met because an escalator handrail probably would not stop suddenly while the escalator continues moving unless someone had been negligent." * * *

In my view, *solely* because the handrail stopped and Mrs. Colmenares fell, without further evidence as to why or how the handrail malfunctioned, does not give rise to an inference of *negligence* by the Ports Authority. * * *

The malfunctioning of an escalator presents [a strong] argument against the raising of an inference of negligence without additional proof as to the cause of the malfunction. Although a court can take notice that an escalator is a complicated piece of machinery, it has no basis of

---

* The court affirmed the portion of the lower court's order refusing to allow the plaintiffs leave to amend their complaint six days before trial to add Westinghouse as a defendant. [Ed.]

common knowledge for inferring that its malfunction is the result of the operator's negligence. Expert testimony is required to establish the basis for such an inference.

* * *

Notes

1. Judge Torruella's dissent may find support in Kmart Corp. v. Bassett, 769 So.2d 282 (Ala. 2000), in which a slim (5–4) majority of the Alabama Supreme Court held that the malfunction of an automatic door at a retail store, which injured the 83–year–old disabled plaintiff, did not support an inference of probable negligence on the part of the store in the absence of supporting expert testimony.

2. Note that the plaintiff sued the tortfeasor's insurer directly. Puerto Rico is not alone in permitting "direct actions" against the insurer. Louisiana and Wisconsin also have "direct action" statutes.

3. *A res ipsa allegation should not prevent plaintiff from attempting to prove negligence the normal way.* A few courts have held that a plaintiff can rely on res ipsa loquitur only if he "is unable to allege or prove the particular act of negligence which caused the injury." Beatty v. Davis, 224 Neb. 663, 665, 400 N.W.2d 850, 852 (1987). These courts require the plaintiff to choose between proving negligence directly and relying on res ipsa loquitur.

Most courts do not put a plaintiff to such a choice, however. For example, in Newing v. Cheatham, 15 Cal.3d 351, 124 Cal.Rptr. 193, 540 P.2d 33 (1975), the plaintiff's decedent was killed when a small plane in which he was a passenger crashed on a clear day. His estate was able to introduce persuasive evidence that the pilot, whose estate was the defendant, had allowed the plane to run out of gas. The court also permitted the plaintiff to rely on res ipsa loquitur.

4. *Defendant's superior access to information is neither necessary nor sufficient for res ipsa.* In addition to the three requirements of res ipsa loquitur addressed in *Colmenares Vivas,* some courts talk about the defendant's better access to information and even the possibility that the defendant is withholding information. This suggests that res ipsa loquitur is a device to force defendants to divulge information. Notwithstanding the language, however, the defendant's having access to information about the accident does not appear to be either a necessary or sufficient predicate for res ipsa loquitur.

5. *The procedural effect of res ipsa.* Some disagreement exists on the procedural effect of res ipsa loquitur. Most courts, including the court in *Colmenares Vivas,* say that res ipsa loquitur raises a "permissive inference" of negligence, which the jury may take or reject, even if the defendant fails to offer evidence. Thus, res ipsa loquitur allows the plaintiff to get the case to the jury by avoiding a directed verdict. A few courts say that res ipsa loquitur raises a "presumption" of negligence, so that the plaintiff is entitled to a directed verdict on the issue of reasonable care if the defendant fails to come forward with evidence. See, e.g., Newing v. Cheatham, note 3, supra.

6. The concept of "nondelegable duty" is explored further in Chapter VII.

Chapter IV

CAUSE IN FACT

The cause–in–fact requirement is typically discussed as an element of the negligence cause of action, and we are staying with that tradition. However, it is important to remember that cause in fact is equally required in intentional tort and strict liability cases. For example, recall that one of the elements of the tort of battery is that defendant must have *caused* physical contact.

As we said in the Introduction to Chapter III, the negligence cause of action requires the plaintiff to establish five elements in order to recover: (1) existence of a duty, usually of reasonable care; (2) breach of that duty (negligence); (3) cause in fact; (4) legal cause; and (5) damages. This chapter addresses the third element.

In all torts cases, normally the plaintiff must prove by a preponderance of the evidence—i.e., that it is more probable than not—that the defendant's substandard conduct was *a* cause of the harm or result complained of. This is typically a jury issue; it will not be decided "as a matter of law," i.e., second–guessed by the trial judge or appellate court, unless reasonable minds could not differ.

Note that the law does not require the plaintiff to prove that defendant's conduct was *the* cause of the harm. This would be an insuperable burden. As was stated in Public Citizen Health Research Group v. Young, 909 F.2d 546, 550 (D.C.Cir.1990), "[e]ver since the first cause brought the world into being, no event has had a single cause." The cause–in–fact requirement is satisfied if defendant's conduct is shown more probably than not to have been among the causes of the result the plaintiff seeks to attribute to the defendant.

Cause in fact is viewed as a bedrock requirement of the law. Sometimes the broad aims of tort law—compensating injured persons and deterring undesirable behavior—might seem to call for dispensing with the requirement in particular cases. But an overarching ideal of *corrective justice*, whereby tort law's central justification is seen in its ability to right wrongs, i.e., to restore the moral balance between injurer and injured, entails the view that the law should hold defendants liable for harms they wrongfully cause and no others.

Cause in fact is the usual name for this issue, but some of the cases refer to it as "proximate cause." More typically, "proximate cause" refers to a different issue, which is treated in Chapter V. In its most frequent usage, "proximate cause"—and its modern and generally preferable synonym "legal cause"—does not refer to factual causation at all, but instead addresses the appropriate scope of responsibility for injuries concededly the factual result of negligent conduct.

A. THE BUT–FOR TEST

EAST TEXAS THEATRES, INC. v. RUTLEDGE

Supreme Court of Texas, 1970.
453 S.W.2d 466.

SMITH, JUSTICE.

This is a damage suit alleging personal injuries were sustained by Sheila Rutledge, on or about September 25, 1966, while attending a midnight movie in a theatre owned and operated by East Texas Theatres, Inc. * * * The jury found the defendant guilty of negligence in failing to remove certain unidentified "rowdy persons" from the theatre and that such negligence was a proximate cause of Sheila's injuries. Damages were assessed by the jury at $31,250.00. Based upon the jury findings, the trial court entered judgment for the plaintiffs. The Court of Civil Appeals has affirmed. 445 S.W.2d 538. We reverse the judgments of both courts and here render judgment that the plaintiffs take nothing.

The defendant presents two major questions for our decision: (1) the error of the Court of Civil Appeals in holding that there was any probative evidence of record to support the jury finding on proximate cause, and (2) the error of the Court of Civil Appeals in holding that the testimony was sufficient to prove a causal connection between the injuries alleged to have been sustained by Sheila and her subsequent complaints of chronic headache, etc. In view of our holding on the first question, it is unnecessary to pass upon the second.

A full and detailed discussion of the evidence bearing on the first question is to be found in the opinion of the Court of Civil Appeals. We briefly summarize the facts. In taking this course, we are mindful of the rule that in deciding whether there is evidence in the record in support of the jury findings, we are required to view the evidence in its most favorable light in support of the verdict.

On September 24 and the early morning of September 25, 1966, Sheila, a paying guest, was attending a special "midnight show" at the Paramount Theatre, one of the several theatres owned by the defendant. The interior of the theatre was arranged with a lower floor and a balcony for the seating of patrons. Sheila and her friends took seats on the lower floor in the left section close to an aisle which ran parallel with the left wall and out beyond the overhang of the balcony. When the picture came to an end, Sheila started making her exit, after the lights were turned on, using the aisle between the left section and the wall. As she proceeded up the aisle toward the front of the building for the purpose of leaving the theatre and just before she walked under the balcony overhang, some unidentified person in the balcony threw a [whiskey] bottle which struck her on the side of her head just above her left ear.

Conduct of the Theatre Patrons

Since the jury found that the patrons in the balcony were acting in a "rowdy" manner and that the defendant, its agents, servants and employees, negligently failed to remove such rowdy persons from the premises and that such negligence proximately caused the injuries sustained by Sheila, we deem it important to particularly point out the evidence bearing on the conduct of the patrons during the evening. The evidence favorable to the verdict is that during the progress of the show, the patrons in the theatre, both on the lower floor and in the balcony, were engaged in "hollering." Sheila, in describing the "hollering," said that "a few slang words" were used. This "hollering" was intermittent; it occurred "off and on" during "parts of" the movie. One witness testified that "* * * they would holler and maybe slack off a few minutes and then holler again." Buddy Henderson testified that he saw paper or cold drink cups either "drifting down" or being thrown down toward the front of the theatre. Sheila did not see throwing of any type. Henderson testified that he did not recall anything drifting down or being thrown down other than the paper cold drink cups. In regard to the duration of the commotion in the theatre, the evidence shows that there was more commotion on the lower floor than in the balcony. Henderson testified that he thought that the "hollering" seemed to get worse toward the end of the show. Sheila was certain that "* * * [a]bout 30 minutes before the show was over it seemed to be quieter; they didn't seem to be as rowdy then." Sheila, Henderson and an officer by the name of Burt, all agreed in their testimony that before the show was over, and, thus, before the accident, all commotion in the theatre had ceased. The last disturbance of any kind before the show was over was not throwing but "hollering." Henderson further testified that nothing happened, whether "hollering" or the throwing of paper cups, to make him think that something bad was going to happen; he was not worried about the safety of himself or the safety of his friends or anybody that was there.

The Balcony Patrons and Their Conduct

The balcony, which would seat 263 people, was "just about full." The witness, Burt, estimated that about 175 of the balcony seats were occupied. The disturbance in the balcony seemed to come from the balcony generally, "just all over it." The evidence does not identify any particular person as being a "rowdy person." No witness could state which persons in the balcony were rowdy and which were not. No witness could identify the person who threw the bottle. Incidentally, there is no evidence that a hard substance of any character was thrown, other than the bottle which struck Sheila. The witness, Henderson, testified that he could not identify the person who threw the bottle, but that out of the corner of his eye, he saw a "movement, a jerking motion" by someone in the balcony and then saw the bottle hit Sheila. No witness testified that the bottle thrower had been engaged in "hollering" or throwing paper cups. * * *

Assuming without deciding that the finding of negligence is supported by evidence of probative force, we go direct[ly] to the question of whether there is in the record evidence of probative force to support the finding of proximate cause. We hold that there is no evidence to support the finding of the jury that the failure of the defendant to remove "rowdy persons" from its premises was a proximate cause of Sheila's injuries.

"Proximate cause" * * * includes two essential elements: (1) there must be cause in fact—a cause which produces an event and without which the event would not have occurred; and (2) foreseeability. * * * We base our decision here on the ground that the plaintiffs have failed to offer evidence of probative force to establish the cause–in–fact element of proximate cause. In particular, the plaintiffs contend that the act of omission in failing to remove "rowdy persons" from the theatre was a proximate cause of the injuries resulting from the throwing of the bottle by an unknown patron of the theatre. We recognize that cause–in–fact covers the defendant's omissions as well as its acts. However, it cannot be said from this record that had the defendant removed the "rowdy persons" from the premises, the bottle thrower would not have thrown the bottle. The record in this case clearly shows a complete lack of proof that the bottle would not have been thrown "but for" the failure of the defendant to remove "rowdy persons" from the premises. There is no evidence that the bottle thrower was one of the "rowdy persons" engaged in "hollering" and throwing paper cups from the balcony. We cannot say from this evidence what persons would have been removed. We agree with the defendant's contention as made in its Motion for Instructed Verdict; Motion for Judgment non obstante veredicto; Amended Motion for New Trial; points in the Court of Civil Appeals and in this Court that the judgment of the trial court cannot be sustained in that there is no evidence that the alleged injuries were proximately caused by any act of commission or omission of the defendant. * * *

The plaintiffs * * * contend that cause in fact was proved on the theory that "it would be considerably more probable that had even minimum supervision, such as a request by theatre employees to cease such rowdy behavior, or for the policeman to even go to the balcony and stand so that he might be seen by the patrons in the balcony, would have prevented the person who did throw the bottle from doing so because of his fear of being apprehended. That the theatre, by and through its employees, in failing to give this minimum supervision or yet, the more burdensome elements submitted [to the jury] upon the part of the plaintiff, failure to oust persons engaging in rowdy behavior, encouraged the wrongdoer by guaranteeing his anonymity in a crowd to the point that he felt he could and did in fact, get away with throwing the bottle." This theory is related in no way to the single act of throwing the bottle. It is purely speculative as to what would have happened had the defendant attempted to remove the "rowdy persons" from the theatre. The bottle thrower may not have been present at a time when the "rowdy persons" were being ejected. If present at the time of removal of the persons who were "hollering" and throwing paper cups, it would be just a guess as to what subjective effect such action may have had upon the bottle thrower. * * * This cannot be permitted. * * *

We recognize that the theatre was under a duty to exercise reasonable care for the safety of its patrons. Marek v. Southern Enterprises, Inc., 128 Tex. 377, 99 S.W.2d 594 (1936). However, operators of theatres are not insurers of their patrons' safety.

The judgments of the Court of Civil Appeals and the trial court are reversed and judgment is here rendered that plaintiffs take nothing.

MAREK v. SOUTHERN ENTERPRISES, INC.

Commission of Appeals of Texas, 1936.
128 Tex. 377, 99 S.W.2d 594.

HICKMAN, COMMISSIONER.

* * * In the trial court plaintiff recovered judgment against defendant for damages for personal injuries sustained by her while a patron at a theatre conducted by defendant in Dallas, known as Palace Theatre. The Court of Civil Appeals reversed that judgment. * * *

The facts show that plaintiff became a patron of the theatre about midnight on December 31, 1931, for a New Year's Eve performance. Shortly after she and the other members of her party were seated some unidentified persons in the theatre began throwing firecrackers and torpedoes promiscuously over the auditorium. One such torpedo or firecracker exploded near plaintiff's head causing her to suffer, among other injuries, the loss of hearing of one ear. * * *

While the plaintiff's petition is drawn in rather general terms, we think that, as against the general demurrer and special exceptions leveled against it, same is sufficient to charge that the defendant was negligent in not taking the proper precaution to prevent plaintiff's injury after the exploding of firecrackers and torpedoes started in the theatre. That was the theory of liability submitted to the jury in the trial court.

Those who conduct places of public amusement to which an admission fee is charged owe the duty to exercise ordinary care for the safety of their patrons. The relationship of proprietor and patron gives rise to that duty. Although the proprietor may be guilty of no negligence in regard to a danger in its incipiency, still, if after it arises he has time to prevent injuries to his patrons, it is his duty to exercise ordinary care to do so. * * *

We have made an independent investigation of the testimony and, while conceding that, on the question of whether defendant could have prevented plaintiff's injury by the exercise of ordinary care after it knew that the throwing of torpedoes and firecrackers had started in the theatre, it is rather meager, still we are unable to say, as a matter of law, that the record is bare of any evidence on the question. There is evidence that the throwing of fireworks had gone on for several minutes before plaintiff was injured, and that defendant did nothing to stop the practice or to protect its patrons from dangers arising therefrom. There is also evidence tending to show that the theatre was in practical darkness, and that after the throwing of fireworks started no lights were turned on and no remonstrance made.

Let it be presumed that the persons who were throwing the torpedoes and firecrackers knew that they were committing acts in violation of the Penal Statutes of this state and penal ordinances of the city of Dallas. That fact would not relieve the defendant of liability. It owed the same duty to protect its patrons from unlawful acts as it did to protect them from boisterous conduct of others not defined as a penal offense. To our minds the fact that the persons throwing these dangerous fireworks knew that their acts were unlawful constitutes some evidence tending to show that, had defendant turned on the lights and remonstrated with them, such throwing would have stopped. We think the jurors had the right, in the exercise of their best judgment based upon their common knowledge and experience, to conclude that, had the lights been turned on, so that the guilty persons could have been seen and identified, they would have desisted from their unlawful conduct. The question presented is one calling for the exercise of the judgment of the jury and is not a question of law for the determination of this court.

* * *

The judgment of the Court of Civil Appeals will be reversed and that of the trial court affirmed.

Opinion adopted by the [Texas] Supreme Court.

Notes

1. *Burden of proof.* As is implicit in *Rutledge* and *Marek,* the plaintiff generally has the burden of establishing the element of cause in fact by a preponderance of the evidence. "Preponderance of the evidence means merely the greater weight of the evidence. * * * That is to say that the facts claimed by the plaintiff must be more likely than not to exist." Dobbs, The Law of Torts § 150, p. 360 (2000).

2. *The but–for test.* The most widely accepted test for cause in fact is the but–for test, which "may be stated as follows: The defendant's conduct is a cause of the event if the event would not have occurred but for that conduct; or conversely, the defendant's conduct is not a cause of the event, if the event would have occurred without it." Rudeck v. Wright, 218 Mont. 41, 709 P.2d 621, 628 (1985). "But–for causation ... is sometimes stated as *sine*

qua non causation, i.e., 'without which not'...." Boeing Co. v. Cascade Corp., 207 F.3d 1177, 1183 (9th Cir. 2000).

Note that the "but for" inquiry addresses a hypothetical situation: what *would have* happened in the absence of the defendant's wrongful conduct. At its core this inquiry is speculative; it asks about a state of affairs that never existed in the world, and never will exist. One way to evaluate the decision in *Rutledge* is to ask why the supreme court justices' speculation was superior to the jury's. Alternatively, one might ask whether the "but for" inquiry was any more speculative in *Rutledge* than in *Marek*.

Because the but–for test calls for speculation about an imagined state of affairs, often there will be room for significant doubt; and indeed, we can never know with absolute certainty what would have happened in the absence of the defendant's wrongful conduct. In recognition of this reality, courts sometimes caution against raising the proof barrier too high. For example, in Reynolds v. Texas and Pac. Ry., 37 La.Ann. 694, 698 (1885), an overweight passenger fell and was injured while hurrying down inadequately lighted stairs leading from defendant's railroad platform to its tracks. The court answered defendant's contention that a person as heavy and in as much of a hurry as the plaintiff might well have fallen even if adequate lighting had been provided by saying:

> [W]here the negligence of the defendant greatly multiplies the chances of accident ... and is of a character naturally leading to its occurrence, the mere possibility that it might have happened without the negligence is not sufficient to break the chain of cause and effect....[1]

See also Kwasny v. United States, 823 F.2d 194, 196 (7th Cir.1987) (Posner, J., for the court, noting "[t]he general tendency of courts in tort cases, once negligence is established, ... to resolve doubts about causation, within reason, in the plaintiff's favor").

Other cases point in the opposite direction from *Reynolds*. See, e.g., McInturff v. Chicago Title & Trust Co., 102 Ill.App.2d 39, 243 N.E.2d 657, 662 (1968), a broadly similar case to *Reynolds* in which the court showed a completely different attitude, holding that the plaintiff had failed to prove that safer stairs would have avoided a fatal fall and stating that "[d]amages cannot be assessed on mere surmise or conjecture...." Cf. Coon v. Ginsberg, 32 Colo.App. 206, 509 P.2d 1293, 1295 (1973) (suggesting that cause in fact needs to be proved "with certainty.") As Professor Dobbs notes, "it is hard to escape the feeling that the but–for rule with its hypothetical alternative case can be applied rigorously in some cases and quite lightly in others." Dobbs, The Law of Torts § 173, p. 422 (2000).

---

1. Judge Calabresi has identified the quoted proposition as a concept that he calls "causal link," which he articulates as follows: "When a defendant's negligent act is deemed wrongful precisely because it has a strong propensity to cause the type of harm that ensued, that very causal tendency is evidence enough to establish a prima facie case of cause–in–fact. The burden then shifts to the defendant to come forward with evidence that its negligence was not such a but–for cause." Liriano v. Hobart Corp., 170 F.3d 264, 271 (2d Cir. 1999); Zuchowicz v. United States, 140 F.3d 381, 390–91 (2d Cir. 1998). According to Judge Calabresi's research, this burden–shifting technique has the status of a rule of law in New York and Connecticut. (Other authorities regard it as less reliable than a rule of law—as something more like a sometimes tendency.)

3. *Expert evidence.* In modern litigation the cause–in–fact issue frequently entails expert testimony, and plaintiffs often lose cases on the basis of complex cause–in–fact questions when their proffered experts cannot be qualified as such or when the experts' opinions are perceived as unconvincing. See, e.g., Oddi v. Ford Motor Co., 234 F.3d 136, 151, 158–159 (3d Cir. 2000) (affirming summary judgment for designer of bread truck when plaintiff's proposed expert "was unable to offer an opinion on ... whether Oddi's injuries [in a wreck of the truck] were exacerbated by the design of the ... truck"); Perkins v. Entergy Corp., 782 So.2d 606 (La. 2001) (reversing as "manifestly erroneous" a bench–trial finding that a voltage disturbance caused an explosion, principally because the plaintiffs' expert's testimony on that point was too equivocal); Marathon Corp. v. Pitzner, 106 S.W.3d 724, 729 (Tex. 2003) (rejecting plaintiff's expert witnesses' testimony out of hand as having "pile[d] speculation on speculation and inference on inference").

The problem of presenting qualified expert cause–in–fact testimony can be particularly acute in cases asserting that toxic substances (e.g. asbestos) caused disease. See generally Restatement (Third) of Torts: Liability for Physical Harm (Basic Principles) § 28, cmt. *c* (Tent. Draft No. 3, April 2003); see also Daubert v. Merrell Dow Pharmaceuticals, Inc., 43 F.3d 1311 (9th Cir.), cert. denied, 516 U.S. 869, 116 S.Ct. 189, 133 L.Ed.2d 126 (1995) (rejecting experts' proffered testimony on the question whether Bendectin, a drug prescribed for morning sickness to about 17.5 million pregnant women in the United States between 1957 and 1982, caused limb reduction birth defects); Mattis v. Carlon Electrical Products, 295 F.3d 856, 861 (8th Cir. 2002) (holding that a medical expert's testimony sufficed to support a finding that plaintiff's exposure to polyvinyl chloride (PVC) cement caused him to suffer reactive airways dysfunction syndrome (RADS) because the testimony was based upon a "proper differential diagnosis," defined as "one that identifies the cause of a medical condition by [systematically ruling out] the likely causes until the most probable cause is isolated").

4. *Common sense.* Amid the flurry of concern about expert testimony and the difficulties of achieving discrimination in its use, it is useful to remember that the ultimate determination of the cause–in–fact issue calls upon the trial judge's and jury's bedrock sense of human reality, their common sense. As the *Daubert* court noted:

> Not knowing the mechanism whereby a particular agent causes a particular effect is not always fatal to a plaintiff's claim. Causation can be proved even when we don't know precisely how the damage occurred, if there is sufficiently compelling proof that the agent must have caused the damage somehow. One method of proving causation in these circumstances is to use statistical evidence. If 50 people who eat at a restaurant one evening come down with food poisoning during the night, we can infer that the restaurant's food probably contained something unwholesome, even if none of the dishes is available for analysis. This inference is based on the fact that, in our health–conscious society, it is highly unlikely that 50 people who have nothing in common except that they ate at the same restaurant would get food poisoning from independent sources.

43 F.3d at 1314. Cf. Kaminsky v. Hertz Corp., 94 Mich.App. 356, 288 N.W.2d 426 (1979) (holding that the plaintiffs' showing that Hertz owned 90% of the yellow trucks bearing the Hertz logo sufficed to establish that Hertz probably owned the otherwise unidentified one that injured them).

5. *The five–step approach.* Under the approach to factual causation detailed in Robertson, The Common Sense of Cause In Fact, 75 Tex.L.Rev. 1765, 1768–73 (1997), properly framing and answering the but–for issue in a lawsuit involves five essential steps. *First,* identify the "injury in suit"—the injury or injuries for which redress is sought. (Normally this first step will present no difficulty. But see the "lost opportunity" cases treated infra in section D.) *Second,* identify the defendant's wrongful conduct. Care is required here. It is not enough for the plaintiff to show that her injuries would not have occurred if the defendant had never been born; the plaintiff must show that her injuries probably would not have occurred if the defendant had not engaged in the particular conduct alleged (and ultimately proved) in the lawsuit as wrongful.

The *third* step is the trickiest. It involves using the imagination to create a counter–factual hypothesis. One creates a mental picture of a situation identical to the actual facts of the case in all respects save one: the defendant's wrongful conduct is now "corrected" to the minimal extent necessary to make it conform to the law's requirements. It is important to stress that the mental operation performed at this third step must be careful, conservative, and modest; the hypothesis must be counter–factual only to the extent necessary to ask the but–for question. Only the defendant's wrongful conduct must be "changed," and that only to the extent necessary to make it conform to the requirements of law.

The *fourth* step asks the key question, whether the injuries that plaintiff suffered would probably still have occurred had the defendant behaved correctly in the sense indicated. The *fifth* and final step is answering the question.

In visualizing the five–step process, a videotape metaphor may be of use. After identifying the injuries in suit and the wrongful conduct, run the tape backward to the period of time immediately preceding the plaintiff's injury. Stop the tape. Change only one thing: change the defendant's conduct to the extent necessary to make it conform to law. In other words, change the accident scene only as necessary to reflect the assumption that the defendant has now been conducting herself properly. *Don't change anything else.* Now, with the defendant behaving properly and lawfully—with defendant's wrongful conduct out of the picture—run the tape forward. Do you see the plaintiff being injured? If so, defendant's wrongful conduct was not a cause in fact of the injury; it was irrelevant. Do you see the plaintiff escaping injury? If you see that clearly enough, then the defendant's wrongful conduct was a cause in fact of the injury. Do you see snow on the screen, no picture, just static? If so, the plaintiff may have failed to meet the burden of proof on the issue of factual causation.

6. *More about step three.* The five–step approach will be useful in focusing your evaluation of *Marek* and *Rutledge.* It may also help to get to

the heart of an interesting disagreement between the majority and dissenting justices in Kernan v. American Dredging Co., 355 U.S. 426, 78 S.Ct. 394, 2 L.Ed.2d 382 (1958). In that case, a Coast Guard regulation required a scow to carry a signal lamp "not less than eight feet above the surface of the water." The signal lamp that was carried on defendant's scow at only three feet above the water ignited fumes lying just above the river's surface and caused a fire that injured the plaintiff. The majority opinion assumed without discussion that the defendant's wrongful conduct—violating the regulation—was a cause in fact of the fire and ensuing injuries. The four dissenters were principally concerned with another point but stated in passing that the majority's cause–in–fact assumption was probably wrong:

> [The finding that the accident was traceable in fact to respondent's violation of the Coast Guard regulation] must rest on the assumption ... that the regulation forbade respondent to carry any signal light at a height of less than eight feet above the water. However, it is questionable whether the regulation had the effect of proscribing a light at three feet, as well as requiring a light at a minimum of eight feet. That is, the violation of the regulation may have consisted solely in the absence of a light at eight feet above the water, not in the presence of a light three feet above the water, in which case the accident could not be attributable to the violation of the regulation.

78 S.Ct. at 402 n. 1. Can you articulate the dissenters' objection in the language of the five–step approach?

7. When struggling with the analytical difficulties occasionally associated with the cause in fact issue, it may be comforting to remember that in most cases the but–for test readily yields an acceptably clear answer. For example, cause in fact was clearly present in most of the cases treated in Chapter III. (Only in T.J. Hooper and Martin v. Herzog was the cause–in–fact issue even worthy of discussion.) Cause in fact can be equally clearly absent. For example, in a suit based on a allegedly inadequate warning in an automobile operator's manual, the plaintiff's admission that he had never read any part of the manual was fatal to his case. Bloxom v. Bloxom, 512 So.2d 839, 850–851 (La. 1987).

When the outcome of the but–for inquiry is honestly debatable, the jury's answer should be respected. See, e.g., Kabzenell v. Stevens, 168 Cal.App.2d 370, 336 P.2d 250, 254 (1959) (holding that even though a bus driver should have sounded his horn when rounding a curve on a mountain road, the jury was justified in finding that this failure played no role in the ensuing accident).

8. A further useful point of perspective is this: A plaintiff who prevails on cause in fact has not thereby won the case. He has merely prevailed on that one issue, and still must contend with the duty, breach, legal cause, and damages issues, as well as with the affirmative defenses potentially available to the defendant.

B. LIMITED–PURPOSE SUBSTITUTES FOR THE STANDARD BUT–FOR TEST: THE SUBSTANTIAL FACTOR TEST

BASKO v. STERLING DRUG, INC.

United States Court of Appeals, Second Circuit, 1969.
416 F.2d 417.

J. Joseph Smith, Circuit Judge.

* * *

The plaintiff, Mrs. Lydia Basko, appeals from a judgment entered [on a general jury verdict] for the defendant drug manufacturers, Sterling Drug, Inc. and Winthrop Laboratories * * *.

* * *

From 1953 to 1961 plaintiff was treated with three different drugs for a skin disease called lupus erythematosus. The drugs were sold under the trade names Aralen, Atabrine, and Triquin, and were manufactured by Winthrop Laboratories, a division of Sterling Drug Co., Inc. The drugs had been prescribed for plaintiff by doctors at Yale–New Haven Hospital. In 1956, plaintiff began experiencing a blurring of her vision * * *. From 1961 to 1965 her vision deteriorated quite badly, and she is now almost totally blind.

At trial plaintiff called a number of medical experts who testified that she was suffering from a form of retinal damage known as chloroquine retinopathy. This is thought to be an idiosyncratic side effect of certain drugs made from chloroquine * * *.

* * *

[Atabrine is not made from chloroquine and could not have contributed to plaintiff's injury. Plaintiff now concedes this. But Aralen and Triquin are both chloroquine–based drugs. According to the records kept by Yale–New Haven Hospital, plaintiff took Aralen from April, 1953 to January, 1957. She took Triquin from November, 1959 to October, 1961. Plaintiff's main theory of liability is that defendant was negligent in failing to warn the medical community of the risk of chloroquine retinopathy. On one permissible view of the facts, this risk did not become known until 1959.]

We [therefore] find reversible error * * * in the way the jury was instructed on the issue of causation. On this issue, the jury was instructed to consider simply whether plaintiff's blindness resulted from her taking one or more of defendant's drugs. More specifically, Judge McLean told the jury that it should decide whether plaintiff's blindness "was caused by Aralen or by Atabrine or by Triquin, or by any two of these, or by all three of them, or by none. * * * If you find that the damage was caused by one or more of these drugs, then you will go on to consider [the question of duty to warn]."

For reasons which will appear, we believe that plaintiff was entitled to more detailed instructions on the law of multiple causation. Suppose, for example, that the jury found (1) that plaintiff's blindness was caused by a combination of Aralen and Triquin, and (2) that the risk of chloroquine retinopathy did not become known until 1959. Suppose also that the jury found (3) that there was no breach of the duty to warn with respect to Aralen, but (4) that defendant gave inadequate warnings with respect to Triquin. On these facts, plaintiff would be entitled to recover if the jury found that either Aralen or Triquin alone would have been sufficient to produce chloroquine retinopathy, and that Triquin was a "substantial factor" in producing her injury. The jury should have been so instructed, and indeed, the court's failure to give explicit instructions may have created the erroneous impression that defendant would not be liable under such circumstances unless there was a breach of the duty to warn with respect to both drugs.[14]

Ordinarily, the concept of proximate cause can be stated in terms of a "but for" test: defendant's negligence is a cause in fact of an injury where the injury would not have occurred but for defendant's negligent conduct. 2 Harper & James, The Law of Torts § 20.2, p. 1110 (1956). The test will not work, however, in the situation where two independent forces concur to produce a result which either of them alone would have produced. In such a situation, either force can be said to be the cause in fact of the harm, despite the fact that the same harm would have resulted from either force acting alone. 2 Harper & James, supra at 1122–1123. See also § 432(2) of the Restatement (Second) of Torts (1965), which provides:

> If two forces are actively operating, one because of the actor's negligence, the other not because of any misconduct on his part, and each of itself is sufficient to bring about harm to another, the actor's negligence may be found to be a substantial factor in bringing it about.

By way of illustration, the Restatement uses the example of a house standing in the path of two fires, one set by the negligence of the A Company and the other of unknown or innocent origins. The fires merge and then destroy the house. Under these circumstances, the Restatement provides that the negligence of the A Company may be considered the legal cause of harm if such negligence is found to be a "substantial factor" in producing the damage.[15]

The reason for imposing liability in such a situation, as Harper and James explain, is that the "defendant has committed a wrong and this

---

14. In instructing the jury, Judge Mc-Lean told the jury that proximate cause meant a cause "without which the injury would not have occurred." This is simply another way of stating the "but for" test.

15. The example is based on Anderson v. Minneapolis, St. Paul & St. Ste. Marie Railway, 146 Minn. 430, 179 N.W. 45 (1920).

has been a cause of the injury; further, such negligent conduct will be more effectively deterred by imposing liability than by giving the wrongdoer a windfall in cases where an all–sufficient innocent cause happens to concur with his wrong in producing the harm." Similarly, in Navigazione Libera T.S.A. v. Newtown Creek Towing Co., 98 F.2d 694, 697 (2d Cir. 1938), Judge Learned Hand stated that "the single tortfeasor cannot be allowed to escape through the meshes of a logical net. He is a wrongdoer; let him unravel the casuistries resulting from his wrong." See also Malone, Ruminations on Cause–In–Fact, 9 Stan.L.Rev. 60, 88–94 (1956). The contrary arguments[16] have been rejected by the Restatement, and there is good reason to believe that the Connecticut courts would follow the Restatement approach.

Assuming arguendo that the risk of chloroquine retinopathy did not become known until 1959, and that plaintiff's blindness could have been caused by either Aralen or Triquin, we have a situation which closely resembles the Restatement example. Since the jury could arguably have found a breach of the duty to warn with respect to Triquin but not Aralen, then the Triquin would be analogous to the negligently started fire, while the Aralen would be analogous to the fire of unknown or innocent origins. We conclude, therefore, that the jury should have been instructed on the "substantial factor" test of multiple causation.

* * *

Reversed and remanded for new trial.

Notes

1. *Uses and misuses of the substantial factor test.* Robertson, The Common Sense of Cause in Fact, 75 Tex. L. Rev. 1765, 1776 (1997), discusses the "uses and misuses of the substantial factor test" as follows:

> The term "substantial factor" has come to have a number of different meanings in the jurisprudence. * * * In the narrowest and only fully legitimate usage, the term describes a cause–in–fact test that is useful as a substitute for the but–for test in a limited category of cases in which two causes concur to bring about an event, and either cause, operating alone, would have brought about the event absent the other cause * * *. [Malone, Ruminations on Cause in Fact, 9 Stan. L.Rev. 60, 88–90 (1956), calls these "combined force" cases.] In a looser and potentially confusing

---

16. The case for non–liability is well stated in Peaslee, Multiple Causation and Damage, 47 Harv. L.Rev. 1127, 1130 (1934):

Where one of the causes is innocent and the other culpable in origin, as of the two fires uniting before reaching and burning the plaintiff's house, must the negligent actor pay the whole loss, or is he responsible for none of it? On the one hand is sufficient wrongful causation of a physical result, and on the other, inevitable loss not decreased by the defendant's wrong. Recovery would make the plaintiff better off than he would have been if the defendant had done no wrong. So long as the innocent cause is in actual, inescapable operation before the wrongful act becomes efficient, it is not apparent how the latter can be considered the cause of the loss. Causation is a matter of fact, and that which is not in fact causal ought not to be deemed so in law.

[Judge Peaslee accepted the substantial factor test in the situation in which the "other fire" had a tortious origin, stating that this application of the test was both "firmly established" and "manifestly just." Id. at 1131–32.]

usage, the substantial factor test is treated as more or less interchangeable with the but–for test; in this usage courts seem to feel that it is appropriate to shift to the substantial factor vocabulary whenever the but–for test is proving difficult to work with for whatever reason. In a third usage, "substantial factor" describes an approach to the issue of legal [proximate] causation or ambit of duty, a matter that should be kept entirely distinct from the cause–in–fact issue.

Basko is an example of what Robertson calls the "narrowest" and "legitimate" use of the substantial factor test. See also Northington v. Marin, 102 F.3d 1564 (10th Cir. 1996) (holding that the conduct of a jailer who was one of several sources of a jailhouse rumor that the plaintiff, a prisoner, was a "snitch" could be treated as a cause in fact of other prisoners' beating the plaintiff, even though the other rumor–spreaders' conduct would have produced the same effect).

2. *The justification for the substantial factor exception to the normal but–for requirement.* Some analysts believe the but–for test captures the essential meaning of factual causation. From this point of view, substituting the more lenient substantial factor test in the "combined force" cases is exceedingly difficult or perhaps even impossible to justify.[2] See, e.g., Callahan v. Cardinal Glennon Hospital, 863 S.W.2d 852, 861–862 (Mo. 1993):

> Some lawyers and judges have come to look upon the "but for" test as a particularly onerous and difficult test for causation. Nothing could be further from the truth. "But for" is an absolute minimum for causation because it *is* merely causation in fact. Any attempt to find liability absent actual causation is an attempt to connect the defendant with an injury or event that the defendant had nothing to do with.

See also Price Waterhouse v. Hopkins, 490 U.S. 228, 282, 109 S.Ct. 1775, 1807, 104 L.Ed.2d 268 (1989) (Kennedy, J., dissenting, stating that using "[a]ny standard less than but–for ... represents a decision to impose liability without causation.")

The opposing viewpoint, which is the traditional one, sees the substantial factor test as an alternative way of establishing the existence of factual causation. This view was elaborated in Boeing Co. v. Cascade Corp., 207 F.3d 1177, 1184–85 (9th Cir. 2000):

> In the special circumstance of causal overdetermination, conduct can be a cause of a result even though it is not a *sine qua non.* [Imagine a kitchen with a light switch at each end. When one person flips up the front switch at precisely the same time another person flips up the rear switch], the light goes on. Neither person's conduct is a *sine qua non* because the light would have gone on anyway. Neither individual's conduct made a difference to the outcome. [Under the but–for test], neither person caused the light to go on. * * * But the light went on. And it did so by human agency, not spontaneously. So the conclusion that [the but–for test] compels, that *no one* caused the light to go on, is false. Because the correct answer has to be the same for the two

---

2. The court in Public Citizen Health Research Group v. Young, 909 F.2d 546, 550 (D.C. Cir. 1990) suggested that "the rationale [for the substantial factor approach] is obscure ... [but it may perhaps be seen as simply denying the defendant] any benefit when a fluke renders his negligence causally redundant."

individuals, by eliminating the false answer we have left only one possible answer which must be true: Each of the two persons caused the light to go on.

See also Judge Posner's opinion in United States v. Feliciano, 45 F.3d 1070, 1075 (7th Cir. 1995):

> A barrel of gasoline is sitting on the street. Through negligence two people toss lighted matches into the barrel at the same time and it explodes. It would have exploded if only one lighted match had been thrown into it; so neither person was a "but for" cause of the explosion; yet both would be held liable in tort (or criminally, if they had acted recklessly or deliberately), both having "caused" the explosion in a perfectly reasonable sense.

3. *The Third Restatement.* Because the term "substantial factor" is so often misused,[3] the Restatement (Third) of Torts: Liability For Physical Harm (Basic Principles) § 27 (Tent. Draft No. 2, March 2002) jettisons the term and substitutes the following provision:

> When an actor's tortious conduct is not a factual cause of physical harm under the [but–for test] only because another causal set exists that is also sufficient to cause the physical harm at the same time, the actor's tortious conduct is a factual cause of the harm.

The thrust of this provision is to uphold factual causation in a considerably broader range of cases than would the traditional view of the substantial factor test.[4]

C. LIMITED–PURPOSE SUBSTITUTES FOR THE STANDARD BUT–FOR TEST: THE ALTERNATIVE LIABILITY, CONCERTED ACTION, AND MARKET SHARE THEORIES

PENNFIELD CORP. v. MEADOW VALLEY ELECTRIC, INC.

Superior Court of Pennsylvania, 1992.
413 Pa.Super. 187, 604 A.2d 1082.

CAVANAUGH, JUDGE.

* * *

3. Perhaps the most notorious example is Mitchell v. Gonzales, 54 Cal.3d 1041, 1 Cal.Rptr.2d 913, 819 P.2d 872 (1991) (jettisoning the but–for test entirely and calling for the use of a substantial factor test for all cause–in–fact issues). For another type of misuse of the substantial factor concept, see Lacy v. District of Columbia, 408 A.2d 985, 990–991 (D.C.App. 1979) (criticizing the trial court for giving a jury instruction requiring the plaintiff to satisfy both the but–for test and a requirement that the defendant's wrongful conduct have been a substantial factor in producing the injury).

4. On its face, § 27 would support cause in fact in cases like City of Piqua v. Morris, 98 Ohio St. 42, 120 N.E. 300 (1918), and Baltimore & O. R. Co. v. Sulphur Springs Ind. School Dist., 96 Pa. 65, 1880 WL 13501 (1880), in which defendants' defective flood–control structures were not treated as factual causes of damage by floods so vast as to overwhelm even the best of such structures. (The proposed Restatement treats these cases in its "Scope of Liability (Proximate Cause)" Chapter, providing in § 36 that "trivial and insubstantial" causes in fact should escape liability on policy—as opposed to factual causation—grounds.)

This action has its origin in the untimely demise of 1,537 swine, who suffocated when an electrically operated ventilation system in their abode failed. The swine were housed at Mountain View Farms, Berks County, Pennsylvania, and were owned by Pennfield Corporation. Pennfield brought an action against Meadow Valley Electric, Inc. [MVE*] the corporation which allegedly performed repair and maintenance services on the electrical equipment at Mountain View Farms. The Pennfield complaint alleged that a defective electrical system installed by MVE caused the ventilation system to fail, thus resulting in the suffocation of the swine.

MVE in turn filed a complaint to join numerous additional defendants including York [Electrical Supply Co.]. MVE's joinder complaint alleged that the ventilation system failed and that the cause of the failure was defective electrical cable purchased either from York or from another distributor, Tri–State Electrical Supply Company. MVE claimed that York was liable * * * on theories of strict liability, negligence, and breach of warranties.[3]

York responded to MVE's joinder complaint with preliminary objections in the nature of a demurrer. The gravamen of York's objections is that to make out a cause of action in strict liability, negligence, or breach of warranties MVE has to specifically identify which defendant supplied the defective cable. York notes specifically that [MVE pleaded that the] "electrical cable installed at Mountain View was bought either from York or Tri–State" and that "[t]he electrical cable bought by MVE from York and Tri–State cannot be identified or distinguished."

* * * [T]he trial court sustained York's preliminary objections [and] dismissed with prejudice [MVE's complaint against York]. This appeal followed.

* * *

MVE's first argument is based on what MVE deems the "alternative liability" theory of Restatement (Second) of Torts, § 433(B)(3) (1965) and Summers v. Tice, [33 Cal.2d 80, 199 P.2d 1 (1948)]. Section 433(B)(3) states * * *:

> Where the conduct of two or more actors is tortious, and it is proved that harm has been caused to the plaintiff by only one of them, but there is uncertainty as to which one has caused it, the burden is upon each actor to prove that he has not caused the harm.

---

* Throughout his opinion Judge Cavanaugh referred to the four entities involved—Meadow Valley Electric, York Electrical Supply, Tri–State Electrical Supply, and Pennfield Corporation—in various ways, sometimes using their names, sometimes abbreviations, and sometimes procedural designations such as plaintiff, defendant, appellant, appellee. In our edited version of the opinion, we call them MVE, York, Tri–State, and Pennfield. We will not further signal this alteration. [Ed.]

3. MVE alleged the same theories of liability against Tri–State as against York. Tri–State answered the complaint but did not file preliminary objections to MVE's complaint as did York.

* * * [MVE argues that under the quoted subsection (3)], because it cannot prove that either York or Tri–State harmed it, the burden is on York or Tri–State to prove that they were not the tortfeasor. This is a mischaracterization of the law. The predicate for applying subsection (3) is that "the conduct of two or more actors is tortious." Subsection (3) is based on the rationale that "injustice [lies in] permitting proved wrong-doers, who among them have inflicted an injury upon the entirely innocent plaintiff, to escape liability merely because the nature of their conduct and the resulting harm has made it difficult or impossible to prove which of them has caused the harm." § 433B(3), cmt. *f*. Here, MVE has not alleged that the conduct of two or more actors is tortious. Rather, MVE asserts one actor may be tortious while admitting the other actor may not be tortious. It is quite obvious from the rule and the rationale that the burden of proof remains on MVE, and subsection (3) does not apply.

* * *

This case is * * * a far cry from the seminal case in this area, the well–known hunting case of Summers v. Tice [supra]. In Summers v. Tice, three persons were hunting fowl when suddenly a bird flew from the brush. Notwithstanding that one of the hunters was in close proximi-ty to the brush, the other two hunters simultaneously fired their weapons, accidentally wounding the hunter. In such circumstances, it was impossible for the injured hunter to determine which party caused the injury. The California Supreme Court felt it was appropriate to shift the burden to the two careless hunters to prove which hunter fired the shot. The court emphasized that both parties were wrongdoers who had brought about a situation where the negligence of one of them had injured their companion. Either of the two was in a better position to know which of them caused the injury, while the nature of their conduct made it difficult or impossible for the injured party to determine who was liable.

MVE implicitly admits in its [complaint] that either York or Tri–State bears no culpability whatsoever in bringing about the suffocation. * * * Thus, unlike in Summers v. Tice or the usual alternative liability theory case, MVE cannot with certainty state that York and Tri–State are * * * tortfeasors.

* * *

* * * [It is essential to refuse to] extend Summers v. Tice * * * to the present fact scenario. Our system of jurisprudence rightly balks at assigning liability to a innocent party. Our reluctance has been overcome only when compelling circumstances demand that we deviate from the rule that a cause of action must fail unless defendant's conduct is shown to have been [a but–for cause] of plaintiff's injury.

We feel the facts of this case highlight the strength of the general rule. * * * Notwithstanding, we believe MVE can amend its complaint * * * to state a viable cause of action. * * * All MVE has to do is to plead facts that, if true, would be legally sufficient to gain [it] relief from York. It is apparent from MVE's complaint that the genesis of legally sufficient facts is present. MVE alleges that York sold it a cable, the cable was defective, and the cable's defect caused [MVE to suffer damages.][15] These alleged facts are the seeds for several causes of action.

It is irrelevant at the demurrer stage * * * whether MVE alleges precisely the same facts against both York and Tri–State. MVE's complaint can allege, at the same time, in the alternative, that it was a cable distributed by York that was defective and that it was a cable distributed by Tri–State that was defective. MVE should then have the opportunity to utilize discovery to pin–point which company distributed the allegedly defective cable. However, if after an opportunity to submit all the relevant evidence, the probabilities are at best still evenly divided between York and Tri–State as to causation, it would be the duty of the trial court to dismiss the complaint at an appropriate dispositional stage in the proceedings upon motion by either or both. * * *

We affirm the trial court's order as to the preliminary objections, but instruct the trial court to allow MVE the opportunity to amend its complaint.

Notes

1. *Dobbs wants to call it "alternative causation."* Professor Dobbs thinks "alternative liability" is a misleading name, because the "liability [that results when the theory is applied] is joint and several,[1] not in the alternative. It is rather causation that is in the alternative, because one or the other but not both tortfeasors are causes of the harm." Dobbs, The Law of Torts § 175, p. 427 (2000).

2. *A remedy–impairment rationale for the alternative liability theory.* Dobbs does not think the "dubious suggestion that defendants might know more than plaintiffs" can explain many of the alternative liability cases. He suggests that a better justification for the theory was set forth in Justice Rand's opinion in Cook v. Lewis, [1951] S.C.R. 830 (Supreme Court of Canada 1951):

> What ... the culpable actor [in cases like Summers v. Tice] has done by his ... negligent act is, first, to have set in motion a dangerous force which embraces the injured person within the scope of its probable mischief; and next, ... to have made more difficult if not impossible the means of proving the possible damaging results of his own act or the similar results of the act of another. He has violated not only the

---

15. MVE apparently feels that it has to allege some sort of "alternative liability" theory to survive a demurrer at this stage because it cannot determine whether York or Tri–State supplied the allegedly defective cable. However, at this stage of the litigation, MVE only has to allege legally sufficient facts, *even if it cannot prove them at this time.* * * *

1. In this usage, "joint and several liability" means that the judgment is for a single sum, representing the total value of the plaintiff's injury, and that the plaintiff is entitled to collect his money from either or both of the defendants, up to but not exceeding the amount of the judgment.

victim's substantive right to security, but he has also culpably impaired the latter's remedial right of establishing liability.

3. *Can the remedy–impairment rationale be used to create a stand–alone exception to the but–for requirement?* Robertson, The Common Sense of Cause in Fact, 75 Tex. L. Rev. 1765, 1787–89 (1997), includes "holding one tortfeasor liable for destroying or impairing plaintiff's case against the other tortfeasor" as one of eight limited–purpose substitutes for the normal but–for test. He maintains that this "deprivation–of–cause–of–action approach" explains Baker v. Willoughby, [1970] A.C. 467 (House of Lords), in which the defendant's negligent driving severely injured plaintiff's leg. Before the case went to trial, the injured leg was shot by a robber, necessitating its amputation. The court held the traffic tortfeasor fully liable for the loss of the use of the leg. Understanding the court's reasoning begins with the realization that a suit against the robber would have been met by the defensive argument that the leg the defendant shot was not worth very much owing to the earlier traffic injury. Thus the negligence of the defendant (the traffic tortfeasor) had effectively deprived the victim of the value of a normal cause of action against the robber. Similarly, the robber's shooting effectively deprived the victim of a normal cause of action with the right of full recovery against the traffic tortfeasor. Each should be liable for tortiously impairing the plaintiff's cause of action against the other.

4. *Alternative liability sometimes applies against product suppliers.* Presumably the alternative liability theory would have been available to MVE if it had been able to show that, while only one of the two suppliers was the source of the particular cable that killed the pigs, both suppliers' cables were identically defective. See Minnich v. Ashland Oil Co., 15 Ohio St.3d 396, 473 N.E.2d 1199 (1984) (holding that each of two suppliers of cleaning fluid—neither of whom provided a proper warning of the product's explosive qualities—had the burden of negating cause in fact in a lawsuit by a worker who had no way of telling which supplier's fluid he was using when hurt in an explosion); Wysocki v. Reed, 222 Ill.App.3d 268, 164 Ill.Dec. 817, 583 N.E.2d 1139 (1991) (similar result against two providers of an allegedly defective drug).

5. *Why should the alternative liability theory require plaintiff to join both tortfeasors as defendants?* Most courts will refuse to apply alternative liability in cases like *Summers* unless both tortfeasors are joined as defendants. We have not found an explanation of this requirement, but it is relatively easy to understand. The ultimate result in *Summers* was a judgment that the two shooters were jointly and severally liable for the plaintiff's injury. From the corrective justice viewpoint, such a result is guaranteed to be unjust as to one of the shooters, whose bullet did not strike the victim. Courts insist that both shooters be in court because they want to be sure they are at least doing something right (holding the true shooter liable) while they are also obviously doing something wrong (imposing liability on the other shooter for a harm that he did not cause).

6. *How many tortfeasors?* Alternative liability gets more and more difficult to justify as the number of defendants increases. Yet courts have used the theory against relatively large groups. See, e.g., Huston v. Konieczny, 52 Ohio St.3d 214, 556 N.E.2d 505 (1990) (five possible furnishers of the

beer that made a teenage driver drunk); Snoparsky v. Baer, 439 Pa. 140, 266 A.2d 707 (1970) (twelve boys, any one of whom might have thrown the rock that struck the plaintiff). In most of the cases in which the alternative liability theory has been used against more than two tortfeasors, there was arguably an element of concerted action that might have provided a better justification for treating each of the tortfeasors' conduct as a cause in fact of the harm. See the next case.

The difficulty of justifying using the alternative liability theory against more than two defendants—i.e., of moving from accepting a 50/50 chance of cause in fact (*Summers*) to a 1/12 chance (*Snoparsky*) or even smaller—was a major reason for the Oregon Supreme Court's total rejection of the alternative liability theory in Senn v. Merrell–Dow Pharmaceuticals, Inc., 305 Or. 256, 751 P.2d 215, 222 (1988).

7. *The Third Restatement.* Restatement (Third) of Torts: Liability for Physical Harm (Basic Principles) § 28(b) (Tent. Draft No. 2, March 2002) embraces the alternative liability theory and suggests that there is no particular problem with using the theory against groups of defendants larger than two.

BICHLER v. ELI LILLY AND CO.

Court of Appeals of New York, 1982.
55 N.Y.2d 571, 436 N.E.2d 182, 450 N.Y.S.2d 776.

MEYER, JUDGE.

* * *

DES [diethylstilbestrol] is a powerful synthetic substance that duplicates the activity of estrogen, a female sex hormone naturally present in all women and, in lesser amounts, present also in men. Invented in 1937 by British researchers, DES was never patented. As a result, it was available for production and marketing to any pharmaceutical manufacturer who obtained Federal Food and Drug Administration (FDA) approval.

DES was first approved for use in the United States in 1941. In that year, 12 pharmaceutical manufacturers, including defendant Eli Lilly and Company, submitted separate new drug applications (NDA's) to the FDA requesting approval of the marketing of DES for the treatment of vaginitis, engorgement of the breasts, excessive menstrual bleeding and symptoms of menopause. Each separate application * * * relied upon a master file of reports and studies compiled by a committee of four drug companies, known as the "Small Committee," which was chaired by Lilly. Three years later the FDA approved several additional NDA's for use of DES in treating cancer of the prostate in males. DES continues to be used to treat some of these non–pregnancy–related medical problems today.

Not until 1947 did the FDA approve DES for the treatment of human miscarriage. Lilly's NDA was the second such application to be approved. Five years later, in 1952, the FDA did away with the need for additional NDA's, at least for previously approved uses, when it declared DES to be "generally recognized ... as safe." In 1971, however, in the face of mounting evidence that DES was ineffective in preventing miscarriage and dangerous to the unborn child as well, the FDA reversed itself and banned the use of DES for the treatment of problems of pregnancy. By that time DES had been taken by perhaps several million pregnant mothers.

In the past decade the link between prenatal DES exposure and the later development in female offspring of clear cell cervical or vaginal adenocarcinoma, a hitherto rare disease involving cancerous growth in glandular tissue, has been unquestionably confirmed. In addition, the FDA estimated in 1975 that 30 to 90% of these offspring develop vaginal adenosis, a noncancerous condition in which glandular tissue normally found only in the cervix is also found in the vagina. Because of the "paramount public importance" of identifying, screening, diagnosing, caring for and treating the estimated more than 100,000 New York women whose health has been endangered by prenatal exposure to DES, the Legislature has enacted section 2500–c of the Public Health Law aimed at locating, monitoring and establishing special programs for these young women.

Plaintiff Joyce Bichler is a DES daughter. Stricken by cervical and vaginal cancer at age 17, she brought suit against Lilly in 1974 for damages sustained in surgically arresting the disease. All of plaintiff's internal reproductive organs and more than half of her vagina were removed. As a result, she can never bear children and will never enjoy normal sexual relations.

In her complaint plaintiff alleged that her 1953 prenatal exposure to DES, ingested by her mother while pregnant with plaintiff, was the proximate cause of the cancer that developed 17 years after her birth in 1954. Lilly, a major American manufacturer of DES, was the only pharmaceutical manufacturer named as defendant, although the pharmacist who filled plaintiff's mother's 1953 prescription stocked DES supplied by at least three of the other 147 drug companies then manufacturing and marketing DES for pregnancy–related problems.

At Lilly's request, the trial was conducted in two stages. The first stage of the trial concerned the identity of the manufacturer of the DES tablets taken by plaintiff's mother. The jury found that plaintiff had not established by a preponderance of the evidence that Lilly was that manufacturer. The second stage of the trial concerned Lilly's liability upon a theory of concerted action. The jury determined that Lilly and other DES manufacturers wrongfully marketed the drug for use in preventing miscarriage without first performing laboratory tests upon pregnant mice. Had those tests been performed, the jury found, the pharmaceutical companies would have learned that DES was capable of causing cancer to develop in female offspring and would not have marketed the drug for problems of pregnancy. The jury awarded plaintiff

$500,000 and the Appellate Division unanimously affirmed the judgment entered upon the jury's verdict.

* * * Lilly seeks reversal on two principal grounds: that the trial court's instructions on concerted action liability were erroneous, and that the evidence before the jury was legally insufficient to support a verdict in plaintiff's favor on the issue of concerted action. For the reasons which follow, we reject these arguments.

II.

In the wake of knowledge about the devastation wrought by DES upon the female offspring of the several million pregnant women who ingested the drug over a 25–year period, an estimated 1000 individual or class action products liability lawsuits have been lodged against pharmaceutical manufacturers. Where the identity of the drug company that manufactured the DES which caused plaintiff's injuries is known, these lawsuits can be prosecuted within well–established principles of products liability as those principles have been adapted to the manufacturing and marketing of prescription drugs. It is, however, the far more usual case that the identity of the drug company whose DES tablets were taken by a plaintiff's mother is unknown and can never accurately be determined. This is because all DES prescribed for pregnant mothers was produced under the identical chemical formula and most of this DES was manufactured and prescribed generically. With the passage of the many years needed for DES–caused vaginal tract abnormalities to appear in prenatally exposed offspring, the patient, physician, pharmacist and drug company records which could have identified the source of the DES have usually disappeared. This same lapse of time has commonly obliterated the individual recollections of those surviving witnesses of any underlying DES transaction. The result is that as a group DES daughters face a dilemma: They have * * * been injured by parallel conduct of a group of pharmaceutical manufacturers. But the practical impossibility for most victims of pinpointing the manufacturer directly responsible for their particular injury threatens to bar any recovery.

Products liability law cannot be expected to stand still where innocent victims face "inordinately difficult problems of proof." Thus, courts as well as commentators have proposed means which permit recovery by prenatally exposed DES daughters. The proposals involve the application of already accepted tort principles of "concerted action" and "alternative liability" to the unusual DES fact pattern as well as resort to more novel theories of "enterprise" and "market share" liability. Here, because only concerted action was pleaded and submitted to the jury, we address only this basis of liability. We expressly leave for another day consideration of whether other theories of liability may in the DES context establish a cause of action.

Concerted action liability rests upon the principle that "[a]ll those who, in pursuance of a common plan or design to commit a tortious act, actively take part in it, or further it by cooperation or request, or who lend aid or encouragement to the wrongdoer, or ratify and adopt his acts done for their benefit, are equally liable with him." An injured plaintiff may pursue any one joint tortfeasor on a concerted action theory. Such tortfeasor may, in turn, seek contribution from others who acted in concert with him. The clearest example of concerted action liability is the drag race. Where two drivers agree to race and one collides with and injures a third party, the other driver is fully responsible for the third party's injuries even though there was no contact between that driver's car and the injured person.

Although Lilly claims it is jurisprudentially unsound to permit full recovery on a concerted action theory against one DES manufacturer for injuries probably sustained by ingestion of DES manufactured by another manufacturer, no motion was ever made by Lilly to dismiss the complaint for failure to state a cause of action, for partial summary judgment limiting plaintiff's recovery to a percentage amount of her injuries corresponding to Lilly's market share, or to join other DES manufacturers as necessary parties. Nor were these issues raised in Lilly's motions to dismiss for failure to make out a prima facie case or for a directed verdict. Rather, Lilly proceeded to trial on a complaint seeking full recovery against Lilly alone among the manufacturers on the basis of concerted action. This, then, has become the controlling law and we look only to the trial court's instructions on concerted action to determine whether, to the extent the issue has been preserved, those instructions were erroneous.

The totality of the trial court's instructions on concerted action was as follows:

[B]y "concerted action," we mean one of two things. First, action taken jointly by drug companies as a result of an express or implied understanding. In this case, other than in connection with the original New Drug Application submitted in 1941 by some twelve companies, in which they expressly agreed to joint submission of clinical data, plaintiff contends that the joint action of the defendant and other drug companies, in testing and marketing DES for use in accidents of pregnancy was by implied or tacit agreement or understanding. That is, it was unspoken, and that this was reflected by the consciously parallel conduct of the companies in these activities.

By the second definition of concerted action, we mean persons acting independently of each other in committing the same wrongful act, but although acting independently, their acts have the effect of substantially encouraging or assisting the wrongful conduct of the other, which, in this case, was the alleged failure to adequately test.

Thus, if you find that defendant and the other drug companies either consciously paralleled each other in failing to test DES on pregnant mice, as a result of some implied understanding, or that they acted independently of each other in failing to do such testing, but that such independent actions had the effect of substantially aiding or encouraging the failure to test by the others, then you should find that the defendant wrongfully acted in concert with the other drug manufacturers in the testing and marketing of DES for use in accidents of pregnancy. Of course, you must also have found that it was wrongful for the defendant and the other drug companies not to have tested DES in pregnant mice because of the state of knowledge that was available to them in 1953.

Lilly's challenge to these instructions separately addresses concerted action by agreement and concerted action by substantial assistance, the two branches of the court's quoted charge. With respect to concerted action by agreement, [Lilly's principal contention is] that the jury should have been instructed that direct evidence or some "plus factor" was needed in addition to conscious parallelism to support a finding of agreement * * *. With respect to concerted action by substantial assistance, [Lilly's principal contention is] that the jury should have been instructed that a finding of agreement was necessary to impose liability * * *. In addition, Lilly claims the court inadequately defined "substantial assistance."

We need not decide the merits of these claims, for none has been preserved for our review * * *. [Lilly's counsel failed to make adequately clear or precise objections to the jury instructions in the trial court.] Accordingly, the court's charge on concerted action is the law governing this case under which the legal sufficiency of the evidence to support the jury's finding of concerted action must be assessed.

III.

Because the trial court submitted two theories of concerted action upon which Lilly's liability for plaintiff's injuries could be premised—concerted action by agreement and concerted action by substantial assistance—and we do not know which theory was accepted by the jury, we must evaluate the sufficiency of the evidence to support recovery under either. As we read the trial court's instructions on concerted action by agreement, the jury is permitted to infer from evidence of consciously parallel behavior that an implied agreement existed between Lilly and other drug companies to market DES for problems of human pregnancy without first conducting tests with DES upon pregnant mice. No "direct evidence" or "plus factor" is required. Consciously parallel conduct by itself is enough. Similarly, the trial court's charge on concerted action by substantial assistance required the jury to find only that Lilly's failure to test DES on pregnant mice before marketing the drug for use by pregnant women substantially aided or encouraged other DES manufacturers to do the same. No express agreement is required. * * *

Review of the evidence, solely on the basis of events beginning in 1947,[7] shows that it was sufficient to support jury findings of both

7. We agree with Lilly that its 1941 collaboration with other pharmaceutical manufacturers to secure initial FDA ap- proval of DES for certain non–pregnancy– related conditions has no bearing upon the concerted action which plaintiff must estab-

conscious parallelism and substantial assistance or encouragement under the jury instructions to which no [acceptably clear or precise] exception was taken. The record shows that eight companies filed NDA's to market DES for problems of pregnancy between April, 1947 and October, 1948. Lilly's application was the second of these, filed only two weeks after the leader. Each of the eight applications relied substantially on the same studies of three research teams that were reported between 1941 and 1947. Each requested approval to market 25 milligram tablets, a dosage five times more powerful than the maximum five milligram tablets approved in 1941. For the jury to infer that this closely parallel conduct was conscious or that Lilly's participation in this first wave of DES pregnancy–related NDA filings substantially encouraged the other 140 companies which were engaged in manufacturing and marketing DES for the same purpose by 1953 is surely within the realm of the fact–finding function.

* * *

We have considered Lilly's remaining arguments and find them to be either unpreserved or without merit. The order of the Appellate Division is therefore affirmed, with costs.

Notes

1. *A "DES–unique version of alternative liability."* In an omitted footnote the court said the alternative liability theory has been used to impose responsibility upon multiple DES manufacturers, citing the decision of an intermediate appellate court in Michigan. The Michigan Supreme Court subsequently modified that decision, explaining that the traditional alternative liability theory rarely fits the facts of multiple–source products cases and that finding causation against the DES manufacturers required the court to create "a new DES–unique version of alternative liability." Abel v. Eli Lilly and Co., 418 Mich. 311, 331, 343 N.W.2d 164, 173 (1984). But cf. Poole v. Alpha Therapeutic Corp., 696 F.Supp. 351, 355 (N.D. Ill. 1988) (approving the use of the alternative liability theory in a case against "all of the defendants that could have possibly caused Poole to contract AIDS" by distributing a virus–infected antihemophilic product and stating that "[w]hen all defendants are present, courts have adopted the [alternative liability] theory" in multiple–source products cases, [citing an asbestos case and an Agent Orange case]).

2. *The concerted action theory seldom works in multiple–source products cases.* The *Bichler* trial judge's instructions on concerted action followed the pattern of Restatement (Second) of Torts § 876 (1979), which reads:

> For harm resulting to a third person from the tortious conduct of another, one is subject to liability if he
>
> (a) does a tortious act in concert with the other or pursuant to a common design with him, or

lish in connection with Lilly's 1947 supple-   DES for problems of pregnancy.
mental application to produce and market

(b) knows that the other's conduct constitutes a breach of duty and gives substantial assistance or encouragement to the other so to conduct himself, or

(c) gives substantial assistance to the other in accomplishing a tortious result and his own conduct, separately considered, constitutes a breach of duty to the third person.

While the Court of Appeals did not approve (nor did it disapprove) the trial judge's instructions, its opinion shows that there is nothing illogical about using the concerted action theory against multiple manufacturers of dangerous products. However, in Hymowitz v. Eli Lilly and Co., 73 N.Y.2d 487, 506, 541 N.Y.S.2d 941, 946, 539 N.E.2d 1069, 1074 (1989), the Court of Appeals said the concerted action theory does not fit the multiple–source products problem:

> [T]he theory of concerted action, in its pure form, [does not] supply a basis for recovery [in a DES case]. This doctrine, seen in drag racing cases, provides for joint and several liability on the part of all defendants having an understanding, express or tacit, to participate in "a common plan or design to commit a tortious act". As we noted in *Bichler* ..., drug companies were engaged in extensive parallel conduct in developing and marketing DES. There is nothing in the record, however, beyond this similar conduct to show any agreement, tacit or otherwise, to market DES for pregnancy use without taking proper steps to ensure the drug's safety. Parallel activity, without more, is insufficient to establish the agreement element necessary to maintain a concerted action claim.

Most courts have agreed that the concerted action theory cannot solve the plaintiffs' causation problems in multiple–source products cases, reasoning that the manufacturers' parallel conduct without more does not indicate tacit agreement nor substantial aid and encouragement to one another.

3. *Standard applications of the concerted action theory.* The concerted action theory has often been applied in multiple–shooter cases (and similar cases such as *Snoparsky*, supra p.135) when the facts show that, while the plaintiff was wounded by only one of the shooters, all were behaving tortiously and engaged in some kind of common or joint activity. (The court in Summers v. Tice could easily have used the concerted action theory, but it did not.)

4. *The concerted action theory is different from vicarious liability.* Dobbs, The Law of Torts § 175, p. 428 (2000), says that when "two defendants are acting in concert, as part of a common plan or design, they are true joint tortfeasors and each is vicariously liable for the other's negligence." But that does not seem quite right, because courts seem to insist that the defendant must himself have engaged in tortious behavior. See, e.g., Orser v. Vierra, 252 Cal.App.2d 660, 60 Cal.Rptr. 708, 713–714 (1967), a two–shooters, single–wound case in which the court quoted approvingly from an early version of the Prosser torts treatise as follows:

> All those who, in pursuance of a common plan or design to commit a tortious act, actively take part in it, or further it by cooperation or request, or who lend aid or encouragement to the wrongdoer, or ratify

and adopt his acts done for their benefit, are equally liable with him. * * * [M]ere knowledge by each party of what the other is doing is [not] sufficient "concert" to make each liable for the acts of the other since one man ordinarily owes no duty to take affirmative steps to interfere with another's activities absent some special relationship. * * * It is . . . essential that each particular defendant who is to be charged with responsibility shall be proceeding tortiously, that is to say with intent to commit a tort, or with negligence.

On this view, the concerted action theory is not full–blown vicarious liability (see Chapter VII) but might instead be termed a theory of "vicarious causal responsibility."

5. *Enterprise liability.* In an omitted footnote, the *Bichler* court explained that the "enterprise liability" theory derives from Hall v. E.I. Du Pont de Nemours & Co., 345 F.Supp. 353 (E.D.N.Y. 1972). "In that case, plaintiffs were unable to identify the manufacturers of allegedly unsafe blasting caps for the simple reason that the caps had been obliterated by explosion. Since the six defendants in that case did, however, comprise virtually the entire American blasting cap industry and since it appeared that their blasting caps were manufactured to meet industry–wide safety standards set by their own trade association, the court held that defendants could be liable for the joint control of the risk of accidental explosion."

Deeming the enterprise liability theory to be a mere "offspring" or "extension" of the concerted action theory, most courts have rejected it as an answer to the plaintiffs' problem in multiple–source products cases. Shackil v. Lederle Laboratories, 116 N.J. 155, 561 A.2d 511, 515 (1989).

6. *The market share theory.* In the multiple–source products context, a court that believes the plaintiff's inability to prove factual causation cannot be relieved by any of the alternative liability, concerted action, and joint enterprise theories must either turn a deserving and tragically helpless plaintiff away empty–handed or devise some new theory of causation. In Sindell v. Abbott Laboratories, 26 Cal.3d 588, 163 Cal.Rptr. 132, 607 P.2d 924 (1980), the California Supreme Court—drawing heavily on an article authored by a law student (Naomi Sheiner), Comment, *DES and a Proposed Theory of Enterprise Liability*, 46 Fordham L. Rev. 963 (1978)—fashioned a "market share" theory that some courts have used against the DES manufacturers. (In *Hymowitz*, supra note 2, the New York Court of Appeals created its own version of a market share theory, emphasizing that the theory was valid for DES cases only. A few other courts have cautiously taken the theory beyond the DES context. See, e.g., Smith v. Cutter Biological, Inc., 72 Haw. 416, 823 P.2d 717 (1991) (antihemophilic factor infected with AIDS virus).)

The Restatement (Third) of Torts: Liability for Physical Harm (Basic Principles) § 28, cmt. *o* (Tent. Draft No. 2, March 2002) takes no position on the validity of the market share theory but offers a helpful explanation:

A number of courts . . . adopted a new "market share" theory that permitted apportionment of liability among defendant–manufacturers based on each one's share of the relevant market for DES. Many of the details of the specific market–share theory adopted vary from court to court, but common to all is that liability is several, rather than joint and several, and is limited to the market share of each defendant, so that in theory each will pay roughly the amount that represents the overall harm caused by that defendant's DES. A roughly equal number of courts have declined to craft a new theory for DES patients, expressing concern that to do so would rend too great a chasm in the tort–law requirement of factual causation. Despite several decades of development, the number of jurisdictions that have addressed and resolved this question for DES victims is quite small; the vast majority of states has not yet been confronted with or decided this issue. However, with DES having been withdrawn from the market in 1971, a latency period of approximately 20 years, and very little judicial activity over the past decade, it appears unlikely that there will be any significant further development of market–share liability in the DES context. Virtually all courts that have considered the question have declined to apply a market–share liability theory to products that are not fungible and therefore do not pose equivalent risks to all of those exposed to the products.

D. LIMITED–PURPOSE SUBSTITUTES FOR THE STANDARD BUT–FOR TEST: THE LOST OPPORTUNITY DOCTRINE

GRANT v. AMERICAN NATIONAL RED CROSS

District of Columbia Court of Appeals, 2000.
745 A.2d 316.

FARRELL, ASSOCIATE JUDGE.

* * *

In July 1982 Calvin Grant * * *, then age twelve, underwent surgery at Children's Hospital in Washington, D.C. to repair a congenital heart defect. During the surgery he received five units of whole blood, which had been provided to Children's Hospital by * * * the American National Red Cross * * *.

All of the five donors whose blood was used on Grant satisfied the blood screening requirements then utilized by the Red Cross. However, in compliance with the Red Cross's procedures at the time, none of the blood had been tested for alanine aminotransferase ("ALT") levels. In September 1993, after a liver biopsy, Grant was found to have the hepatitis C virus. He filed a complaint in the Superior Court charging the Red Cross with negligence in not having screened the blood administered to him during the 1982 surgery for ALT. During the litigation, it was determined that one of the five donors of the donated blood had been positive for hepatitis C. At the Red Cross's request, blood samples from the positive donor and [Grant] were tested by means of DNA, and it was confirmed that [Grant] had been infected with the virus during the 1982 transfusion.

In 1982, when Grant underwent surgery, scientists and doctors were aware that besides hepatitis A and hepatitis B there was a form referred to as "non–A, non–B" (or "NANB") hepatitis. Although today scientists know that most NANB hepatitis is caused by the hepatitis C virus ("HCV"), that virus was not isolated until 1989, and the first test to screen blood for HCV antibodies was not available until 1990. In his suit Grant asserted, nonetheless, that the Red Cross should have tested all donor blood for ALT levels as a "surrogate test" for NANB hepatitis,[2] because blood containing elevated levels of ALT has an increased chance of carrying the NANB hepatitis virus. According to [Grant], at the time of his surgery ALT testing could identify a significant portion (up to 40%) of the blood supply infected with the NANB hepatitis, and—he asserted—the Red Cross itself believed that ALT testing might prevent as many as a third of the expected serious cases of NANB hepatitis cases annually, yet made a "business" (or cost–benefit) decision to forgo the testing.

The Red Cross defended by asserting that in 1982, all of the available data and the practice of national blood suppliers counseled against routine screening by ALT donor testing. It proffered evidence that, according to the consensus of leading experts nationwide, ALT testing would not have detected approximately 70 percent of donors infected with the then–unknown viral agent HCV; that the same percentage of the donors excluded on the basis of ALT testing would have been healthy and not affected by that agent; and that as a result routine ALT testing would have annually excluded many thousands of units of healthy blood from donors not carrying hepatitis, while failing to detect the vast majority of donors carrying NANB hepatitis.

Grant responded by conceding that he could not prove by greater than 50% (more likely than not) that he would not have been infected even if ALT testing had been performed. Specifically, he admitted that his expert testimony would be able to establish no more than a 40 percent correlation between ALT levels and infection with the NANB hepatitis * * *.[3] Grant argued nonetheless—as he does on appeal—that a jury should be allowed to decide whether the Red Cross's negligence in not screening for elevated ALT levels "depriv[ed] him of an opportunity to avoid" the infection he incurred even if that "opportunity" were measured at less than fifty–percent likelihood. Citing decisions of other courts that have applied the so–called "loss of chance" doctrine, he argued that it was "a jury question whether the Red Cross's negligent

2. A surrogate test, while not testing directly for the causative agent of a disease or its antibodies, may reveal a statistical association between a disease and a particular agent.

3. * * * In her deposition Grant's expert witness, Dr. Johanna Pindyck, acknowledged that Grant's chance of not being infected would have improved by "at least 30 percent" had ALT testing been used, but that she could not "say for certain whether it would have been greater than that." This approximated the affidavit

of Dr. Thomas Zuck, past president of the Council of Community Blood Centers, that in 1982 there was "only a 30% chance that the implicated donor would have had an elevated ALT level and his blood discarded" as a result of ALT testing. Similarly, a study performed by the National Institutes of Health at about the same time confirmed that ALT testing "would fail to detect about 70% of the blood that would infect recipients with non–A, non–B hepatitis" (Affidavit of Dr. Paul V. Holland).

failure to test proximately caused Calvin Grant's injury by increasing his chances of getting NANB infected blood by at least 30%." The trial court, on the strength of decisions of this court cited by the Red Cross, concluded as a matter of law that Grant had failed to present triable issues of fact on both negligence and proximate causation. It therefore granted summary judgment to the Red Cross.

* * *

Grant concedes, as he did in the trial court, his inability to prove that the Red Cross's assumed negligence more likely than not caused his hepatitis infection, i.e., that blood testing for ALT levels would—as a matter of probability—have detected the donor carrying the hepatitis C virus, leading to rejection of that blood donation. Instead Grant urges us to depart from that standard and accept the view of some courts in cases such as this that a plaintiff makes out a triable issue on causation by showing that the defendant's conduct deprived him of a substantial, though less than fifty percent, chance of a better outcome had due care been exercised. * * *

Grant argues * * * that this court has already applied the "loss of chance" doctrine in Ferrell v. Rosenbaum, [691 A.2d 641 (D.C. 1997)] * * *. Upon analysis, we do not read *Ferrell* as deviating from the basic standard of proof of causation by probability. In that case, the plaintiff sued her physician and hospital for misdiagnosing her infant child's potentially fatal blood disorder of Fanconi anemia. She proffered evidence that the child's best hope of survival into adulthood had been through a bone marrow transplant from a compatible donor sibling. Indeed, her expert witness would have testified that, according to recent scientific reports, "*70 to 90 percent* of Fanconi anemia patients can be cured of their hematological disease if transplanted with a matched sibling at an early age." The plaintiff's theory was that the defendants' negligence in misdiagnosing the child's condition deprived her of the opportunity she would have seized—but which she later lost through circumstances—to bear a child or children who could have donated the necessary bone marrow. In reversing summary judgment to the defendants, we acknowledged that 't]he bare possibility that the Ferrells could have had another child, or children, that could have been a suitable bone marrow donor' would not suffice * * *. But we held that, given the proffered testimony that the mother "would have done anything to help [the affected child], including having another child or children," the "significant" chances that this "would have yielded a suitable donor" for the child, and the even stronger evidence (cited above) of correlation between a transplant and likely cure, the plaintiff had presented a triable issue on whether the alleged negligence "substantial[ly]" contributed to the child's reduced chances for survival. * * * Id. at 651–52 (citing and relying on conclusion of the court in Daniels v. Hadley Mem'l Hosp., 185 U.S.App.D.C. 84, 93, 566 F.2d 749, 758 (1977), "that there was an 'appreciable chance' that [the] patient's life would have been saved, after [a] bench trial includ[ed] testimony that 75–80% of patients survived if given proper treatment").

The "lost chance" recognized in *Ferrell* was thus the opportunity for the plaintiff to avail herself of a medical procedure with a high likelihood (a 70–90 percent chance) of success if carried out. No similar claim is made in the present case, given Grant's inability to offer proof that screening blood for ALT levels would have offered a more than thirty-percent–plus chance of detecting a donor's hepatitis. *Ferrell* thus synchronizes with the standard of probability required by our decisions, whereas Grant's proof does not.

* * *

Grant's conceded inability to prove that the Red Cross's assumed negligence more likely than not caused his injury required the entry of summary judgment for the Red Cross. Accordingly, the judgment of the Superior Court is affirmed.

Notes

1. *The genesis of the lost opportunity doctrine.* The lost opportunity doctrine came out of cases grappling with the normal requirement of expert testimony to establish factual causation in medical malpractice and other cases involving medical causation. The law's burden–of–proof standard on factual causation is "by a preponderance of the evidence," meaning "more probably than not." But medical and other scientific experts are often loath to give an opinion that "X probably caused Y." They seem more comfortable with expressing their opinions in the form of estimates of the mathematical chances that avoiding X would have avoided Y. At one time courts were inclined to regard such estimates as too conjectural to serve as evidence of factual causation in medical cases, sometimes suggesting that "even a conjecture that a better than fifty percent chance of [medical] recovery would have been in prospect but for the defendant's negligence will not justify a submission [of the cause–in–fact] issue to the jury." Malone, Ruminations on Cause–in–Fact, 9 Stan.L.Rev. 60, 88 (1956).

In Hamil v. Bashline, 481 Pa. 256, 392 A.2d 1280 (1978), expert testimony established that an emergency room physician's failure to diagnose and treat a patient's heart attack—which proved fatal—deprived the patient of a 75% chance of surviving. Reversing a jury verdict for the defendant, the Pennsylvania Supreme Court held, in effect, that such testimony is readily translatable into terms with which the law is comfortable: When a medical witness gives an expert opinion that "X deprived the patient of a 75% chance of avoiding Y," courts can take that to mean "X probably caused Y."

That's all there was to *Hamil*. Nevertheless, courts in cases like Herskovits v. Group Health Co–op., 99 Wash.2d 609, 664 P.2d 474 (1983), picked up on *Hamil* and used it as authority for allowing damages when the medical testimony put the chance of survival that the defendant's negligent conduct cost the patient at less than 50%. The experts in *Herskovits* testified that the defendant's negligent failure to timely diagnose and begin treating a patient's lung cancer lowered the patient's chances of surviving the cancer from 39% to 25%. In a divided opinion, the court held that damages should be awarded (presumably calculated at 14% of whatever the damages would have been if plaintiff had been able to prove the defendant's negligent conduct caused the death). *Herskovits* became the leading case for the "lost opportunity" doctrine.

2. *The lost opportunity doctrine in medical malpractice cases.* The arguments for using the lost opportunity doctrine in the medical malpractice context are very strong. In Murrey v. United States, 73 F.3d 1448 (7th Cir. 1996), the plaintiffs could not show that a V.A. Hospital's delay in administering surgical treatment caused their decedent's death, but they did have evidence that prompt treatment would have given decedent a 5 to 10 percent chance of surviving. Chief Judge Posner's opinion for the court explained why the hospital's negligent destruction of this small chance was actionable:

> It does not matter, as far as liability is concerned, how good or bad [the patient's] prospects were (obviously it matters greatly to the amount of damages). The government does not deny that under the law of Illinois, which governs the substantive issues here * * *, the loss of a chance is compensable. Actually, the question is unsettled in Illinois. But the government is bound by its concession, and our guess is that the Supreme Court of Illinois, should the question ever be put to it, will answer in favor of liability.[1] A loss is a loss even if it is only probable, as are most things in life. No doubt Murrey would have paid a lot (if he had a lot to pay) for a 5 percent chance of survival if the alternative was a certainty of immediate death. This shows that he lost something by being deprived of that chance. If 200 people were in Murrey's situation and received improper care, we would expect 10 to have survived if all 200 had received proper care, so that if none of the 200 was entitled to any damages the hospital would have escaped liability for malpractice that had caused a number of deaths in a realistic sense of "cause." Damages for loss of a chance are necessary to prevent the underdeterrence of medical negligence.

Despite the strength of these arguments—which seem convincing on compensation, deterrence, *and* corrective–justice grounds—the lost opportunity doctrine is controversial. In Smith v. State Dep't of Health & Hosp., 676 So.2d 543, 547 (La.1996) (adopting the doctrine), the court said "it has been recognized by a majority of the states." But in an omitted footnote the *Grant* court said the majority of jurisdictions have rejected the doctrine. The Restatement (Third) of Torts: Liability for Physical Harm (Basic Principles) § 26, cmt. n (Tent. Draft. No. 2, March 2002) "takes no position" on the validity of the lost opportunity doctrine.

3. *The lost opportunity doctrine outside the medical malpractice context?* In the above cited comment, the proposed Restatement indicates that the lost opportunity doctrine has "almost universally" been confined to medical malpractice cases, explaining:

> Three features of that context are significant: (1) a contractual relationship exists between patient and physician (or physician's employer), in

---

1. This was a good guess. See Holton v. Memorial Hospital, 176 Ill.2d 95, 223 Ill.   Dec. 429, 679 N.E.2d 1202 (1997). [Ed.]

which the *raison d'etre* of the contract is that the physician will take every reasonable measure to obtain an optimal outcome for the patient; (2) reasonably good empirical evidence is available about the general statistical probability of the lost opportunity; and (3) frequently the consequences of the physician's negligence will deprive the patient of a less–than–50–percent chance for recovery.

In Daugert v. Pappas, 104 Wash.2d 254, 262, 704 P.2d 600, 605 (1985), the same court that decided *Herskovits* (supra note 1) held that "clearly the loss of chance analysis ... is inapplicable in a legal malpractice case." See also Hardy v. Southwestern Bell Telephone Co., 910 P.2d 1024 (Ok.1996) (refusing to extend the doctrine to a case in which the 911 emergency system "locked up" because of the telephone company's decision to allow the sale of Garth Brooks concert tickets by phone, bringing about a delay in summoning emergency medical assistance to a heart attack victim).

4. *The measure of damages in lost opportunity cases.* In the jurisdictions that recognize the lost opportunity doctrine, Dobbs, The Law of Torts § 178, pp. 435–437 (2000), has identified three approaches to measuring damages in cases in which the plaintiff shows loss of a chance of 50% or less: "[a] [O]ne group of courts permits the jury to find causation and make an award for the whole of the loss, disregarding the fact that the patient was likely to die regardless of the doctor's negligence. * * * [b] [Under a second method], the plaintiff recovers * * * only an amount representing the value of the chance destroyed by the defendant's negligence. * * * When the plaintiff's chances for survival are quantified by testimony, the easiest calculation is one that discounts total damages by the plaintiff's chance. If the patient had only a 40% chance of living even when given proper medical treatment, and the defendant's negligence deprived her of all that chance, the defendant should be liable for 40% of the total damages. * * * [c] [A third approach rejects] any automatic use of the quantified chance to discount full damages [and instead instructs the jury] to consider all the evidence, including the testimony assigning numerical values to the plaintiff's chances, and come up with its own valuation." Both Professor Dobbs and the proposed Restatement (Third) can be read to indicate that the second of the three approaches is the most sensible.

In a state that has adopted the lost opportunity doctrine and the second of Professor Dobbs's damages–measurement approaches, what should the recovery be in a wrongful death action in which the experts testify that defendant's medical negligence deprived the decedent of a 90% chance of survival? In Gordon v. Willis Knighton Medical Center, 661 So.2d 991 (La.App. 1995), the majority's answer was 90% of full damages. A dissenting judge maintained:

> When a plaintiff ... has lost a 50% or better chance of survival, full damages, rather than a percentage, should be awarded. Common sense dictates that conduct depriving a person of a 90% chance of survival is the probable cause of death.

The Restatement (Third), § 26, cmt. *n* (Tent. Draft No. 2, March 2002) signals agreement with the *Gordon* dissent, stating that plaintiffs who "show that the probability of a better outcome was in excess of 50% ... *of course* recover the entirety of their damages." (Emphasis supplied.)

5. *An innovative "increased risk" theory.* Stating that "theories of lost chance of recovery and increased risk of future injury have similar underpinnings," the court in Dillon v. Evanston Hospital, 199 Ill.2d 483, 503, 264 Ill.Dec. 653, 666, 771 N.E.2d 357, 370 (2002), held that a patient should be able to recover the value of a small but significant chance of future injury brought about by the negligence of a physician who installed a 16–centimeter catheter in the plaintiff's upper chest and then removed only seven centimeters of it. The nine–centimeter fragment migrated to the patient's heart. The court explained the patient's situation:

> On medical advice, plaintiff chose not to attempt removal of the fragment. All the expert witnesses but one believed that the risks of injury from an attempted removal of the fragment outweighed the risks that would exist if the catheter remained in the heart. The attendant risks of the catheter remaining were infection, perforation of the heart, arrhythmia, embolization, and further migration of the fragment. At the time of trial, plaintiff had not suffered from any of these conditions, although she did suffer from anxiety over the fragment's presence.[2]

> The evidence was that it was not reasonably certain that plaintiff would in the future suffer the injuries for which she was at risk due to the fragment's presence in her heart. Several physicians testified about the risk of infection, with the lowest estimated risk being close to zero and the highest being 20%. The risk of arrhythmia was less than 5%. The risks of perforation and migration were also small. The risk of embolization was low to nonexistent. [771 N.E.2d at 366.]

In approving the patient's right to recover the value of these risks, the *Dillon* court relied significantly on Petriello v. Kalman, 215 Conn. 377, 576 A.2d 474 (1990), which held that a patient was entitled to recover damages when medical negligence created a risk of future bowel obstruction that was "somewhere between 8 and 16 percent." The *Petriello* court acknowledged that it was breaking new ground.

The "increased risk" reasoning of *Dillon* and *Petriello* is very much a minority viewpoint. And probably the approach is even less likely than the lost opportunity doctrine to be used outside the medical malpractice context. In Mauro v. Raymark Industries, 116 N.J. 126, 561 A.2d 257 (1989), the majority opinion argued strongly for the traditional (more probable than not) requirement in refusing to permit recovery against the manufacturers of asbestos–containing products whose wrongful conduct caused the presently healthy plaintiff to sustain a 20–43% chance of future fatal cancer. Both the majority and dissenting opinions in *Mauro* provide good discussions of the competing policy considerations.

---

2. The emotional suffering—fear, anxiety, and anger—resulting from medical negligence that deprives a patient of an opportunity of a medical cure (or creates a risk of future harm) must be carefully distinguished from the lost opportunity (or future risk) itself. Under the principles discussed in Section D of Chapter VI, infra p. 235, recovery for the emotional consequences in these cases is not particularly problematic. [Ed.]

E. APPORTIONING DAMAGES ACCORDING TO CAUSATION

"Causation in fact is an all–or–nothing proposition. * * * [S]pecific conduct is either a cause in fact, or it is not."[1] A single indivisible injury—no matter how many causes in fact it has—cannot be apportioned by causation. Thus, for example, in Summers v. Tice, supra p. 132, the wound to the plaintiff's eye was a single indivisible injury, and each of the tortious shooters was treated as a cause in fact of the entirety.[2]

But obviously damages should be apportioned by causation whenever there is a reasonable basis for doing so, because otherwise, the bedrock cause–in–fact tenet—that no one should be held responsible for consequences that she had nothing to do with—will be offended. Thus, if the evidence in *Summers* had shown that one shooter wounded the plaintiff's eye and the other simultaneously wounded his knee, each shooter's liability would have been limited to the consequences that could be traced to his conduct, i.e., to the wound that he produced.[3]

We have just discussed a clear case of a single indivisible injury and a clear case of separate injuries that can and should be apportioned. The subject of this section is a large middle ground between these two poles. Quite often the injuries of which the plaintiff complains will be theoretically separate and divisible, but as a practical matter it will be impossible to sort out which injuries stemmed from which causes. Broadly speaking, the question addressed in this section is this: When the plaintiff can show that the defendant's tortious conduct was a cause in fact of some significant part (but probably not all) of an inextricable tangle of injuries, how do and should the courts respond?

1. APPORTIONING HARM CAUSED BY MULTIPLE TORTFEASORS

PINER v. SUPERIOR COURT

Supreme Court of Arizona, 1998.
192 Ariz. 182, 962 P.2d 909.

FELDMAN, JUSTICE.

* * *

On his way to work on Friday, October 12, 1990, William Piner stopped his truck to let a pedestrian cross the street. While he was stopped, a car driven by Billy Jones hit Piner's truck from behind. Police were called to investigate the incident. Piner waited for the police to finish their investigation before calling his physician to complain of pain in his neck, upper back, left arm, and head. The doctor's staff told Piner

---

1. Waste Management, Inc. v. South Central Bell Tel. Co., 15 S.W.3d 425, 433 (Tenn.App. 1997).

2. Only one of them actually caused it, but the alternative liability doctrine legitimated treating each as though he had done so.

3. This would be true unless the concerted action theory applied to make each shooter responsible not only for his own shot but also for the other's.

that the doctor was unavailable but would call him back later that day. Piner then fixed the broken tail lights on his truck and went to work.

Later that day, Piner was driving to lunch when the car ahead of him stopped to let some pedestrians cross the street. Piner stopped and was again hit from the rear, this time by a vehicle driven by Cynthia Richardson. Feeling similar pain symptoms after this accident, Piner called his doctor's office and was again told that the doctor was occupied and would contact him later.

Piner was unable to see his physician until Monday. After examination, the doctor concluded that Piner suffered a number of injuries as a result of the collisions. Due to the nature of the injuries, however, neither she nor any other physician has been able to attribute any particular part of Piner's total injuries to one accident or the other.

Piner filed an action against Jones and Richardson * * * alleging indivisible injuries resulting from the successive impacts. Neither defendant has asserted that he or she could apportion the particular physical harm Piner suffered between the separate accidents. Apparently, all parties agree that both collisions contributed to Piner's total physical injuries.

Piner moved for partial summary judgment, arguing that because his injuries are indivisible, defendants should be held jointly and severally liable. According to Piner, in a successive accident, indivisible injury case, defendants have the burden of proving apportionment; if neither defendant can demonstrate what portion of the total damage he or she caused, they should be held jointly and severally liable for the entire amount. [The trial judge denied Piner's motion, ruling that] A.R.S. § 12–2506 abolished the system of joint and several liability * * * "and that the plaintiff has to prove which accident caused which injuries, and if not, the plaintiff loses." [We granted Piner leave to file this interlocutory appeal.]

* * *

THE INDIVISIBLE INJURY RULE IN ARIZONA

A. *Evolution of the Rule of Joint and Several Liability: Causation and Apportionment of Damages*

Black–letter tort law tells us that as an essential element of the action, the plaintiff must provide evidence that the defendant's conduct caused plaintiff's damage. [Thus a] plaintiff's case failed if that plaintiff was unable to establish the damage attributable to a defendant's conduct. [But the] law eventually recognized an exception for multiple, culpable actors if the plaintiff, through no fault of his own, was unable to apportion causation * * *.

* * *

The evolution of Arizona law on the subject [began in 1928, when] Arizona recognized joint and several liability as a well–settled rule but one that applied only in cases involving tortious injury brought about by concerted action of two or more tortfeasors. See White v. Arizona Eastern R. Co., 26 Ariz. 590, 594, 229 P. 101, 102 (1924). Salt River Valley Water Users' Ass'n v. Cornum further limited the definition of joint tortfeasors, holding only those tortfeasors who pursued a "community of purpose" jointly and severally liable to the plaintiff. 49 Ariz. 1, 8, 63 P.2d 639, 643 (1937).

* * *

* * * *Cornum* recognized one exception: when the negligence of different tortfeasors "coincided in time, place, and character" [so as to produce a single indivisible result], joint and several liability could be applied even though the defendants' actions were not concerted.* When the plaintiff's case fell outside the exception, the plaintiff would have to apportion damage by causation or prove that one of the tortfeasors was the proximate cause of the entire injury. If the plaintiff was unable to do so, the case failed.

In 1966, Holtz [v. Holder, 101 Ariz. 247, 418 P.2d 584 (1966)] recognized another circumstance in which a plaintiff could be excused from apportioning damages. The facts in *Holtz* are similar to those in * * * the present case. Holtz, like Piner, suffered [injuries] from separate [traffic] accidents. [Holtz's injuries resulted from two collisions separated by five to ten minutes. Like Piner's, Holtz's injuries were theoretically divisible, but Holtz's doctor testified that it was "medically impossible to determine which impact caused which injuries," and that "the only way to tell would have been an examination of the plaintiff immediately after the first collision."] We held that the tortfeasors were jointly and severally liable for Holtz's entire damage. Such a result was "desirable as a matter of policy" even though it extended the exception recognized in * * * *Cornum* to include incidents of successive injury.

To reach this result, *Holtz* actually applied two different rules. First, when the injury was indivisible, even though caused by successive accidents, the plaintiff could assert a claim against all wrongdoers without having the burden of "proving the extent of damage or injury caused by each...." We described this as the "single indivisible injury rule." *Holtz* shifted the burden of apportionment to the defendants and gave them incentive to apportion cause by holding each liable for the entire amount of unapportioned damages. Successive tortfeasors are responsible for the entire amount of damages if "their acts occur closely

---

* For typical examples of such cases—in which the conduct of each of two independently acting tortfeasors was a but–for cause of an indisputably single and indivisible injury—see Austin Electric Ry. Co. v. Faust, 133 S.W. 449 (Tex.Civ.App. 1910) (holding a streetcar company and an ice company jointly and severally liable when a collision between a negligently operated street car and the ice company's negligently operated horse–drawn wagon caused the ice company's horses to bolt into a second collision with a nearby buggy in which the plaintiff was sitting at the time); Baylor University v. Bradshaw, 52 S.W.2d 1094 (Tex.Civ.App. 1932) (holding that a bus passenger hurt in a collision between the negligently operated bus and a negligently speeding train could recover in full from the bus company, which could then recover over in a third party action for contribution against the railroad). [Ed.]

in time and place" and the plaintiff receives successive injuries that "the trier of fact determines to be unapportionable between or among the several tortfeasors." * * *

Holtz's [second rule was that] damages were not to be apportioned on the basis of fault. Thus, all defendants were jointly and severally liable for the whole amount of damage. At common law, degrees of fault were never assigned to the parties involved and were unnecessary because they were unrelated to the damages assessed. * * * This, [then], was the common law in Arizona—each tortious actor was jointly and severally liable for all of the damage caused by his conduct, even if one was much more at fault than another.

B. *The Impact of UCATA*

Defendants claim the Uniform Contribution Among Tortfeasors Act (UCATA) overruled *Holtz* and its progeny, thus requiring the factfinder to apportion damages between multiple actors and making each tortfeasor severally liable only for the portion of damages caused by his conduct. If the plaintiff is unable to provide enough evidence to form a basis for apportionment of damages, then, defendants argue, the claim must be dismissed. We disagree with this view because UCATA does not require limiting liability by apportioning damages but by apportioning fault.

The Arizona Legislature enacted its first version of UCATA in 1984. These provisions replaced [the common law rule of contributory negligence, whereby a plaintiff's negligent conduct barred his recovery entirely, with a statutory regime of comparative fault, under which a plaintiff's negligent conduct diminishes his recovery on a percentage–fault basis but no longer automatically bars all recovery. The 1984 UCATA also] abolished the rule forbidding contribution between joint tortfeasors. Under this new regime, the factfinder allocated a percentage of fault to each culpable actor. Even though the culpable defendants were still jointly and severally liable for all damages, the legislature established a right of contribution that allowed a defendant held liable for more than his share of fault to recover from the other tortfeasors in proportion to their several contributions of fault.** This change was intended to bring about a system in which each tortfeasor would eventually contribute only a portion of damage equal to the percentage of fault attributed to that tortfeasor by the factfinder. But Arizona's negligence law still produced harsh results when one defendant was insolvent, thus leaving the others unable to obtain contribution. See, e.g., Gehres [v. City of Phoenix, 156 Ariz. 484, 753 P.2d 174 (1987)] (defendants assigned five percent of fault held jointly and severally liable for one hundred percent of damages).

In response, the Arizona Legislature amended UCATA, abolishing joint liability and replacing it with a system that requires the courts to

---

** In the pre–comparative fault era, contribution in cases like *Austin Electric* and *Bradshaw*, supra note *, was on a per capita (head count) basis. [Ed.]

allocate responsibility among all parties who caused the injury, whether or not they are present in the action. A.R.S. § 12–2506(B). Under the present [statute], "the liability of each defendant is several only and not joint." § 12–2506(D). Taken in isolation, this wording tends to support defendants' argument, but several factors militate against such an interpretation. First, the legislative intent was to cure the *Gehres* "deep pocket" problem of a defendant only minimally at fault yet liable for the full amount of damages.

A second factor is that the old [pre–*Holtz*] rule [often] conditioned the plaintiff's recovery on the impossible: if unable to divide the indivisible, the plaintiff was denied relief and the culpable parties were relieved of all responsibility. The injustice inherent in this policy has been repeatedly recognized by our courts. We do not believe that when the legislature attempted to eliminate the injustice it perceived in the deep pocket problem, it also intended to reestablish an unfair regime under which an innocent victim is denied any relief because the damages caused by independent wrongdoers result in an indivisible, unapportionable injury.

Most important, the clear text of [§ 12–2506] does not require that a defendant's liability be limited by apportioning damages, but only by apportioning fault:

> A. In an action for personal injury, property damage or wrongful death, the liability of each defendant for damages is several only and is not joint.... *Each defendant is liable only for the amount of damages allocated to that defendant in direct proportion to that defendant's percentage of fault.... [T]he trier of fact shall multiply the total amount of damages recoverable by the plaintiff by the percentage of each defendant's fault,* and that amount is the maximum recoverable against the defendant....

> B. In assessing percentages of fault the trier of fact shall consider the fault of all persons who contributed to the alleged injury....

* * *

> F. (2) "Fault" means an actionable breach of legal duty, act or omission *proximately causing or contributing to injury or damages sustained by a person seeking recovery * * *.*

Thus, while [§ 12–2506] requires the plaintiff to prove that a defendant's conduct was a cause of injury, it does not instruct us to limit liability by apportioning damages. Instead, each tortfeasor whose conduct caused injury is severally liable only for a percentage of the total damages recoverable by the plaintiff, the percentage based on each actor's allocated share of fault.

We conclude, therefore, that [§ 12–2506] has left intact the rule of indivisible injury, relieving the plaintiff of apportioning damage according to causal contribution. When the tortious conduct of more than one defendant contributes to one indivisible injury, the entire amount of damage resulting from all contributing causes is the total amount "of damages recoverable by the plaintiff," as that term is used in § 12–2506(A). The second part of the *Holtz* rule, however, was abrogated by § 12–2506(A). Contrary to the common law and cases such as *Gehres*, the fault of all actors is compared and each defendant is severally liable for damages allocated "in direct proportion to that defendant's percentage of fault." § 12–2506(A). To determine each defendant's liability "the trier of fact shall multiply the total amount of damages recoverable by the plaintiff by the percentage of each defendant's fault, and that amount is the maximum recoverable against the defendant."

Thus in an indivisible injury case, the factfinder is to compute the total amount of damage sustained by the plaintiff and the percentage of fault of each tortfeasor. Multiplying the first figure by the second gives the maximum recoverable against each tortfeasor. This result conforms not only with the intent of the legislature and the text of the statute but also with common sense. When damages cannot be apportioned between multiple tortfeasors, there is no reason why those whose conduct produced successive but indivisible injuries should be treated differently from those whose independent conduct caused injury in a single accident. Like our predecessors in *Holtz*, we see no reason to employ a different rule if the injuries occur at once, five minutes apart or, as in the present case, several hours apart. The operative fact is simply that the conduct of each defendant was a cause and the result is indivisible damage.

* * *

CONCLUSION

In the present case, the trial judge erred in placing the burden of proof on apportionment on Piner. Assuming Piner proves that the conduct of both Jones and Richardson contributed to the final result, the burden of proof on apportionment is on them. If the judge concludes there is no evidence that would permit apportionment, then the case should be treated as one involving indivisible injuries. If the judge * * * concludes there is [evidence that might provide a basis for apportionment], the jurors should be instructed that if they are able to apportion damages, they should do so, allocating fault and damages for each accident separately. They should also be instructed that if they are unable to apportion damages, then they are to determine Piner's total damages resulting from both accidents. In such case, the indivisible injury rule will apply. * * * [But the jurors will also] be instructed to allocate fault in accordance with § 12–2506. The judge is then to multiply each tortfeasor's percentage of fault by the [total damages]. Each tortfeasor in an indivisible injury case is then severally liable for the product of that calculation.

* * *

The trial court's * * * order denying Piner's motion for partial summary judgment and * * * ruling regarding jury instruction content are vacated. The trial court may proceed in accordance with this opinion.

Notes

1. *Joint and several liability (and the "one satisfaction" rule).* The term "joint and several liability" describes the feature of a judgment against multiple defendants—as to each of whom cause in fact has been established under the normal but for test or one of the established limited–purpose alternatives—that enables the plaintiff to collect the entire amount from any one or any combination of them. A judgment imposing joint and several liability "means that each defendant is liable to the plaintiff for the whole of the plaintiff's damages, except that the plaintiff may not collect, from all of the defendants together, more than those damages." McKinnon v. City of Berwyn, 750 F.2d 1383, 1387 (7th Cir.1984). The principal function of the joint and several liability doctrine is to protect the plaintiff against the risk of "uncollectability," i.e., the risk that one or more of the tortfeasors may be insolvent or otherwise unable to satisfy its liability.

Ordinarily each defendant held subject to joint and several liability has a right of *contribution* from the other(s). The right of contribution means "that a defendant forced to pay a disproportionate amount of the plaintiff's damages [can ordinarily] insist that other defendants (or even nondefendant tortfeasors) reimburse him for some of the cost. [T]he whole point of contribution is to mitigate the effect of joint and several liability, which allows liability to fall disproportionately on one or some of a group of joint tortfeasors." *McKinnon,* 750 F.2d at 1387. Judgments imposing joint and several liability and recognizing contribution rights shift the risk of uncollectability from the plaintiff to the group of tortfeasors.

2. *The single indivisible injury rule.* The appropriateness of shifting the apportionment burden to defendants in what the *Piner* court variously calls "multiple culpable actors" cases and "single indivisible injury" cases is widely accepted. It is endorsed by Restatement (Third) of Torts: Apportionment of Liability § 26, cmt. *h* (2000) and by the proposed Restatement (Third) of Torts: Liability for Physical Harm (Basic Principles) § 28, cmt. *d(1)* (Tent. Draft No. 2, March 2002). The leading case for the approach is probably Maddux v. Donaldson, 362 Mich. 425, 108 N.W.2d 33 (1961), in which the plaintiff's tangle of injuries resulted from two collisions separated by about 30 seconds. The court allowed recover in full from the second motorist. (The first, impecunious and uninsured, was not pursued.)

3. *How far apart is too far?* There is no agreement on how far apart in time the two accidents can be before the "single indivisible injury" burden–shifting rule loses its plausibility and gives way to the normal allocation of the burden of proof. Pang v. Minch, 53 Ohio St.3d 186, 559 N.E.2d 1313 (1990), applied the burden–shifting rule against traffic tortfeasors responsible for three separate wrecks spread over a five–month period. But the court in Potts v. Litt, 171 Ariz. 98, 828 P.2d 1239 (App. 1991), thought two wrecks 13 days apart were outside the legitimate applicability of the rule, stating that "[w]e have been unable to find a case that was submitted to a jury

under the indivisible injury rule in which the successive accidents were as distant in time as the accidents involved here."

4. *Distinguishing apportionment by causation from apportionment by percentage fault.* The analytically crucial line the *Piner* court drew between apportionment by causation and apportionment by percentage fault is more fully treated in Chapter XI. The distinction is clear enough, but litigants often seek to obscure it. See, e.g., Ravo v. Rogatnick, 70 N.Y.2d 305, 520 N.Y.S.2d 533, 514 N.E.2d 1104 (1987), in which a medical malpractice defendant unsuccessfully argued that the jury's assignment of 20% fault to him (and 80% to another physician defendant had worked with) amounted to a finding that defendant had caused only 20% of the patient's injury.

2. APPORTIONING HARM CAUSED BY A COMBINATION OF TORTIOUS CONDUCT AND OTHER CAUSES

FOLLETT v. JONES

Supreme Court of Arkansas, 1972.
252 Ark. 950, 481 S.W.2d 713.

HOLT, JUSTICE.

* * * Chauncy G. Jones was driving a pick–up truck when a collision occurred between it and a car driven by [Frank Follett]. Jones sustained three nondisplaced broken ribs, contusions, abrasions, and a blow to his head as a result of the accident. He was taken to a hospital where he died 17 days later. Prior to the date of the accident, Jones had regularly worked at his job and, also, on his farm. However, it is undisputed that on the date of the accident, unbeknownst to the deceased, he had terminal cancer of the lung. The cancerous condition was discovered from the x–rays taken to determine the extent of the injuries to his chest. An autopsy report listed the cancer as the cause of his death. A jury found * * * that [Follett] was negligent in causing the accident and that [Follett's] negligence was the proximate cause of Jones' death. The jury awarded $3,867.89 damages to [Jones's estate in compensation for Jones's 17 days of suffering from the broken ribs, etc.] and $8,000.00 to [Jones's widow in wrongful death damages. Follett has appealed the award of wrongful death damages.] * * *

We first consider [Follett's] assertion * * * that the trial court erred in not directing a verdict in his favor as to the wrongful death because the evidence failed to establish that the "accident was the proximate cause of the decedent's death." Medical testimony from two physicians was presented to establish that the death was proximately caused by the accident. One of the doctors testified that "the injuries received in the automobile accident hastened his death" and, further, the death was a result of "a combination" of the injuries and the cancer. However, decedent would have eventually died of the cancer had the accident never occurred. The other medical expert testified: "I believe that his injuries hastened his death." This evidence when viewed most favorably to the appellees, as we must do on appeal, is sufficient to present a question of fact for a jury's determination as to whether the accident proximately caused Jones's death.

We next consider [Follett's] contention that the jury's award for wrongful death is based upon speculation in that the record is void of any evidence relating to the "period of time that the accident shortened the life span of the decedent." Although the evidence as adduced is sufficient to present a jury question as to proximate causation, there is no evidence * * * from which the jury could determine the relative time span that this accident "shortened" Jones's life. In the absence of such evidence the jury's award is without a reasonable basis and is, therefore, speculative. * * *. However, * * * upon a retrial it is not impossible that the deficiency of proof as to decedent's "shortened" life span could be supplied. In such a situation a remand [for a new trial] is proper.* * * [T]he judgment is reversed and the cause remanded [for a new trial].

LANCASTER v. NORFOLK AND WESTERN RAILWAY CO.

United States Court of Appeals, Seventh Circuit, 1985.
773 F.2d 807.

POSNER, CIRCUIT JUDGE.

This [is an] appeal by the Norfolk and Western from a judgment for $850,000 in a suit under the Federal Employers' Liability Act (45 U.S.C. §§ 51–60)* by a former employee of the railroad, Gary Lancaster * * *.

The jury could have found the following facts in favor of Lancaster. In 1975 he was a 30–year–old mechanic working in the railroad's locomotive shop in Decatur, Illinois. Lachrone, a short–tempered foreman in the shop who had once been disciplined for roughing up a worker, became angry at Lancaster and several other workers who Lachrone thought were soldiering on the job. After flipping over a table on which one of the workers (not Lancaster) was sleeping, and smashing a bench, Lachrone grabbed a broom handle, approached Lancaster in a menacing fashion, screamed at him for about 15 seconds, and shook the broomstick in his face. * * *

The incident upset Lancaster abnormally. He thought people were following him, thought his phone was tapped, felt that the pressures of working for the railroad were too much, and went to Georgia to look for a new job. But after a couple of months his distress subsided and he went back to the old one. He was assigned to another foreman, Funderburk, who liked to "goose" workers, pull their hair, and hit them on the arms. He did these things to Lancaster, over the latter's protest. This

---

* Most workplace injury claims by employees against employers are taken out of the tort system by workers' compensation statutes, which impose a limited responsibility upon the employer regardless of fault and immunize the employer against tort liability. The Federal Employers' Liability Act (FELA) is an unusual (and important) alternative approach; it enables injured railway employees to sue their employers in tort. The Jones Act, 46 U.S.C. app. § 688(a), does the same thing for seamen. [Ed.].

behavior culminated in an incident in 1976 when Funderburk twice stuck his hand down the back of Lancaster's pants—once squeezing a buttock, the other time sticking his finger into Lancaster's anus. Lancaster became very upset, had trouble working, consulted a doctor, and on the doctor's advice took a leave of absence. [Lancaster was exhibiting definite symptoms of mental illness—most notably in the form of a hallucination in which he thought he saw a bug–like creature, almost a foot long, that had humanoid hands, feet, and face.] The doctor diagnosed Lancaster as suffering from anxiety * * *.

Lancaster returned to work early in 1977 and worked uneventfully until an incident in 1979 involving another supervisor, Boyd. Lancaster and another worker were repairing a locomotive under Boyd's supervision when Boyd picked up a sledgehammer—though as a supervisor he was not supposed to wield a sledgehammer—and swung it at a pin that was stuck. The sledgehammer flew out of Boyd's hands when he completed his swing, and struck Lancaster. Although only bruised, Lancaster became very upset because he thought Boyd had thrown the sledgehammer at him ("I swear before God the man throwed that sledgehammer, because when he throwed it, it went right where my head was back, and when I moved back is the only thing that saved my life").

Two months later Lancaster found himself working under another hot–tempered supervisor, like Lachrone—Tynan, a burly six–footer, who while fondling a pickax handle told Lancaster that if he didn't "keep on the job and do it right, I'll put your name on it." About a week later Lancaster happened to deliver some papers to Tynan that were folded. Tynan said, "I told you not to fold the papers," to which Lancaster replied that he had not folded them, they had been folded when he had received them to give to Tynan. Tynan, enraged, charged Lancaster with pickax handle in hand ("I turned around, and here's Jack [Tynan] coming at me, and I says, don't Jack, don't") and struck the door frame over Lancaster's head with the handle ("I heard his pickax handle hit the door frame, and I turned around, and there's Jack, and he wasn't smiling"). Lancaster became even more upset than after the previous incidents. Indeed his mental condition deteriorated rapidly. His doctor referred him to a psychiatrist who, two weeks after the incident with Tynan, diagnosed Lancaster as schizophrenic. Lancaster quit work, tried unsuccessfully to return, and is expected never to be well enough to work again.

A psychologist who testified for the railroad opined that Lancaster's latent schizophrenia would surely have been triggered by some other traumatic event if no supervisor misconduct had occurred. The two psychiatrists who testified for Lancaster thought this unlikely, among other reasons because Lancaster had got through two divorces before 1970 without incident. They thought that Lancaster's sense of self–worth was bound up with his work for the railroad and that his supervisors' hostile acts had exerted unbearable psychological pressure on him. All three expert witnesses agreed that the incident with Tynan, coming on top of the earlier incidents, had precipitated a descent into madness from which Lancaster will never recover.

Surprisingly, the railroad does not dispute the reasonableness of the damage award (which is made up of $40,000 in medical expenses, $200,000 in past and future pain and suffering, and $610,000 in lost earnings), although it does challenge one of the instructions on damages.

* * *

[The railroad also argues that most of the incidents that allegedly precipitated Lancaster's psychosis—the assault by Lachrone, the batteries by Funderburk, the battery or negligent infliction of personal injury by Boyd—are time–barred under the FELA's three–year statute of limitations. However, it is clear that the assault by Tynan—the pickax-handle episode—is not time–barred.] It was [Tynan] (the jury could have found) who pushed Lancaster over the edge. That Lancaster may have been made especially susceptible to such misconduct by earlier acts for which the railroad might or might not be liable would be no defense. Under the "thin skull," or more colorfully the "eggshell skull," rule, the railroad would be fully liable for the consequences of Tynan's assault.

* * *

Suppose the jury had been instructed that the only tortious conduct that it could consider was Tynan's assault in 1979, which clearly was not time–barred. The expert witnesses seem agreed that it was that assault which triggered the schizophrenia on which Lancaster's entire claim of damages rests. The fact that the railroad had weakened Lancaster by earlier misconduct for which it could not be held liable would be irrelevant to its liability for Tynan's assault and to the amount of damages it would have to pay. The tortfeasor takes his victim as he finds him (emphatically so if the victim's weakened condition is due to earlier, albeit time–barred, torts of the same tortfeasor); that is the eggshell-skull rule. The single act of Tynan made the railroad fully liable for all the damages that Lancaster sought and the jury awarded.

* * *

The last issue relates to the judge's refusal to instruct the jury to reduce Lancaster's damages by the probability that he would have become schizophrenic even if the railroad's supervisors had not misbehaved. Lancaster points out that since the tortfeasor takes his victim as he finds him, if the victim is highly vulnerable that is the tortfeasor's bad luck; there is no discount to average damages. This is a thoroughly sensible principle, by the way. If a tortfeasor never had to pay more than the average victim's damages, victims as a class would be systematically undercompensated and tortfeasors as a class therefore systematically underdeterred, because victims with above–average injuries would get their damages cut down while victims with below–average injuries would not get an offsetting increase.

But a corollary to this principle is that the damages of the "eggshell skull" victim must be reduced to reflect the likelihood that he would have been injured anyway, from a nonliable cause, even if the defendant had not injured him. The purpose of this corollary is transparent in a case like Dillon v. Twin State Gas & Elec. Co., 85 N.H. 449, 163 A. 111 (1932). The estate of Dillon, who was electrocuted by the defendant's negligence on his way down from the bridge he had just jumped off, was allowed to get damages only for the short time Dillon would have lived had it not been for the defendant's negligence. But the principle also applies to cases such as this where the tort victim is highly vulnerable to injury and the damages he suffered must therefore be discounted (multiplied) by the probability, distinctly less than one, that but for the tort he would have lived a normal life.

It is desirable in such cases to direct the jury's attention to the issue by a specific instruction. But the failure to give such an instruction in this case was not reversible error. The judge's instruction on damages was sufficiently general to allow (though it did not compel, as it should have done) the jury to adjust damages downward for the probability that something other than tortious misconduct would have triggered Lancaster's latent schizophrenia; for he told the jury simply that they should award Lancaster the damages proximately caused by the alleged wrongdoing if they found the railroad liable. In its closing argument the railroad reminded the jurors of the psychologist's testimony that, had it not been for the alleged wrongdoing, something else in Lancaster's life would have set him off. Lancaster's counsel argued the contrary evidence of his expert witnesses but did not suggest that it would be improper for the jury to apportion damages according to the probability that Lancaster would have gone through the rest of his life without incident if he had not been victimized by the railroad. The jury was thus at least apprised of the issue.

More important, the railroad failed to offer a specific instruction. In a civil case it is not enough for a party, especially a sophisticated litigant like the Norfolk and Western Railway, merely to point out a subtle omission in the instructions and leave it to the plaintiff and the district judge to figure out as best they can how to repair it. A failure to offer a correct instruction normally will excuse the trial judge's giving an incorrect alternative, and the same principle should apply to the failure to offer any instruction. Furthermore, the defendant put in no evidence that would have enabled the jury to make a sensible apportionment of damages between the defendant's conduct and the normal vicissitudes of life that would have confronted Lancaster, and might have precipitated his madness, even if his supervisors had behaved. The instruction that the defendant requested, even if given, would thus have left the jury up in the air. It is the defendant's own fault that the jury was allowed to bring in a verdict that, given Lancaster's preexisting vulnerability to psychosis, may seem high.

Affirmed.

Notes

1. *The eggshell skull rule and its flip side.* The eggshell skull rule means that the victim's pre–accident vulnerability, however extreme, affords the tortfeasor no excuse. Thus, if the victim has unusually fragile bones, the injuries may be far more extensive than would have been those of an average person, but the tortfeasor is nevertheless responsible for the full extent of the injuries she culpably brought about. See, e.g., McNabb v. Green Real Estate Co., 62 Mich.App. 500, 233 N.W.2d 811 (1975) (contemplating full recovery for the extensive consequences of a "brittle diabetic's" fall on defendant's defective stairway).

By the same token, the victim may have unusually strong bones, so that his or her injuries are less extensive than would have been those of an average person. Here, too, the tortfeasor's responsibility is measured by the actual consequences. This is the flip side of the eggshell skull rule. Both sides flow from the premise that our tort law is a system of corrective justice. The maxim repeatedly recited by Judge Posner—"the tortfeasor takes his victim as he finds him"[4]—succinctly captures that premise.

2. *The cause–in–fact rule applied in Follett and Lancaster.* The eggshell rule does not address cause in fact; it deals with the scope of a defendant's responsibility for consequences that concededly resulted from defendant's tortious conduct. But the rule that Judge Posner termed a "corollary" of the eggshell rule *is* a manifestation of the basic cause–in–fact requirement. In holding that the railroad's liability should have been limited to the value of the difference between the schizophrenia Tynan induced and the schizophrenia that Lancaster's preexisting mental illness would eventually have brought about regardless of Tynan's attack, the court was applying the basic rule that a tortfeasor should not be held accountable for consequences that would have befallen the victim regardless of the tortfeasor's wrongful conduct. This same rule was applied in *Follett*, supra p. 157, to protect the tortfeasor from liability for the death that the victim's preexisting cancer would have brought about regardless of the traffic accident.

3. *The problem presented by Dillon v. Twin States.* Dillon v. Twin States, supra p. 161, is arguably different from *Follett* and *Lancaster* in that Dillon (who did not jump, by the way; it was an accidental fall) was not suffering from a preexisting illness at the time of the tort. But the difference seems slight, because Dillon was at least as certain to die from the fall that was already in progress when the tort occurred as Follett was from the cancer (and probably more certain to die than Lancaster was to become schizophrenic).

But once the principle of the preexisting condition cases is extended to a case like *Dillon*—in which the problem is not a preexisting condition but a looming threat—the question arises, why shouldn't a defendant who kills a person in a car accident get a big discount if the decedent was on her way to catch an airplane that crashed on takeoff? Dobbs, The Law of Torts § 177, p. 433 (2000), suggests courts are adamantly resistant to such arguments because "it is both impractical and logically improper to devalue the plain-

---

4. For an alternative phrasing of the maxim, see Vaughn v. Nissan Motor Corp., 77 F.3d 736, 738 (4th Cir. 1996): "[The tortfeasor] must take its victim as it finds her."

tiff's life, limb, or property in the light of subsequent losses from extraneous forces that no one present at the time would have taken into account." King, Causation, Valuation, and Chance in Personal Injury Torts Involving Preexisting Conditions and Future Consequences, 90 Yale L.J. 1353, 1356–57 (1981), gets at the difference between *Dillon* and the plane–crash hypothetical as follows:

> [A] tortfeasor should be charged only with the value of the interest he destroyed. In determining what that value is, the preinjury condition of the victim should be taken into account. Valuation therefore requires that there be a workable definition of preexisting conditions—those conditions that should be considered in assessing the value of the interest destroyed. * * * Generally, a preexisting condition may be defined as a disease, condition, or force that has become sufficiently associated with the victim to be factored into the value of the interest destroyed, and that has become so before the defendant's conduct has reached a similar stage. A threatening force or condition should qualify when it has "attached' "—that is, its association with the value of the interest in question could not be avoided even if the victim were aware of its existence * * *.

See also Robertson, The Common Sense of Cause In Fact, 75 Tex.L.Rev. 1765, 1797–98 (1997).

4. *Note that Lancaster was an intentional tort case. Lancaster* is an important reminder that the cause–in–fact requirement is fully applicable in intentional tort cases.

5. *Assigning the burden of proof.* In noting that the railroad "put in no evidence that would have enabled the jury to make a sensible apportionment of damages," Judge Posner may suggest that the apportionment burden should be on the defendant in the present context, just as it is in the multiple–tortfeasor context. The next case indicates that the suggestion is somewhat controversial.

BLATZ v. ALLINA HEALTH SYSTEM

Court of Appeals of Minnesota, 2001.
622 N.W.2d 376.

LANSING, JUDGE.

Allina Health System, doing business as HealthSpan Transportation Services, contracts [with Scott County] to provide paramedic and ambulance services to Jordan, Minnesota, and surrounding communities.

* * *

In the summer of 1995, Mary Blatz lived at 18555 Halifax Lane in Jordan with her husband, Patrick Sherman, and their two children. On the morning of June 18, 1995, shortly after awakening, Blatz told Sherman she was having trouble breathing. * * * Sherman dialed 911.

The Scott County 911 tape indicates that Sherman's call was received at approximately 8:50 a.m. Sherman told the dispatcher that his wife was "having severe chest pains in a bad way right now." The dispatcher confirmed the family's address and telephone number, notified the Scott County Sheriff's Office, and notified the HealthSpan dispatcher. The HealthSpan dispatcher, in turn, notified HealthSpan paramedics, and the ambulance was en route at 8:53 a.m.

* * *

[Scott County Deputy Brian Wondra was not familiar with the immediate area but had no trouble finding the Blatz–Sherman residence. He arrived between 9:03 and 9:04 a.m. and began administering CPR to Blatz. The paramedics—who did have trouble finding the house—did not arrive until five or six minutes later. By then, Blatz had no heartbeat and was not breathing.] The paramedics inserted an oropharyngeal airway and gave Blatz 100% oxygen; they also established an IV line. One paramedic testified that within three minutes of their arrival, the monitor showed perfusion—that the heart was pumping and the blood was flowing. The other paramedic testified that Blatz's color improved within 30 to 60 seconds and her pulse returned within one to two minutes.

Blatz remained in a coma for approximately four weeks. No one has been able to determine what caused her initial cardiopulmonary arrest. But the arrest caused an anoxic brain injury that resulted in a severe loss of mental and physical capacity. Blatz is permanently disabled, is incapable of caring for herself, and lives in a nursing home. The medical evidence uniformly indicated that her condition will not improve. By January 2000, Blatz had incurred medical expenses of about $469,000.

Blatz's theory of [liability was that the paramedics were negligent] because "a reasonably prudent driver" would have [avoided the navigational mistakes made by the paramedics and therefore reached the Sherman residence significantly sooner. Blatz presented evidence that if the paramedics had not been delayed by their mistakes, they would have arrived at the Blatz–Sherman household approximately two to five minutes earlier. Blatz's theory of causation was based on the testimony of a physician who works as assistant director of a hospital's emergency department. He testified that the two–to–five minute] time period was within the window of opportunity in which Blatz could have been revived and irreversible brain damage could have been prevented.

Allina's defense theory rested on the testimony of two expert witnesses, a physician specializing in neurology and a physician specializing in pulmonary and respiratory disorders. Both expressed the opinion that the irreversible brain damage was complete before the deputy's arrival, and thus the paramedics' initial inability to locate the house had no effect on the brain injury Blatz suffered. * * *

The jury found that Allina was negligent in responding to the 911 call and that this negligence was a direct cause of Blatz's injuries. [It awarded $11 million in damages.] Allina brought post–trial motions for JNOV and a new trial. * * * The district court denied the motions, and Allina [has appealed, contending that the evidence does not support a finding of negligence or causation. Allina also challenges a jury instruction relating to damages.]

* * *

[We believe the evidence supports the jury's finding of negligence and causation and thus turn to Allina's challenge to the jury instruction.] Allina alleges that the district court's instruction on a pre–existing condition, based on CIVJIG 91.40, misstates the law. See 4A Minnesota Practice, CIVJIG 91.40 (1999). Allina argues that the last sentence [of the instruction] impermissibly shifts the burden of proving causal damages from the plaintiffs to the defendants. The instruction given at trial reads:

> Now, there is evidence that Mary Blatz had a pre–existing medical condition prior to the arrival of the Allina ambulance. Allina Health Systems is liable only for the damages that you find to be directly caused by the negligence, if any. *If you cannot separate damages caused by the pre–existing medical condition from those caused by Allina's negligence, if any, then Allina is to be held liable for all of the damages.*

4A Minnesota Practice, CIVJIG 91.40 (1999) (emphasis added). * * *

CIVJIG 91.40 is intended to take the place of CIVJIG 163 from the 1986 edition of the Jury Instruction Guides, which read:

> A person who has a defect or disability at the time of an accident is nevertheless entitled to damages for any aggravation of such pre–existing condition, even though the particular results would not have followed if the injured person had not been subject to such pre–existing condition. Damages are limited, however, to those results which are over and above those which normally followed from the pre–existing condition, had there been no accident.

[It is argued that CIVJIG 91.40's last sentence is consistent with the treatment of liability apportionment among at–fault defendants in] Mathews v. Mills, 288 Minn. 16, 22, 178 N.W.2d 841, 845 (1970). Analyzing liability for a passenger's injuries in a multiple–impact collision, the court held that "unless the damage caused by each [tortfeasor] is clearly separable, permitting the distinct assignment of responsibility to each, each is responsible for the entire damage." The burden of proving that the harm is capable of being divided lies with each defendant who contends it can be divided. If the court determines the harm is divisible, the actual apportionment is a fact question for the jury. The court, relying on principles of joint and several liability, reasoned that placing the burden of proof on the defendant "is a result of a choice made as to where a loss * * * shall fall—on an innocent plaintiff or on defendants who are clearly proved to have been at fault."

CIVJIG 91.40 extends beyond *Mathews* * * *. [I]t embraces the [appropriateness of] apportioning harm not just among at–fault defendants, but between a pre–existing condition and an at–fault defendant. [And] it places the burden of proof for the apportionment of aggravation on the at–fault defendant. Because the apportionment of aggravation of an injury is not between two at–fault defendants, as in *Mathews*, but rather between a pre–existing condition and an at–fault defendant, the principles underlying joint and several liability have thus been extended to circumstances in which they do not apply.

There is precedent in other states for placing the burden of proof on the at–fault defendant when apportioning damages between an at–fault defendant and an innocent or pre–existing cause. [The most frequently cited case in this line may be] Newbury v. Vogel, 151 Colo. 520, 379 P.2d 811, 813 (1963) (holding that defendant was responsible for the entire damage when court found it impossible to apportion between damages from accident and damages from pre–existing arthritic condition). * * * See generally Dan B. Dobbs, The Law of Torts § 174, at 425 (2000).

* * *

* * * With some rewording, [CIVJIG 91.40] may be a correct statement of the law in a case apportioning damage among two or more defendants whose combined conduct causes a plaintiff harm. But applying the instruction to aggravation of a pre–existing medical condition to apportion damage between that pre–existing condition and an at–fault defendant not only extends Minnesota law but also conflicts with existing caselaw. * * *

In this case, however, the instruction neither destroyed the substantial correctness of the charge nor created substantial prejudice on a vital issue. First, the district court crafted the instruction to state that Allina was liable only for damages directly caused by "its negligence, if any," rather than "any damages" caused by "the accident." The instruction is narrowed to the pre–existing medical condition and Allina's negligence, not incorporating any theoretical injuries "caused by the accident" that might not result from Allina's negligence or a pre–existing condition. Second, the effect of the instruction is limited by the facts of the case. Blatz's expert testified that Blatz sustained irreversible brain injury in the time period between arrival of the deputy at 9:03 to 9:04 a.m. and the paramedics' arrival at 9:08 to 9:09 a.m. Allina's causation experts both testified that Blatz sustained brain damage before the deputy arrived; thus, under Allina's theory of the case, an earlier arrival of the paramedics would not have made a difference because the irreversible injury was completed before 9:03–9:04 when the deputy arrived. The jury was thus presented two alternative theories of causation; those theories were separate, and the evidence did not overlap in a way that resulted in a shifting of the burden of proof. Furthermore, Allina did not argue for apportionment. The jury instruction, while not helpful to the jury, was not prejudicial. Allina is not entitled to a new trial because of the jury instruction on a pre–existing condition.

* * *

Affirmed.

Notes

1. *Restatements.* The Restatement (Third) of Torts: Liability for Physical Harm (Basic Principles) § 28, cmt. *d(2)* (Tent. Draft No. 2, March 2002) puts cases like *Blatz* in a category it labels "apportioning harm between tortious conduct and innocent causes or nonparty actors," describes a split in the jurisprudence on the placement of the burden of proving up a basis for apportionment in these cases (Reporters' Note), and "takes no position on who should bear the burden of proof." The Restatement (Third) of Torts: Apportionment of Liability § 26, cmt. *h* (2001) endorses placing the burden on the defendant. The Reporters' Note acknowledges that the burden-placement question here is more difficult than in the multiple-tortfeasors context.

2. *Why is burden–shifting more controversial here than in multiple-tortfeasor cases?* We have found no clear explanation of the widely shared view that placing the burden on the defendant in cases like *Follett, Lancaster*, and *Blatz* is less readily justified than in cases like *Piner*, supra p. 150. But it may be as simple as this: Our tort law is a system of corrective justice, which means that tortfeasors can routinely take advantage of their victims' extraneous bad luck—e.g., in being old, sick, poor, and/or unable to prove up a case. But allowing tortfeasors to benefit from one another's bad conduct just seems too powerfully unfair to countenance. (A similar intuition may be at the heart of Judge Peaslee's view—which is fairly widely shared—that the substantial factor test is appropriate for the case of the two tortious fires but not for the case of the innocent fire and the tortious fire. See p. 128, fn. 16 supra.)

3. *The apportionment burden should never be very heavy.* The Restatement (Third) of Torts: Liability for Physical Harm (Basic Principles) § 28, cmt. *d* persuasively state: "However the burden of proof is allocated ..., the preferred approach is to employ a modest threshold for the party with the burden of proof to satisfy the burden of production on the magnitude of harm." Cf. Robertson, The Common Sense of Cause in Fact, 75 Tex.L.Rev. 1765, 1794 (1997):

> In traditional judicial thinking, we must guard against holding a defendant responsible when he has caused no harm [to the plaintiff], but once we know that he has caused [the plaintiff] some harm, we need not worry overmuch about making him pay too much. As Judge Posner has written, "a tort plaintiff's burden of proving the extent of his injury is not a heavy one. Doubts are resolved against the tortfeasor." (DePass v. United States, 721 F.2d 203, 209 (7th Cir.1983) (Posner, J., dissenting).

4. *An alternative approach to apportionment.* The Reporters' Note to Restatement (Third) of Torts: Apportionment of Liability § 26 cmt. *h* (2001) discusses with apparent approval a "per capita" approach to damages apportionment, but the Restatement stops short of endorsing it. (The Reporters' Note says that some commentators like the approach but that the caselaw support is "sparse.") The approach is traceable to Loui v. Oakley, 50 Haw. 272, 438 P.2d 393 (1968), in which the defendant's negligent conduct injured the plaintiff in a traffic accident occurring on August 4, 1961. Before the case went to trial, plaintiff had three more wrecks (in February 1962, November 1962, and January 1965) that caused injuries to the same area of

the body hurt in the first accident. The trial judge instructed the jury that if they could not determine how much damage resulted from the first accident, they should hold the defendant for all the damages from all four accidents. Reversing, the appellate court stated that the jury should be told to try hard to apportion by causation. The jury should be further told that if it could not find a basis for apportionment by causation, it should allocate 1/4 of the damages to each of the four wrecks. See also Montalvo v. Lapez, 77 Haw. 282, 884 P.2d 345 (1994), in which the plaintiff suffered from a tangle of injuries stemming from four traffic accidents, two "assaults" (batteries), and four additional incidents in which the plaintiff injured himself. These events covered the period from 1964 through most of 1991. The defendant was a negligent motorist who contributed to the injuries in a 1988 traffic accident. The court said that if causal apportionment was not possible—"if the jury is unable to apportion, even roughly"—then it must divide the damages equally among the various causes." The opinion is unclear as to whether this would entitle the plaintiff to only 1/10 of his damages or perhaps to as much as 1/3 (on the view that the various causes should be grouped as pre–accident events, the accident in suit, and post–accident events).

Industry–Specific Bodies of Law

In *Bichler*, supra p. 135, and the notes following it, we saw an example of courts' developing a specialized causation rule for DES cases. There are some "special" causation rules for asbestos–exposure cases. Menne v. Celotex Corp., 861 F.2d 1453, 1455 (10th Cir. 1988).[5] Medical malpractice cases entail some industry–specific causation rules. See Chapter XIII, infra. Perhaps legal malpractice cases do too. (Coon v. Ginsberg, supra p. 122, was a legal malpractice case.) Many of the cases in which traffic accident victims seek recovery for enhanced injuries from safety deficiencies in the vehicles (so–called "crashworthiness" cases) arguably turn on specialized causation rules. (For a good run–down on the cause–in–fact jurisprudence in crashworthiness cases, see Stecher v. Ford Motor Co., 779 A.2d 491 (Pa.Super. 2001)). And there are probably other examples.

Whether special rules for (or against) particular types of defendants is desirable (or even constitutionally permissible) is probably outside this casebook's appropriate scope. But when reading cases and treatises—and when constructing legal briefs and arguments—students and practitioners have to maintain a steady alertness to the coverage of any proposition under scrutiny: Is it (and should it be) part of the general law of factual causation, or is it an industry–specific mutation?

---

5. Cf. Pustejovsky v. Rapid–American Corp., 35 S.W.3d 643 (Tex. 2000) (relaxing the "single–injury rule"—the rule that generally requires a plaintiff to combine all of the claims arising from an injurious event in a single lawsuit—for asbestos–exposure plaintiffs only). For a useful discussion of why asbestos litigation is widely regarded as *sui generis*, see In Re Owens Corning, 305 B.R. 175, 217–219. (D.Del. 2004). The court begins its discussion by noting that "the sheer size of the asbestos litigation makes it unlike any other mass tort," and end it by stating that "statistically, fifteen asbestos claimants die every day."

Chapter V

THE "LEGAL CAUSE" ISSUE

A. THE STRUCTURAL VOCABULARY OF NEGLIGENCE LAW

As we have repeatedly said, the plaintiff's prima facie case in negligence law comprises five issues or elements: duty, breach, cause in fact, legal cause, and damages. In traditional thinking, the duty element is regarded as an issue of law for the trial judge to decide. The other four elements are loosely classified as issues of "fact," for the jury to decide unless reasonable minds could not differ.

"Legal cause" is a preferable (but not widely enough accepted) name for the fourth element. The main competitor is "proximate cause." As we saw in Chapter IV, "proximate cause" has also been used with some frequency as a synonym for cause in fact. "Proximate cause" is an old term with a murky history and a large amount of cumbersome baggage. In the notes and questions in this book we try to avoid the term "proximate cause" in favor of the vocabulary set forth above. We hope the term will eventually disappear.[1] Meanwhile, when you encounter the term "proximate cause" in reading a case, you must always examine the context to see whether the court is using it to mean cause in fact, legal cause, or both.

The key to mastery of negligence law is understanding the function of each of the five elements and the boundaries separating them from one another. This is a challenging assignment, because courts differ—among themselves and over time—in their usages. The best approach is to read a few thousand cases, distill from them a basic structural model, and then use that model as an analytical grid for understanding and evaluating particular decisions. In evaluating the conceptual structure reflected in any particular decision, a dominant focus should be the allocation of authority among the jury, the trial judge, and the appellate

---

1. The Restatement (Second) of Torts worked hard to inculcate the "legal cause" usage, but the authors of the proposed Restatement (Third) (Third) of Torts: Liability for Physical Harm (Basic Principles)—while deploring the term "proximate cause"—believe that "legal cause" is no better. We continue to think "legal cause" is better or at least not as bad.

court. Because of the tradition that treats duty issues as "law" and the others as "fact," deciding how to classify a particular disputed matter—deciding whether it is a duty issue, a breach issue, or a causation issue—is potentially determinative of whether the trial judge or the jury is the proper decision maker. The classification also determines the scope and nature of appellate review.

The essential features of the basic structural model reflected in this book are as follows.[2] Analysis of the *duty* issue begins by accepting the following generalization from Heaven v. Pender, [1883] 11 Q.B.D. 503, 509:

> [W]henever one person is by circumstances placed in such a position with regard to another that every one of ordinary sense who did think would at once recognise that if he did not use ordinary care and skill in his own [affirmative] conduct with regard to those circumstances he would cause danger of [physical] injury to the person or property of the other, a duty arises to use ordinary care and skill to avoid such danger.

(As we will see in Chapter VI, the new Restatement (Third) of Torts: Liability for Physical Harm (General Principles) generally reflects this perspective.) From this perspective, a defendant whose activities have brought about physical injury to another normally owes a duty of reasonable care unless some rule of law provides otherwise. (Chapter VI treats some of these "no–duty" rules.) In our view, it is potentially misleading to say "defendant had no duty" unless the situation is controlled by a rule of law of enough breadth and clarity to permit the trial judge in most cases raising the problem to dismiss the complaint or award summary judgment for the defendant on the basis of the rule. If the case is of a sort that typically the judge will need to know the details of the occurrence before ruling for the defendant—i.e., if the case is of a type that must normally reach the directed verdict (or later) stage before defendant can expect to prevail—then the appropriate formulation is in terms of plaintiff's failure to establish breach or legal cause rather than "no duty."

As we learned in Chapter III, the *breach* issue addresses whether the defendant violated the duty of reasonable care that has been established or is provisionally assumed to be owed. To determine whether the defendant violated the duty of reasonable care, we ask whether (from the perspective of a person of ordinary prudence in the defendant's situation) the seriousness of expectable injury multiplied by the probability of such injury's occurrence outweighed the burden of taking precautions against it.

---

2. These matters are treated at much greater length in Powers, Judge and Jury in the Texas Supreme Court, 75 Tex.L.Rev. 1699 (1997); Robertson, The Vocabulary of Negligence Law: Continuing Causation Confusion, 58 La.L.Rev. 1 (1997); and Robertson, Allocating Authority Among Institutional Decision Makers in Louisiana State–Court Negligence and Strict Liability Cases, 57 La.L.Rev. 1079 (1997).

Chapter IV taught that the *cause in fact* element addresses the causal connection between the defendant's wrongful conduct and the plaintiff's injury. The most widely used test for assessing that connection is the but–for inquiry. This test asks whether the injury in suit would have occurred if the defendant had avoided the wrongful conduct at issue in the lawsuit.

The *legal cause* element is the ordinary negligence law's analog to the threshold criteria for imposing liability (under the rubric of "negligence per se") on the basis of defendant's violation of a penal statute. (See Gorris v. Scott, supra p. 104; Potts v. Fidelity Fruit, supra p. 106.) The ultimate question addressed by both the negligence per se criteria and the legal cause issue is this: Was the rule of law violated by the defendant designed to protect people like the plaintiff against harm of the sort the plaintiff suffered? In an ordinary negligence case, it is a bit less easy than in a negligence per se case to identify the rule of law violated by the defendant. But the difficulty is manageable. In an ordinary negligence case, the plaintiff establishes that the defendant violated the law by satisfying the breach element, i.e., by proving that the defendant engaged in conduct that was less than reasonable care under the circumstances. In order to establish that the defendant's conduct fell below reasonable care, the plaintiff must show that the defendant's conduct created or exacerbated one or more foreseeable risks of harm to others. That array of risks—the array of foreseeable risks of harm that the defendant should have guarded against—identifies and defines the rule of law the defendant violated. The legal cause issue then becomes: was the injury that befell the plaintiff among the array of foreseeable risks the existence of which called upon the defendant to alter his or her conduct?

Restatement (Third) of Torts: Liability for Physical Harm (Basic Principles) (Tent. Draft. No. 3, April 2003) puts the foregoing basic test for legal cause as follows:

§ 29. An actor is not liable for harm different from the harms whose risks made the actor's conduct tortious.

§ 30. An actor is not liable for harm when the tortious aspect of the actor's conduct did not increase the risk of [that] harm.

In comments *b* and *d* to § 29,the Restatement explains that jury instructions on legal (proximate) cause should convey the idea that "the harm that occurred must be one that results from the hazards that made the defendant's conduct tortious in the first place," and thus that "the jury should be told in deciding whether plaintiff's harm is within the scope of liability, it should go back to the reasons for finding the defendant engaged in negligence or other tortious conduct."[3]

---

3. Current practice does not give the jury this information. Typically, the jury is told only that "a proximate cause of an injury is that which in a natural and continuous sequence produces the injury and without which the injury would not have occurred." Torres v. El Paso Electric Co., 127 N.M. 729, 987 P.2d 386, 393 (1999).

The *damages* element—treated infra in Chapter VIII—reflects the negligence law's requirement that the plaintiff be able to show actual loss or damage. Nominal damages, to vindicate a technical right, cannot be recovered in a negligence action.

B. LEGAL CAUSE: BASIC CONCEPTS

Dobbs, The Law of Torts § 193, p. 484 (2000) wryly notes that "a good deal of [the] terminology in proximate cause cases is . . . superfluous." Having fun with this idea, Leon Green once spun out a list of what he deemed utterly useless "ruffles and decorations" that have been attached in front of the word *cause*, including "remote, proximate, direct, immediate, adequate, efficient, operative, inducing ,moving, active, real, effective, decisive, supervening, primary, original, contributory, ultimate, concurrent, causa causans, legal, responsible, dominating, natural, probable, and others."[1] Courts often make the same point:

> No legal question has been more discussed in the cases than this one of legal cause, or, as it has commonly been termed, proximate cause. Very many attempts have been made to frame a definition or state a test which will determine whether there is or is not liability in all cases. None of these attempts have been successful.[2]

Despite the difficulty of penetrating the jungle of legal cause vocabulary, we believe that one who reads a significant number of cases with a close eye on what courts actually do—in a sense relegating to secondary importance what they say[3]—will see them most often using an approach that *allows the trier of fact to find legal cause whenever the plaintiff's injury was among the array of risks the creation or exacerbation of which led to the conclusion that the defendant's conduct was negligent.* The new Restatement states that this approach "has proved increasingly attractive to courts, and [that] a trend toward its ascendancy as the predominant standard employed to limit liability, with necessary adjustments at the margins, continues. . . ."[4] In studying each case below, one useful focus will be whether the court's (a) result and (b) language are consistent with the suggested approach.

THE GLENDOLA

Circuit Court of Appeals, Second Circuit, 1931.
47 F.2d 206.

L. Hand, Circuit Judge.

The [plaintiff's] steamer, Tilford, on the twenty–third day of April, 1925, was bound up the Cape Fear river for her pier in the city of

1. Leon Green, Rationale of Proximate Cause 135–36 (1927).

2. Derosier v. New England Tel. & Tel. Co., 81 N.H. 451, 130 A. 145, 152 (1925).

3. As Judge Friendly put it, "what courts do in [legal cause] cases makes bet-ter sense than what they, or others, say." In re Kinsman Transit Co., 338 F.2d 708, 725–26 (2d Cir. 1964).

4. Restatement (Third) of Torts: Liability for Physical Harm (Basic Principles) § 29, cmt. *e* (Tent. Draft No. 3, April 2003).

Wilmington, North Carolina. When about two miles below the city she came into collision with the [defendant's] ship, Glendola, bound out, in which she was injured on her port bow, her plates being so bent that the seams opened, and her cargo of gasoline began to spurt from her side into the water. The circumstances were such as to persuade us that the Glendola was alone at fault, and we [uphold the trial judge's determination that she is liable to the Tilford's owners. We must now determine whether the trial judge was correct in imposing liability for both the results of the collision itself and also for the subsequent harms that befell the Tilford.]

After [the collision] the Tilford kept on to her berth, leaking gasoline as she went, and a serious menace to herself, to nearby steamers, and to the wharves and the buildings upon them, after she reached her berth. Her ordinary way of berthing on the flood, which was [then] making, was to drop her anchor after a tug had come alongside her port bow. * * *

On the day in question it was not safe to order the tug, which was in attendance upon the steamer, upon her port bow, where the gasoline was leaking, for a spark on the surface of the water might have started a disastrous fire. Instead, a line was heaved from the starboard bow of the steamer to the bow of the tug, on which she backed with all her power, thus relieving the strain on the port anchor, which had been let go at the proper time. The two did not, however, serve to hold her, and she drifted upstream, though canting somewhat to starboard, until she [went aground] astern in shallow water, thus suffering additional damages. Being thus fast astern, her bow, floating upstream, collided with the end of the pier, still further damaging her * * *.

* * *

The * * * question is whether the Glendola is liable not only for the injuries caused by the collision down the river, but also for the [grounding] and the collision with the wharf. Her faulty navigation having caused the first collision, she was a wrongdoer, and nothing is more unsatisfactory than the discussion in the books and by legal writers as to the limits of liability in such cases. It is commonly agreed that the * * * care [required] towards others depends upon the likelihood that its omission may cause injury. The extent of the [care required] is not measured actuarially, that is, only in terms of [an injury's] probability; it varies with the gravity of the injury which may result. One may be liable for mutilating or killing another, though the risk one takes is less probable of realization than greater risks, from the consequences of which one would be immune, if the results must be trivial. The law does not establish a zone of consequences, fixed merely by their probability, and impose liability upon any one whose acts bring to pass anything within it. Along with other considerations, it balances the interests at stake, and restricts the foresight required, as the damage to be apprehended diminishes. Thus the excuse for the act is itself a factor in determining the consequences with which the actor is chargeable.

However, there is much uncertainty in the books as to whether liability should be extended to remote consequences once the actor is shown to have been at fault. On the one hand are the greater number of decisions, of which In re Polemis, (1921) L.R. 3 K.B. 560, is an extreme instance, in which, because the omission was in any case likely to cause some damage, liability is extended to injuries for which the defendant would not have been responsible if they alone were to be apprehended. The wrong, once established, involves the wrongdoer in all its consequences. On the other hand are those decisions which treat remote consequences as though the wrong consisted in causing these alone, and which hold the actor only for such as he should have foretold. * * * The broader liability seem to rest upon punitive notions, extending responsibility because the actor is at fault, not in respect of what actually happens, but of something nearer. Perhaps this better satisfies the demands of history, but we must confess ourselves in doubt as to its consistency with usual notions.

In the case at bar, however, that question does not really arise, because it appears to us that, judged by either rule, the Glendola is liable for the strand and second collision. Even if we accept the narrower doctrine, and find it necessary that the later injuries must be reasonably apprehended at the outset, they were such. The Tilford was a tanker, and her cargo was visibly either oil or gasoline. To break her sides was to cripple her more seriously than other ships. If her cargo leaked, as well it might, she became a menace to herself and all about her, and her navigation, disabled as she was, would be embarrassed whenever it required the approach of other steamers. She was bound to a pier and must soon dock; docking, especially in such a narrow berth, requires tugs and tugs carry fire. It did not require powers of divination to foresee that she would thus have trouble in docking, and while we agree that nobody could foretell exactly how this might arise, that was not necessary, if it was likely that it might include a strand in such narrow waters, under which she might swing with the tide against one shore or the other. These are what injured her, and these might fairly be predicted.

* * *

Notes

1. *The Glendola* was an admiralty case in which the trial judge, sitting without a jury, was the trier of fact. At the time, appellate review of factual determinations in such cases was much more aggressive than is true today. Little if any deference was afforded the trial judge's fact findings.

2. Judge Hand's paragraph treating the "probability" and "gravity" of threatened injury should be compared with his later formulation in *Carroll Towing,* supra p. 81.

3. *Polemis and the directness test for legal cause. In re Polemis* was an action for extensive fire damage to a ship that resulted when a heavy plank that defendant's employees dropped into the hold of plaintiff's ship caused an unusual spark and an unexpected fire. Defendant's employees' conduct

was negligent because of the risk of impact damage to the ship, but no one could have foreseen the fire. The English Court of Appeal held that foreseeability of the fire was irrelevant to the question presented, stating:

> The presence or absence of reasonable anticipation of damage determines the legal quality of the act as negligent or innocent. If it be thus determined to be negligent, then the question whether particular damages are recoverable depends only on the answer to the question whether they are the direct consequences of the act.

Polemis was not interpreted quite as broadly as the opinion in *The Glendola* suggests; its "direct consequences" language was taken as a limit. Nevertheless, *Polemis* laid down a broad rule for scope of liability,[5] and it was effectively overruled in the following case.

OVERSEAS TANKSHIP LTD. v. MORTS DOCK & ENGINEERING CO. LTD. (WAGON MOUND I)

Privy Council 1961.
[1961] A.C. 388, [1961] 2 W.L.R. 126, [1961] 1 All E.R. 404.

VISCOUNT SIMONDS.

[Plaintiffs were Sydney shipbuilders who owned and operated Sheerlegs Wharf. While plaintiffs were engaged in welding operations there, defendant's negligence caused a large quantity of furnace oil to escape from defendant's ship Wagon Mound, moored 600 feet from Sheerlegs Wharf. The oil spilled into the bay and spread beneath the wharf. Plaintiffs stopped welding for a time, but resumed after investigating and forming the belief that furnace oil would not ignite on the surface of the water. Welding operations continued for the rest of that day and until 2 p.m. the following day (November 1, 1951), when a fire started in the oil beneath plaintiff's wharf. The wharf was destroyed.

[In a bench trial, the trial judge found that the fire occurred because sparks from the welding operations set fire to cotton waste or rags floating in the water; this in turn ignited the furnace oil. The trial judge also specifically found that the defendants "did not know and could not reasonably be expected to know that [the oil] was capable of being set afire when spread on water." Nevertheless, the trial judge held that plaintiffs were entitled to recover, reasoning that the release of the furnace oil was negligence because of the pollution damage it could be expected to cause, and that the rule of the *Polemis* case [supra p. 174] mandated recovery on concluding that the fire was a direct consequence of the release of the oil.

5. While the directness approach generally permits a wider scope of liability than the foreseeability approach, the criterion of "directness" is vague enough to be pointed in the other direction from time to time. A court operating under the directness approach that wishes to limit liability can almost always do so by finding that some "intervening," "supervening," or "superseding" force has "broken the chain of causation."

[Defendants appealed to the Supreme Court of New South Wales, which affirmed the trial judge's judgment in favor of plaintiff. Defendants then appealed to the Privy Council in England.]

[The trial judge] made the all important finding, which must be set out in his own words: "The *raison d'etre* of furnace oil is, of course, that it shall burn, but I find the defendant did not know and could not reasonably be expected to have known that it was capable of being set afire when spread on water." This finding was reached after a wealth of evidence which included that of a distinguished scientist, Professor Hunter. * * *

One other finding must be mentioned. The learned judge held that apart from damage by fire the [plaintiffs] had suffered some damage from the spillage of oil in that it had got upon their slipways and congealed upon them and interfered with their use of the slips. He said: "The evidence of this damage is slight and no claim for compensation is made in respect of it. Nevertheless it does establish some damage which may be insignificant in comparison with the magnitude of the damage by fire, but which nevertheless is damage which beyond question was a direct result of the escape of the oil." It is upon this footing that their Lordships will consider the question whether the [defendants] are liable for the fire damage. * * *

It is inevitable that first consideration should be given to the [*Polemis* case]. For it was avowedly in deference to that decision and to decisions of the Court of Appeal that followed it that the [court below] was constrained to decide the present case in favor of the [plaintiffs]. * * *

* * *

[T]he decision of the Court of Appeal in *Polemis* plainly asserts that, if the defendant is guilty of negligence, he is responsible for all the consequences whether reasonably foreseeable or not. The generality of the proposition is perhaps qualified by the fact that each of the Lords Justices refers to the outbreak of fire as the direct result of the negligent act. There is thus introduced the conception that the negligent actor is not responsible for consequences which are not "direct," whatever that may mean. * * *

* * *

If the line of relevant authority had stopped with *Polemis,* [we] might, whatever [our] own views as to its unreason, have felt some hesitation about overruling it. But it is far otherwise. * * *

* * *

[T]he authority of *Polemis* has been severely shaken though lip–service has from time to time been paid to it. In [our] opinion it should no longer be regarded as good law. It is not probable that many cases will for that reason have a different result, though it is hoped that the law will be thereby simplified, and that in some cases at least palpable injustice will be avoided. For it does not seem consonant with current ideas of justice or morality that for an act of negligence, however slight or venial, which results in some trivial foreseeable damage the actor should be liable for all consequences however unforeseeable and however grave, so long as they can be said to be "direct". It is a principle of civil liability, subject only to qualifications which have no present relevance, that a man must be considered to be responsible for the probable consequences of his act. To demand more of him is too harsh a rule, to demand less is to ignore that civilised order requires the observance of a minimum standard of behaviour.

* * * [I]f some limitation must be imposed upon the consequences for which the negligent actor is to be held responsible—and all are agreed that some limitation there must be—why should that test (reasonable foreseeability) be rejected which, since he is judged by what the reasonable man ought to foresee, corresponds with the common conscience of mankind, and a test (the "direct" consequence) be substituted which leads to nowhere but the never ending and insoluble problems of causation. * * *

* * *

In the same connexion may be mentioned the conclusion to which the [court below] finally came in the present case. Applying the rule in *Polemis* and holding, therefore, that the unforeseeability of the damage by fire afforded no defence, [the court below] went on to consider the remaining question. Was it a "direct" consequence? Upon this Manning, J., said: "Notwithstanding that, if regard is had separately to each individual occurrence in the chain of events that led to this fire, each occurrence was improbable and, in one sense, improbability was heaped upon improbability, I cannot escape from the conclusion that if the ordinary man in the street had been asked, as a matter of common sense, without any detailed analysis of the circumstances, to state the cause of the fire at Mort's Dock, he would unhesitatingly have assigned such cause to spillage of oil by the appellants' employees." Perhaps he would, and probably he would have added: "I never should have thought it possible." But with great respect to the [court below] this is surely irrelevant, or, if it is relevant, only serves to show that the *Polemis* rule works in a very strange way. After the event even a fool is wise. But it is not the hindsight of a fool; it is the foresight of the reasonable man which alone can determine responsibility. The *Polemis* rule by substituting "direct" for "reasonably foreseeable" consequence leads to a conclusion equally illogical and unjust.

* * *

* * * Suppose an action brought by *A* for damage caused by the carelessness (a neutral word) of *B,* for example a fire caused by the careless spillage of oil. It may, of course, become relevant to know what duty *B* owed to *A,* but the only liability that is in question is the liability for damage by fire. It is vain to isolate the liability from its context and to say that *B* is or is not liable and then to ask for what damage he is liable. For his liability is in respect of that damage and no other. If, as admittedly it is, *B*'s liability (culpability) depends on the reasonable foreseeability of the consequent damage, how is that to be determined except by the foreseeability of the damage which in fact happened—the damage in suit? And, if that damage is unforeseeable so as to displace liability at large, how can the liability be restored so as to make compensation payable?

But, it is said, a different position arises if *B*'s careless act has been shown to be negligent and has caused some foreseeable damage to *A*. [We] have already observed that to hold *B* liable for consequences however unforeseeable of a careless act, if, but only if, he is at the same time liable for some other damage however trivial, appears to be neither logical nor just. This becomes more clear if it is supposed that similar unforeseeable damage is suffered by *A* and *C* but other foreseeable damage, for which *B* is liable, by *A* only. A system of law which would hold *B* liable to *A* but not to *C* for the similar damage suffered by each of them could not easily be defended. Fortunately the attempt is not necessary. For the same fallacy is at the root of the proposition. It is irrelevant to the question whether *B* is liable for unforeseeable damage that he is liable for foreseeable damage, as irrelevant as would the fact that he had trespassed on Whiteacre be to the question whether he had trespassed on Blackacre. * * *

* * *

[We] will humbly advise Her Majesty that this appeal should be allowed and the respondents' action so far as it related to damage caused by the negligence of the appellants be dismissed with costs * * *.

Notes

1. *Wagon Mound II.* The tight logic of the *Wagon Mound I* opinion got peculiar treatment in a second case arising out of the same fire, Overseas Tankship (U.K.) Ltd. v. Miller Steamship Co. (*Wagon Mound II*), [1967] 1 A.C. 617, [1967] 2 All E.R. 709 (P.C.). The fire that destroyed Sheerlegs Wharf had also damaged two ships, whose owners brought consolidated negligence actions against the Wagon Mound owners. When that case came to trial, *Wagon Mound I* had already been decided by the Privy Council. The trial judge again found that the ignition of the furnace oil was unforeseeable, and on that basis (following the rule of *Wagon Mound I*), denied recovery in the negligence actions. This time around the Privy Council held there *should* be negligence liability, reasoning that the fire was not so unforeseeable as all that. The Privy Council explained that the *Wagon Mound I* plaintiffs had been inhibited from proving the foreseeability of the fire because such a finding would have convicted them of contributory negligence (then a bar to recovery in New South Wales) for continuing the welding, whereas "[this] difficulty * * * does not affect the present plaintiffs."

2. *Judge Friendly's view.* In Petition of Kinsman Transit Co., 338 F.2d 708 (2d Cir.1964), the defendants relied heavily on *Wagon Mound I*. A dissenting judge was convinced by the argument, but not Judge Friendly.

Kinsman was a Cleveland, Ohio, company that owned five ships. During the winter of 1958–59, four of its ships were tied up in the Buffalo River for the winter awaiting the thaw of Lake Erie and the resumption of navigation on the lake. Because it was not securely enough fastened to its winter mooring in the river, one of Kinsman's ships broke away under the pressure of an especially heavy current in the river, drifted downstream, struck other moored ships and broke them loose, and ended up causing the collapse of the City of Buffalo's drawbridge. The ships and the collapsed bridge combined to dam up the river, causing extensive flooding and property damage for many miles upstream. The dissenting judge characterized the accident as "an extraordinary concatenation of ... extraordinary events, not unlike the humorous and almost–beyond–all–imagination sequences depicted by the famous cartoonist Rube Goldberg." Unpersuaded, the majority held that Kinsman should be liable for the damages shown. Judge Friendly's opinion for the court evaluated *Wagon Mound I* as follows:

> We have no difficulty with the result of *The Wagon Mound,* in view of the finding that the appellant had no reason to believe that the floating furnace oil would burn * * * On that view the decision simply applies the principle which excludes liability where the injury sprang from a hazard different from that which was improperly risked. [But] some language in the [*Wagon Mound I* opinion] goes beyond this * * * (Id. at 723.)

The *Wagon Mound I* language that Judge Friendly disagreed with was probably the paragraph of *Wagon Mound* that begins, "Suppose an action brought by A for damage...." (supra p. 177). That paragraph seems to call for collapsing the breach and legal cause issues into a single inquiry, whereby the B<PL inquiry would address solely the particular injury that befell the plaintiff rather than the general array of foreseeable risks made to appear by the evidence. Judge Friendly flatly rejected the *Wagon Mound* court's suggestion that such a limitation on negligence liability is morally compelled:

> We see no reason why an actor engaging in conduct which entails a large risk of small damage and a small risk of other and greater damage, of the same general sort, from the same forces, and to the same class of persons, should be relieved of responsibility for the latter simply because the chance of its occurrence, if viewed alone, may not have been large enough to require the exercise of care. By hypothesis, the risk of the lesser harm was sufficient to render his disregard of it actionable; the existence of a less likely additional risk that the very forces against whose action he was required to guard would produce other and greater damage than could have been reasonably anticipated should inculpate him further rather than limit his liability. (338 F.2d at 725.)

See also Fazzolari v. Portland School Dist., 303 Or. 1, 734 P.2d 1326, 1331 n.9 (1987) (agreeing with Judge Friendly in rejecting the *Wagon Mound I* moral calculus because "aggregate risks may make conduct negligent [and thus blameworthy] even though the specific risk to the particular plaintiff might in isolation be neither sufficiently unreasonable nor foreseeable [by itself to call for precautions]").

3. *The eggshell skull rule. Wagon Mound I* turned out to work a smaller change in the law than it seemed to proclaim. See, e.g., Smith v.

Leech Brain & Co. Ltd., [1962] 2. Q.B. 405 (Q.B.), in which a worker suffered a burned lower lip while handling molten metal in defendant's factory. The defendant was negligent for not having an adequate shield between the worker and the metal. The burn developed into a cancerous condition from which the worker died. Answering the defendant's argument that *Wagon Mound I* defeated liability because the cancer and death were highly unforeseeable consequences, the court said: " * * * I am quite satisfied that the [Privy Council] in the *Wagon Mound* case did not have what I may call, loosely, the thin skull cases in mind. It has always been the law of this country that a tortfeasor takes his victim as he finds him. * * * The [Privy Council] were [holding] that a man is no longer liable for the *type* of damage which he could not reasonably anticipate. [They] were not * * * saying that a man is only liable for the *extent* of damage which he could anticipate * * *." (Emphasis supplied.)

We encountered the foregoing idea—that defendant will be liable if some injury of the general type plaintiff sustained was a foreseeable consequence of defendant's negligent conduct, although the extent of the injuries may be quite unexpected—in Chapter IV (the *Lancaster* case, supra p. 158). The concept has various names, including the "eggshell skull rule" and "the extent rule." It has wide currency. See, e.g., Hammerstein v. Jean Development West, 111 Nev. 1471, 907 P.2d 975 (1995), which imposed liability on a hotel whose fire alarm kept going off needlessly. The twelfth or so false alarm in a three–month period caused a 70–year–old diabetic guest to hurry down the stairs; he twisted his ankle, which eventually led to a very serious gangrenous infection. The court said the plaintiff did not have to establish the foreseeability of either "the extent of [his] harm or the manner in which the harm occurred."

4. *The mechanism rule.* The preceding quotation from *Hammerstein* combines the extent rule with a concept sometimes called "the mechanism rule," which was put by Justice Holmes in Munsey v. Webb, 231 U.S. 150, 156, 34 S.Ct. 44, 58 L.Ed. 162 (1913) (a seemingly clear case for imposing liability on a building owner whose dangerous elevator killed a passenger) as follows: "It was not necessary that the defendant should have had notice of the particular method in which an accident would occur, if the possibility of an accident was clear to the ordinarily prudent eye." What Justice Holmes meant was this: If the plaintiff and the general type of harm sustained by the plaintiff were foreseeable, recovery is usually permitted, even though the particular way in which the harm came about—the *manner of occurrence* of the harm—may be quite bizarre. E.g., in Hughes v. Lord Advocate, [1963] A.C. 837, [1963] 1 All E.R. 705 (H.L.), defendants' workmen went to tea and left a manhole in an Edinburgh street surrounded by paraffin lamps and unattended. An 8–year–old boy entered the tent around the manhole and knocked or lowered one of the lamps into the hole. There was an explosion, and the boy was badly hurt. The lower courts held for defendants, reasoning that while it was foreseeable that a child might enter the unattended tent and suffer burns from the lamps, the explosion and consequent injuries were not foreseeable. Reversing, the House of Lords held that the *Wagon Mound I* principle exonerates a defendant only "if the damage [that occurred] can be regarded as *differing in kind* from what was foreseeable. * * * [The] mere

fact that the *way in which the accident happened* could not be anticipated is [not] enough to exclude liability * * *." (Lord Reid) (emphasis added.)

The mechanism (or manner–of–occurrence) rule is widely recited, and it makes sense. But it is a relatively weak analytical tool, because whenever a court perceives that the mechanism is just too weird, it is free to characterize the situation as one involving a different type of harm than was put at risk by the defendant's negligent conduct. See, e.g., Doughty v. Turner, [1964] 1 Q.B. 518 (Court of Appeal 1963), an action by a worker who was burned when the defendant negligently knocked the heavy cover of a large vat of molten liquid (800 degrees centigrade) into the vat, bringing about a chemical eruption that flung the liquid onto the worker. The court held that the worker could not recover, because, while knocking the cover into the vat had caused a foreseeable risk of causing injuries through simple splashing, the chemical eruption—a violent one—was not foreseeable.

5. *Some rules of thumb.* The courts have developed some consensus on the proper treatment of "foreseeability" problems of certain recurrent types.

(a) *Subsequent medical injuries:* A defendant who is liable for negligently causing a personal injury will generally be held liable for subsequent injuries done by rescue and medical personnel in responding to and treating the injury. Unless there is something fairly extraordinary about the subsequent injury, it is *deemed* foreseeable. This is true although the medical personnel may be negligent and liable in their own right. The Restatement (Third) of Torts: Liability for Physical Harm (Basic Principles) (Tent. Draft No.3, April 2003), puts the rule as follows:

> § 35.   Enhanced Harm Due to Efforts to Render Medical or Other Aid.
>
> An actor whose tortious conduct is a factual cause of physical harm to another is subject to liability for any enhanced harm suffered due to the efforts of third persons to render aid reasonably required by the other person's injury, so long as the enhanced harm arises from a risk that inheres in the effort to render aid.

The rule has a fairly broad sweep. See, e.g., Younger v. Marshall Industries, Inc., 618 So.2d 866 (La. 1993) (holding the original injurer liable when a defective seat in a hospital shower bath collapsed, causing further injury to the victim); Smith v. Hardy, 144 Ga.App. 168, 240 S.E.2d 714 (1977) (contemplating liability of a negligent motorist when the traffic accident caused plaintiff's pre–existing ulcer to flare up 27 days later, necessitating a blood transfusion—negligently administered—that caused the victim to lose her eyesight); Pridham v. Cash & Carry Bldg. Ctr., 116 N.H. 292, 359 A.2d 193 (1976) (holding original injurer liable for victim's death in ambulance wreck).

Courts have not been as ready to hold the original wrongdoer for the subsequent negligence of mechanics and repairers. In Exner Sand & Gravel Corp. v. Petterson Lighterage & Towing Corp., 258 F.2d 1 (2d Cir.1958), the defendant negligently caused $500 worth of bow damage to the plaintiff's barge. While that was being fixed, the repairer negligently caused $11,000 worth of bottom damage. Denying recovery against the original negligent party for the bottom damage, the court distinguished the "subsequent medical negligence" cases by saying that "the risks which in view of 'human fallibility' are 'normally recognized as inherent in the necessity of submitting to medical, surgical or hospital treatment' [are not] 'normally recognized as inherent' in the services of the repairman." (Another justification for this distinction might be that it is much easier to successfully sue a negligent repairer than a negligent physician. See infra Chapter XIII.)

(b) *Rescuers:* Within broad limits, they are deemed foreseeable. The most famous rescuer case is Wagner v. International Ry. Co., 232 N.Y. 176, 133 N.E. 437 (1921), in which negligence in the operation of defendant's train caused plaintiff's cousin to be thrown out. Plaintiff walked along the trestle to look for his cousin's body and fell off. Judge Cardozo's opinion reversed the trial judge for having told the jury to find for defendant unless they concluded that there was separate negligent conduct directed toward the plaintiff himself, stating:

> Danger invites rescue. The cry of distress is the summons to relief. The law does not ignore these reactions of the mind in tracing conduct to its consequences. It recognizes them as normal. It places their effects within the range of the natural and probable. The wrong that imperils life is a wrong to the imperiled victim; it is a wrong also to his rescuer. * * * The risk of rescue, if only it be not wanton, is born of the occasion. The emergency begets the man. The wrongdoer may not have foreseen the coming of a deliverer. He is accountable as if he had.

This is another rule that sweeps pretty broadly. It applies in actions against tortfeasors who put innocent victims at risk as well as against those who negligently or intentionally put themselves at risk. See, e.g., Thomas v. Garner, 284 Ill.App.3d 90, 219 Ill.Dec. 737, 672 N.E.2d 52 (1996) (9–year–old girl, trying to cross the street to fetch her little brother from where defendant school bus driver had let him off on the wrong side of the street from the house, treated as rescuer); Thompson v. Summers, 567 N.W.2d 387 (S.D. 1997) (hot air balloon pilot was subject to liability under the rescue doctrine when he brought the balloon too close to a high–voltage power line, causing a bystander who was trying to help to sustain serious electrical burns); Talbert v. Talbert, 22 Misc.2d 782, 199 N.Y.S.2d 212 (Sup.Ct. 1960) (man trying to commit suicide in his garage held liable to his son for the injuries the son sustained in breaking into the garage).

In many states, a doctrine often called the "fireman's rule" prevents firefighters, police officers, and similar professional risk takers from invoking the rescue doctrine. See, e.g., Maltman v. Sauer, 84 Wash.2d 975, 530 P.2d 254 (1975) (denying the benefits of the rescue doctrine to the crew of an army helicopter that crashed while en route to the scene of a traffic accident).[6]

(c) *Suicide:* When the defendant negligently hurts a person who later commits suicide as a result of the injuries, the general rule imposes liability for the death only if it can be said that the injured person took his or her own life while insane or during unconsciousness or delirium. If the injured person was lucid when the suicide occurred, this counts as an "abnormal" voluntary act which insulates defendant from responsibility. See Cleveland v. Rotman, 297 F.3d 569 (7th Cir. 2002) (Ill. law) (tax lawyer not liable for

---

6. The fireman's rule has applications beyond the context of the rescue doctrine. See infra p. 283; Dobbs, The Law of Torts §§ 284–287, pp. 767–779 (2000).

suicide of 74–year–old client, in despair over a 30–year losing fight with the Internal Revenue Service that was allegedly made hopeless by defendant's bad advice); Exxon Corp. v. Brecheen, 526 S.W.2d 519 (Tex.1975) (concluding that trucker whom defendant negligently sprayed in the face with gasoline was rendered mentally ill by the experience and was not lucid when he committed suicide almost three years later).[7]

6. *Scope of liability for intentional tortfeasors.* A traditional viewpoint was expressed by Justice Marshall as follows:

> Although many legal battles have been fought over the extent of tort liability for remote consequences of *negligent* conduct, it has always been assumed that the victim of an *intentional* tort can recover from the tortfeasor if he proves that the tortious conduct was a cause in fact of his injuries. An inquiry into proximate cause has traditionally been deemed unnecessary in suits against intentional tortfeasors.

Associated Gen. Contractors v. California State Council of Carpenters, 459 U.S. 519, 547–48, 103 S.Ct. 897, 74 L.Ed.2d 723 (1983) (Marshall, J., dissenting; emphasis in original). The Restatement (Third) of Torts: Liability for Physical Harm (Basic Principles) (Tent. Draft No. 3, April 2003), treats the matter as follows:

> § 33. Scope of Liability for Intentional and Reckless Tortfeasors
>
> (a) An actor who intentionally causes physical harm is subject to liability for that harm even if it is unlikely to occur.
>
> (b) An actor who intentionally or recklessly causes physical harm is subject to liability for a broader range of harms than the harms for which that actor would be liable if acting negligently. In general, the moral culpability of the actor, as reflected in the reasons for and intent in committing the tortious acts, the seriousness of harm intended and threatened by those acts, and the degree to which the actor's conduct deviated from appropriate care, are important factors in determining the scope of liability.
>
> (c) An actor who intentionally or recklessly causes harm is, nevertheless, not subject to liability for harm when the risk of that harm was not increased by the actor's intentional or reckless conduct.

The doctrine of transferred intent (see supra p. 18) is one manifestation of the law's tendency toward an extensive scope of liability for intentional torts.

PALSGRAF v. LONG ISLAND R. CO.

Court of Appeals of New York, 1928.
248 N.Y. 339, 162 N.E. 99.

CARDOZO, C.J.

Plaintiff was standing on a platform of defendant's railroad after buying a ticket to go to Rockaway Beach. A train stopped at the station,

---

7. Obviously the suicide rule should not apply in actions against defendants whose negligent conduct consists in failing to guard against suicide. See Hickey v. Michigan State University, 439 Mich. 408, 487 N.W.2d 106, 119 (1992) (jailer could be liable for prisoner's suicide because the jailer's negligent conduct "consist[ed] in a failure to protect the plaintiff against the very risk that occur[red]"); Joseph v. State, 26 P.3d 459 (Alaska 2001) (same); Edwards v. Tardif, 240 Conn. 610, 692 A.2d 1266 (1997) (same principle applied against psychiatrist engaged to treat patient for depression and suicidal tendencies).

bound for another place. Two men ran forward to catch it. One of the men reached the platform of the car without mishap, though the train was already moving. The other man, carrying a package, jumped aboard the car, but seemed unsteady as if about to fall. A guard on the car, who had held the door open, reached forward to help him in, and another guard on the platform pushed him from behind. In this act, the package was dislodged, and fell upon the rails. It was a package of small size, about fifteen inches long, and was covered by a newspaper. In fact it contained fireworks, but there was nothing in its appearance to give notice of its contents. The fireworks when they fell exploded. The shock of the explosion threw down some scales at the other end of the platform many feet away. The scales struck the plaintiff, causing injuries for which she sues.

The conduct of the defendant's guard, if a wrong in its relation to the holder of the package, was not a wrong in its relation to the plaintiff, standing far away. Relatively to her it was not negligence at all. Nothing in the situation gave notice that the falling package had in it the potency of peril to persons thus removed. Negligence is not actionable unless it involves the invasion of a legally protected interest, the violation of a right. * * * The plaintiff, as she stood upon the platform of the station, might claim to be protected against intentional invasion of her bodily security. Such invasion is not charged. She might claim to be protected against unintentional invasion by conduct involving in the thought of reasonable men an unreasonable hazard that such invasion would ensue. These, from the point of view of the law, were the bounds of her immunity, with perhaps some rare exceptions, survivals for the most part of ancient forms of liability, where conduct is held to be at the peril of the actor. If no hazard was apparent to the eye of ordinary vigilance, an act innocent and harmless, at least to outward seeming, with reference to her, did not take to itself the quality of a tort because it happened to be a wrong, though apparently not one involving the risk of bodily insecurity, with reference to some one else. "In every instance, before negligence can be predicated of a given act, back of the act must be sought and found a duty to the individual complaining, the observance of which would have averted or avoided the injury." "The ideas of negligence and duty are strictly correlative." The plaintiff sues in her own right for a wrong personal to her, and not as the vicarious beneficiary of a breach of duty to another.

A different conclusion will involve us, and swiftly too, in a maze of contradictions. A guard stumbles over a package which has been left upon a platform. It seems to be a bundle of newspapers. It turns out to be a can of dynamite. To the eye of ordinary vigilance, the bundle is abandoned waste, which may be kicked or trod on with impunity. Is a passenger at the other end of the platform protected by the law against the unsuspected hazard concealed beneath the waste? If not, is the result to be any different, so far as the distant passenger is concerned, when the guard stumbles over a valise which a truckman or a porter has left upon the walk? The passenger far away, if the victim of a wrong at all, has a cause of action, not derivative, but original and primary. His claim to be protected against invasion of his bodily security is neither greater nor less because the act resulting in the invasion is a wrong to another far removed. In this case, the rights that are said to have been violated, the interests said to have been invaded, are not even of the same order. The man was not injured in his person nor even put in danger. The purpose of the act, as well as its effect, was to make his person safe. If there was a wrong to him at all, which may very well be doubted, it was a wrong to a property interest only, the safety of his package. Out of this wrong to property, which threatened injury to nothing else, there has passed, we are told, to the plaintiff by derivation or succession a right of action for the invasion of an interest of another order, the right to bodily security. The diversity of interests emphasizes the futility of the effort to build the plaintiff's right upon the basis of a wrong to some one else. The gain is one of emphasis, for a like result would follow if the interests were the same. Even then, the orbit of the danger as disclosed to the eye of reasonable vigilance would be the orbit of the duty. One who jostles one's neighbor in a crowd does not invade the rights of others standing at the outer fringe when the unintended contact casts a bomb upon the ground. The wrongdoer as to them is the man who carries the bomb, not the one who explodes it without suspicion of the danger. Life will have to be made over, and human nature transformed, before prevision so extravagant can be accepted as the norm of conduct, the customary standard to which behavior must conform.

The argument for the plaintiff is built upon the shifting meanings of such words as "wrong" and "wrongful," and shares their instability. What the plaintiff must show is "a wrong" to herself; i.e., a violation of her own right, and not merely a wrong to some one else, nor conduct "wrongful" because unsocial, but not "a wrong" to any one. We are told that one who drives at reckless speed through a crowded city street is guilty of a negligent act and therefore of a wrongful one, irrespective of the consequences. Negligent the act is, and wrongful in the sense that it is unsocial, but wrongful and unsocial in relation to other travelers, only because the eye of vigilance perceives the risk of damage. If the same act were to be committed on a speedway or a race course, it would lose its wrongful quality. The risk reasonably to be perceived defines the duty to be obeyed, and risk imports relation; it is risk to another or to others within the range of apprehension. This does not mean, of course, that one who launches a destructive force is always relieved of liability, if the force, though known to be destructive, pursues an unexpected path. "It was not necessary that the defendant should have had notice of the particular method in which an accident would occur, if the possibility of an accident was clear to the ordinarily prudent eye." Some acts, such as shooting, are so imminently dangerous to any one who may come within reach of the missile however unexpectedly, as to impose a duty of prevision not far from that of an insurer. Even today, and much oftener in earlier stages of the law, one acts sometimes at one's peril. Under this head, it may be, fall certain cases of what is known as transferred intent, an act willfully dangerous to A resulting by misadventure in injury to B. These cases aside, wrong is defined in terms of the natural or probable, at least when unintentional. The range of reasonable apprehension is at times a question for the court, and at times, if varying inferences are possible, a question for the jury. Here, by concession, there was nothing in the situation to suggest to the most cautious mind that the parcel wrapped in newspaper would spread wreckage through the station. If the guard had thrown it down knowingly and willfully, he would not have threatened the plaintiff's safety, so far as appearances could warn him. His conduct would not have involved, even then, an unreasonable probability of invasion of her bodily security. Liability can be no greater where the act is inadvertent.

Negligence, like risk, is thus a term of relation. Negligence in the abstract, apart from things related, is surely not a tort, if indeed it is understandable at all. Negligence is not a tort unless it results in the commission of a wrong, and the commission of a wrong imports the violation of a right, in this case, we are told, the right to be protected against interference with one's bodily security. But bodily security is protected, not against all forms of interference or aggression, but only against some. One who seeks redress at law does not make out a cause of action by showing without more that there has been damage to his person. If the harm was not willful, he must show that the act as to him had possibilities of danger so many and apparent as to entitle him to be protected against the doing of it though the harm was unintended. Affront to personality is still the keynote of the wrong. * * * The victim does not sue derivatively, or by right of subrogation, to vindicate an interest invaded in the person of another. Thus to view his cause of action is to ignore the fundamental difference between tort and crime. He sues for breach of a duty owing to himself.

The law of causation, remote or proximate, is thus foreign to the case before us. The question of liability is always anterior to the question of the measure of the consequences that go with liability. If there is no tort to be redressed, there is no occasion to consider what damage might be recovered if there were a finding of a tort. We may assume, without deciding, that negligence, not at large or in the abstract, but in relation to the plaintiff, would entail liability for any and all consequences, however novel or extraordinary; Ehrgott v. Mayor, etc., of City of New York, 96 N.Y. 264, 48 Am.Rep. 622 [1884];* cf. Matter of Polemis, [supra

---

* Proceeding with proper care on a cold rainy night on a New York City street, Mr. Ehrgott drove his horse–drawn carriage into a ditch for which defendant was negligently responsible, breaking the carriage's axle and dragging Ehrgott over the dashboard. It took Ehrgott several hours to report the matter to the police, procure another carriage, and drive several miles to his home. The wreck plus the prolonged exposure to the cold and rain left Ehrgott with a permanent disease of the spine. The court rejected defendant's efforts to attribute the disease to Ehrgott's own post–accident decisions, stating that "[t]he best statement of the rule is that a wrong–doer is responsible for the natural and proximate consequences of his misconduct; and what

p. 174]. There is room for argument that a distinction is to be drawn according to the diversity of interests invaded by the act, as where conduct negligent in that it threatens an insignificant invasion of an interest in property results in an unforeseeable invasion of an interest of another order, as, e.g., one of bodily security. Perhaps other distinctions may be necessary. We do not go into the question now. The consequences to be followed must first be rooted in a wrong.

The judgment of the Appellate Division and that of the Trial Term should be reversed, and the complaint dismissed, with costs in all courts.

ANDREWS, J., dissenting.

* * *

* * * The result we shall reach depends upon our theory as to the nature of negligence. Is it a relative concept—the breach of some duty owing to a particular person or to particular persons? Or, where there is an act which unreasonably threatens the safety of others, is the doer liable for all its proximate consequences, even where they result in injury to one who would generally be thought to be outside the radius of danger? This is not a mere dispute as to words. We might not believe that to the average mind the dropping of the bundle would seem to involve the probability of harm to the plaintiff standing many feet away, whatever might be the case as to the owner or to one so near as to be likely to be struck by its fall. If, however, we adopt the second hypothesis, we have to inquire only as to the relation between cause and effect. We deal in terms of proximate cause, not of negligence.

Negligence may be defined roughly as an act or omission which unreasonably does or may affect the rights of others * * *.

* * *

But we are told that "there is no negligence unless there is in the particular case a legal duty to take care, and this duty must be one which is owed to the plaintiff himself and not merely to others." This I think too narrow a conception. Where there is the unreasonable act, and some right that may be affected there is negligence whether damage does or does not result. That is immaterial. Should we drive down Broadway at a reckless speed, we are negligent whether we strike an approaching car or miss it by an inch. The act itself is wrongful. It is a wrong not only to those who happen to be within the radius of danger, but to all who might have been there—a wrong to the public at large. Such is the language of the street. * * *

* * *

are such consequences must generally be left for the determination of the jury." It held that the trial judge did not err in refusing to instruct the jury that the defendant was liable "only for such damages as might reasonably be supposed to have been in the contemplation of the plaintiff and defendant as the probable result of the accident." [Ed.]

Due care is a duty imposed on each one of us to protect society from unnecessary danger, not to protect *A, B,* or *C* alone.

* * *

The proposition is this: Every one owes to the world at large the duty of refraining from those acts that may unreasonably threaten the safety of others. Such an act occurs. Not only is he wronged to whom harm might reasonably be expected to result, but he also who is in fact injured, even if he be outside what would generally be thought the danger zone. There needs be duty due the one complaining, but this is not a duty to a particular individual because as to him harm might be expected. Harm to some one being the natural result of the act, not only that one alone, but all those in fact injured may complain. * * * Unreasonable risk being taken, its consequences are not confined to those who might probably be hurt.

If this be so we do not have a plaintiff suing by "derivation or succession." Her action is original and primary—not that she is subrogated to any right of action of the owner of the parcel or of a passenger standing at the scene of the explosion.

* * * [W]hen injuries * * * result from our unlawful act, we are liable for the consequences. It does not matter that they are unusual, unexpected, unforeseen, and unforeseeable. But there is one limitation. The damages must be so connected with the negligence that the latter may be said to be the proximate cause of the former.

* * *

* * * What we * * * mean by the word "proximate" is that, because of convenience, of public policy, of a rough sense of justice, the law arbitrarily declines to trace a series of events beyond a certain point. This is not logic. It is practical politics. * * *

Take the illustration given in an unpublished manuscript by a distinguished and helpful writer on the law of torts. A chauffeur negligently collides with another car which is filled with dynamite, although he could not know it. An explosion follows. *A*, walking on the sidewalk nearby, is killed. *B*, sitting in a window of a building opposite, is cut by flying glass. *C*, likewise sitting in a window a block away, is similarly injured. And a further illustration: A nursemaid, ten blocks away, startled by the noise, involuntarily drops a baby from her arms to the walk. We are told that *C* may not recover while *A* may. As to *B* it is a question for court or jury. We will all agree that the baby might not. Because, we are again told, the chauffeur had no reason to believe his conduct involved any risk of injuring either *C* or the baby. As to them he was not negligent.

But the chauffeur, being negligent in risking the collision, his belief that the scope of the harm he might do would be limited is immaterial. His act unreasonably jeopardized the safety of any one who might be affected by it. *C*'s injury and that of the baby were directly traceable to the collision. Without that, the injury would not have happened. *C* had the right to sit in his office, secure from such dangers. The baby was entitled to use the sidewalk with reasonable safety.

The true theory is, it seems to me, that the injury to *C,* if in truth he is to be denied recovery, and the injury to the baby, is that their several injuries were not the proximate result of the negligence. And here not what the chauffeur had reason to believe would be the result of his conduct, but what the prudent would foresee, may have a bearing—may have some bearing, for the problem of proximate cause is not to be solved by any one consideration. It is all a question of expediency. There are no fixed rules to govern our judgment. There are simply matters of which we may take account. * * * There is in truth little to guide us other than common sense.

* * * We draw an uncertain and wavering line, but draw it we must as best we can.

[I]t is all a question of fair judgment, always keeping in mind the fact that we endeavor to make a rule in each case that will be practical and in keeping with the general understanding of mankind.

* * *

* * * The act upon which defendant's liability rests is knocking an apparently harmless package onto the platform. The act was negligent. For its proximate consequences the defendant is liable. If its contents were broken, to the owner; if it fell upon and crushed a passenger's foot, then to him; if it exploded and injured one in the immediate vicinity, to him also as to *A* in the illustration. Mrs. Palsgraf was standing some distance away. How far cannot be told from the record—apparently 25 or 30 feet, perhaps less. Except for the explosion, she would not have been injured. We are told by the appellant in his brief, "It cannot be denied that the explosion was the direct cause of the plaintiff's injuries." So it was a substantial factor in producing the result—there was here a natural and continuous sequence—direct connection. The only intervening cause was that, instead of blowing her to the ground, the concussion smashed the weighing machine which in turn fell upon her. There was no remoteness in time, little in space. * * *

Under these circumstances I cannot say as a matter of law that the plaintiff's injuries were not the proximate result of the negligence. That is all we have before us. * * *

The judgment appealed from should be affirmed, with costs.

Pound, Lehman, and Kellogg, JJ., concur with Cardozo, C.J.

Andrews, J., dissents in opinion in which Crane and O'Brien, JJ., concur.

Notes

1. *The railroad's negligent conduct.* Judge Cardozo states that it "may very well be doubted" whether defendant's employees were guilty of any

negligent conduct. This is a puzzling remark, given the facts of the case. In the intermediate appellate court (the "Appellate Division"), the decision (by a 3–2 vote) was to affirm the plaintiff's judgment. Palsgraf v. Long Island R. Co., 222 App.Div. 166, 225 N.Y.S. 412 (1927). The majority opinion in that court justified the jury finding of negligent conduct as follows:

> Two of the defendant's employees undertook to help [the man with the bundle to board] the train while it was in motion, one of them the trainman and the other the man on the platform. During their efforts to assist the man onto the moving train, these men knocked the bundle out from under the passenger's arm, and it fell under the train. * * * The sole question of defendant's negligence submitted to the jury was whether the defendant's employees were 'careless and negligent in the way they handled this particular passenger after he came upon the platform and while he was boarding the train.' This question of negligence was submitted to the jury by a fair and impartial charge, and the verdict was supported by the evidence. The jury might well find that the act of the passenger in undertaking to board a moving train was negligent, and that the acts of the defendant's employees in assisting him while engaged in that negligent act were also negligent. Instead of aiding or assisting the passenger engaged in such an act, they might better have discouraged and warned him not to board the moving train. It is quite probable that without their assistance the passenger might have succeeded in boarding the train, and no accident would have happened, or without the assistance of these employees the passenger might have desisted in his efforts to board the train. (225 N.Y.S. at 413).

The dissenting judges in the Appellate Division did not dispute the existence of negligent conduct: "[The] door of the train should have been closed before the train started, which would have prevented the passenger making the attempt." Id. at 414.

2. *Mrs. Palsgraf's lawyer's theory of the case.* Aside from res ipsa loquitur cases, a plaintiff's lawyer proves the breach element by identifying questionable conduct of the defendant and using the evidence to convey a picture of an array of risks created or exacerbated by that conduct. It has always been a mystery why Helen Palsgraf's lawyer chose to paint such a picture that didn't have his client in it. Perhaps counsel overestimated the health and strength of the directness test for legal causation.

3. *Unforeseeable plaintiffs.* Judge Cardozo choice of a no–duty articulation for the decision creates the powerful impression that there must be a rule of law saying unforeseeable plaintiffs can't win. But there has never been such a rule.[8] See Jackson v. B. Lowenstein & Bros., 175 Tenn. 535, 136 S.W.2d 495 (1940), in which the court criticized the *Palsgraf* majority opinion—stating that "appellate courts should not lightly" take the legal cause issue away from the jury—in the course of holding a large Memphis department store exposed to liability to a plaintiff who was no more foreseeable than Helen Palsgraf. Mrs. Jackson was coming up the stairs approaching a landing and a right–angle turn when a man (Atkins) suddenly

8. Some analysts would say that Judge Cardozo was justified in *creating* such a rule. Others—including the authors of this book (and the framers of the new Restatement) disagree. See infra p. 295.

tumbled down the stairs and knocked her over. The defendant's negligent conduct consisted in the maintenance of a defective rubber mat at the top of the stairs. Atkins's daughter had tripped on the mat and fallen to the landing, baby in arms. Atkins ran down the stairs to try to help his daughter and granddaughter. He was then knocked from the landing and on down into the plaintiff by other customers who had crowded onto the landing in response to Atkins's daughter's accident. The court concluded that a reasonable jury could find that the injury to Mrs. Jackson was a more–or–less natural outcome of Atkins's daughter's accident and hence of defendant's negligent conduct.

Restatement (Third) of Torts: Liability for Physical Harm (Basic Principles) § 29, cmt. *m* (Tent. Draft No. 3, April 2003) states: "No express limitation in this section places harm to unforeseeable plaintiffs outside the scope of an actor's liability. * * * Ordinarily, the risk standard contained in this section will, without requiring any separate reference to the foreseeability of the plaintiff, preclude liability for harm to such plaintiffs."

4. *The superseding cause doctrine.* The dissenting judges in the Appellate Division argued for reversal on the basis of proximate cause, stating:

> [T]he negligence of defendant was not a proximate cause of the injuries to plaintiff. Between the negligence of defendant and the injuries there intervened the negligence of the passenger carrying the package containing an explosive. This was an independent, and not a concurring, act of negligence. The explosion was not reasonably probable as a result of defendant's act of negligence. The negligence of defendant was not a likely or natural cause of the explosion, since the latter was such an unusual occurrence. Defendant's negligence was a cause of plaintiff's injury, but too remote. (225 N.Y.S. at 414–15.)

That serious misconduct by someone other than the defendant—or any other causal force that might be similarly deemed dramatic and highly unexpected—might "intervene" between the defendant's negligent conduct and the injury in such a way as to become a "superseding" or a "supervening" cause, insulating the defendant from liability, is a plausible concept of long standing. See, e.g., Watson v. Kentucky & Indiana Bridge & R. Co., 137 Ky. 619, 126 S.W. 146 (1910) (holding that a rail carrier that negligently spilled gasoline that was then ignited by a man trying to light a cigar, causing an explosion that harmed the innocent plaintiff, could be liable if the cigar man was merely negligent but not if his act was "wanton or malicious"); Minor v. Zidell Trust, 618 P.2d 392 (Ok. 1980) (holding that the conduct of an 86–year–old motorist, who passed out at the wheel of his car and then drove it through the second–story wall of defendant's parking garage was a superseding and thus the "sole proximate" cause of the motorist's injuries, although the wheel curb may have been too low and/or the wall too weak). The Restatement (Third) of Torts: Liability for Physical Harm (Basic Principles) (Tent. Draft No. 3, April 2003), states the superseding cause doctrine as follows:

§ 34. Intervening Acts and Superseding Causes

An actor is not subject to liability for harm, for which a force of nature or an independent act is also a factual cause of the harm, if the harm is different from the harms whose risks made the actor's conduct tortious.

5. *Judge Posner on legal cause.* Judge Posner sees the suicide rule, supra p. 182, as a specific application of the superseding cause concept and offers the following explanation of both the rule and the concept:

> [T]he general rule is that the negligent actor is not liable for the victim's decision to kill himself. The suicide is said to be a supervening cause of the victim's loss of his life, breaking the chain of responsibility that would otherwise link the loss to the negligent act. Of course, this is just a conclusion, not reasoning; but it is a conclusion sustained by reasoning about the unforeseeability of most suicides and the role of foreseeability in determining tort liability. If an employer refuses an employee's request for a raise, the latter may respond by killing himself, and yet the employer even if somehow negligent in failing to give the employee the raise would not be legally responsible for the death, just as if through the carelessness of the driver a truck spilled a toxic substance and a passerby scraped it up and poisoned his mother–in–law with it the driver would not be liable to the mother–in–law's estate; the son–in–law's criminal act would be deemed a supervening cause.
>
> A person is not liable for such improbable consequences of negligent activity as could hardly figure in his deciding how careful he should be. Liability in such circumstances would serve no deterrent, no regulatory purpose; it would not alter behavior and increase safety. Nothing would be gained by imposing liability in such a case but compensation, and compensation can be obtained more cheaply by insurance.
>
> But by the same token the doctrine of supervening cause is not applicable when the duty of care claimed to have been violated is precisely a duty to protect against ordinarily unforeseeable conduct. A risk unforeseeable to an ordinary person is foreseeable to a specialist who assumes a duty to prevent the risk from materializing. The duty is a recognition that the unforeseeable has become foreseeable to the relevant community. And so a hospital that fails to maintain a careful watch over patients known to be suicidal is not excused by the doctrine of supervening cause from liability for a suicide, any more than a zoo can escape liability for allowing a tiger to escape and maul people on the ground that the tiger is the supervening cause of the mauling. In both cases there is a foreseeable, in the sense of probable, hazard which precautions can and should be taken in order to lessen.

Jutzi–Johnson v. United States, 263 F.3d 753, 755–56 (7th Cir. 2001) (citations omitted; paragraph break added).

The third paragraph of Judge Posner's explanation is his version of the "very risk" concept that we encountered in footnote 7, supra p. 183. This *core risk* idea explains the cases that hold automobile owners liable for leaving the keys in the ignition when a car thief runs over the plaintiff and on policemen who bring about traffic accidents by instigating high–speed chases. (In both situations, courts are divided.)

In the following case, Judge Posner expands the thought in the second paragraph of his above–quoted explanation and uses it to explain the entire doctrine of legal cause.

EDWARDS v. HONEYWELL, INC.

United States Court of Appeals, Seventh Circuit, 1995.
50 F.3d 484.

Posner, Chief Judge.

A fireman's widow has sued Honeywell, the provider of an alarm system intended to protect the house where her husband was killed in the line of duty. The suit, filed in an Indiana state court, charges that David John Edwards died because of Honeywell's negligence in failing to call the fire department promptly upon receiving a signal from the alarm. As a result of the delay, the floor of the burning house was in a severely weakened condition by the time the firemen entered, and it collapsed beneath Edwards, plunging him to his death. The district court, to which the suit had been removed under the diversity jurisdiction, granted summary judgment for Honeywell. The court held that Honeywell owed no duty of care to fireman Edwards under the common law of Indiana. * * *

In 1982 Honeywell had made a contract with a couple named Baker to install (for $1,875) and monitor (for $21 a month) an alarm system in the Bakers' house. The house is a wood–frame house located in a suburb of Indianapolis and ordinary in every respect except that the Bakers conducted an interior–decorating service out of the basement. The contract limited Honeywell's liability to the Bakers for the consequences of any failure of the system to $250. The validity of this limitation is not questioned.

The alarm system was of a type that has become common. If the house was entered while the alarm was turned on, and the alarm was not promptly disarmed, or if someone in the house pushed either a "panic button" or a button on the alarm console labeled fire, police, or emergency medical service, a signal was automatically transmitted over the telephone lines to a central station maintained by Honeywell. The person manning the station (called the "alarm monitor") would call the fire department if the fire or medical–emergency button had been pressed, and otherwise would call the police department. * * *

Six years passed. It was now an afternoon in the winter of 1988, and Mrs. Baker was working in the basement with two of the employees of the decorating service when she heard a sound. She looked up and noticed an orange glow in the furnace room. One of the employees opened the door to the room, revealing a shelving unit in the furnace room already engulfed in flames from floor to ceiling. Mrs. Baker ran upstairs and tried to dial 911 but misdialed. She gave up on the phone and pushed two buttons on the control panel of the alarm system. One was the fire button, the other the police button. Then she grabbed her dog and ran out the front door. The two people who had been working in the basement with her fled at the same time; they were the only other people in the house. * * *

The signals from the Bakers' house [came] into [Honeywell's] central station at 2:54 p.m., triggering an audible alarm. The alarm monitor, hearing it, * * * pressed a function key, causing the relevant information about the Bakers to flash on the screen of her computer. The display told her to call the Indianapolis Fire Department * * *. So she pushed the "direct fire button" to the Indianapolis Fire Department, connecting her immediately with the department's dispatcher. She gave the dispatcher the Bakers' address. The dispatcher told her that it was within the jurisdiction of a different fire department, that of the City of Lawrence, to which the dispatcher transferred the call. That was wrong too. It was the fire department of Lawrence Township that had jurisdiction over the Bakers' house. So the dispatcher for the City of Lawrence transferred the call that had been relayed to the City of Lawrence's fire department.

Had Honeywell's operator called the township's fire department first, rather than reaching that department as it were on the third try, it would have taken no more than 45 seconds for the department to learn of the fire at the Bakers' house. Because of the jurisdictional error, it was not until 2:58 that the department received the call. The 45 seconds had been stretched to four minutes because of the misinformation in Honeywell's computer. The plaintiff claims, and for purposes of this appeal we accept, that Honeywell was careless in not having a procedure for verifying and updating such essential information as which fire department to call in the event of a fire in a subscriber's premises, since the boundaries between fire districts are shifted from time to time.

A Lawrence Township fire chief arrived at the scene at 3:00 p.m. (This was remarkably prompt, the call having come in only two minutes earlier. But the Bakers' residence was only a mile or a mile and a half from the firehouse. This shows by the way the importance of notifying the right fire department.) He saw dark smoke but no flames. Mrs. Baker was there and told him that she thought her furnace had exploded. The chief did not ask her when the fire had started but assumed that, because Mrs. Baker had been at home, she had notified the fire department immediately. This implied that the fire was less than three minutes old. Five minutes later, at 3:05 p.m., two parties of firemen began leading hoses into the house, entering through the front door and the garage (which was on the side of the house) respectively. The floor was hot to the touch (firemen customarily enter a burning building on all fours because smoke and heat rise), and the group that had entered through the front door quickly withdrew, fearing that the floor would collapse. The smoke thickened. Fire was seen darting from the roof. Edwards, an experienced fireman, was one of two men who had entered the house from the garage. Sometime between 3:10 and 3:15, before he could withdraw from the house, the floor collapsed and he fell into the basement and was asphyxiated.

The house was severely damaged by the fire, and the Bakers have since moved to another house. They no longer subscribe to Honeywell's alarm service.

We may assume that the firemen would have arrived a little more than three minutes earlier (to be exact, four minutes minus 45 seconds earlier) had Honeywell's call gone to the right fire department directly rather than having to be relayed. Whether fireman Edwards' life would have been saved is obviously a highly speculative question. It depends on what the firemen would have done with the extra three minutes and 15 seconds. If they would have brought the fire under control in that time, then the floor might not have collapsed. But if at the end of that period they would still have been laying their hoses (no water had yet been applied to the fire when the firemen withdrew and the floor collapsed), the floor would have collapsed just as it did and Edwards would have been killed just as he was. Absence of evidence that the delay of which the plaintiff complains made any difference to Edwards' fate was not, however, the ground on which the district judge dismissed the suit. Nor does Honeywell urge it as an alternative ground for affirming the judgment.

* * *

As the premise of our further discussion, we may assume without having to decide not only that Honeywell breached its duty of care to the Bakers by not updating the information in its computer on which fire department to call if the Bakers' house caught on fire, but also that as a consequence of this breach fireman Edwards died. We are speaking of a tort duty of care * * *, not a contractual duty; there is no suggestion that Edwards was a third–party beneficiary of the contract between Honeywell and the Browns.

The question we must decide, therefore, is whether Honeywell's duty of care extended to firemen who might be summoned to fight the blaze, for, if not, the plaintiff's suit was properly dismissed. Why duty should be an issue in a negligence case is not altogether clear, however, and the quest for an answer may guide us to a decision.

* * * [O]riginally negligence signified carelessness only in the performance of * * * a duty arising from an undertaking (for example that of a surgeon) or a [specific] duty imposed by law, such as an innkeeper's duty to look after his guests' goods. It was not until the nineteenth century that a general principle of liability for the careless infliction of harm was securely established. But as liability for negligence expanded, the judges felt a need to place limitations on its scope and to rein in juries, and the concept of duty was revived to name some of these limitations and to exert some control over juries. Negligence was redefined as the breach of a duty running from the injurer to the injurer's victim to exercise due care, and the question whether there was such a duty in the particular case or class of cases was, and remains, a matter for the judge to decide, not the jury. * * *

Should a passerby be liable for failing to warn a person of a danger? The courts thought not, and therefore said there is no tort duty to rescue. Even if the defendant had acted irresponsibly or even maliciously in failing to warn or rescue the [victim], the plaintiff could not obtain damages. This limitation on the scope of the duty of care has stood but others have fallen by the wayside in most or all states, such as the nonduty of care of a manufacturer to users of his defective products other than the first purchaser, Winterbottom v. Wright, 10 M. & W. 109, 152 Eng.Rep. 402 (Ex. 1842), the nonduty of care of an accountant to persons who rely on his audit report but have no contractual relation with him, Ultramares Corp. v. Touche, 255 N.Y. 170, 174 N.E. 441 (1931) (Cardozo, J.), and the nonduty of care of railroads in avoiding fire damage to anyone other than the owner of buildings or other property actually struck by the railroad's sparks, as opposed to owners of property to which the fire that had been started by those sparks spread. Ryan v. N.Y. Central R.R., 35 N.Y. 210 (1866).

Of particular relevance to the present case are two lines of precedent. Indeed the present case could be said to lie at their intersection. One concerns the duty of care to an unforeseeable victim. The classic case is *Palsgraf* * * * The Indiana courts accept *Palsgraf's* exclusion of liability to unforeseeable victims. So if fireman Evans [sic] was an unforeseeable victim of Honeywell's negligence, this suit must fail.

The other line of cases concerns the duty of care of water companies, telephone companies, and other providers of services of the public utility type—today including alarm services—to the general public as opposed to customers. Again the most famous cases are Judge Cardozo's. H.R. Moch Co. v. Rensselaer Water Co., 247 N.Y. 160, 159 N.E. 896 (1928), held that a company which had contracted to supply water to a city and its residents was not liable for the consequences of a fire that the fire department was unable to bring under control (with resulting damage to the plaintiff's property) because the water company failed through carelessness to maintain adequate pressure in the water mains. Kerr S.S. Co. v. Radio Corp. of America, 245 N.Y. 284, 157 N.E. 140 (1927), held that careless failure to transmit the plaintiff's telegram, a failure that caused the plaintiff to lose a valuable contract, was not a tortious wrong to the plaintiff. Telegraph companies have gone by the board. But there have been cases which hold that telephone companies can be liable for fire damage resulting from an operator's failure to transmit a distress call, and an equal number of cases rejecting such liability.

We do not know the standing of the public utility cases in Indiana law. The courts of Indiana recognize as do all common law courts the duty limitation on tort liability, but they pitch the criterion for it at so high a level of generality that their position on those cases cannot be inferred from it. Other states do not have crisper formulations. The matter may not lend itself to precise verbal formation. Even so, if the rest of the states were in agreement on the scope of the limitation with respect either to a case such as the present one or to the class of cases illustrated by *Moch* and *Kerr*, we could assume that Indiana would fall into line. They are not. The principle of these cases is accepted in some jurisdictions, rejected in others. The split is mirrored in the cases closest to the present one—cases involving the liability of alarm services to noncustomers (none of them, however, firemen, policemen, or other rescue workers) for the consequences of the service's negligence. There are no Indiana cases concerning the liability of alarm services to noncustomers.

The basic criticism of both the *Palsgraf* and *Moch–Kerr* lines of decisions, articulated with characteristic force by Judge Friendly in Petition of Kinsman Transit Co., [supra p. 178], is that since by assumption the defendant was careless (for the concept of duty would have no liability–limiting function otherwise), why should its carelessness be excused merely because either the particular harm that occurred as a consequence, or the person harmed as a consequence, was unforeseeable? If the Long Island Railroad's employees had avoided jostling the passenger carrying the bundle of fireworks, as due care required them to do, Mrs. Palsgraf would not have been injured. If the water company had kept up the pressure, as it was contractually obligated to do, the fire would not have raged out of control. And if Honeywell had used due care in identifying the fire department with jurisdiction over a fire in the Bakers' house, Edwards (we are assuming for purposes of this appeal) would not have been killed. In none of these cases would the defendant, in order to prevent the injury of which the plaintiff was complaining, have had to exercise more care than it was required by law to exercise anyway.

The arguments on the other side, the arguments in favor of the duty limitation in these cases, are twofold. The first arises from the fact that a corporation or other enterprise does not have complete control over its employees, yet it is strictly liable under the principle of respondeat superior for the consequences of their negligent acts committed in the scope of their employment. [See Chapter VII.] It is not enough to say to the enterprise be careful and you have nothing to fear. The carelessness of its employees may result in the imposition of a crushing liability upon it. In order to know how many resources (in screening new hires and in supervising and disciplining workers after they are hired) to invest in preventing its employees from being careless, the employer must have some idea, some foresight, of the harms the employees are likely to inflict. Imposing liability for unforeseeable types of harm is unlikely, therefore, to evoke greater efforts at preventing accidents; it is likely merely to constitute the employer an insurer. The railroad in *Palsgraf* did not know that conductors who jostle boarding passengers pose a threat of injury by explosion to people standing elsewhere on the platform, and the water company in *Moch* did not know the likelihood of fires or the value of the property that might be damaged by them.

The second argument in favor of using the concept of duty to limit the scope of liability for careless acts, an argument relevant to *Moch* and *Kerr* though not to *Palsgraf*, is that the defendant may not be in the best position to prevent a particular class of accidents, and placing liability on it may merely dilute the incentives of other potential defendants. In most cases the best way to avert fire damage is to prevent the fire from starting rather than to douse it with water after it has started. The water company represents a second line of defense, and it has no control over the first. It cannot insist that people not leave oil–soaked rags lying about or that they equip their houses and offices with smoke detectors and fire extinguishers.

How far in general these arguments outweigh the consideration emphasized by Judge Friendly [in *Kinsman*] is a matter of fair debate; but they are especially powerful in this case, and remember that Indiana is a jurisdiction that follows *Palsgraf*. The provider of an alarm service not only has no knowledge of the risk of a fire in its subscribers' premises, and no practical ability to reduce that risk (though we suppose an alarm service like a fire insurer could offer a discount to people who installed smoke detectors in their premises); it also lacks knowledge of the risk of a fire to firemen summoned to extinguish it. That risk depends not only on the characteristics of the particular premises but also on the particular techniques used by each fire department, the training and qualifications of the firemen, and the quality of the department's leadership. The alarm company knows nothing about these things and has no power to influence them.

The death of a fireman in fighting a residential fire appears to be a rare occurrence. And we have not been referred to a single case in which such a death was blamed on a malfunction, human or mechanical, in an alarm system. The problem of proving causation in such a case is * * * a formidable one, and the plethora of potential defendants makes it difficult (we should think) for an alarm company to estimate its likely liability even if it does foresee the kind of accident that occurred here. If "unforeseeable" is given the practical meaning of too unusual, too uncertain, too unreckonable to make it feasible or worthwhile to take precautions against, then this accident was unforeseeable. Honeywell would have difficulty figuring out how careful it must be in order to satisfy its legal obligations or how much more it ought to charge its subscribers in order to cover its contingent liability to firemen and to any others who might be injured in a fire of which the alarm company failed to give prompt notice. Similar problems of debilitating legal uncertainty would arise if the person injured were a police officer or a paramedic rather than a firefighter.

The alarm service constitutes, moreover, not a first or second line of defense against fire but a third line of defense—and in this case possibly a fourth, fifth, or ... nth. The first is the homeowner. We do not know why the Bakers' furnace exploded—whether it was because of a defect in the furnace or a failure by the Bakers or others to inspect or maintain it properly. The second line of defense is the fire department. Potential defendants in this case included not only the alarm service and the fire department (though presumably the plaintiff's only remedy against the department would be under Indiana's public employees' compensation law), but the Bakers, the manufacturer of the furnace, any service company that inspected or maintained the furnace, possibly even the supplier of the wood for the floor that collapsed or the architect or builder of the house. The plaintiff has chosen to sue only the alarm service. Of course none of the others may be negligent. And if any of the others are, conceivably the alarm service might implead them so that liability could come to rest on the most culpable. Yet it is also possible that the principal attraction of the alarm service as a defendant is that it is a large out–of–state firm with deep and well–lined pockets. We can only speculate. All things considered, however, the creation of a duty of care running from the alarm service to Edwards is likely to make at best a marginal contribution to fire safety and one outweighed by the cost of administering such a duty. That at least is our best guess as to how the Supreme Court of Indiana would evaluate this case were it before that court.

Pointing to the $250 limitation of the alarm service's liability to the Bakers, the plaintiff argues that if Honeywell prevails in this suit, alarm services will have no incentive to take care. But they will. Honeywell lost the Bakers' business. Our society relies more heavily on competition than on liability to optimize the quality of the goods and services supplied by the private sector of the economy. A case such as this does Honeywell's customer relations no good even if it wins the case—as we think it must.

* * *

AFFIRMED.

Notes

1. Judge Posner cast his opinion in duty terms, but we consider *Edwards* to be a legal cause case for the same reason that we put *Palsgraf* in this category: The decision does not apply or establish any categorical (general) rule respecting "unforeseeable" plaintiffs but only determines that the particular plaintiff was not (in some sense or another) foreseeable enough.

2. *"No duty" versus "no legal cause as a matter of law."* Courts often act as though it makes no difference whether a scope–of–responsibility issue is framed in duty language or legal cause language. See, e.g., Sakon v. Pepsico, Inc., 553 So.2d 163 (Fla. 1989). Sakon was a 14–year–old boy who broke his neck trying to emulate a dangerous bicycle stunt he saw performed in a televised soft drink commercial. The federal court where the boy's action against the advertiser was lodged certified to the Florida Supreme Court the question whether Florida law recognized "a duty owed by a television advertiser to its targeted audience of young viewers" under the described circumstances. The Florida Supreme Court couched its negative response primarily in proximate cause terminology.

But of course it does make a difference. If Judge Posner had not determined that "[t]he Indiana courts accept *Palsgraf*[]"[9] he probably would

9. Under the influence of *Palsgraf*, many courts treat the unforeseeable plain-   tiff problem as a duty issue and the remaining categories (type of harm, manner of

have been led to discuss Honeywell's responsibility to fireman Edwards under the rubric of legal cause and to explain why Edwards's case failed as a matter of law to establish legal causation. The normal meaning of the phrase "no legal cause as a matter of law" is that no reasonable juror could find that the harm to the plaintiff was among the array of risks the creation or exacerbation of which led to the conclusion that the defendant's conduct was negligent. This might have been difficult to say with a straight face under the facts of *Edwards*. (Does Judge Posner's undocumented and seemingly casual remark that "[t]he death of a fireman in fighting a residential fire appears to be a rare occurrence" seem plausible to you?)

Our point is that the choice between the *duty* and *legal cause* approaches to particular scope–of–responsibility issue has potentially determinative rhetorical consequences. A defendant who succeeds in characterizing a scope–of–responsibility issue as one of duty benefits from the tradition that duty issues are for the judge, not the jury, and the court's concomitant freedom to soar far above the facts of the case into a high realm of legal theory. A plaintiff's successful characterization of such an issue as one of legal cause invokes the presumption that that juries get such issues unless reasonable minds could not differ and the concomitant implication that the answer ought to be sensitive to the particular facts of the case.

3. *The shift–of–responsibility cases.* It is questionable whether a policy of steering plaintiffs toward the most obviously and immediately responsible tortfeasors and away from others (expressed by Judge Posner as a caution against "dilut[ing] the incentives of other potential defendants") can justify the result in *Edwards*. But it does seem to justify some cases in which defendants escape liability because the plaintiff's harm occurs after responsibility for the danger has shifted in a meaningful sense from the defendant to another responsible actor. See, e.g., Kent v. Commonwealth, 437 Mass. 312, 771 N.E.2d 770 (2002) (state parole board's negligent release of dangerous murderer to the federal INS was not a legal cause of a violent crime by the murderer eight years later); Braun v. New Hope Township, 646 N.W.2d 737 (S.D. 2002) (farmer who broke a road–hazard sign was not responsible for an accident that occurred after township had negligently repaired the sign); Sisco v. Broce Mf'g, Inc., 1 Fed. Appx. 420, 2001 WL 45590 (6th Cir. 2001) (Tenn. law) (unpublished) (plaintiff's employer's negligent failure to repair brakes of highway sweeper was a supervening act between the manufacturer's defective design or manufacture of the brakes and the brake–failure accident).

4. *An advocacy perspective.* It is probably obvious by now that, even when it is carefully articulated and applied, "the principle of proximate [legal] cause is hardly a rigorous analytical tool."[10] Courts are cognizant, and sometimes admit, that many of their legal cause decisions could reasonably have come out the other way. This means that it is often difficult to predict the outcome of close legal cause contests, and that it is not always easy for

---

occurrence, extent of harm) under the rubric of legal or proximate cause.

10. Blue Shield v. McCready, 457 U.S. 465, 102 S.Ct. 2540, 2548 n. 13, 73 L.Ed.2d 149 (1982).

an observer to understand why seemingly very similar cases have reached different results.[11]

Legal cause doctrine may do a better job of guiding the efforts of counsel than of predicting judicial behavior. Indeed, it is clear enough what plaintiff's counsel must do: the plaintiff's lawyer must either show the court that the defendant was negligent because of the very risk that befell the plaintiff or present the court with an array of risks—unjustifiably created or exacerbated by the defendant—that at least arguably has the injury to the plaintiff somewhere within the array. As we saw in note 2 following *Palsgraf*, supra p. 190, Helen Palsgraf's lawyer failed to do that. If the plaintiff's lawyer can show the court that the plaintiff's injury is within the array of risks that leads to the conclusion that the defendant's conduct was negligent, the legal cause issue should go to the jury regardless of how unusual the particular accident and/or particular injury might seem.

5.   *Some exercises.* In the following decisions, defendants prevailed with "no legal cause as a matter of law" arguments. If given the chance to try again as counsel for the plaintiff in each case, what additional evidence would you be hoping to find?

Di Ponzio v. Riordan, 89 N.Y.2d 578, 657 N.Y.S.2d 377, 679 N.E.2d 616 (1997). The defendant self–service gasoline station did not comply with an ordinance requiring it to insist that customers turn off their engines before pumping gas. A customer left his car's engine running while he pumped gas and then went inside to pay. The car rolled backward and struck the plaintiff, another customer. In holding that the gas station was entitled to summary judgment, the court stated: "When a vehicle's engine is left running in an area where gasoline is being pumped, there is a natural and foreseeable risk of fire or explosion because of the highly flammable properties of the fuel. * * * The occurrence that led to plaintiff's injury was clearly outside of this limited class of hazards."

Newton v. South Carolina Public Rys. Comm'n, 319 S.C. 430, 462 S.E.2d 266 (1995). The defendant was responsible for the maintenance of a train crossing signal. The signal was out of order for several days, constantly signaling an imminent train. Newton, who was unaware of the malfunction, stopped at the signal and was promptly rear–ended by a closely following motorist (Ross). In holding that the trial judge was correct in dismissing Newton's complaint against the Commission, the court stated: "[I]t was foreseeable that an individual who, like Ross, knew of the malfunction would ignore the signal, fail to stop, and be hit by a train while crossing the track. This type of accident is a natural and probable consequence of the Commission's negligence. On the other

---

11. See, e.g., Estates of Morgan v. Fairfield Family Counseling Ctr., 77 Ohio St.3d 284, 673 N.E.2d 1311 (1997) (allowing the legal cause issue to reach the jury in an action against a psychiatrist who negligently withdrew medication and terminated the care of a psychotic patient, who murdered his parents nine months later); Williamson v. Liptzin, 141 N.C.App. 1, 539 S.E.2d 313 (2000) (very similar case awarding judgment as a matter of law to the psychiatrist when the plaintiff–patient—a deeply disturbed law student—shot two people and was himself wounded and incarcerated eight months after the psychiatrist's negligent actions).

hand, the negligence of Ross in failing to watch the roadway before the crossing is not chargeable against the Commission."

Schneider v. Esperanza Transmission Co., 744 S.W.2d 595, 597 (Tex.1987): An employer's entrusting its employee with a truck for his personal use—negligent because of the employee's record of dangerous driving—was not a legal cause of injuries plaintiff incurred when the employee's friend was driving the truck. "The risk that caused the entrustment to be negligent did not cause the collision."

C. LEGAL CAUSE: CURRENT FERMENT

HUNLEY v. DuPONT AUTOMOTIVE

United States Court of Appeals, Sixth Circuit, 2003.
341 F.3d 491.

MARBLEY, DISTRICT JUDGE.

* * *

Defendant–Appellee, DuPont Automotive, Division of E.I. DuPont de Nemours and Co., Inc. ("DuPont"), operates a paint factory in Mount Clemens, Michigan. At approximately 9:34 p.m., on January 27, 1997, DuPont suffered one of the largest paint spills in the history of the plant. At that time, a DuPont employee was in the process of filling a shipping container with paint to ship to an automobile manufacturer. As she was moving the container toward a holding tank, she struck the bottom of the tank with the top of the container, thereby dislodging the filling valve of the tank. Within the next few minutes, the tank emptied its 2400 gallons of paint onto the worker and the surrounding work area.

DuPont mandates that any chemical spill of more than one–quarter cup necessitates an emergency response. Therefore, at 9:35 p.m. on the evening of the spill, DuPont employees initiated emergency procedures. In particular, a DuPont fire brigade member working in the production area sounded the alarm, calling into action a plant–wide emergency response. Upon hearing the alarm, DuPont's internal fire brigade members donned their protective gear and entered the spill area. According to DuPont, within minutes, all non–fire brigade employees had evacuated the production area and reported to their assigned evacuation sites, closing the fire doors between the production area and the shipping warehouse as they left. One door, however, [may have been left open].
* * *

DuPont contracts with Pinkerton, a private security company, to provide security at the plant. At the time of the spill, Plaintiff–Appellant Jerome Hunley ("Hunley") was employed as a Pinkerton security guard at the DuPont plant in Mount Clemens. Pinkerton security guards are obligated to follow Pinkerton's Site Post Orders. Those orders specify that, in the event of a spill, Pinkerton security guards are to provide a head count report to the fire brigade captain. The Pinkerton Site Post

Orders also expressly state: "Security does not respond to the scene of a spill."

According to Plaintiffs–Appellants, upon Hunley's arrival at work on the evening of the spill, he was told by his supervisor, Bill Maynard, to deliver the head–count report to the fire brigade captain. Hunley printed out the report, and then delivered it to the fire brigade captain, whom he found in the area of the spill. Hunley claims that he gained access to the area of the spill by entering through an open door. When he entered the area of the spill to deliver the report, he was not wearing protective clothing, nor was he breathing through a respirator; none of these protective items had been issued to him by DuPont. The fire brigade members in the vicinity of the spill, however, were all wearing protective clothing, including masks.

Hunley states that, shortly after delivering the report to the fire captain, he began to have "rushing thoughts," which he describes as "too many thoughts running through [his] head at once," and that he also began feeling dizzy. After working the night of the spill, Hunley went home and tried to sleep. While trying to sleep, however, he began hallucinating. In particular, he claims that he heard "whale sounds" and saw "upside down people." Hunley then drove to his grandmother's home, thinking that would help calm him.

On the drive back home from his grandmother's house, Hunley's hallucinations continued. In response to one of the hallucinations, Hunley began driving his truck at speeds estimated to be between sixty and ninety miles per hour against rush hour traffic in Troy, Michigan. Ultimately, his car became airborne, and then landed on top of the car of a nineteen–year–old woman, who was pronounced dead at the scene of the accident. Immediately following the accident, Hunley was transported to a nearby hospital, where he was initially diagnosed with brief reactive psychosis, a temporary diagnosis used to explain his acute psychotic symptoms.

Prior to the car accident, Hunley had no recorded medical history of mental illness, nor did he have a criminal record. He was twenty–four years old at the time. After a series of mental evaluations following the accident, Hunley was ultimately diagnosed with schizophrenia, an organic mental disease that frequently manifests itself when sufferers are in their late teens or early twenties. He has also been diagnosed as suffering from an "acute psychotic break" accompanied by auditory and visual hallucinations at the time of the accident. Hunley's expert, Dr. Gerald Shiener, M.D., opines that Hunley's psychotic break was brought on by the stress of knowing that he had been exposed to toxins in the area of the spill by being in the area without protective gear while all others in the vicinity of the spill were protected by special clothing and masks.

Following one year of hospitalization, Hunley was tried on a charge of manslaughter for the death of the nineteen–year–old woman in the car accident. At the conclusion of the trial, he was found guilty but mentally ill. He is currently incarcerated, serving a term of four to fifteen years.

* * *

[In this action—brought on Hunley's behalf by his guardian—plaintiff alleges that DuPont was guilty of negligent conduct that was a cause in fact and a legal (proximate) cause of his psychosis and related injuries. After discovery had been completed, the district court granted DuPont's motion for summary judgment. Hunley has appealed.]

The district court granted summary judgment to DuPont on the ground that Hunley failed to set forth a prima facie case of negligence. To state a prima facie case of negligence in Michigan, the plaintiff must establish the following four elements: (1) that the defendant owed the plaintiff a duty; (2) that the defendant breached that duty; (3) that the defendant's breach caused the plaintiff's harm, which includes (a) cause in fact and (b) legal, or proximate, cause; and (4) damages to the plaintiff. The district court premised its ruling on its finding that, although DuPont owed a duty to Hunley, DuPont did not breach that duty through its conduct. Based on the analysis set forth below, we conclude that, although Plaintiffs–Appellants raised a genuine issue of fact with respect to both duty and breach, summary judgment was nonetheless proper because they failed, as a matter of law, to establish a genuine issue of material fact as to the existence of proximate cause.

1. EXISTENCE OF A DUTY

DuPont argues that Plaintiffs–Appellants have failed to establish the duty element of the prima facie case because it had neither a duty to provide Hunley with personal protective equipment, nor a duty to warn him that a psychotic break was a danger associated with visual exposure to a paint spill. DuPont errs, however, by viewing the issue of duty so narrowly. Although it may not have owed these particular duties to Hunley, it did have a general duty to exercise due care to protect its security guards, including Hunley, from certain dangers associated with paint spills. This duty arises from the relationship between DuPont and Hunley of premises owner and invitee.

* * *

2. BREACH

Plaintiffs–Appellants assert that DuPont breached its duty to Hunley by failing to provide him with protective gear, by failing to warn him about the nature of the hazards associated with paint spills, and by failing to warn him about the risks inherent in delivering the head count to the fire brigade captain. [We agree with the district court that DuPont's management were entitled to rely on the fact that Hunley's Site Post Orders prohibited him from responding to the scene of a spill. Therefore, DuPont had no reason to issue protective gear to him or to warn him about spill–exposure risks. The district court was correct in concluding that DuPont was not negligent in these particulars.]

[Plaintiff–Appellants also argue that DuPont breached its duty to protect Hunley from the dangers of paint spills by leaving open a door to the spill area. Here, questions of fact exist, precluding summary judgment.] DuPont asserts that all doors to the area of the spill were closed upon evacuation of the employees who had been working in the area prior to the spill. Hunley, on the other hand, alleges that he entered the area to deliver the head count through an open door. Thus, an issue of fact exists with respect to whether a door was, in fact, left open.

Assuming the door was left open, a jury might find that this fact constitutes a breach of DuPont's duty. Although DuPont understood that Pinkerton security guards were not to enter the area of the spill, a jury might find that DuPont should have foreseen that a security guard would nonetheless enter the area if a door were left open. In particular, the risk of a security guard entering the area of the spill through an open door might have been foreseeable in light of the fact that the security guard was told to deliver a head count to the fire brigade captain, wherever he may be. Moreover, although DuPont's other failures do not in and of themselves constitute a breach of DuPont's duty, those failures certainly become factually significant if DuPont could have foreseen that, by leaving a door open, Hunley might enter the area of the spill despite his Site Post Orders to the contrary.

Therefore, we conclude that the Plaintiffs–Appellants satisfied the breach element of their prima facie case to the extent necessary to survive summary judgment.

3. CAUSATION

We now turn to the question of whether Plaintiffs–Appellants have raised a genuine issue of material fact with respect to the issue of causation. To satisfy this element, Plaintiffs–Appellants must demonstrate both cause in fact and legal, or proximate, cause. Based on our conclusion that Plaintiffs–Appellants have failed to demonstrate proximate cause as a matter of law, we need not reach the issue of cause in fact.

Relying on La Pointe v. Chevrette, 264 Mich. 482, 250 N.W. 272 (1933), Hunley asserts that, under Michigan law, proximate cause requires only that the harm suffered by the plaintiff be the natural and probable result of the defendant's negligence, not that the particular harm suffered be foreseeable. In *La Pointe*, a young boy suffered an unusual infection of the bone in his leg after his employer forced him to work outdoors in inclement weather without the proper protective clothing. In ruling that the employer could be liable for the boy's disease, even though it was not foreseeable that such a severe illness would result from working outside in inclement weather, the court stated:

> Where an act is negligent, to render it the proximate cause, it is not necessary that the one committing it might have foreseen the

particular consequence or injury, or the particular manner in which it occurred, if by the exercise of reasonable care it might have been anticipated that some injury might occur.

Although this language in *La Pointe* suggests that the particular harm suffered by the plaintiff need not have been foreseen for there to be proximate cause, more recent Michigan case law sets forth a different standard of law. Recent cases indicate that Michigan courts have shifted their analysis of this issue and, under the current view, the determination of proximate cause involves an examination of the foreseeability of the harm suffered by the plaintiff, and whether the defendant should be held responsible for such harm. * * *

Accordingly, we will apply Michigan's more recent principle of proximate cause in examining whether Plaintiffs–Appellants have raised a genuine issue of material fact with respect to this element.[5] Applying this standard, it is clear that Plaintiffs–Appellants have failed to establish this element of their prima facie case because no reasonable mind could find that it was foreseeable that Hunley would suffer an acute psychotic break, and, ultimately, schizophrenia, as a result of DuPont's having left the door to the spill area open. Even if it was foreseeable that a security guard not clothed in protective gear would enter the area of the spill and see other individuals in the area wearing protective gear, it was not reasonably foreseeable that, as a result of doing so, he would suffer the harm incurred by Hunley. Hunley's own expert, Dr. Shiener, stated simply that he believed that some of the mental health literature indicated that there was a relationship between the onset of psychosis and exposure to stressful situations. This statement does not indicate that exposure to stressful situations is certain to cause psychosis, or that even mental health experts can foresee which stressful situations will cause psychosis. Accordingly, no reasonable mind could find that it was foreseeable that exposure to this stressful situation would have resulted in Hunley's illness.

Furthermore, we are of the opinion that Hunley failed to establish proximate cause even under the more lenient standard of foreseeability that he contends applies under these circumstances. It may have been foreseeable that some physical harm might result from exposure to the paint spill. Plaintiffs–Appellants, however, argue not that Hunley's psychotic break resulted from exposure to the spill itself, but that it resulted from Hunley's exposure to the stress of knowing that he had been in the area of the spill while he was not wearing protective gear, although others in the area were wearing such gear. We conclude, as a matter of law, that it was not reasonably foreseeable that any harm, let alone the particular harm suffered by Hunley, would have resulted from this stress.[6]

---

5. Although proximate cause often must be resolved by the jury, the Court may decide this issue as a matter of law if reasonable minds could not disagree with respect to the resolution of this issue.

6. It is worth noting that this case is distinguishable from *La Pointe*. In *La Pointe*, although the particular harm suffered was not necessarily foreseeable, it was

Therefore, we affirm the district court's ruling granting summary judgment to DuPont * * *

* * *

Notes

1. *Multiple doctrinal explanations were available. Hunley* is a good corroboration of Leon Green's observation that "[l]egal theory is too rich in content not to afford alternative ways, and frequently several of them, for stating an acceptable judgment." Green, Mahoney v. Beatman: A Study in Proximate Cause, 39 Yale L.J. 532, 533 (1930). Nothing prevented the *Hunley* court from justifying its result—summary judgment for defendant— on the no–duty basis urged by DuPont, on the no–breach basis used by the trial judge, or on cause–in–fact grounds. Moreover, the no–duty rule treated in section D of Chapter VI, infra p. 235, might have presented yet another choice. In a case like this, counsel must try to lead the court to see the case in the most client–friendly of the multiple doctrinal contexts into which it might be fitted.

2. *Too much richness?* Sometimes the "richness" of legal doctrine produces decisions whose grounds are hard to identify. In Perez v. Lopez, 74 S.W.3d 60 (Tex. App. 2002), a young boy killed himself with a 30.06 bolt action rifle after persuading defendant, a locksmith, to pick the trigger lock so that the rifle could be fired. The rifle belonged to the boy's adult brother. The boy took it from his brother's house to the locksmith—who picked the lock—and then to his own house, where it lay around for more than a week, during which the boy's father discovered it, discovered that the lock was picked, and then left it lying in an available spot. (On the day of the suicide, the boy's father had taken the rifle to work to try to sell it to a fellow worker and then put it back under the bed.) In reversing a judgment for the plaintiff and holding that the trial judge should have directed a verdict or granted judgment notwithstanding the verdict for defendant, the court left it unclear whether it was relying on the suicide cases (supra p. 182) the shift–of–responsibility cases (supra p. 200) or no–breach grounds. The lack of clarity as to the basis for the decision is significant for legal analysts—it makes it harder to evaluate the correctness of the decision, and one doesn't know for what proposition(s) the case might be cited—but it is even more significant for the parties. Obviously the defendant would be happier with a no–breach explanation, and the boy's father—the plaintiff in the case—certainly would not like a shift–of–responsibility explanation.

3. *Distinguishing La Pointe.* Evidently the *Hunley* court saw *La Pointe* as an eggshell skull (extent–of–harm) case. Why wasn't *Hunley* in the same category? Does the court's concluding paragraph convert an eggshell–skull issue into a type–of–harm issue?

foreseeable that some physical harm would result from being forced to work outdoors in inclement weather. Here, on the other hand, it was not foreseeable that any harm would result to Hunley from the stress of knowing that he was in the area of the toxic spill without protective gear. Furthermore, because security guards are expected to react to situations that would likely cause stress, it was not foreseeable that stress would cause this type of reaction.

MEYERING v. GENERAL MOTORS CORPORATION

Court of Appeal, Fourth District, Division 1, California, 1990.
275 Cal.Rptr. 346.

WIENER, ACTING PRESIDING JUSTICE.

Plaintiff Kurt Meyering was severely injured when he was struck on the head by a chunk of concrete thrown from a freeway overpass by two juveniles. At the time of his injury, Meyering was driving a 1984 Chevrolet Corvette recently purchased by his girlfriend, Jane Casey. The concrete chunk struck him after penetrating the car's sunroof. The Corvette was designed and manufactured by defendant General Motors Corporation (GM) * * *.

Meyering's complaint alleges * * * that [GM was] negligent in the design, manufacture and distribution of the automobile. * * * Meyering's theory is that the sunroof was made from a type of plexiglass which was too thin and too weak. He contends there is a relatively inexpensive alternative—lexan polycarbonate sheeting—which is shatterproof and would have prevented the injury he suffered in this case.

In sustaining [GM's demurrer], the trial court accepted [GM's] argument that the criminal conduct of the two juveniles constituted an unforeseeable intervening act which the manufacturer * * * of the vehicle had no duty to guard against.

* * *

The role played by "foreseeability" in a negligence cause of action has proven to be a confusing one for courts grappling with questions of duty, negligence and proximate cause. * * * [I]n Ballard v. Uribe (1986) 41 Cal.3d 564, 715 P.2d 624, the California Supreme Court * * * caution[ed] lower courts against deciding fact–specific issues of foreseeability in the guise of determining whether the plaintiff has pleaded a valid cause of action. "[A] court's task—in determining 'duty'—is not to decide whether a *particular* plaintiff's injury was reasonably foreseeable in light of a *particular* defendant's conduct, but rather to evaluate more generally whether the category of negligent conduct at issue is sufficiently likely to result in the kind of harm experienced that liability may appropriately be imposed on the negligent party." [*Ballard* court's emphasis.]

The trial court's comments here in sustaining defendant's demurrer do not make clear whether it understood the limited nature of the foreseeability question before it. To the extent the court was focusing on the particular facts of this incident, *Ballard* makes clear it is an inappropriate basis for denying a plaintiff the opportunity to plead a cause of action. Moreover, it must be remembered that a defendant "may be liable if his conduct was a 'substantial factor' in bringing about the harm, though he neither foresaw nor should have foreseen the extent of the harm or the manner in which it occurred." Thus here, even if one could consider fact–specific foreseeability issues at the pleading stage, it is not necessary that GM anticipate that someone might throw a rock off a freeway overpass. Rather, in designing the Corvette's sunroof, it is only necessary that GM foresee the possibility that objects could fall from above a car and thus pose a danger to its occupants. (See Green v. Denney (1987) 87 Or.App. 298, 742 P.2d 639 (affirming judgment against auto manufacturer relating to freak accident where horse fell on top of car, collapsing roof).)

Meyering points out that objects can fall from trucks onto cars below; roadside signs frequently warn of the danger of falling rocks; indeed, the rock in question here could have been accidentally or negligently kicked off the overpass and onto a passing car. In addition, it may well be that the sunroof in question would provide inadequate protection to the car's occupants during rollover accidents. It is certainly a question of fact as to the extent of the risk posed by the sunroof's design and whether GM was negligent in failing to use stronger materials.

It may be, however, the trial court truly understood that fact–specific foreseeability was not an issue at the demurrer stage. The court may have reasoned—and GM certainly argues—that regardless of how foreseeable the risk of falling objects may be and how negligent GM may have been in failing to take account of that risk, policy considerations dictate a limitation on GM's liability for its negligence. In more familiar but perhaps less useful terms, GM claims it had no "duty" to guard against the criminal acts of third persons.[1]

* * * GM's argument anachronistically recalls a view long rejected by California courts as well as most other jurisdictions. "The view ... that an intervening criminal act is by its very nature a superseding cause ... is rejected by many courts and writers as an illogical and undesirable formula. They point out that in a large number of situations the very reason why the defendant's conduct is negligent is that it creates the risk of the particular intervening criminal act, and that it is absurd to invoke the very fact which establishes negligence to absolve the negligent person from liability.... The later California cases have fully accepted this theory as to both negligent and intentional intervening acts." See, e.g., Richardson v. Ham (1955) 44 Cal.2d 772, 285 P.2d 269 (lack of an ignition lock permits intoxicated persons to joyride in a 26–ton bulldozer); Bigbee v. Pacific Tel. & Tel. Co. (1983) 34 Cal.3d 49, 665 P.2d 947 (improper siting of a phone booth causes injury to caller when booth is struck by a drunk driver); Peterson v. San Francisco Community College Dist. (1984) 36 Cal.3d 799, 685 P.2d 1193 (untrimmed foliage

1. As the opinions of Judges Cardozo and Andrews in the venerable case of Palsgraf v. Long Island R. Co., (1928) 248 N.Y. 339,162 N.E. 99, illustrate, the concepts of "duty" and "proximate cause" are effectively interchangeable ideas addressing the identical issue: At what point do external policy considerations require that a concededly negligent defendant's liability be restricted? Having previously expressed our concerns with the "duty" rubric, we nonetheless employ that formulation as the lesser of two evils. * * *

provides hiding place for potential rapist); Isaacs v. Huntington Memorial Hospital (1985) 38 Cal.3d 112, 695 P.2d 653 (inadequate lighting and security contributes to shooting of doctor in hospital parking lot).

It is well established that manufacturers must design their products to perform in a reasonably safe manner. This obligation includes taking into account the possibility that foreseeable negligence or misconduct of the user or third persons may contribute to causing the injury. Illustrative of this principle and particularly relevant to the facts of this case is the Ninth Circuit Court of Appeals decision in d'Hedouville v. Pioneer Hotel Co. (9th Cir.1977) 552 F.2d 886. Plaintiff's decedent in *d'Hedouville* was killed in a hotel fire started by an arsonist. Plaintiff sued Monsanto Company, the manufacturer of the hotel carpet, for wrongful death alleging that the fiber in the carpet ignited readily, did not self–extinguish and contributed to the outbreak and rapid spread of the fire. Applying Arizona law, the Ninth Circuit affirmed a jury verdict in plaintiff's favor. Monsanto had argued, as does GM here, that the arsonist's criminal act constituted a superseding cause of the victim's death which cut off any liability on its part. Rejecting this argument, the Ninth Circuit observed that "[w]hile this appears to have been the rule stated in early Arizona cases, more recent decisions apply the general principle of foreseeability to intervening criminal acts." The court went on to explain that Monsanto could foresee the possibility of fires in buildings in which its carpeting was installed and had the obligation to design its product with these hazards in mind. * * *

The obligations of automobile manufacturers have been particularly well defined by case law. In what is perhaps the seminal case nationally on the issue, the Eighth Circuit Court of Appeals rejected GM's argument that it had no duty to design a car to withstand collisions because the intended purpose of an automobile is not to crash into other vehicles or objects. "This duty of reasonable care in design rests on common law negligence that a manufacturer of an article should use reasonable care in the design and manufacture of his product to eliminate any unreasonable risk of foreseeable injury. The duty of reasonable care in design should be viewed in light of the risk. While all risks cannot be eliminated nor can a crash–proof vehicle be designed under the present state of the art, there are many common–sense factors in design, which are or should be well known to the manufacturer that will minimize or lessen the injurious effects of a collision. The standard of reasonable care is applied in many other negligence situations and should be applied here." Larsen v. General Motors Corporation (8th Cir.1968) 391 F.2d 495, 503.

It is perhaps unnecessary to add that these principles apply regardless of whether the car is colliding with some other object or, as in this case, some other object is colliding with the car. * * *

* * *

Our conclusion does not suggest that an intentional criminal act can never be a superseding cause of injury. [GM refers] us to Restatement Second of Torts section 442B which [indicates that an intervening force will relieve a negligent actor of liability for resulting harm when] "the harm is intentionally caused by a third person and is not within the scope of the risk created by the actor's conduct." * * * The facts here do not present a similar issue. There is no suggestion that Meyering's juvenile assailants were intent on harming him, knew of the defective sunroof and deliberately took advantage of his vulnerability. It appears, rather, that the boys were engaged in reckless behavior * * * likely with no intent to cause personal injury. There is certainly no superseding cause on these facts which can be resolved as a matter of law.[4]

* * *

The judgment of dismissal is reversed. The trial court is directed to overrule GM's demurrer * * *.

FROEHLICH, ASSOCIATE JUSTICE, dissenting.

The majority here determines that a willfully tortious, criminal act which concurs with the antecedent negligence of another party is not a superseding cause of the resulting damage when the occurrence and the injury are foreseeable by the first actor in terms of noncriminal conduct. The majority * * * elects to expand the scope of tort liability in California * * *.

* * *

The majority cites and relies upon cases and authority which, I respectfully suggest, are inapposite. * * * Where one's conduct can specifically be anticipated to induce criminal conduct, he will be held to foresee it. * * * [This explains] Richardson v. Ham (lack of an ignition lock permits intoxicated persons to joyride in a 26–ton bulldozer). * * * Our case does not fit this category. Nothing General Motors did can be deemed to have induced or made more likely the subsequent tortious act of the rock thrower. Our record discloses no evidence suggesting the tortfeasor selected Meyering's car because it had a sunroof, or that he had some knowledge that it was a defective sunroof.

* * *

[Another] line of cases which is distinguishable is that which deals with superseding *negligence*, as opposed to superseding intentional or criminal acts. Typical of these is *Bigbee*, in which liability of the telephone company was found possible when the plaintiff, using its telephone booth, was injured by a drunk driver who ran into it. Although drunk driving may be a crime, its civil nature is essentially that of negligence. * * *

---

4. We wholeheartedly agree with the dissent that the facts of this case and our status as an intermediate appellate court do not call for the creation of expansive new theories of tort liability. Our point of disagreement is that we believe the result we reach is compelled by existing—indeed well–established—precedent. As a result, we eschew reliance on "enlightened" legal thought (see, e.g., Huber, Liability, The Legal Revolution And Its Consequences (1988)) which fervently exhorts a substantial change in the legal status quo because of perceived disastrous consequences caused by existing legal rules). * * *

The authority asserted by the majority to be definitively in point consists [principally] of *d'Hedouville*, which involved the liability of Monsanto Company for furnishing a hotel with flammable carpet. One of Monsanto's defenses was that the fire which damaged the plaintiffs was the result of arson, contending the arson was a superseding cause. The only portion of the lengthy opinion directed to the issue before us is the brief paragraph as follows:

> Monsanto argues that under Arizona decisions the criminal act of a third person constitutes a superseding cause as a matter of law. While this appears to have been the rule stated in early Arizona cases, more recent decisions apply the general principle of foreseeability to intervening criminal acts.

It is to be noted that this brief passage makes no reference to Restatement principles, nor does it cite any California cases. * * * [This was a federal court's interpretation of Arizona law, and it] should not be deemed controlling in that little or no consideration or discussion is devoted to the question, and the [Arizona] authority it cites does not support the broad proposition espoused.

* * *

If one is to go out of state, he will find considerable authority which supports the concept that criminality (absent the special circumstances set forth above) constitutes a superseding cause of damage. This authority is relatively current and certainly not an anachronism. * * *

* * *

* * * [T]he ruling of the majority is a departure from current law. * * * Saying this, the logical next question is "Why shouldn't we depart from current law?" Admittedly, there is no binding Supreme Court authority on the subject. Since the majority avers that it is simply applying existing law, it provides little by way of argument for its position. * * * [However the majority has effectively reached] a policy decision favoring recovery by plaintiffs from remote actors, increasing the potential scope of liability for manufacturers, and fostering claims and litigation. Is this the direction in which we are presently headed in the California judiciary? I think not, and therefore dissent from the policy decision implicit in the majority's opinion.

Whether plaintiffs' litigation potential vis–a–vis manufacturers of products should be increased or decreased is no doubt a matter of politics and philosophy, presumably best determined by the legislature. The function of an intermediate appellate court is, I contend, not to determine such philosophy but simply to reflect it. We have known periods of great expansion in the rights of plaintiffs. We are not now in one of those periods. * * * We should not now in the Court of Appeal be expanding grounds for liability in negligence * * *. The Supreme Court has [repeatedly] recognized * * * that litigation is not and cannot be the ultimate answer to all grievances. We are in a trend of restriction, not expansion, of litigation rights. This, I suggest, is in harmony with enlightened legal thought.[5]

* * *

Notes

1.   The California Supreme Court granted a writ of review. It did not reverse the Court of Appeal's decision, but it designated the Court of Appeal's opinion as "unpublished" and thus—under California practice—not citable as authority.

2.   *Liberalizing (or abolishing) the superseding cause doctrine.* The trend detected and relied on by the *Meyering* majority—toward liberalizing the doctrine of superseding cause—has been noted by other courts and observers, many of whom attribute it to the influence of tort law's wholesale shift into the regime of comparative fault. (We encountered the comparative-fault phenomenon in the *Piner* case in Chapter IV, supra p. 150. See also Chapters IX and XI, infra.) For example, Restatement (Third) of Torts: Liability for Physical Harm (Basic Principles) § 34, cmt. *c* (Tent. Draft No. 3, April 2003) states: "Just as comparative responsibility has * * * ameliorate[d] the harshness of contributory negligence, * * * the advent of comparative principles has reduced the role for superseding cause. * * * [T]he need for aggressive use of superseding cause to absolve a tortfeasor from liability has subsided in light of the * * * trend toward permitting comparative responsibility to be apportioned among * * * tortfeasors. Comparative responsibility permits liability to be apportioned among multiple tortfeasors * * * to take account of the causal relationship between each tortfeasor's conduct and the harm as well as the culpability of each tortfeasor." The court in Barry v. Quality Steel Products, 263 Conn. 424, 820 A.2d 258 (2003), took this idea to the limit, stating that in light of the adoption of comparative fault, "the doctrine of superseding cause no longer serves a useful purpose in our jurisprudence."

3.   *Further on the effects of the adoption of comparative fault.* In Reynolds v. Kansas Department of Transportation, 273 Kan. 261, 43 P.3d 799 (2002), a passenger in a car that crashed into a cow on a controlled-access highway sued the state highway department and showed that the department's negligently maintained fence allowed the cow to get onto the road. The jury found the cow's owner 45% at fault, plaintiff's host driver 20% at fault, and the defendant highway department 35% at fault. The court

---

5. See, for instance, Huber, Liability, The Legal Revolution and Its Consequences (1988) where it is persuasively argued that our system of determination of compensation for injuries through tort litigation is haphazard, poorly directed, excessively expensive, and generally detrimental to our competitive world position. Huber states at page 221:

Applied as it has been in recent years, open–ended tort law serves only as an engine of social destruction. Sometimes the effect is to alienate individuals from each other. The freedom of contract is

undermined, private bilateral deals are curtailed. Sometimes the effect is to alienate the individual from community and state. Each individual is issued his own quiver of claims against the state and the publicly risky activities it has sanctioned; the state strikes back with more and more paternalistic legislation to protect citizens willy–nilly from injury. The unchecked inflation of the nonnegotiable right to sue eventually undercuts a panoply of other freedoms.

* * *

rejected the department's argument that the escape of the cow was the sole proximate cause of the accident and made this startling pronouncement: "With the adoption of comparative fault, Kansas has moved beyond the concept of proximate cause in negligence." (Having said that, the court immediately backpedaled: "Intervening and superseding causes, which cut off liability for earlier negligence, are still recognized in extraordinary cases.")

4. *In a comparative fault system, can the plaintiff's negligent conduct still sometimes constitute a superseding (sole proximate) cause of the accident?* As we will see in Chapter IX, the essential aim of all comparative fault regimes is to abolish the contributory negligence doctrine, under which the victim's negligent conduct was a total bar to recovery. In a comparative fault regime, when a court says that the plaintiff should lose because his own conduct was a superseding cause (or the "sole proximate cause") of the accident, has it smuggled the contributory negligence doctrine back into the law? Judge Posner thinks so:

> [Arguing that the plaintiff's negligent conduct was the superseding or sole proximate cause of the accident is] a transparent effort to circumvent Indiana's comparative negligence statute, by relabeling contributory negligence as proximate cause and thereby using a victim's negligence to eliminate his cause of action rather than merely to reduce the size of the damages award to which he is entitled.

Justice v. CSX Transp., Inc., 908 F.2d 119, 124 (7th Cir. 1990). Dobbs, The Law of Torts § 196 (2000), tends to agree with Judge Posner but notes that the courts are divided on the question. Paul T. Hayden, Butterfield Rides Again: Plaintiff's Negligence as Superseding or Sole Proximate Cause in Systems of Pure Comparative Responsibility, 33 Loy. L.A. L.Rev. 887, 945 (2000), is an extensive study of the jurisprudence, concluding that the majority of courts will sometimes allow the plaintiff's negligent conduct to serve as a superseding cause that insulates a negligent defendant from liability and that this is a good thing whenever the plaintiff's fault "is truly extraordinary, overwhelming, or gross compared to that of the defendant."

5. *Intervening crimes and intentional torts.* The *Meyering* case was inherently difficult because of the perception that a criminal and intentionally tortious act (the juveniles' throwing of the chunk of concrete) had intervened between the defendant's negligent conduct (marketing a car with a weak roof) and the plaintiff's injury. As we will see in Galanti v. United States, infra p. 229, and in Section G of Chapter VI, infra p. 295, this is a problem that give the courts a great deal of trouble. The jurisprudence is chaotic. Compare Kitchen v. K–Mart Corp., 697 So.2d 1200 (Fla.1997), holding that K–Mart could be liable for selling a .22 rifle to a visibly drunk man who then used the weapon to intentionally shoot the plaintiff, with Buczkowski v. McKay, 441 Mich. 96, 490 N.W.2d 330 (1992), holding that K–Mart had "no duty" to avoid selling .410 ammunition to a visibly drunk man who then used the shells to intentionally shoot the plaintiff.

6. *Ad hoc no–duty rules.* The defendants in *Meyering* and *Hunley* fought hard to frame the dispositive issues in such a way as to call for determination by the judge rather than a jury. GM argued that it had no duty to guard against the risk that someone would throw concrete from an

overpass onto the sun roof of a Corvette. DuPont argued that it had "neither a duty to provide Hunley with personal protective equipment nor a duty to warn him that a psychotic break was a danger associated with visual exposure to a paint spill." From the viewpoint of the traditional analysis set out in Section A of this chapter, GM's argument was an attempt to convert a legal cause issue into a duty issue and DuPont's was an attempt to convert a breach issue into a duty issue. As we saw, neither of these arguments succeeded. But such arguments frequently do succeed. See Chapter VI, Section G, infra p. 295.

Chapter VI

THE DUTY ISSUE

A. INTRODUCTION: THE PRINCIPLE OF HEAVEN v. PENDER

As we saw in Section A of Chapter V, analysis of the negligence cause of action traditionally begins with the broad proclamation of Heaven v. Pender, supra p. 170, that anyone engaged in an activity that potentially places others at risk of physical harm has a duty to use to use reasonable care to minimize the risk. The law of most—perhaps all—states includes some version of the Heaven v. Pender principle. The versions range from the facially overbroad pronouncement that "[i]n Wisconsin, everyone has a duty to the whole world"[1] to the considerably more informative formulation that Michigan's law of negligence "imposes on every person engaged in the prosecution of any undertaking an obligation to use due care, [i.e.,] to so govern his actions as not to unreasonably endanger the person or property of others."[2] As we will see, the principle is subject to exceptions, but it has the useful practical meaning that "[i]n the usual run of cases, a general duty to avoid negligence is assumed, and there is no need for the court to undertake detailed analysis of precedent and policy" in order to conclude that a duty exists.[3]

Restatement (Third) of Torts: Liability for Physical Harm (Basic Principles) § 6(a) (Tent. Draft No. 2, March 2002), embraces the Heaven v. Pender principle, stating: "An actor ordinarily has a duty to exercise reasonable care when the actor's conduct poses a risk of physical harm." Comment *b* explains that this principle means that normally the existence–of–duty issue "does not require attention from the court;" in most cases, the existence of a duty of care may be assumed. Comment *d* provides two compelling justifications for the principle:

1. Miller v. Wal–Mart Stores, 219 Wis.2d 250, 580 N.W.2d 233, 238 (1998).

2. Doe v. Johnson, 817 F.Supp. 1382, 1386 (W.D. Mich. 1993).

3. Dobbs, The Law of Torts § 227, p. 578 n. 1 (2000) (quoting from Hamilton v. Accu–Tek, 62 F.Supp.2d 802 (E.D.N.Y. 1999).

One justification for imposing liability for negligent conduct that causes physical harm is corrective justice: imposing liability remedies an injustice done by the defendant to the plaintiff. An actor who permits [his] conduct to impose a risk of harm on others that exceeds the burden the actor would bear in avoiding that risk impermissibly ranks personal interests ahead of the interests of others. This, in turn, violates an ethical norm of equal consideration. Imposing liability seeks to remedy this violation.

Another justification for imposing liability for negligence is to give actors appropriate incentives to engage in safe conduct. The actor's adoption of appropriate precautions improves the overall welfare and thereby advances broad economic goals.

Seemingly at odds with the Heaven v. Pender principle is the frequently–encountered statement that "[i]n order for negligence liability to attach, the parties must have a relationship recognized by law as the foundation of a duty of care."[4] The idea that the existence of a duty of care depends on a relationship between tortfeasor and victim can be reconciled with the *Heaven* principle, but only by engaging in the redundancy that, under *Heaven*, the defendant (by engaging in an activity with the potential for harm to others) has created a relationship with those the activity foreseeably endangers. See Donoghue v. Stevenson, 1932 S.L.T. 317, 323 (House of Lords 1932) (Lord Atkin), in which the court held that the manufacturer of a bottle of ginger beer containing a decomposed snail should be liable to a sickened consumer whose friend had bought the beverage for her and explained:

> [I]n English law there must be, and is, some general conception of relations giving rise to a duty of care * * * The rule that you are to love your neighbour becomes in law, you must not injure your neighbour * * * Who, then, in law is my neighbour? The answer seems to be—persons who are so closely and directly affected by my act that I ought reasonably to have them in contemplation as being so affected when I am directing my mind to the acts or omissions which are called in question. This appears to me to be the doctrine of Heaven v. Pender * * *

The Heaven v. Pender principle is subject to at least two types of qualifications or exceptions. The first type comprises the group of general–category no–duty rules that are treated in Sections B through F of this Chapter. The second—consisting in courts' intermittent assertions of the authority to create new no–duty rules–is treated in Section G. These limitations on the Heaven v. Pender principle are not static. Limitations of the sort discussed in Section G are still very much in dispute. Those discussed in Sections C through F are fairly well settled, although they can be narrowed or broadened from time to time and place to place. The privity limitation discussed in Section B is largely vestigial, but it still has some force.

4. Huggins v. Citibank, N.A., 355 S.C. 329, 585 S.E.2d 275 (2003).

When a duty is found to exist, it is usually a duty to use reasonable care, but it can be a lesser or greater duty. In Section F we shall see that occupiers of land are often held to something less than the full duty of reasonable care. Common carriers are sometimes said to owe their passengers a duty of utmost care. See, e.g., Markwell v. Whinery's Real Estate, Inc., 869 P.2d 840 (Okla. 1994).

B. PRIVITY OF CONTRACT

At one time English law took the idea that the existence of a duty of care depended on the existence of a relationship between the defendant and the plaintiff more seriously than it came to be treated in Donoghue v. Stevenson. The principal manifestation of the relationship requirement was a doctrine of "privity of contract." That doctrine can be seen at work in Langridge v. Levy, 2 M. & W. 510, 50 E.R. 863 (1836), in which a young man was hurt by a defective gun that his father had bought for him. The court held the seller of the gun liable for fraud—he had lied about the identity of the gun's maker—but stated that negligence liability could not be imposed because the plaintiff could not show "a breach of a public duty [flowing from a recognized public calling such as that of surgeon or blacksmith] or a violation of a private right existing between himself and the defendant." In Winterbottom v. Wright, 10 M. & W. 109, 152 E.R. 402 (1842)—the seminal privity–of–contract case— the court held that the defendant's negligence in the performance of his contract with the owner of a mail coach to keep the coach in safe running condition could not serve as the basis for liability to a driver of the coach who was "lamed for life" when the coach collapsed. The *Winterbottom* court explained its ruling:

> There is no privity of contract between [defendant and plaintiff]; and if the plaintiff can sue, every passenger, or even any person passing along the road, who was injured by the upsetting of the coach, might bring a similar action. Unless we confine the operation of such contracts as this to the parties who entered into them, the most absurd and outrageous consequences, to which I can see no limit, would ensue. * * * By permitting this action, we should be working this injustice, that after the defendant had done everything to the satisfaction of [the coach's owner], and after all matters between them had been adjusted, and all accounts settled on the footing of their contract, we should subject them to be ripped open by this action of tort being brought against him.

As we will spell out in a bit more detail in Chapter XV, Section A, the privity–of–contract doctrine worked to insulate manufacturers of defective products from any responsibility to consumers who did not buy the product directly from the manufacturer. In MacPherson v. Buick Motor Co., 217 N.Y. 382, 111 N.E. 1050 (1916), Judge Cardozo effectively abolished the privity rule in the products–liability context. (Recall Judge Posner's inclusion of Winterbottom v. Wright among the no–duty rules that have "fallen by the wayside" in *Edwards*, supra p. 196 However, vestiges of *Winterbottom's* "privity" idea can still be found in other areas of negligence law. Consider the following case.

BUSH v. SECO ELECTRIC CO.

United States Court of Appeals, Seventh Circuit, 1997.
118 F.3d 519.

CUDAHY, CIRCUIT JUDGE.

The law of Indiana has long held that once an owner accepts a piece of construction work from an independent contractor, the owner takes full responsibility for it. The contractor's duty of care to a third party for personal injury thereby ceases, for the contractor and the third party are not in privity. And with the contractor's duty goes its liability as well. In embracing this "acceptance rule," Indiana has not been alone. In the related area of warranties in sales of personal property, American courts many years ago shed a requirement of privity between injured parties and manufacturers. MacPherson v. Buick Motor Co., [supra p. 218]. But, in the world of construction contracts, courts have been much slower to relax the privity strictures of the nineteenth–century common law.

Defendants SECO Electric Company and Jack Satkamp (collectively SECO) argue that the acceptance rule remains potent in Indiana and that it blocks any liability to plaintiff Jerri Bush. Bush was a temporary employee at an Indianapolis recycling plant owned by Rumpke Recycling, Inc. (Rumpke). The plant recycled aluminum cans; Bush's main job was "densifying" the cans inside the plant building. Delivery trucks would drop cans into a deep pit, and a giant conveyor contraption would pick them up and deposit them in a hopper. (Rumpke had hired SECO to install the wiring of the conveyor.) The conveyor sometimes failed to gather all the aluminum cans, which then needed to be cleaned up. The proper way to do this was to go down into the pit, pick the cans up, dump them in big garbage bins and haul the bins out. The safety protocol called for shutting off the conveyor with controls located outside the pit. A yellow safety guard was supposed to be fitted on the conveyor's mouth, making it impossible to feed cans into the conveyor. There was no emergency shut–off button actually in the pit.

Bush was picked to go clean the pit. Bush says she knew nothing of the safety protocol, and it was her first day on pit duty. She began shoveling cans onto the conveyor while it was still running. The safety guard was not on, apparently taken off to be cleaned or repaired. The conveyor snagged her clothes and Bush lost her arm.

* * *

SECO moved for summary judgment, raising the acceptance rule as its defense. That Rumpke had accepted the wiring job was not in dispute: the conveyor had been operating for four weeks when Bush was injured, and Rumpke's control over the conveyor was beyond doubt. Bush argued that the acceptance rule did not defeat her action, because she fitted into a narrow "humanitarian" exception. Under this exception, lack of privity could be overlooked if a contractor produced "a product or work in a condition that was dangerously defective, inherently dangerous or imminently dangerous such that it created a risk of imminent personal injury"—but mere negligence would not suffice. The absence of an emergency stop–button in the pit itself constituted such a condition, Bush argued. The district court thought not. Because SECO therefore owed no duty of care to Bush, the district court granted summary judgment to SECO. Bush appeals. * * *

While this appeal was awaiting oral argument, the Indiana Supreme Court in Blake v. Calumet Construction Corp., 674 N.E.2d 167 (Ind. 1996), recast the acceptance rule. In her briefs before this court, Bush forecast that the Indiana Supreme Court would overrule the privity–based acceptance rule for personal injuries in favor of a negligence standard rooted in foreseeability. In this, Bush was disappointed: the acceptance rule survives in Indiana.*

Yet in its explication of the "imminent personal injury" exception upon which Bush relied in the district court, *Blake* may have delivered what Bush seeks. *Blake* is peppered with words like "expectable," "reasonable," and "foreseeable," words alien to the privity analysis of the acceptance rule. In spirit, it seems, *Blake* looks to the granddaddy of negligence cases, *Palsgraf* [supra p. 183]. *Blake* goes so far as to remark upon the advantages of junking the acceptance rule in favor of a "*Palsgraf*–like foreseeability standard." Such a standard, *Blake* notes, would "obviate[] possible confusion caused by terms like 'acceptance' or 'imminently dangerous.' " Yet rather than trace this logic to its implicit conclusion, *Blake* in the end declines to set aside the acceptance rule.

So the acceptance rule survives; but in what form? For the humanitarian exception widens enough in *Blake* to re–shape the acceptance rule itself. Where a contractor hands over work "in a defective or dangerous state," "important considerations of deterrence and prevention militate in favor of imposing an ongoing duty of care." And *Blake* grounds this view on a foundation that is positively Palsgrafian: "The possibility of harm from the condition is foreseeable by the contractor." The spirit of *Palsgraf* is evident as well in *Blake's* elaboration of the humanitarian exception. The exception applies to contractors' work that is (1) dangerously defective, (2) inherently dangerous, or (3) imminently dangerous. *Blake* supplies definitions for each. Because the "inherently dangerous" sub–exception best applies to "dangerous activities such as blasting, rather than conditions or instrumentalities" (like SECO's wiring), we quote only the first and third definitions. SECO's wiring would be " 'dangerously defective' if the work is turned over in a condition that has a propensity for causing physical harm to foreseeable third parties using it in reasonably expectable ways." Or its work might be " 'imminently dangerous' if it 'is reasonably certain to place life or limb in peril.' "

* Not any more. See Peters v. Forster, 804 N.E.2d 736 (Ind. 2004). [Ed.]

In *Blake*, the defendant contractor had built a loading dock attached to a maintenance building. The contractor had not put up a guardrail. Wrapping up some work in the building, plaintiff Blake took a break mid–evening and exited onto the darkened loading dock. Stepping off the edge, Blake fell four feet to the concrete below and broke his hip. The trial court invoked the acceptance rule and granted summary judgment to the defendant contractor. The Court of Appeals affirmed. Equipped with the re–visited humanitarian exception, the Indiana Supreme Court decided that Blake should have survived summary judgment. "[T]he lack of a safety device on a darkened construction site," the *Blake* court held, "is enough to present a jury question on the loading dock's status as an imminently dangerous condition."

The district court decided against Bush under pre–*Blake* law. Whether Bush can surmount summary judgment under current Indiana law is puzzling. Maybe a reasonable jury could conclude that the absence of an emergency stop–button down in the pit was "reasonably certain to place life or limb in peril." We do not know. The acceptance rule has shifted enough to make extrapolating from the district court's decision little more than divination. We believe the district court must take a second look in light of *Blake*. Additional submissions might lead to summary judgment. And, if not, a trial would seem appropriate.

The opinion of the district court is vacated and this case remanded for further proceedings.

Notes

1. Even when the lack of privity is not the direct basis for a "no–duty" ruling, it can be an influential factor. For example, in Strauss v. Belle Realty Co., 65 N.Y.2d 399, 492 N.Y.S.2d 555, 482 N.E.2d 34 (1985), the court held that even though the ConEd Power Company was guilty of gross negligence in bringing about a massive 25–hour power failure in New York City (the blackout of 1977), the company's liability for injuries caused by the blackout was limited to persons with whom the company had a contractual relationship. Thus, the complaint of a tenant of a ConEd customer, who lost running water because of the blackout and then fell on darkened basement stairs while seeking an alternative water source, was properly dismissed by the lower court. The *Strauss* court stated that "while the absence of privity does not foreclose recognition of a duty, * * * [c]onsiderations of privity are not entirely irrelevant in implementing policy." 482 N.E.2d at 36. The court defined its policy goal as "extend[ing] defendant's duty to cover specifically foreseeable parties but at the same time [containing] liability to manageable levels." Id. at 37.

The privity concept also helps to account for the significant number of cases insulating physicians from liability for negligence in facilitating or failing to prevent their patients' infecting or otherwise harming others. See, e.g., McNulty v. City of New York, 100 N.Y.2d 227, 762 N.Y.S.2d 12, 792 N.E.2d 162 (2003) (doctors who treated a patient with infectious meningitis owed no duty of care to the patient's friend, who stuck close to the patient after the doctors led her to believe she was not at great risk of infection);

Schmidt v. Mahoney, 659 N.W.2d 552 (Iowa 2003) (physician who negligently told his epileptic patient that it was safe to drive a car had no duty to a person the patient injured in a car wreck during a seizure).

2. In reading *Bush,* were you surprised to see "the spirit of *Palsgraf* " working for a plaintiff?

C. DUTY TO ACT? NONFEASANCE vs. MISFEASANCE

"There is no distinction more deeply rooted in the common law and more fundamental than that between misfeasance and nonfeasance, between active misconduct working positive injury to others and passive inaction, a failure to take positive steps to benefit others, or to protect them from harm not created by any wrongful act of the defendant." Bohlen, The Moral Duty to Aid Others as a Basis of Tort Liability, 56 U.Pa.L.Rev. 217, 219 (1908). Calling the misfeasance/nonfeasance line "the most definite boundary of negligence law," Leon Green sought to explain the basis of the distinction:

> Broadly speaking no person is under a duty to another unless he has entered upon some course of conduct towards such other. As long as a person does nothing he comes under no duty imposed by law. This is one of the most dependable limitations upon duties * * *. [I]n the tort field at least, this power we call law is merely designed to *control* conduct and not to *compel* it. We have enough to do to keep our activities within control, without attempting to regulate the directions the latent energies of individuals should take.

Green, the Duty Problem in Negligence Cases, 28 Colum.L.Rev. 1014, 1026–27 (1928).

In the following cases and notes we will see the nonfeasance rule applied, challenged, and tested, and we will observe the courts struggling toward designing appropriate limits and exceptions to it. As announced by Professors Bohlen and Green, the rule is easy to understand and perhaps even to appreciate. But in application it is often controversial[1] and sometimes significantly complex. One recurrent complexity is that "the line between 'active misconduct' and 'passive inaction' is not easily drawn. The range of human conduct theoretically susceptible of tort consequence runs from the zenith of clearly affirmative misconduct (misfeasance) to the nadir of clear inaction (nonfeasance), but there exists an area of shadowland where misfeasance and nonfeasance coalesce." McNiece and Thornton, Affirmative Duties in Tort, 58 Yale L.J. 1272, 1272 (1949). Moreover, even when it is clear that the conduct in suit constituted nonfeasance, a case may present difficult questions

---

1. "Some of the decisions [holding no liability for nonfeasance] have been shocking in the extreme" and "revolting to any moral sense." Prosser and Keeton on Torts, § 56, pp. 375–76 (5th ed. 1984).

respecting the applicability of one or more of four loosely delineated exceptions to the nonfeasance rule.[2]

LACEY v. UNITED STATES

United States District Court, District of Massachusetts, 1951.
98 F.Supp. 219.

SWEENEY, CHIEF JUDGE.

* * * [T]he administrator of the estate of a pilot who lost his life in Massachusetts Bay after his plane had fallen into the water seeks to recover against the United States * * * by reason of the allegedly negligent failure of the Coast Guard to rescue his decedent. * * *

It is well settled common law that a mere bystander incurs no liability where he fails to take any action, however negligently or even intentionally, to rescue another in distress. [Plaintiff urges] here that the Coast Guard is charged by statute with the responsibility of saving lives at sea, and a civil tort liability for negligence is thereby created which would be otherwise non–existent. With this I cannot agree. The statute, 14 U.S.C.A. § 1 et seq., invokes a military discipline of rewards and punishments to promote the proper performance of their duties by Coast Guard personnel, but nowhere in the statute is there created a right to be rescued in the sense of an award of civil damages for the negligent failure of the Coast Guard to attempt to rescue a person in distress. It is not for the Court to create this right where such a novel tort liability is neither contemplated by the basic statute nor recognized by prior law. It is true that, while the common law imposes no duty to rescue, it does impose on the Good Samaritan the duty to act with due care once he has undertaken rescue operations. The rationale is that other would–be rescuers will rest on their oars in the expectation that effective aid is being rendered. Under this theory it is argued here that the Coast Guard is liable because it did undertake to rescue the deceased but negligently failed to reach [him] while [he was] still alive. That the Government does not come within the Good Samaritan rule is demonstrated by the fact that the complaint does not show that the Coast Guard's rescue attempt reached the stage where other would–be rescuers were induced to cease their efforts in the belief that the Coast Guard had

---

2. It is contemplated that the Restatement (Third) of Torts: Liability for Physical Harm (Basic Principles) will include a Chapter 7 dealing with the nonfeasance rule and its exceptions. That chapter is not yet available for citation or discussion. The treatment of the area in the Restatement (Second) of Torts is only somewhat helpful; it is vague at critical junctures and puzzlingly repetitious at others. For those who may be interested in trying to make sense of it, here is one way of organizing the Restatement (Second) treatment: Section 314 sets forth *the basic nonfeasance rule*. Sections 323, 324, and 324A treat what we will call the *volunteer exception*. Sections 314A and 314B set forth certain "special relations" between defendant and plaintiff that may generate an affirmative duty of care; we will call this the *relationship with victim exception*. Sections 321 and 322 treat the *prior conduct exception*. Sections 315 through 319 deal with the situation in which the plaintiff is injured by the affirmative conduct of a third person and set forth certain relationships between defendant and the third person that may generate an affirmative duty of care; we will call this the *relationship with perpetrator exception*.

the situation in hand. Since the deceased [was] in no way deprived of other available help by the Coast Guard operations, there is no tort liability on the Coast Guard for its allegedly negligent failure to save the deceased. * * *

[T]he Government's * * * motion to dismiss is allowed.

Notes

1. *No common law duty to rescue.* The cases holding that "the common law imposes no duty to rescue" constitute the most controversial application of the nonfeasance rule. Statutes in many European countries make it a misdemeanor to refuse assistance to a person in serious or mortal danger. See also Vt.Stat.Ann. tit. 12 § 519, which provides as follows:

(a) A person who knows that another is exposed to grave physical harm shall, to the extent that the same can be rendered without danger or peril to himself or without interference with important duties owed to others, give reasonable assistance to the exposed person unless that assistance or care is being provided by others.

(b) A person who provides reasonable assistance in compliance with subsection (a) of this section shall not be liable in civil damages unless his acts constitute gross negligence or unless he will receive or expects to receive remuneration. Nothing contained in this subsection shall alter existing law with respect to tort liability of a practitioner of the healing arts for acts committed in the ordinary course of his practice.

(c) A person who willfully violates subsection (a) of this section shall be fined not more than $100.00.

Note that this statute imposes no tort–law duty to rescue.

2. *Does the law need a nonfeasance rule?* The nonfeasance rule is controversial in applications like *Lacey*, but courts seem to regard it as fundamental. Wisconsin is unusual in not having such a rule. In Rockweit v. Senecal, 197 Wis.2d 409, 541 N.W.2d 742 (1995), the Rockweit family— father, mother, and 18–month–old Anthony—were camping at a proprietary campground. One night they were joined around their campfire by a number of friends, including Ann Tynan, a friend who was camping several sites away. Everyone eventually went to bed—Tynan was one of the last—and nobody put out the fire. The next morning, Anthony Rockweit slipped away from his mother and slid into the fire pit, sustaining severe burns. One of the defendants was Tynan—allegedly negligent for going to bed without dousing the fire—and the lower court determined that she should share in the responsibility for the child's injuries. In reviewing that decision, the Wisconsin Supreme Court said that a jury could find that Tynan's conduct was negligent and that it was a legal cause of Anthony's injuries. It also said that Tynan's argument—that because her conduct was pure nonfeasance, she owed no duty of care—was "incorrect" and "without merit." The court—which has frequently stated that Wisconsin has no nonfeasance rule—explicitly held that Tynan owed a duty of care and breached it. But it then turned to a "public policy" analysis that led it to stress a number of factual considerations—Tynan's conduct was an "omission," she did not select the fire site nor start the fire, she never had any custody or control

over Anthony, she "did not create the hazard," she did not "assume any responsibility to maintain the fire pit"—in support of the conclusion that Anthony's injury was "too remote from any alleged negligence on [Tynan's] part to impose liability."

3. *The volunteer exception to the nonfeasance rule.* The "Good Samaritan rule"—unsuccessfully invoked by the *Lacey* plaintiff—is one of several well recognized exceptions to the nonfeasance rule. The Good Samaritan exception is sometimes also called the "volunteer" exception or the "undertaking" exception. The essence of it is that one who volunteers to assist another thereby undertakes a duty of reasonable care not to make the situation worse. This exception led to liability for a failed Coast Guard rescue mission in United States v. Gavagan, 280 F.2d 319 (5th Cir.1960), on the finding that reliance on the Coast Guard's effort had induced the friends and families of the imperiled fishermen to forego private efforts "which, in all probability, would have been successful."

The thrust of subsection (b) of the Vermont duty–to–rescue statute is to change the Good Samaritan rule by relieving the volunteer rescuer of the duty of reasonable care to avoid worsening the situation and substituting a more lenient duty to avoid grossly negligent conduct. Many states have so-called "Good Samaritan statutes" that—without imposing any duty to rescue—seek to encourage it by giving voluntary rescuers similar protection.

SCHENK v. MERCURY MARINE DIVISION

Court of Appeals of Michigan, 1986.
155 Mich.App. 20, 399 N.W.2d 428, lv. to appeal denied (April 1, 1987).

MOES, JUDGE.

Plaintiff appeals as of right from the October 10, 1984, order granting defendant Robert Langeland's motion for summary judgment in this negligence action. * * *

For some period of time prior to October 12, 1981, Venessa Vilcans, plaintiff's decedent, and defendant Robert Langeland were involved in a very close social relationship. Langeland was married; decedent was a widow. Langeland can be best generally termed an experienced outdoorsman. Decedent was not.

Langeland, for some fourteen years, went duck hunting with a friend, Donald Verberkmoes. Such a hunting trip was scheduled by Langeland and Verberkmoes for October 12, 1981, on the Muskegon River. Decedent invited herself along on the duck hunting trip and advised Langeland that she had purchased a duck stamp, a federal stamp, and low hip waders for the hunting trip.

Early on the morning of October 12, 1981, the three met at a restaurant and went to the boat launching site. The boat and motor were owned by Verberkmoes and were carried to the site on Langeland's truck. The boat, with the motor mounted on it, was placed in the water. Langeland put on his full length water waders, but removed them for decedent to use, decedent's hip waders being too short. The waders were insulated and had adjustable shoulder straps. A leather belt was placed around the top of the waders decedent was wearing. Langeland used another pair of full–length waders. The high waders were utilized because the river had overflowed and the water was high. Verberkmoes got into the boat first and went to the rear. Langeland next went to the middle of the boat and decedent pushed the boat from shore and jumped in.

Verberkmoes attempted to start the motor. It stalled and more gas was given. The motor started fast. Langeland told Verberkmoes to shut it off or they would sink. Upon the motor being stopped, the front end of the boat went down and water came in and filled the boat.

Langeland told everyone to remain where they were. Verberkmoes tried, however, to step past Langeland. The weight in the boat was shifted and all three fell into the water. The weight of Langeland's waders caused him to go under water; however, he cut the wader straps and surfaced. Verberkmoes and decedent were heard some fifteen to twenty feet distant. Verberkmoes and decedent drowned.

Plaintiff claims on appeal that the trial court erred by holding that no legal duty existed between decedent and Langeland as a matter of law. Plaintiff alleged that Langeland, in allowing decedent to use his full–length waders, owed decedent a duty of care and further alleged that it was breached in four ways: he allowed decedent to wear waders that were too large; he failed to warn and instruct her of the proper and safe use of waders; he failed to warn and instruct her of the proper use of a life jacket; and he failed to act when decedent complained that the waders were cumbersome and clumsy.

* * *

* * * It is a general rule of common law that a person has no duty to render assistance to another if he is not liable for the initial injury in the absence of a special relationship.

Further, every person who engages in the performance of an under-taking has an obligation to use due care or to act so as not to unreasonably endanger the person or property of another.

It is not enough that an individual simply acts. The act must have been one to render service to another. Smith v. Allendale Mutual Ins. Co., 410 Mich. 685, 303 N.W.2d 702 (1981). In the instant case, Langeland simply loaned more appropriate waders to replace the waders which had been purchased and were being worn by decedent. This cannot be considered the rendering of a service or an undertaking which would have been performed for Langeland's [sic] benefit. It was a reasonable act under the situation that existed and did not increase any danger accepted by the decedent. It was a gratuitous act in which defendant did not assume an obligation or render a service. No special relationship existed requiring Langeland to be more affirmative in his actions and requiring Langeland to instruct decedent. It was a simple act of allowing another person to utilize a more appropriate piece of water equipment.

To impose a duty would fly in the face of all commonly accepted codes of conduct.

* * *

Affirmed.

Kelly, Presiding Judge, dissenting.

I respectfully dissent on this close and difficult legal issue. * * *

[T]he law imposes upon every individual "a duty to refrain from conduct of a character likely to injure a person with whom he comes in contact * * *, and to use his property so as not unreasonably to injure others." 57 Am.Jur.2d, Negligence, § 37, p. 385. In Sponkowski v. Ingham County Road Comm., 152 Mich.App. 123, 393 N.W.2d 579 (1986), a group of Michigan State University students planned a hayride event at stables located in Mason, Michigan. Four or more privately owned automobiles set out from East Lansing, with one driver leading the way. The leader, who was familiar with the route and who was a named defendant in the action, lost control of his vehicle at a sharp turn and ended up in a ditch. The car behind him also left the road at the same curve and struck a tree which resulted in the decedent's death. The trial court concluded as a matter of law that defendant owed no duty to the plaintiff's decedent and thus dismissed plaintiff's action for failure to state a claim. We reversed, holding that "where a person voluntarily assumes the performance of a duty (i.e., to lead another motor vehicle to an unfamiliar destination), he is required to perform it carefully, not omitting to do what an ordinary prudent person would do in accomplishing the task."

In this case, plaintiff alleges in his second amended complaint that defendant, an experienced fisherman, advised the decedent that her own waders were inadequate, loaned her oversized waders of his own, and secured them around her waist with a belt. Plaintiff alleges that defendant knew decedent was inexperienced in the outdoors and knew that her use of these waders was dangerous. Plaintiff further alleges that defendant never warned the decedent of the risks associated with the use of the waders nor advised her of the need for a life jacket. Although there may be difficulties in proving this case, particularly with regard to the causation element * * *, it is clear to me that plaintiff has sufficiently pled a cause of action in that defendant loaned decedent an item of personal property knowing that decedent's use of that property under the circumstances loaned was dangerous. In effect, he put on her waders which were a trap if she fell in the water. I conclude that the complaint should have survived defendant's motion for summary judgment * * *.

Notes

1. *Was Langeland's allegedly negligent conduct nonfeasance, or was it misfeasance?* Judging from the way the majority opinion paraphrased the argument on appeal, the plaintiff's complaint may not have been entirely clear on the theory of the case. But surely the most straightforward view

would take the plaintiff as asserting that Langeland was negligent in equipping Vilcans with ill–fitting waders without taking adequate precautions. This is the interpretation that the dissenter eventually came to in the third–to–last sentence of his opinion. On this view, *Schenk* should have been treated as a garden–variety negligent entrustment case. (Recall Schneider v. Esperanza Transmission Co., supra p. 202.)

2. *The application of the volunteer exception in Schenk.* Having chosen to treat the case as a nonfeasance case, the court then took the plaintiff as asserting two exceptions to the nonfeasance rule. In rejecting the applicability of the volunteer exception, the court cited Smith v. Allendale Mutual for the proposition that the exception is inapplicable in Michigan unless the volunteer's conduct was intended solely for the recipient's benefit. *Smith* arguably does support that proposition, but it certainly does not compel it. The *Smith* decision—and the story leading up to it—is worth explaining. Here is the chronology:

(a) Industrial workers are typically precluded by workers' compensation statutes from suing their employers in tort. Workers' compensation benefits are relatively modest as compared to damages in tort. Consequently injured workers often pursue what is called "third party liability," meaning tort liability of some non–employer entity whose culpable conduct may have contributed to the injuries. A line of Michigan cases held workers' compensation insurers liable for negligent safety inspections of insured employers' premises on the basis of the volunteer exception to the nonfeasance rule. See, e.g., Ray v. Transamerica Ins. Co., 10 Mich.App. 55, 158 N.W.2d 786 (1968).

(b) The *Ray* line of cases was legislatively overruled in 1972 by M.C.L.A. § 418.827(8), providing:

> The furnishing of, or failure to furnish, safety inspections or safety advisory services incident to providing workmen's compensation insurance ... shall not subject the insurer ... to third party liability for damages for injury, death or loss resulting therefrom.

(c) Then came *Smith*, which can best be understood as driven by the need to plug a loophole inadvertently left open by the legislature. The court in *Smith* upheld JNOV on behalf of a *fire* insurer whose inspections in a feed mill failed to detect fire hazards that eventually caused an explosion, killing three workers and seriously hurting three others. The court based its holding on the nonfeasance rule, stating: "The law does not impose a duty on insurers to inspect the premises of their insureds, although such an obligation may be undertaken." The workers' argument that in the case at hand the obligation *was* undertaken was rejected with the following explanation:

> It is not enough that the insurer acted. It must have undertaken to render services to another. Its acts do not constitute such an undertaking unless it agreed or intended to benefit the insured or its employees by the inspections. * * * [The volunteer exception] does not apply to an actor following a self–serving course of conduct.

3. *The application of the "relationship with victim" exception in Schenk.* Restatement (Second) of Torts §§ 314A and 314B list the following

"special relations" as potentially giving rise to a duty of affirmative care on the part of the first–named in each pair: common carrier–passenger; inn-keeper–guest; occupier of land–public invitee; custodian–ward or charge; and employer–employee. The Restatement (Second) "expresses no opinion as to whether there may not be other relations which impose a similar duty." The Langeland–Vilcans relationship did not fit neatly into any of the Restatement's listed categories. But the Michigan Supreme Court had gone well beyond the Restatement list in Farwell v. Keaton, 396 Mich. 281, 240 N.W.2d 217 (1976), in holding that the sixteen–year–old social companion of an eighteen–year–old boy left injured and semi–conscious after a fight with a gang the two boys had encountered "knew or should have known of the peril Farwell was in and could render assistance without endangering himself [and thus] had an affirmative duty to come to Farwell's aid." Note that in concluding that "[n]o special relationship existed requiring Langeland to be more affirmative in his actions," the *Schenk* court seemingly ignored *Farwell*.

GALANTI v. UNITED STATES

United States Court of Appeals, Eleventh Circuit, 1983.
709 F.2d 706, cert. denied, 465 U.S. 1024, 104 S.Ct. 1279, 79 L.Ed.2d 683 (1984).

MORGAN, SENIOR CIRCUIT JUDGE.

Vivian W. Galanti, plaintiff–appellant, brought this action against the government in the District Court for the Northern District of Georgia under the Federal Tort Claims Act (FTCA), 28 U.S.C. § 1346(b), claiming that her husband, Isaac N. Galanti, died as a result of negligence committed by an agent of the Federal Bureau of Investigation (FBI). The district court concluded that no actionable negligence exists under the pertinent facts and granted the government's motion to dismiss for failure to state a claim. We affirm the district court's order for the following reasons.

The facts giving rise to appellant's claim are undisputed.[1] In October of 1978, Isaac N. Galanti and Roger Dean Underhill were shot to death on a secluded tract of undeveloped property in Fulton County, Georgia. Galanti was interested in purchasing the property from Underhill, and the two men were inspecting it at the time of their deaths. Unknown to Galanti, Underhill was a key witness in the government's investigation into the criminal activity of Michael G. Thevis. Thevis, a convicted felon, had escaped from federal custody six months earlier and was still a fugitive at the time of the murders. He was apprehended a month later and eventually convicted in federal court of violating Underhill's civil rights by having him murdered, along with the innocent bystander Galanti, in order to prevent Underhill's testimony in the government's case.

For several months before his death, Underhill traveled a great deal and kept a low profile, although he frequently contacted F.B.I. Agent

---

1. Our statement of the facts is taken from a detailed stipulation which the parties prepared and submitted to the district court.

Paul V. King, Jr. King was in charge of the Thevis investigation and knew that Thevis had made earlier attempts to kill Underhill. King considered Underhill to be in extreme danger at all times. For this reason, the government arranged for Underhill to enter a witness protection program in which Underhill would be given a permanent, new identity with government assistance, but Underhill refused to enter the program until he sold the undeveloped property in Fulton County. He ignored advice to retain a real estate agent and insisted on personally handling the sale of his property. In the week preceding his death, Underhill repeatedly visited the property even though King advised him of the needless danger involved. On the night before the murders, Underhill called and informed King that he would be showing the property the next day to Galanti who had answered a newspaper advertisement. King made no attempt to contact and warn Galanti of the potential danger, nor did he arrange for surveillance of the property. This is the conduct which formed the basis of appellant's suit in the district court. She claimed that King's failure to warn or protect Nicholas Galanti against a specific, foreseeable danger was a negligent act and the proximate cause of her husband's death.[2]

This action was necessarily filed in federal court under the provisions of the FTCA since appellant seeks to hold the government liable for the negligence of its employee, but both parties agree that Georgia law controls the negligence issue. In Georgia there are four essential elements of a negligence action: (1) A legal duty to conform to a standard of conduct raised by the law for the protection of others against unreasonable risks of harm; (2) a breach of this standard; (3) a legally attributable causal connection between the conduct and the resulting injury; and (4) some loss or damage flowing to the plaintiff's legally protected interest as a result of the alleged breach of the legal duty. It is the first element with which we are concerned in this appeal. The court below concluded that under no circumstances could appellant establish a legal duty owed by King to Nicholas Galanti, and accordingly granted the government's motion to dismiss for failure to state a claim. Appellant vigorously challenges this conclusion and relies on a large number of state and federal cases, some very recent, in order to support her argument. After a careful review of the various claims and the relevant law, we find that the district court's order must be affirmed.

The general rule in Georgia is that one has no duty to warn or protect another person from a foreseeable risk of harm simply because of one's knowledge of the danger. In other words, the mere foreseeability of injury to another person does not of itself create a duty to act. This rule is not applicable in three distinct factual situations, however, and appellant contends that each of the three exceptions is present here. First, the duty to protect or warn against danger will arise if the defendant has in

---

2. Mrs. Galanti also argued below that the government was negligent in allowing Thevis to escape from custody, but the district court concluded that this theory of relief was not properly included in the pleadings and refused to consider it. Appellant does not challenge that decision in this appeal.

any way taken an affirmative step to create the danger. In the recent case of United States v. Aretz, 248 Ga. 19, 26, 280 S.E.2d 345, 350 (1981), the Georgia Supreme Court held that "where one by his own act, although without negligence on his part, creates a dangerous situation, he is under a duty to remove the hazard or give warning of the danger so as to prevent others from being injured where it is reasonably foreseeable that this will occur." In that case, the United States Army provided one of its contractors with mistaken information concerning the appropriate storage classification of explosive materials. The Army later realized the mistake, but failed to communicate it to the contractor, and the materials exploded causing injury and death to several of the contractor's employees. The Georgia court, upon certification from the Fifth Circuit Court of Appeals, held that the Army's failure to inform the contractor of the change in classification was a breach of duty which arose when the Army mistakenly classified the materials in the first place. The *Aretz* decision relied heavily on an earlier Georgia case, Hardy v. Brooks, 103 Ga.App. 124, 118 S.E.2d 492 (1961), where the defendant hit and killed a cow without negligence while driving his car on a public road. The Georgia Court of Appeals held that the defendant's act of killing the cow created the duty to act in the face of foreseeable danger to other drivers on the road. Therefore, *Aretz* and *Hardy* stand for the proposition that a duty to warn or protect a third person from danger will arise if the defendant affirmatively contributes to the creation of the danger. In the present case, FBI Agent King did nothing to create the foreseeable danger. He was merely aware of the risk to Galanti and for whatever reason chose not to act. Georgia law does not hold him legally responsible for knowledge alone.

A second exception to the general rule concerns the defendant's failure to properly exercise his ability to control the foreseeably dangerous instrument. The most recent Georgia decision involving this principle is Bradley Center, Inc. v. Wessner, 250 Ga. 199, 296 S.E.2d 693 (1982). In that case, a private mental hospital released one of its patients despite its ability to keep the patient confined, and despite its knowledge that the patient might cause harm to a specific third party. Under these facts the Georgia court held that the hospital owed a legal duty to the third party even in the absence of the usual doctor–patient privity. Appellant argues that *Bradley* stands for the proposition that one must always warn or protect a third person from a foreseeable criminal act, but this argument is incorrect. *Bradley*, and other cases like it, hold that the legal duty arises only if the defendant failed to exercise his ability to control the potential criminal. This is not the situation we are faced with here. Appellant has not alleged, and the relevant facts do not support the theory, that FBI Agent King or his associates had the ability and failed to control Michael Thevis.[5] Thevis was a wanted fugitive beyond King's control during the relevant time period, and thus King had no duty to warn or protect Galanti merely because of the danger posed by Thevis' known criminal intent.

5. See note 2, supra.

Finally, law enforcement officials may have the legal duty to warn or protect against danger if they have voluntarily assumed or incurred that duty to a specific individual. However, this duty, if at all applicable here, would extend only to Roger Dean Underhill, and he repeatedly ignored warnings and refused protection. Appellant cannot cite to any Georgia statute or case which charges law enforcement officials with the duty to warn or protect members of the general public simply upon learning of a possible danger.

We recognize that the result in this case may appear harsh because Galanti's death very likely would have been avoided if King had chosen to act rather than to remain silent. Nonetheless, Georgia law did not impose any legal duty on King to act on behalf of Galanti, and therefore appellant's complaint did not establish a viable claim. For this reason, the order of the district court is affirmed.

Notes

1. The Federal Tort Claims Act is the principal waiver of the federal government's "sovereign immunity" from tort liability. It is set forth in Chapter XII, infra pp. 475.

2. *Identifying the arguments in Galanti.* The court's sentence at footnote signal 2 might be read to indicate that Mrs. Galanti was arguing that King's negligent conduct was misfeasance rather than nonfeasance. The second–to–last paragraph of the opinion indicates that she was also urging the relationship–with–victim exception to the nonfeasance rule. But it is reasonably clear that her main hopes were (a) the exception illustrated by *Aretz* and *Hardy* and (b) the exception illustrated by *Bradley Center.*

3. *The prior conduct exception. Aretz* and *Hardy* applied a principle sometimes called the "prior conduct" exception to the nonfeasance rule. As phrased in Restatement (Second) of Torts § 321(1), its thrust is that "an actor [who] does an act, and subsequently realizes or should realize that it has created an unreasonable risk of causing physical harm to another, * * * is under a duty to exercise reasonable care to prevent the risk from taking effect."

It is useful to see this exception as containing two ingredients: the defendant's prior conduct, which is not itself being asserted as a basis for liability; and the defendant's subsequent failure to take steps to deal with a danger that has arisen out of the prior conduct, which failure *is* being asserted as the basis for liability. (Another way to say this: the plaintiff in a prior conduct case is not claiming that the original conduct was actionable misfeasance, but that its existence makes the later nonfeasance actionable.)

The government's prior conduct in *Galanti* included allowing Thevis to escape from custody, but let's assume that the court's footnote 2 takes that conduct completely out of the case. The other prior conduct candidate was King's use of Underhill as an informant. Why didn't that conduct suffice to bring the plaintiff under the prior conduct exception? In pondering this question, consider notes 4 and 6 below.

4. *Informative applications and rejections of the prior conduct exception.* The prototypical application of the prior conduct exception holds the

motorist who non–negligently creates a highway obstruction to a duty of reasonable care to try to alleviate the problem. Cases like *Hardy,* holding such motorists liable for negligently failing to remove the obstruction or take other reasonable steps to protect highway users, are numerous. However, even in this situation, some courts have seemed inclined to keep the exception narrow by refusing to apply it when the defendant's contribution to the creation of the highway obstruction was in some fashion indirect or attenuated. For example, in Dubus v. Dresser Industries, 649 P.2d 198 (Wyo.1982), two W.S. Hatch Company trucks became disabled on a wind-swept highway during a blizzard. A short time later a Dresser Industries pickup had to swerve to avoid colliding with the Hatch trucks and spilled boxes of drill bits from the bed of the pickup onto the highway. All three drivers left the scene without clearing away the drill bits. Plaintiff came along shortly thereafter, stopped to investigate the tangle of vehicles, and tripped and fell on one of the drill bits. The court held that the Dresser driver had a duty of reasonable care to clear away the drill bits, but upheld summary judgment on behalf of the Hatch drivers, stating that "the record [does not] reflect that Hatch is responsible for the dropping and scattering of the boxes from the Dresser vehicle." See also Buchanan v. Rose, 138 Tex. 390, 159 S.W.2d 109 (1942), holding that a trucker was free to drive away and do nothing about a bridge that broke down under the weight of his vehicle because the bridge was in such bad shape that "it is hardly fair to say that the [trucker] created the dangerous situation."

5. *The relationship–with–perpetrator exception.* The principle applied in *Bradley Center* exposes the defendant to liability on the basis of the relationship between the defendant and the person who was the active and immediate cause of the harm. "Generally a [defendant] does not have a duty to control the conduct of another [X] to prevent harm to [the plaintiff] unless a special relationship [between the defendant and X] is shown. The special relationships [between defendant and X] giving rise to such a duty are parent–minor child, master–servant, possessor of land–licensee, and a person in [voluntary or official] charge of another with dangerous propensities, as listed in sections 315 through 319 of the Restatement (Second)."[3]

This exception to the nonfeasance rule enabled the plaintiffs to survive defendant's motion for summary judgment in Texas Home Management, Inc. v. Peavy, 89 S.W.3d 30 (Tex. 2002), in which a dangerous 17–year–old committed a murder while on authorized home leave from defendant's facility that was supposed to be maintaining court–mandated control over the mentally retarded youngster. But the courts seem grudging with this exception and show no tendency to move beyond the Restatement (Second) list. See, e.g., Daniel v. Webb, 110 S.W.3d 708 (Tex.App. 2003) (woman had no duty to keep her obviously dangerous 92–year–old grandfather from driving his car); Remsburg v. Montgomery, 376 Md. 568, 831 A.2d 18 (2003) (man who accompanied his 27–year–old son during a deer hunt had no duty to supervise even though he had told his son to "shoot the first thing that moves").

---

3. Ventura v. Picicci, 227 Ill.App.3d 865, 169 Ill.Dec. 881, 592 N.E.2d 368, 369 (1992).

6. *Responsibility for others' crimes and intentional torts. Galanti* was an inherently difficult case for the same reason that *Meyering*, supra p. 208, was: courts do not feel confident in their handling of lawsuits (increasingly prevalent) in which crime victims seek to pin responsibility for the results of a crime on someone other than the criminal. In such cases the arguments for liability can often be strong. But in any case asserting that the defendant should be held liable for his negligence in failing to prevent or guard against another's crime or intentional tort, if the issue is at all close the judge will be inclined to characterize the defendant's conduct as nonfeasance rather than misfeasance and to construe any potentially applicable exceptions to the nonfeasance rule pretty narrowly.

We take up this problem again in Section G, infra p. 295.

7. *An advocacy perspective.* Plaintiffs seem fairly often to mischaracterize their cases. In *Schenk*, supra p. 225, the plaintiff may have acquiesced in a nonfeasance characterization of the case when the argument for a misfeasance characterization was strong. In Ventura v. Picicci, 227 Ill.App.3d 865, 169 Ill.Dec. 881, 592 N.E.2d 368 (1992), a mother whose adult son habitually engaged in violent and crazy behavior let him live with her, bought him cocaine and a gun, and let him keep ammunition in the house. When the man eventually shot his girlfriend, the girlfriend sued the mother, evidently treating the case as a nonfeasance case and relying principally or solely on the relationship–with–perpetrator exception. The complaint was dismissed.

In Lauer v. City of New York, 95 N.Y.2d 95, 711 N.Y.S.2d 112, 733 N.E.2d 184 (2000), the City Medical Examiner (ME) wrongly diagnosed the death of a three–year–old as a homicide and so noted on the autopsy report and death certificate. The police suspected the child's father and immediately began investigating and harassing him. A month or two later the ME discovered his mistake—the child had died of a ruptured brain aneurysm, not a beating—but the ME notified no one, and the police investigation of the father continued for another couple of years before a newspaper expose finally brought the truth to light. The father, whose life was completely ruined, sued the City (as vicariously liable for the ME's negligent conduct). Because of a doctrine of governmental immunity, the ME's original mistake was not actionable, so the lawsuit necessarily focused on the ME's subsequent failure to let the police know as soon as the mistake was discovered. A divided court exonerated the city, holding that the complaint should be dismissed. From reading the several opinions in the case, it appears that the plaintiff relied principally on the relationship–with–victim exception (perhaps on the view that the nature of the ME's office generated that kind of relationship with the family of the murdered child). The prior conduct exception does not seem to have been emphasized.

The introductory note to this Section warned that the exceptions to the nonfeasance rule are loosely delineated, and by now you are probably convinced. But trying to keep them separated is usually worth the effort. Consider Zylka v. Leikvoll, 274 Minn. 435, 144 N.W.2d 358 (1966). In winter darkness at 30 degrees below zero, Leikvoll, who owned and operated a wrecker service, was using his wrecker to push Traphagan's disabled car. A vehicle driven by Bounds came along and collided with Traphagan's right front fender. Other traffic piled up, and eventually plaintiff, a pedestrian, was struck by a car. The jury found that Leikvoll was not negligent respecting the Traphagan–Bounds collision but that he was negligent thereafter in not doing a better job of lighting and flagging the scene. Leikvoll argued that he was entitled to a directed verdict because "his position was that of a volunteer and * * * [t]hus * * * unless his conduct increased the danger to plaintiff, he is not liable." Wrong, said the court; "Leikvoll was a participant in the creation of the first accident * * *, not * * * a volunteer but * * * one called upon to exercise reasonable care, either to remove the hazard or give adequate warning to others." Translation: The court saw through Leikvoll's attempt to characterize the case against him as confined to the volunteer exception. In the court's view, the proper characterization was the prior conduct exception.

D. MENTAL AND EMOTIONAL HARM

A defendant held liable for an intentional tort will usually be required to compensate for attendant emotional suffering, even in the absence of physical injury. Furthermore, when the defendant has caused a bodily injury compensable under negligence law, emotional pain is a recognized element of damages. In the latter case, the emotional suffering damages are often said to be "parasitic" to the physical injury.

The present section addresses the courts' treatment of negligently–inflicted emotional suffering that is not parasitic to a compensable physical harm. The movement of the law has been from a rule prohibiting recovery toward cautious recognition of some kinds of emotional suffering claims. The law on emotional injuries varies from state to state, but the Pennsylvania cases in this section illustrate a typical pattern.

Note that abolition of the broad no–duty rule for emotional injuries does not mean that such injuries will be treated identically with physical harms. Virtually all courts recognize a need for some special restrictions for non–physical injuries.

BOSLEY v. ANDREWS

Supreme Court of Pennsylvania, 1958.
393 Pa. 161, 142 A.2d 263.

BELL, JUSTICE.

Defendant's cattle strayed onto plaintiffs' farm and injured their crops, for which the jury gave plaintiffs a verdict of $179.99. Mrs. Mary Louise Bosley, the wife–plaintiff, sought to recover damages for a heart disability which resulted from her fright and shock upon being chased by a Hereford bull owned by defendant. The bull did not strike or touch plaintiff, and plaintiff suffered no physical injury. The Superior Court sustained the entry of a nonsuit. * * *

* * *

[T]he evidence does not show that [the bull] got any nearer to Mrs. Bosley than approximately 25 feet. Plaintiff collapsed on the ground and had an attack of coronary insufficiency—shortness of breath, pain in her chest and an insufficiency of blood flowing into the artery into the heart. * * *

* * *

The rule is long and well established in Pennsylvania that there can be no recovery of damages for injuries resulting from fright or nervous shock or mental or emotional disturbances or distress, unless they are accompanied by physical injury or physical impact.

In the leading case of Koplin v. Louis K. Liggett Co., 322 Pa. 333, 185 A. 744 [1936], plaintiff claimed damages because she became nauseated by the presence of a centipede in the spoon with which she was eating her soup, and was made sick for several weeks. This Court denied recovery * * *.

In Morris v. Lackawanna & Wyoming Valley Railroad Co., 228 Pa. 198, 77 A. 445 [1910], plaintiff claimed damages for a miscarriage resulting from a nervous shock occasioned by the electric car in which she was riding *bumping* over the track at an open switch. This Court denied recovery * * *.

In Ewing v. Pittsburgh, C. & St. L. Ry. Co., 147 Pa. 40, 23 A. 340, 14 L.R.A. 666 [1892], plaintiff's statement of claim averred that by a collision on defendant's railroad which occurred through the negligence of defendant's employees, defendant's cars were derailed and thrown against plaintiff's dwelling and she was thereby subjected to great fright, fear and nervous distress, became sick and disabled and was unable to attend to her usual work and duties. A demurrer to the statement of claim was sustained * * *.

In Fox v. Borkey, 126 Pa. 164, 17 A. 604 [1889], plaintiff was husking [corn] with her husband. An explosion occurred which was caused by defendant's blasting; the earth trembled and dirt blew over them as if it were hail. Plaintiff fell to the ground, trembling all over with shock; she became very nervous and had heart trouble * * *. The Court denied recovery.

In Potere v. City of Philadelphia, 380 Pa. 581, 112 A.2d 100 [1955], a contractor and the city were held jointly liable for a cave–in of a city street as the result of which plaintiff suffered physical injuries and a severe shock to his nervous system which was diagnosed as an anxiety neurosis. The Court said:

> It has been well established that in the absence of physical injury or physical impact, mental or emotional distress is not the subject of legal redress. However, where, as here, a plaintiff sustains *bodily injuries,* even though trivial or minor in character, *which are accompanied by fright or mental suffering directly traceable* to the peril in which the defendant's negligence placed the plaintiff, then mental suffering is a legitimate element of damages.

* * *

Plaintiff cites a number of decisions of this Court to support her claim but fails to realize that in those cases where recovery was allowed for nervous shock, *the nervous shock was accompanied by physical injuries,* and that all of her cases recognized and reiterate the above mentioned well settled rule. What plaintiff is really asking us to do is to review and change the rule which has been so long and clearly established by our cases * * *.

To allow recovery for fright, fear, nervous shock, humiliation, mental or emotional distress—with all the disturbances and illnesses which accompany or result therefrom—where there has been no physical injury or impact, would open a Pandora's box. * * * [A]ny one of a dozen * * * every–day events can cause or aggravate fright or nervous shock or emotional distress or nervous tension or mental disturbance. Such an event, if compensable, may cause normal people, as well as nervous persons and persons who are mentally disturbed or mentally ill, to honestly believe that the sudden and unexpected event caused them fright or nervous shock or nervous tension with subsequent emotional distress or suffering or pain or miscarriage or heart attack, or some kind of disease. * * * For every wholly genuine and deserving claim, there would likely be a tremendous number of illusory or imaginative or "faked" ones. Medical science * * * could not prove that these could not have been caused or precipitated or aggravated by defendant's alleged negligent act.

We have considered all of the contentions of the plaintiffs but find no merit in them.

The judgment of the Superior Court is affirmed * * *.

Musmanno, Justice, dissenting.

* * *

The great fear of the Majority seems to be that if we should allow the plaintiff in this case to submit her case to a jury, and, incidentally, *that is all she is seeking,* the courts would be besieged with "faked" cases. * * *

But are our courts so naive, are they so gullible, are they so devoid of worldly knowledge, are they so childlike in their approach to realities that they can be deceived and hoodwinked by claims that have no factual, medical, or legalistic basis? If they are, then all our proud boasts of the worthiness of our judicial system are empty and vapid indeed.

The Majority's apprehension that if we should allow the instant case to go to a jury for factual determination, the Courts would be engulfed in a tidal wave of lawsuits, is to look upon a raindrop and visualize an inundation. Many jurisdictions now permit recovery where physical disablement tortiously caused is not made manifest through visible trauma, and I have seen no report that in those States the Courts are awash in trumped–up cases. * * *

* * *

Notes

1. The rule permitting recovery for emotional suffering only if it was "accompanied by physical injury or physical impact" does not insist that the physical injury or impact cause the emotional harm. For example, in the *Potere* case discussed by the *Bosley* majority, the plaintiff suffered a sprained ankle and a bruised elbow when his truck fell into a 19–foot–deep hole in the street. These were indisputably physical injuries. He also suffered a much more serious "anxiety neurosis", which clearly resulted from the fall and not from the physical injuries. Recovery for the anxiety neurosis was allowed.

2. At the same time it was clear that physical injuries *caused by* the emotional stress did not qualify. Mrs. Bosley had a heart ailment, and the plaintiffs in *Koplin, Morris, Ewing,* and *Fox* got physically sick. None was permitted recovery.

3. What exactly was required to constitute an *impact* under the "physical injuries or impact" rule? Mrs. Bosley fell to the ground; the plaintiff in *Fox* was showered with dirt falling "as if it were hail"; neither was good enough. What if Mrs. Bosley had run into a tree while fleeing the bull, and then fallen to the ground with an emotionally induced heart ailment? What if she had run into a tree, breaking her nose, and then had the emotionally induced heart ailment?

NIEDERMAN v. BRODSKY

Supreme Court of Pennsylvania, 1970.
436 Pa. 401, 261 A.2d 84.

ROBERTS, JUSTICE.

Appellant, Harry Niederman, alleges that on November 4, 1962 he was walking with his son at the corner of 15th and Market Streets in Philadelphia. At that time * * * appellee was driving a motor vehicle in a reckless and negligent manner as a result of which the automobile skidded onto the sidewalk and destroyed or struck down a fire hydrant, a litter pole and basket, a newsstand and appellant's son, who at that time was standing next to appellant. Almost immediately after this destructive path was cut by appellee's car, appellant claims that he suffered severe chest pain and that upon examination in the hospital, where he was confined for five weeks, appellant was diagnosed to have sustained acute coronary insufficiency, coronary failure, angina pectoris, and possible myocardial infarction. Consequently, appellant sought recovery from appellee for both these severe disabilities and the accompanying shock and mental pain.

Appellant's complaint was reluctantly dismissed on preliminary objections for failing to state a cause of action under the "impact rule" which provides that there can be no recovery for the consequences of fright and shock negligently inflicted in the absence of contemporaneous impact. * * *

Today we decide that on the record before us, appellant may go to trial and if he proves his allegations, recovery may be had from a negligent defendant, despite the fact that appellant's injuries arose in the absence of actual impact. * * * By our holding today Pennsylvania proceeds along the path recently followed by our neighboring jurisdictions and removes this ancient roadblock to appellant's recovery.

* * *

An analysis of the prior case law indicates that there have been three basic arguments which in the past would have defeated appellant. The first deals with medical science's difficulty in proving causation between the claimed damages and the alleged fright. The second involves the fear of fraudulent or exaggerated claims. Finally, there is the concern that such a rule will precipitate a veritable flood of litigation.

* * * While we agree that [the first argument might once] have been an appropriate conclusion because of the lack of sophistication in the medical field * * *, it would presently be inappropriate for us to ignore all of the phenomenal advances medical science has achieved in the last eighty years. * * *

* * *

The logical invalidity of this objection to medical proof can be demonstrated further by noting that the rule has *only* been applied where there is absolutely no impact whatsoever. Once there is even the slightest impact, it has been held that the plaintiff can recover for any damages which resulted from the accompanying fright, even though the impact *had no causal connection* with the fright–induced injuries. [The court here quoted *Potere*. See note 1 after *Bosley*, supra p. 237.]

It appears completely inconsistent to argue that the medical profession is absolutely unable to establish a causal connection in the case where there is no impact at all, but that the slightest impact (e.g., a bruised elbow and sprained ankle in *Potere*) suddenly bestows upon our medical colleagues the knowledge and facility to diagnose the causal connection between emotional states and physical injuries. * * *

Finally, even if we assume *arguendo* that a great deal of difficulty still remains in establishing the causal connection, this still does not represent sufficient reason to deny appellant an *opportunity* to prove his case to a jury. There is no reason to believe that the causal connection involved here is any more difficult for lawyers to prove or for judges and jurors to comprehend than many others which occur elsewhere in the law. * * *

The second major objection includes the fear of fictitious injuries and fraudulent claims. * * *

The charge that fraudulent claims will arise is not unique to this Commonwealth. Every court that has been confronted with a challenge to its impact rule has been threatened with the ominous spectre that an avalanche of unwarranted, trumped–up, false and otherwise unmeritorious claims would suddenly cascade upon the courts of the jurisdiction. The virtually unanimous response has been that (1) the danger of illusory claims in this area is no greater than in cases where impact occurs and that (2) our courts have proven that any protection against such fraudulent claims is contained within the system itself—in the integrity of our judicial process, the knowledge of expert witnesses, the concern of juries and the safeguards of our evidentiary standards.

* * *

The last argument urged by the proponents of the impact rule is that: "If we permitted recovery in a case such as this, our Courts would be swamped by a virtual avalanche of cases for damages for many situations and cases hitherto unrecoverable in Pennsylvania." However, it is our view that this argument is currently refuted on two grounds. First, it is not at all clear that the flood of litigation has occurred in states without the impact rule. * * *

Secondly, and more compelling * * * is the fundamental concept of our judicial system that any such increase should not be determinative or relevant to the availability of a judicial forum for the adjudication of impartial individual rights. "It is the business of the law to remedy wrongs that deserve it, even at the expense of a 'flood of litigation'; and it is a pitiful confession of incompetence on the part of any court of justice to deny relief upon the ground that it will give the courts too much work to do." Prosser, Intentional Infliction of Mental Suffering: A New Tort, 37 Mich.L.Rev. 874 (1939). * * *

* * *

We today choose to abandon the requirement of a physical impact as a precondition to recovery for damages proximately caused by the tort in only those cases like the one before us where the plaintiff was in personal danger of physical impact because of the direction of a negligent force against him and where plaintiff actually did fear the physical impact. Since appellant's complaint alleges facts which if proven will establish that the negligent force was aimed at him and put him in personal danger of physical impact, and that he actually did fear the force, this case must proceed to trial.

The order of the Court of Common Pleas of Philadelphia County is reversed and appellee's preliminary objections are dismissed.

BELL, CHIEF JUSTICE, dissenting.

The Majority too often forget that an emotionally appealing or heart–rending claim often produces bad law and sets a dangerous precedent.

* * *

The majority Opinion commits three tremendous and grievous errors in overruling Pennsylvania's "impact rule." The first regrettable and disastrous error is that they open Pandora's famous Box, out of which will flow a multiplicity of trespass suits for personal injuries and/or diseases. These will include the most fictitious or false or exaggerated claims that the imagination can conceive * * *.

The second major error of the Majority is that they not only substitute a "medical guessing game" for Pennsylvania's clear and definite and well–established "impact rule," but add a "Judicial guessing game." Few writers and few States can agree on a clear and definite formula for recovery, and the Majority itself cannot formulate a clear, specific, definite and boundarized rule or standards for recovery in this so–called "impact" field, which the Majority now abolish. * * *

The third major error of the Majority is that they deal another fatal or nearfatal blow to stare decisis. Once again a majority of the present Supreme Court has cavalierly buried or ignored the basic principle and the fundamental precept upon which the House of Law was built and maintained. Upon this Rock of Gibraltar, all Judges and all public officials, as well as all the people of Pennsylvania, can see and know and rely on their respective rights, their powers, their duties, their obligations and limitations. It is regrettable to be compelled to say that a decision of the present Court of Pennsylvania is good "for this day and this train only." What a catastrophe, and what a mockery of Law and of Justice!

* * *

Notes

1. When judges change the law by moving from no–duty rules toward legal cause treatment of particular issues, the stated justifications are usually much like those of the *Niederman* majority. And the objections to such movement are likewise similar from area to area.

2. What if Mr. Niederman had pleaded that his emotional suffering resulted from fear and anguish over the injuries to his son, standing right beside him, rather than fear for his own safety? See the following case.

SINN v. BURD

Supreme Court of Pennsylvania, 1979.
486 Pa. 146, 404 A.2d 672.

Nix, Justice.

At issue in this appeal is the vexing and complex question of when a plaintiff should be allowed to recover damages for negligently caused mental trauma. The specific question presented for our review is whether the trial court properly sustained appellee's demurrer to the fourth count of appellant's complaint in which she sought to recover damages for physical and mental injuries incurred when she saw her minor daughter struck and killed by an automobile, although the plaintiff herself was not within any zone of personal physical danger and had no reason to fear for her own safety. * * *

* * *

The averred facts are as follows. Appellant JoAnne Marie Sinn lived with her husband and two minor children in Elizabeth Township, Allegheny County. On June 12, 1975, at approximately 5:53 p.m., the deceased, Lisa Sinn, and her sister, Deborah, were standing by the Sinn's mail box located alongside the Greenock–Buena Vista Road, approximately 36 feet from the nearest intersection. An automobile operated by the appellee struck Lisa and hurled her through the air, causing injuries which resulted in her death. Deborah was not struck by the vehicle, although it narrowly missed her. Appellant witnessed the accident from a position near the front door of her home. * * * The fourth count was brought by appellant for damages she sustained from the emotional stress of witnessing her daughter's death. * * *

* * *

Since the *Niederman* decision, experience has taught us that the zone of danger requirement can be unnecessarily restrictive and prevent recovery in instances where there is no sound policy basis supporting such a result. It has unquestionably not been effective in every instance of assuring that one may "seek redress for every substantial wrong." The restrictiveness of the zone of danger test is glaringly apparent where it is allowed to deny recovery to a parent who has suffered emotional harm from witnessing a tortious assault upon the person of his or her minor child. A majority of the commentators and a growing number of jurisdictions have considered this problem in recent years and have concluded that it is unreasonable for the zone of danger requirement to exclude recovery in such cases.

This new awareness of the unfairness of the zone of danger requirement in these cases is based upon the implicit acceptance that the emotional impact upon a parent witnessing the killing of a minor child is at least as great and as legitimate as the apprehension that is inspired by a plaintiff being personally within the zone of danger. * * *

* * *

In an attempt to still the concerns of those troubled by "the fear of unlimited liability" the Supreme Court of Hawaii [in Leong v. Takasaki, 55 Haw. 398, 520 P.2d 758 (1974), which allowed recovery by a 10–year–old boy who saw his stepgrandmother struck and killed by an automobile] suggested the limiting of recovery "to claims of serious mental distress." We believe this is a reasonable response to the concern. * * *

The *Leong* court attempted to achieve an objective standard by defining serious mental distress as being properly found where a reasonable person "normally constituted, would be unable to adequately cope with the mental stress engendered by the circumstances" of the event. Such a test focuses upon the situation producing the emotional stress and requires it to be [of] a nature that would be likely to produce a response in a person of average sensitivities. In this determination factors such as the context in which the trauma occurred, the development of physical ramifications, and the duration and severity of the emotional distress are available to make the judgment an objective—as opposed to a subjective—one.

* * *

[One of the policy arguments against bystander recovery has been the difficulty of reasonably circumscribing the area of liability.] This issue raises the question of the extent to which bystander recovery will be permitted. We are confident that the application of the traditional tort concept of foreseeability will reasonably circumscribe the tortfeasor's liability in such cases. Foreseeability enters into the determination of liability in determining whether the emotional injuries sustained by the plaintiff were reasonably foreseeable to the defendant.

[Dillon v. Legg, 68 Cal.2d 728, 441 P.2d 912 (1968), is the seminal case in this area. In determining that a mother who saw her daughter struck and killed by an automobile should be allowed to recover], the California Supreme Court identified three factors determinative of whether the injury to the plaintiff [in such a case] was reasonably foreseeable: (1) whether plaintiff was located near the scene of the accident as contrasted with one who was a distance away from it; (2) whether the shock resulted from a direct emotional impact upon plaintiff from the sensory and contemporaneous observance of the accident, as contrasted with learning of the accident from others after its occurrence; [and] (3) whether plaintiff and the victim were closely related, as contrasted with an absence of any relationship or the presence of only a distant relationship. In elaborating upon these factors, the court stated:

> The evaluation of these factors will indicate the *degree* of the defendant's foreseeability: obviously defendant is more likely to foresee that a mother who observes an accident affecting her child will suffer harm than to foretell that a stranger witness will do so. Similarly, the degree of foreseeability of the third person's injury is far greater in the case of his contemporaneous observance of the accident than that in which he subsequently learns of it. The defendant is more likely to foresee that shock to the nearby, witnessing mother will cause physical harm than to anticipate that someone distant from the accident will suffer more than a temporary emotional reaction. All these elements, of course, shade into each other; the fixing of obligation, intimately tied into the facts, depends upon each case.

> In light of these factors the court will determine whether the accident and harm was *reasonably* foreseeable. Such reasonable foreseeability does not turn on whether the particular defendant as an individual would have in actuality foreseen the exact accident and loss; it contemplates that courts, on a case–to–case basis, analyzing all the circumstances, will decide what the ordinary man under such circumstances should reasonably have foreseen. The

courts thus mark out the areas of liability, excluding the remote and unexpected.

* * *

* * * Since we have determined that a tortfeasor's liability for mental distress is not to be denied solely because the plaintiff was beyond the zone of physical danger, we must examine whether the injuries sustained by appellant were reasonably foreseeable. It is clear that appellant's injuries were of a nature reasonably foreseeable under the circumstances alleged. Where the bystander is a mother who witnessed the violent death of her small child and the emotional shock emanated directly from personal observation of the event, we hold as a matter of law that the mental distress and its effects is a foreseeable injury.[21]

* * *

ROBERTS, JUSTICE, dissenting.

* * * The depth and inconsolable nature of a parent's loss at the death of a child is unique in human experience. And where that death is caused by another's irresponsible act, it is not unexpected that parents turn to the law to seek redress for the harm done to them. * * * Yet * * * the law must recognize that not every human loss arising out of another's conduct constitutes a legal injury for which compensation shall be available.* * *

* * *

The central problem this kind of action brings before the courts is not that of the genuineness of the emotional distress, but that of rationally limiting defendant's liability. The opinion of Mr. Justice Nix disingenuously would have us believe that today we need not consider whether it is possible to limit recovery solely to plaintiff's class. If, however, there is no principled means of distinguishing this plaintiff from any other, then to decide her case is to decide the question the majority claims is not before us. One can say that question is not before us only by assuming its answer.

Mr. Justice Nix asserts that he sufficiently limits liability by narrowing recovery to "foreseeable injuries." But what constitutes a foreseeable injury is the conclusion of legal analysis, not its principal tool. Indeed there is remarkable disagreement about how to distinguish the "foreseeable" from the "unexpected." In Massachusetts one who does not witness an accident to a third party may still suffer foreseeable emotional distress from learning of the death. In Hawaii, such injuries are not foreseeable. In Connecticut, seeing an accident will foreseeably cause

---

21. * * * We need not here consider the case where the mother is notified of the accident by another. Nor do we consider the situation where the relationship between the plaintiff–bystander and the accident victim is more remote. These are questions which may properly be left to another day. Jurisprudentially, the remote and unexpected can best be excluded by reaching these issues on a more appropriate record.

emotional distress, while hearing one will not. In California, witnessing a negligent stillbirth does not create a foreseeable injury, while coming upon an already injured victim may.

In Rhode Island a mother may recover, but not a close personal friend. In Arizona, anyone who was a close friend of the victim may suffer a foreseeable injury. In Hawaii, not every one who is close will suffer a foreseeable injury, but a step–grandson's emotional distress is foreseeable. This variety of rules "limiting" recovery is eloquent testimony that there is no natural non–arbitrary way to limit liability for this injury.

* * *

Mr. Justice Nix's foreseeable injury "test," adopted from *Dillon,* predicates recovery upon plaintiff's (1) witnessing an accident, (2) close–up (3) in which a "close" relative is injured. This test, ostensibly simple, will produce monumental problems both of application and fair limitation. If recovery is extended in the present case, can the law close its eyes to the emotional distress of bystanders who recently witnessed the traumatic amputation of a young woman's hand by a subway car? Does the majority's "rule" give us any principle at all in the following situation? Three siblings get off a bus. Two attempt to cross the street. The third begins to walk away from them down the block. A moment later he hears screeching car brakes, screams and one of his siblings yelling, "My God, Jim is dead." Does the brother have a foreseeable injury? Is there any way to judge whether his emotional distress "resulted from a direct emotional impact upon the plaintiff from the sensory and contemporaneous observance of the accident" or from "learning of the accident from others after its occurrence?" How many steps down the street distinguish immediate observation from indirect learning? * * *

* * *

Notes

1. The California Supreme Court's *Dillon* decision has been so influential that the uninjured bystander problem is also often called the Dillon v. Legg problem.

2. Some of the Pennsylvania bystander cases after Sinn v. Burd are described in the following case.

ARMSTRONG v. PAOLI MEMORIAL HOSPITAL

Superior Court of Pennsylvania, 1993.
430 Pa.Super. 36, 633 A.2d 605, appeal denied, 538 Pa. 663, 649 A.2d 666 (1994).

CIRILLO, JUDGE.

In this appeal we are asked to consider whether the trial court erred when it ruled that a jury award of $1,000 on a claim of negligent infliction of emotional distress warranted a new trial on the damages question alone and whether the trial court erred when it refused to enter a judgment *non obstante veredicto* (j.n.o.v.). On both questions, we reverse.

As she was dressing her young son for a birthday party one morning, Dawn Armstrong received a telephone call from Paoli Memorial Hospital, informing her that her husband had been in an accident and asking her to come to the hospital.

The hospital had summoned Mrs. Armstrong because a critically injured accident victim named Thomas Armstrong had been brought in unconscious by ambulance. Following a hospital policy to notify the next–of–kin as quickly as possible, an emergency room employee asked information for a telephone number of Thomas Armstrong in Chester. Based on that information, she called Dawn Armstrong.

Once at the hospital, Dawn Armstrong met with a neurosurgeon and examined X–rays of a man with a crushed cranium. She was not allowed to see the patient. Only after she had been at the hospital for more than an hour did her sister see the accident victim's driver's license. Then, it was clear the accident victim was not Dawn Armstrong's husband, Thomas *J.* Armstrong, but Thomas *H.* Armstrong, also of Chester. Dawn Armstrong testified that when she heard the injured man was not her husband, "I just lost it. I urinated, defecated, and I just lost it completely."

As a result of the misidentification, Dawn Armstrong testified she suffers from depression, nightmares, insomnia and unreasonable fears about the safety and whereabouts of her husband and son for which she has undergone psychological counseling.

The Armstrongs filed suit against Paoli Memorial Hospital, alleging negligent infliction of emotional distress, intentional infliction of emotional distress and asking for compensatory and punitive damages. The count of intentional infliction of emotional distress and the request for punitive damages were dismissed by the trial judge at the close of testimony. Only the question of negligent infliction of emotional distress went to the jury. The claims for intentional infliction of emotional distress and punitive damages were not revived in post–trial motions. In response to post–trial motions the trial court entered a single order granting a new trial as to damages, calling a verdict of $1,000 "inadequate, indeed supremely embarrassing," and denying the hospital a j.n.o.v.

* * *

Not every wrong constitutes a legally cognizable cause of action. Lubowitz v. Albert Einstein Med. Center, 424 Pa.Super. 468, 472, 623 A.2d 3, 5, (1993) (false report of exposure to AIDS is not a legally cognizable injury). The law cannot be expected to compensate for every minor psychic shock incurred in the course of everyday living. Not every loss constitutes a legal injury for which compensation is available.

The fundamental question underlying this appeal is whether Pennsylvania recognizes an independent tort of negligent infliction of emotional distress.

* * *

The tort of negligent infliction of emotional distress has evolved almost exclusively in the context of those who observe injury to close family members and are as a consequence of the shock emotionally distressed. To state a cause of action for negligent infliction of emotional distress the plaintiff must demonstrate that she is a foreseeable plaintiff and that she suffered a physical injury as a result of the defendant's negligence.

Physical injury must be averred to sustain a cause of action for negligent infliction of emotional distress. See Covello v. Weis Markets, Inc., 415 Pa.Super. 610, 610 A.2d 50 (1992), appeal denied, 533 Pa. 644, 622 A.2d 1376 (1993), (policeman who was unable to extricate a child from a trash compactor failed to allege physical harm to himself); Abadie v. Riddle Memorial Hospital, 404 Pa.Super. 8, 589 A.2d 1143 (1991) (demurrer sustained for failure to state a cause of action when plaintiff failed to allege physical harm from a raucous hospital staff birthday celebration while she was being treated); Wall by Lalli v. Fisher, 388 Pa.Super. 305, 565 A.2d 498, allocatur denied, 526 Pa. 636, 584 A.2d 319 (1990) (mother who witnessed a dog bite her child failed to aver physical injury to herself); Banyas v. Lower Bucks Hospital, 293 Pa.Super. 122, 437 A.2d 1236 (1981) (plaintiff who was charged with murder after hospital records were altered to blame him for a death and to conceal malpractice failed to aver physical harm and, thus, stated no cause of action for negligent infliction of emotional distress).

The requirement that physical harm must accompany emotional distress to state a cause of action is based on the Restatement (Second) of Torts § 436A. Temporary fright, nervous shock, nausea, grief, rage, and humiliation if transitory are not compensable harm; but, long continued nausea or headaches, repeated hysterical attacks or mental aberration are compensable injuries. This court applied the Restatement standards to a case in which the plaintiff averred "headaches, shaking, hyperventilation, nightmares, shortness of breath, lack of control over the bowels, and tightening of the muscles in the neck, back and chest" and found that she had stated a cause of action for negligent infliction for emotional distress when her employer wrongfully coerced her to enter an abusive substance abuse program. Crivellaro v. Pennsylvania Power and Light, 341 Pa.Super. 173, 491 A.2d 207 (1985). Relying on Comment c to § 436A, a panel of this court held that "symptoms of severe depression, nightmares, stress and anxiety, requiring psychological treatment, and * * * ongoing mental, physical and emotional harm" sufficiently stated physical manifestations of emotional suffering to sustain a cause of action. Love v. Cramer, 414 Pa.Super. 231, 606 A.2d 1175 (1992). Cases which the Crivellaro court collected from other jurisdictions cite depression, nightmares, nervousness, insomnia and hysteria as physical symptoms warranting recovery.

In this case, Armstrong's allegation of loss of continence when she learned the accident victim coupled with her claim of depression, nightmares and insomnia meet the requirement of allegation of physical injury.

While physical injury is necessary to recovery, it is not sufficient. Armstrong must still demonstrate that she was a foreseeable plaintiff towards whom the hospital acted negligently.

The requirement that a plaintiff allege physical injury is intrinsic to the question of who is a foreseeable plaintiff. The original test for whether a tortfeasor was liable for the emotional distress of another was the "impact rule." There was no recovery for emotional disturbance unless it was accompanied by physical injury or physical impact. The impact rule yielded to a zone of danger test in *Niederman* [supra p. 238]. When *Niederman* 's "zone of danger" rule became unworkable, Pennsylvania adopted the foreseeability test of Sinn v. Burd [supra p. 241.]

* * *

* * * Since Sinn v. Burd, the debate has centered on the meaning of "sensory and contemporaneous observance." In Yandrich v. Radic, 495 Pa. 243, 433 A.2d 459 (1981), the state supreme court held that a father who arrived on the accident scene after his son had been taken to the hospital had not stated a cause of action. Five years later the court reached the same conclusion in Mazzagatti [v. Everingham, 512 Pa. 266, 516 A.2d 672 (1986)] regarding a mother who arrived on the scene minutes after the accident and saw her child's body in the street. *Mazzagatti,* 512 Pa. at 280, 516 A.2d at 679. The court reasoned that where the close relative is not present at the scene of the accident, but instead learns of the accident from a third party, the close relative's prior knowledge of the injury to the victim serves as a buffer against the full impact of observing the accident scene. By contrast the relative who contemporaneously observes the tortious conduct has no time in which to brace his or her emotional system. The negligent tortfeasor inflicts upon this bystander an injury separate and apart from the injury to the victim.

In Brooks v. Decker, 512 Pa. 365, 516 A.2d 1380 (1986), our Supreme Court held that a father who followed an ambulance to the scene of an accident and saw his injured son in the street failed to state a cause of action. And, in Bloom v. Dubois Regional Medical Center, 409 Pa.Super. 83, 597 A.2d 671 (1991), this court denied recovery to a husband who found his wife hanging by her neck in a hospital room, allegedly due to the failure of the hospital and her doctor to treat her suicidal tendencies. The panel held that the husband had not witnessed the tortious conduct, only its aftermath.

The next year, a panel of this court allowed recovery by a woman whose mother died in her arms after a doctor failed to diagnose or treat a serious heart ailment. The daughter had taken her mother for treatment and was present when the doctor was dismissive of the woman's symptoms. Love v. Cramer, supra (Cirillo, J., dissenting). This court has also allowed a wife to recover when she saw a speeding vehicle heading for her husband's car, heard the collision, and immediately realized her husband had been struck. Neff v. Lasso, 382 Pa.Super. 487, 555 A.2d 1304 (1989). Most recently, this court *en banc* allowed recovery for negligently inflicted emotional distress to a mother who was standing at the head of a supermarket checkout line near a plate glass window when her children were terribly injured by a drunken driver just outside the window. Krysmalski v. Tarasovich, 424 Pa.Super. 121, 622 A.2d 298 (1993) (Cirillo, J., dissenting).

Thus, the impact rule became the zone of danger test, *Niederman,* supra, and finally the three–part test of Sinn v. Burd, supra. In the evolution, the change was not in the need to allege physical harm but in the expansion of the proximate cause of the harm. Originally the law required that the harm be caused by the impact; today we recognize that the shock of apprehending an injury to a loved one can cause physical manifestation of emotional disturbance.

In the case at hand, Dawn Armstrong fails to meet the bystander test of Sinn v. Burd because she was not related to the accident victim and she did not have a contemporaneous perception of the accident. She posits her theory of recovery on a separate and independent tort, that which was allegedly committed when she was mistakenly summoned to the hospital.

Only two appellate cases in Pennsylvania have held that the question of negligent infliction of emotional distress in a context other than bystander recovery should go to the jury. In Stoddard v. Davidson, 355 Pa.Super. 262, 513 A.2d 419 (1986), the question was whether there was sufficient "impact" to allow recovery when the plaintiff was emotionally distressed after he ran over the body of a woman whom the defendant killed and left lying in the road. The plaintiff alleged that his distress arose when he had to hold a cover over the corpse for three hours during the police investigation of the victim's death. The panel, with one concurrence and one dissent, found sufficient impact alleged to allow a jury to decide if there was negligent infliction of emotional distress.

In the second case, *Crivellaro,* supra, the question was whether an employee who was coerced by her employer into entering an controversial drug and alcohol rehabilitation program has alleged sufficient physical manifestation of her injury to recover. A panel of this court found that she had.

This case asks us to expand the tort of negligent infliction of emotional distress beyond the fact situations of liability to close family members who actually witness an accident, something which, with the exception of *Stoddard,* supra, and *Crivellaro,* supra, Pennsylvania has consistently refused to do.

Among the cases in which this court has refused to recognize an independent tort of negligent infliction of emotional distress is *Lubowitz,* supra, in which a false report of exposure to AIDS was insufficient to support a cause of action for negligent infliction of emotional distress. *Lubowitz* followed the reasoning of the asbestos cases in Pennsylvania in which this court has found that fear of disease is not a compensable wrong. * * *

* * *

Few if any jurisdictions recognize an independent cause of action for negligent infliction of emotional distress. More often the tort of negligent infliction of emotional distress is premised on the violation of a pre-existent duty based on a contractual or implied contractual relationship. Cf. *Crivellaro,* supra, (pre-existent employer–employee relationship).

California experimented with allowing recovery on an independent tort of negligent infliction of emotional distress. The Armstrongs argue that Molien v. Kaiser Foundation Hospitals, 27 Cal.3d 916, 167 Cal.Rptr. 831, 616 P.2d 813 (1980), is persuasive. In *Molien,* the California Supreme Court held that a general duty to refrain from inflicting serious mental distress was based on the foreseeability of the plaintiff. The *Molien* case allowed a husband to recover for his mental distress after his wife was wrongly diagnosed as having syphilis. Only a few years later, the same court expressed reservations about the "limitless exposure to liability." Thing v. LaChusa, 48 Cal.3d 644, 771 P.2d 814, 821 (Cal.1989). A second California appellate court decision found that *Molien* created a "quagmire of novel claims." Andalon v. Superior Court, 162 Cal.App.3d 600, 208 Cal.Rptr. 899, 903 (1984). By 1992, California had abolished negligent infliction of emotional distress as an independent tort and had narrowed its scope to include only those cases in which a contractual relationship existed, Burgess v. Superior Court, 2 Cal.4th 1064, 831 P.2d 1197 (1992), or those in which a bystander witnessed an injury to a loved one.

* * *

The law is not the guarantor of an emotionally peaceful life. Tort law cannot protect any of us from the emotional slings and arrows of daily living. Not every mistake that happens will be legally cognizable. Were we to allow Dawn Armstrong to collect, we would risk opening the floodgates of litigation in Pennsylvania, something we decline to do.

Factually, Dawn Armstrong is in a particularly perilous position. Had the telephone call from Paoli Memorial Hospital been accurate, she could not have stated a cause of action for any emotional distress she suffered learning of her husband's injuries. Consequently, Dawn Armstrong is forced to argue that she was injured when she learned it was not her husband who was injured, information which foreseeably would cause relief, not distress. Indeed, Armstrong testified that it was when she learned it was not her husband in the hospital that she "lost it."

Our review of the law of Pennsylvania and our sister states makes it clear that to state a cause of action for negligent infliction of emotional distress, Dawn Armstrong must demonstrate that she is a bystander who meets the criteria of Sinn v. Burd, supra, or that the defendant, Paoli Memorial Hospital, owes her a pre–existing duty of care, either through contract or fiduciary duty. *Crivellaro,* supra. This she cannot do. Dawn Armstrong was not a bystander who witnessed an injury to a close family member, nor did Paoli Memorial Hospital owe her a pre–existing duty of care.

Since we find that the Armstrongs have not stated a cause of action, we reverse the trial court's denial of a j.n.o.v. and order judgment in favor of the defendant. The trial court's order of a new trial on damages alone is also reversed.

Notes

1.   Did subsequent developments vindicate Justice Roberts's dissent in Sinn v. Burd?

2.   *The "physical manifestation" requirement. Armstrong* states that in addition to other requirements, "physical injury" is necessary to recover for negligently caused emotional distress, but the requirement is satisfied by depression, nightmares and insomnia. A more common and precise term in this context is "physical manifestation," meaning a physical ailment consequent to the emotional distress, and thereby corroborative of its severity (to be distinguished from physical trauma resulting directly from an impact). Most jurisdictions likewise require physical manifestation but are lenient in interpreting the condition. A number of jurisdictions have abandoned the requirement. The Texas Supreme Court gave five reasons for doing this: (a) "The requirement is overinclusive because it permits recovery for mental anguish when the suffering * * * results in any physical impairment, regardless of how trivial the injury." (b) "[T]he requirement is underinclusive because it arbitrarily denies court access to persons with valid claims they could prove if permitted to do so." (c) "[T]he requirement is defective because it 'encourages extravagant pleading and distorted testimony.' '[I]n most instances of severe mental disturbance some deleterious physical consequence can, with a little ingenuity, be found * * *' and characterization of an injury as physical or mental may depend on the ingenuity of counsel in framing the pleadings." (d) "[T]he concept of 'physical manifestation' has been expanded to the point where the term has lost much of its former significance." (e) "[M]edical research has provided modern mankind with a much more detailed and useful understanding of the interaction between mind and body. It is well recognized that certain psychological injuries can be just as severe and debilitating as physical injuries." St. Elizabeth Hospital v. Garrard, 730 S.W.2d 649, 652–53 (Tex.1987).

3.   *The Dillon factors.* As illustrated by the Pennsylvania bystander cases surveyed in *Armstrong,* many cases have encountered problems with the first two *Dillon* factors, whether plaintiff was located near the scene of the accident and whether the plaintiff experienced direct sensory perception of it. The third factor, whether plaintiff and the victim were closely related, has less often been at issue but has presented its own difficulties. See, e.g.,

Elden v. Sheldon, 46 Cal.3d 267, 250 Cal.Rptr. 254, 758 P.2d 582 (1988) (unmarried cohabitant lacked sufficiently close relationship); Dunphy v. Gregor, 136 N.J. 99, 642 A.2d 372 (1994) (unmarried cohabitant had sufficiently close relationship); Blanyar v. Pagnotti Enterprises, Inc., 451 Pa.Super. 269, 679 A.2d 790 (1996), aff'd, 551 Pa. 313, 710 A.2d 608 (1998) (plaintiff who witnessed drowning of cousin lacked sufficiently close relationship). See also Roman v. Carroll, 127 Ariz. 398, 621 P.2d 307 (Ariz.App.1980) (no bystander recovery for plaintiff who witnessed dismemberment of her poodle by defendant's St. Bernard).

4. *Thing v. La Chusa*. In Thing v. La Chusa [cited in *Armstrong* at p. 250], the California Supreme Court slightly modified the *Dillon* factors and turned them into formal requirements for bystander recovery. Citing the need to limit liability and provide predictability, the court expressly abandoned any case–by–case determination of foreseeability as the test.

5. Stoddard v. Davidson, described in *Armstrong* at p. ___, indicates that at least in Pennsylvania "impact" survives as an alternative theory available to a plaintiff who fails to make out the elements of bystander recovery or zone of danger. At least two more recent Pennsylvania cases agree. See Brown v. Philadelphia College of Osteopathic Medicine, 449 Pa.Super. 667, 674 A.2d 1130 (1996); Tomikel v. Commonwealth Dept. of Transp., 658 A.2d 861 (Pa.Cmwlth.1995).

6. *Fear of disease*. The cases cited in *Armstrong* denying recovery for fear of a disease are in accord with most decisions elsewhere with similar facts. See, e.g., Metro–North Commuter R.R. Co. v. Buckley, 521 U.S. 424, 117 S.Ct. 2113, 138 L.Ed.2d 560 (1997) (railroad worker negligently exposed to carcinogen but without symptoms of disease cannot recover under Federal Employers' Liability Act for negligently inflicted emotional distress because facts fail to make out zone of danger or physical impact); Potter v. Firestone Tire & Rubber Co., 6 Cal.4th 965, 25 Cal.Rptr.2d 550, 863 P.2d 795 (1993) (no recovery for fear of cancer in a negligence action for exposing plaintiffs to carcinogens unless plaintiff is "more likely than not" to develop cancer). With *Metro–North*, compare Norfolk & Western Railway Co. v. Ayers, 538 U.S. 135, 123 S.Ct. 1210, 155 L.Ed.2d 261 (2003), permitting (5–4) recovery for fear of cancer as part of pain and suffering by plaintiffs who had actually contracted asbestosis, which increases the risk of cancer.

A number of cases involve "fear of AIDS." The cases present a great variety of facts and outcomes. A number of courts have required that the plaintiff show "actual exposure" to the virus. See, e.g., K.A.C. v. Benson, 527 N.W.2d 553 (Minn.1995). Some courts further require that plaintiff prove a medically possible "channel of transmission" of the virus. See, e.g., Brown v. New York City Health & Hosp. Corp., 225 A.D.2d 36, 648 N.Y.S.2d 880 (1996). California requires, in addition to actual exposure, that plaintiff show that he is more likely than not to contract AIDS. See Kerins v. Hartley, 27 Cal.App.4th 1062, 33 Cal.Rptr.2d 172 (1994). On the other hand, a few courts require only that plaintiff show a reasonable fear of AIDS. See, e.g., Williamson v. Waldman, 150 N.J. 232, 696 A.2d 14 (1997) (fear must be reasonable based upon accurate generally available public knowledge about AIDS transmission); Faya v. Almaraz, 329 Md. 435, 620 A.2d 327 (1993).

In many of the fear–of–disease cases denying recovery, a toxic substance has come into actual contact with the plaintiff's body, or plaintiff has been touched with possibly contaminated medical equipment. What do these outcomes indicate about the current content of the zone of danger and impact doctrines? Can you formulate those doctrines so as to incorporate these cases?

Suppose that as a result of defendant's negligence, plaintiff is pricked by a needle that might be contaminated. Plaintiff suffers fear of AIDS and other diseases (and perhaps physical manifestations resulting from the mental distress) but develops no infectious disease and repeatedly tests negative for HIV. No "actual exposure" or "channel of transmission" is shown. On these facts, some courts have denied any recovery. See, e.g., Carroll v. Sisters of St. Francis Health Services, 868 S.W.2d 585 (Tenn.1993); Babich v. Waukesha Memorial Hospital, Inc., 205 Wis.2d 698, 556 N.W.2d 144 (App.1996). Others have allowed recovery based upon "impact." See, e.g., Marchica v. Long Island R.R. Co., 31 F.3d 1197 (2d Cir.1994), cert. denied, 513 U.S. 1079, 115 S.Ct. 727, 130 L.Ed.2d 631 (1995).

E. ECONOMIC LOSS WITHOUT PHYSICAL INJURY

Tort law has no general problem with awarding recovery for economic loss. Economic loss is recoverable in the torts of intentional misrepresentation and intentional interference with contract. It is recoverable in wrongful death actions, see Chapter VIII, infra. It is sometimes recoverable, though severely limited, in negligent misrepresentation. Even in ordinary negligence–based personal injury cases, all of the traditional elements of damages, aside from the pain and suffering portions, are designed to compensate for economic loss. This includes damages for medical expenses and lost earnings. See generally Chapter VIII.

But a special problem arises when a person who has not suffered an injury to his person or tangible property seeks recovery for financial detriment allegedly produced by defendant's negligent conduct. Such an injury is called *pure economic loss*. Traditional Anglo–American tort law denied recovery in negligence for such losses, and there is still a pronounced reluctance to redress them. Perlman, Interference With Contract and Other Economic Expectancies: A Clash of Tort and Contract Doctrine, 49 U.Chi.L.Rev. 61, 70–72 (1982) offers useful speculation about one of the principal reasons for that reluctance:

> The consequences of any act can be traced indefinitely, but tort law has never made a defendant pay for all harm caused by his tortious act * * *. At some point, it is generally agreed that the defendant's act cannot fairly be singled out from the multitude of other events that combine to cause loss. A number of doctrinal devices—proximate cause, intervening cause, and duty—have served to limit liability.

* * *

There is little agreement on where to draw the line. * * * Moreover, courts faced with the problem of limiting liability in individual cases have concerns beyond locating the limit at precisely the right point. They can be expected to search for a rule that can be applied consistently and articulated sensibly to guide future cases and to avoid the appearance of arbitrariness.

In cases of physical injury to persons or property, the task of defining liability limits is eased, but not eliminated, by the operation of the laws of physics. Friction and gravity dictate that physical objects eventually come to rest. The amount of physical damage that can be inflicted by a speeding automobile or a thrown fist has a self–defining limit. Even in chain reaction cases, intervening forces generally are necessary to restore the velocity of the harm–creating object. These intervening forces offer a natural limit to liability.

The laws of physics do not provide the same restraints for economic loss. Economic relationships are intertwined so intimately that disruption of one may have far–reaching consequences. Furthermore, the chain reaction of economic harm flows from one person to another without the intervention of other forces. Courts facing a case of pure economic loss thus confront the potential for liability of enormous scope, with no easily marked intermediate points and no ready recourse to traditional liability–limiting devices such as intervening cause.

In another large group of cases, the principal reason for denying recovery for pure economic losses seems to be a reluctance to allow a tort remedy when the plaintiff could have secured (or perhaps did secure) a remedy contractually. The next two cases assay the considerations for and against the no–duty rule in these contexts.

There is a great deal of jurisprudence addressing the problem of finding principled ways to limit liability for pure economic loss in the business torts in which it is routinely compensated. Negligent misrepresentation, for example, differs from other negligence actions primarily in the additional rules it employs to restrict the scope of liability. Our objective here is only to suggest the scope and operation of the economic loss rule in ordinary negligence cases.

STATE OF LA. EX REL. GUSTE v. M/V TESTBANK

United States Court of Appeals, Fifth Circuit (En Banc), 1985.
752 F.2d 1019, cert. denied, 477 U.S. 903, 106 S.Ct. 3271, 91 L.Ed.2d 562 (1986).

HIGGINBOTHAM, CIRCUIT JUDGE.

We are asked to abandon physical damage to a proprietary interest as a prerequisite to recovery for economic loss in cases of unintentional maritime tort. We decline the invitation.[1]

In the early evening of July 22, 1980, the M/V Sea Daniel, an inbound bulk carrier, and the M/V Testbank, an outbound container

---

1. We do not address intentional tort or ultrahazardous activity, such as blasting.

ship, collided at approximately mile forty–one of the Mississippi River Gulf outlet. [This channel is a 66–mile, man–made shortcut between New Orleans and the Gulf of Mexico.*] At impact, a white haze enveloped the ships until carried away by prevailing winds, and containers aboard Testbank were damaged and lost overboard. The white haze proved to be hydrobromic acid and the contents of the containers which went overboard proved to be approximately twelve tons of pentachlorophenol, PCP, assertedly the largest such spill in United States history. [Pentachlorophenol (PCP) is toxic to both human and marine life in even moderate quantities. PCP contains dioxin, which has been tentatively linked to cancer in humans and other mammals. This PCP is not phencyclidine [(phenycyolohexyl) piperidine], or "angel dust", which is also designated by the initials PCP.] The United States Coast Guard closed the outlet to navigation until August 10, 1980 and all fishing, shrimping, and related activity was temporarily suspended in the outlet and four hundred square miles of surrounding marsh and waterways. [Civil Defense and local authorities evacuated all residents within a ten–mile radius of the collision.]

Forty–one lawsuits were filed and consolidated before the same judge in the Eastern District of Louisiana. These suits presented claims of shipping interests, marina and boat rental operators, wholesale and retail seafood enterprises not actually engaged in fishing, seafood restaurants, tackle and bait shops, and recreational fishermen. * * *

Defendants moved for summary judgment as to all claims for economic loss unaccompanied by physical damage to property. The district court granted the requested summary judgment as to all such claims except those asserted by commercial oystermen, shrimpers, crabbers and fishermen who had been making a commercial use of the embargoed waters. The district court found these commercial fishing interests deserving of a special protection akin to that enjoyed by seamen. [524 F.Supp. 1170 (E.D.La.1981). The claims of the commercial fishing interests went to trial and the Sea Daniel was held liable. That part of the case was not appealed.]

On appeal a panel of this court affirmed, concluding that claims for economic loss unaccompanied by physical damage to a proprietary interest were not recoverable in maritime tort. 728 F.2d 748 (5th Cir.1984). * * * We then took the case en banc * * *. * * *

* * *

The meaning of Robins Dry Dock v. Flint, 275 U.S. 303, 48 S.Ct. 134, 72 L.Ed. 290 (1927) (Holmes, J.) is the flag all litigants here seek to capture. We turn first to that case and to its historical setting.

Robins broke no new ground but instead applied a principle, then settled both in the United States and England, which refused recovery for negligent interference with "contractual rights." Stated more broadly, the prevailing rule denied a plaintiff recovery for economic loss if that

---

*The bracketed material in this paragraph is from the dissenting opinion. [Ed.]

loss resulted from physical damage to property in which he had no proprietary interest. [ ]. *See also* James, *Limitations on Liability for Economic Loss Caused by Negligence: A Pragmatic Appraisal,* 25 Vand. L.Rev. 43, 44–46 (1972) (discussing history of the rule); Carpenter, *Interference with Contract Relations,* 41 Harv.L.Rev. 728 (1928). Professor James explains this limitation on recovery of pure economic loss: "The explanation * * * is a pragmatic one: the physical consequences of negligence usually have been limited, but the indirect economic repercussions of negligence may be far wider, indeed virtually open–ended."

* * *

In *Robins,* the time charterer of a steamship sued for profits lost when the defendant dry dock negligently damaged the vessel's propeller. The propeller had to be replaced, thus extending by two weeks the time the vessel was laid up in dry dock, and it was for the loss of use of the vessel for that period that the charterer sued. The Supreme Court denied recovery to the charterer, noting:

> . . . no authority need be cited to show that, as a general rule, at least, a tort to the person or property of one man does not make the tort–feasor liable to another merely because the injured person was under a contract with that other unknown to the doer of the wrong. [ ] The law does not spread its protection so far.

* * *

The principle that there could be no recovery for economic loss absent physical injury to a proprietary interest was not only well established when *Robins Dry Dock* was decided, but was remarkably resilient as well. Its strength is demonstrated by the circumstance that *Robins Dry Dock* came ten years after Judge Cardozo's shattering of privity in MacPherson v. Buick Motor Co., 217 N.Y. 382, 111 N.E. 1050 (1916).* Indeed this limit on liability [has] stood against a sea of change in the tort law. * * *

Plaintiffs would confine *Robins* to losses suffered for inability to perform contracts between a plaintiff and others, categorizing the tort as a species of interference with contract. [H]owever, it is apparent that *Robins Dry Dock* represents more than a limit on recovery for interference with contractual rights. * * * If a time charterer's relationship to its negligently injured vessel is too remote, other claimants without even the connection of a contract are even more remote. * * * If a plaintiff connected to the damaged chattel by contract cannot recover, others more remotely situated are foreclosed a fortiori. * * *

* * *

Plaintiffs urge that the requirement of physical injury to a proprietary interest is arbitrary, unfair, and illogical, as it denies recovery for foreseeable injury caused by negligent acts. At its bottom the argument

---

* On the "shattering of privity" in physical injury cases, see section B, supra. [Ed.]

is that questions of remoteness ought to be left to the trier of fact. Ultimately the question becomes who ought to decide—judge or jury— and whether there will be a rule beyond the jacket of a given case. The plaintiffs contend that the "problem" need not be separately addressed, but instead should be handled by "traditional" principles of tort law. Putting the problem of which doctrine is the traditional one aside, their rhetorical questions are flawed in several respects.

Those who would delete the requirement of physical damage have no rule or principle to substitute. Their approach fails to recognize limits upon the adjudicating ability of courts. We do not mean just the ability to supply a judgment; prerequisite to this adjudicatory function are preexisting rules, whether the creature of courts or legislatures. Courts can decide cases without preexisting normative guidance but the result becomes less judicial and more the product of a managerial, legislative or negotiated function.[11]

Review of the foreseeable consequences of the collision of the Sea Daniel and Testbank demonstrates the wave upon wave of successive economic consequences and the managerial role plaintiffs would have us assume. The vessel delayed in St. Louis may be unable to fulfill its obligation to haul from Memphis, to the injury of the shipper, to the injury of the buyers, to the injury of their customers. Plaintiffs concede, as do all who attack the requirement of physical damage, that a line would need to be drawn—somewhere on the other side, each plaintiff would say in turn, of its recovery. Plaintiffs advocate not only that the lines be drawn elsewhere but also that they be drawn on an ad hoc and discrete basis. The result would be that no determinable measure of the limit of foreseeability would precede the decision on liability. We are told that when the claim is too remote, or too tenuous, recovery will be denied. Presumably then, as among all plaintiffs suffering foreseeable economic loss, recovery will turn on a judge or jury's decision. There will be no rationale for the differing results save the "judgment" of the trier of fact. Concededly, it can "decide" all the claims presented, and with comparative if not absolute ease. The point is not that such a process cannot be administered but rather that its judgments would be much less the products of a determinable rule of law. In this important sense, the resulting decisions would be judicial products only in their draw upon judicial resources.

The bright line rule of damage to a proprietary interest, as most, has the virtue of predictability with the vice of creating results in cases at its edge that are said to be "unjust" or "unfair." Plaintiffs point to seemingly perverse results, where claims the rule allows and those it disallows are juxtaposed—such as vessels striking a dock, causing minor

---

11. * * * "When asked, cajoled, and finally forced to try to solve unadjudicable problems, courts will inevitably respond in the only manner possible—they will begin exercising managerial authority and the discretion that goes with it. Attempts will be made to disguise the substitution, to preserve appearances, but the process which evolves should (and no doubt eventually will) be recognized for what it is—not adjudication, but an elaborate, expansive masquerade." Henderson, Expanding the Negligence Concept: Retreat From the Rule of Law, 51 Ind.L.J. 467, 476–77 (1976).

but recoverable damage, then lurching athwart a channel causing great but unrecoverable economic loss. The answer is that when lines are drawn sufficiently sharp in their definitional edges to be reasonable and predictable, such differing results are the inevitable result—indeed, decisions are the desired product. But there is more. The line drawing sought by plaintiffs is no less arbitrary because the line drawing appears only in the outcome—as one claimant is found too remote and another is allowed to recover. The true difference is that plaintiffs' approach would mask the results. The present rule would be more candid, and in addition, by making results more predictable, serves a normative function. It operates as a rule of law and allows a court to adjudicate rather than manage.[12]

That the rule is identifiable and will predict outcomes in advance of the ultimate decision about recovery enables it to play additional roles. Here we agree with plaintiffs that economic analysis, even at the rudimentary level of jurists, is helpful both in the identification of such roles and the essaying of how the roles play. Thus it is suggested that placing all the consequence of its error on the maritime industry will enhance its incentive for safety. While correct, as far as such analysis goes, such in terrorem benefits have an optimal level. Presumably, when the cost of an unsafe condition exceeds its utility there is an incentive to change. As the costs of an accident become increasing multiples of its utility, however, there is a point at which greater accident costs lose meaning, and the incentive curve flattens. When the accident costs are added in large but unknowable amounts the value of the exercise is diminished.

With a disaster inflicting large and reverberating injuries through the economy, as here, we believe the more important economic inquiry is that of relative cost of administration, and in maritime matters administration quickly involves insurance. Those economic losses not recoverable under the present rule for lack of physical damage to a proprietary interest are the subject of first party or loss insurance. The rule change would work a shift to the more costly liability system of third party insurance. For the same reasons that courts have imposed limits on the concept of foreseeability, liability insurance might not be readily obtainable for the types of losses asserted here. As Professor James has noted, "[s]erious practical problems face insurers in handling insurance against potentially wide, open–ended liability. From an insurer's point of view it is not practical to cover, without limit, a liability that may reach catastrophic proportions, or to fix a reasonable premium on a risk that does not lend itself to actuarial measurement." [ ] By contrast, first party insurance is feasible for many of the economic losses claimed here.

---

12. Fuller, The Forms and Limits of Adjudication, 92 Harv.L.Rev. 353, 396 (1978). This case illustrates how our technocratic tradition masks a deep difference in attitudes toward the roles of a judiciary. The difference between the majority and dissenting opinions is far more than a choice between competing maritime rules. The majority is driven by the principle of self ordering and modesty for the judicial role; the dissent accepts a role of management which can strain the limits of adjudication.

Each businessman who might be affected by a disruption of river traffic or by a halt in fishing activities can protect against that eventuality at a relatively low cost since his own potential losses are finite and readily discernible. Thus, to the extent that economic analysis informs our decision here, we think that it favors retention of the present rule.

* * *

In conclusion, having reexamined the history and central purpose of the doctrine of *Robins Dry Dock* as developed in this circuit, we remain committed to its teaching. Denying recovery for pure economic losses is a pragmatic limitation on the doctrine of foreseeability, a limitation we find to be both workable and useful. * * *

Accordingly, the decision of the district court granting summary judgment to defendants on all claims for economic losses unaccompanied by physical damage to property is affirmed.

[Judge Higginbotham's opinion was joined by nine other judges, two of whom filed the following additional opinion.]

GEE, CIRCUIT JUDGE, with whom CLARK, CHIEF JUDGE, joins, concurring.

Both the majority opinion and the dissent do our Court proud, joining a few others on that relatively short list of truly distinguished and thoughtful legal writings of which it or any court can boast. Neither opinion, however, confronts explicitly what is for me the overarching issue in the appeal. That issue, a legal one only in the broadest sense and only implicitly presented, is perhaps best addressed in a brief collateral writing such as this will be.

The issue to which I refer is, *who* should deal with questions of such magnitude as the rule for which the dissent contends would, again and again, draw before the courts? An oil spill damages hundreds, perhaps thousands, of miles of coastal area. A cloud of noxious industrial gas leaks out, kills thousands, and injures thousands more. A commonly-used building material is discovered, years after the fact, to possess unforeseen lethal qualities affecting thousands who have worked with it. The long–term effects of inhaling coal dust are found to be disabling to a significant proportion of veteran miners. None of these illustrations is fanciful; each has arisen in recent times and presented itself for resolution to our body politic. Congress has dealt effectively with Black Lung; it has signally failed to deal with the ravages of asbestosis—a scourge, I suspect, far more general and widespread—and a swelling wave of individual asbestosis claims, to be resolved on a case by case basis, pushes slowly through our court system, threatening to inundate it and to consume in punitive damage awards to early claimants the relatively meager assets available to compensate the general class affected, many of whom have not yet suffered the onset of symptoms. It is my thesis that the dispute–resolution systems of courts are poorly equipped to manage disasters of such magnitude and that we should be wary of adopting rules of decision which, as would that contended for by the dissent, encourage the drawing of their broader aspects before us.

* * *

WISDOM, CIRCUIT JUDGE, with whom RUBIN, POLITZ, TATE, and JOHNSON, CIRCUIT JUDGES, join, dissenting.

* * * This Court's application of *Robins* is out of step with contemporary tort doctrine, works substantial injustice on innocent victims, and is unsupported by the considerations that justified the Supreme Court's 1927 decision.

Robins was a tort case grounded on a contract. Whatever the justification for the original holding, this Court's requirement of physical injury as a condition to recovery is an unwarranted step backwards in torts jurisprudence. The resulting bar for claims of economic loss unaccompanied by any physical damage conflicts with conventional tort principles of foreseeability and proximate cause. I would analyze the plaintiffs' claims under these principles, using the "particular damage" requirement of public nuisance law* as an additional means of limiting claims. Although this approach requires a case–by–case analysis, it comports with the fundamental idea of fairness that innocent plaintiffs should receive compensation and negligent defendants should bear the cost of their tortious acts. Such a result is worth the additional costs of adjudicating these claims, and this rule of liability appears to be more economically efficient. * * *

* * *

* * * It is, of course, axiomatic in tort law that those who have been proximately and foreseeably injured should recover. Although cause and effect can be carried to limitless and unknowable lengths, courts have chosen to deal with these concepts in a restrained manner that is practical and within the scope of ordinary human understanding. These arbitrary limits are delineated by "proximate" or "natural" causes. One must admit that the line between recovery and nonrecovery may appear as arbitrary under a rule of proximate cause as a line created by a requirement for physical damages. In a sense, any line that the courts draw to limit recovery is arbitrary. But this dissent attempts to draw lines which comport more closely with principles of intrinsic fairness than the line based on physical damage.

* * *

First, the damage must be proximately caused by the accident. Although this requirement will preclude some claims, it provides relief for many of the claims for economic losses at issue here because of the great interdependence of the elements in the maritime industry. Hardly any claim escapes its imprimatur, and its overinclusiveness in defining the class of proper plaintiffs in this case limits its traditional utility. We

* See Chapter XVI, infra. [Ed.]

therefore concentrate instead on the principles of foreseeability and "particular" damage, which are more useful here in delimiting recovery.

Foreseeability provides a mechanism for limiting claims that are proximately related to the accident. The requirement of foreseeability precludes recovery for damages resulting from gains that are allegedly lost because the accident altered the course of events upon which the expected gain was predicated. For example, the law should not compensate a shipper for purely speculative profits. Such predictions of the future are limitless in variety and incalculable in scope. Foreseeability requires that we confine the scope of claims to those arising from activities in process at the time of the accident or to claims that can be proven with certainty.

Finally, a plaintiff must assert a "particular" damage that distinguishes him from the general population. This requirement of "particular" damage, basic in the law of public nuisance, developed as a response to widespread losses. It was formulated to compensate those plaintiffs most seriously aggrieved by a tort while preventing open–ended liability. The distinction is useful here. In a maritime accident, a business suffers "particular" damages to the extent that the accident prevents the business from engaging in primary maritime activities, such as fishing or use of the waterways, or supplying commodities or services vital to primary maritime activities, such as those of bait and tackle shops, drydocks, marinas, and seafood wholesalers or processors. All other losses that are not peculiar to maritime activities are part of the general economic dislocation caused by the accident and are therefore not "particular".

A plaintiff must meet all three criteria for recovery. This test should provide a reasonably satisfactory equilibrium among compensation to plaintiffs, foreclosure of open–ended liability, and imposition of incentives on defendants to obtain insurance and to exercise due care.

PARTIES ENTITLED TO RECOVER UNDER THE TEST

Shrimpers, crabbers, oystermen, and other commercial fishermen who routinely operated in those parts of the Mississippi River Gulf Outlet and the surrounding areas that were temporarily closed by the Coast Guard should recover. It is foreseeable that a ship carrying PCP might be in a collision and that some of the PCP containers might be lost overboard. It is also foreseeable that a PCP spill would result in the closure of fishing areas. Commercial fishermen have suffered damages that are proximately caused by this closure. Finally, they have suffered "particular" damages because, unlike members of the general public, the tort has denied them their livelihood in the maritime industry.

Ships that were trapped or delayed by the closure of the Gulf Channel Outlet are also entitled to recovery. It is foreseeable that a PCP spill would result in closure of the river to navigation. Such closure proximately caused shippers to incur additional expenses. The damage is "particular" because the operators of these ships have incurred additional pecuniary outlays in the course of their maritime activities. Ships that can alter their routes to reduce or eliminate losses should be denied recovery *pro tanto* because of their duty to mitigate damages. [ ] If the rerouting of ships caused delays in an alternate route from crowding, ships that would have taken the alternate route in any event should not recover their delay expenses.

The land–based businesses that have claimed damages include dry-docks, marinas, bait and tackle shops, seafood processors, seafood whole-salers, and restaurants. It is here that drawing the line becomes difficult, for these businesses have been affected by the PCP spill, but all would agree that a seafood restaurant in New Orleans should not recover for a loss of business from consumers' concern over contaminated products.

The general test of recovery for these claimants is whether their business of supplying a vital commodity or service to those engaged in the maritime industry has been interrupted by the collision, the closure, or the embargo. Marinas, for example, in the afflicted area should be allowed to recover. If all shipping and boating is suspended, then a marina or drydock in the area affected is unable to supply docking or repair services to users of the waterway. No mitigation of damages is possible. The same would be true for similarly situated boat charterers who supply marine "common carrier" services. Bait and tackle shops present a similar situation: The condemnation of a large fishing area damages or destroys the livelihood of those shops whose business is exclusively predicated upon supplying direct inputs (bait, fuel) to those whose commercial undertakings have been foreclosed by the quarantine and embargo. Finally, seafood processors and seafood wholesalers that provide services for the condemned area should recover.

There is a point beyond which we cannot allow recovery. Seafood restaurants, for example, are not providers of a vital service to the afflicted area. Their damage is not sufficiently distinguishable from general economic dislocation to allow for recovery. They are too removed from the tortious act. A plaintiff may also be barred because it is not sufficiently involved with the afflicted area as a supplier of vital inputs peculiar to maritime activities. The bar would arise, for example, if a bait and tackle shop were only partially connected with a foreclosed area. Basically, a claim for damages that is indistinguishable from a general grievance furnishes no basis for recovery.

* * *

The advantages of this alternate rule of recovery are that it compensates damaged plaintiffs, imposes the cost of damages upon those who have caused the harm, is consistent with economic principles of modern tort law, and frees courts from the necessity of creating a piecemeal quilt of exceptions to avoid the harsh effects of the *Robins* rule.

EXTRINSIC NOTIONS OF FAIRNESS AND CASE–BY–CASE ADJUDICATION

If tort law fails to compensate plaintiffs or to impose the cost of damages on those who caused the harm, it should be under a warrant clear of necessity. When a rule of law, once extended, leads to inequitable results and creates principles of recovery that are at odds with the great weight of tort jurisprudence, then that rule of law merits scrutiny. A strict application of the extension denies recovery to many plaintiffs who should be awarded damages. Conventional tort principles of foreseeability, proximate causation, and "particular" damages would avoid such unfairness.

It is true that application of foreseeability and proximate causation would necessitate case–by–case adjudication. But I have a more optimistic assessment of courts' ability to undertake such adjudication than the majority.[38] Certainly such an inquiry would be no different from our daily task of weighing such claims in other tort cases.

The majority opinion also states that the *Robins* rule, being free from the vagaries of factual findings in a case–by–case determination, serves an important normative function because it is more predictable and more "candid". Normative values would also be served, however, by eliminating a broad categorical rule that is insensitive to equitable and social policy concerns that would support allowing the plaintiffs' claims in many individual cases. In assessing "normative concerns", the courts' compass should be a sense of fairness and equity, both of which are better served by allowing plaintiffs to present their claims under usual tort standards. It is not clear, moreover, that a jury's finding of negligence in a case–by–case determination is "less the product of a determinable rule of law" when the finder of fact is guided in its determination by rules of law. The jury's finding of liability in this case would be no more "lawless" than a finding of proximate cause, foreseeability, and particular damages in a physical damage case.

THE ECONOMIC ARGUMENTS

The economic arguments regarding allocation of loss that purportedly favor the *Robins* rule of nonliability are not as clear to me as they appear to be to the majority. It is true that denial of recovery may effectively spread the loss over the victims. It is not certain, however, that victims are generally better insurors against the risk of loss caused by tortious acts having widespread consequences. Although the victims do possess greater knowledge of their circumstances and their potential damages, we do not know whether insurance against these types of losses is readily available to the businesses that may be affected. We do know that insurance against this kind of loss is already available for shippers. Imposition of liability upon the shippers helps ensure that the potential tortfeasor faces incentives to take the proper care. The majority's point is well taken that the incentives to avoid accidents do not

---

38. * * * The majority opinion favors a bright line rule, as opposed to a case–by–case determination of liability, because it enables courts to "adjudicate" rather than to "manage". A bright line rule such as the one the majority proposes, however, requires no adjudication whatsoever. Judges need merely to preside over a self–executing system of limited liability where recovery is predicated upon an easily determined physical injury. The application of such a rule, rather than a case–by–case determination, seems more "management" than adjudication.

increase once potential losses pass a certain measure of enormity. But in truth we have no idea what this measure is: Absent hard data, I would rather err on the side of receiving little additional benefit from imposing additional quanta of liability than err by adhering to *Robins'* inequitable rule and bar victims' recovery on the mistaken belief that a "marginal incentive curve" was flat, or nearly so. If a loss must be borne, it is no worse if a "merely" negligent defendant bears the loss than an innocent plaintiff absorb the damages.

* * *

RUBIN, CIRCUIT JUDGE, with whom WISDOM, POLITZ and TATE, CIRCUIT JUDGES, join, dissenting.

* * *

Judge Gee's view, in which Chief Judge Clark joins, is that, while we should not go beyond the physical–injury requirement, the question of scope of liability for damages should be resolved by legislative action. If, however, the limited–recovery rule is fair, it does not require Congressional consideration.

I agree with Judge Gee and Chief Judge Clark that the subject calls for legislative consideration and that the necessary application of principle accompanied by suitable line drawing can be better accomplished by statute. However, I would not await such action, for, in default of it, every time we reject a claim we act as decisively and finally as if we had allowed it—as definitively as if we were adhering to a statutory command not to allow damages when no such command has been given. The constitutional grant of jurisdiction to federal courts over cases and controversies not only empowers but requires us to review the constitutionality of legislation, as the Court held in Marbury v. Madison a century and a half ago. It equally empowers and requires us to decide other cases within our jurisdiction whether or not Congress has provided a rule of decision and even when we think Congress should have acted and has not done so.

Robins should not be extended beyond its actual holding and should not be applied in cases like this, for the result is a denial of recompense to innocent persons who have suffered a real injury as a result of someone else's fault. We should not flinch from redressing injury because Congress has been indifferent to the problem.

Notes

1. In allowing the claims of the commercial fishermen, the district judge in *Testbank* explained that the fishermen "have established a course of business conduct which makes *commercial* use of a public right with which the defendant interfere[d]." He relied on cases like Union Oil Co. v. Oppen, 501 F.2d 558 (9th Cir.1974), in which the court distinguished commercial fishing interests on the ground that they "directly make use of a resource of the sea, *viz.* its fish, in the ordinary conduct of their business." Does either

of those explanations successfully distinguish shore–based business such as seafood processors?

2.   Because *Testbank* articulates federal maritime law, it is not necessarily controlling for tort law generally, but it is an influential decision. Moreover, since maritime law governs most claims arising out of oil spills, *Testbank's* interpretation of *Robins Dry Dock* controls a great many economic loss cases.

3.   *The Exxon Valdez case.* At this writing, state law claims for pure economic loss resulting from the Exxon Valdez disaster in Alaska are still alive. A federal district judge held that such claims by shore-based businesses such as boat charterers, fishing lodges, and fish processors were preempted by the maritime law rule announced in *Robins Dry Dock* and applied in *Testbank*. But the Ninth Circuit held that Alaska law allows for recovery of pure economic losses as long as they are not too remote, and said federal maritime law does not preempt state law claims based on that rule. In re Exxon Valdez, 270 F.3d 1215 (9th Cir. 2001). In addition, Exxon spent $2.1 billion on clean-up activities and paid the state and federal governments more than $900 million for environmental damage. A $4.5 billion punitive damage award against Exxon was not yet final as of this writing. See p. ___ infra.

4.   *Physical damage.* Under the rule espoused by the *Testbank* majority, everything turns on proof of physical damage. A marina owner whose docks are damaged recovers for all the lost profits that can be attributed to the dock damage, while another who suffers no such damages but is just as effectively shut down recovers nothing. Earnings lost when a railroad negligently caused bombs to explode, thereby shutting down the nearby plant where the plaintiff worked, were not recoverable; see Adams v. Southern Pacific Transportation, 50 Cal.App.3d 37, 123 Cal.Rptr. 216 (1975). But when a driver negligently hit a power pole, disrupting current to the plaintiff's plant, the court permitted recovery for earnings lost because the disruption caused a power surge that damaged a transformer in the plant. See George A. Hormel & Co. v. Maez, 92 Cal.App.3d 963, 155 Cal.Rptr. 337 (1979).

Because the *Testbank* rule "capriciously showers compensation along the path of physical destruction, regardless of the status or circumstances of individual claimants," the New Jersey Supreme Court rejected the rule and adopted a "particular foreseeability" approach similar to that of the *Testbank* dissenters. See People Express Airlines, Inc. v. Consolidated Rail Corp., 100 N.J. 246, 495 A.2d 107 (1985).

5.   *Disproportionate liability?* When the facts do not raise the spectre of massive liability to numerous claimants, the grip of the no–duty rule is not as strong. In a leading California case, a building contractor engaged by an airport owner to renovate the air conditioning system negligently failed to

complete the work on time, causing a lessee who operated a restaurant in the airport to lose profits. The California Supreme Court recognized a cause of action for "negligent loss of expected economic advantage." See J'Aire Corp. v. Gregory, 24 Cal.3d 799, 598 P.2d 60, 157 Cal.Rptr. 407 (1979).

One commentator argues that the prospect of widespread liability disproportionate to the defendant's fault is the only explanation for the economic loss rule. See Robert L. Rabin, Tort Recovery for Negligently Inflicted Economic Loss: A Reassessment, 37 Stan.L.Rev. 1513 (1985). The *Moransais* case, infra, suggests at least one other explanation.

6. *Economic Analysis.* In the *Testbank* case, both Judge Higginbotham and Judge Wisdom rely on economic arguments. As is true of traditional legal arguments, persuasive economic arguments usually can be found on both sides of any question tough enough to lead to serious litigation. The acceptance of economic analysis has been one of the most influential developments in torts scholarship in the past generation. Today no one doubts that economic analysis is a useful and revealing way of looking at particular torts issues; the question is whether economic analysis is the principal, or perhaps even only, useful analytical tool. Some "law and economics" thinkers have come to believe that using the "tools of economic analysis" is the only sensible way, or at least much the best way, of thinking about *all* of tort law. R. Posner, Tort Law, Cases and Economic Analysis xviii (1982). For a criticism of this viewpoint as a form of "reductionism," see Powers, On Positive Theories of Tort Law, 66 Tex.L.Rev. 191 (1987). See also Balkin, Too Good to Be True: The Positive Economic Theory of Law, 87 Colum.L.Rev. 1447 (1987).

Despite the argument that the "law and economics" thinkers purport to explain too much with a too–narrow view, their tools and perspectives are often extremely illuminating. There is now a vast "law and economics" literature, including the Journal of Legal Studies and the Journal of Law & Economics. The seminal piece was Coase, The Problem of Social Cost, 3 J.L. & Economics 1 (1960). In simple terms, the "Coase theorem" holds that, in any situation in which a potential tortfeasor and a potential victim are free to bargain without cost in advance of any harm about the risks created by their respective activities, the ultimate allocation of resources will be the same (in all important respects) whether the legal system imposes liability or not.

MORANSAIS v. HEATHMAN

Supreme Court of Florida, 1999.
744 So.2d 973.

[Plaintiffs contracted with an engineering corporation to inspect a house they wanted to buy. The inspection report allegedly was deficient in failing to report defects in the house's air conditioning, electrical system, and roof. After buying the house, the plaintiffs found that the defects made it uninhabitable. They brought suit for breach of contract against the engineering firm and also brought individual suits in tort against the firm's engineering employees who did the inspection, asserting that the employees were guilty of professional malpractice. They alleged no bodily injury or property damage. The trial court granted the employees' motions to dismiss the tort complaints. Affirming, the district court of appeal held that the suit for breach of contract against the firm was viable, but that the plaintiffs had no cause of action in the tort suits because of the economic loss rule.]

* * *

The essence of the early holdings discussing the rule is to prohibit a party from suing in tort for purely economic losses to a product or object provided to another for consideration, the rationale being that in those cases "contract principles [are] more appropriate than tort principles for resolving economic loss without an accompanying physical injury or property damage."

* * * In [Florida Power & Light Co. v. Westinghouse Elec. Corp., 510 So.2d 899 (Fla.1987)], the seminal case on the applicability of the economic loss rule, Florida Power & Light (FPL) sued Westinghouse for breach of express warranties in the contract and for negligence, all arising from leaks discovered in six steam generators manufactured by Westinghouse for sale to FPL. In its analysis and conclusion that the negligence claim was barred, this Court relied on the reasoning in two cases, both of which involved damages to defective products. See East River Steamship Corp. v. Transamerica Delaval, Inc., 476 U.S. 858, 871, 106 S.Ct. 2295 (1986) (holding that a manufacturer of a defective steam turbine is not liable under a theory of negligence or strict liability where the only injury is to the product itself); Seely v. White Motor Co., 63 Cal.2d 9, 403 P.2d 145, 151 (1965) (holding that a manufacturer of a defective product is not subject to strict liability where the damages are purely economic). We agreed with the economic loss rule discussed in those cases and held that the rule barred FPL's negligence claim where there was no physical injury or property damage other than to the generators themselves, and that contract principles rather than tort principles would be adequate and fair to resolve any claims for the purely economic losses to the products provided by Westinghouse. We reasoned that the contracting parties were in the best position to have anticipated potential problems with the items provided and could have adequately protected their respective interests through measures such as the applicable warranty law, "negotiation and contractual bargaining," or insurance. Our holding in *Florida Power & Light* remains sound in its adherence to the fundamental precedents we relied upon in applying the so–called economic loss rule.

Unfortunately, however, our subsequent holdings have appeared to expand the application of the rule beyond its principled origins and have contributed to applications of the rule by trial and appellate courts to situations well beyond our original intent. For example, in [AFM Corp. v. Southern Bell Tel. & Tel. Co., 515 So.2d 180 (Fla.1987)] we extended the economic loss rule to preclude a negligence claim arising from breach of a service contract in a nonprofessional services context. In that case, AFM contracted with Southern Bell for a referral service for AFM's customers. However, Southern Bell mistakenly listed the wrong telephone number in its yellow pages and inadvertently disconnected the referral system by giving a different customer AFM's old telephone number. Because AFM's damages resulted from a breach of the underlying contract and not any independent tort, we held that AFM was limited to contractual remedies only. In other words, we held that a purchaser of services could not recover purely economic loss due to negligence arising from a breach of contract where the purchaser has not shown the commission of a tort independent of the breach itself. While we continue to believe the outcome of that case is sound, we may have been unnecessarily over–expansive in our reliance on the economic loss rule as opposed to fundamental contractual principles.

* * *

* * * Today, we again emphasize that by recognizing that the economic loss rule may have some genuine, but limited, value in our damages law, we never intended to bar well–established common law causes of action, such as those for neglect in providing professional services. Rather, the rule was primarily intended to limit actions in the product liability context,[13] and its application should generally be limited to those contexts or situations where the policy considerations are substantially identical to those underlying the product liability–type analysis. We hesitate to speculate further on situations not actually before us. The rule, in any case, should not be invoked to bar well–established causes of actions in tort, such as professional malpractice.

We agree with the observations of those who have noted that because actions against professionals often involve purely economic loss without any accompanying personal injury or property damage, extending the economic loss rule to these cases would effectively extinguish such causes of action. * * *

Accordingly, we hold that the economic loss rule does not bar a cause of action against a professional for his or her negligence even though the damages are purely economic in nature and the aggrieved party has entered into a contract with the professional's employer.* * *.

* * *

Wells, J., concurring.

[T]he economic loss rule should be limited to cases involving a product which damages itself by reason of a defect in the product. I

---

13. We note that other jurisdictions have addressed the economic loss rule in relation to professional malpractice claims against architects and have reached contrary results. See City Express, Inc. v. Express Partners, 87 Hawai'i 466, 959 P.2d 836 (1998) (holding that plaintiff may not recover purely economic losses against architect for professional negligence where plaintiff contracted with architect); 2314 Lincoln Park West Condominium Ass'n. v. Mann, Gin, Ebel & Frazier, Ltd., 136 Ill.2d 302, 144 Ill.Dec. 227, 555 N.E.2d 346 (1990) (holding that economic loss rule bars cause of action in tort for professional malpractice against architect); but see Robinson Redevelopment Co. v. Anderson, 155 A.D.2d 755, 547 N.Y.S.2d 458 (1989) (holding that economic loss rule does not bar negligence claim against architect).

would recede from AFM Corp. v. Southern Bell Telephone & Telegraph Co., because that opinion erroneously applies the economic loss rule and has given rise to confusion as to the rule's applicability.

OVERTON, SENIOR JUSTICE, dissenting.

* * *

In [Casa Clara Condominium Ass'n., Inc. v. Charley Toppino and Sons, Inc., 620 So.2d 1244 (Fla.1993)] the defendant had contracted to supply concrete for the construction of condominiums. That concrete contained a high salt content that caused reinforcing rods to rust and the concrete to break off. The plaintiff Casa Clara Condominium Association brought tort actions against the supplier of that concrete. The trial court, district court of appeal, and, finally, this Court applied the economic loss rule in dismissing those causes of action. This Court [affirmed, holding that] "contract principles [are] more appropriate than tort principles for recovering economic loss without an accompanying physical injury or property damage." If we held otherwise, "contract law would drown in a sea of tort." *East River*, 476 U.S. at 866. We refuse[d] to hold that homeowners are not subject to the economic loss rule.[8]

* * *

In my view, there is absolutely no logical basis to justify a recovery in tort to the property owners in this case when no tort recovery was allowed to the property owners against the concrete supplier for defective concrete in *Casa Clara*.

It appears to me that the majority has substantially obliterated the distinction between contract and tort causes of action, and, in addition, has effectively overruled our rather recent decision in *Casa Clara* without saying so.

* * *

If I understand the majority opinion correctly, it means that if there is an express written contract for legal services with a law firm then the aggrieved client may bring causes of action upon the same facts on the basis of (1) a breach of contract and (2) multiple tort claims for malpractice individually against each lawyer who had anything to do with the case.

* * *

* * * *Casa Clara* explained the economic loss rule and made clear that it helped make the demarcation between contract and tort. After this decision, for all practical purposes, there will be no real distinction

8. Numerous other jurisdictions have also refused to give greater tort remedies to homeowners. [Justice Overton cited cases from Delaware, Illinois, Virginia, and Washington.]

except that tort will be the preferred basis for a cause of action with a contract action being just a collateral proceeding.

* * *

Notes

1. *Pure economic loss in products liability cases.* The majority of courts agree that when a defective product causes damage only to the product itself, tort recovery is barred. See Chapter XV, section E, infra p. 567. Such cases are classified as pure economic loss cases (rather than physical property damage cases) because of policy reasons for believing they should be controlled by contract law.

2. *Tort or contract?* A similar choice between tort and contract law arises when the case involves not a defective product but a claim of negligent performance of a service contract. Again, there is general agreement that tort law should not supplant contract law, but here courts are receptive to arguments that the existence of a contract should not always preclude tort liability. The majority opinion in the principal case mentions a number of possible justifications for intervention by tort law:

(a) there is a tort independent of the breach;

(b) the economic loss rule only applies where the considerations are substantially identical to those underlying product liability analysis;

(c) well–established causes of action in tort are exempted from the rule;

(d) professional malpractice claims are exempted from the rule because otherwise those would be extinguished.

Which of these, if any, justifies the application of tort law in the principal case?

3. In Kennedy v. Columbia Lumber & Mfg. Co., 299 S.C. 335, 384 S.E.2d 730 (1989), the court held that a builder is liable only in contract if the only duties it breaches are contractual, but is liable in tort if it breaches a "legal duty," e.g., builds a house that it should know will pose a serious risk of physical harm or violates a building code (assuming the applicable building code imposes duties on the builder). Is this different from the "independent tort" concept mentioned in Note 2? Is it a workable way of restricting tort liability to cases in which there is something more than a mere breach of contract?

4. Should tort liability be permitted only when the plaintiff does not have (or could not have secured) a contractual remedy against the culpable party? In the *Casa Clara* case (see Justice Overton's dissent), homeowners were denied recovery against the subcontractor who supplied the defective concrete. The court argued that they could bring breach of warranty claims against the third parties who sold them their homes–parties who presumably were as ignorant of the defect as the buyers were. Does it make sense to prefer the contractual remedy when the effect of doing so shifts the loss from the culpable party to an innocent party?

5. One observer argues that it is futile to try to resolve economic loss issues by classifying them as either contract or tort problems. Instead, he

proposes a new classification, "economic negligence," which would be neither but would try to refocus the analysis in each case on the policies of both tort and contract law and the problem of indeterminate liability. See Feinman, Doctrinal Classification and Economic Negligence, 33 San Diego L.Rev. 137 (1996).

F.   OWNERS AND OCCUPIERS OF LAND

The Anglo–American tort law treating injuries caused by activities and conditions on private land derives historically "from a culture deeply rooted to the land, a culture which traced many of its standards to a heritage of feudalism." Kermarec v. Compagnie Generale Transatlantique, 358 U.S. 625, 630, 79 S.Ct. 406, 410, 3 L.Ed.2d 550 (1959). This body of law is complex and changing, but it generally remains a central feature of it that owners and occupiers of land owe limited duties, i.e., are not fully subject to the normal operation of the requirements of reasonable care.

Traditionally ownership as such entailed almost no responsibility. Only when the owner of land was also its occupier (also called possessor) did the tort law address him significantly. The occupier of land owed limited duties to guard against injuries to persons outside the premises, and his or her responsibility to those injured on the premises differed according to the circumstances of the victim's presence there. In determining whether the defendant was treated as an occupier, the key concept was possession, defined by Restatement (2d) of Torts § 328E as follows:

A possessor of land is

(a) a person who is in occupation of the land with intent to control it or

(b) a person who has been in occupation of land with intent to control it, if no other person has subsequently occupied it with intent to control it, or

(c) a person who is entitled to immediate occupation of the land, if no other person is in possession under clauses (a) and (b).

Typically, unless the land has been leased to another, the owner is treated as the occupier. Land under lease is typically regarded as occupied by the lessee, not the owner. See Section F–4, infra p. 291.

1.   OCCUPIER'S LIABILITY FOR INJURIES OFF THE LAND

When activities or artificial conditions on the defendant's land injure neighbors or users of adjacent highways, ordinary principles of negligence apply: the occupier owes a duty of reasonable care, and will be liable if negligence, cause in fact, legal cause, and damages are established. But injuries caused by natural conditions traditionally were excluded from the occupier's responsibility. The "natural conditions" limitation, which probably originated as an application of the basic nonfeasance concept (see section C, supra p. 222), may be changing, as the following decision suggests.

SPRECHER v. ADAMSON COMPANIES

Supreme Court of California, 1981.
30 Cal.3d 358, 178 Cal.Rptr. 783, 636 P.2d 1121.

BIRD, CHIEF JUSTICE.

* * *

[Respondents own] a 90–acre parcel of land in Malibu, California. The parcel is bounded on the north by the Pacific Coast Highway and on the south by Malibu Road. Across Malibu Road and opposite the parcel are a number of beach front homes, including the home of appellant, Peter Sprecher.

Respondents' parcel of land contains part of an active landslide which extends seaward from the parcel for some 1,700 feet along Malibu Road and beyond the boundaries of respondents' property. The Sprecher property is situated within the toe of this slide. The landslide, which has been evident since the area was first developed in the early 1900s, is classified as active because it exhibits periodic cycles of activity and dormancy. The parties agree that the slide is a natural condition of the land which has not been affected by any of respondents' activities on the 90–acre parcel.

In March 1978, heavy spring rains triggered a major movement of the slide which caused appellant's home to rotate and to press against the home of his neighbor, Gwendolyn Sexton. As a result, Sexton filed an action against appellant, seeking to enjoin the encroachment of his home upon hers. Appellant cross–complained against Sexton, the County of Los Angeles and respondents.[1] Specifically, appellant sought damages for the harm done to his home by the landslide. He alleged that such damage proximately resulted from respondents' negligent failure to correct or to control the landslide condition.

Respondents moved for summary judgment, arguing primarily that a possessor of land has no duty to remedy a natural condition of the land in order to prevent harm to property outside his premises. Since the landslide was a natural condition, they argued that they were not liable for the damage to appellant's home.

In opposition, appellant challenged the present validity of the common law rule of nonliability for a natural condition, arguing that the rule is neither premised upon sound public policy nor in accord with modern principles of tort liability.

* * *

The trial court ruled in favor of respondents and this appeal followed.

---

1. Neither Sexton nor the County of Los Angeles is a party to this appeal.

There appear to be only five California cases which refer to or deal with the distinction between artificial and natural conditions on land. Three of these decisions were concerned with the question of liability for damage caused by a natural, as opposed to an artificial, condition. [Boarts v. Imperial Irrigation Dist., 80 Cal.App.2d 574, 578, 182 P.2d 246 (1947)] relied on this distinction to deny recovery; [Wisher v. Fowler, 7 Cal.App.3d 225, 229, 86 Cal.Rptr. 582 (1970)] questioned its applicability in an urban setting; and [Harris v. De La Chapelle, 55 Cal.App.3d 644, 648, 127 Cal.Rptr. 695 (1976)] held that in an urban area, "a landowner is liable for conditions occurring where he fails to exercise reasonable care to [prevent] an unreasonable risk of harm to users of the highway from trees on his property". This court has not previously addressed the wisdom of the common law rule of nonliability for harm caused by a natural condition to persons outside the premises. * * *

This progression of the law in California mirrors what appears to be a general trend toward rejecting the common law distinction between natural and artificial conditions. Instead, the courts are increasingly using ordinary negligence principles to determine a possessor's liability for harm caused by a condition of the land. The early case of Gibson v. Denton (1896) 4 A.D. 198, 38 N.Y.S. 554 was a precursor of this trend. In *Gibson,* the court held a possessor of land liable for damage caused when a decayed tree on her premises fell on the home of her neighbor during a storm. * * *

In more recent years, at least 13 other states and the District of Columbia have begun applying ordinary negligence principles in determining a possessor's liability for harm caused by a natural condition.

Not surprisingly, all these cases involved an injury caused by a fallen tree. However, the principles expressed by these courts are not so limited. * * *

The courts are not simply creating an exception to the common law rule of nonliability for damage caused by trees and retaining the rule for other natural conditions of the land. Instead, the courts are moving toward jettisoning the common law rule in its entirety and replacing it with a single duty of reasonable care in the maintenance of property. * * *

Furthermore, the courts are not imposing the duty of reasonable care only on possessors of land located in urban and suburban areas. The cases indicate that the duty of reasonable care for the protection of those outside the premises against natural conditions applies even in rural areas. Some of the cases, however, have drawn a distinction between the standard of care owed with respect to natural conditions in urban areas and the standard owed in rural areas.

While the courts have imposed liability for harm caused by a natural condition where the possessor of land located in a rural area knew or had reason to know of the danger it posed, some courts have refused to impose a duty of inspection on the possessor of rural land. Other courts have questioned the efficacy of a "rural" versus "urban" distinction even as regards the standard of care, noting that with the growth of suburbs and the increase in traffic through rural areas, it has become less workable. * * *

The latest formulation of the duty owed by a possessor of land to persons outside his premises with regard to natural conditions which is set forth in the Restatement Second of Torts still limits the reach of the duty to persons traveling on the public streets and highways. (Rest.2d Torts, § 840, subd. (2).) * * * It is difficult to discern any reason to restrict the possessor's duty to individuals using the highways. To do so would create an unsatisfying anomaly: a possessor of land would have a duty of care toward strangers but not toward his neighbor.

* * *

Historically, the consideration most frequently invoked to support the rule of nonliability for natural conditions was that it was merely an embodiment of the principle that one should not be obligated to undertake affirmative conduct to aid or protect others. * * *

* * *

Whatever the rule may once have been, it is now clear that a duty to exercise due care can arise out of possession alone. One example is provided by modern cases dealing with the duty of a possessor of land to act affirmatively for the protection of individuals who come upon the premises. * * *

* * *

[T]he possessor's control and supervisory power over the land has been expressly relied upon by some courts in imposing a duty of reasonable care with regard to a natural condition of the land. Husovsky v. United States, 590 F.2d 944 [D.C.Cir.1978], involved a motorist's suit for injuries he sustained when a poplar tree fell on his automobile while he was driving through a public park. * * *

* * *

Thus, it becomes clear that the traditional characterization of a defendant's failure to take affirmative steps to prevent a natural condition from causing harm as nonactionable nonfeasance conflicts sharply with modern perceptions of the obligations which flow from the possession of land. Possession ordinarily brings with it the right of supervision and control. * * *

Another deficiency of the historical justification of the rule of nonliability is simply that it proves too much. Under the traditional analysis, a possessor of land should be excused from any duty to prevent harm to persons outside his land whenever he has played no part in the creation of the condition which threatens the harm, be it artificial or natural. However, most courts recognize that the possessor is under an affirmative duty to act with regard to a dangerous artificial condition even though the condition was created solely by some predecessor in title or possession; or by the unauthorized conduct of some other third person. "To impose such a duty is to cross the line from misfeasance to nonfeasance" unless the present possessor somehow aggravates the danger.

[I]n the cases holding that a possessor has an affirmative duty to prevent harm by a dangerous artificial condition created solely by another, the liability of the defendant has been predicated upon his possession and control of the artificial condition which caused the harm. Thus, these cases confirm that mere possession with its attendant right to control conditions on the premises is a sufficient basis for the imposition of an affirmative duty to act. In sum, the historical justification for the rule of nonliability for natural conditions has lost whatever validity it may once have had.

* * *

* * * All this leads to but one conclusion. The distinction between artificial and natural conditions should be rejected. * * *

* * *

Respondents next contend that the summary judgment must be affirmed because appellant failed to introduce admissible evidence sufficient to raise a triable issue of fact regarding the reasonableness of respondent's failure to take affirmative steps to control the landslide condition on the 90–acre parcel. * * *

Respondents' expert witness testified, by affidavit, that it ordinarily would be quite expensive for respondents even to determine the measures required to correct the landslide condition on the 90–acre parcel. Construction of the corrective measures would entail even greater expense. Moreover, it would not be possible for respondents totally to control the landslide. A full solution would require that measures also be taken upon the property of other landowners in the slide area. Finally, respondents' geologist asserted that the measures proposed for control of the slide by appellant's expert witness would be, at best, only slightly effective and that the cost of implementing them, therefore, would not be justified by the benefit to appellant.

On the other hand, that portion of appellant's evidence which is conceded to be admissible establishes that respondents knew or had reason to know of the landslide but did nothing to abate the condition. Further, proper excavation and sloping at the head of the slide together with dewatering might have been effective in preventing the landslide from harming appellant's home.

Construing appellant's evidence liberally and respondents' narrowly, as this court must [because respondents seek summary judgment], a rational inference can be drawn that effective measures for the control of the slide were within respondents' reach and that such measures would have entailed a substantial expense. Although the cost of implementing only slightly effective measures would not be justified by the benefit to appellant, it can be inferred that the cost of implementing effective measures might (or might not) be justified by the benefit to appellant and to respondents. Although the case is a close one, the evidence does not conclusively establish that no rational inference of negligence can be drawn under the circumstances of this case.

* * *

The judgment of the trial court is reversed and the cause remanded to the trial court for further proceedings consistent with the views expressed in this opinion.

RICHARDSON, JUSTICE, concurring.

* * *

* * * I find it exceedingly difficult to imagine what respondents reasonably could have done to prevent or reduce the damage caused by the natural condition here present.

* * *

Nonetheless, I agree that appellant should be entitled before a fact finder to explore the propriety of respondents' conduct referable to the geological condition.

Notes

1. As the *Sprecher* opinion suggests, the jurisdictions that have held the occupier responsible for natural conditions vary considerably. Some limit the duty to highway injuries; some, to injuries from trees; some, to urban land occupiers. The narrowest possible extension would presumably relax the no–duty rule only when an urban tree harms a highway user. What would you expect Alaska's position to be? New Jersey's? According to Prosser & Keeton, "England, thickly settled, requires reasonable care as to all trees." Prosser & Keeton on Torts § 57, p. 391 n. 58 (5th ed. 1984).

2. Does the Coase theorem furnish a useful perspective for thinking about the wisdom of *Sprecher*? (See the Economic Analysis note following *Testbank*, supra p. 266.) Assuming that economic analysis would not provide any useful support for imposing liability for the mudslide on the defendant, is there a compelling fairness argument for doing so?

2. OCCUPIER'S LIABILITY FOR INJURIES ON THE PREMIS-ES

This note summarizes a cumbersome and complex body of material. Simplification, always likely to falsify, is especially dangerous here. In the standard treatments of this area, duty and breach factors have become inextricably commingled. The law everywhere is confused and changing. *Caveat lector*. No textual summary of this area is an adequate substitute for close study of the decisions of particular jurisdictions. What follows is a sketch of the traditional view.

Persons who enter land and get hurt there find their rights contingent upon the circumstances of their entry. Depending on those circumstances, the injured person may have been a trespasser, a licensee, or an invitee. Unless reasonable minds could not differ, the jury should determine which category the plaintiff belongs in.

The definitions designed to delineate among the three categories are complex and detailed. Here is the gist of it. A trespasser is one who enters (or stays) without any right or privilege to do so. A licensee is one whose only privilege derives from the occupier's consent; social guests are licensees. An invitee comes on some errand of potential economic benefit to the occupier or under circumstances implying a representation by the occupier that reasonable care has been used to make the place suitably safe.

If the plaintiff was a trespasser, at one time it was held that the occupier owed no duty at all. This was said to be true whether the injury was caused by an activity, an artificial condition, or a natural condition. This monolithic protection of landed interests soon yielded to the rule as normally stated today: The occupier "owes no duty to a trespasser except to refrain from injuring him by 'willful or wanton' conduct." Prosser & Keeton on Torts § 58, p. 397 (5th ed. 1984).

There are two significant exceptions or qualifications to the general trespasser rule. The most important set of qualifications benefit injured children. This matter is set aside for separate treatment in section F–3, infra p. 284. Second, when the occupier knows that significant numbers of trespassers habitually frequent a particular and limited part of the land, or when a trespasser's presence on the land has actually been discovered by the occupier, most courts hold the occupier to a duty of reasonable care in conducting activities on the premises.

The early decisions involving licensee plaintiffs treated them much like trespassers, imposing liability only for injuries caused by the occupier's intentional, willful, wanton, or reckless conduct. Soon most jurisdictions expanded the occupier's duty to licensees to include reasonable care (1) in the conduct of activities on the premises if the danger is not apparent to the licensee, and (2) to warn the licensee of dangerous conditions (both natural and artificial) if the occupier knew or "had reason to know" of the condition and the condition was not known or likely to be discovered by the licensee.

The invitee plaintiff is owed a duty of reasonable care with respect to activities and with respect to conditions about which the occupier "should have known." This means conditions about which the occupier would have known had he or she used reasonable care; in other words, conditions unknown to the occupier can give rise to liability if the occupier should have discovered them. (It is sometimes said that as to an invitee, the occupier has a duty to inspect, but that is true only if reasonable care would require inspection.)

The implications of the foregoing summary are that invitees' rights are superior to those of licensees in two respects: (a) As to injuries from activities on the land, the occupier owes the invitee a full–blown duty of reasonable care, whereas the duty owed to the licensee is somewhat circumscribed by the invitee's obligation to look out for himself. (b) As to injuries from conditions on the land, the invitee is owed a duty respecting conditions about which the occupier "should have known" whereas the licensee is owed a duty with respect to conditions about which the occupier "had reason to know." This means the while the occupier can't escape liability to the licensee by claiming no knowledge of the risk if he or she knew the facts that made the condition dangerous, the occupier has no duty to discover such facts even if reasonable care would require it. See, e.g., Fleck v. Nickerson, 239 Or. 641, 399 P.2d 353 (Or.1965). Recall that Sprecher v. Adamson Companies, supra p. 272, mentioned this distinction in connection with harm caused by natural conditions, noting that some courts would impose liability on urban occupiers if they "should have known" but on rural occupiers only if they "had reason to know" of the danger.

Because it is easier to show that the occupier *should have known* of the danger than it is to show that he or she *had reason to know* of it, classification of the plaintiff as an invitee or a licensee is often outcome–determinative. The following case involves one aspect of the classification issue.

STITT v. HOLLAND ABUNDANT LIFE FELLOWSHIP

Supreme Court of Michigan, 2000.
462 Mich. 591, 614 N.W.2d 88.

YOUNG, J.

In this premises liability case the plaintiff, Violet Moeller, was injured when she tripped over a concrete tire stop in defendant church's parking lot. Plaintiff was [not a member of the church but] was visiting the church to attend bible study. Plaintiff sued the church, alleging that the defendant negligently placed the tire stops and failed to provide adequate lighting in the parking lot. [She died before this decision and her personal representative was substituted as the named plaintiff.]

At trial, the jury was instructed on the obligations property owners owe to licensees. The jury returned a verdict in favor of the church. The Court of Appeals reversed and remanded the case for a new trial after determining that the trial court erred by instructing the jury on the obligations owed to licensees rather than "public invitees" as defined in Restatement (2d) of Torts, § 332.

We granted leave to appeal in this case to determine the proper standard of care owed to individuals on church property for noncommercial purposes. We hold that the trial court correctly instructed the jury that such individuals are licensees and not invitees. Accordingly, we reverse the Court of Appeals decision and reinstate the trial court judgment in favor of the church.

* * *

III

ANALYSIS

A. The Common–Law Classifications

Historically, Michigan has recognized three common–law categories for persons who enter upon the land or premises of another: (1) trespasser, (2) licensee, or (3) invitee. Michigan has not abandoned these common–law classifications. Each of these categories corresponds to a different standard of care that is owed to those injured on the owner's premises. Thus, a landowner's duty to a visitor depends on that visitor's status.

A "trespasser" is a person who enters upon another's land, without the landowner's consent. The landowner owes no duty to the trespasser except to refrain from injuring him by "willful and wanton" misconduct.

A "licensee" is a person who is privileged to enter the land of another by virtue of the possessor's consent. A landowner owes a licensee a duty only to warn the licensee of any hidden dangers the owner knows or has reason to know of, if the licensee does not know or have reason to know of the dangers involved. The landowner owes no duty of inspection or affirmative care to make the premises safe for the licensee's visit. Typically, social guests are licensees who assume the ordinary risks associated with their visit.

The final category is invitees. An "invitee" is "a person who enters upon the land of another upon an invitation which carries with it an implied representation, assurance, or understanding that reasonable care has been used to prepare the premises, and make [it] safe for [the invitee's] reception." * * * Thus, an invitee is entitled to the highest level of protection under premises liability law.

A possessor of land is subject to liability for physical harm caused to his invitees by a condition on the land if the owner: (a) knows of, or by the exercise of reasonable care would discover, the condition and should realize that the condition involves an unreasonable risk of harm to such invitees; (b) should expect that invitees will not discover or realize the danger, or will fail to protect themselves against it; and (c) fails to exercise reasonable care to protect invitees against the danger.

The Court of Appeals correctly recognized that invitee status is commonly afforded to persons entering upon the property of another for business purposes. In this case, we are called upon to determine whether invitee status should extend to individuals entering upon church property for *non* commercial purposes. Because invitee status necessarily turns on the existence of an "invitation," we must examine our common law in order to ascertain the meaning of that term.

B. The Meaning of Invitation in Michigan's Common Law

[The court concluded that earlier Michigan decisions were inconsistent, but that none squarely addressed the question whether a mere "public invitee" such as a churchgoer is entitled to invitee status.]

C. The Restatement

We begin by noting that a large number of jurisdictions have adopted § 332 of the Restatement:

(1) An invitee is either a public invitee or a business visitor.

(2) A public invitee is a person who is invited to enter or remain on land as a member of the public for a purpose for which the land is held open to the public.

(3) A business visitor is a person who is invited to enter or remain on land for a purpose directly or indirectly connected with business dealings with the possessor of the land.

Subsection (2) of § 332 of the Restatement creates an invitee status that does not depend on a commercial purpose. * * *

* * *

[W]e decline to adopt § 332 of the Restatement here. [The court overruled its own 1970 decision "to the extent [it] purported to adopt the Restatement definition."]

D. Business Purpose As A Precondition of Invitee Status

Given the divergence of our cases on what circumstances create invitee status, we must provide some form of reconciliation in this case. In harmonizing our cases, we conclude that the imposition of additional expense and effort by the landowner, requiring the landowner to inspect the premises and make them safe for visitors, must be directly tied to the owner's commercial business interests. It is the owner's desire to foster a commercial advantage by inviting persons to visit the premises that justifies imposition of a higher duty. In short, we conclude that the prospect of pecuniary gain is a sort of quid pro quo for the higher duty of care owed to invitees. Thus, we hold that the owner's reason for inviting persons onto the premises is the primary consideration when determining the visitor's status: In order to establish invitee status, a plaintiff must show that the premises were held open for a *commercial* purpose.

With regard to church visitors, we agree with the court in McNulty v. Hurley, 97 So.2d 185 (Fla., 1957), that such persons are licensees.[10] In *McNulty,* a churchgoer was injured when, as she was leaving the church, she was pushed to the ground by a crowd of people. The lower court granted the defendant church's motion to dismiss on grounds that the plaintiff failed to state a cause of action. The defendant contended that one entering church premises for the purpose of attending religious services is a mere licensee. Thus, the only duty of the church was to refrain from wanton negligence or willful misconduct and to refrain from intentionally exposing her to danger. The plaintiff, on the other hand, argued that she was on the church premises by invitation and that most

---

10. The Florida Supreme Court has since moved away from *McNulty* and has adopted § 332 of the Restatement. See Post v. Lunney, 261 So.2d 146 (Fla., 1972). However, we continue to find *McNulty's* reasoning persuasive.

religions urge members and others to enter their churches and hold their doors open as a standing invitation. The Florida Supreme Court disagreed, stating:

> [A]n invitation to enter and worship, whether it be either express or implied, does not constitute one who accepts the invitation an invitee in the legal sense. In order for such relationship to arise the person entering onto the premises, i.e., the invitee, must have done so for purposes which would have benefited the owner or occupant of the premises, i.e., the invitor, or have been of mutual benefit to the invitee and the invitor. And as we view it this benefit must be of a material or commercial rather than of a spiritual, religious, or social nature.

* * *

[W]hether the plaintiff in the instant case previously gave an offering to the church has no bearing on whether she was a licensee or an invitee. Absent a showing that the church's invitation to attend its services was for an essential commercial purpose, Ms. Moeller should be considered a licensee and not an invitee. A person who attends church as a guest enjoys the "unrecompensed hospitality" provided by the church in the same way that a person entering the home of a friend would. We conclude that church visitors who are attending church for religious worship are more like social guests (licensees) than business visitors (invitees).

IV

CONCLUSION

We recognize that a majority of jurisdictions considering the issue have adopted the public invitee definition set forth in § 332 of the Restatement. However, in exercising our common–law authority, our role is not simply to "count heads" but to determine which common–law rules best serve the interests of Michigan citizens. We believe that Michigan is better served by recognizing that invitee status must be founded on a commercial purpose for visiting the owner's premises.

* * *

WEAVER, C.J., and TAYLOR, CORRIGAN, and MARKMAN, JJ. concurred.

KELLY, J.,(joined by CAVANAGH, J.), dissenting.

* * *

For over a century, Michigan has recognized that one can be classified as an invitee when on an invitor's property for a commercial purpose *or* pursuant to an invitation. Thus, the *McNulty* decision runs contrary to recognized principles of Michigan law by imposing a commercial purpose requirement to the designation of an invitee. This Court has expressly stated, "Invitation is sufficient. Pecuniary profit to the owner is not essential." Therefore, the majority's reliance on *McNulty* is misplaced.

Furthermore, Florida itself has rejected the *McNulty* decision. See Post v. Lunney, 261 So.2d 146 (Fla., 1972). In *Post,* the Florida Supreme Court adopted § 332, including the public invitee provision. It pointed out that the *McNulty* mutual benefit test was too narrow and had the potential to cause unjust results. "For example, it would prohibit recovery for damages due to ordinary negligence to a 'window–shopping' visitor to a store, while permitting recovery to a person who made a purchase, however small. To avoid these and similar results, 'the economic benefit theory has been strained to the breaking point.' " The Florida court applied the public invitee provision of § 332 to the case. It concluded that the plaintiff was an invitee because she had been invited to enter property opened to members of the public for tours.

The recognized law of Michigan is more consistent with the decision in *Post* than it is with the decision in *McNulty.* We have long recognized that one could be an invitee without benefiting the owner or being on the property for a commercial purpose. That principle is contained in the public invitee provision of § 332. Therefore, as the Florida court did in *Post,* this Court should find that the public invitee provision of § 332 is applicable to this plaintiff.

* * *

I agree with the Indiana Court of Appeals [opinion in Fleischer v. Hebrew Orthodox Congregation, 504 N.E.2d 320, 323 (Ind.App. 1987)]:

> The public invitee test set out in Restatement section 332(2) would require that the occupant open his premises to the public or to some broad segment of it. Thus, it would not extend invitee status to social guests. When premises are opened to the public, their use and condition begin to affect the public interest, so that it is reasonable for courts to impose upon the occupant a standard of reasonable care toward those members of the public who enter for the purpose for which they were invited. The occupant does not lose control of his property; he can withdraw the invitation or restrict entry as he sees fit. Neither does he owe a duty of reasonable care to the public in general. The test would further require that the visitor enter the premises for the particular purpose for which the occupant has encouraged the public to do so. It is this latter fact which raises the inference that the occupant will use reasonable care to keep the premises safe for the visitor.

* * *

> Given the public interest involved and our recognition of the implication of safety which arises when the public is encouraged to enter premises for a particular purpose, we conclude that the public invitee test is a proper guide for determining invitee status.

* * *

The public invitee provision of § 332 accurately reflects the common law of Michigan. * * * [I]t reflects the sound public policy of protecting members of the public when premises are open to them.

* * *

Notes

1. *Judicial politics.* The principal case is a useful reminder that courts are not necessarily bound by historical trends, consensus views, or even their own precedents. All of those indicated Ms. Moeller would be treated as a public invitee. The view that only business visitors are invitees was generally rejected long ago, and the Restatement's definition, which gives public invitees the same status as business invitees, has been embraced virtually universally. See Dan Dobbs, The Law of Torts 599 (2000). Treating Ms. Moeller as a licensee required the court to overrule at least strong dicta in its own precedents. But something else was also at work in Michigan. In the late 1990's the Republican governor appointed three new justices to vacancies on the Michigan Supreme Court, creating for the first time in 50 years a conservative majority committed to reducing tort liability. *Stitt* was one of twenty–five cases from 1998–2000 in which this new majority overturned long–standing precedents. In the 2000 election, when the three Republican appointees were up for election, the Democrats tried to win the court back but failed after a campaign in which both sides spent $15 million. See Sarah K. Delaney, Stare Decisis v. the "New Majority": the Michigan Supreme Court's Practice of Overruling Precedent, 1998–2000, 66 Albany L. Rev. 871 (2003).

2. Courts usually construe the business–visitor branch of the invitee definition broadly. See, e.g., Wal–Mart Stores, Inc. v. Lerma, 749 S.W.2d 572 (Tex. App. 1988)(holding shopper's child to be invitee); Wieseler v. Sisters of Mercy Health Corp., 540 N.W.2d 445 (Iowa 1995)(holding hospital patient's visitor to be invitee).

3. *Open and obvious risks.* Even as to invitees, some states absolve the landowner from liability if the condition causing the plaintiff's injury was "open and obvious." See, e.g., Tichenor v. Lohaus, 212 Neb. 218, 322 N.W.2d 629 (1982). Some jurisdictions never employed this limitation, and in most that did it has now been subsumed into comparative negligence analysis and no longer acts as a complete bar to recovery. See, e.g., Ward v. K–Mart Corp., 136 Ill.2d 132, 143 Ill.Dec. 288, 554 N.E.2d 223 (1990).

4. *Recreational use statutes.* The occupier of rural land generally owes licensees a lesser duty than whatever is imposed by the common law, because of "recreational use statutes." See generally Dobbs, supra note 1 (stating that all or virtually all states have such statutes). These vary from state to state, but generally require the plaintiff to show something like willful and wanton conduct in order to recover. It may be that the courts are inclined to construe these statutes narrowly, i.e., to hold the occupier to the common law duties whenever possible. See, e.g., Harrison v. Middlesex Water Co., 80 N.J. 391, 403 A.2d 910 (1979).

5. *The Fireman's Rule.* Under the "Fireman's Rule," firefighters and police entering premises to assist the occupier get classified as licensees and

find their protection against injuries limited accordingly, on the theory that they are present by virtue of a privilege rather than an invitation. The rule is widely criticized but seems to be entrenched.

6. *Evaluating burdens.* The majority in the principal case argues that treating church visitors as invitees would impose "additional expense and effort by the landowner, requiring the landowner to inspect the premises and make them safe for visitors." But other visitors who use the parking lot surely would be classed as invitees (e.g., the minister or other paid employees, tradesmen), so the church presumably would have to inspect to protect them anyway. Some courts appear to take this consideration into account in deciding whether to classify a plaintiff as an invitee. See, e.g., Rivas v. Oxon Hill Joint Venture, 130 Md.App. 101, 744 A.2d 1076 (2000)(noting that treating subpoena–server as invitee would require no more care by owner of apartment complex parking lot than it would obliged to exercise anyway for benefit of its tenants.) Is this a legitimate consideration? A more relevant consideration than whether the visitor confers economic benefit?

7. *Rethinking occupier liabilities.* Because of the complexity and uncertainty involved in applying the traditional rules based on categories of plaintiffs, as well as doubts as to the continued wisdom of giving so much protection to landed interests, a movement began in 1957 to abolish the categories and hold the occupier of land to a general duty of reasonable care. England and about half the states have abandoned the tripartite classification scheme in favor of imposing a general duty of care, at least as to all except trespassers. This is not a clear trend, however, because in recent years about as many states have decided to adhere to the scheme as have modified it. In Pinnell v. Bates, 838 So.2d 198 (Miss. 2002) the court listed 25 states that have abolished the categories at least in some respects, 19 that have expressly refused to do so, and six that retain them but have not expressly considered the question.

3. OCCUPIER'S LIABILITY TO CHILDREN INJURED ON THE PREMISES

Even for 19th century courts, the traditional rules of occupiers' liability were too harsh when applied to trespassing children. Two cases in which children trespassed on railroad land and were hurt playing on turntables spawned the *attractive nuisance doctrine.* (Sioux City & Pacific Railroad Co. v. Stout, 84 U.S. (17 Wall.) 657, 21 L.Ed. 745 (1873); Keffe v. Milwaukee & St. Paul Railway Co., 21 Minn. 207 (1875).) This doctrine, which originated as a way of "promoting" the injured child out of the trespasser category, had a complicated and colorful life until "restated" in Restatement (2d) of Torts § 339 (1965). Among the Restatement's more influential provisions, § 339 "has been cited so frequently, and has received such general acceptance on the part of the courts, that it has become the new point of departure." Prosser & Keeton on Torts § 59, p. 402 (5th ed. 1984). It is quoted and applied in the following decision.

THUNDER HAWK v. UNION PACIFIC R.R. CO.

Supreme Court of Wyoming, 1992.
844 P.2d 1045.

Macy, Chief Justice.

Alexander Thunder Hawk, Jr. (Alex) suffered a traumatic below–the–knee amputation of his left leg as a result of a rail yard accident. Alex, by and through his guardian ad litem and conservators, sued Union Pacific Railroad Company for negligent, grossly negligent, and willful and wanton misconduct. * * * The district court granted summary judgments in favor of Union Pacific on all claims.

* * *

The issues which we must address on appeal are:

(1) Whether the district court erred by granting a summary judgment adverse to Alex's claim that Union Pacific owed a duty of reasonable care to him under the attractive nuisance doctrine;

(2) Whether the district court erred by granting a summary judgment adverse to Alex's claim that Union Pacific acted in willful or wanton disregard for his safety on July 20, 1989 * * *.

* * *

On July 20, 1989, Alex, who was then six years old, went with two friends to play in Crow Creek near the Ames Overpass in west Cheyenne, Wyoming. After playing for an undetermined period of time, Alex and his friends climbed up the embankment adjacent to the creek. Four sets of Union Pacific railroad tracks, which run longitudinally east and west, lie on top of that embankment. Alex crossed the northernmost tracks, as well as the adjacent tracks, and began playing on a train located on the third set of tracks. Unbeknown to Alex, the train on the third set of tracks, later identified as the NPSE1–20, had been stopped by the train operations manager for the purpose of removing transient riders. Once three transient riders were located and removed, the manager cleared the NPSE1–20 for departure. When the NPSE1–20 began to leave, Alex jumped from the car on which he was playing. His left leg landed in the path of the train and was severed just below the knee.

Alex, by and through his guardian ad litem and conservators, filed a complaint against Union Pacific on June 29, 1990, alleging that his injuries were proximately caused by Union Pacific's negligent, grossly negligent, and willful and wanton misconduct.

* * * By an order entered on November 4, 1991, * * * the district court ruled that Alex was a trespasser or at most a bare licensee to whom Union Pacific owed a duty not to willfully or wantonly harm and that the attractive nuisance doctrine could not be invoked under the facts of the case to elevate the standard of care. By an order entered on

April 16, 1992, * * * the district court ruled that no evidence existed to show that Union Pacific breached its duty not to willfully or wantonly harm Alex * * *.

NOVEMBER 4, 1991, ORDER

The real battle in this case is over what duty of care Union Pacific owed to Alex on July 20, 1989. In its November 4, 1991, order, the district court determined that Union Pacific owed no duty to Alex other than not to injure him willfully or wantonly. Alex does not contend on appeal that he was other than a trespasser or bare licensee on the date in question; however, he does contend that the district court erred by granting a summary judgment adverse to his claim that Union Pacific owed a duty of reasonable care to him under § 339 of the Restatement (Second) of Torts, popularly referred to as the attractive nuisance doctrine.[1]

We * * * adopt what is now the most widely accepted statement of the doctrine. * * * The Restatement (Second) of Torts § 339 (1965) provides:

A possessor of land is subject to liability for physical harm to children trespassing thereon caused by an artificial condition upon the land if

(a) the place where the condition exists is one upon which the possessor knows or has reason to know that children are likely to trespass, and

(b) the condition is one of which the possessor knows or has reason to know and which he realizes or should realize will involve an unreasonable risk of death or serious bodily harm to such children, and

(c) the children because of their youth do not discover the condition or realize the risk involved in intermeddling with it or in coming within the area made dangerous by it, and

---

1. The term "attractive nuisance" originated from early cases which espoused the theory that land possessors "impliedly invited" children onto their premises when they maintained thereon a dangerous condition or instrumentality which they knew or had reason to know would be attractive to children. Consistent with common–law rules of premises liability, the courts held under such circumstances that the land possessor would be held to a duty of due care. See, e.g., Keffe v. Milwaukee and St. Paul Railway Company, 21 Minn. 207, 18 Am.Rep. 393 (Minn.1875). A land possessor would be held liable under the theory of "implied invitation," however, only when a child was injured by the particular condition or instrumentality which initially attracted him to the premises. United Zinc & Chemical Co. v. Britt, 258 U.S. 268, 42 S.Ct. 299, 66 L.Ed. 615 (1922).

Today, the term "attractive nuisance" is somewhat of a misnomer. Section 339 of the Restatement (Second) of Torts does not require that a child be attracted to the land possessor's premises by a dangerous condition or instrumentality and that he be injured by the particular attraction. Nor does § 339 rely upon the legal fiction of "implied invitation" to elevate a land possessor's duty of care to child trespassers. Despite these recognized differences, the courts, including this one, continue to refer to injured–child–trespasser cases popularly as "attractive nuisance" cases.

(d) the utility to the possessor of maintaining the condition and the burden of eliminating the danger are slight as compared with the risk to children involved, and

(e) the possessor fails to exercise reasonable care to eliminate the danger or otherwise to protect the children.

As the attractive nuisance doctrine is an exception to the common law, it is strictly construed by the courts. To recover under § 339, a child trespasser must first demonstrate by a preponderance of the evidence at trial the existence of elements (a) through (d). If the child trespasser is successful in doing so, the duty of reasonable care under element (e) attaches to the land possessor. The child trespasser must then, as in any other negligence case, prove the elements of breach, proximate causation, and damages by a preponderance of the evidence.

In the instant case, our own review of the record discloses that genuine issues of material fact existed as to elements (a) and (b). Thus, the focus of the present dispute concerns the district court's determinations as to elements (c) and (d). The district court granted a summary judgment in favor of Union Pacific on the basis of the following two findings:

> Plaintiff fails to present specific facts showing that a genuine issue of material fact does exist as to [element] (c) of the doctrine; i.e., that [Alex], because of his youth, did not realize the risk involved in playing on the trains. The depositions of [Alex], his mother and his father clearly show that [Alex] knew that the trains were dangerous.

> Additionally, Plaintiff fails to present facts showing that a genuine issue of material [fact] does exist as to [element] (d); i.e., that the utility of maintaining the railroad property condition and the burden of eliminating the danger are slight as compared to the risk to children.

Union Pacific advances both legal and evidentiary arguments as to why the district court's findings and order should be affirmed. Initially, Union Pacific asks this Court to hold, as a matter of law, that the attractive nuisance doctrine is inapplicable to trains because even young children appreciate that trains are dangerous. Exemplary of the cases relied upon by Union Pacific is Herrera v. Southern Pacific Railway Company, 188 Cal.App.2d 441, 10 Cal.Rptr. 575 (1961), wherein the court stated: "Nothing could be more pregnant with warning of danger than the noise and appearance of a huge, rumbling, string of railroad cars."

In contrast to *Herrera* and other similar cases, Alex was not attracted to a moving train "pregnant with warning of danger." Alex was attracted to and played upon the NPSE1–20, which, prior to the time of Alex's injury, was stopped in the rail yard. We are persuaded that it would be a bad policy to adopt a rule which would eliminate any legal incentive for railroads to take reasonable measures to protect young children from foreseeable, train–related injuries.[3] We believe that the attractive nuisance doctrine strikes an appropriate balance between a railroad's land–use rights and Wyoming's policy of "throw[ing] a protective arm [a]round children of tender years." We hold that a determination of whether a particular child appreciates the risk of playing on or about a train should be made on a case–by–case basis.

Union Pacific's first evidentiary argument is that the undisputed facts of this case support the district court's determination that, contrary to the requirement of element (c), Alex knew prior to his accident that trains were dangerous. Union Pacific directs our attention to the depositions of Alex and his parents which were submitted with its partial summary judgment motion. A review of Alex's deposition reflects that he admitted his parents warned him about trains and that he knew they were dangerous on the date of his injury. Alex's testimony is confirmed, in part, by his parents' depositions. They both testified that they told Alex that trains were dangerous.

Alex's counsel argues that Alex's deposition statement that he knew at the time of his accident that trains were dangerous should not be given preclusive effect. His counsel argues that Alex certainly had a clearer perspective of a train's potential danger when he was deposed, as he sat in a chair with a prosthesis strapped to his left leg, than he had some two years earlier when he boarded the NPSE1–20. His counsel also argues that the district court ignored contrary evidence which raised a genuine issue of material fact regarding Alex's knowledge of the danger. Our attention is directed to the depositions of Alex's primary resource teacher, his school social worker, and his regular school teacher, which he relied upon in opposing Union Pacific's partial summary judgment motion. From these depositions, we discover that Alex was and continues to be learning disabled. He has trouble paying attention and suffers from a severe delay in language processing skills. His school teacher explained:

> [Alex is] the kind of child who you could say, ["]You're not to play on this tire swing with the water,["] if there's water below. And you can go through and explain the whole thing to him, and it may not have any meaning. And he's the child who, the next day, gets in trouble, and says, ["]I don't understand why I'm in trouble, I'm just playing out here for recess.["]

In light of Alex's learning disabilities, we do not believe that the fact that Alex had been warned generically that trains were dangerous can support a finding that he "realize[d] the risk" of intermeddling with the

---

3. Our position is apparently in accord with that of the Wyoming Legislature. Wyo. Stat. § 37–9–1101 (Supp.1992), enacted in 1991, provides:

Except in cases of attractive nuisance, no person owning, operating, loading or unloading a railroad car or train shall be liable for any damages for the accidental death or injury of a person occurring while the person was riding the railroad car or train in violation of W.S. 37–12–104, or while the person was boarding or unboarding from the railroad car or train without the consent of the owner or operator of the railroad car or train.

NPSE1–20 on the date of his injury, as required by element (c). We hold that sufficient evidence was presented, when viewed from the vantage point most favorable to Alex, to create a genuine issue of material fact as to whether Alex really understood the risks on July 20, 1989, involved in playing on or about trains.

Union Pacific's second evidentiary argument is that the district court correctly determined that, contrary to element (d), Alex failed to present evidence that "the utility to the possessor of maintaining the condition and the burden of eliminating the danger are slight as compared with the risk to children involved." The fallacy of this argument is that Alex did not, under the circumstances of this case, have the burden of presenting evidence at this stage of the proceeding. Orthodox summary judgment rules require the movant to first make a prima facie case that no issue of material fact exists before the burden shifts to the nonmoving party to come forward with conflicting evidence. A review of the record reveals that Union Pacific failed to present any competent evidence on the burden–benefit issue with its partial summary judgment motion. Therefore, the burden to present conflicting evidence never shifted to Alex. On appeal, Union Pacific merely alleges that taking preventative measures would require an "enormous commitment of resources" and would require "hundreds of additional employees." These broad allegations come too late and are insufficient to rescue the district court's erroneous finding. We hold that element (d)'s burden–benefit analysis remains as a viable issue.

Genuine issues of material fact exist as to elements (a) through (d) of § 339. We reverse the November 4, 1991, order granting a partial summary judgment. Should the fact finder resolve the issues as to elements (a) through (d) in Alex's favor, Union Pacific will be held to a standard of reasonable care under element (e), and liability will be determined as in any negligence case.

APRIL 16, 1992, ORDER

* * *

Union Pacific contends that the district court correctly granted a summary judgment on the willful and wanton misconduct issue because no evidence was present in the record to show that Union Pacific employees knew that Alex was on the NPSE1–20 on July 20, 1989. Union Pacific argues that, if the employees did not know Alex was present, they could not act in conscious disregard for his safety.

Alex counters that a genuine issue of material fact exists regarding the willful and wanton misconduct issue because Union Pacific had notice that children played on the tracks and yet failed to take measures to protect these children from injury. To support this position, Alex relied, in part, upon the deposition of a Union Pacific employee who saw and reported children in the rail yard on several occasions. Alex also relied upon the deposition and affidavit of an expert in railroad safety. The expert stated that it was his opinion that, in light of Union Pacific's knowledge, its policies demonstrated a "conscious disregard" for the safety of children. These policies included Union Pacific's failure to secure the rail yard, its failure to enforce existing operating rules for the detection of persons on or near trains, and its failure to supplement existing rules with a bulletin to warn crews of the potential presence of children.

In Mayflower Restaurant Company v. Griego, 741 P.2d 1106, 1115 (Wyo.1987), we gave the definition of willful and wanton misconduct:

> Willful and wanton misconduct is the intentional doing of an act, or an intentional failure to do an act, in reckless disregard of the consequences and under circumstances and conditions that a reasonable person would know, or have reason to know that such conduct would, in a high degree of probability, result in harm to another.

We believe that Alex submitted evidence which, viewed from the vantage point most favorable to his position, was sufficient to create a genuine issue of material fact concerning Union Pacific's safety policy. We reverse that portion of the April 16, 1992, order which granted a summary judgment adverse to Alex's willful and wanton misconduct claim.

* * *

Notes

1. On remand, the case was tried to a jury, which found in favor of the railroad. See Thunder Hawk v. Union Pacific R. Co., 891 P.2d 773 (Wyo. 1995).

2. Anyone who is on the land without the owner's consent (and without a privilege such as the one accorded emergency personnel) is a trespasser for purposes of premises liability law. Intent, which would be a requisite to finding the interloper guilty of the tort of trespass, is not a requisite here.

3. *Attractive nuisance in the Restatement.* The attractive nuisance doctrine originated as an exception to the limited–duty rule that otherwise applies to trespassers. Section 339 of the Restatement undertakes to describe the circumstances under which an occupier of land owes a duty of reasonable care to trespassing children. But subsection (e) addresses the question of reasonable care. The explanation is that drafters of the Restatement were not always careful to segregate different elements of the negligence case; sometimes, as in § 339, they lump two or more issues into a single section. Note that the section purports to state the requisites not merely for finding the existence of a duty, but for finding "liability." But of course the section is incomplete for that purpose, because it omits mention of other elements, such as legal cause and damages, which would be equally essential to a finding of liability. The court in the principal case solves this problem by treating only subsections (a) through (d) as relevant to the duty issue, leaving (e) to be handled "as in any negligence case." Should subsection (d) also be treated as relevant to the breach issue rather than the duty issue?

4. Note that the court assumes the attractive nuisance doctrine applies in the principal case whether plaintiff is a trespasser or a "bare licensee." Although the doctrine is most frequently invoked by trespassers, it is also available to child licensees and child invitees to the extent it improves their chances.

5. What are the implications of the statute quoted in footnote 3 of the opinion? Obviously the legislature intended to exclude attractive nuisance cases from its general ban on railroad liability to unauthorized riders. Why isn't that dispositive of the railroad's argument that the attractive nuisance doctrine should not apply to trains, rather than merely "in accord with" the court's decision?

4. OWNER'S LIABILITY FOR INJURIES ON LEASED LAND

At common law a lease of real property was regarded as equivalent to a sale for the term. This characterization had many consequences, two of which are important in premises liability cases. With respect to injuries to third persons (whether occurring on the premises or outside), it generally meant that the owner was regarded as lacking possession and control of the land and therefore under no responsibility. With respect to injuries to the lessee, it generally meant that the doctrine of caveat emptor protected the owner.

These were harsh doctrines, and the courts found a number of ways around them. Some of the standard "exceptions"—ways of finding owner liability—as well as a more radical approach to the problem are set forth in the following decision.

SARGENT v. ROSS

Supreme Court of New Hampshire, 1973.
113 N.H. 388, 308 A.2d 528.

KENISON, CHIEF JUSTICE.

The question in this case is whether the defendant landlord is liable to the plaintiff in tort for the death of plaintiff's four–year–old daughter who fell to her death from an outdoor stairway at a residential building owned by the defendant in Nashua. The defendant resided in a ground–floor apartment in the building, and her son and daughter–in–law occupied a second story apartment serviced by the stairway from which the child fell. At the time of the accident the child was under the care of the defendant's daughter–in–law who was plaintiff's regular baby–sitter.

Plaintiff brought suit against the daughter–in–law for negligent supervision and against the defendant for negligent construction and maintenance of the stairway which was added to the building by the defendant about eight years before the accident. There was no apparent cause for the fall except for evidence that the stairs were dangerously steep, and that the railing was insufficient to prevent the child from falling over the side. The jury returned a verdict for the daughter–in–law but found in favor of the plaintiff in her action against the defendant landlord. [The landlord now appeals, urging that the trial judge erred in denying her motions for directed verdict and judgment n.o.v.]

Claiming that there was no evidence that the defendant retained control over the stairway, that it was used in common with other tenants, or that it contained a concealed defect, defendant urges that there was accordingly no duty owing to the deceased child for the defendant to breach. This contention rests upon the general rule which has long obtained in this and most other jurisdictions that a landlord is not liable, except in certain limited situations, for injuries caused by defective or dangerous conditions in the leased premises. The plaintiff does not directly attack this rule of nonliability but instead attempts to show, rather futilely under the facts, defendant's control of the stairway. She also relies upon [another] exception to the general rule of nonliability, to wit, that a landlord is liable for injuries resulting from his negligent repair of the premises. The issue, as framed by the parties, is whether the rule of nonliability should prevail or whether the facts of this case can be squeezed into the negligent repair or some other exception to the general rule of landlord immunity.

General principles of tort law ordinarily impose liability upon persons for injuries caused by their failure to exercise reasonable care under all the circumstances. * * * But, except in certain instances, landlords are immune from these simple rules of reasonable conduct which govern other persons in their daily activities. This "quasi–sovereignty of the landowner" finds its source in an agrarian England of the dark ages. Due to the untoward favoritism of the law for landlords, it has been justly stated that "the law in this area is a scandal." * * * [C]ourts and legislatures alike are beginning to reevaluate the rigid rules of landlord–tenant law in light of current needs and principles of law from related areas. * * *

* * * Thus, a landlord is now generally conceded to be liable in tort for injuries resulting from defective and dangerous conditions in the premises if the injury is attributable to (1) a hidden danger in the premises of which the landlord but not the tenant is aware, (2) premises leased for public use, (3) premises retained under the landlord's control, such as common stairways, or (4) premises negligently repaired by the landlord.

[T]he parties in this action concentrated at trial and on appeal on whether any of the exceptions applied, particularly whether the landlord or the tenant had control of the stairway. The determination of the question of which party had control of the defective part of the premises causing the injury has generally been considered dispositive of the landlord's liability. This was a logical modification to the rule of nonliability since ordinarily a landlord can reasonably be expected to maintain the property and guard against injuries only in common areas and other areas under his control. A landlord, for example, cannot fairly be held responsible in most instances for an injury arising out of the tenant's negligent maintenance of the leased premises. [ ] But the control test is insufficient since it substitutes a facile and conclusive test for a reasoned consideration of whether due care was exercised under all the circumstances.

There was evidence from which the jury could find that the landlord negligently designed or constructed a stairway which was dangerously steep or that she negligently failed to remedy or adequately warn the deceased of the danger. A proper rule of law would not preclude recovery in such a case by a person foreseeably injured by a dangerous hazard solely because the stairs serviced one apartment instead of two. But that would be the result if the control test were applied to this case, since this was not a "common stairway" or otherwise under the landlord's control. While we could strain this test to the limits and find control in the landlord, as plaintiff suggests, we are not inclined to so expand the fiction since we agree that "it is not part of the general law of negligence to exonerate a defendant simply because the condition attributable to his negligence has passed beyond his control before it causes injury * * *."

The anomaly of the general rule of landlord tort immunity and the inflexibility of the standard exceptions, such as the control exception, is pointedly demonstrated by this case. A child is killed by a dangerous condition of the premises. Both husband and wife tenants testify that they could do nothing to remedy the defect because they did not own the house nor have authority to alter the defect. But the landlord claims that she should not be liable because the stairs were not under her control. Both of these contentions are premised on the theory that the other party should be responsible. So the orthodox analysis would leave us with neither landlord nor tenant responsible for dangerous conditions on the premises. This would be both illogical and intolerable, particularly since neither party then would have any legal reason to remedy or take precautionary measures with respect to dangerous conditions. In fact, the traditional "control" rule actually discourages a landlord from remedying a dangerous condition since his repairs may be evidence of his control. Nor can there be serious doubt that ordinarily the landlord is best able to remedy dangerous conditions, particularly where a substantial alteration is required.

* * *

[P]laintiff's reliance on the negligent repairs exception to the rule of nonliability would require us to broaden the exception to include the negligent construction of improvements to the premises. We recognize that this would be no great leap in logic, but we think it more realistic instead to consider reversing the general rule of nonliability. * * * The emphasis on control and other exceptions to the rule of nonliability, both at trial and on appeal, unduly complicated the jury's task and diverted effort and attention from the central issue of the unreasonableness of the risk.

In recent years, immunities from tort liability affording "special protection in some types of relationships have been steadily giving way" in this and other jurisdictions. * * * We think that now is the time for the landlord's limited tort immunity to be relegated to the history books where it more properly belongs.

This conclusion springs naturally and inexorably from our recent decision in Kline v. Burns, 111 N.H. 87, 276 A.2d 248 (1971). *Kline* was an apartment rental claim suit in which the tenant claimed that the premises were uninhabitable. Following a small vanguard of other jurisdictions, we modernized the landlord–tenant contractual relationship by holding that there is an implied warranty of habitability in an apartment lease transaction. As a necessary predicate to our decision, we discarded from landlord–tenant law "that obnoxious legal cliche, caveat emptor." [ ] In so doing, we discarded the very legal foundation and justification for the landlord's immunity in tort for injuries to the tenant or third persons. * * *

To the extent that Kline v. Burns did not do so, we today discard the rule of "caveat lessee" and the doctrine of landlord nonliability in tort to which it gave birth. We thus bring up to date the other half of landlord–tenant law. Henceforth, landlords as other persons must exercise reasonable care not to subject others to an unreasonable risk of harm. * * * The questions of control, hidden defects and common or public use, which formerly had to be established as a prerequisite to even considering the negligence of a landlord, will now be relevant only inasmuch as they bear on the basic tort issues such as the foreseeability and unreasonableness of the particular risk of harm. * * *

* * *

Our decision will shift the primary focus of inquiry for judge and jury from the traditional question of "who had control?" to a determination of whether the landlord, and the injured party, exercised due care under all the circumstances. Perhaps even more significantly, the ordinary negligence standard should help insure that a landlord will take whatever precautions are reasonably necessary under the circumstances to reduce the likelihood of injuries from defects in his property. * * *

Although the trial court's instructions to the jury in the instant case were cast according to the traditional exceptions of control and hidden danger, the charge clearly set forth the elements of ordinary negligence which were presented by the court as a prerequisite to a finding of liability on either issue. Thus, the jury could find that the defendant was negligent in the design or construction of the steep stairway or in failing to take adequate precautionary measures to reduce the risk of injury. We have carefully reviewed the record and conclude that there is sufficient evidence, on the basis of the principles set forth above, to support the verdict of the jury which had the benefit of a view. Both plaintiff and the wife tenant testified that the stairs were too steep, and the husband tenant testified that his wife complained to him of this fact. While the defendant landlord did not testify, the jury could find that she knew that this steep stairway was frequently used by the young children for whom her daughter–in–law was the regular, daily babysitter. In any event, the use of these steps by young children should have been anticipated by the defendant.

* * *

Note

Several states have followed the *Sargent* decision; others continue to expand the exceptions to the owner–lessor's "immunity." Particularly regarding lessors of urban dwellings, the issue has been influenced by statutes and decisions implying a warranty of habitability into residential leases. Prosser & Keeton on Torts § 63, p. 435 (5th ed. 1984).

G. DUTY TO PROTECT AGAINST THIRD–PARTY TORTS AND CRIMES

As we suggested in the introduction to this chapter, the concept of duty can shrink as well as expand. In recent years, new no–duty rules have emerged as a major tool for "rein[ing] in juries"[1] and thereby limiting the scope of negligence liability. The Restatement (Third) of Torts: Liability for Physical Harm (Basic Principles) § 7 (Tent. Draft No. 2, March 2002), acknowledges the potential legitimacy of such newly–created no–duty rules, but it sets forth fairly demanding criteria for their creation. Section 7 provides in pertinent part :

> A court may determine that an actor has no duty or a duty other than the ordinary duty of reasonable care. Determinations of no duty and modifications of the duty of reasonable care are unusual and are based on special problems of principle or policy that warrant denying liability or limiting the ordinary duty of care in a particular class of cases. * * *

Comment *a* cautions that "[n]o–duty rules are appropriate only when a court can promulgate relatively clear, categorical, bright–line rules of law applicable to a general. class of cases." Comment *i* states that "without a broad, categorical duty rule, courts do not properly use no–duty determinations to substitute their own evaluation of the competing risks and burdens in a specific case for that of the factfinder. . . ."

From Section 7 and the comments, one might glean four Restatement criteria for the legitimacy of a newly–created no–duty rule: (a) the judge should acknowledge that a new rule is being created; (b) the new rule should be justified on the basis of principle or policy; (c) something about the lawsuit must be "unusual" enough to call for "special" treatment; and (d) the rule must be clear and broad enough to cover an identifiable class of cases;[2] it must not be an *ad hoc (i.e.,* for this case only) no–duty rule.

1. Recall Judge Posner's discussion of the duty concept in *Edwards, supra* p. 193.

2. Formulating this criterion is somewhat challenging because of the tension between Section 7's use of the term "particular class of cases" and the language of generality and breadth in comments *a* and *d.*

For cases that acknowledge and attempt to justify the creation of the new rules they announced, see Pelman v. McDonald's Corp., 237 F.Supp.2d 512 (S.D.N.Y. 2003), holding that the only way class–action plaintiffs complaining of childhood obesity as a result of fast–food consumption could state a valid cause of action would be to allege "either that the attributes of McDonald's products are so extraordinarily unhealthy that they are outside the reasonable contemplation of the consuming public or that the products are so extraordinarily unhealthy as to be dangerous in their intended use;" Doe v. Johnson, 817 F.Supp. 1382 (W.D.Mich. 1993), holding that a complaint against a sexually promiscuous celebrity who infected the plaintiff (and ultimately her infant child) with the HIV virus might state a cause of action if it could allege that the defendant knew or had strong reason to suspect that he had the virus, but that much of the complaint as it stood had to be dismissed because "without more, a defendant who has had unprotected sexual encounters with multiple partners does not have a legal duty to inform a plaintiff of his or her past sexual activity;" and Creasy v. Rusk, 730 N.E.2d 659 (Ind. 2000), holding that, while Alzheimer's patients are subject to the normal (i.e., Vaughan v. Menlove) standard of care, Alzheimer's patients who have no capacity to control their conduct do not owe a duty to their caregivers to refrain from violent conduct.

Other cases create new no–duty rules without acknowledging that anything unusual is happening or articulating a policy–or principle–based justification for the departure. These cases are subject to criticism, because a plaintiff who is being deprived of the application of the *Heaven* principle deserves an explanation for being treated differently than usual (and also because they make it tough for those who work daily at trying to make sense of the law to figure out what is going on[3]). Examples include Lawlor v. Orlando, 795 So.2d 147 (Fla.App. 2001) (announcing that psychotherapists ordinarily have no duty to guard against the risk of suicide of outpatients); Leach v. Mountain Lake, 120 F.3d 871 (8th Cir. 1997) (holding that pleasure–boat marinas that rent boats have no duty to advise their customers of impending bad weather); and Coburn v. City of Tucson, 143 Ariz. 50, 691 P.2d 1078 (1984) (holding that a municipality ordinarily has no liability for partially obscuring visibility at a street intersection if all law–abiding motorists can still see one another.)

---

3. Also troublesome from this point of view are cases that recognize the existence of a duty of care only after struggling as though each plaintiff in each new situation must make an affirmative and convincing showing that she should be owed a duty. See, e.g., In re September 11 Litigation, 208 F.Supp.2d 279 (S.D.N.Y. 2003) (holding that the airlines and airport security companies owed to persons injured on the ground by the hijacked and deliberately crashed planes a duty of reasonable care in screening passengers); Bajwa v. Metropolitan Life Ins. Co., 208 Ill.2d 414, 281 Ill.Dec. 554, 804 N.E.2d 519 (2004) (holding "as a matter of first impression" that a life insurance company must exercise reasonable care not to insure a life for the benefit of someone who means to murder the insured); Northern Indiana Pub. Serv. Co. v. Sharp, 790 N.E.2d 462 (Ind. 2003) (indicating that it was clear that an electrical utility with an overhead high–voltage wire had a duty of reasonable care to avoid electrocuting people on the ground only because of prior case law holding electric companies to such a duty).

One of the principal areas in which courts have created new no–duty rules in recent years is in connection with liability of defendants who are alleged to have done something (or failed to do something) that caused the plaintiff to be harmed by the crime or intentional tort of a third person. In the *Meyering* case, supra p. 208, we saw a court reject an attempt to treat the third person's act as a superseding cause. *Galanti,* supra p. 229, was another third–party crime case, but there the defendant invoked the established principle of no duty for nonfeasance. In this section we consider cases in which courts are asked to create new no–duty rules to preclude liability for third–party crimes or intentional torts. (Technically speaking, *Stagl* may not fit into this category, but it lays a necessary foundation.)

STAGL v. DELTA AIRLINES, INC.

United States Court of Appeals, Second Circuit, 1995.
52 F.3d 463.

CALABRESI, CIRCUIT JUDGE.

* * *

Plaintiff, Eleanor M. Stagl, appeals from a judgment * * * granting summary judgment to defendant, Delta Air Lines, Inc., and dismissing her personal injury action against Delta which was based upon the airline's alleged negligent supervision and management of its baggage retrieval system. * * *

On May 1, 1993, Mrs. Stagl, then 77 years old, was a passenger on a Delta flight from Orlando, Florida to LaGuardia Airport in New York City. The plane was delayed for approximately one–half hour, and Mrs. Stagl noted that upon its arrival in New York the passengers were visibly upset. After disembarking from the aircraft, Mrs. Stagl proceeded to a designated baggage carousel located in Delta's terminal in order to retrieve her luggage.

In her affidavit in opposition to Delta's motion for summary judgment, Mrs. Stagl describes the Delta terminal as "bedlam." According to her, "[p]eople were crowded around the baggage carousel and everyone seemed in a hurry to get out of the airport." Moreover, they were "rowdy and unruly, pushing and shoving each other, grabbing their luggage from the moving carousel by whatever means possible." She further claims that Delta did not provide any personnel, or make any cautionary announcement to quell the turmoil; nor did the airline cordon off a separate area in which elderly and disabled passengers could safely obtain their luggage.

In an attempt to reclaim her own belongings, Mrs. Stagl made her way to the "front rank" of the throng surrounding the baggage carousel. Apparently, an unidentified man to one side of her reached across the conveyor belt, grabbed his satchel with great force, and unwittingly triggered a domino effect. His bag collided with another's suitcase, which, in turn, fell off the carousel, toppling Mrs. Stagl. As a result, she suffered a broken hip.

Mrs. Stagl brought this diversity action in the district court, claiming that Delta did not exercise reasonable care to ensure her safety. She complained that the airline negligently failed to take any crowd–control measures or to provide a safe method by which elderly and disabled people could retrieve their luggage. Mrs. Stagl alleged that her physical injuries were the proximate result of Delta's inaction.

* * *

[T]he district court granted Delta summary judgment * * * [concluding] that, under New York law, Mrs. Stagl had "failed to establish that Delta's duty as an air carrier encompasses a duty to control the crowd at the baggage retrieval area or designate a separate area for elderly passengers." The district judge further determined that Delta had, in any event, fulfilled its duty to act reasonably under the circumstances. * * *

* * *

A.   DELTA'S DUTY OF REASONABLE CARE

The district court ruled that "Delta owed no duty to protect [Mrs. Stagl] from the particular injury involved here." * * * [T]he district court concluded that Delta had no obligation "to protect against or warn of potential negligent conduct by third persons within the terminal building." This was error.

There is no question that Delta, as an owner or occupier of the premises, owed a duty to take reasonable steps in maintaining the safety of its baggage retrieval area. * * *

This duty is a broad one, and it includes the obligation "to take reasonable precautions to protect [patrons] from dangers which are foreseeable from the arrangement or use of the property," [ ] as well as to exercise reasonable care in protecting visitors from the foreseeable, injurious actions of third parties. * * *

* * *

In the present case, the district judge refused to impose an obligation upon Delta to safeguard passengers against the foreseeable risks created by its concentration of allegedly unruly travelers around a congested baggage carousel. In the district court's opinion, such a duty would "offer little if any real public benefit, and yet would impose upon the airline burdensome and costly obligations." Although we appreciate that, under New York law, the "existence and scope of an alleged tortfeasor's duty is usually a policy–laden declaration reserved for Judges" that, in part, weighs competing socioeconomic factors in an attempt to distribute "burdens of loss and reparation on a fair, prudent basis," we also note that New York courts do not exercise this authority on an ad hoc basis.

[W]here, as here, the applicable duty relationship is well established, we do not believe New York law condones the limitation of a familiar liability rule simply to avoid placing a disproportionate burden on a defendant in a particular case. The law deals with that problem not by redefining the defendant's duties in each case, but by asking whether— considering all the circumstances of the particular case—the defendant breached its duty of care.

B. Delta's Alleged Breach of Duty

Apparently as an alternative basis for its decision, the district court determined that "Delta fulfilled its duty to act reasonably under the circumstances." This, of course, raises the age–old debate as to when it is appropriate for a court to decide the question of a defendant's due care as a matter of law, rather than allowing a jury to resolve it as an issue of fact. The problem was perhaps best presented in Lorenzo v. Wirth, 170 Mass. 596, 49 N.E. 1010 (1898), the noted case that posed the burning question of whether a court may rule that an open coalhole in the sidewalk, with a pile of recently delivered coal upon it, is so obviously hazardous to all pedestrians that the exercise of ordinary care does not require the placement of additional warnings.

Answering in the affirmative, then–Judge Holmes [held that the trial judge should have directed a verdict for the defendant and] stated that "[i]n simple cases of this sort, courts have felt able to determine what, in every case, however complex, defendants are bound at their peril to know, namely, whether the given situation is on one or the other side of the line [of the defendant's duty of care]." Judge Knowlton took the opposite view in *Lorenzo*, and insisted that the

> kind of conduct ... required under complex conditions, to reach the usual standard of due care, namely, the ordinary care of persons of common prudence, is a question of fact, to be determined according to the observation and experience of common men. Even when there is no conflict in testimony, if there are acts and omissions, of which some tend to show negligence, and others do not, the question whether there was negligence or not is, in my judgment, a question for the jury.

Although vestiges of this polemic survive, see, e.g., Akins v. Glens Falls City School Dist., 53 N.Y.2d 325, 441 N.Y.S.2d 644, 424 N.E.2d 531 (1981) (concluding, over strong dissent, that the installation of a standard backstop fence fulfills a baseball park owner's duty of reasonable care to protect spectators from foul balls as a matter of law), Holmes' view—"that standards of conduct ought increasingly to be fixed by the court for the sake of certainty—has been largely rejected." See Richard M. Nixon, Changing Rules of Liability In Automobile Accident Litigation, 3 Law & Contemp.Probs. 476, 477 (1936).[4] Indeed, the New York Court

---

4. It may be worth noting that Mr. Nixon wrote this article when he was a law student at Duke University Law School.

Long before he became a significant political figure, Mr. Nixon's article was recognized as a leading piece on the Holmes–

of Appeals has concluded [in Havas v. Victory Paper Stock Co., 49 N.Y.2d 381, 426 N.Y.S.2d 233, 402 N.E.2d 1136, 1139 (1980)] that it is

> particularly appropriate to leave [a finding of negligence] to the jury, not only because of the idiosyncratic nature of most tort cases ..., or because there was room for a difference of view as to whether [the defendant's] conduct in the particular circumstances of this case did or did not evidence a lack of due care, but, perhaps above all, because in the determination of issues revolving about the reasonableness of conduct, the values inherent in the jury system are rightfully believed an important instrument in the adjudicative process. . . .

* * *

In support of her contention that Delta was careless in managing its baggage carousel and the crowd around it, Mrs. Stagl submitted the affidavit of an engineer named Grahme Fischer. Mr. Fischer enumerated several ways in which, in his opinion, Delta could have made the baggage carousel area safer for passengers like Mrs. Stagl. Without expressing any views regarding the reasonableness of the proposed measures contained in this affidavit, we conclude that, when read in the light most favorable to Mrs. Stagl, Mr. Fischer's statement clearly raises issues of fact as to whether Delta sufficiently discharged its duty of care. * * *

* * *

C. Proximate Causation and Third Party Intervenors

Since Delta's alleged negligence is a jury question, the district court should not have dismissed the case unless it could say, as a matter of law, that Delta's actions were not the proximate cause of Mrs. Stagl's injuries. According to Delta, the proximate cause of Mrs. Stagl's injuries was the rogue passenger at the baggage carousel—that is, his luggage–wielding behavior was a superseding event that now insulates the airline from liability. This contention has no merit.

The governing rule in New York has long been settled and is perfectly clear: an intervenor's actions will not break the necessary chain of causation where they are "a normal or foreseeable consequence of the situation created by the defendant's negligence." * * * Conversely, "[i]f the intervening act is extraordinary under the circumstances, not foreseeable in the normal course of events, or independent of or far removed from defendant's conduct, it may well be a superseding act which breaks the causal nexus." Furthermore, in order for the causal link to remain intact, a defendant need not foresee the precise intervening act; its occurrence need only fall within the general category of reasonably anticipated consequences of the defendant's actions.

Knowlton controversy because it was one of the first to apply "legal realism" to the debate. Nixon suggested the desirability of the Holmes position because of the per- ceived tendencies of juries to be biased in favor of plaintiffs. Despite his own viewpoint, however, Nixon recognized that, by and large, Holmes had lost out.

In light of these principles, Delta's causation argument immediately fails. An impatient, suitcase–swinging traveler at a crowded airport baggage carousel hardly seems an extraordinary event. * * *

Indeed, the appearance of a rude and hurried passenger at Delta's LaGuardia terminal is highly unlikely to break the causal connection between the airline's alleged negligence and Mrs. Stagl's injury—particularly since Mrs. Stagl's theory of negligence rests on Delta's claimed failure to mitigate the very risks generated by such people. [As was stated in Derdiarian v. Felix Contracting Corp., 51 N.Y.2d 308, 434 N.Y.S.2d 166, 414 N.E.2d 666, 671 (1980):] "An intervening act may not serve as a superseding cause, and relieve an actor of responsibility, where the risk of the intervening act occurring is the very same risk which renders the actor negligent." It certainly does not do so as a matter of law. * * * The question of proximate cause in this case remains an issue for the jury to determine.

* * *

[We reverse the summary judgment and remand the case for further proceedings.]

Notes

1. Judge Calabresi's belief that courts should not announce no–duty rules "on an ad hoc basis" is fairly widely shared. As we saw in the introductory note to this section, that is the Restatement (Third) view. See also Sugarman, *Assumption of Risk,* 31 Val.U.L.Rev. 833, 872 (1997) (deploring "ad hoc, free–standing [duty] doctrines"); Dobbs, The Law of Torts § 227, p.580 (2000). Cf. Moning v. Alfono, 400 Mich. 425, 254 N.W.2d 759, 762 (1977): "It obscures the separate issues in a negligence case (duty, proximate cause and ... standard of care) to combine and state them together in terms of whether there is a duty to refrain from particular conduct."

2. *The Goodman–Pokora story.* After writing *Lorenzo,* Justice Holmes was appointed to the United States Supreme Court, where he engaged in the same battle over how to formulate and decide breach issues, eventually losing. In Baltimore & Ohio R. Co. v. Goodman, 275 U.S. 66, 48 S.Ct. 24, 72 L.Ed. 167 (1927)—holding that a motorist's action in driving across a railroad track constituted contributory negligence as a matter of law, necessitating a directed verdict for the defendant railroad—Justice Holmes announced for the Court that motorists in general are negligent as a matter of law when they traverse grade crossings without stopping, looking, listening, and if necessary getting out of the vehicle to reconnoiter. The key passage in Justice Holmes' opinion was this:

> It is true ... that the question of due care very generally is left to the jury. But we are dealing with a standard of conduct, and when the standard is clear it should be laid down once for all by the Courts.

Only a few years later, the Court found it necessary to overrule *Goodman.* Justice Cardozo wrote for the Court in Pokora v. Wabash Ry. Co., 292 U.S. 98, 104–06, 54 S.Ct. 580, 582–83, 78 L.Ed. 1149 (1934):

Standards of prudent conduct are declared at times by courts, but they are taken over from the facts of life. To get out of a vehicle and reconnoitre is an uncommon precaution, as everyday experience informs us. Besides being uncommon, it is very likely to be futile, and sometimes even dangerous. * * * Illustrations such as this bear witness to the need for caution in framing standards of behavior that amount to rules of law. The need is the more urgent when there is no background of experience out of which the standards have emerged. They are then, not the natural flowerings of behavior in its customary forms, but rules artificially developed, and imposed from without. * * * The opinion in Goodman's Case has been a source of confusion in the federal courts to the extent that it imposes a standard for application by the judge, and has had only wavering support in the courts of the states.* We limit it accordingly.

3. *Another argument for maintaining the jury's authority over the breach issue.* The temptation for courts to decide for themselves what reasonable care requires has not disappeared. For example, in Kentucky Fried Chicken v. Superior Court, 14 Cal.4th 814, 59 Cal.Rptr.2d 756, 927 P.2d 1260 (1997), a KFC customer taken hostage during an armed robbery was injured when the robber turned violent after the store clerk failed to promptly comply with the robber's demand to turn over the store's cash. The majority held that KFC was entitled to summary judgment. It said imposing a duty to comply with a robber's unlawful demand to turn over money in order to protect others would be against the state's policy of allowing owners to defend their property.

In dissent Justice Kennard, joined by Justice Werdegar, said the majority mischaracterized the issue as one of duty. The dissent, which sets forth the conventional view of the relationship between duty and breach, is worth reading in full. A highly condensed extract follows:

By framing the issue as a question of duty, the majority usurps the jury's historic function in a negligence case to determine the reasonableness of defendant's conduct under the surrounding circumstances. * * * The "inherently situational" reasonable person standard of conduct * * * gives business proprietors a wide latitude of discretion in responding to robberies, while nonetheless allowing for liability in those few cases where the proprietor acts unreasonably and causes harm to a customer. * * * The focus of the duty analysis should not be on the details of a defendant's conduct. The [proper duty] inquiry is whether a defendant must take steps to avoid causing a given type of harm to the victim. [ ] *What* steps a defendant must take to avoid the harm is a question of whether the defendant has met the standard of care by acting reasonably under the circumstances; also, it is a question that arises only after a duty has been found to exist.

It is always possible to recast any question of whether the standard of care has been breached as a question of "duty," as the majority does

---

* Goodman and Pokora were decided under the regime of Swift v. Tyson, 41 U.S. (16 Pet.) 1, 10 L.Ed. 865 (1842), whereby the Supreme Court felt itself authorized to declare nationwide tort rules binding on all federal courts. Subsequently, Erie R.R. Co. v. Tompkins, 304 U.S. 64, 58 S.Ct. 817, 82 L.Ed. 1188 (1938), held that federal courts have no authority to declare general rules of common law. [Ed.]

here. Thus, instead of asking whether an automobile driver who failed to stop in time used the care of a reasonable driver under like circumstances, we could ask whether the driver had a "duty" to begin braking sooner; instead of asking whether a doctor treated a feverish patient with the care of a reasonable physician we could ask whether the doctor had a "duty" to administer penicillin. If a court does so, however, it abandons the flexibility inherent in the application of the reasonable person standard and instead dictates a rigid, inflexible rule of conduct that applies not only to the defendant in the case before it but also to all defendants in future cases who are confronted by a risk of the same type of harm to another, regardless of differences in the surrounding circumstances. For good reason, most courts have rejected this course.

* * *

There are at least three good reasons why negligence law has allocated the judgment of the reasonableness of a defendant's conduct to the jury as a matter for case–by–case determination, rather than having courts, under the rubric of "duty," establish as a matter of law fixed and unvarying rules of conduct for various categories of human activity. The first reason arises from the irreducible variety of circumstances which may surround an event that causes harm to someone. Because of this variety, an individualized rather than categorical determination of what constitutes reasonable care to avoid a particular type of harm usually will provide a more precise measure of what conduct is reasonable under the circumstances.

Justice Kennard's second reason was that leaving the question to the jury "allows successive juries to reassess what precautions are reasonable as social, economic, and technological conditions change over time." The third was that the jury brings a wider array of practical experience and knowledge to that task than does a judge. "The jury is a repository of collective wisdom and understanding concerning the conditions and circumstances of everyday life that it can bring to bear on the determination of what conduct is reasonable."

Compare Justice Kennard's view with that expressed in Moning v. Alfono, 400 Mich. 425, 254 N.W.2d 759, 763 (1977): "The preference for jury resolution of the issue of negligence is not ... simply an expedient reflecting the difficulty of stating a rule that will readily resolve all cases; rather, it is rooted in the belief that the jury's judgment of what is reasonable under the circumstances of a particular case is more likely than the judicial judgment to represent the community's judgment of how reasonable persons would conduct themselves." Cf. Leon Green, The Duty Problem in Negligence Cases, 28 Colum.L.Rev. 1014, 1029 (1928): "[T]he very purpose of jury trial is to give a new deal in each case."

McCARTHY v. OLIN CORPORATION

United States Court of Appeals, Second Circuit, 1997.
119 F.3d 148.

MESKILL, CIRCUIT JUDGE.

Plaintiffs include two surviving victims and the estate of one deceased victim of the December 7, 1993 assault on the 5:33 p.m. Long Island Railroad commuter train. * * *

* * *

On December 7, 1993, Colin Ferguson boarded the Long Island Railroad's 5:33 p.m. commuter train departing from New York City and opened fire on the passengers. Six people, including Dennis McCarthy, were killed and nineteen others, including Kevin McCarthy and Mary-anne Phillips, were wounded in the vicious attack. Ferguson was armed with a 9mm semiautomatic handgun, which was loaded with Winchester "Black Talon" bullets (Black Talons). The injuries to Dennis and Kevin McCarthy and Maryanne Phillips were enhanced by the ripping and tearing action of the Black Talons because, unfortunately, the bullets performed as designed.

The Black Talon is a hollowpoint bullet designed to bend upon impact into six ninety–degree angle razor–sharp petals or "talons" that increase the wounding power of the bullet by stretching, cutting and tearing tissue and bone as it travels through the victim. The Black Talon bullet was designed and manufactured by Olin Corporation (Olin) through its Winchester division and went on the market in 1992. Although the bullet was originally developed for law enforcement agencies, it was marketed and available to the general public. In November 1993, following public outcry, Olin pulled the Black Talon from the public market and restricted its sales to law enforcement personnel. Colin Ferguson allegedly purchased the ammunition in 1993, before it was withdrawn from the market.

Plaintiffs brought this action against Olin * * *.

Olin moved to dismiss the complaint pursuant to Fed.R.Civ.P. 12(b)(6) for failure to state a claim upon which relief can be granted. The district court granted the motion. First addressing the issue of negligence, the court held that plaintiffs' negligence theories must fail because Olin owed no duty to plaintiffs to protect them from criminal misuse of the Black Talon ammunition.* * *

Plaintiffs appeal the dismissal of their complaint, claiming that the issue of whether they will ultimately prevail is a matter to be determined on a factual basis and not merely on the pleadings. In the alternative, plaintiffs request that because the complaint is based on novel theories of liability under New York law, we certify the questions raised in this case to the New York Court of Appeals.

* * *

Recently, the New York courts have had the opportunity to address issues almost identical to those raised in this case. See Pekarski v. Donovan, Nos. 95–11161, 95–1175, 95–1187, slip op. (N.Y.Sup.Ct. Oneida County Sept. 27, 1995); Forni v. Ferguson, 232 A.D.2d 176, 648 N.Y.S.2d 73 (1st Dep't 1996). Basing their decisions on well–settled principles of

New York tort law, the New York courts held that the plaintiffs could not state a cause of action upon which relief could be granted against Olin for the manufacture and marketing of the Black Talon bullet. [Many federal courts have stated that "while a federal court is not bound by lower state court decisions, they do have great weight in informing the court's prediction on how the highest court of the state would resolve the question."] Although the New York Court of Appeals has not addressed the issue of ammunition manufacturer liability, the *Forni* and *Pekarski* decisions, as well as existing precedents in New York law, provide us with sufficient guidance to analyze the district court's dismissal of this case. Therefore, we decline to certify any questions of law to New York's highest court. We will now address the merits of plaintiffs' appeal.

* * *

[The court held that the trial judge had properly dismissed plaintiffs' claims based on strict products liability.]

* * *

In their complaint, appellants also asserted causes of action for the negligent marketing and manufacture of Black Talon bullets. On appeal, appellants do not appear to pursue their negligent manufacturing claim but rather focus their argument on Olin's negligent marketing of the ammunition. For the reasons discussed below, appellants cannot assert a cause of action under either theory of negligence.

The crux of appellants' negligence theory is that Olin negligently marketed and placed the Black Talon ammunition for sale to the general public. Appellants argue that because of the severe wounding power of the bullets, Olin should have restricted sales to law enforcement agencies, for whom the bullet was originally designed. They also argue that Olin should have known that their advertising, which highlighted the ripping and tearing characteristics of the bullet, would attract "many types of sadistic, unstable and criminal personalities," such as Ferguson.

To state a cause of action for negligence, the plaintiffs must show: (1) that Olin owed them a "duty, or obligation, recognized by law", (2) a breach of the duty, (3) a "reasonably close causal connection between [defendant's] conduct and the resulting injury" and (4) loss or damage resulting from the breach. * * *

* * * The existence of a duty is a question of law to be decided by the court. New York courts are reluctant to impose a duty of care where there is little expectation that the defendant could prevent the actions of a third party. * * * While there are of course many exceptions to this rule, we find that none of them is applicable here.

New York courts do not impose a legal duty on manufacturers to control the distribution of potentially dangerous products such as ammunition. Accordingly, although it may have been foreseeable by Olin that criminal misuse of the Black Talon bullets could occur, Olin is not legally liable for such misuse. As the district court pointed out, appellants have not alleged that any special relationship existed between Olin and Ferguson. Here, Olin could not control the actions of Ferguson. * * *

* * * To impose a duty on ammunition manufacturers to protect against criminal misuse of its product would likely force ammunition products—which legislatures have not proscribed, and which concededly are not defectively designed or manufactured and have some socially valuable uses—off the market due to the threat of limitless liability. Because Olin did not owe a legal duty to plaintiffs to protect against Colin Ferguson's horrible action, appellants' complaint does not state a cause of action for negligence and the claim was properly dismissed.

* * *

CALABRESI, CIRCUIT JUDGE, dissenting.

* * *

In cases that are dramatic and involve "hot" issues, there is a tendency for the parties to describe themselves as raising new issues that are remarkable in their legal context.[9] But in fact, such cases are usually best looked at in the most traditional of ways. Courts must see how these cases fit into old categories before considering whether it is either necessary or proper to expand those old categories or to create new ones. And so it is with the case before us. For this reason, I begin with the most traditional of the causes of action that the plaintiffs have raised— negligence—and address it in its most "black letter" terms. * * * In doing this I do not, of course, seek to determine whether liability for negligence lies in a case like this one in New York. I examine the issue only to discern whether the question is sufficiently open to warrant certification.

* * *

To hold a defendant liable in negligence in New York, a plaintiff must show: 1) a duty on the part of the defendant; 2) a breach of that duty by conduct involving an "unreasonable risk of harm"; 3) damages suffered by the plaintiff; and 4) causation, both in fact and proximate, between the breach and the plaintiff's harm. So viewed, three of the four elements of a cause of action for negligence—damages, causation, and conduct involving an unreasonable risk of harm—are either readily present or sufficiently cognizable under New York law on the facts of this case that a federal court would err mightily to hold on its own to the contrary. * * *

* * *

* * * The only aspect of this case—viewed as a negligence action— that is problematic is the existence of a duty. * * * [Under New York

---

9. The plaintiffs in the instant case are guilty of this mistake. See McCarthy v. Sturm, Ruger and Co., 916 F.Supp. 366, 372 (S.D.N.Y.1996) ("Plaintiffs candidly argue that I should expand existing tort doctrines to cover this case....").

law as set forth in Waters v. New York City Housing Authority, 69 N.Y.2d 225, 513 N.Y.S.2d 356, 505 N.E.2d 922, 923–24 (1987)]:

> The question of the scope of an alleged tortfeasor's duty is, in the first instance, a legal issue for the court to resolve. In this analysis, not only logic and science, but policy play an important role. The common law of torts is, at its foundation, a means of apportioning risks and allocating the burden of loss. While moral and logical judgments are significant components of the analysis, we are also bound to consider the larger social consequences of our decisions and to tailor our notion of duty so that the legal consequences of wrongs are limited to a controllable degree.

* * *

This does not mean that the court is required—or even permitted—to weigh such policy considerations to determine the existence of a duty in each individual New York negligence case. Once the New York Court of Appeals has established that the relationship between plaintiffs and defendants in certain circumstances or categories of cases suffices to establish a duty of due care, all cases of like kind are covered by that finding, and there is no warrant to take a case from the jury for a separate judicial examination of duty.

It follows that, before we can be confident that there is a jury question as to negligence in this case, we must find precedents that establish a duty between the parties in cases akin to this one. I am not prepared to make such a finding. Nor, however, am I prepared to say that the New York Court of Appeals would not find that such a precedent exists or create one in this case. I am not, in other words, satisfied that the New York Court of Appeals has made a policy determination, one way or the other, in circumstances akin to those here.

* * *

* * * New York law is * * * quite clear that the defendant in many circumstances can be under a duty to the plaintiff that makes him liable for the harm caused by the intervening negligent acts of a third party. * * *

* * *

In fact, under appropriate conditions, a defendant can even be held liable for the intervening criminal acts of a third party. See, e.g., [ ] Nallan v. Helmsley–Spear, Inc., 50 N.Y.2d 507, 429 N.Y.S.2d 606, 612–13, 407 N.E.2d 451, 457–58 (1980) (holding that a commercial landlord has a duty to take reasonable precautionary measures to minimize the risk of foreseeable criminal activity and to make the premises safe for the visiting public); Stevens v. Kirby, 86 A.D.2d 391, 450 N.Y.S.2d 607, 610 (1982) ("A tavern owner owes a duty to his patrons to protect them from personal attack when he has reasonable cause to anticipate conduct on the part of third persons which is likely to endanger their safety.").

* * *

What of this case? On the one hand, it seems that the defendant could have substantially reduced the harm caused by these unusually destructive bullets by not marketing them to the general public. And the danger of exposing the defendant to liability beyond sound public policy might not be present here, especially if the New York courts were to conclude that marketing Black Talons to the general public causes more harm than benefit. On the other hand, this case may well involve "the expansion . . . of new channels of liability" since it involves a criminal intervenor in a case where no direct relationship exists between the injured plaintiff and the defendant. * * *

Under the circumstances, it is hard to know whether the New York Court of Appeals would find a duty. The fact that the foreseeable intervenor behaved in a criminal, rather than a negligent, manner does not change matters for the purposes of proximate cause.* * * * Does it do so for purposes of duty? That is a question to which the New York Court of Appeals has given us no answer * * * Since the Court of Appeals has neither countenanced nor foreclosed liability in cases involving a criminal intervenor and the absence of a direct relationship, I believe that we are bound to allow that Court to make a policy determination of duty in the instant case.

In this respect, the argument that, because it is legal to sell and advertise Black Talons, there can be no liability, is misplaced. * * * There is all of the difference in the world between making something illegal and making it tortious. Making an activity tortious forces the people who derive benefit from it to internalize the costs associated with it, thereby making sure that the activity will only be undertaken if it is desired by enough people to cover its costs.[22] It does not proscribe it altogether. As a result, very different policy considerations go into the decision of whether to forbid something and the decision of whether to find a duty that permits liability for the harm it causes. The fact that the New York legislature has failed to prohibit Black Talons is certainly one factor that the New York Court of Appeals is likely to consider in deciding the "policy–laden declaration reserved for Judges" that it must make in resolving whether a duty exists. [ ] But the weight to be given to this factor is just the sort of thing that only the New York Court of Appeals itself can determine.

* * *

* In an edited–out portion of the opinion, Judge Calabresi explained this statement by quoting from Derdiarian v. Felix Contracting Corp., 51 N.Y.2d 308, 414 N.E.2d 666, 671 (1980): "An intervening act may not serve as a superseding cause . . . where the risk of the intervening act occurring is the very same risk which renders the actor negligent." [Ed.]

22. Cf. Note, Absolute Liability for Ammunition Manufacturers, 108 Harv.L.Rev. 1679, 1691 (1995) ("The primary advantage of [imposing tort liability on ammunition manufacturers] is that it will force consumers of ammunition to internalize costs that have heretofore been borne by third parties and society in general. Such internalization will provide manufacturers and consumers with the proper incentives to choose care and activity levels that more closely equate costs and benefits.") (footnote omitted); Id.at 1690 (noting that, unlike banning ammunition, imposing liability "does not reflect any moral or ethical condemnation of ammunition manufacturers").

Notes

1. *Certified questions.* When a federal court encounters a question of state law the answer to which is not clear, it has two choices: it can make an educated guess as to how the state courts would rule, or it can seek an answer from a state court. Most states have established procedures which permit the state court of last resort to answer certified questions submitted by federal courts (and sometimes lower state courts). In the principal case, the Second Circuit could have asked the New York Court of Appeals whether New York law imposed a duty on the manufacturer of Black Talons, but the majority thought it unnecessary to do so.

2. In response to a number of lawsuits against manufacturers for deaths and injuries caused by handguns, the California legislature passed a statute precluding product liability claims based on findings that the risks created by certain weapons outweighed their benefits. See Cal. Civ. Code § 1717.4. In a suit against the manufacturer of a semiautomatic assault weapon used to murder eight people in San Francisco, the California Supreme Court held that the legislature intended this statute to also immunize manufacturers against claims that they negligently marketed their products. See Merrill v. Navegar, Inc., 26 Cal.4th 465, 28 P.3d 116, 110 Cal.Rptr.2d 370 (2001).

BRAUN v. SOLDIER OF FORTUNE, INC.

United States Court of Appeals, Eleventh Circuit, 1992.
968 F.2d 1110.

ANDERSON, CIRCUIT JUDGE.

[Michael Savage placed the following personal service advertisement in Soldier of Fortune Magazine:

> GUN FOR HIRE: 37 year old professional mercenary desires jobs. Vietnam veteran. Discrete and very private. Body guard, courier, and other special skills. All jobs considered. (The ad then gave an address and telephone number.)

Savage said he received thirty to forty calls per week during the ten months that the ad ran, most of them seeking his help in perpetrating criminal acts such as murder, kidnapping, and assault. One call was from a man who employed Savage to murder his business partner, Richard Braun. Savage and two other men shot Braun to death and wounded his son Michael.

[Michael Braun and his brother sued under Georgia law for the wrongful death of their father and Michael sued for his own personal injuries, alleging that the magazine had been negligent in publishing the ad.

[The plaintiffs introduced evidence showing that a number of news-papers and magazines had reported instances of murder, kidnapping, and extortion that had resulted from other Soldier of Fortune ads before Braun's murder. The publisher, managing editor, and advertising man-ager of Soldier of Fortune testified that they were not aware of any previous criminal acts resulting from their ads and did not understand Savage's ad as referring to criminal activity.

A jury awarded the plaintiffs $2.375 million in compensatory and $10 million in punitive damages. The district court reduced the punitive award to $2 million. The magazine and its parent corporation (collectively "SOF") appealed.]

* * *

A. Duty Under Georgia Law

* * *

Georgia courts recognize a "general duty one owes to all the world not to subject them to an unreasonable risk of harm." Accordingly, the district court properly found that SOF had a legal duty to refrain from publishing advertisements that subjected the public, including appellees, to a clearly identifiable unreasonable risk of harm from violent criminal activity. To the extent that SOF denies that a publisher owes any duty to the public when it publishes personal service ads, its position is clearly inconsistent with Georgia law. We believe, however, that the crux of SOF's argument is not that it had no duty to the public, but that, as a matter of law, the risk to the public presented when a publisher prints an advertisement is "unreasonable" only if the ad openly solicits criminal activity.

1. Risk–Utility Balancing

To determine whether the risk to others that an individual's actions pose is "unreasonable," Georgia courts generally apply a risk–utility balancing test. A risk is unreasonable if it is "of such magnitude as to outweigh what the law regards as the utility of the defendant's alleged negligent conduct." Simply put, liability depends upon whether the burden on the defendant of adopting adequate precautions is less than the probability of harm from the defendant's unmodified conduct multiplied by the gravity of the injury that might result from the defendant's unmodified conduct. United States v. Carroll Towing Co., 159 F.2d 169, 173 (2d Cir.1947).

For the reasons stated below, we find that the district court properly struck the risk–utility balance when it instructed that the jury could hold SOF liable for printing Savage's advertisement only if the advertisement on its face would have alerted a reasonably prudent publisher to the clearly identifiable unreasonable risk of harm to the public that the advertisement posed.* * *

SOF relies heavily on Eimann v. Soldier of Fortune Magazine, Inc., 880 F.2d 830 (5th Cir.1989), cert. denied, 493 U.S. 1024, 110 S.Ct. 729, 107 L.Ed.2d 748 (1990), to support its contention that the district court erred in its application of risk–utility balancing to this case. In *Eimann*, the son and mother of a murder victim brought a wrongful death action under Texas law against SOF, seeking to hold SOF liable for publishing a personal service ad through which the victim's husband hired an assassin to kill her. The advertisement in question read:

> EX–MARINES–67–69 'Nam Vets, Ex–DI, weapons specialist—jungle warfare, pilot, M.E.*, high risk assignments, U.S. or overseas. (404) 991–2684.

The district court instructed the jury that it could find SOF liable if "(1) the relation to illegal activity appears on the ad's face; or (2) 'the advertisement, embroidered by its context, would lead a reasonable publisher of ordinary prudence under the same or similar circumstances to conclude that the advertisement could reasonably be interpreted' as an offer to commit crimes." The jury found for plaintiffs and awarded them $1.9 million in compensatory damages and $7.5 million in punitive damages.

The Fifth Circuit reversed the jury's verdict. After applying Texas risk–utility balancing principles similar to Georgia's, the court concluded that "[t]he standard of conduct imposed by the district court against SOF is too high...." * * *

SOF's reliance on *Eimann* is misplaced. We distinguish *Eimann* from this case based on the instructions to the respective juries.[3] In *Eimann*, the district court violated risk–utility balancing principles when it allowed the jury to impose liability on SOF if a reasonable publisher would conclude "that the advertisement could reasonably be interpreted" as an offer to commit crimes. The Fifth Circuit correctly observed that virtually anything might involve illegal activity, and that applying the district court's standard would mean that a publisher "must reject all [ambiguous] advertisements," or risk liability for any "untoward consequences that flow from his decision to publish" them.

In this case, the district court stressed in its instructions that the jury could hold SOF liable only if the ad on its face contained a "clearly identifiable unreasonable risk" of harm to the public. We are convinced that the district court's use of phrases like "clear and present danger" and "clearly identifiable unreasonable risk" properly conveyed to the jury that it could not impose liability on SOF if Savage's ad posed only an unclear or insubstantial risk of harm to the public and if SOF would bear a disproportionately heavy burden in avoiding this risk. The jury instructions in *Eimann*, in contrast, did not preclude the jury from imposing liability on the basis of an ambiguous advertisement that presented only an unclear risk of harm to the public.

---

* Testimony in the *Eimann* case indicated that "M.E." meant "multi–engine planes." [Ed.]

3. Appellees also argue that *Eimann* is distinguishable from the present case because the advertisement at issue in *Eimann* was "facially innocuous" and "ambiguous in its message" while Savage's advertisement clearly conveyed that the advertiser was "ready, willing and able" to use his gun to commit crimes. We agree. The adver-tisement in *Eimann* merely listed the advertisers' qualifications and indicated a willingness to accept risky assignments in the United States or overseas. Unlike Savage's ad, the ad in *Eimann* did not contain language that would alert a reasonable publisher to the clearly identifiable unreasonable risk that the advertisers were offering criminal services.

Furthermore, in *Eimann*, the district court instructed that, even if the face of the ad did not reveal its connection to illegal activity, the jury could hold the publisher liable if a reasonably prudent publisher would discover the connection to crime through investigation of the advertisement's "context." It is significant that the district court in this case did not impose such a duty. The district court here stressed that the jury could find SOF liable only if Savage's ad "on its face" would convey to a reasonable publisher that the ad created a "clearly identifiable unreasonable risk" of harm to the public.

[The court held that liability based on this "modified negligence standard" did not violate the magazine's First Amendment rights.]

* * *

B. Proximate Cause

SOF's sole remaining claim is that the jury erred in finding that SOF's publication of Savage's ad was the proximate cause of appellees' injuries. SOF argues that the events that intervened between its publication of Savage's ad and the carrying out of the murder plot were entirely unforeseeable and, therefore, that SOF's publication of Savage's ad was too remote in the chain of events leading to appellees' injuries for the jury to hold SOF liable. Since the proximate cause issue does not implicate any constitutional values, we review the jury's factual finding under the traditional standard of deference to the fact finder.

We find that the jury had ample grounds for finding that SOF's publication of Savage's ad was the proximate cause of appellees' injuries. Georgia law recognizes that, "[g]enerally, the intervening criminal act of a third party, without which the injury would not have occurred, will be treated as the proximate cause of the injury, superseding any negligence of the defendant...." If, however, "the criminal act was a reasonably foreseeable consequence of the defendant's conduct, the casual connection between that conduct and the injury is not broken." We have already held that the language of Savage's ad should have alerted a reasonably prudent publisher to the clearly identifiable unreasonable risk that Savage was soliciting violent and illegal jobs. It follows that a reasonable jury could conclude that the criminal act that harmed appellees was reasonably foreseeable and, accordingly, that the chain of causation was not broken.

Affirmed.

[Eschbach, Senior Circuit Judge, dissented on the ground that the ad was ambiguous rather than a clear solicitation for criminal activity, and that the majority's reasoning therefore could not dispose of First Amendment concerns.]

Notes

1. *Duty or breach?* One way of viewing this decision is as the creation of a new limited–duty rule: a publisher need not use reasonable care to *discover* risks of this sort in all the ads submitted to it, but must use

reasonable care as to ads that on their face pose a "clearly identifiable unreasonable risk"—a limited duty somewhat like that owed by an occupier to a licensee in traditional premises liability law. But the same result can be reached by breach analysis. The court could say: as a matter of law, it is not unreasonable for publishers to run ads of this sort unless the risk is apparent on the face of the ad. It is not entirely clear which route the court believes it is taking. The court seems to believe that the issue is one of duty, but the discussion of risk–utility balancing is more appropriate on the question of breach. Note that the court characterizes SOF's position not as a no–duty argument, but as a claim that the risk it had created was unreasonable only if the ad openly solicited criminal activity. Does that argument properly raise a duty issue? If the court intends to create a general rule to cover publishers' liability for crimes facilitated by their ads, should it treat the matter as a limited–duty rule?

2. *First Amendment influence.* This decision was influenced by First Amendment considerations. Any analysis that would allow juries to hold publishers liable on ordinary negligence principles would have been subject to serious First Amendment objections, based on the law's effects on free speech generally, even if the judgment this particular case did not violate the publisher's free speech rights. So if the court wanted to uphold the judgment in this case, it was important to employ a categorical rule that would give some protection to all publishers, rather than an ad hoc rule that applied to this case only.

For a discussion of *Braun* and other cases involving media liability for crimes of third parties, see David A. Anderson, *Incitement and Tort Law*, 37 Wake Forest L. Rev. 957 (2002).

Chapter VII

VICARIOUS LIABILITY

When the defendant's employee, contractor, or child hurts someone, the defendant may be liable on the basis of defendant's own negligence. Thus, the company that hires an obviously incompetent driver to operate a heavy truck is subject to liability when the driver runs over someone. The developer who engages a contractor with a terrible job–safety record may be liable when the contractor hurts a construction worker. The parent who entrusts a reckless teenager with a powerful vehicle may be liable for harm the child does with the machine. Indeed, anyone whose substandard conduct enables another person to hurt the plaintiff may be liable for the resulting injuries, on familiar principles of negligence law.

Vicarious liability is something different. When *A* is held *vicariously* liable for damages done by *B*, the liability is not based on any view that *A* has been at fault; it is imposed solely on the basis that *B* was at fault and that the relationship between *A* and *B* justifies holding *A* responsible.

The most important instance of vicarious liability, often called "respondeat superior," is the liability of an employer ("master") for the tort of an employee ("servant") who was acting in the scope of the employment. As a general rule, one who employs an independent contractor, rather than an employee, is not subject to vicarious liability for the contractor's torts. There are exceptions to this general rule, however, which are introduced in this chapter.

Whether the employed party is characterized as an employee or an independent contractor depends upon the nature of the relationship. If the employer exercises or has the right to exercise control over the physical conduct ("manner and means") of the work, the one employed is an employee or servant. If the relationship is such that the employer directs only the result, and the party employed is free to determine the manner and means, then the relationship is one of independent contractor. See Restatement (Second) of Agency § 220 (1958). Many factors may be considered in determining whether the relationship is one of employee or independent contractor, including the length of time of the employment; who provides the tools, instrumentalities, and place of work; the method of payment (by time or by the job); and the degree of skill and judgment required. See id. (listing ten nonexclusive factors).

Under the common law, parents are not vicariously liable for the torts of their children. Many jurisdictions have imposed limited vicarious liability upon parents by statute. These "parental liability" statutes vary widely, but typically they cap liability at a fairly low amount, apply only to children in a specified age range, and often apply only to acts in the nature of malicious mischief (vandalism).

Other relationships that have supported vicarious liability under certain circumstances include partnerships and joint enterprises. Vicarious liability has also sometimes been imposed on the basis of statutes making the owner of a car liable for the fault of anyone driving it with the owner's permission.

IRA S. BUSHEY & SONS, INC. v. UNITED STATES

United States Court of Appeals, Second Circuit, 1968.
398 F.2d 167.

FRIENDLY, CIRCUIT JUDGE.

While the United States Coast Guard vessel Tamaroa was being overhauled in a floating drydock located in Brooklyn's Gowanus Canal, a seaman returning from shore leave late at night, in the condition for which seamen are famed, turned some wheels on the drydock wall. He thus opened valves that controlled the flooding of the tanks on one side of the drydock. Soon the ship listed, slid off the blocks and fell against the wall. Parts of the drydock sank, and the ship partially did—fortunately without loss of life or personal injury. The drydock owner sought and was granted compensation by the District Court for the Eastern District of New York [in a bench trial]; the United States appeals.

* * *

Seaman Lane, whose prior record was unblemished, returned from shore leave a little after midnight on March 14. He had been drinking heavily; the quartermaster made mental note that he was "loose." For reasons not apparent to us or very likely to Lane[4], he took it into his head, while progressing along the gangway wall, to turn each of three large wheels some twenty times; unhappily, as previously stated, these wheels controlled the water intake valves. After boarding ship at 12:11 A.M., Lane mumbled to an off-duty seaman that he had "turned some valves" and also muttered something about "valves" to another who was standing the engineering watch. Neither did anything; apparently Lane's condition was not such as to encourage proximity. At 12:20 A.M. a crew member discovered water coming into the drydock. By 12:30 A.M. the ship began to list, the alarm was sounded and the crew were ordered

---

4. Lane disappeared after completing the sentence imposed by a court–martial and being discharged from the Coast Guard.

ashore. Ten minutes later the vessel and dock were listing over 20 degrees; in another ten minutes the ship slid off the blocks and fell against the drydock wall.

The Government attacks imposition of liability on the ground that Lane's acts were not within the scope of his employment. It relies heavily on § 228(1) of the Restatement of Agency 2d which says that "conduct of a servant is within the scope of employment if, but only if: * * * (c) it is actuated, at least in part by a purpose to serve the master." Courts have gone to considerable lengths to find such a purpose, as witness a well–known opinion in which Judge Learned Hand concluded that a drunken boatswain who routed the plaintiff out of his bunk with a blow, saying "Get up, you big son of a bitch, and turn to," and then continued to fight, might have thought he was acting in the interest of the ship. Nelson v. American–West African Line, 86 F.2d 730 (2 Cir.1936), cert. denied, 300 U.S. 665, 57 S.Ct. 509, 81 L.Ed. 873 (1937). It would be going too far to find such a purpose here; while Lane's return to the Tamaroa was to serve his employer, no one has suggested how he could have thought turning the wheels to be, even if— which is by no means clear—he was unaware of the consequences.

In light of the highly artificial way in which the motive test has been applied, the district judge believed himself obliged to test the doctrine's continuing vitality by referring to the larger purposes *respondeat superior* is supposed to serve. He concluded that the old formulation failed this test. We do not find his analysis so compelling, however, as to constitute a sufficient basis in itself for discarding the old doctrine. It is not at all clear, as the court below suggested, that expansion of liability in the manner here suggested will lead to a more efficient allocation of resources. As the most astute exponent of this theory has emphasized, a more efficient allocation can only be expected if there is some reason to believe that imposing a particular cost on the enterprise will lead it to consider whether steps should be taken to prevent a recurrence of the accident. Calabresi, The Decision for Accidents: An Approach to Non–fault Allocation of Costs, 78 Harv.L.Rev. 713, 725–34 (1965). And the suggestion that imposition of liability here will lead to more intensive screening of employees rests on highly questionable premises.[5] The unsatisfactory quality of the allocation of resource rationale is especially striking on the facts of this case. It could well be that application of the traditional rule might induce drydock owners, prodded by their insurance companies, to install locks on their valves to avoid similar incidents in the future, while placing the burden on shipowners is much less likely to lead to accident prevention.[7] It is true, of course, that in many cases the plaintiff will not be in a position to insure, and so expansion of liability will, at the very least, serve *respondeat superior's* loss spreading

5. We are not here speaking of cases in which the enterprise has negligently hired an employee whose undesirable propensities are known or should have been.

7. Although it is theoretically possible that shipowners would demand that dry-dock owners take appropriate action, see Coase, The Problem of Social Cost, 3 J.L. & Economics 1 (1960), this would seem unlikely to occur in real life.

function. But the fact that the defendant is better able to afford damages is not alone sufficient to justify legal responsibility, and this overarching principle must be taken into account in deciding whether to expand the reach of *respondeat superior.*

A policy analysis thus is not sufficient to justify this proposed expansion of vicarious liability. This is not surprising since *respondeat superior,* even within its traditional limits, rests not so much on policy grounds consistent with the governing principles of tort law as in a deeply rooted sentiment that a business enterprise cannot justly disclaim responsibility for accidents which may fairly be said to be characteristic of its activities. It is in this light that the inadequacy of the motive test becomes apparent. Whatever may have been the case in the past, a doctrine that would create such drastically different consequences for the actions of the drunken boatswain in *Nelson* and those of the drunken seaman here reflects a wholly unrealistic attitude toward the risks characteristically attendant upon the operation of a ship. We concur in the statement of Mr. Justice Rutledge in a case involving violence injuring a fellow–worker, in this instance in the context of workmen's compensation:

> Men do not discard their personal qualities when they go to work. Into the job they carry their intelligence, skill, habits of care and rectitude. Just as inevitably they take along also their tendencies to carelessness and camaraderie, as well as emotional make–up. In bringing men together, work brings these qualities together, causes frictions between them, creates occasions for lapses into careless-ness, and for fun–making and emotional flare–up. * * * These expressions of human nature are incidents inseparable from working together. They involve risks of injury and these risks are inherent in the working environment.

* * *

Put another way, Lane's conduct was not so "unforeseeable" as to make it unfair to charge the Government with responsibility. We agree with a leading treatise that "what is reasonably foreseeable in this context [of *respondeat superior*] * * * is quite a different thing from the foreseeably unreasonable risk of harm that spells negligence * * *. The foresight that should impel the prudent man to take precautions is not the same measure as that by which he should perceive the harm likely to flow from his long–run activity in spite of all reasonable precautions on his own part. The proper test here bears far more resemblance to that which limits liability for workmen's compensation than to the test for negligence. The employer should be held to expect risks, to the public also, which arise 'out of and in the course of' his employment of labor." 2 Harper & James, The Law of Torts 1377–78 (1956). See also Calabresi, Some Thoughts on Risk Distribution and the Law of Torts, 70 Yale L.J. 499, 544 (1961). Here it was foreseeable that crew members crossing the drydock might do damage, negligently or even intentionally, such as pushing a Bushey employee or kicking property into the water. Moreover, the proclivity of seamen to find solace for solitude by copious resort to the bottle while ashore has been noted in opinions too numerous to warrant citation. Once all this is granted, it is immaterial that Lane's precise action was not to be foreseen. Consequently, we can no longer accept our past decisions that have refused to move beyond the *Nelson* rule, since they do not accord with modern understanding as to when it is fair for an enterprise to disclaim the actions of its employees.

One can readily think of cases that fall on the other side of the line. If Lane had set fire to the bar where he had been imbibing or had caused an accident on the street while returning to the drydock, the Government would not be liable; the activities of the "enterprise" do not reach into areas where the servant does not create risks different from those attendant on the activities of the community in general. We agree with the district judge that if the seaman "upon returning to the drydock, recognized the Bushey security guard as his wife's lover and shot him," vicarious liability would not follow; the incident would have related to the seaman's domestic life, not to his seafaring activity, and it would have been the most unlikely happenstance that the confrontation with the paramour occurred on a drydock rather than at the traditional spot. Here Lane had come within the closed–off area where his ship lay, to occupy a berth to which the Government insisted he have access, and while his act is not readily explicable, at least it was not shown to be due entirely to facets of his personal life. The risk that seamen going and coming from the Tamaroa might cause damage to the drydock is enough to make it fair that the enterprise bear the loss. It is not a fatal objection that the rule we lay down lacks sharp contours; in the end, as Judge Andrews said in a related context, "it is all a question [of expediency,] * * * of fair judgment, always keeping in mind the fact that we endeavor to make a rule in each case that will be practical and in keeping with the general understanding of mankind." Palsgraf v. Long Island R.R. Co., (dissenting opinion).

Since we hold the Government responsible for the damage resulting from Lane's turning the wheels, we find it unnecessary to consider Bushey's further arguments that liability would attach in any event because of later inaction of Lane and others on the Tamaroa * * *.

Affirmed.

Notes

1. Note there is no suggestion that defendant itself did anything wrong. (See text and footnote 5 of the opinion.) Further, Judge Friendly seemed to believe that leaving the risk on the plaintiff would be at least as "likely to lead to accident prevention" as imposing liability. (See text and footnote 7.) What, then, is the argument for liability?

2. In connection with the court's footnote 7, see the note 6 following the *Testbank* case in Chapter VI, section E, supra p. 266.

3. The "scope of the employment" criterion is vague and therefore quite flexible in operation. Decisions dealing with employees' intentional

torts are especially unpredictable. See, e.g., Lisa M. v. Henry Mayo Newhall Memorial Hosp., 12 Cal.4th 291, 48 Cal.Rptr.2d 510, 907 P.2d 358 (1995) (hospital technician who sexually molested patient while performing ultrasound procedure was acting outside scope of employment); Mary M. v. City of Los Angeles, 54 Cal.3d 202, 285 Cal.Rptr. 99, 814 P.2d 1341 (1991) (police officer's rape of detainee was within scope of employment); Houston Transit Co. v. Felder, 146 Tex. 428, 208 S.W.2d 880 (1948) (bus company liable when, after a slight collision, the bus driver hit the other motorist in the face with a money–changing box).

4.　In most common–law jurisdictions, when an innocent employer is held vicariously liable for the tort of an employee, the employer is entitled to indemnity from the employee. See, e.g., Lister v. Romford Ice Co., [1957] A.C. 555 (H.L.). Although well settled, this rule is controversial, especially so when the true party at interest seeking indemnity is the employer's liability insurer. See the dissenting opinions in *Lister*. Reported decisions in which employers seek indemnity from errant employees are rare; evidently the right is seldom exercised.

PUSEY v. BATOR

Supreme Court of Ohio, 2002.
94 Ohio St.3d 275, 762 N.E.2d 968.

DOUGLAS, JUSTICE.

[Greif Brothers Corporation, a steel drum manufacturer, owned and operated a manufacturing plant in Youngstown, Ohio. In early 1987, Greif Brothers experienced several thefts from its parking lot. Lowell Wilson, the superintendent at Greif Brothers' Youngstown plant, decided to hire a security company to guard Greif Brothers' property. He engaged] Youngstown Security Patrol, Inc. ("YSP") to supply a uniformed security guard to "deter theft [and] vandalism" on Greif Brothers' property during specified hours. Wilson told YSP's owner and president, Carl Testa, that he wanted the security guard to periodically check the parking lot and the inside of the building. Other than those instructions, Wilson did not instruct Testa in the manner that YSP was to protect Greif Brothers' property.

The written security contract did not specify whether the guard was to be armed or unarmed, and Wilson and Testa both later testified that they never discussed the subject. At least some of the YSP security guards that were assigned to watch Greif Brothers' property carried firearms. Wilson was [well] aware of this * * *.

On June 30, 1991, Testa hired Eric Bator as a YSP security guard. Notes written on the bottom of Bator's application indicate that Bator was hired as an unarmed guard but that he would take the necessary training required by the state to become certified as an armed guard. Nevertheless, because he felt uneasy performing his security duties without a weapon, Bator took his gun, in a briefcase, to work with him. Bator testified that his supervisor, Bill Kissinger, knew that Bator carried a gun while working as a YSP guard and that Bator was not licensed to work as an armed guard. Kissinger testified that he had seen Bator's gun but denied knowing that Bator carried the gun while working as a YSP guard.

YSP employed several security guards but only one guard per shift was assigned to guard Greif Brothers' property. Bator was the guard assigned to Greif Brothers' property from 11:00 p.m., August 11 to 7:00 a.m., August 12, 1991. At approximately 1:00 a.m., Bator looked out through a window in the guard office and saw two individuals, later identified as Derrell Pusey and Charles Thomas, walking through Greif Brothers' parking lot. Bator used the radio in the office to inform a YSP guard on duty at another location that two people were on Greif Brothers' property. [He then went outside, unarmed, to investigate. Because Thomas's and Pusey's responses seemed suspicious and potentially belligerent, Bator soon returned to the office to get his pistol. He then attempted to apprehend the two men. The situation deteriorated, and it ended in tragedy when Bator shot and killed Derrell Pusey.]

* * *

* * * [P]laintiff–appellant, Ethel Pusey, Derrell's mother, individually and as executor of Derrell's estate, filed a wrongful death and survivorship action against Bator, YSP, and Greif Brothers. YSP and Bator settled with Pusey soon after the jury trial began, leaving Greif Brothers as the only defendant.

After Pusey rested her case, Greif Brothers moved for a directed verdict * * *. The trial court granted Greif Brothers' motion. The court held that even if Derrell's death was the result of YSP's negligence, Greif Brothers was not liable because YSP was an independent contractor and, as a general rule, an employer is not liable for the negligent acts of its independent contractor. The court rejected Pusey's assertion that the nature of the work contracted for in this case qualified as an exception to the general rule.

Pusey appealed the trial court's decision to the Seventh District Court of Appeals. The court of appeals, in a split decision, affirmed the trial court's ruling and Pusey appealed to this court. The case is before this court upon our allowance of a discretionary appeal.

The issue for our determination in this case is whether the court of appeals erred in affirming the trial court's ruling directing a verdict in favor of Greif Brothers. A decision granting a directed verdict should be affirmed on appeal if, when the evidence is viewed most strongly in favor of the nonmoving party, reasonable minds could only find against the nonmoving party. In making its determination that Greif Brothers was not liable for the damages resulting from Derrell's death, the trial court first determined that YSP was an independent contractor and not an employee of Greif Brothers. This was an important factor in the court's ultimate decision because, whereas an employer is liable for the negligent acts of its employees committed within the scope of employment, an employer of an independent contractor generally is not liable for the negligent acts of the independent contractor. Because this finding was a pivotal factor in the trial court's decision, we review it first.

The chief test in determining whether one is an employee or an independent contractor is the right to control the manner or means of performing the work. If such right is in the employer, the relationship is that of employer and employee; but if the manner or means of performing the work is left to one responsible to the employer for the result alone, an independent contractor relationship is created.

We find that, even when viewed in the light most favorable to Pusey, the evidence clearly established YSP's status as an independent contractor. Greif Brothers specified the result to be accomplished, i.e., to deter vandals and thieves, but the details of how this task should be accomplished, with the exception noted above regarding periodic patrolling of the property, were left to YSP. Moreover, YSP, not Greif Brothers, hired the guards, supplied them with uniforms and equipment, paid them, and assigned them to their posts, and was responsible for training them and ensuring that they were state–certified as security guards. For the foregoing reasons, we agree with the trial court's conclusion, affirmed by the court of appeals, that YSP was an independent contractor.

As stated previously, an employer is generally not liable for the negligent acts of an independent contractor. There are, however, exceptions to this general rule, several of which stem from the nondelegable duty doctrine. Nondelegable duties arise in various situations that generally fall into two categories: (1) affirmative duties that are imposed on the employer by statute, contract, franchise, charter, or common law and (2) duties imposed on the employer that arise out of the work itself because its performance creates dangers to others, i.e., inherently dangerous work. Prosser & Keeton, The Law of Torts (5 Ed.1984) 511–512, Section 71; Albain v. Flower Hosp. (1990), 50 Ohio St.3d 251, 260–261, 553 N.E.2d 1038, 1047–1048. If the work to be performed fits into one of these two categories, the employer may delegate the *work* to an independent contractor, but he cannot delegate the *duty*. In other words, the employer is not insulated from liability if the independent contractor's negligence results in a breach of the duty.

Pusey claims that hiring armed guards to protect property creates a nondelegable duty because the work is inherently dangerous. Consequently, Pusey argues, even if YSP is an independent contractor, that status does not relieve Greif Brothers from liability for the damages arising from Derrell's death resulting from the alleged negligence of Bator.

Work is inherently dangerous when it creates a peculiar risk of harm to others unless special precautions are taken. Under those circumstances, the employer hiring the independent contractor has a duty to see that the work is done with reasonable care and cannot, by hiring an independent contractor, insulate himself or herself from liability for injuries resulting to others from the negligence of the independent contractor or its employees.

To fall within the inherently–dangerous–work exception, it is not necessary that the work be such that it cannot be done without a risk of harm to others, or even that it be such that it involves a high risk of such harm. It is sufficient that the work involves a risk, recognizable in advance, of physical harm to others, which is inherent in the work itself.

The exception does not apply, however, where the employer would reasonably have only a general anticipation of the possibility that the contractor may be negligent in some way and thereby cause harm to a third party. For example, one who hires a trucker to transport his goods should realize that if the truck is driven at an excessive speed, or with defective brakes, some harm to persons on the highway is likely to occur. An employer of an independent contractor may assume that a careful contractor will take routine precautions against all of the ordinary and customary dangers that may arise in the course of the contemplated work.

The inherently–dangerous–work exception does apply, however, when special risks are associated with the work such that a reasonable man would recognize the necessity of taking special precautions. The work must create a risk that is not a normal, routine matter of customary human activity, such as driving an automobile, but is rather a special danger to those in the vicinity arising out of the particular situation created, and calling for special precautions. 2 Restatement of the Law 2d, Torts, at 385, Section 413, Comment b; Prosser & Keeton at 513–514, Section 71.

Greif Brothers argues that hiring armed guards to protect property does not create a peculiar risk of harm to others and, therefore, does not fit within the inherently–dangerous–work exception. The common pleas court agreed with Greif Brothers and relied on the Twelfth District Court of Appeals' holding in Joseph v. Consol. Rail Corp. (Oct. 30, 1987), unreported, 1987 WL 19481, to support its decision.

In *Joseph,* the defendant, Conrail, hired an independent contractor to perform surveillance of an employee of Conrail to determine the validity of the employee's claim that he had injured his back. The investigators were consequently detected and confronted by the employee. In a subsequent action by the employee against Conrail for alleged damages resulting from the confrontation, the trial court granted summary judgment in favor of Conrail. [Affirming, the court of appeals rejected the plaintiff's contention that the inherently–dangerous–work exception was applicable and stated that that exception "is limited to dangerous work, and cannot be extended to proper work dangerously done."]

Although we agree with the holding in *Joseph,* we disagree with the trial court's determination that it is applicable to the facts of this case. One crucial difference between the work at issue in *Joseph,* i.e., surveillance, and the work at issue herein, i.e., an armed guard deterring thieves and vandals, is that an *armed* confrontation with a suspicious person may be *required* by the latter. Surveillance work, as emphasized by the *Joseph* court, is not inherently dangerous to the person being investigated because the purpose of the investigator is to remain undetected and unobtrusive. In contrast, *armed* YSP guards were instructed to "deter" thieves and vandals. Thus, the work contracted for contemplates a confrontation between an armed guard and persons entering the property. For the foregoing reasons, we do not agree with the trial court's determination that *Joseph* supports its conclusion that hiring armed guards to protect property is not inherently dangerous to those entering the property.

In affirming the trial court's decision, the court of appeals did not consider whether armed security satisfied the inherently–dangerous–work exception. * * * We find that work such as YSP was hired to perform does create a peculiar risk of harm to others. When armed guards are hired to deter vandals and thieves it is foreseeable that someone might be injured by the inappropriate use of the weapon if proper precautions are not taken. Thus, such an injury is one that might have been anticipated as a direct or probable consequence of the performance of the work contracted for, if reasonable care is not taken in its performance. Also, the risk created is not a normal, routine matter of customary human activity, such as driving an automobile, but is instead a special danger arising out of the particular situation created and calling for special precautions. We therefore hold that when an employer hires an independent contractor to provide armed security guards to protect property, the inherently–dangerous–work exception is triggered such that if someone is injured by the weapon as a result of a guard's negligence, the employer is vicariously liable even though the guard responsible is an employee of the independent contractor.

We do not mean to suggest by the foregoing that we have determined that Derrell's death resulted from YSP's negligence. That issue is to be determined by a finder of fact. If the fact finder so finds, however, then, pursuant to our holding herein, Greif Brothers is liable for the damages even though the negligence was that of an employee of an independent contractor.

For the foregoing reasons, we reverse the judgment of the court of appeals and remand the cause to the trial court for a fact–finder's determination whether Derrell's death was a result of YSP's negligence.

Judgment reversed and cause remanded.

COOK, JUSTICE, concurring in judgment only.

A majority of this court holds that the provision of "armed security guards to protect property" triggers, as a matter of law, the "inherently–dangerous–work exception" to the general rule that an employer is not vicariously liable for the negligence of its independent contractor.[3] Accordingly, the majority decides that Greif Brothers may be vicariously

---

3. At least three courts have held that the provision of armed security personnel is *not,* in and of itself, an inherently dangerous activity. See Ross v. Texas One Partnership (Tex.App.1990), 796 S.W.2d 206, 214–215; Brien v. 18925 Collins Avenue Corp. (Fla.App.1970), 233 So.2d 847, 38 A.L.R.3d 1328; Schreiber v. Camm (D.N.J. 1994), 848 F.Supp. 1170, 1177–1180.

liable if the jury finds that Eric Bator acted negligently in shooting Derrell Pusey. Although I agree with the majority's decision to reverse the judgment and remand the cause, I would decline to hold that the work contracted by Greif Brothers to Youngstown Security Patrol ("YSP") was "inherently dangerous" to others as a matter of Ohio law. * * *

* * *

If an independent contractor's work is "generically hazardous," such that the activity poses an inherent danger to others regardless of the skill with which the contractor performs the work, * * * a court may find that the work falls within the inherently–dangerous–work exception as a matter of law. * * * [The inherently–dangerous–work exception can also be applied to activities that are not "generically hazardous"— because they *can* be performed safely by taking proper precautions— when the employer has reason to know that his independent contractor is likely, *under particular circumstances,* to endanger others absent reasonable precautions. When the activity at issue is not "generically hazardous," the applicability of the exception depends the fact–specific, particular circumstances under which any task is to be performed.]

I do not view the work YSP contracted to perform—providing security guards to protect Greif Brothers property—as falling within the "generically hazardous" branch of the inherently–dangerous–work exception. Whether the presence of security guards poses a peculiar risk to others depends on the particular circumstances of the job, such as the location of the guarded premises and the likelihood of the guards being armed. * * * [W]e should allow the trier of fact to decide whether the facts and circumstances surrounding this case bring YSP's work within the purview of the "peculiar risk"/"special danger" branch of the inherently–dangerous–work exception.

* * *

Notes

1. As explained in the opinion of the court in *Pusey*, the concept of nondelegable duty may be applied in situations other than inherently dangerous work. An example is Colmenares Vivas v. Sun Alliance Insurance Co., Chapter III, section E, p. 111 supra). See also Maloney v. Rath, 69 Cal.2d 442, 71 Cal.Rptr. 897, 445 P.2d 513 (1968), in which a statute requiring motor vehicles to have adequate brakes was construed to impose a "nondelegable duty" on an automobile owner, justifying liability against the owner when the car's brakes failed solely because the repair job was inadequate.

2. There are other exceptions to the general rule of nonliability of one who employs an independent contractor. See, e.g., Jackson v. Power, 743 P.2d 1376 (Alaska 1987), subjecting a hospital to liability for the negligence of an independent contractor physician working in its emergency room because it had held him out to the public as its employee. (The court found support in both the agency and torts restatements. See Restatement (Second) of Agency § 267 (1958); Restatement (Second) of Torts § 429 (1965).)

Chapter VIII

DAMAGES

A. INTRODUCTION

The law of damages is complex and demanding. It is addressed in depth in upper–level law school courses on remedies. This chapter does no more than introduce the general principles and examine selected problems that are particularly important in modern torts litigation.

The three broad categories of damages that may be awarded in torts cases are nominal damages, compensatory damages, and punitive damages.

The cause of action for some intentional torts—e.g., battery, assault, false imprisonment, and trespass to land—is complete without proof of actual damages. When a plaintiff wins such a case without proving any damages, the court awards *nominal damages,* which may be defined as "a trivial sum of money awarded to a litigant who has established a cause of action but has not established that he is entitled to compensatory damages." Restatement (2d) of Torts § 907.

Compensatory damages "are the damages awarded to a person as compensation, indemnity, or restitution for harm sustained by him." Restatement (2d) of Torts § 903. The basic theory of compensatory damages in tort cases is restoration of the plaintiff to his or her pre–injury condition, to the extent that an award of money can do that. (By way of rough contrast, a basic theory of damages for breach of contract is said to be giving the plaintiff the reasonably expectable benefits of the bargain.)

In causes of action based on negligence and strict liability, the plaintiff must prove compensatory damages as part of the prima facie case. This is true of some intentional torts, as well. Even when the plaintiff can establish a cause of action without proving damages, it is rarely worthwhile to do so. In practice, the amount of damages is often the most important and intensely contested part of the case.

Punitive damages "are damages, other than compensatory or nominal damages, awarded against a person to punish him for his outrageous conduct and to deter him and others like him from similar conduct in the future." Restatement (2d) of Torts § 908(1).

B. COMPENSATORY DAMAGES FOR PHYSICAL HARMS TO PROPERTY

The law of damages for physical harms to property is fairly technical. But the basic principles are simple. For an invasion of land, the basic measure of recovery is any diminution in the land's value caused by the invasion (or, at plaintiff's election, the reasonable costs of restoration), plus the value of the plaintiff's loss of use of the land (the rental value).

When a chattel has been converted or destroyed, the basic measure of damages is its entire value at the time and place of the tort. Obviously in such cases, it would be duplicative to allow the plaintiff to recover lost rental value as well.

In cases in which a chattel has been damaged but not destroyed, the basic measure of damages is the diminution in value caused by the tort. Insurance policies, especially for automobile coverage, often measure the loss by the cost of repair, but that is not the tort measure, though it may be highly relevant.

In cases in which the plaintiff has merely lost the use of the chattel for a time, the basic measure of damages is the value of the use of which the plaintiff has been deprived.

In all these cases, "consequential" or "incidental" damages may also be awarded. For example, the victim of a trespass to land may recover for bodily harm or damage to chattels caused by the invasion. As we have already seen in Ch. VI Sec. E, supra p. 253, an owner whose property is damaged is generally entitled to recover for a resulting loss of business profits if the amount can be shown with reasonable certainty.

C. COMPENSATORY DAMAGES IN PERSONAL INJURY CASES

There are some differences in detail among Anglo–American jurisdictions in their treatment of personal injury damages. Such differences may become highly significant in particular cases. But in broad outline, all jurisdictions recognize three main types of personal injury compensatory damages:

medical (and related) expenses (past and future);

loss of earning capacity (past and future); and

physical and mental pain and suffering (past and future).

The first two categories are sometimes called "special damages" or "specials", and the third category is sometimes called "general damages." These terms, which once had a technical meaning, have become debased and probably no longer serve any useful purpose. Today one is more likely to encounter the terms "pecuniary damages," referring to the first two categories, and "nonpecuniary damages," referring to pain and suffering and other losses that cannot be easily measured in dollars.

Damages issues may come up on appeal in any of the procedural contexts discussed in Chapter I. One highly visible impact of the law of damages on torts cases is the judge's instructions to the jury. A fairly typical jury instruction is set forth below. Like all such pattern jury charges, the following—which is a modification of those promulgated by the California Bar Association—will be tailored and streamlined by the trial judge to fit the circumstances of particular cases.

If you find that plaintiff is entitled to a verdict against defendant, you must then award plaintiff damages in an amount that will reasonably compensate her for each of the following elements of claimed injury:

(a) The reasonable value of medical, hospital, and nursing care, services, and supplies reasonably required and actually given in the treatment of the plaintiff to the present time, and the present cash value of the reasonable value of similar items reasonably certain to be required and given in the future.

(b) The reasonable value of working time lost to date. In determining this amount, you should consider evidence of plaintiff's earning capacity, her earnings, how she ordinarily occupied herself, and find what she was reasonably certain to have earned in the time lost if she had not been injured. A person's ability to work may have a monetary value even though she is not employed by another. In determining this amount, you should also consider evidence of the reasonable value of services performed by another in doing things for the plaintiff which, except for her injury, plaintiff would ordinarily do for herself.

(c) The present cash value of earning capacity reasonably certain to be lost in the future as a result of the injury in question.

(d) Reasonable compensation for any pain, discomfort, fears, anxiety, and other mental and emotional distress suffered by the plaintiff and of which her injury was a proximate cause, and for similar suffering reasonably certain to be experienced in the future from the same cause. No definite standard or method of calculation is prescribed by law by which to fix reasonable compensation for pain and suffering. Nor is the opinion of any witness required as to the amount of such reasonable compensation. Furthermore, the argument of counsel as to the amount of damages is not evidence of reasonable compensation. In making an award for pain and suffering you shall exercise your authority with calm and reasonable judgment and the damages you fix shall be just and reasonable in the light of the evidence.

RODRIGUEZ v. McDONNELL DOUGLAS CORP.

California Court of Appeal, 1978.
87 Cal.App.3d 626, 151 Cal.Rptr. 399.

JEFFERSON, JUSTICE.

[Plaintiff Richard Rodriguez was a sprinkler fitter's apprentice for a fire protection company engaged as a subcontractor on a major construction project to modify a McDonnell Douglas hangar. Through the negligence of another subcontractor and the general contractor, a 630–pound pipe fell on Rodriguez, striking the back of his helmet, his back, and his legs. The accident happened in 1970. At the conclusion of the trial in 1975, the jury exonerated McDonnell Douglas but found the negligent contractors liable to Rodriguez for more than $4 million and to his wife, Mary Anne, for $500,000. On appeal the defendants argued that the trial judge should have granted their motion for a new trial on the ground (among others) that the size of the awards suggested that the jury acted on passion and prejudice.]

* * *

VI

THE ISSUE OF WHETHER THE DAMAGES AWARDED WERE EXCESSIVE

A. *The Nature of the Injuries*

As the contention is made on appeal that the award of damages was excessive, we summarize here the relevant medical testimony presented on behalf of plaintiff Richard Rodriguez. Eight doctors described to the jury various aspects of the massive injuries sustained by the plaintiff Richard and problems encountered as a result thereof.

Prior to the accident, Richard Rodriguez had been a happy and healthy young man 22 years of age. He was approximately six feet tall, and engaged in an active life with family and friends. He had been married to Mary Anne, aged 20 years, for sixteen months.

Dr. Christos Papatheodorou, a neurosurgeon, treated Rodriguez from the date of the accident until March 1971. The plaintiff's brain had been severely injured by the falling pipe; his spine was fractured and there was substantial, irreparable damage to the spinal cord. Richard's mind gradually became clear, although he does not remember the events surrounding the accident. It was Dr. Papatheodorou's task to advise Richard and his wife Mary Anne, that Richard would never walk again nor would he ever regain any function in the lower part of his body. Plaintiff Richard is triplegic as a result of this accident, paralyzed from the middle of the chest down. He has lost all bladder, bowel and sexual function. In addition, there are complications associated with the left side of his entire body, ranging from his left eye to a left arm which is practically useless.

The consequences of the spinal cord injury and the resultant paralysis have been tremendously heavy. Shortly after his admission to the hospital after the accident, Richard developed bleeding ulcers which were life–threatening. Dr. John Sweeney, a surgeon, performed a partial gastectomy, removing part of his patient's stomach.

Surgery was later performed on plaintiff's left hand by an orthopedic surgeon, Dr. Eric Widell, in an effort to restore some function. The "tendon transplant surgery" resulted in limited improvement in the left hand, but the arm is still significantly impaired.

Dr. Alan Shanberg, a urologist, was called upon in December 1970, to take charge of bladder, kidney and bowel problems. Richard was experiencing serious infection in these areas. The first surgery performed to provide an alternative method of disposing of urine was a suprapubic cystotomy which involved placing a tube in the stomach, to which a bag could be attached. The operation was unsuccessful. It was then necessary to form an urethroileo conduit, and an ileostomy was performed. This is a method of urinary diversion effected by opening a hole in the stomach, a stoma, to which a bag–type "artificial bladder" is attached. At some point in time, it may be necessary to repeat this surgical procedure, if the stoma should close. Richard requires enemas and laxatives relative to bowel care; there have been problems with impaction from time to time. Kidney stones and other kidney complications regularly occur in patients with spinal cord injuries; prevention requires a carefully prescribed diet.

In addition, a major area of concern to a triplegic are ulcerated pressure sores, decubitis. Simple weightbearing produces these sores; while the triplegic cannot feel them, such sores may extend from the surface of the skin down to the bone, and osteomyelitis may develop, requiring amputation of the legs. The triplegic must shift position constantly and must avoid such small pressures as those resulting from wrinkled clothing. Dr. Billy De Shazo, a plastic surgeon, testified that he had operated on three extensive pressure sores developed by Richard, plugging the holes with skin taken from other parts of the body.

Since 1973, Dr. Frederick Amerongen has been the neurosurgeon who has cared for plaintiff Richard. Certain procedures were undertaken to block the constant pain in plaintiff's left arm. Surgery was performed to remove ganglia, but the operation was not successful. Pain remains, particularly when the arm is cold. Dr. Amerongen testified that Richard has clonics (spasms) beyond his control on occasion. Richard must wear a support corset in order to sit up; he cannot bathe himself, nor can he dress and undress himself.

Thomas Gucker III, M.D., an orthopedic specialist, has been the coordinator of Richard's medical care. He operated on Richard to remove a bone deposit which had formed near the right hip; he has also treated Richard with a brine pool immersion technique to heal recurring pressure sores. Dr. Gucker enumerated the various medical specialists who must see Richard several times a year for the rest of his life.

Psychiatrist James McGinnis testified at trial concerning two in-depth interviews he had conducted with plaintiff and his wife, Mary Anne, in 1973 and just prior to trial in 1975. Richard expressed his desire to live. While he and his wife have remained devoted to one another, the details of their daily lives involve matters physically and psychologically overwhelming. By 1975, the burden had become evident.

Several of the treating physicians expressed the opinion that plaintiff Richard has a normal life expectancy, despite his injuries. However, from the date of the accident to time of trial, Richard had been hospitalized fourteen times.

B. The Amount of the Award

Defendants assert that the size of the award suggests that the jury acted on the basis of passion and prejudice. Upon appeal, we apply the familiar rule that "[a] reviewing court must uphold an award of damages whenever possible and all presumptions are in favor of the judgment * * *." The fact that an award may set a precedent by its size does not in and of itself render it suspect. The determination of the jury can only be assessed by examination of the particular circumstances involved. It was cogently stated in *Niles v. City of San Rafael*, (1974) 42 Cal.App.3d 230, 241, 116 Cal.Rptr. 733, 739: "The determination of damages is primarily a factual matter on which the inevitable wide differences of opinion do not call for the intervention of appellate courts. An appellate court, in reviewing the amount of damages, must determine every conflict in the evidence in respondent's favor and give him the benefit of every reasonable inference. An appellate court may not interfere with an award unless 'the verdict is so large that, at first blush, it shocks the conscience and suggests passion, prejudice or corruption on the part of the jury.'"]

In *Niles*, an eleven-year old boy had been rendered mute and quadraplegic due to the negligence of the defendants. The award of damages was $4,025,000. As is true in the case at bench, such items as lost earnings and the need for attendant care were properly considered by the jury in the *Niles* case. It is argued here that since plaintiff Richard Rodriguez is not as limited in movement as was Kelly Niles, the plaintiff in Niles, an award larger than the *Niles* award is subject to criticism. On the other side, seeking to justify the award in the case before us, plaintiffs point to other large personal injury judgments obtained in specific cases in California and in other jurisdictions. This species of argument is not helpful to a reviewing court. For us to measure the validity of an award of damages by making a comparison with other cases would constitute a "serious invasion into the realm of factfinding" specifically disapproved of by the California Supreme Court. There is no merit in a principle that would countenance measuring a monetary distinction to be applied to triplegia, as opposed to quadraplegia.

The injuries sustained herein can only logically be described as catastrophic. Plaintiff Richard was a young person just beginning a happy and productive life. The power to enjoy sexual relations and to father children has been taken from him. The ability to take care of personal needs is not his to enjoy. Without dispute, the record establishes the unalterable tragic consequences of the injuries the intense pain and suffering and the recurrent need for hospitalization as well as the permanent limitations all of this places on the task of just existing and living. As difficult as it may appear to place a monetary value on such a loss, the trier of fact, under our judicial system, must do so. We conclude that the award in this case was within the jury's discretion.

C. The Economic Evidence

Defendants challenge the amount of the award of damages on the ground that the evidence offered by the plaintiffs with respect to wages lost by Richard Rodriguez from the date of the accident to time of trial, and with respect to the loss of future earning capacity, militates against the sufficiency of the evidence to support the judgment.

Plaintiffs did not introduce evidence of the actual amount plaintiff Richard had earned as an apprentice sprinkler fitter prior to the accident. We know of no rule of law that requires that a plaintiff establish the amount of his actual earnings at the time of the injury in order to obtain recovery for loss of wages although, obviously, the amount of such earnings would be helpful to the jury in particular situations.

In the instant case, Richard was an apprentice, without an economic track record of any consequence; information concerning actual earnings at the time of the accident could well have been misleading. The plaintiffs did introduce into evidence the union contract applicable to Richard's employment, which showed, along with other information, the annual increase in wages earned by sprinkler fitters from 1970 forward. This financial data was offered on the assumption that plaintiff would have continued to work at his chosen trade had he not been injured, a reasonable assumption to make.

With respect to loss of future earnings, the decisional law and other authorities carefully point out that "[l]oss of earning power is an element of general damages which can be inferred from the nature of the injury, without proof of actual earnings or income either before or after the injury, and damages in this respect are awarded for the loss of ability thereafter to earn money."

"[O]ne's earning capacity is not a matter of actual earnings. The impairment of the power to work is an injury wholly apart from any pecuniary benefit the exercise of such power may bring and if the injury has lessened this power, the plaintiff is entitled to recover * * *. In short, the test is not what the plaintiff would have earned, but what he could have earned." The important distinction just discussed is particularly applicable when the plaintiff is a student or an apprentice.]

* * *

In *Niles v. City of San Rafael, supra*; the award was based upon statistics of the United States Department of Labor showing the average lifetime earnings of an American male.

In the case before us, in addition to the evidence of the union contract (past and present), the plaintiffs offered the testimony of an expert economist, Robert Edward Schultz, a professor at the graduate school of business at the University of Southern California. He possessed solid educational qualifications and had taught at the University of Southern California since 1952. Schultz's expert qualifications included varied experience as an economic consultant and having been involved as an expert witness in considerable litigation, making projections of future economic trends.

Schultz was asked to make certain economic projections concerning Richard's lost earnings, both past and future, based upon certain assumptions. He had been provided with the union data; it showed that in 1969, a journeyman sprinkler fitter was earning $8.69 per hour, excluding fringe benefits, while in 1976, the same individual would earn $14.66 per hour, exclusive of fringe benefits. Schultz determined that the wages of such a worker had increased during the 1969–1976 period at a rate of 9 percent per year. Schultz also took into account the fact that an apprentice sprinkler fitter's wages constituted a percentage of the journeyman's wages, a percentage which would increase as the apprentice progressed from one apprentice period to the next.

Schultz assumed that Richard would have continued as an apprentice during the period of past lost wages (from 1970 until time of trial) and also assumed that he would have been fully employed; Schultz arrived at a figure for wages lost to time of trial of $111,646. No objection to this testimony was made by the defendants.

With respect to future loss of wages—loss of earning capacity—Schultz arrived at an annual base wage for 1975 of $16.62 per hour, including fringe benefits, totaling $34,569 per year. He then projected this figure into the future on the basis that (1) Richard would have become a journeyman in 1976; (2) he would have worked at his trade for 35 years until he was 62 years of age; (3) he would have received wages increasing annually at a rate of 7 percent; and (4) the [future wage estimates should be] discounted at a rate of 6 percent. Schultz also assumed that, had he not been injured, Richard would have worked full time, 40 hours per week, 52 weeks of the year (including a paid vacation period), with the exception of the year 1975, as the evidence had established that during that particular year, a 32–hour week was the norm.

By projecting the union wages at a strict hourly rate, without allowance for overtime or "moonlighting" (secondary employment capacity), Schultz calculated that by the year 2010, Richard would have had annual earnings of over $300,000. Schultz arrived at a lost earnings figure, or a loss of earning capacity, of $1,440,144. No objection was made by the defendants to this testimony given on direct examination by Schultz.

On cross–examination, the defendants explored with Schultz the assumptions upon which he had made his calculations. It developed that Schultz had not been informed of what Richard's actual earnings had been prior to the accident, nor did he know what were the average annual earnings of a sprinkler fitter, past or present. Defendants elicited from Schultz the estimate that, in the construction industry generally, the average worker was only employed in Southern California 80 percent of the year at the union rate. Schultz testified that he had not taken this circumstance into account when making his calculations; he did not know if sprinkler fitters followed the construction industry average, commenting that the nature of the work (often inside buildings) was not as subject to weather limitations as some construction work would be. Defendants also cross–examined Schultz with respect to the potential impact on future earnings of strikes, use of nonunion labor and business recession.

* * *

* * * [D]efendants moved to strike the testimony of Schultz, on the ground that his assumptions in making his calculations had no evidentiary support. * * *

* * *

* * * [W]e find no error in the trial court's ruling refusing to strike the testimony of Schultz; the cross–examination of Schultz exposed the full–employment fallacy upon which his calculations were based, and there was no timely objection to his testimony given on direct or cross–examination; in addition, the jury verdict was not returned in a form from which it can be determined what actual sum the jury allocated for Richard's earnings loss. Unlike *Niles,* supra, the jury was not required to specify particular sums for the various items of damage sought by plaintiffs. But the jury may well have rejected the amounts claimed by the plaintiffs as lost earnings; the verdict was considerably less than the total requested. Furthermore, the gravity of the injuries and the pain and suffering of the plaintiff are of such magnitude that the award is easily justified.

D.   Attendant Care

Defendants assert that the jury should not have been provided, as it was, with information concerning the past and future cost of attendant care, because the evidence was insufficient to establish the need for such care on the part of plaintiff Richard. This assertion lacks merit.

Dr. Gucker testified that Richard should presently have one and one–half shifts of attendant care, and that, when he reached 45 years of age, two shifts of attendant care were indicated. Dr. McGinnis, a psychiatrist, expressed an opinion that, in years to come, the mental health of Richard and his wife, Mary Anne, would be protected, as would be their interpersonal relationship, if an attendant could provide certain personal care for plaintiff, particularly with respect to problems of bladder and bowel.

From the date of the accident to the time of trial, with the exception of periods of hospitalization, 24–hour–a–day attendant care has been provided to Richard by his wife, Mary Anne. For this care, Richard has received an allowance of $280 per month from the State [Workers' Compensation] Fund. It is not too clear from the record why Mary Anne has provided such care without outside assistance; she testified that she had, on occasion, attempted, without success, to find an adequate attendant for her husband. While all of the doctors who testified expressed their admiration for this wife's devotion in caring for her husband, there was evidence that the burden placed upon her has become overwhelming. Dr. Amerongen testified that just prior to trial he had hospitalized Mary Anne for a few days of sleep.

We reject the premise that the cost of attendant care, past or future, should not have been an item for consideration by the jury because of the presence of Mary Anne. It is not part of her duties as a wife to render 24–hour–a–day attendant care. As to past care, the jury was entitled to determine that the sum of $280 per month was not anywhere near enough for the services rendered, in light of the evidence presented by plaintiffs on this issue.

No attack has been made here on the estimate testified to by Schultz concerning the cost of attendant care from the time of the accident to the time of trial, based upon the wage history of such attendants during that period of time, $124,586.

Projecting present wages into the future ($4.50 per hour) and assuming a 5 percent annual increase in those wages, reduced to present value, the economist expressed an opinion that a fund of $693,733 would be required to provide one and one–half shifts of attendant care per day for plaintiff Richard's life (43.8 years from time of trial); a total of $924,978 would be required if another half–shift were added.

* * *

[T]he necessity for attendant care and the reasonable value thereof are questions for jury determination.

* * *

E. *Admissibility of Evidence of Inflation*

It is claimed that, in making its award, it was improper for the jury to take into account inflationary trends. California law has long approved consideration of the factor of inflation as a matter of economic reality. * * * No claim has been made here that the percentages employed by plaintiffs' economist in varying contexts had no basis in fact. We therefore reject this claim of error asserted by defendants.

*F. The Claim that the Awards Were Excessive
as a Result of Inflammatory Evidence*

Defendants contend that the jury awards of $4,235,996 to Richard and $500,000 to Mary Anne were excessive because the jury was prejudicially affected by the introduction into evidence of certain photographs of plaintiff Richard and by the receipt into evidence of certain testimony concerning Richard's physical condition.

We have examined the photographs which were introduced into evidence. The claim is made that they were "gory," "gruesome" depictions, unnecessarily cumulative of other evidence concerning plaintiff Richard's injuries. While they are not pleasant photographs, they served a relevant function in the fact–finding process. These photographs were relevant on the issue of the nature and extent of plaintiff Richard's injuries to guide the jury in making a fair assessment of adequate compensation for such injuries. The photographs show different portions of the body of plaintiff Richard—the scars, the pressure sores, the opening in his stomach, and the useless legs. * * *

* * *

It is also asserted that the testimony of eight doctors was unnecessarily cumulative. The assertion is without merit. Each doctor called by the plaintiffs testified in substantial part to different aspects of the medical care that had been provided from the time of the accident to time of trial. That testimony, too, was highly relevant on the issue of damages.

Finally, it is asserted that undue emphasis was placed on plaintiff Rodriguez' impotence, pressure sores, and the problems resulting from disfunction of bladder and bowel. We know of no delicate way of approaching these subjects, with which plaintiffs must concern themselves on a daily basis.

In connection with the jury award of $500,000 to plaintiff Mary Anne, we take note of the fact that " '[t]he concept of (loss of) consortium includes not only loss of support or services, it also embraces such elements as love, companionship, affection, society, sexual relations, solace and more.' " Considering the youth of plaintiffs, the deprivation to be suffered by Mary Anne will extend over an inordinately long period of time.

We conclude that, in light of the evidence, the awards to plaintiffs were reasonable. The injuries to Richard were exceedingly grave and grievous. The defendants make no showing that the amounts of the two awards reflect passion and prejudice as a result of any cumulative or inflammatory evidence. The evidentiary support for the jury's awards is immune from any valid attack.

* * *

Notes

1. Loss of consortium, the theory on which Rodriguez's wife recovered, is discussed further in the notes following McDavid v. United States, infra p. 359.

2. *Reducing awards.* If the trial or appellate court believes that the award is excessive, it usually has three options: grant a new trial on all issues, grant a new trial on the damage issues only, or order a remittitur, whereby a (partial or complete) new trial is ordered unless the plaintiff agrees to remit a specified amount of the award. If a court grants a remittitur, the plaintiff is under considerable pressure to accept, even if the plaintiff thinks the amount left after remittitur is too low, because if the plaintiff declines he or she faces new trial (or appeal) before a court that has already expressed a view as to what the maximum award should be. Moreover, plaintiffs' lawyers generally dislike new trials on damage issues only, because in those the focus of attention is on the plaintiff and his or her claimed losses rather than on the defendant's misconduct. Some jurisdictions require a complete new trial on all issues even if the error in the first trial related only to the amount of damages.

3. *Present Value.* Note that the economic expert's projection of Rodriguez's loss of future earning capacity was "discounted at a rate of 6 per cent" and also that the projected cost of future attendant care was "reduced to present value." These are both references to a standard accounting adjustment reflecting the time value of money. When he collects the judgment, Rodriguez will receive a lump sum, part of it representing compensation for future lost earning capacity and future costs of attendant care. As the court observes, in arriving at the estimates for such future losses, it is appropriate to take expectations about inflation into account. But they also need to be adjusted downward, to take into account the fact that Rodriguez will receive all the money immediately.

Suppose, for example, his award includes $10,000 for attendant care for the year 1998; if the judgment is paid in 1978, he has the use of the money for 20 years before he has to spend it on attendants. If he invests it prudently, the $10,000 will have increased substantially when the time comes to pay the attendants. For example, if he invests the $10,000 in U.S. Treasury bonds at 6 per cent interest and invests each year's dividends similarly, he will have $32,071 in 20 years (ignoring the tax payable on the dividends). This is simply the effect of compounding interest; each year he earns interest not only on the $10,000 but also on the previous years' earnings.

Discounting to present value is the reverse of compounding interest. The question it addresses is, "what sum of money, awarded today, will equal $10,000 in 20 years?" The answer depends, of course, on the rate of interest that the money can be expected to return over the 20–year period. This rate is called the discount rate. The higher that rate, the less the money that needs to be awarded today to reach the $10,000 goal in 20 years. Once a discount rate is chosen, reduction to present value is a purely mathematical task. For most lawyers, the easiest way to make this calculation is to use a present value table, which can be found in most standard financial reference books, or a financial calculator that has a present value function. (In our example, if we use a discount rate of 6 per cent, the present value of $10,000 due in 20 years is $3,118.) Following is a portion of a typical present value table, showing what $1, to be paid in the future, is worth today, assuming annual compounding:

YEAR	4%	5%	6%	7%	8%	9%	10%
1	.9615	.9524	.9434	.9346	.9259	.9174	.9091
2	.9246	.9070	.8900	.8734	.8573	.8417	.8264
3	.8890	.8638	.8396	.8163	.7938	.7722	.7513
4	.8548	.8227	.7921	.7629	.7350	.7084	.6830
5	.8219	.7835	.7473	.7130	.6806	.6499	.6209
6	.7903	.7462	.7050	.6663	.6302	.5963	.5645
7	.7599	.7107	.6651	.6227	.5835	.5470	.5132
8	.7307	.6768	.6274	.5820	.5403	.5019	.4665
9	.7026	.6446	.5919	.5439	.5002	.4604	.4241
10	.6756	.6139	.5584	.5083	.4632	.4224	.3855
11	.6496	.5847	.5268	.4751	.4289	.3875	.3505
12	.6246	.5568	.4970	.4440	.3971	.3555	.3186
13	.6006	.5303	.4688	.4150	.3677	.3262	.2897
14	.5775	.5051	.4423	.3878	.3405	.2992	.2633
15	.5553	.4810	.4173	.3624	.3152	.2745	.2394
16	.5339	.4581	.3936	.3387	.2919	.2519	.2176
17	.5134	.4363	.3714	.3166	.2703	.2311	.1978
18	.4936	.4155	.3503	.2959	.2502	.2120	.1799
19	.4746	.3957	.3305	.2765	.2317	.1945	.1635
20	.4564	.3769	.3118	.2584	.2145	.1784	.1486

In jury trials, reduction to present value usually is handled as it was in *Rodriguez*: the expert witnesses incorporate the present value calculation into their estimates of the plaintiff's losses, and are free to challenge each other's assumptions as to the appropriate discount rate. It is for the jury to decide which expert's assumptions to accept. In bench trials judges sometimes do the reduction themselves.

There is general agreement that awards for future pecuniary losses, such as medical expenses and loss of earning capacity, should be reduced to present value. Awards for future nonpecuniary losses, such as pain and suffering and loss of enjoyment, often are not reduced, probably in the belief that these calculations are so imprecise to begin with that reduction to present value would add only an illusion of accuracy. The California pattern jury charges quoted at the beginning of this chapter reflect this view.

McDOUGALD v. GARBER

New York Court of Appeals, 1989.
73 N.Y.2d 246, 538 N.Y.S.2d 937, 536 N.E.2d 372.

WACHTLER, CHIEF JUDGE.

This appeal raises fundamental questions about the nature and role of nonpecuniary damages in personal injury litigation. By nonpecuniary damages, we mean those damages awarded to compensate an injured person for the physical and emotional consequences of the injury, such as pain and suffering and the loss of the ability to engage in certain activities. Pecuniary damages, on the other hand, compensate the victim for the economic consequences of the injury, such as medical expenses, lost earnings and the cost of custodial care.

The specific questions raised here deal with assessment of nonpecuniary damages and are (1) whether some degree of cognitive awareness is a prerequisite to recovery for loss of enjoyment of life and (2) whether a jury should be instructed to consider and award damages for loss of enjoyment of life separately from damages for pain and suffering. We answer the first question in the affirmative and the second question in the negative.

I.

On September 7, 1978, plaintiff Emma McDougald, then 31 years old, underwent a Caesarean section and tubal ligation at New York Infirmary. Defendant Garber performed the surgery; defendants Armengol and Kulkarni provided anesthesia. During the surgery, Mrs. McDougald suffered oxygen deprivation which resulted in severe brain damage and left her in a permanent comatose condition. This action was brought by Mrs. McDougald and her husband, suing derivatively, alleging that the injuries were caused by the defendants' acts of malpractice.

A jury found all defendants liable and awarded Emma McDougald a total of $9,650,102 in damages, including $1,000,000 for conscious pain and suffering and a separate award of $3,500,000 for loss of the pleasures and pursuits of life. The balance of the damages awarded to her were for pecuniary damages—lost earnings and the cost of custodial and nursing care. Her husband was awarded $1,500,000 on his derivative claim for the loss of his wife's services. On defendants' posttrial motions, the Trial Judge reduced the total award to Emma McDougald to $4,796,728 by striking the entire award for future nursing care ($2,353,374) [on the ground that the evidence did not show that plaintiff would require future nursing services above and beyond those provided for by the award for custodial care] and by reducing the separate awards for conscious pain and suffering and loss of the pleasures and pursuits of life to a single award of $2,000,000 [on the ground of excessiveness]. Her husband's award was left intact. On cross appeals, the Appellate Division affirmed and later granted defendants leave to appeal to this court.

II.

We note at the outset that the defendants' liability for Emma McDougald's injuries is unchallenged here * * *.

Also unchallenged are the awards in the amount of $770,978 for loss of earnings and $2,025,750 for future custodial care—that is, the pecuniary damage awards that survived defendants' posttrial motions.

What remains in dispute, primarily, is the award to Emma McDougald for nonpecuniary damages. At trial, defendants sought to show that Mrs. McDougald's injuries were so severe that she was incapable of either experiencing pain or appreciating her condition. Plaintiffs, on the other hand, introduced proof that Mrs. McDougald responded to certain stimuli to a sufficient extent to indicate that she was aware of her circumstances. Thus, the extent of Mrs. McDougald's cognitive abilities, if any, was sharply disputed.

The parties and the trial court agreed that Mrs. McDougald could not recover for pain and suffering unless she were conscious of the pain. Defendants maintained that such consciousness was also required to support an award for loss of enjoyment of life. The court, however, accepted plaintiffs' view that loss of enjoyment of life was compensable without regard to whether the plaintiff was aware of the loss. Accordingly, because the level of Mrs. McDougald's cognitive abilities was in dispute, the court instructed the jury to consider loss of enjoyment of life as an element of nonpecuniary damages separate from pain and suffering. The court's charge to the jury on these points was as follows:

"If you conclude that Emma McDougald is so neurologically impaired that she is totally incapable of experiencing any unpleasant or painful sensation, then, obviously, she cannot be awarded damages for conscious pain * * *.

"It is for you to determine the level of Emma McDougald's perception and awareness. Suffering relates primarily to the emotional reaction of the injured person to the injury. Thus, for an injured person to experience suffering, there, again, must be some level of awareness. If Emma McDougald is totally unaware of her condition or totally incapable of any emotional reaction, then you cannot award her damages for suffering. If, however, you conclude that there is some level of perception or that she is capable of an emotional response at some level, then damages for pain and suffering should be awarded * * *.

"Damages for the loss of the pleasures and pursuits of life, however, require no awareness of the loss on the part of the injured person. Quite obviously, Emma McDougald is unable to engage in any of the activities which constitute a normal life, the activities she engaged in prior to her injury * * * Loss of the enjoyment of life may, of course, accompany the physical sensation and emotional responses that we refer to as pain and suffering, and in most cases it does. It is possible, however, for an injured person to lose the enjoyment of life without experiencing any conscious pain and suffering. Damages for this item of injury relate not to what Emma McDougald is aware of, but rather to what she has lost. What her life was prior to her injury and what it has been since September 7, 1978 and what it will be for as long as she lives."

We conclude that the court erred, both in instructing the jury that Mrs. McDougald's awareness was irrelevant to their consideration of damages for loss of enjoyment of life and in directing the jury to consider that aspect of damages separately from pain and suffering.

III.

We begin with the familiar proposition that an award of damages to a person injured by the negligence of another is to compensate the victim, not to punish the wrongdoer. The goal is to restore the injured party, to the extent possible, to the position that would have been occupied had the wrong not occurred. To be sure, placing the burden of compensation on the negligent party also serves as a deterrent, but purely punitive damages—that is, those which have no compensatory purpose—are prohibited unless the harmful conduct is intentional, malicious, outrageous, or otherwise aggravated beyond mere negligence.

Damages for nonpecuniary losses are, of course, among those that can be awarded as compensation to the victim. This aspect of damages, however, stands on less certain ground than does an award for pecuniary damages. An economic loss can be compensated in kind by an economic gain; but recovery for noneconomic losses such as pain and suffering and loss of enjoyment of life rests on "the legal fiction that money damages can compensate for a victim's injury" We accept this fiction, knowing that although money will neither ease the pain nor restore the victim's abilities, this device is as close as the law can come in its effort to right the wrong. We have no hope of evaluating what has been lost, but a monetary award may provide a measure of solace for the condition created.

Our willingness to indulge this fiction comes to an end, however, when it ceases to serve the compensatory goals of tort recovery. When that limit is met, further indulgence can only result in assessing damages that are punitive. The question posed by this case, then, is whether an award of damages for loss of enjoyment of life to a person whose injuries preclude any awareness of the loss serves a compensatory purpose. We conclude that it does not.

Simply put, an award of money damages in such circumstances has no meaning or utility to the injured person. An award for the loss of enjoyment of life "cannot provide [such a victim] with any consolation or ease any burden resting on him * * *. He cannot spend it upon necessities or pleasures. He cannot experience the pleasure of giving it away".

We recognize that, as the trial court noted, requiring some cognitive awareness as a prerequisite to recovery for loss of enjoyment of life will result in some cases "in the paradoxical situation that the greater the degree of brain injury inflicted by a negligent defendant, the smaller the award the plaintiff can recover in general damages". The force of this argument, however—the temptation to achieve a balance between injury and damages—has nothing to do with meaningful compensation for the victim. Instead, the temptation is rooted in a desire to punish the defendant in proportion to the harm inflicted. However relevant such retributive symmetry may be in the criminal law, it has no place in the law of civil damages, at least in the absence of culpability beyond mere negligence.

Accordingly, we conclude that cognitive awareness is a prerequisite to recovery for loss of enjoyment of life. We do not go so far, however, as to require the fact finder to sort out varying degrees of cognition and determine at what level a particular deprivation can be fully appreciated. With respect to pain and suffering, the trial court charged simply that there must be "some level of awareness" in order for plaintiff to recover. We think that this is an appropriate standard for all aspects of nonpecuniary loss. No doubt the standard ignores analytically relevant levels of cognition, but we resist the desire for analytical purity in favor of simplicity. A more complex instruction might give the appearance of greater precision but, given the limits of our understanding of the human mind, it would in reality lead only to greater speculation.

We turn next to the question whether loss of enjoyment of life should be considered a category of damages separate from pain and suffering.

IV.

There is no dispute here that the fact finder may, in assessing nonpecuniary damages, consider the effect of the injuries on the plaintiff's capacity to lead a normal life. Traditionally, in this State and elsewhere, this aspect of suffering has not been treated as a separate category of damages; instead, the plaintiff's inability to enjoy life to its fullest has been considered one type of suffering to be factored into a general award for nonpecuniary damages, commonly known as pain and suffering.

Recently, however, there has been an attempt to segregate the suffering associated with physical pain from the mental anguish that stems from the inability to engage in certain activities, and to have juries provide a separate award for each.

Some courts have resisted the effort, primarily on the ground that duplicative and therefore excessive awards would result. Other courts have allowed separate awards, noting that the types of suffering involved are analytically distinguishable. Still other courts have questioned the propriety of the practice but held that, in the particular case, separate awards did not constitute reversible error.

In [two decisions of the Appellate Division], courts were persuaded that the distinctions between the two types of mental anguish justified separate awards and that the potential for duplicative awards could be mitigated by carefully drafted jury instructions. In addition, the courts opined that separate awards would facilitate appellate review concerning the excessiveness of the total damage award.

We do not dispute that distinctions can be found or created between the concepts of pain and suffering and loss of enjoyment of life. If the term "suffering" is limited to the emotional response to the sensation of pain, then the emotional response caused by the limitation of life's activities may be considered qualitatively different. But suffering need not be so limited—it can easily encompass the frustration and anguish caused by the inability to participate in activities that once brought pleasure. Traditionally, by treating loss of enjoyment of life as a permissible factor in assessing pain and suffering, courts have given the term this broad meaning.

If we are to depart from this traditional approach and approve a separate award for loss of enjoyment of life, it must be on the basis that such an approach will yield a more accurate evaluation of the compensation due to the plaintiff. We have no doubt that, in general, the total award for nonpecuniary damages would increase if we adopted the rule. That separate awards are advocated by plaintiffs and resisted by defendants is sufficient evidence that larger awards are at stake here. But a larger award does not by itself indicate that the goal of compensation has been better served.

The advocates of separate awards contend that because pain and suffering and loss of enjoyment of life can be distinguished, they must be treated separately if the plaintiff is to be compensated fully for each distinct injury suffered. We disagree. Such an analytical approach may have its place when the subject is pecuniary damages, which can be calculated with some precision. But the estimation of nonpecuniary damages is not amenable to such analytical precision and may, in fact, suffer from its application. Translating human suffering into dollars and cents involves no mathematical formula; it rests, as we have said, on a legal fiction. The figure that emerges is unavoidably distorted by the translation. Application of this murky process to the component parts of nonpecuniary injuries (however analytically distinguishable they may be) cannot make it more accurate. If anything, the distortion will be amplified by repetition.

Thus, we are not persuaded that any salutary purpose would be served by having the jury make separate awards for pain and suffering and loss of enjoyment of life. We are confident, furthermore, that the trial advocate's art is a sufficient guarantee that none of the plaintiff's losses will be ignored by the jury.

The errors in the instructions given to the jury require a new trial on the issue of nonpecuniary damages to be awarded to plaintiff Emma McDougald. * * *

Accordingly, the order of the Appellate Division, insofar as appealed from, should be modified, with costs to defendants, by granting a new trial on the issue of nonpecuniary damages of plaintiff Emma McDougald, and as so modified, affirmed.

TITONE, JUDGE, dissenting.

* * *

The capacity to enjoy life—by watching one's children grow, participating in recreational activities, and drinking in the many other pleasures that life has to offer—is unquestionably an attribute of an ordinary healthy individual. The loss of that capacity as a result of another's negligent act is at least as serious an impairment as the permanent destruction of a physical function, which has always been treated as a compensable item under traditional tort principles. Indeed, I can imagine no physical loss that is more central to the quality of a tort victim's continuing life than the destruction of the capacity to enjoy that life to the fullest.

Unquestionably, recovery of a damage item such as "pain and suffering" requires a showing of some degree of cognitive capacity. Such a requirement exists for the simple reason that pain and suffering are wholly subjective concepts and cannot exist separate and apart from the human consciousness that experiences them. In contrast, the destruction of an individual's capacity to enjoy life as a result of a crippling injury is an objective fact that does not differ in principle from the permanent loss of an eye or limb. As in the case of a lost limb, an essential characteristic of a healthy human life has been wrongfully taken, and, consequently, the injured party is entitled to a monetary award as a substitute, if, as the majority asserts, the goal of tort compensation is "to restore the injured party, to the extent possible, to the position that would have been occupied had the wrong not occurred."

Significantly, this equation does not suggest a need to establish the injured's awareness of the loss. The victim's ability to comprehend the degree to which his or her life has been impaired is irrelevant, since, unlike "conscious pain and suffering," the impairment exists independent of the victim's ability to apprehend it. Indeed, the majority reaches the conclusion that a degree of awareness must be shown only after injecting a new element into the equation. Under the majority's formulation, the victim must be aware of the loss because, in addition to being compensatory, the award must have "meaning or utility to the injured person." This additional requirement, however, has no real foundation in law or logic. "Meaning" and "utility" are subjective value judgments that have no place in the law of tort recovery, where the primary goal is to find ways of quantifying, to the extent possible, the worth of various forms of human tragedy.

* * *

Notes

1. There is disagreement among the states on both of the issues decided in the principal case. Some courts hold that the plaintiff need not be conscious to recover damages for loss of enjoyment of life. See, e.g., Holston v. Sisters of the Third Order of St. Francis, 247 Ill.App.3d 985, 187 Ill.Dec. 743, 618 N.E.2d 334 (1993). Some permit a separate award for loss of enjoyment in addition to the award for pain and suffering. See, e.g., Fantozzi v. Sandusky Cement Products Co., 64 Ohio St.3d 601, 597 N.E.2d 474 (1992).

2. *Hedonic damages*. Damages for loss of enjoyment of life are sometimes called "hedonic" damages. Note that these damages are not mentioned by any name in the California jury instructions reproduced at the beginning of this section. California is one of the states that does not allow a separate award for these losses. Even in such states, however, loss of enjoyment is compensable (at least in theory) as part of the plaintiff's suffering. These damages can constitute the major portion of the plaintiff's loss in some

cases, such as an injury to an amateur athlete or musician to whom the ability to perform is the major reward in life.

3. *Quantifying nonpecuniary losses.* Once the jury has determined what pain and suffering the plaintiff has suffered, or what enjoyment has been lost, how does it go about translating those losses into dollar amounts? The judge's instructions usually are as vague as the language of the California instructions: "reasonable compensation," "no definite standard," "calm and reasonable judgment," "just and reasonable." At one time plaintiff's lawyers were allowed to suggest dollar amounts in their pleadings and these could be read to the jury. But tort reform rules in many jurisdictions now forbid the pleading of specific figures for nonpecuniary losses. Evidence of awards by other juries in similar cases is inadmissible. Because jurors are given little information during the trial about appropriate awards, it is easy to see why the plaintiffs' bar and defense interests engage in public relations battles to shape public attitudes about tort recoveries.

4. Most jurisdictions permit lawyers to propose in their arguments to the jury some amount for nonpecuniary losses, often with the limitation that the amount suggested must be one that the evidence would support. See Braun v. Ahmed, 127 A.D.2d 418, 515 N.Y.S.2d 473 (1987) (canvassing positions of various states). But the tort reform prohibitions on pleading specific amounts sometimes are construed to also preclude arguing specific amounts. See, e.g., Bechard v. Eisinger, 105 A.D.2d 939, 481 N.Y.S.2d 906 (1984).

5. *Unit of time arguments.* The most controversial method of proposing specific amounts for nonpecuniary losses is the unit–of–time argument. Plaintiffs' attorneys like to propose that juries award a suggested rate per day, hour, or minute. By this method, a modest rate can produce a substantial award. For example, $5 per hour for pain and suffering and $5 per hour for loss of enjoyment, multiplied times 16 waking hours per day for ten years, would produce a total award of $584,000. This technique is criticized on the ground that it tends to create an illusion of precision, but it is frequently permitted, at least if accompanied by an instruction from the judge reminding the jury that the formula suggested is just argument, not evidence. See, e.g., Westbrook v. General Tire and Rubber Co., 754 F.2d 1233 (5th Cir.1985).

Collateral Benefits

Accident victims often receive payments or other benefits from sources other than the tortfeasor—health insurance, disability payments, and workers compensation, to name a few. These are called collateral source payments or collateral benefits. Should they be deducted from the victim's tort recovery? If they are not deducted and the victim receives a complete tort recovery, he or she will receive more than full compensation. On the other hand, deducting them gives the tortfeasor, rather than the victim, the benefit of payments that were earned by or provided for the welfare of the victim.

In general, the common law does not deduct collateral benefits. This principle, "the collateral source rule," has been a target of tort reform, and many states now have statutes requiring that some collateral payments be deducted from tort awards. Even in the absence of a statute, courts now seem inclined to define collateral benefits narrowly, as in the following case.

HAYNES v. YALE–NEW HAVEN HOSPITAL

Supreme Court of Connecticut, 1997.
243 Conn. 17, 699 A.2d 964.

BORDEN, ASSOCIATE JUSTICE.

[Barbara Freeman, a rural mail carrier, was injured when her vehicle was struck head–on by a vehicle driven by Alan G. Perrier. She was taken to Yale–New Haven's emergency department and was treated for a fractured left leg and a fractured pelvis. After approximately one and one–half hours, the emergency room doctors noticed that the decedent was experiencing " 'an expanding abdominal girth.' " She was taken to surgery, where the surgeon discovered large amounts of blood in her abdomen as a result of laceration of her spleen. During the surgery her circulation failed and she went into cardiac arrest and died.

[Freeman's daughter, Susan Haynes, brought a wrongful death suit against Perrier, the other driver, and received from his insurance company a settlement of $20,000, the limits of his liability insurance coverage. Haynes then made a claim under the underinsured motorist coverage that Freeman had purchased from her own insurer, Covenant. Although the state required motorists to carry only $20,000 in underinsured motorist coverage, Freeman had bought $900,000 worth of coverage. An arbitration panel fixed the total damages at $650,000 and Covenant paid Haynes $630,000 after deducting the $20,000 she had received from Perrier's insurance carrier.

[Haynes then initiated a medical malpractice claim against the hospital and the surgeon. The trial court granted the defendants' motion for summary judgment on the ground that the plaintiff had already received full compensation for the harm suffered by her decedent.]

We first address the plaintiff's argument that underinsured motorist benefits, because of their contractual nature, are not within the ambit of the common law rule precluding double recovery for the same harm,[6] but, rather, come within the common law collateral source rule.[7] * * *

* * *

6. The rule precluding double recovery is a "simple and time–honored maxim that [a] plaintiff may be compensated only once for his just damages for the same injury * * *. Plaintiffs are not foreclosed from suing multiple defendants, either jointly or separately, for injuries for which each is liable, nor are they foreclosed from obtaining multiple judgments against joint tortfeasors * * *. The possible rendition of multiple judgments does not, however, defeat the proposition that a litigant may recover just damages only once. Double recovery is foreclosed by the rule that only one satisfaction may be obtained for a loss that is the subject of two or more judgments."

7. The collateral source rule provides that a defendant is not entitled to be relieved from paying any part of the compensation due for injuries proximately resulting from his act where payment [for such injuries or damages] comes from a collateral source, wholly independent of him.... The basis of [this] rule is that a wrongdoer shall not benefit from a windfall from an outside source. That rule is applicable ... in any tort case.

* * * She argues that, because Covenant's liability was based entirely upon its contract with the decedent, all payments made pursuant to the underinsured motorist policy should be viewed as purely contractual in nature. Thus, according to the plaintiff, the collateral source rule should apply.

* * *

* * * Although in form first party insurance, underinsured motorist insurance operates in part as a surrogate for a third party who lacks sufficient liability insurance. It provides benefits only upon proof that a third party, namely, an underinsured motorist for whose liability it acts as a surrogate, was a tortfeasor who injured the insured. Moreover, the amount of an underinsured motorist payment is determined, within contractual limits, by the measure of tort damages. * * *

* * *

[W]e need to go beyond labels in resolving the question posed by this case. Put another way, the question is not whether underinsured motorist benefits *are* a collateral source; the question is whether they *should be treated* as a collateral source, in the present factual context. * * * We conclude that, for the particular purpose of characterizing underinsured motorist payments, the relationship in the present case between the underinsured carrier and the defendant may be viewed as analogous to that of joint tortfeasors, and thus that the general tort rule precluding double recovery from joint tortfeasors should apply.

We begin with the fundamental principle that the purpose of underinsured motorist insurance is to place the insured in the *same* position as, but *no better* position than, the insured would have been had the underinsured tortfeasor been fully insured. * * * The plaintiff's argument, however, would have her recover *more* than her full damages— indeed, that is the whole point of her action against the defendants— *solely* because of her decedent's underinsured motorist coverage. * * *

Furthermore, the plaintiff's putative right to recover against the defendants in the present case, for the loss that her decedent's underinsured motorist carrier has already paid, depends *solely* on the order of litigation in this case. * * * Under the plaintiff's argument * * * when she pursues her underinsured motorist policy *first*, as she in fact did, she can recover, not only the $650,000 that she received from her decedent's underinsured motorist carrier, but an additional amount for the same damages when she then brings an action against the defendants. Had the exact same claims been presented in a different order, however—namely, an action against the defendants *first*, rather than *second*—she agrees that she could recover only a total of $650,000. Stating the plaintiff's position in this manner demonstrates why it must fail, for it would be bizarre to say that the law permits a double recovery depending on the order of litigation of the plaintiff's claims. Put another way, it cannot be the law that underinsured motorist benefits are, or are not, a "collateral source" depending solely on *when* they are sought.

Finally, the equities do not weigh substantially in favor of the plaintiff's position. Precluding the plaintiff from obtaining double recovery does not deprive the decedent of the benefit for which she paid her underinsured motorist premium, namely, a guaranteed recovery of her wrongful death damages, subject to contractual limits, despite the fact that she was hit by an underinsured motorist, and whether there was a joint tortfeasor who could also be held liable. The only thing she is deprived of is the opportunity to recover *more* than she paid for. Moreover, although we acknowledge the general notion that a defendant, if indeed negligent, should be held accountable, our conclusion does not create an inappropriate windfall for the defendants. * * * *Whenever* the principle against double recovery is applied as between various tortfeasors, or tortfeasor surrogates, one of the parties escapes at least some degree of liability. In such cases, however, the policy behind the fundamental principle barring double recovery is, therefore, not a windfall under the law, but rather a necessary consequence of a fundamental policy choice.

* * *

Berdon, Associate Justice, with whom Katz and McDonald, Associate Justices, join, dissenting.

* * *

* * * The majority's reasoning stands underinsured motorist law on its head by transforming *the decedent's insurance,* for which she paid the premiums for coverage substantially in excess of that required by law, *into the underinsured motorist tortfeasor's* insurance. * * *

* * *

My conclusion that underinsured motorist benefits is a collateral source is further buttressed by [recent tort reform statutes] which provide that an award of economic damages, based on personal injury or wrongful death, shall be reduced by the trial court, after liability is determined and damages are awarded, by certain enumerated payments of "collateral sources" (statutory collateral source credits) to the plaintiff. Notwithstanding this limited abrogation of the collateral source rule by statute, the legislature has, up to this point in time, chosen not to include underinsured motorist benefits in [the statutory list of payments that must be credited against the judgment], * * * which demonstrates an intent on its part to limit the encroachment on the collateral source rule.[6]

* * *

6. I am aware that there is a school of thought that the collateral source rule should be abandoned or restricted. Those who advocate the elimination of the collateral source rule, to the extent that a tortfeasor is relieved of all liability, however,

* * * The overarching flaw in the majority's reasoning is that it concludes that "underinsured motorist benefits, although contractual in nature, operate in part as a liability insurance surrogate for the underinsured motorist third party tortfeasor." * * * [T]his state's insurance regulation and our established case law have rejected this "surrogate" argument. * * * Once the majority made the leap that underinsured motorist benefits are a "liability insurance surrogate" for the underinsured tortfeasor motorist, it was able to treat the underinsured motorist carrier as a joint tortfeasor, alongside the defendants, in which case the general tort rule precluding double recovery from joint tortfeasors would apply. I have no quarrel with the single recovery rule being applied faithfully to actual joint tortfeasors. But underinsured motorist carriers *are not joint tortfeasors,* and should not be viewed as such. * * *

* * *

In what it finds as further support for its position, the majority asserts that the plaintiff's right to recover depends solely on the order of litigation. The thrust of the majority's reasoning is that if the plaintiff had first brought an action against the defendants, she would not be entitled to recover the underinsured motorist benefits. As I see it, the answer to that reasoning is that the contractual relationship between insurer and insured allows the insured to promptly seek benefits from its insured. The underinsured motorist carrier is required to make *prompt* payment of a claim that it finds to be clearly payable. * * * The fact that the plaintiff, as administratrix of the decedent's estate, was able to recover a prompt payment, based upon the decedent's contractual arrangement with her insurer, before the plaintiff brought an action against the defendants in this case should not be used to create a windfall for the defendants. * * *

With respect to the order of litigation, allowing the plaintiff to recover in this case makes sense for another reason. The conclusion that underinsured motorist benefits are not a collateral source jeopardizes the subrogation rights of underinsured motorist carriers and also impermissibly interferes with the contractual relationship of the insurer and insured. An underinsured motorist carrier, based on the insurance contract or a settlement agreement, after fulfilling its duty of making prompt payment, would surely seek reimbursement of all or part of a payment if the insured later recovers from the tortfeasor. This is common practice in the world of underinsured motorist benefits. * * *

---

lose sight of an important aspect of the law of torts. "The 'prophylactic' factor of preventing future harm has been quite important in the field of torts. The courts are concerned not only with compensation of the victim, but with admonition of the wrongdoer. When the decisions of the courts become known, and defendants realize that they may be held liable, there is of course a strong incentive to prevent the occurrence of the harm. Not infrequently one reason for imposing liability is the deliberate purpose of providing that incentive." [ ] In other words, with respect to the alleged facts of this case, the policy of the law must also be concerned with discouraging further conduct of hospital emergency room personnel from negligently allowing patients to bleed to death. [Footnote relocated].

The underinsured motorist carrier's assertion of its rights to reimbursement for payments made to an insured greatly reduces the prospects of double recovery.[26] * * *

* * *

Notes

1. The disagreement revealed by the majority and dissenting opinions in the principal case is widespread. The dissenting opinion cited decisions in ten jurisdictions agreeing with its position and three adopting the majority's view. The majority acknowledged that more states agreed with the dissent's position.

2. *Subrogation.* The rights of reimbursement referred to in the dissenting opinion arise from subrogation clauses that are found in most insurance policies. Health insurance policies, for example, usually provide that if the policy holder recovers a judgment or settlement from a tortfeasor (or a tortfeasor's insurance company), the health insurance company has a subrogation right in that recovery—i.e., is entitled to recoup from those funds whatever it has paid to hospitals or doctors. As a practical matter, that often means that the first–party insurer (the victim's own health or auto insurance carrier) pays the victim and then brings suit against the tortfeasor to enforce its subrogation rights.

3. As the dissent in *Haynes* noted, rights of subrogation have an important bearing on collateral source questions. If benefits such as health insurance payments are deducted from the recovery, allowing subrogation against what remains of the plaintiff's recovery defeats the purpose of health insurance, while disallowing subrogation defeats the objective of transferring the loss to the victim's insurance company to wrongdoer's. To avoid this, the statutes requiring deduction of collateral payments often contain an exception for payments that are subject to a right of subrogation.

4. *Insurance implications.* The real parties in interest in tort cases are often insurance companies. For example, in the principal case, the real winners are the insurance carriers for the doctor and the hospital; they do not even have to defend the malpractice suit. The real loser (assuming the plaintiff was full compensated by the $650,000 she received) was the underinsured motorist carrier: if the plaintiff had won, the underinsured motorist carrier presumably would have asserted subrogation rights to any recovery the plaintiff obtained from the malpractice claim—or modified its policy

26. Professor Tait has noted that "[o]dd as it may seem, to reap the fruits of subrogation requires a continued recognition of the Collateral Source Rule. This is so because if the tortfeasor's liability to the plaintiff is reduced by the amount of the collateral benefits, the plaintiff will have no cause of action for that amount to which the collateral source can be subrogated." C. Tait, "Connecticut's Collateral Source Rule: Stepchild of the Law of Damages," 1 Conn. L.Rev. 93, 116 (1968). As Professor Tait aptly stated, subrogation creates a *middle ground* between abolishing the collateral source rule and allowing absolute double recovery: "[Subrogation] offers a recognized alternative to [double recovery, a solution] that would further the basic tort principles of compensation and indemnity within the concept of fault liability. As long as ... fault remains the keystone of our tort law, it is subrogation that merits the attention of our courts and legislature, and its adoption in appropriate new areas should help legitimize the Collateral Source Rule within the law of damages." Id., 123. I cannot agree more.

language to make sure it had such rights in the future. Courts rarely discuss the insurance ramifications of their tort decisions. Should they?

Tort Reform

The collateral source rule has been a target of the tort reform movement. Statutes in many states now require deduction of items that under the common law rule would be treated as collateral payments. For example, one of the tort reform statutes referred to in the dissenting opinion requires deduction of amounts the plaintiff receives under health insurance or HMO agreements. See Conn. G.S. § 52–225. Statutes requiring deduction of collateral benefits have sometimes been held unconstitutional. See, e.g., Thompson v. KFB Insurance Co., 252 Kan. 1010, 850 P.2d 773 (Kan.1993), holding that a statute giving defendants a credit for insurance, workers compensation, social security, or similar payments when the claim exceeded $150,000 violated the equal protection clause of the Kansas constitution. (This was the third legislative attack on the collateral source rule to be held unconstitutional in Kansas.)

The tort reform movement has generated many modifications of tort law. Most of them do not change the basic elements of negligence law, as you might surmise from the fact that we have not encountered them until this point in the book. In this and succeeding chapters, however, we shall see their effects frequently. The movement began in the 1980s, largely in response to rapidly rising premiums for medical malpractice insurance. It burgeoned in the 1990s, fueled by a perception that tort law was inflating insurance costs, inhibiting economic growth, and creating windfalls for greedy plaintiffs and their lawyers. It became a major political issue in many states and in Congress, pitting insurance companies and business interests against trial lawyers, labor unions, and consumer groups. It eventually extended beyond the field of tort law and became to some extent a campaign against lawsuits generally. The perceptions and emotions it generated produced not only legislative action, but also changes in judicial politics that have made many courts less hospitable to plaintiffs' claims, particularly novel ones. Whatever the merits of these changes, it is clear that the expansion of tort law that occurred over the last half of the 20th century has been halted and in many respects reversed.

Whether these changes were necessary, whether they are really reforms or merely special pleading, and whether they have been or will be effective are questions that continue to be contested. Although there have been many empirical studies, very few of those have generated conclusions that are generally accepted. We urge students to keep an open mind, try to understand how the law operated before and after the change, and evaluate each modification on its merits.

D. WRONGFUL DEATH AND SURVIVAL ACTIONS

The common law permitted no recovery for a tort that caused death. The explanation generally given is the "felony–merger rule," an early English doctrine premised on the notion that any intentional or negligent killing was a felony. The primary offense was the breach of the King's peace rather than the wrong to the victim, so the tort was considered "merged" into the crime. Moreover, as in all felonies, the punishment was death for the felon and forfeiture of his estate to the Crown; thus there was no defendant left to sue and no assets from which a recovery might be had. See, e.g., Moragne v. States Marine Lines, 398 U.S. 375, 90 S.Ct. 1772, 26 L.Ed.2d 339 (1970). Another explanation may be that the law generally does not give one person a cause of action for a tort committed against another.

Whatever the explanation, the rule created the untenable result that a tortfeasor whose victim died was better off than one whose victim was merely injured. Beginning in the mid–nineteenth century, England and every American jurisdiction adopted statutes permitting actions for "wrongful death." These specified who could recover (usually spouse and children, sometimes also parents and siblings, sometimes all the decedent's legal heirs), and who could bring suit (usually the person authorized to administer the decedent's estate, sometimes any of the persons authorized to recover). At first the statutes permitted recovery only for pecuniary losses, such as loss of support, and often they had fixed dollar ceilings, e.g., $5,000, but gradually most states dropped these limitations, and now nonpecuniary losses such as loss of the decedent's guidance and companionship are an important part of wrongful death recovery.

Although wrongful death is a very large exception to the general rule that one person has no cause of action for a tort committed on another, it is still an exception. When an entertainer, an entrepreneur, or a star athlete is tortiously injured or killed, the tort can cause millions of dollars in losses to employers, employees, shareholders, promoters, or agents, but the law denies them any recovery. See, e.g., Cole, Raywid & Braverman v. Quadrangle Development Corp., 444 A.2d 969 (D.C.App. 1982) (law firm has no cause of action for wrongful death of managing partner).

It is difficult to generalize about wrongful death because the cause of action remains almost entirely statutory and courts generally adhere to the specific dictates of the statute even when those seem inconsistent with the general principles that the statute is supposed to embody. For example, it is often said that the purpose of wrongful death recovery is to provide for the decedent's dependents, and the statutes usually name classes of survivors that the legislature probably assumed would be dependents (e.g. spouses and children). Nevertheless, courts routinely deny recovery to dependents who do not fit the statutory description (e.g. unadopted stepchildren). See, e.g., Klossner v. San Juan County, 21 Wash.App. 689, 586 P.2d 899 (1978), aff'd 93 Wash.2d 42, 605 P.2d 330 (1980). (In California a similar decision led the legislature to amend the statute to allow recovery by stepchildren and other dependent minors who lived in decedent's household. See Cal.Civ.Proc. Code § 377.60.) On the other hand, persons who fit the statutory classification but are not dependent (e.g. adult children) routinely recover.

The following case shows the grip of the wrongful death statute in a similar context.

ASPINALL v. McDONNELL DOUGLAS CORP.

United States Court of Appeal, Ninth Circuit, 1980.
625 F.2d 325.

CHAMBERS, CIRCUIT JUDGE.

Appellant Aspinall, individually and as personal representative of the estate of Anthony Price, appeals from the district court's order for summary judgment holding that she and her children are not his "heirs" for the purposes of the California wrongful death act (Section 377, California Code of Civil Procedure).

Price was killed in March 1974, with 345 other passengers and crew members, when a DC–10 * * * crashed at Paris. The plane had been manufactured by appellee McDonnell Douglas Corporation and it had been designed in part by appellee General Dynamics Corporation. At the time of his death Price, a resident of England, was unmarried and had no issue. His parents were deceased and he had no collateral heirs. But he and appellant had lived together in the roles of husband and wife for over four years and Price left his entire estate to appellant by will. He had been the sole support (except for a small pension) of appellant and her children during the four years, but he had never married appellant and he had never adopted her children.

* * *

[On defendants' motion for summary judgment, the district court] held that appellant and her children were not eligible for relief under California's wrongful death statute as they did not qualify as "heirs" for the purpose of that statute.[2]

Under California law the right of a survivor to recover under the wrongful death theory is purely statutory; the Legislature's intent in adopting the statute was to create an entirely new cause of action where none existed theretofore. At the time that the cause of action arose in this case, the courts of California defined "heirs," as used in Section 377, as those "who would have been eligible to inherit from the decedent's estate had he died intestate," i.e. under the intestacy provisions of the California Probate Code. Nowhere in those Probate Code provisions, as worded at the time this cause of action arose, would appellant come within the definition of an "heir," entitled to succeed to decedent's estate. And nowhere in those Probate Code provisions would her children be considered his "heirs."

2. Section 377, as worded at the time that this cause of action arose, stated:

"When the death of a person * * * is caused by the wrongful act or neglect of another, his heirs, and his dependent parents, if any, who are not heirs, or personal representatives on their behalf may maintain an action for damages against the person causing the death * * *."

Appellant contends that she would be entitled to succeed to some of decedent's estate because she was his "putative spouse." Even if we were to accept, for purposes of argument, her interpretation of the rights of putative spouses under California case law, it is clear that she was not a "putative spouse" according to the California definition, i.e. a surviving spouse of a marriage that was "solemnized in due form and celebrated in good faith by at least one of the parties but which, by reason of some legal infirmity, is either void or voidable." In this case there is no claim of any marriage, whether legal, void or voidable.

* * *

Appellant also urges this Court to extend the California wrongful death statute to her and her children on some equitable basis. While we might like to do so, our hands are tied. We cannot legislate this change in California's statute law. Finally, we cannot accept appellant's argument that the California statute denies her and her children equal protection.

Affirmed.

Note

A survey of caselaw showed that all reported decisions reached the same result as *Aspinall*, including one case in which the cohabitants had been engaged to be married a few days after the death and another in which they had cohabited for 24 years. See Note, The Right of a Cohabitant to Recover in Tort: Wrongful Death, Negligent Infliction of Emotional Distress and Loss of Consortium, 32 U.Louisville J.Fam.L. 531 (1994) (observing that the 1990 census found almost 3 million unmarried couples cohabiting in the United States and concluding that wrongful death statutes embody an obsolete vision of family relationships).

In the principal case, note that the plaintiff was the beneficiary of the decedent's will. Suppose Price's estate had a cause of action for his death; if it did, that recovery would eventually go to the plaintiff. If Price had lived long enough to file a suit for the injuries he suffered in the crash, his estate would have been permitted to maintain that suit after his death. California and virtually all other jurisdictions have "survival statutes" providing that pending actions survive the death of either the plaintiff or defendant. Some of the statutes go further, providing that a claim survives even if it had not yet been filed at the time of death. In many states, the distinction between wrongful death and survival actions has become blurred, as the following case shows.

McDAVID v. UNITED STATES

Supreme Court of Appeals of West Virginia, 2003.
213 W.Va. 592, 584 S.E.2d 226.

STARCHER, CHIEF JUSTICE.

[Plaintiff's husband died while being treated at a Veteran's Administration hospital. She sued in federal court, alleging that negligence by government physicians caused his death, and sought damages under West Virginia law for his emotional distress and pain and suffering from the time of the negligence until his death, and for his loss of enjoyment of life. The government moved to dismiss the claim for pain and suffering. The federal court submitted to the state supreme court the following certified question: "Whether a decedent's beneficiaries may recover damages for a decedent's pain and suffering, incurred between the time of injury and the time of death, where the injuries result in death but the decedent did not institute an action for personal injury prior to his or her death?"]

* * *

In Estate of Helmick by Fox v. Martin, 188 W.Va. 559, 425 S.E.2d 235 (1992), we concluded that under the wrongful death act a decedent's beneficiaries could recover damages for a decedent's pain and suffering, if the decedent initiated a personal injury action prior to his or her death. We left unanswered the question raised by the parties in this case, stating that "[w]e need not resolve at this time the remaining question of whether pain and suffering is recoverable where the action is not filed until after the decedent's death."

The defendant argues that the wrongful death act, and our interpretation of those laws in *Helmick*, requires a decedent to initiate a personal injury action before death in order to recover for losses incurred by the decedent's estate during the time period between the wrongful act, neglect or default of the defendant and the decedent's death. The defendant argues that if the decedent does not file a personal injury action for those losses prior to death, then the cause of action dies with the decedent.

The plaintiff argues that the defendant is urging a harsh and absurd construction to the wrongful death act. The plaintiff asserts that the logical outcome of the defendant's argument is that plaintiffs' lawyers will rush to file lawsuits whenever a client is injured and there is a chance the client will die, and that those lawsuits will be filed before the plaintiffs' lawyers have a chance to properly investigate and determine whether the lawsuits have any merit. The plaintiff suggests that a decedent's failure to file a lawsuit before dying—whether born of the decedent's disdain for litigation, or an inability to reach the courthouse before dying—should not affect the beneficiaries' ability to recover the full damages that the decedent could have recovered, had he or she survived the defendant's wrongful act, neglect or default.

* * *

B.

Damages under other States' Wrongful Death Acts and Survival Statutes

* * *

The majority of wrongful death acts, particularly those patterned after Lord Campbell's Act, award damages based upon a "loss–to–survivors" theory. Under these statutes, damages generally are to be assessed in accordance with the loss to the decedent's survivors, with many states limiting recovery to the pecuniary losses of the decedent's survivors caused by the decedent's death.

The minority of wrongful death acts measure damages by the loss to the decedent's estate. These wrongful death acts allow for the estate to recover its losses—such as lost income, funeral expenses, medical expenses, or any other damages related to the decedent's fatal injury.

States enacted wrongful death acts as a response to the failure of the common law to provide a remedy for wrongful death. However,

> . . . there was a corresponding failure in the common law to provide a remedy for personal injuries to a person who died either before bringing or before completing a personal injury action. At common law, the action or cause of action for such injury would abate and be forever lost if the injured person died before the action was commenced or before judgment was entered therein.

States responded by enacting "survival" statutes to allow a decedent's survivors to pursue a cause of action that belonged to a decedent, but was not pursued or completed when the decedent died. Most survival statutes provide that "an action for personal injuries . . . does not abate upon the death of either the injured party or the person liable. . . . Such statutes do not usually make any distinction between actions for fatal injuries (where the injury sued upon causes death) and actions for non–fatal (where the injured person dies from a cause other than the injury sued upon) injuries."

There are substantial conceptual differences between the remedies provided by a wrongful death act and a survival statute. "Wrongful death acts compensate either the survivors, or the estate of the deceased, for losses they have sustained. Survival statutes * * * permit recovery * * * for damages which the decedent could have recovered had he lived * * *. [T]he survival statute merely continues in existence the injured person's claim after death as an asset of his estate, while the usual wrongful death statute creates a new cause of action * * * based upon the death itself."

The majority of states now hold that the representative of a decedent's estate may contemporaneously bring both a wrongful death action—to recover for losses to the decedent's survivors—and an action under the survival statute, to recover for losses to the decedent's estate. The majority of jurisdictions allow an action to recover losses to the decedent's estate that occurred in the lapse of time between the injury–causing wrongful act, and the decedent's death—and include such elements as the decedent's "pain and suffering, mental anguish, impairment of earning capacity, medical expenses, and, of course, funeral expenses, since the injury did cause these to be incurred.[5]

* * * "It is the rule in a numerical majority of jurisdictions that damages for decedent's conscious pain and suffering prior to death may be recovered under both the survival statutes and the hybrid type of enlarged survival–wrongful death statute [of the sort described in the preceding paragraph]."

* * *

[The court recounted the history of the West Virginia wrongful death statute which, like most, originally provided limited remedies but was gradually broadened. The original 1863 statute allowed recovery only for pecuniary losses to the widow and next of kin; in 1868 a limit of $5,000 was set; that was raised to $10,000 in 1868, $20,000 in 1955, $25,000 in 1961, and $100,000 in 1965. Amendments in 1965 allowed recovery for hospital and medical expenses in addition to the survivors' losses. In 1976 the legislature removed the monetary cap altogether and provided that the damages should be distributed under the decedent's will if there were no surviving family members. In 1982 the court held that punitive damages were recoverable. The current version of the statute, W.Va.Code 55–7–6 (1992), provided for damages including, but not limited to, "(A) Sorrow, mental anguish, and solace which may include society, companionship, comfort, guidance, kindly offices and advice of the decedent; (B) compensation for reasonably expected loss of (i) income of the decedent, and (ii) services, protection, care and assistance provided by the decedent; (C) expenses for the care, treatment and hospitalization of the decedent incident to the injury resulting in death; and (D) reasonable funeral expenses."]

* * *

The effect of these amendments has been to allow juries to award damages for all losses flowing from the wrongful act, neglect or default of a defendant. The Legislature has enlarged the damages recoverable under [the statute] to permit juries to award damages that the deceased might have recovered had he or she survived the injury and brought the action, in addition to the damages resulting from the wrongful death. Juries are now clearly required * * * to consider awarding fair and just damages for all losses—including but not limited to—losses to both the decedent's beneficiaries and to the decedent's estate. But of course, it is axiomatic that the jury is only allowed to award the decedent's beneficiaries one recovery for each loss.

* * *

5. Murphy v. Martin Oil Co., 56 Ill.2d 423, 308 N.E.2d 583 (1974) represents an example of a case brought under both a wrongful death act and survival statute. The decedent was severely burned in a fire at the defendant's gasoline station, and died nine days later. The decedent's beneficiaries sought wrongful death damages, and under the survival statute sought "damages for the decedent's physical and mental suffering, for loss of wages for the nine–day period following his injury and for the loss of his clothing worn at the time of injury." 56 Ill.2d at 425, 308 N.E.2d at 584. The Illinois court permitted the recovery of these damages.

The defendant argues that W.Va.Code, 55–7–8[9] and our holding in *Helmick* clearly and unambiguously provides that damages for pain and suffering of the decedent may be pursued only if the decedent instituted a personal injury action prior to his or her death. We disagree, because W.Va.Code, 55–7–8 is silent regarding the situation presented by the present case, and because the defendant's argument fails to take into account the expansive damages that juries can award as compensation for losses caused by a defendant's wrongful act * * *.

* * *

We therefore hold that under the wrongful death act, W.Va.Code, 55–7–6, a jury's verdict may include damages for the decedent's pain and suffering endured between the time of injury and the time of death, where the injury resulted in death but the decedent did not institute an action for personal injury prior to his or her death. * * *

* * *

[Opinion of MAYNARD, J., dissenting, omitted]

Notes

1. *Terminology.* Sec. 55–7–6 is identifiable as a wrongful death statute; it allows recovery for the survivors' loss of the decedent's society, companionship, guidance, services, and care. It differs from many wrongful death statutes in two respects: most states do not permit recovery for the survivors' grief or mental anguish, and most measure the pecuniary losses in terms of the support the survivors would have received from the decedent, rather than the decedent's income. Sec. 55–7–8 might be called a nonabatement statute; it provides that an action filed by the decedent does not abate at his or her death. Most courts do not use that term, however; like West Virginia Supreme Court they use the same term—"survival statute"—to describe this sort of statute as they use to describe those that allow the estate to sue even if the claim was not filed before the decedent's death. By holding that suits of the latter type could be brought under sec. 55–7–6, the court made that section into what it calls a "hybrid" or "enlarged" wrongful death claim. Such blurring of the distinction between the wrongful death and survival concepts has little to commend it, but it is fairly widespread.

2. The dissent argued that the majority's interpretation of W.Va.Code § 55–7–6 made § 55–7–8 meaningless—if losses such as the decedent's pain and suffering can be recovered in the wrongful death action, there is no need for a separate survival statute. Is that a persuasive reason for denying such recoveries if suit was not filed before the decedent's death?

3. *Evidentiary considerations.* Because major elements of wrongful death recovery require predictions about the support and services the decedent would have given the survivors, some delicate evidentiary questions arise. The jury is entitled to know how much money the decedent was likely

---

9. W.Va.Code, 55–7–8 [1989] states, in pertinent part:

Where an action is brought by a person injured for damage caused by the wrong-ful act, neglect or default of any person or corporation, and the person injured dies as a result thereof, the action shall not abate by reason of his or her death * * *.

to make and how generous and attentive the decedent was to the needs of the survivors. To that extent, evidence of decedent's frugality or profligacy and sobriety or intemperance is admissible, as is evidence (positive and negative) about the decedent's relationships with the survivors. On the other hand, courts often exclude evidence about the decedent's moral transgressions, such as marital infidelities, apparently in the belief that they are likely to be more prejudicial than probative. See, e.g., Gamble v. Hill, 208 Va. 171, 156 S.E.2d 888 (1967) (excluding evidence of decedent's two extramarital pregnancies on the ground that such immoralities would not diminish survivors' losses). With similar reservations, it can be said that the character and habits of the survivors may be admissible to show how long or how much the decedent was likely to support and nurture them.

A recurring issue is remarriage of the surviving spouse; is the defendant entitled to show that the spouse is better off with his or her new mate? Many states do not allow the jury even to be told of the remarriage, apparently on the theory that what the survivor does after the death should not benefit the tortfeasor. See, e.g., Gilmer v. Carney, 608 N.E.2d 709 (Ind.App.1993).

4. *Proving pain and suffering in death cases.* In an omitted portion of the opinion in *McDavid,* the court discussed the circumstances under which an award of pain and suffering is permissible:

> In order for a jury to award damages for pain and suffering, most courts hold that there must be actual evidence of conscious pain and suffering of the decedent; conjecture will not suffice. * * *

> For example, in Morrissey v. Welsh Co., 821 F.2d 1294, 1301 (8th Cir.1987), the decedent was buried under a collapsed wall, but was conscious, able to communicate with her would–be rescuers, and was aware of the fact that she had literally been buried alive. The decedent died before being removed from the rubble. The court concluded, applying Missouri law, that the decedent's survivors could recover damages for the decedent's premortem pain and suffering. See also, Phillips v. Mazda Motor Mfg. (USA) Corp., supra, (decedent's legs were "crushed like an accordion" by 17 ton truss; pain and suffering award proper because decedent remained conscious under truss for 30 minutes); Bolton v. Massachusetts Bay Transp. Auth., 32 Mass.App.Ct. 654, 593 N.E.2d 248 (1992) (pain and suffering award proper because paramedic who accompanied decedent to the hospital testified that she was able to respond to verbal commands); Higgins v. State, 192 A.D.2d 821, 596 N.Y.S.2d 479 (1993) (award for conscious pain and suffering allowed when decedent received electrical shock after entering a lake; decedent contemplated death for several minutes because electrical shock rendered him unable to escape the water, then caused him to come into contact with a more intense source of electricity); Smith v. Printup, 254 Kan. 315, 866 P.2d 985 (1993) (award allowed when lay testimony of first person on the scene of automobile accident showed decedent was breathing erratically, and seemed to respond with a two–syllable word and body movement when told help was on the way).

> Courts generally hold that in those situations where death is instantaneous, or where there is no evidence that the decedent con-

sciously perceived pain and suffering before death, no damages for pain and suffering are allowed. [ ] See, e.g., * * * Baker v. Slack, 319 Mich. 703, 30 N.W.2d 403 (1948) (evidence failed to show that decedent–pedestrian struck by automobile was conscious at any time during a thirty–minute interval before death, though she did make an outcry at the moment she was struck).

Losses to the Decedent's Estate

The West Virginia wrongful death statute—§ 55–7–6—allows recovery for "loss of income of the decedent." Usually wrongful death recovery gives the survivors only the portion of the decedent's income that he or she would have spent on them—the financial support they lost by virtue of the wrongful death. If the statute was meant to allow more than this, does it mean loss of income between the time of injury and the time of death, or loss of income for the decedent's entire expected working life?

Most survival statutes limit recovery to losses sustained before death, but that can put the tortfeasor whose victim dies in better position than one whose victim is permanently disabled. The victim who is permanently disabled is entitled to recover for lost earning capacity for the remainder of his or her expected life. When the victim is killed, in most states the tortfeasor has to pay (as support damages under the wrongful death statute) only the portion of the earnings that the decedent would have contributed to survivors plus (under the survival statute) the decedent's lost earnings from the tort until death. The tortfeasor escapes liability for (a) earnings the decedent would have spent on himself or herself and (b) earnings the decedent would have saved and thus passed on to his or her estate.

Suppose the decedent is a professional with rising earnings, two grown children who are eligible to recover under the wrongful death statute, and a long–term companion who is ineligible under the wrongful death statute but is the beneficiary of decedent's will. Since the decedent's years of supporting the children are over, their wrongful death recovery is likely to be modest. The loss to the companion is likely to be substantial because the decedent had reached a point where he or she was able to accumulate wealth. The damages–before–death limitation assures that in this situation the tortfeasor will pay considerably less than the true cost of the death.

A few states avoid this situation by construing their survival statutes to permit the estate to recover for the wealth the decedent would have likely accumulated during his or her natural lifetime. See, e.g., Weil v. Seltzer, 873 F.2d 1453 (D.C.Cir.1989) (allowing recovery under survival action for decedent's probable future earnings less decedent's projected personal expenses and amounts decedent would have contributed to those entitled to recover under the wrongful death statute).

Loss of Consortium in Non–Fatal Cases

Once courts began allowing recovery for loss of society in wrongful death cases, the question naturally arose whether family members of seriously injured persons could recover such damages in non–fatal cases. The traditional law had treated husbands (and later, wives) differently from other family members in this respect. From early times the common law recognized a husband's cause of action for "loss of consortium" produced by non–fatal injury to the spouse. The traditional rule denied a similar cause of action to the wife. See, e.g., Best v. Samuel Fox & Co., Ltd., [1952] A.C. 716 (H.L.). Most of the modern American cases confronting the issue have eliminated the discrimination by recognizing a wife's cause of action for lost consortium.

The recovery for loss of consortium is similar to the survivors' recovery for loss of society in wrongful death actions, and in the latter parents and children usually are allowed to recover for their loss of the decedent's society. Nevertheless, the majority of jurisdictions confine the cause of action in non–fatal cases to spouses. Influenced by the trend to allow recovery for loss of society in wrongful death cases, some recent decisions have allowed children's claims for loss of an injured parent's consortium and parents' claims for loss of an injured child's consortium. But these cases remain a minority (though a substantial one), and at least as many recent decisions have rejected these claims as have accepted them. Compare Gallimore v. Children's Hospital Medical Center, 67 Ohio St.3d 244, 617 N.E.2d 1052 (1993) (recognizing both parents' and childrens' consortium claims) with Dearborn Fabricating & Engineering Corp. v. Wickham, 551 N.E.2d 1135 (Ind.1990) (denying child's claim) and Roberts v. Williamson, 111 S.W.3d 113 (Tex. 2003) (denying parent's claim).

Recall that in Rodriguez v. McDonnell Douglas Corp., supra p. 328, the victim's wife recovered for loss of consortium. Before that decision, in a different appeal arising from the same case, Mary Anne Rodriguez had persuaded the California Supreme Court to recognize a spouse's right to recover for loss of consortium. See Rodriguez v. Bethlehem Steel Corp., 12 Cal.3d 382, 115 Cal.Rptr. 765, 525 P.2d 669 (1974). Three years later, however, the same court refused to recognize such a right for either parents or children. See Borer v. American Airlines, Inc., 19 Cal.3d 441, 138 Cal.Rptr. 302, 563 P.2d 858 (1977), and Baxter v. Superior Court, 19 Cal.3d 461, 138 Cal.Rptr. 315, 563 P.2d 871 (1977). (In some states, statutes grant parents a right to recover for the loss of an injured child's society).

E. OTHER COMPENSATORY DAMAGE ISSUES

Many damages issues apply to nonfatal and fatal cases alike. We discuss a few of them here.

Interest

Once a judgment is entered in a personal injury case, the amount normally is treated as a debt owed by the defendant and interest begins to accrue at a rate that is usually set by statute.

As to prejudgment interest, there is less uniformity of treatment. The traditional view was that since the amount of the debt was "unliquidated," i.e., not known until judgment, no interest should accrue until that time. Increasingly, however, courts have been inclined (or directed by legislatures) to award prejudgment interest on the theory that the tortfeasor's obligation to make the victim whole arises when the injury occurs, or at least when suit is filed. See, e.g., McCrann v. United States Lines, Inc., 803 F.2d 771 (2d Cir.1986).

Taxation

Punitive damages are subject to federal income tax, but compensatory damages are not. See 26 U.S.C. § 104(a). There is little agreement as to what jurors should be told about this. In Rodriguez v. McDonnell Douglas Corp., supra p. 328, the trial court forbade the parties from introducing evidence relating to taxation. In a portion of the opinion not reproduced in the casebook, the court of appeals approved that procedure and said most jurisdictions agree that jurors should be told nothing about taxation. Will that produce correct results?

In O'Gilvie v. United States, 519 U.S. 79, 117 S.Ct. 452, 136 L.Ed.2d 454 (1996), the Supreme Court said Congress intended plaintiffs to receive the benefit of the exclusion. That result will be achieved if jurors ignore the effects of taxation in fixing the compensatory award. But what if they assume the award is taxable? Suppose the jury believes the plaintiff has suffered a $100,000 loss of earning capacity and mistakenly believes the award will be taxed at 33 per cent; the jury might award $150,000 to make sure the plaintiff gets $100,000 after taxes. In that event, the plaintiff would get not only the tax break that Congress presumably intended, but an additional $50,000 that overcompensates the plaintiff at the defendant's expense. To prevent that, the Supreme Court has held that defendants in Federal Employers Liability Act (FELA) cases are entitled to have the jury told that compensatory damages will not be taxed. Norfolk & W. Ry. Co. v. Liepelt, 444 U.S. 490, 100 S.Ct. 755, 62 L.Ed.2d 689 (1980). Two dissenting justices thought the possibility that the jury would mistakenly assume taxability was no more relevant than the possibility that the jury might act on mistaken assumptions about the defendant's insurance or the plaintiff's attorney fee obligations—matters about which the jury normally is told nothing. Some states require that juries be told whether their awards will be subject to taxation. See, e.g., Tex. Civ. Prac. & Rem. Code § 18.091.

Is the knowledge that compensatory damages are not taxable helpful to juries if they do not know why Congress exempted them? Suppose jurors assume the purpose is to reduce the aggregate cost of tort liability; logically, they would then reduce the award by the amount they think would have been payable in taxes but for the exclusion—to $66,667 in the example above.

It is said that most state courts ignore *Liepelt* and do not tell juries anything about the taxability of damage awards. See Janson v. North Valley Hospital, 93 Wash.App. 892, 971 P.2d 67 (1999). A related problem is whether the jury should be given pre–tax or after–tax estimates of the plaintiff's earnings losses. The *Liepelt* majority held that it was error, under the FELA, to exclude evidence of the tax that would have been payable on the earnings. But if the jury bases its award on after–tax earnings, will the result be consistent with *O'Gilvie's* theory as to the purpose of Sec. 104(a)(2)? Reducing both the earnings estimate and the award on account of taxation would subject the plaintiff to double taxation; reducing either denies the plaintiff the windfall that *O'Gilvie* says Congress intended.

Periodic Payments

As we saw above, supra p. 336, awards for pecuniary losses usually are reduced to present value on the theory that the plaintiff can use the award to make more money by investing it. Of course, the successful plaintiff need not invest the award, prudently or otherwise. If the plaintiff chooses to fritter away the money, the tort system's objective of making the injured plaintiff self-sufficient is frustrated. This is only one of the weaknesses of the traditional lump sum judgment. Another is that it requires all future losses to be calculated at one moment in time, precluding future adjustments for changes in earnings, medical costs, treatment methods, inflation, and most importantly, the plaintiff's condition. But courts have shown little interest in retaining jurisdiction to permit such ongoing adjustments and seem firmly committed to the finality of a one-time determination of all these variables. That does not preclude paying the one-time sum out periodically, however, and there has been some movement in that direction. A number of states permit or even require the court to arrange for periodic payment of certain types of judgments, for example, judgments for medical malpractice or against governmental entities. See, e.g., *American Bank & Trust Co. v. Community Hospital*, 36 Cal.3d 359, 204 Cal.Rptr. 671, 683 P.2d 670 (1984); *Bernier v. Burris*, 113 Ill.2d 219, 100 Ill.Dec. 585, 497 N.E.2d 763 (1986); *Smith v. Myers*, 181 Ariz. 11, 887 P.2d 541 (Ariz.1994).

Structured settlements

Far more common are settlement agreements providing for periodic payments rather than (or in addition to) a lump sum. Parties often negotiate "structured settlements" in which the defendant typically agrees to buy the plaintiff an annuity that guarantees the plaintiff a specified monthly or annual payment for a specified period such as the rest of the plaintiff's life, a fixed number of years, or until the plaintiff's children reach a certain age. Because of the time value of money, this arrangement costs the defendant less than the total the plaintiff ultimately receives. The annuity provider (usually a life insurance company) in effect manages the money until it is time to pay it to the plaintiff. These arrangements are so popular—and sometimes so intricate—that they have spawned a new profession, the structured settlement broker. Lawyers employ these brokers to advise them on the many annuity options available.

Caps on Damages

In more than half the states, legislatures have imposed caps on compensatory damages. In some states the cap applies only to certain types of cases or certain types of damages. In California, for example, damages in medical malpractice cases for noneconomic losses (including pain and suffering, disfigurement, physical impairment, and inconvenience) are capped at $250,000, Cal. Civ. Code § 3333.2; in Utah total damages against liquor providers are capped at $500,000. Utah Code. Ann. 32A–14a–102. The cap in Maryland applies to all personal injury cases, and limits noneconomic damages to $500,000 (with a $15,000 adjustment upward each year). Md. Ann. Code, Ct. & Jud. Proc. § 11–108. Colorado limits damages against health care providers to $300,000 for noneconomic damages and $1 million total for all categories of damages. Colo. Rev. Stat. § 13–64–302.l.

Opponents of caps argue that they make the most seriously injured plaintiffs bear the costs of tortious conduct while leaving whatever imperfections are thought to require modification of the common law damages rules unaffected in the vast majority of cases where damages do not reach the cap. Proponents say they are a simple way of reducing the cost of tort liability, and therefore of insurance premiums. Both sides agree that caps affect far more cases than those in which recovery is actually reduced to conform to the cap, because the existence of the cap reduces settlement value of cases by giving defendants a ceiling on their potential losses if they refuse to settle.

Alternative Compensation Schemes

The best–known alternative to tort liability as a means of compensating personal injuries or wrongful death is workers' compensation. All states and the federal government have statutes giving employers immunity from most tort liability for on–the–job injuries or occupational diseases in exchange for their contributions to a fund or insurance plan which pays injured workers benefits in amounts that are administratively determined. Benefits are payable without regard to the fault of either the employer or the employee, usually do not cover the full amount of employee's lost earnings, and do not include anything for pain and suffering. There are numerous exclusions, e.g., for intentional torts, and attempts by employees to get out of the workers' compensation scheme and into the tort scheme generate considerable litigation. See, e.g., KAREN A. LERNER, WORKERS' COMPENSATION LAW AND PRACTICE (1989).

Another alternative, much–publicized but not widely adopted, is no-fault insurance. The idea is that certain classes of injuries, e.g., from auto accidents, are compensated by the victim's own insurance, at least up to a specified threshold amount. The theory is that this is less costly than a system in which the defendant's insurance pays only after the victim establishes the defendant's liability under tort law. The plan was advanced in ROBERT E. KEETON AND JEFFREY O'CONNELL, BASIC PROTECTION FOR THE TRAFFIC VICTIM (1965), and is often called the Keeton–O'Connell plan. A few states have employed such plans with apparent success for a number of years, but the idea has not caught on nationally. See Roger C. Henderson, No–Fault Insurance for Automobile Accidents: Status and Effect in the United States, 56 Or. L. Rev. 287 (1977).

Occasionally Congress creates ad hoc compensation plans to bypass tort liability in specific situations. For example, to encourage manufacturers to quickly produce enough vaccine for mass immunization campaigns, Congress created a federal compensation fund to pay those who suffer injurious side effects from the vaccinations. Benefits are limited and procedures for establishing entitlement are standardized. See, e.g., National Childhood Vaccine Injury Act, 42 U.S.C. § 300aa–1 et seq. For a description of the statutory scheme, see Schafer v. American Cyanamid Co., 20 F.3d 1 (1st Cir. 1994).

The most notable recent example of an ad hoc federal plan is the Victim Compensation Fund created for survivors and relatives of those killed in the September 11, 2001, attacks on the World Trade Center and the Pentagon. Congress hastily created the Fund in the aftermath of the attacks to protect airlines, insurance companies, and building owners from tort claims that they claimed would bankrupt them. In exchange for waiving the right to sue in tort, the plan offered an average of $1.8 million to families of those killed, with some receiving as much as $6.9 million. Payments to those injured varied widely, from $500 to $7.9 million. About 95 per cent of those eligible opted to take the federal payment. The ultimate cost to the government was expected to be about $3 billion. See Applicants Rush to Meet Deadline for Sept. 11 Fund, N.Y. Times, Dec. 23, 2003, at A1.

Critics noted that the Fund provided no compensation to victims of previous terrorist activities, offered no promise of similar treatment for future victims, and in many cases compensated people who were already wealthy. Despite the general hostility of Congress and the Bush Administration to tort damages, the Fund adopted generous tort–law concepts of damages, including not only economic losses but also "physical and emotional pain, suffering, inconvenience, physical impairment, mental anguish, disfigurement, loss of enjoyment of life, loss of society and companionship, loss of consortium (other than loss of domestic service), hedonic damages, injury to reputation, and all other nonpecuniary losses of any kind or nature." Air Transportation Safety Act, 115 Stat. 236, § 402(7). "[T]he Fund steers a somewhat uncertain course between collective principles that would emphasize timely compensation and filling the gaps of unmet need, on the one hand, and individualized recovery that would pull in the direction of the tort model, on the other." Robert L. Rabin, The Quest for Fairness in Compensating Victims of September 11, 49 Clev. St. L. Rev. 573, 578 (2001). For an extensive discussion of the 9/11 Fund, see Symposium, After Disaster: The September 11th Compensation Fund and the Future of Civil Justice, 53 De Paul L.Rev. 205 (2003).

F. PUNITIVE DAMAGES

STATE FARM MUTUAL AUTO. INS. CO. v. CAMPBELL

Supreme Court of the United States, 2003.
538 U.S. 408, 123 S.Ct. 1513, 155 L.Ed.2d 585.

JUSTICE KENNEDY.

[In 1981, Campbell was involved in a head–on collision in which another driver, Ospital, was killed and a third, Slusher was permanently disabled. Campbell's liability insurance company, State Farm, decided to contest liability, declined offers by Slusher and Ospital's estate to settle the claims for the policy limit of $50,000, and took the case to trial. A jury determined that Campbell was 100 percent at fault and returned a judgment for $185,849.

[State Farm eventually paid the entire $185,849, eight years after the accident, but the Utah courts held that State Farm had acted in bad faith in failing to promptly settle the suit against the Campbells in the face of early determinations by the company's investigators that Campbell was at fault and that a large judgment was likely if the case went to trial. The Utah Supreme Court upheld an award of $1 million in compensatory damages for the Campbells' emotional distress resulting from the fear that they would lose all their assets because of the judgment exceeding their insurance coverage. It also upheld an award of $145 million in punitive damages based largely on findings that State Farm's refusal to settle the case against the Campbells was part of a nationwide scheme to meet corporate financial goals by underpaying claims, formalized in a company document called the "Performance, Planning and Review" (PPR) policy. The Supreme Court granted certiorari on State Farm's claim that the punitive damage award was excessive and in violation of the due process clause of the Fourteenth Amendment.]

* * *

II

[I]n our judicial system compensatory and punitive damages, although usually awarded at the same time by the same decisionmaker, serve different purposes. Compensatory damages "are intended to redress the concrete loss that the plaintiff has suffered by reason of the defendant's wrongful conduct." By contrast, punitive damages serve a broader function; they are aimed at deterrence and retribution.

While States possess discretion over the imposition of punitive damages, it is well established that there are procedural and substantive constitutional limitations on these awards. The Due Process Clause of the Fourteenth Amendment prohibits the imposition of grossly excessive or arbitrary punishments on a tortfeasor. * * *

[In BMW of North America, Inc. v. Gore, 517 U.S. 559, 116 S.Ct. 1589 (1996)] we instructed courts reviewing punitive damages to consider three guideposts: (1) the degree of reprehensibility of the defendant's misconduct; (2) the disparity between the actual or potential harm suffered by the plaintiff and the punitive damages award; and (3) the difference between the punitive damages awarded by the jury and the civil penalties authorized or imposed in comparable cases. We reiterated the importance of these three guideposts in [Cooper Industries, Inc. v. Leatherman Tool Group, Inc., 532 U.S. 424, 121 S.Ct. 1678 (2001)] and mandated appellate courts to conduct de novo review of a trial court's application of them to the jury's award. * * *

* * *

III

Under the principles outlined in * * * *Gore*, this case is neither close nor difficult. * * * We address each guidepost of *Gore* in some detail.

A

"[T]he most important indicium of the reasonableness of a punitive damages award is the degree of reprehensibility of the defendant's conduct." *Gore*, 517 U.S. at 575. We have instructed courts to determine the reprehensibility of a defendant by considering whether: the harm caused was physical as opposed to economic; the tortious conduct evinced an indifference to or a reckless disregard of the health or safety of others; the target of the conduct had financial vulnerability; the conduct involved repeated actions or was an isolated incident; and the harm was the result of intentional malice, trickery, or deceit, or mere accident. The existence of any one of these factors weighing in favor of a plaintiff may not be sufficient to sustain a punitive damages award; and the absence of all of them renders any award suspect. It should be presumed a plaintiff has been made whole for his injuries by compensatory damages, so punitive damages should only be awarded if the defendant's culpability, after having paid compensatory damages, is so reprehensible as to warrant the imposition of further sanctions to achieve punishment or deterrence.

Applying these factors in the instant case, we must acknowledge that State Farm's handling of the claims against the Campbells merits no praise. The trial court found that State Farm's employees altered the company's records to make Campbell appear less culpable. State Farm disregarded the overwhelming likelihood of liability and the near-certain probability that, by taking the case to trial, a judgment in excess of the policy limits would be awarded. State Farm amplified the harm by at first assuring the Campbells their assets would be safe from any verdict and by later telling them, postjudgment, to put a for-sale sign on their house. While we do not suggest there was error in awarding punitive damages based upon State Farm's conduct toward the Campbells, a more modest punishment for this reprehensible conduct could have satisfied the State's legitimate objectives, and the Utah courts should have gone no further.

This case, instead, was used as a platform to expose, and punish, the perceived deficiencies of State Farm's operations throughout the country. The Utah Supreme Court's opinion makes explicit that State Farm was being condemned for its nationwide policies rather than for the conduct direct toward the Campbells. * * *

A State cannot punish a defendant for conduct that may have been lawful where it occurred. Nor, as a general rule, does a State have a legitimate concern in imposing punitive damages to punish a defendant for unlawful acts committed outside of the State's jurisdiction. Any proper adjudication of conduct that occurred outside Utah to other persons would require their inclusion, and, to those parties, the Utah courts, in the usual case, would need to apply the laws of their relevant jurisdiction.

* * * Lawful out–of–state conduct may be probative when it demonstrates the deliberateness and culpability of the defendant's action in the State where it is tortious, but that conduct must have a nexus to the specific harm suffered by the plaintiff. A jury must be instructed, furthermore, that it may not use evidence of out–of–state conduct to punish a defendant for action that was lawful in the jurisdiction where it occurred. A basic principle of federalism is that each State may make its own reasoned judgment about what conduct is permitted or proscribed within its borders, and each State alone can determine what measure of punishment, if any, to impose on a defendant who acts within its jurisdiction.

For a more fundamental reason, however, the Utah courts erred in relying upon this and other evidence: The courts awarded punitive damages to punish and deter conduct that bore no relation to the Campbells' harm. A defendant's dissimilar acts, independent from the acts upon which liability was premised, may not serve as the basis for punitive damages. A defendant should be punished for the conduct that harmed the plaintiff, not for being an unsavory individual or business. Due process does not permit courts, in the calculation of punitive damages, to adjudicate the merits of other parties' hypothetical claims against a defendant under the guise of the reprehensibility analysis, but we have no doubt the Utah Supreme Court did that here.

The same reasons lead us to conclude the Utah Supreme Court's decision cannot be justified on the grounds that State Farm was a recidivist. Although "[o]ur holdings that a recidivist may be punished more severely than a first offender recognize that repeated misconduct is more reprehensible than an individual instance of malfeasance," in the context of civil actions courts must ensure the conduct in question replicates the prior transgressions.

* * * In this case, because the Campbells have shown no conduct by State Farm similar to that which harmed them, the conduct that harmed them is the only conduct relevant to the reprehensibility analysis.

B

Turning to the second *Gore* guidepost, we have been reluctant to identify concrete constitutional limits on the ratio between harm, or potential harm, to the plaintiff and the punitive damages award. We decline again to impose a bright–line ratio which a punitive damages award cannot exceed. Our jurisprudence and the principles it has now established demonstrate, however, that, in practice, few awards exceeding a single–digit ratio between punitive and compensatory damages, to a significant degree, will satisfy due process.* * * Single–digit multipliers are more likely to comport with due process, while still achieving the State's goals of deterrence and retribution, than awards with ratios in range of 500 to 1, or, in this case, of 145 to 1.

Nonetheless, because there are no rigid benchmarks that a punitive damages award may not surpass, ratios greater than those we have previously upheld may comport with due process where "a particularly egregious act has resulted in only a small amount of economic damages." The converse is also true, however. When compensatory damages are substantial, then a lesser ratio, perhaps only equal to compensatory damages, can reach the outermost limit of the due process guarantee. The precise award in any case, of course, must be based upon the facts and circumstances of the defendant's conduct and the harm to the plaintiff.

In sum, courts must ensure that the measure of punishment is both reasonable and proportionate to the amount of harm to the plaintiff and to the general damages recovered. In the context of this case, we have no doubt that there is a presumption against an award that has a 145–to–1 ratio. The compensatory award in this case was substantial; the Campbells were awarded $1 million for a year and a half of emotional distress. This was complete compensation. The harm arose from a transaction in the economic realm, not from some physical assault or trauma; there were no physical injuries; and State Farm paid the excess verdict before the complaint was filed, so the Campbells suffered only minor economic injuries for the 18–month period in which State Farm refused to resolve the claim against them. The compensatory damages for the injury suffered here, moreover, likely were based on a component which was duplicated in the punitive award. Much of the distress was caused by the outrage and humiliation the Campbells suffered at the actions of their insurer; and it is a major role of punitive damages to condemn such conduct. Compensatory damages, however, already contain this punitive element.

* * *

C

The third guidepost in *Gore* is the disparity between the punitive damages award and the "civil penalties authorized or imposed in comparable cases." * * *

* * * The most relevant civil sanction under Utah state law for the wrong done to the Campbells appears to be a $10,000 fine for an act of fraud, an amount dwarfed by the $145 million punitive damages award. The Supreme Court of Utah speculated about the loss of State Farm's business license, the disgorgement of profits, and possible imprisonment, but here again its references were to the broad fraudulent scheme drawn from evidence of out–of–state and dissimilar conduct. This analysis was insufficient to justify the award.

IV

An application of the *Gore* guideposts to the facts of this case, especially in light of the substantial compensatory damages awarded (a portion of which contained a punitive element), likely would justify a punitive damages award at or near the amount of compensatory damages. The punitive award of $145 million, therefore, was neither reasonable nor proportionate to the wrong committed, and it was an irrational and arbitrary deprivation of the property of the defendant. The proper calculation of punitive damages under the principles we have discussed should be resolved, in the first instance, by the Utah courts.

The judgment of the Utah Supreme Court is reversed, and the case is remanded for proceedings not inconsistent with this opinion.

Justice Ginsburg, dissenting.

* * *

I

The large size of the award upheld by the Utah Supreme Court in this case indicates why damage–capping legislation may be altogether fitting and proper. Neither the amount of the award nor the trial record, however, justifies this Court's substitution of its judgment for that of Utah's competent decisionmakers. In this regard, I count it significant that, on the key criterion "reprehensibility," there is a good deal more to the story than the Court's abbreviated account tells.

Ample evidence allowed the jury to find that State Farm's treatment of the Campbells typified its "Performance, Planning and Review" (PP & R) program; implemented by top management in 1979, the program had "the explicit objective of using the claims–adjustment process as a profit center." "[T]he Campbells presented considerable evidence," the trial court noted, documenting "that the PP & R program * * * has functioned, and continues to function, as an unlawful scheme * * * to deny benefits owed consumers by paying out less than fair value in order to meet preset, arbitrary payout targets designed to enhance corporate profits." That policy, the trial court observed, was encompassing in scope; it "applied equally to the handling of both third–party and first–party claims."

Evidence the jury could credit demonstrated that the PP & R program regularly and adversely affected Utah residents. Ray Summers, "the adjuster who handled the Campbell case and who was a State Farm employee in Utah for almost twenty years," described several methods used by State Farm to deny claimants fair benefits, for example, "falsifying or withholding of evidence in claim files." A common tactic, Summers recounted, was to "unjustly attac[k] the character, reputation and credibility of a claimant and mak[e] notations to that effect in the claim file to create prejudice in the event the claim ever came before a jury." State Farm manager Bob Noxon, Summers testified, resorted to a tactic of this order in the Campbell case when he "instruct[ed] Summers to write in the file that Todd Ospital (who was killed in the accident) was speeding because he was on his way to see a pregnant girlfriend." In truth, "[t]here was no pregnant girlfriend." Expert testimony noted by the trial court described these tactics as "completely improper."

The trial court also noted the testimony of two Utah State Farm employees, Felix Jensen and Samantha Bird, both of whom recalled "intolerable" and "recurrent" pressure to reduce payouts below fair value. When Jensen complained to top managers, he was told to "get out of the kitchen" if he could not take the heat; Bird was told she should be "more of a team player." At times, Bird said, she "was forced to commit dishonest acts and to knowingly underpay claims." Eventually, Bird quit. Utah managers superior to Bird, the evidence indicated, were improperly influenced by the PP & R program to encourage insurance underpayments. For example, several documents evaluating the performance of managers Noxon and Brown "contained explicit preset average payout goals."

Regarding liability for verdicts in excess of policy limits, the trial court referred to a State Farm document titled the "Excess Liability Handbook"; written before the Campbell accident, the handbook instructed adjusters to pad files with "self–serving" documents, and to leave critical items out of files, for example, evaluations of the insured's exposure. Divisional superintendent Bill Brown used the handbook to train Utah employees. While overseeing the Campbell case, Brown ordered adjuster Summers to change the portions of his report indicating that Mr. Campbell was likely at fault and that the settlement cost was correspondingly high. The Campbells' case, according to expert testimony the trial court recited, "was a classic example of State Farm's application of the improper practices taught in the Excess Liability Handbook."

The trial court further determined that the jury could find State Farm's policy "deliberately crafted" to prey on consumers who would be unlikely to defend themselves. In this regard, the trial court noted the testimony of several former State Farm employees affirming that they were trained to target "the weakest of the herd"—"the elderly, the poor, and other consumers who are least knowledgeable about their rights and thus most vulnerable to trickery or deceit, or who have little money and hence have no real alternative but to accept an inadequate offer to settle a claim at much less than fair value.''

The Campbells themselves could be placed within the "weakest of the herd" category. The couple appeared economically vulnerable and emotionally fragile. At the time of State Farm's wrongful conduct, "Mr. Campbell had residuary effects from a stroke and Parkinson's disease."

To further insulate itself from liability, trial evidence indicated, State Farm made "systematic" efforts to destroy internal company documents that might reveal its scheme, efforts that directly affected the Campbells. For example, State Farm had "a special historical department that contained a copy of all past manuals on claim–handling practices and the dates on which each section of each manual was changed." Yet in discovery proceedings, State Farm failed to produce any claim–handling practice manuals for the years relevant to the Campbells' bad–faith case.

State Farm's inability to produce the manuals, it appeared from the evidence, was not accidental. Documents retained by former State Farm employee Samantha Bird, as well as Bird's testimony, showed that while the Campbells' case was pending, Janet Cammack, "an in–house attorney sent by top State Farm management, conducted a meeting . . . in Utah during which she instructed Utah claims management to search their offices and destroy a wide range of material of the sort that had proved damaging in bad–faith litigation in the past—in particular, old claim–handling manuals, memos, claim school notes, procedure guides and other similar documents." "These orders were followed even though at least one meeting participant, Paul Short, was personally aware that these kinds of materials had been requested by the Campbells in this very case."

Consistent with Bird's testimony, State Farm admitted that it destroyed every single copy of claim–handling manuals on file in its historical department as of 1988, even though these documents could have been preserved at minimal expense. Fortuitously, the Campbells obtained a copy of the 1979 PP & R manual by subpoena from a former employee. Although that manual has been requested in other cases, State Farm has never itself produced the document.

* * *

II

The Court dismisses the evidence describing and documenting State Farm's PP & R policy and practices as essentially irrelevant, bearing "no relation to the Campbells' harm." It is hardly apparent why that should be so. What is infirm about the Campbells' theory that their experience with State Farm exemplifies and reflects an overarching underpayment scheme, one that caused "repeated misconduct of the sort that injured them"? The Court's silence on that score is revealing: Once one recognizes that the Campbells did show "conduct by State Farm similar to that which harmed them," it becomes impossible to shrink the reprehensibility analysis to this sole case, or to maintain, at odds with the determination of the trial court, that "the adverse effect on the State's general population was in fact minor".

* * *

III

When the Court first ventured to override state–court punitive damages awards, it did so moderately. The Court recalled that "[i]n our federal system, States necessarily have considerable flexibility in determining the level of punitive damages that they will allow in different classes of cases and in any particular case." Today's decision exhibits no such respect and restraint. * * * In a legislative scheme or a state high court's design to cap punitive damages, the handiwork in setting single–digit and 1–to–1 benchmarks could hardly be questioned; in a judicial decree imposed on the States by this Court under the banner of substantive due process, the numerical controls today's decision installs seem to me boldly out of order.

* * *

[Justices Scalia and Thomas dissented on the ground that the constitution does not constrain the size of punitive damage awards.]

Notes

1. Is the disparity between Justice Kennedy's and Justice Ginsburg's appraisal of reprehensibility an argument for or against constitutional scrutiny of punitive damage awards?

2. Modern tort litigation often involves side agreements among the parties. In the principal case, after State Farm refused to post bond so Campbell could appeal, Campbell obtained his own lawyer who negotiated a settlement with Slusher and Ospital's estate in which they agreed not to demand payment of the $135,849 not covered by Campbell's insurance. In return, Campbell agreed to give them 90 per cent of any recovery on the bad–faith claim against State Farm and to allow their lawyers to take over that litigation. This agreement, described in an omitted portion of the majority opinion, was reached a year and a half after the judgment was entered against Campbell, which accounts for the majority's statement that the Campbells were only at risk of losing their assets for 18 months. There is no indication it had any effect on the Court's decision. Should it?

3. In England and in some states, damages of this sort are called exemplary rather than punitive. See, e.g., David W. Robertson, Punitive Damages in American Maritime Law, 28 J. Maritime L. & Commerce 73, 83 (1997). In the principal case, the majority objects that the case "was used as a platform to expose and punish the perceived deficiencies of State Farm's operations throughout the country." If the objective is to make an example of a defendant who commits an egregious wrong, is that a valid objection? Is the objective impermissible?

4. *State law limitations.* In addition to the federal constitutional restrictions, punitive damages are subject to many state law limitations. Some states do not permit them at all. In all states that permit them, they are awardable only against defendants who are guilty of some elevated level of fault, such as conscious disregard for the safety or welfare of others, and sometimes that must be shown by clear and convincing proof. Some states require bifurcated trials to prevent evidence that is relevant to punitive damages from affecting decisions as to liability and compensatory damages. Some states cap the amount. See, e.g., N.J. Stat. Ann. 2A:15–5.14, limiting punitive damages to the greater of $350,000 or five times the compensatory award; Kan. Stat. Ann. § 60–3701(e), limiting punitive damages to the lesser of $5 million or the defendant's highest annual gross income in the past five years. Some require that the amount be fixed by a judge rather than a jury, or that they be carefully controlled by appellate courts. Some give a substantial portion of any punitive damage award to the state rather than the plaintiff. Many of these restrictions are documented in an appendix to Justice Ginsburg's dissenting opinion in BMW of North America, Inc. v. Gore, 517 U.S. 559, 614, 116 S.Ct. 1589, 134 L.Ed.2d 809 (1996).

5. *Empirical evidence.* Punitive damages are awarded in only a small fraction of the cases. A study by the U.S. Justice Department found that even before the most recent round of restrictions, only 4 per cent of the plaintiffs who won their tort claims received punitive damages, and only 2 per cent received more than $36,000 in punitive damages. Plaintiffs won punitive damages in only 2 per cent of the product liability cases they won and 3 per cent of the medical malpractice cases. See Plaintiffs Rarely Win Punitives, Study Says, ABA Journal Oct. 1995 at 26. See also Theodore Eisenberg, *Damage Awards in Perspective: Behind the Headline–Grabbing Awards in* Exxon Valdez *and* Engle, 36 Wake Forest L. Rev. 1129 (2001) (concluding that behind the headlines, "It is a world of rare, modest awards and of reduced or reversed large awards"). Nonetheless, business interests and some academics contend that large punitive damage awards, even if rare, raise the cost of litigation and make settlement more difficult. See A. Mitchell Polinsky, *Are Punitive Damages Really Insignificant, Predictable, and Rational? A Comment on Eisenberg, et al.,* 26 J. Legal Stud. 663 (1997).

6. *Academic warriors.* The war over punitive damages has extended into academia. Exxon–Mobil Corp., facing a $5.3 billion punitive damage award arising from the massive oil spill from the supertanker Exxon Valdez in Alaska in 1989, funded at least 13 studies by law school and business school professors, psychologists, and economists. The studies generally concluded that juries award punitive damages erratically and that punitive damages are harmful to the economy. These studies, published in law reviews and other academic publications, were cited by Exxon–Mobil in its own appeals, and were also cited by corporate amici curiae in the *Cooper Industries* and *State Farm* cases in the Supreme Court. See, e.g., Brief of Certain Leading Business Corporations as Amici Curiae in Support of Petitioner, 2002 WL 1964582. In the *State Farm* case, a group of academics not involved in the Exxon–funded studies filed their own amicus brief challenging the objectivity and validity of those studies and citing numerous other studies that contradicted their findings. See Brief Amici Curiae of

Certain Leading Social Scientists and Legal Scholars in Support of Respondents, 2002 WL 31409923.

At this writing the $5.3 billion award against Exxon–Mobil has been reduced to $4.5 billion, see In re Exxon Valdez, 296 F.Supp.2d 1071 (D. Alaska 2004), with further appeals to the Ninth Circuit and the Supreme Court expected.

Chapter IX

AFFIRMATIVE DEFENSES BASED ON PLAINTIFF'S CONDUCT

A. INTRODUCTION

The five elements of the plaintiff's prima facie case in a cause of action based on negligence are duty, breach, cause in fact, legal cause, and damages. If the plaintiff establishes these elements, there will be a recovery unless the defendant can establish an affirmative defense.

The term "affirmative defense" is not peculiar to negligence law. In its general usage it means any matter that, if pleaded and proved by the defendant, will defeat or reduce the liability that plaintiff has otherwise established. Rule 8(c) of the Federal Rules of Civil Procedure requires a defendant wishing to rely on an affirmative defense to "affirmatively" plead it, and lists as the affected defenses:

> accord and satisfaction, arbitration and award, assumption of risk, contributory negligence, discharge in bankruptcy, duress, estoppel, failure of consideration, fraud, illegality, injury by fellow servant, laches, license, payment, release, res judicata, statute of frauds, statute of limitations, waiver, and any other matter constituting an avoidance or affirmative defense.

This chapter addresses the traditional affirmative defenses to negligence that are based on some aspect of the plaintiff's conduct: contributory or comparative negligence, failure to avoid consequences, failure to mitigate damages, and assumption of risk.

The procedural rules that allocate the burden of pleading and proving these defenses vary somewhat from state to state. In most states, the defendant must plead and prove contributory or comparative negligence and assumption of risk.[1]

---

1. "Students are often confused on one point. To say that the defendant has the burden of proving an affirmative defense like contributory fault is not to say that the evidence on that topic must originate with the defendant. The plaintiff's own evidence or admissions may suffice to show such fault. To say that the defendant has the burden is to say that the defendant will be the party who suffers if the evidence is not

B. CONTRIBUTORY AND COMPARATIVE NEGLIGENCE

Under the traditional common law doctrine of contributory negligence, defendants who were indisputably guilty of seriously negligent conduct often escaped liability. If such a defendant could prove a negligence case against the plaintiff—i.e., if the defendant could prove that the plaintiff, too, was guilty of negligent conduct that was a cause in fact and a legal cause of the injuries—the defendant would not be liable. This was true even though the defendant's negligence may have been far worse—more extreme or more blameworthy—than the plaintiff's. The theory of the contributory negligence rule was that any legally relevant negligence of the plaintiff, no matter how slight, would bar recovery completely.

The rule often produced obvious injustice, and over time the courts devised many ways of avoiding its harshest effects. These ameliorations were of two principal types. First, courts sometimes applied the general rules and doctrines of negligence law in ways that made it difficult for the defendant to prove the necessary case against the plaintiff. Sometimes courts would use a "double standard" on the breach issue; conduct that would plainly have charged the party with primary negligence would somehow not be substandard enough to constitute contributory negligence. Other courts would refuse to find that the plaintiff's conduct was a legal cause of the injuries even though identical conduct causing injury to someone else would certainly have led to liability. For example, in Laird v. Travelers Ins. Co., 263 La. 199, 267 So.2d 714 (1972), the plaintiff stopped his car in the traffic lane of a narrow, crooked, busy highway, and was struck from the rear by a speeding truck. Plaintiff's conduct in stopping at that place was clearly negligent, as a nearby driveway afforded a safe place to stop. Had a passenger in plaintiff's car been hurt and sued him, his conduct would certainly have been held a legal cause of the injuries. But in plaintiff's suit against the speeding truck, the court exonerated him of contributory negligence, concluding that his conduct was not a legal cause of his being struck.

Second, the courts developed a number of specific doctrines that operated as exceptions to the contributory negligence rule. The most important of these ameliorative doctrines was "last clear chance." This doctrine, which took many confusing forms, had at its core the idea that the negligent plaintiff should still recover if he could show that the defendant had a later opportunity to avoid the accident. Another such doctrinal exception to contributory negligence was a rule that ignored the victim's negligence if the defendant's conduct was "willful and wanton."

All of these ameliorations had the same flaw that the contributory negligent rule itself had—they were "all or nothing" approaches. When

forthcoming, so that the defendant must be sure that, from whatever source, evidence on the issue does in fact appear." Dobbs, The Law of Torts § 198, p. 493 (2000).

the contributory negligence rule obtained, the plaintiff bore the entire loss, although it was a product of the combined negligence of plaintiff and defendant; when one of the ameliorations obtained, the defendant bore the entire loss.

A generally more satisfactory state of affairs had long been in force in civil law systems and in the maritime law; in those systems, plaintiffs and defendants generally shared losses produced by their combined negligence. This loss sharing approach is usually called "comparative negligence" or "comparative fault." It may also be called "comparative responsibility."

The comparative negligence philosophy began to appeal to common law systems after World War II. England, whose courts had invented the rule of contributory negligence, abolished contributory negligence by statute in 1945. The Law Reform (Contributory Negligence) Act, 1945, provided in pertinent part:

> Where any person suffers damage as the result partly of his own fault and partly of the fault of any other person or persons, a claim in respect of that damage shall not be defeated by reason of the fault of the person suffering the damage, but the damages recoverable in respect thereof shall be reduced to such extent as the court thinks just and equitable having regard to the claimant's share in the responsibility of the damage * * *.

Beginning in the 1960's, a movement toward replacing the contributory negligence rule with some version of comparative negligence began to pick up steam in this country. Today, only five American jurisdictions—Alabama, Maryland, North Carolina, Virginia, and the District of Columbia—still use contributory negligence as an absolute bar to recovery. Thirty-five states adopted comparative negligence by statute. Eleven states adopted comparative negligence by judicial decision, but one of these states now has a statute. The following decision was the first judicial adoption.

HOFFMAN v. JONES

Supreme Court of Florida, 1973.
280 So.2d 431.

Adkins, Justice.

[Plaintiff's husband was killed in a traffic accident that resulted from a combination of his own negligence and the negligence of the other driver. The trial judge denied plaintiff's request to instruct the jury on comparative negligence. The trial judge gave the standard contributory negligence instruction, and the jury returned a verdict for the defendant. Plaintiff appealed to the intermediate appellate court, which certified the following question to the state supreme court]:

> Whether or not the Court should replace the contributory negligence rule with the principles of comparative negligence?

* * *

Prior to answering the question certified, we must * * * consider our * * * power and authority to replace the rule of contributory negligence with that of comparative negligence. It has been suggested that such a change in the common law of Florida is properly within the province only of the Legislature, and not of the courts. We cannot agree.

The rule that contributory negligence is an absolute bar to recovery was—as most tort law—a judicial creation, and it was specifically judicially adopted in Louisville and Nashville Railroad Co. v. Yniestra, 21 Fla. 700 (1886). Most scholars attribute the origin of this rule to the English case of Butterfield v. Forrester, 11 East 60, 103 Eng.Rep. 926 (K.B.1809) * * *. * * *

* * *

* * * The rule of contributory negligence as a complete bar to recovery was imported into the law by judges. Whatever may have been the historical justification for it, today it is almost universally regarded as unjust and inequitable to vest an entire accidental loss on one of the parties whose negligent conduct combined with the negligence of the other party to produce the loss. If fault is to remain the test of liability, then the doctrine of comparative negligence which involves apportionment of the loss among those whose fault contributed to the occurrence is more consistent with liability based on a fault premise.

* * *

The demise of the absolute–bar theory of contributory negligence has been urged by many American scholars in the law of torts. It has been abolished in almost every common law nation in the world, including England—its country of origin—and every one of the Canadian Provinces. Some form of comparative negligence now exists in Austria, France, Germany, Portugal, Switzerland, Italy, China, Japan, Persia, Poland, Russia, Siam and Turkey.

Also, our research reveals that sixteen states have so far adopted some form of the comparative negligence doctrine.

One reason for the abandonment of the contributory negligence theory is that the initial justification for establishing the complete defense is no longer valid. It is generally accepted that, historically, contributory negligence was adopted "to protect the essential growth of industries, particularly transportation." Modern economic and social customs, however, favor the individual, not industry.

We find that none of the justifications for denying any recovery to a plaintiff, who has contributed to his own injuries to any extent, has any validity in this age.

Perhaps the best argument in favor of the movement from contributory to comparative negligence is that the latter is simply a more equitable system of determining liability and a more socially desirable method of loss distribution. The injustice which occurs when a plaintiff suffers severe injuries as the result of an accident for which he is only slightly responsible, and is thereby denied any damages, is readily apparent. The rule of contributory negligence is a harsh one which either places the burden of a loss for which two are responsible upon only one party or relegates to Lady Luck the determination of the damages for which each of two negligent parties will be liable. When the negligence of more than one person contributes to the occurrence of an accident, each should pay the proportion of the total damages he has caused the other party.

In an effort to ameliorate the harshness of contributory negligence, other doctrines have evolved in tort law such as "gross, willful, and wanton" negligence, "last clear chance" and the application of absolute liability in certain instances. Those who defend the doctrine of contributory negligence argue that the rule is also not as harsh in its practical effect as it is in theory. This is so, they say, because juries tend to disregard the instructions given by the trial judge in an effort to afford some measure of rough justice to the injured party. We agree with [Maloney, From Contributory to Comparative Negligence: A Needed Law Reform, 11 U.Fla.L.Rev. 135, 151–52 (1958)] that,

> [T]here is something basically wrong with a rule of law that is so contrary to the settled convictions of the lay community that laymen will almost always refuse to enforce it, even when solemnly told to do so by a judge whose instructions they have sworn to follow * * *.

> [T]he disrespect for law engendered by putting our citizens in a position in which they feel it is necessary to deliberately violate the law is not something to be lightly brushed aside; and it comes ill from the mouths of lawyers, who as officers of the courts have sworn to uphold the law, to defend the present system by arguing that it works because jurors can be trusted to disregard that very law.

* * *

[W]e feel the time has come for this Court to join what seems to be a trend toward almost universal adoption of comparative negligence. A primary function of a court is to see that legal conflicts are equitably resolved. In the field of tort law, the most equitable result that can ever be reached by a court is the equation of liability with fault. Comparative negligence does this more completely than contributory negligence, and we would be shirking our duty if we did not adopt the better doctrine.

Therefore, we now hold that a plaintiff in an action based on negligence will no longer be denied any recovery because of his contributory negligence.

If it appears from the evidence that both plaintiff and defendant were guilty of negligence which was, in some degree, a legal cause of the injury to the plaintiff, this does not defeat the plaintiff's recovery entirely. The jury in assessing damages would in that event award to the plaintiff such damages as in the jury's judgment the negligence of the defendant caused to the plaintiff. In other words, the jury should apportion the negligence of the plaintiff and the negligence of the defendant; then, in reaching the amount due the plaintiff, the jury should give the plaintiff only such an amount proportioned with his negligence and the negligence of the defendant.

* * *

If plaintiff and defendant are both at fault, the former may recover, but the amount of his recovery may be only such proportion of the entire damages plaintiff sustained as the defendant's negligence bears to the combined negligence of both the plaintiff and the defendant. For example, where it is found that the plaintiff's negligence is * * * equal to that of the defendant, the amount awarded to the plaintiff should be reduced by one–half from what it otherwise would have been.

The doctrine of last clear chance would, of course, no longer have any application in these cases.

We decline herein to dissect and discuss all the possible variations of comparative negligence which have been adopted in other jurisdictions. Countless law review commentaries and treatises can be found which have covered almost every conceivable mutation of the basic doctrine. Suffice it to say that we consider the "pure form" of comparative negligence * * * to be the most equitable method of allocating damages in negligence actions.

In the usual situation where the negligence of the plaintiff is at issue, as well as that of the defendant, there will undoubtedly be a counterclaim filed. The cross–plaintiff (just as plaintiff in the main suit) guilty of some degree of negligence would be entitled to a verdict awarding him such damages as in the jury's judgment were proportionate with his negligence and the negligence of cross–defendant. This could result in two verdicts—one for plaintiff and one for cross–plaintiff. In such event the Court should enter one judgment in favor of the party receiving the larger verdict, the amount of which should be the difference between the two verdicts. This is in keeping with the long recognized principles of "set off" in contract litigation. The Court's primary responsibility is to enter a judgment which reflects the true intent of the jury, as expressed in its verdict or verdicts.

In rare cases the net result of two such claims will be that the party more responsible for an accident will recover more than the party less responsible. On the surface, this might seem inequitable. However, using an extreme example, let us assume that a plaintiff is 80 per cent responsible for an automobile accident and suffers $20,000 in damages, and that the defendant—20 per cent responsible—fortunately suffers no damages. The liability of the defendant in such a case should not depend upon what damages he suffered, but upon what damages he caused. If a jury found that this defendant had been negligent and that his negligence, in relation to that of the plaintiff, was 20 per cent responsible for causing the accident then he should pay 20 per cent of the total damages, regardless of the fact that he has been fortunate enough to not be damaged personally.

Petitioners in this cause, and various amicus curiae who have filed briefs, have raised many points which they claim we must consider in adopting comparative negligence, such as the effects of such a change on the concept of "assumption of risk," and [on] "contribution" between joint tortfeasors. We decline to consider all those issues * * *.

[I]t is not the proper function of this Court to decide unripe issues, without the benefit of adequate briefing, not involving an actual controversy, and unrelated to a specific factual situation.

We are fully confident that the trial court judges of this State can adequately handle any problems created by our change to a comparative negligence rule as these problems arise. The answers to many of the problems will be obvious in light of the purposes for which we adopt the rule stated above:

(1) To allow a jury to apportion fault as it sees fit between negligent parties whose negligence was part of the legal and proximate cause of any loss or injury; and

(2) To apportion the total damages resulting from the loss or injury according to the proportionate fault of each party.

In accomplishing these purposes, the trial court is authorized to require special verdicts to be returned by the jury and to enter such judgment or judgments as may truly reflect the intent of the jury as expressed in any verdict or verdicts which may be returned.

We recognize the thousands of pending negligence cases affected by this decision. In fact, the prospect of a general upheaval in pending tort litigation has always been a deterring influence in considering the adoption of a comparative negligence rule. We feel the trial judges of this State are capable of applying this comparative negligence rule without our setting guidelines in anticipation of expected problems. The problems are more appropriately resolved at the trial level in a practical manner instead of a theoretical solution at the appellate level. The trial judges are granted broad discretion in adopting such procedure as may accomplish the objectives and purposes expressed in this opinion.

* * *

Notes

1. *Three types of comparative–fault systems.* Comparative negligence rules vary considerably from state to state, but there are three main versions, exemplified by the following statutes:

N.Y.Civ.Prac.Law § 1411: In any action to recover damages for personal injury, injury to property, or wrongful death, the culpable conduct attributable to the claimant or to the decedent, including contributory negligence or assumption of risk, shall not bar recovery, but the amount of damages otherwise recoverable shall be diminished in the proportion which the culpable conduct attributable to the claimant or decedent bears to the culpable conduct which caused the damages.

Wis.Stat. § 895.045: Contributory negligence does not bar recovery in an action by any person or the person's legal representative to recover damages for negligence resulting in death or injury to person or property, if that negligence was not greater than the negligence of the person against whom recovery is sought, but any damages allowed shall be diminished in the proportion to the amount of negligence attributed to the person recovering. The negligence of the plaintiff shall be measured separately against the negligence of each person found to be causally negligent. * * *

Ark.Stat. § 16–64–122:

(a) In all actions for damages for personal injuries or wrongful death or injury to property in which recovery is predicated upon fault, liability shall be determined by comparing the fault chargeable to a claiming party with the fault chargeable to the party or parties from whom the claiming party seeks to recover damages.

(b)(1) If the fault chargeable to a party claiming damages is of less degree than the fault chargeable to the party or parties from whom the claiming party seeks to recover damages, then the claiming party is entitled to recover the amount of his damages after they have been diminished in proportion to the degree of his own fault.

(b)(2) If the fault chargeable to a party claiming damages is equal to or greater in degree than any fault chargeable to the party or parties from whom the claiming party seeks to recover damages, then the claiming party is not entitled to recover such damages.

(c) The word "fault" as used in this section includes any act, omission, conduct, risk assumed, breach of warranty, or breach of any legal duty which is a proximate cause of any damages sustained by any party.

(d) In cases where the issue of comparative fault is submitted to the jury by an interrogatory, counsel for the parties shall be permitted to argue to the jury the effect of an answer to any interrogatory.

States with comparative negligence rules resembling New York's are referred to as "pure" comparative negligence systems. States that follow the Wisconsin approach are often called "modified (51%)" systems. States that follow the Arkansas approach are often called "modified (50%) systems." The numbers are useful short–hand designations of the cut–off point—the point at which the plaintiff's fault is too great to allow any recovery—in simple two–party cases. (But be careful with them. In some systems, a plaintiff can be cut off from recovery for fault assessed at less than 50% in multiparty cases. See, e.g., note 3 infra.)

Most of the judicial decisions inaugurating comparative negligence regimes, like *Hoffman,* opted for a "pure" version. Most of the statutes are modified forms. The Restatement (Third) of Torts: Apportionment of Liability § 7 (2000) provides:

Plaintiff's negligence (or the negligence of another person for whose negligence the plaintiff is responsible) that is a legal cause of an indivisible injury to the plaintiff reduces the plaintiff's recovery in proportion to the share of responsibility the factfinder assigns to the plaintiff (or other person for whose negligence the plaintiff is responsible).

Comment *a* refers to this provision as "a pure comparative–responsibility system."

2. *Special verdicts.* In many states, the establishment of a comparative negligence system called for changes in trial court procedure. For example, note that *Hoffman* recommends "special verdicts" in comparative negligence cases. Thus, instead of instructing the jurors on the law of comparative negligence and leaving its application entirely to them, a Florida trial judge will require the jury to make specific findings as to (a) the total amount of plaintiff's damages, (b) the defendant's degree or percentage of negligence, and (c) the plaintiff's degree or percentage of negligence. (Remember that neither defendant's nor plaintiff's negligent conduct will "count" unless it was a cause in fact and a legal cause of the injuries.) The trial judge will then reduce the damages by the plaintiff's percentage of negligence and enter judgment in the reduced amount.

3. *Should the jury be told what the effects of its findings will be?* Section (d) of the Arkansas statute reflects a fairly recent trend toward letting the jury know how its fault assessments will affect the parties. (For further attention to this issue, see Kaeo v. Davis, infra p. 439.) Can you see why the argument for such a provision is stronger in Arkansas than in New York?

4. *In modified systems, what is the cut–off point in multiple–defendant cases?* Suppose the jury returns a verdict finding the plaintiff 40% at fault and each of two defendants 30% at fault. Under the Arkansas statute quoted above, can the plaintiff recover anything from each defendant? What about Wisconsin?

The Restatement (Third) of Torts: Apportionment of Liability, § 7, cmt. n (Reporters' Note) (2000) says the Wisconsin provision on this point is unique. Comment *n* implies that a court confronted with a statute that is ambiguous on the point—e.g., a statute identical to the first sentence of the Wisconsin statute—should interpret it not to bar the plaintiff in the situation posited in this note.

5. *The percentage vocabulary.* Dobbs, The Law of Torts § 203, p. 511 (2000), says "[t]he language of percentage is exactly the right language for fault apportionment under comparative fault rules * * *." The Restatement (Third) of Torts: Apportionment of Liability (2000), contemplates the use of percentages to express what it calls the "comparative responsibility" of the parties. Almost all states use the percentage vocabulary.[1] It has its critics.

---

1. But see Maine's statute, 14 M.R.S.A. § 156 (1980), which provides that in cases in which a comparative–fault reduction in the plaintiff's recovery is appropriate, "the court shall instruct the jury to find and record the total damages which would have been recoverable if the claimant had not been at fault, and further instruct the jury to reduce the total damages by dollars and cents, and not by percentage, to the extent deemed just and equitable, having regard to the claimant's share in the responsibility for the damages, and instruct the jury to return both amounts with the knowledge that the lesser figure is the final verdict in the case." The statute also contemplates instructing the jury that "[if the] claimant is found by the jury to be equally at fault, the claimant shall not recover."

In Pelletier v. Fort Kent Golf Club, 662 A.2d 220 (Me. 1995), the plaintiff was play-

See Robertson, Eschewing Ersatz Percentages: A Simplified Vocabulary of Comparative Fault, 45 St. Louis U. L.J. 831 (2001). But it is deeply entrenched.

6. *New substantive issues created by the adoption of comparative fault.* "[T]he nearly universal adoption of comparative responsibility by American courts and legislatures has had a dramatic impact. * * * Comparative responsibility has a potential impact on almost all areas of tort law."[2] This is a huge phenomenon. Here we will look briefly at two of the multitude of instances in which the advent of comparative fault is necessitating the reexamination of situations that were relatively nonproblematic in the contributory negligence era.

a.   Suppose you negligently leave your car unlocked with the key in the ignition and an intoxicated person steals the car and injures himself in a wreck. In the contributory negligence era, he wouldn't have sued you— obviously, he would have been barred by his own fault. In a comparative fault system, especially a pure one, some new doctrine may be needed. (You may well win on the merits, but what you need is something that gets the complaint thrown out.) The New York judiciary has named its response to this kind of problem—i.e., an action by a plaintiff whose injury stems from the combination of defendant's negligent conduct and the plaintiff's illegal or highly immoral conduct—the "preclusion doctrine" and has used it to dismiss complaints by a bombmaker, a burglar, a car thief, a fleeing felon, and an unlicensed dentist. See generally Alami v. Volkswagen of America, Inc., 97 N.Y.2d 281, 739 N.Y.S.2d 867, 766 N.E.2d 574 (2002). Dobbs, The Law of Torts § 208 (2000), says this "preclusion" principle has been applied "selectively" around the country and intimates that it engages the courts in making distinctions—as to which kinds of victim fault are illegal or immoral enough to kill the lawsuit at the threshold—that may be difficult to justify.

b.   Suppose your preoccupation with a cellular phone conversation causes you to wreck your car, producing personal injuries that require hospitalization, and the negligence of an emergency–room physician makes your injuries worse. If your medical malpractice action had been brought during the contributory negligence era, the physician would not have been able to invoke your negligent driving against you; the last clear chance doctrine would readily have prevented it. Here again, the switch to comparative fault seems to necessitate the creation of new legal doctrine. The Restatement (Third) of Torts: Apportionment of Liability § 7, cmt. *m* (2000) provides that "in a case involving negligent rendition of a service, including

ing golf on a course that had a railroad track running across it. Her second shot from the tee landed 43 feet short of the tracks. Her third shot hit the tracks and ricocheted back into her face. The jury found that plaintiff and the golf club were both negligent, that plaintiff's total damages were $250,000, and that because of her negligence the plaintiff should have her recovery reduced to $40,000. The plaintiff appealed—a bold strategy under the circumstances—and argued that the verdict was incoherent because the relationship between the total damages and the damages

awarded meant the jury was assessing her with 210/250ths of the fault, whereas under the statute she should have been cut off from all recovery at 125/250ths. Nonsense, said the court: "The plain meaning of the statutory language allows a jury to award damages in disproportion to its determination of liability. * * * [W]hat a jury deems 'just and equitable' does not have to be proportionate to the claimant's fault."

2.   Restatement (Third) of Torts: Apportionment of Liability § 1, cmt. *a* (2000).

medical services, a factfinder does not consider any plaintiff's conduct that created the situation the service was employed to remedy." For a discerning application and discussion of this proposition, see the majority and dissenting opinions in Aden v. Fortsh, 169 N.J. 64, 776 A.2d 792 (2001) (action against insurance broker).

7. *Set off.* Presumably thinking only about automobile accident litigation, the *Hoffman* court assumed that it will be "usual" for both parties to be hurt and file claims against each other. It held that in such situations—i.e., when the jury returns verdicts awarding damages to both the plaintiff and the defendant/counterclaimant—the court should "set off" the verdicts and enter one net judgment. This was not a good idea.[3] In Jess v. Herrmann, 26 Cal.3d 131, 161 Cal.Rptr. 87, 604 P.2d 208, 211–12 (1979), the court explained:

> The facts of the instant case illustrate the problem. [Jess sustained $100,000 in damages and was 40% at fault. Herrmann sustained $14,000 in damages and was 60% at fault.] If both Jess and Herrmann carry adequate automobile insurance, in the absence of a mandatory setoff rule, Jess would receive $60,000 from defendant Herrmann's insurer to partially compensate her for the serious injuries caused by Herrmann's negligence, and Herrmann would receive $5,600 from Jess' insurer to partially compensate her for the injuries suffered as a result of Jess' negligence. Under the setoff rule applied by the trial court, however—despite the fact that both Jess' and Herrmann's injuries, financial losses and insurance coverage remain in fact unchanged—Jess' recovery from Herrmann's insurer is reduced to $54,400 and Herrmann is denied any recovery whatsoever from Jess' insurer.

> As these facts demonstrate, a mandatory setoff rule in the typical setting of insured tortfeasors does not serve as an innocuous accounting mechanism or as a beneficial safeguard against an adversary's insolvency but rather operates radically to alter the parties' ultimate financial positions. Such a mandatory rule diminishes both injured parties' actual recovery and accords both insurance companies a corresponding fortuitous windfall at their insureds' expense. Indeed, in this context, application of a mandatory setoff rule produces the anomalous situation in which a liability insurer's responsibility under its policy depends as much on the extent of the injury suffered by its own insured as on the amount of damages sustained by the person its insured has negligently injured.

The Restatement (Third) of Torts: Apportionment of Liability § 9 (2000) provides:

> If two parties are liable to each other in the same suit, each party is entitled to a setoff of any recovery owed by the other party, except that, in cases in which one or both of the parties has liability insurance, setoff does not reduce the payment of a liability insurer unless an applicable rule or law or statute so provides.

3. Subsequently the court changed its mind. See Stuyvesant Ins. Co. v. Bournazi-an, 342 So.2d 471 (Fla. 1976).

WASSELL v. ADAMS

United States Court of Appeals, Seventh Circuit, 1989.
865 F.2d 849.

POSNER, CIRCUIT JUDGE.

The plaintiff, born Susan Marisconish, grew up on Macaroni Street in a small town in a poor coal–mining region of Pennsylvania—a town so small and obscure that it has no name. * * * After graduating from high school she worked briefly as a nurse's aide, then became engaged to Michael Wassell, also from Pennsylvania. Michael joined the Navy in 1985 and was sent to Great Lakes Naval Training Station, just north of Chicago, for basic training. He and Susan had decided to get married as soon as he completed basic training. The graduation was scheduled for a Friday. Susan, who by now was 21 years old, traveled to Chicago with Michael's parents for the graduation. The three checked into a double room at the Ron–Ric Motel, near the base, on the Thursday (September 22, 1985) before graduation. The Ron–Ric is a small and inexpensive motel that caters to the families of sailors at the Great Lakes Naval Training Station a few blocks to the east. The motel has 14 rooms and charges a maximum of $36 a night for a double room. The motel was owned by Wilbur and Florena Adams, the defendants in the case.

Four blocks to the west of the Ron–Ric Motel is a high–crime area: Murder, prostitution, robbery, drugs—the works. The Adamses occasionally warned women guests not to walk alone in the neighborhood at night. They did not warn the Wassells or Susan.

Susan spent Friday night with Michael at another motel. On Saturday the Wassells checked out and left for Pennsylvania, and at the Wassells' suggestion Susan moved from the double room that she had shared with them to a single room in the Ron–Ric. Michael spent Saturday night with her but had to return to the base on Sunday for several days. She remained to look for an apartment where they could live after they were married (for he was scheduled to remain at the base after completing basic training). She spent most of Sunday in her room reading the newspaper and watching television. In the evening she went to look at an apartment.

Upon returning to her room at the motel, she locked the door, fastened the chain, and went to bed. She fell into a deep sleep, from which she was awakened by a knock on the door. She turned on a light and saw by the clock built into the television set that it was 1:00 a.m. She went to the door and looked through the peephole but saw no one. Next to the door was a pane of clear glass. She did not look through it. The door had two locks plus a chain. She unlocked the door and opened it all the way, thinking that Michael had come from the base * * *. It was not Michael at the door. It was a respectably dressed black man whom Susan had never seen before. He asked for "Cindy" (maybe "Sidney," she thought later). She told him there was no Cindy there.

Then he asked for a glass of water. She went to the bathroom * * * to fetch the glass of water. When she came out of the bathroom, the man was sitting at the table in the room. [He then raped her.]

* * *

The rapist was never prosecuted; a suspect was caught but Susan was too upset to identify him. There had been a rape at the motel several years previously * * *. There had also been a robbery, and an incident in which an intruder kicked in the door to one of the rooms. These were the only serious crimes committed during the seven years that the Adamses owned the motel.

Susan married Michael, but the rape had induced post–trauma stress that has, according to her testimony and that of a psychologist testifying as her expert witness, blighted her life. She brought this suit against the Adamses on January 21, 1986. It is a diversity suit that charges the Adamses with negligence in failing to warn Susan or take other precautions to protect her against the assault. The substantive issues are governed by the law of Illinois. A jury composed of four women and three men found that the Adamses had indeed been negligent and that their negligence had been a proximate cause of the assault, and the jury assessed Susan's damages at $850,000, which was the figure her lawyer had requested in closing argument. But in addition the jury found that Susan had been negligent too—and indeed that her negligence had been 97 percent to blame for the attack and the Adamses' only 3 percent. So, following the approach to comparative negligence laid down in Alvis v. Ribar, 85 Ill.2d 1, 421 N.E.2d 886 (1981)—the decision in which the Supreme Court of Illinois abolished the common law rule that contributory negligence is a complete bar to a negligence suit—the jury awarded Susan only $25,500 in damages. This happens to be approximately the midpoint of the psychologist's estimate—$20,000 to $30,000—of the expense of the therapy that the psychologist believes Susan may need for her post–traumatic stress.

Susan's lawyer asked the district judge to grant judgment in her favor notwithstanding the verdict, on the ground either that she had been nonnegligent as a matter of law or that her negligence was immaterial because the Adamses had been not merely negligent but willful and wanton in their disregard for her safety. In the alternative, counsel asked the judge to grant a new trial on the ground that the jury's apportionment of negligence was contrary to the manifest weight of the evidence. * * * The judge denied the motion[s], and Susan appeals.

Had she filed her suit after November 25, 1986, she could not have recovered any damages, assuming the jury would have made the same apportionment of responsibility between her and the Adamses. Illinois' new comparative negligence statute (Ill.Rev.Stat. ch. 110, ¶ 2–1116; see also ¶ 2–1107.1) bars recovery in negligence (or strict liability product) cases in which the plaintiff's "fault ... is more than 50% of the proximate cause of the injury or damage for which recovery is sought." But as her suit was filed before that date, the new statute is inapplicable.

Susan Wassell's counsel argues that the jury's verdict "reflected a chastened, hardened, urban mentality—that lurking behind every door is evil and danger, even if the guest is from a small town unfamiliar with the area." He takes umbrage at the defendants' argument that Susan's "antennae" should have been alerted when she didn't see anyone through the peephole. He rejects the metaphor, remarking unexceptionably that human beings do not have antennae and that this case is not a Kafka story about a person who turned into an insect (i.e., is not *The Metamorphosis*). He points out that a person awakened from a deep sleep is not apt to be thinking clearly and that once Susan opened the door the fat was in the fire—if she had slammed the door in the rapist's face he might have kicked the door in, as had happened once before at this motel, although she didn't know that at the time.

* * * Susan's counsel insists that Susan was not negligent at all but that, if she was, she was at most 5 percent responsible for the catastrophe, which, he argues, could have been averted costlessly by a simple warning from the Adamses. To this, the Adamses' counsel replies absurdly that a warning would have been costly—it might have scared guests away! The loss of business from telling the truth is not a social loss; it is a social gain.

The common law refused to compare the plaintiff's and the defendant's negligence. The negligent plaintiff could recover nothing, unless the defendant's culpability was of a higher degree than simple negligence. Susan argues that the defendants were willful and wanton, which, she says, would make her negligence as irrelevant under a regime of comparative negligence as it would be in a jurisdiction in which contributory negligence was still a complete defense.

Both the premise (that the Adamses were willful and wanton) and the conclusion (that if so, her own negligence was irrelevant) are wrong. As we guessed in Davis v. United States, 716 F.2d 418, 429 (7th Cir.1983), that it would, Illinois appears to be lining up with the states that allow the plaintiff's simple negligence to be compared with the defendant's "willful and wanton conduct." See State Farm Mut. Auto. Ins. Co. v. Mendenhall, 517 N.E.2d 341 (Ill.App. 1987). We say "appears to be" because * * * *Mendenhall* * * * is not a decision of the Illinois Supreme Court, and because a critical premise of the decision may be shaky. That is the proposition that "willful and wanton" under Illinois law denotes merely a heightened form of negligence, so that there is only a small difference between simple negligence and willful and wanton misconduct despite the ominous sound of the words "willful" and "wanton." As we noted in *Davis*, there are two lines of "willful and wanton" decisions in Illinois. One, which seemed to be in the ascendancy when we wrote *Davis*, * * * regards "willful and wanton" as merely a heightened form of "negligent." * * * But the cases since *Davis* appear to have swung round to the narrower concept, under which willful and wanton conduct denotes "conscious disregard for ... the safety of others" or "knowledge that [the defendant's] conduct posed a high probability of serious physical harm to others." * * *

If the more recent formulations are authoritative, this would undermine the argument in *Davis* and *Mendenhall* for allowing a plaintiff's simple negligence to be compared with a defendant's willful and wanton misconduct. But it would not help Susan Wassell win her case. No rational jury could find that the Adamses *consciously* disregarded a *high* probability of *serious* physical harm. * * *

[So the] district judge was right to deny Susan's request for judgment notwithstanding the verdict. But was he right to deny her [motion] for a new trial? [In support of her new trial motion, Susan argues that the jury's finding that her negligence was so great as to outweigh the Adamses' by a factor or more than 30 was contrary to the manifest weight of the evidence.] * * *

The old common law rule barring the contributorily negligent plaintiff from recovering any damages came eventually to seem too harsh. That is why it has been changed in most jurisdictions, including Illinois. It was harsh, all right, at least if one focuses narrowly on the plight of individual plaintiffs, but it was also simple and therefore cheap to administer. The same cannot be said for comparative negligence, which far from being simple requires a formless, unguided inquiry, because there is no methodology for comparing the causal contributions of the plaintiff's and of the defendant's negligence to the plaintiff's injury. In this case, either the plaintiff or the defendants could have avoided that injury. It is hard to say more, but the statute requires more—yet without giving the finder of facts any guidance as to how to make the apportionment.

We have suggested in previous cases that one way to make sense of comparative negligence is to assume that the required comparison is between the respective costs to the plaintiff and to the defendant of avoiding the injury. If each could have avoided it at the same cost, they are each 50 percent responsible for it. According to this method of comparing negligence, the jury found that Susan could have avoided the attack at a cost of less than one thirty–second the cost to the Adamses. Is this possible?

It is careless to open a motel or hotel door in the middle of the night without trying to find out who is knocking. Still, people aren't at their most alert when they are awakened in the middle of the night, and it wasn't crazy for Susan to assume that Michael had returned without telling her, even though he had said he would be spending the night at the base. So it cannot be assumed that the cost—not to her (although her testimony suggests that she is not so naive or provincial as her lawyer tried to convince the jury she was), but to the reasonable person who found himself or herself in her position, for that is the benchmark in determining plaintiff's as well as defendant's negligence—was zero, or even that it was slight. As innkeepers (in the increasingly quaint legal term), the Adamses had a duty to exercise a high degree of care to protect their guests from assaults on the motel premises. And the cost to the Adamses of warning all their female guests of the dangers of the neighborhood would have been negligible. Surely a warning to Susan would not have cost the Adamses 32 times the cost to her of schooling herself to greater vigilance.

But this analysis is incomplete. It is unlikely that a warning would have averted the attack. Susan testified that she thought the man who had knocked on the door was her fiance. Thinking this, she would have opened the door no matter how dangerous she believed the neighborhood to be. The warning that was not given might have deterred her from walking alone in the neighborhood. But that was not the pertinent danger. Of course, if the Adamses had told her not to open her door in the middle of the night under any circumstances without carefully ascertaining who was trying to enter the room, this would have been a pertinent warning and might have had an effect. But it is absurd to think that hoteliers are required to give so obvious a warning, any more than they must warn guests not to stick their fingers into the electrical outlets. Everyone, or at least the average person, knows better than to open his or her door to a stranger in the middle of the night. The problem was not that Susan thought that she should open her bedroom door in the middle of the night to anyone who knocked, but that she wasn't thinking clearly. A warning would not have availed against a temporary, sleep–induced lapse.

Giving the jury every benefit of the doubt, as we are required to do * * *, we must assume that the jury was not so muddle–headed as to believe that the Adamses' negligence consisted in failing to give a futile warning. Rather, we must assume that the jury thought the Adamses' negligence consisted in failing to have a security guard, or telephones in each room, or alarms * * *. The only one of these omitted precautions for which there is a cost figure in the record was the security guard. A guard would have cost $50 a night. That is almost $20,000 a year. This is not an enormous number. * * * [But it] might be much greater than the monetary equivalent of the greater vigilance on the part of Susan that would have averted the attack.

The assumption that the jury was clear–thinking and instruction–abiding is artificial, of course. During its deliberations, the jury sent the judge a question about the duty to warn (the judge did not answer it). This is some indication that the jury thought that the Adamses' negligence consisted in failing to warn Susan. But it is equally plausible that the jury didn't think the Adamses were negligent at all toward Susan, but, persuaded that she had suffered terribly, wanted to give her a token recovery. Concern with sympathy verdicts appears to lie behind Illinois' new statute barring the plaintiff from recovering any damages if he is more than 50 percent negligent. * * * It may be more than coincidence that the jury awarded Susan just enough money to allow her to undertake the recommended course of psychological therapy. We are not supposed to speculate about the jury's reasoning process, and we have just seen that it would not necessarily strengthen Susan's case if we did. The issue for us is not whether this jury was rational and law–abiding but whether a rational jury could, consistently with the evidence, have returned the verdict that this jury did. If we were the trier of fact, persuaded that both parties were negligent and forced to guess about the relative costs to the plaintiff and to the defendants of averting the assault, we would assess the defendants' share at more than 3 percent. But we are not the trier of fact, and are authorized to upset the jury's apportionment only if persuaded that the trial judge abused his discretion in determining that the jury's verdict was not against the clear weight of the evidence. We are not so persuaded. It seems probably wrong to us, but we have suggested an interpretation of the evidence under which the verdict was consistent with the evidence and the law. And that is enough to require us to uphold the district judge's refusal to set aside the verdict.

AFFIRMED.

Notes

1. *The ameliorative doctrines.* Most states adopting comparative negligence have done away with the old ameliorative or avoidance doctrines. Note that *Hoffman* jettisons last clear chance. See also Davila v. Sanders, 557 S.W.2d 770 (Tex.1977) (abolishing an "imminent peril" doctrine); Turner v. New Orleans Public Service, Inc., 476 So.2d 800 (La.1985) (abolishing a "humanitarian doctrine" that had permitted negligent pedestrians to recover full damages from negligent motorists). The question in all these decisions has been whether the particular doctrine under scrutiny had independent validity or was merely "directed to the old choice between total victory and total defeat for the injured plaintiff." *Davila,* 557 S.W.2d at 770.

2. *Should the ameliorative doctrines be retained in modified comparative fault systems?* One way to view the modified comparative fault systems is as hybrid systems in which the contributory negligence defense remains in force for cases in which the victim's fault exceeds a certain level. In these systems, do the ameliorative doctrines still have a legitimate role in the cases in which the plaintiff will otherwise be barred? The Restatement (Third) of Torts: Apportionment of Liability § 7 cmt. *o* (2000) answers with a firm no. The reasoning is somewhat as follows.

The core case in which an ameliorative doctrine was needed to escape the harsh efforts of contributory negligence was when a plaintiff was only slightly negligent, compared with the far greater culpability of the defendant. By definition, such a case does not arise under modified comparative responsibility, because the plaintiff is barred only if the jury assigns the plaintiff a percentage of responsibility at or above 50%. Moreover, it would be difficult administratively to retain the ameliorative doctrines to escape the effect of barring a plaintiff under modified comparative responsibility without also forgiving the plaintiff of the negligent behavior even when the plaintiff would still be below 50% or 51% and, consequently, would not be barred. (Trying to draw this distinction would greatly complicate the jury submission, and courts should avoid this unless there is good reason for doing so.) Finally, one of the unspoken rationales for the ameliorative doctrines seems to have been that contributory negligence as an absolute bar was itself disreputable. It is more difficult for a court to conclude that modified comparative responsibility, especially when it has been legislatively adopted, is similarly disreputable.

3. *Should the plaintiff's negligence reduce recovery in intentional tort cases?* The *Wassell* plaintiff did not sue the rapist. If she had, would her negligence have been a legitimate defense? In answering such a question, the first place to look is the state's comparative fault statute. (See, e.g., the three that are quoted in note 1 following *Hoffman*, supra p. 381.) If that inquiry doesn't yield a clear "yes," most courts are likely to answer no. The Restatement (Third) of Torts: Apportionment of Liability § 1, cmt. *c* (2000) says that "[a]lthough some courts have held that a plaintiff's negligence may serve as a comparative defense to an intentional tort, most have not. This Restatement takes no position on that issue." For further attention to this question, see Chapter XI, Section E.

4. *The multiple meanings of "willful and wanton."* Judge Posner's opinion in *Wassell* demonstrates that interpreting a particular state's "willful and wanton" doctrine can be difficult. If the doctrine meant that the plaintiff could escape the effects of his negligence by showing that the defendant's negligence was significantly greater, it was only an ameliorative doctrine that should disappear once a comparative fault regime is adopted. But if it meant that a plaintiff's negligence should not constitute a defense when the defendant's conduct was qualitatively different from negligence— because it included the element of *conscious* disregard of a highly unacceptable risk and thus seemed more like an intentional wrong than like negligence—then perhaps "mere" negligence on the victim's part should not affect the recovery (just as most courts seem to think it shouldn't in standard intentional tort cases). For other courts struggling with this difficulty, see Martel v. Montana Power Co., 231 Mont. 96, 752 P.2d 140, (1988) (jettisoning a "willful and wanton" doctrine); Danculovich v. Brown, 593 P.2d 187 (Wyo. 1979) (jettisoning the last clear chance doctrine but keeping a "willful and wanton" doctrine). Cf. Weaver v. Lentz, 348 S.C. 672, 561 S.E.2d 360 (App.2002) (holding that damages were properly reduced to reflect the plaintiff's decedent's negligence even though the defendant may have acted "recklessly").

5. *What is being "compared?"* Judge Posner's approach to the validity of the 97% assignment to Susan Wassell is intriguing, but it has not been influential; perhaps it was too tightly focused on only the "B" element in the Hand B<PL formula. It is doubtful whether the 97% assignment could have been upheld in a system following the view of Restatement (Third) of Torts: Apportionment of Liability § 8 (2000):

> Factors for assigning percentages of responsibility to each person whose legal responsibility has been established include
>
> (a) the nature of the person's risk–creating conduct, including any awareness or indifference with respect to the risks created by the conduct and any intent with respect to the harm created by the conduct; and
>
> (b) the strength of the causal connection between the person's risk–creating conduct and the harm.

The assignment of 97% to Susan Wassell would have been even less likely to withstand scrutiny in Louisiana, where the Supreme Court has provided:

> In determining the percentages of fault, the trier of fact shall consider both the nature of the conduct of each party at fault and the extent of the causal relation between the conduct and the damages claimed. In assessing the nature of the conduct of the parties, various factors may influence the degree of fault assigned, including (1) whether the conduct resulted from inadvertence or involved an awareness of the danger, (2) how great a risk was created by the conduct, (3) the significance of what was sought by the conduct, (4) the capacities of the actor, whether superior or inferior, and (5) any extenuating circumstances which might require the actor to proceed in haste, without proper thought.

Watson v. State Farm Fire and Cas. Ins. Co., 469 So.2d 967, 974 (La. 1985). See also Eaton v. McLain, 891 S.W.2d 587, 592–93 (Tenn. 1994), where the court provides a multi–factor formulation very similar to that in *Watson*. Dobbs, The Law of Torts § 202, p. 508 (2000), cautions that formulations like those in *Watson* and *Eaton* are "merely familiar instances of the fundamental negligence analysis" and that "[i]nstructions that specify particular instances of the general principle may run risks of overemphasizing particular facets of the negligence issue."

In thinking about the way in which juries are supposed to arrive at percentage–fault assessments,[4] it may help to realize that there is no need (nor indeed does it even seem possible) to directly compare one party's conduct with that of the other. "The jury makes no such comparison; instead, it estimates each actor's extent of departure from the norm appropriate to that actor's situation and registers that normative estimation in numerical form. Regardless of whether the estimate is called a 'percentage' or a 'normative assignment,' it is plain on reflection that it does not result from comparing one actor's conduct with another's but rather from comparing each actor's conduct with that actor's own behavioral norm."[5] The Restatement (Third) of Torts: Apportionment of Liability § 8, cmt. *a* (2000) states that " 'assigning shares of responsibility' may be a less confusing phrase [than 'comparing conduct'] because it suggests that the factfinder, after considering the relevant factors, *assigns* shares of responsibility rather than *compares* incommensurate qualities." But the term "comparative responsibility" or "comparative fault" is deeply entrenched.

C. FAILURE TO AVOID CONSEQUENCES; FAILURE TO MITIGATE DAMAGES

DARE v. SOBULE

Supreme Court of Colorado, 1984.
674 P.2d 960.

ERICKSON, CHIEF JUSTICE.

* * *

4. Possibly we do not want to think too much about what may actually be going on in the jury room. See, e.g., Quady v. Sickl, 260 Wis. 348, 51 N.W.2d 3 (1952), where the court made no comment on the seemingly impossible precision of jury assignments of fault to four participants in a multi–vehicle traffic accident as: 14.17%, 15.42%, 23.33%, 47.08%.

5. Robertson, Eschewing Ersatz Percentages: A Simplified Vocabulary of Comparative Fault, 45 St. Louis U. L.J. 831, 855 (2001).

On July 30, 1977, Tracy Dare (decedent) was riding a motorcycle eastward on Mississippi Avenue in Jefferson County when respondent, who was driving his automobile westward on that street, made a left turn in front of the motorcycle. The motorcycle struck the car and the decedent was thrown over the car by the impact, landed on his head, and died as a result of head injuries.

Petitioners brought this action against respondent to recover damages for the wrongful death of their son. At trial, two witnesses testified that decedent was not wearing a protective helmet at the time of the accident. Petitioners did not object to the introduction of the evidence. * * *

Petitioners tendered the following proposed jury instruction: "To operate a motorcycle without wearing a helmet is not contributory negligence." The trial court, however, refused to give the tendered instruction on the ground that the instruction would give undue emphasis to one factor in the negligence equation. In refusing to give the instruction, the trial court ruled that, in presenting their closing arguments, neither side was to make reference to the failure of the decedent to wear a protective helmet.

The jury returned a verdict finding that both the decedent and the respondent were negligent, the negligence of each was a proximate cause of the claimed damages, and the percentage of negligence attributable to decedent was 80% and to respondent 20%. The jury also found that the amount of the petitioners' damages which were proximately caused by the collision was $4,089.14. [Because Colorado is a modified comparative fault state, the judge ordered that plaintiffs take nothing, and they appealed.]

The Court of Appeals affirmed the verdict for respondent, and held that it would have been improper to give an additional instruction stressing the helmet issue, particularly where, as here, "defendant [respondent] did not assert [the failure of the decedent to wear a helmet] as a defense, and the issue was not presented to the jury."

* * *

Petitioners contend that the trial court's refusal to instruct the jury that failure to wear a helmet when riding a motorcycle did not constitute contributory negligence was reversible error. We agree.

* * *

When contributory negligence was a total bar to recovery for negligence, we held that failure to wear a seat belt was not contributory negligence. Fischer v. Moore, 183 Colo. 392, 517 P.2d 458 (1973). [W]e said there was no statutory duty to wear an available seat belt and held:

In short, the seat belt defense, under the laws that existed prior to the adoption of our comparative negligence statute, is not an affirmative defense to an action for negligence, and evidence that the injured party failed to wear a seat belt may not be brought before the jury *in any form* to establish contributory negligence or to reduce the amount of the injured person's damages.

183 Colo. at 396, 517 P.2d at 460. (Emphasis added.) In that case, however, we expressly limited our holding to the situation where evidence of plaintiff's failure to wear a seat belt was offered to show plaintiff's contributory negligence, stating:

[B]ecause contributory negligence acts as a complete bar to recovery and rests upon different policy considerations, the conclusions reached in this decision should not be construed to apply as a bar to the seat belt defense, in a similar factual setting under the Colorado comparative negligence statute.

In our view, under the law of comparative negligence in Colorado, evidence of a plaintiff's failure to wear a protective helmet is inadmissible to show negligence on the part of the plaintiff or to mitigate damages.[4]

Both contributory negligence and comparative negligence are premised on negligence. Contributory negligence bars recovery; comparative negligence takes into account the negligence which caused the injury and reduces damages proportionately. Under either theory, however, we consider the plaintiff's negligence in the balance.

* * *

Our General Assembly has not mandated the use of protective helmets as a standard of conduct. In 1977, the General Assembly expressly repealed the portion of section 42–4–231, C.R.S.1973 (1982 Supp.), which required that all persons operating motorcycles wear protective helmets.

The critical inquiry then is whether this court should impose a standard of conduct upon all persons riding motorcycles. We decline to impose such a standard for several reasons.

First, a defendant should not diminish the consequences of his negligence by the failure of the injured party to anticipate defendant's negligence in causing the accident itself. Second, a defense premised on an injured party's failure to wear a protective helmet would result in a windfall to tortfeasors who pay only partially for the harm their negligence caused. Third, allowing the defense would lead to a veritable battle of experts as to what injuries would have or have not been avoided had the plaintiff been wearing a helmet.

We hold, therefore, that, under the Colorado Comparative Negligence Act, evidence of plaintiff's failure to wear a protective helmet is

4. In our view, decedent's failure to wear a protective helmet in this case is analogous to plaintiff's failure to fasten his seat belt in *Fischer,* supra.

inadmissible to show negligence on the part of the injured party or to mitigate damages. * * *

* * *

As a matter of substantive law, it makes no difference that the evidence of failure to wear a protective helmet was not challenged by objection or a motion to strike at trial. Huddleston v. Fergeson, 564 S.W.2d 448 (Tex.Civ.App.1978) (testimony violative of parol evidence rule, a rule of substantive law, is without probative force whether objected to or not). In our view, the giving of petitioners' tendered instruction would not only have been proper, but was necessary in the light of our holding in Fischer v. Moore, supra * * *. The improper admission of evidence of failure to wear a protective helmet provides a rational explanation for the jury's findings that decedent was 80% negligent and respondent was 20% negligent. We, accordingly, reverse and remand this case to the Court of Appeals with directions to remand to the trial court for a new trial.

HUTCHINS v. SCHWARTZ

Supreme Court of Alaska, 1986.
724 P.2d 1194.

COMPTON, JUSTICE.

Charles Hutchins and Donna Hutchins (Hutchins) appeal a jury verdict which awarded Hutchins $1,937.09 damages for injuries sustained in an automobile collision with Robert Schwartz (Schwartz). The jury determined that Hutchins was 40% comparatively negligent. On appeal Hutchins claims that the trial court erred 1) by admitting evidence of Hutchins' failure to wear a seat belt; [and] 2) by denying his motion for judgment notwithstanding the verdict (JNOV) and/or new trial * * * .

* * *

Hutchins was not wearing a seat belt at the time of the accident. He sustained cuts on his head, bruises on his chest, knee and wrist, and a broken big toe. * * *

Hutchins sued Schwartz for $275,000 compensatory damages. He filed a motion *in limine* to exclude evidence of his non–use of a seat belt. Judge Milton M. Souter denied the motion, ruling that evidence of Hutchins' failure to wear a seat belt could be used by Schwartz to argue for a reduction of damages.

At the end of the trial, Judge Souter granted Hutchins' motion for directed verdict on the seat belt issue. The jury was instructed to disregard all evidence relating to Hutchins' non–use of a seat belt.

The jury returned a verdict finding Schwartz 60% negligent and Hutchins 40% comparatively negligent. It awarded Hutchins $1,937.09 in damages.

Hutchins moved for JNOV and/or a new trial. The motion was denied. * * *

Hutchins claims that the trial court erred by denying his motion *in limine* and allowing evidence on Hutchins' non–use of a seat belt. He contends that this error was not cured by the trial court's subsequent instruction telling the jury to disregard the seat belt evidence. Hutchins urges the court to follow the jurisdictions which reject evidence of non–use of seat belts.

* * *

We have not addressed whether failure to use a seat belt can be used in a personal injury action as evidence of comparative negligence.

* * *

The question is whether we should impose a duty upon a person to wear a seat belt when driving a car equipped with one.

Most jurisdictions, whether they have adopted comparative or contributory negligence, have rejected the proposition. In [Amend v. Bell, 89 Wash.2d 124, 570 P.2d 138 (1977)], the Washington Supreme Court stated the reasons upon which most courts rely when declining to impose a duty upon all persons riding in a car equipped with seat belts.

First, the defendant should not diminish the consequences of his negligence by the plaintiff's failure to anticipate defendant's negligence. Plaintiffs are not required to predict a defendant's negligence.

Second, seat belts are not required in all vehicles.

Third, a majority of motorists do not habitually use their seat belts.

Fourth, admission of evidence of non–use would lead to a "battle of experts" as to what injuries would have or have not been avoided if plaintiff had worn a seat belt.

Other courts have declined because the legislature has not mandated seat belt use. The decision as to whether people should wear seat belts is one of policy and best left to the legislature.

Other courts have declined because the duty to avoid a defendant's negligence and mitigate one's own damages does not arise until after the accident and injury have occurred. Hutchins argues that a defendant must take his plaintiff as he finds him under the "eggshell skull" theory.

The supreme courts of Florida and Wisconsin, however, have taken a contrary view.

In Bentzler v. Braun, 34 Wis.2d 362, 149 N.W.2d 626 (1967), the Wisconsin Supreme Court recognized that there was a demonstrable link between wearing seat belts and minimizing injuries. The failure to wear seat belts was not negligence per se but

> where seat belts are available and there is evidence before the jury indicating causal relationship between the injuries sustained and the failure to use seat belts, it is proper and necessary to instruct the

jury in that regard. A jury in such case could conclude that an occupant of an automobile is negligent in failing to use seat belts.

In a subsequent case, [Foley v. City of West Allis, 113 Wis.2d 475, 335 N.W.2d 824 (1983)], the Wisconsin court stated that the seat belt defense

> is this court's recognition that in light of the realities of the frequency of automobile accidents and the extensive injuries they cause, the general availability of seat belts, and the public knowledge that riders and drivers should "buckle up for safety," those who fail to use available seat belts should be held responsible for the incremental harm caused by their failure to wear available seat belts.

The Wisconsin court suggested that the so called "seat belt defense" comports with the principles underlying comparative negligence. A plaintiff only recovers damages for injuries caused by defendant and not for those that plaintiff could have prevented by wearing a seat belt.

In Insurance Co. of North America v. Pasakarnis, 451 So.2d 447, 453 (Fla.1984), the Florida Supreme Court stated:

> As we have already expressly acknowledged, automobile collisions are foreseeable as are the so-called "second collisions" with the interior of the automobile. The seat belt has been a safety device required by the federal government for nearly twenty years. In a 1982 study by the United States Department of Transportation, it is reported that the evidence for the effectiveness of safety belts in reducing deaths and injury severity is substantial and unequivocal.

In light of the importance of the seat belt as a safety precaution and the minimal effort required to fasten an available seat belt, the court concluded that failure to wear one could be a pertinent factor for the jury to consider in determining damages.

We agree with the reasoning of the Florida and Wisconsin courts. These courts persuasively rebut the arguments of those holding the contrary.

Automobile accidents are foreseeable. The fact that many motorists do not wear seat belts may suggest that a failure to use a seat belt does not violate a standard of care. However, the fact that a majority of people act in a certain manner does not make that conduct reasonable especially when that conduct involves an unnecessary risk.

Most studies indicate that seat belt use is more advantageous than non-use since it prevents serious injuries.

As to a "battle of experts", juries are constantly evaluating expert testimony. This is not unique to the seat belt issue.

In *Pasakarnis,* the court responded to the argument that it should reject evidence of non-use absent specific legislation requiring the use of seat belts. The court stated that it has a duty to ensure that the law remains both fair and realistic as society and technology change. The court primarily modernized the law of torts as seen in its decisions of comparative negligence and loss of consortium. Additionally, the absence of a legislative mandate to wear seat belts means only that the failure to use one cannot constitute negligence per se.

Regarding a plaintiff's duty to mitigate damages before the injury occurs, the *Foley* court stated that when the plaintiff's pre–injury conduct does not cause the accident but aggravates the ensuing damages, then damage reduction is "the better view unless we are to place an entirely artificial emphasis upon the moment of impact, and the pure mechanics of causation."

We conclude that the failure to wear a seat belt is relevant evidence for the purpose of damage reduction. However, we do not choose to categorize such evidence as a "seat belt defense." Rather, the concept of comparative negligence contemplates the inclusion of all relevant factors in arriving at the appropriate damage award and non–use of a seat belt is a relevant factor for apportioning damages. We find it unnecessary to wait for legislative action on this subject.

Therefore, if under the facts and circumstances of the case a reasonably prudent person would have used a seat belt and if plaintiff suffered more severe injuries as a result of not wearing a seat belt, then the jury should be permitted to consider this factor in assessing damages.

In this case, we do not need to determine the extent to which seat belt evidence is relevant since the trial court directed a verdict against Schwartz on this issue.

We conclude that the trial court did not abuse its discretion by admitting evidence of Hutchins' failure to wear a seat belt. The court gave a subsequent jury instruction to disregard such evidence since it found that Schwartz presented insufficient evidence that the seat belt system actually worked and that Hutchins' injuries were caused by his failure to wear a seat belt. The subsequent instruction removed any possibility of jury confusion or prejudice.

* * *

Hutchins contends that the trial court erred in denying his motion for JNOV and/or new trial because there is no evidence showing that he was 40% comparatively negligent * * *.

* * *

After reviewing the evidence * * *, we conclude that reasonable minds could differ as to whether Hutchins' headlights were on or off. * * * Additionally, the jury could have concluded that Hutchins was traveling too fast for the road conditions. We conclude that there is an evidentiary basis for the jury's finding that Hutchins was 40% comparatively negligent.

* * *

[Affirmed.]

Notes

1. *Distinguishing among failure to avoid consequences, failure to mitigate damages, and contributory or comparative negligence.* The law of negligence traditionally precluded recovery of any damages that the plaintiff could have avoided by taking prudent measures *after* the accident to prevent or reduce the severity of his injuries. This rule is known as the doctrine of mitigation of damages. In some jurisdictions this is not a full–fledged affirmative defense, because the defendant is not required to plead it. But in most respects the mitigation of damages rule functions as an affirmative defense; in practice the defendant must introduce evidence and persuade the trier of fact that reasonable care by the plaintiff after the accident would have avoided some of the damages.

The doctrine of mitigation of damages is sometimes also called the "doctrine of avoidable consequences." But in the recent cases and commentary, the "avoidable consequences" terminology is applied to the issue raised in *Dare* and *Hutchins*. Most of these cases involve the plaintiff's failure to wear an automobile safety belt. A defendant who contends that the plaintiff should not be permitted to recover any damages that could have been avoided by wearing a seat belt is making an argument closely resembling the standard mitigation of damages argument, but the issue is different in this respect: the traditional mitigation of damages doctrine focuses on the victim's conduct after the accident, whereas the "avoidable consequences" argument in the seat belt and similar cases focuses on pre–accident conduct. Many recent judicial opinions have regarded that difference as an important one. Therefore, it seems best to highlight it by confining the term *mitigation of damages* to inquiries into the victim's post–accident conduct, and using the term *avoidable consequences* to refer to pre–accident conduct.

For clarity of analysis, avoidable consequences issues should also be distinguished from comparative (or contributory) negligence issues. Both terms focus on pre–accident conduct; but the difference—a clear and important one—is that conduct constituting comparative or contributory negligence was a cause in fact and a legal cause of the accident and hence of all of the victim's injuries, whereas conduct violative of the avoidable consequences doctrine will normally have been a cause in fact of only some of the injuries.

In summary, the preferred terminology in this area is as follows:

Comparative (or contributory) negligence: Pre–accident conduct by the victim that was a cause of the accident and hence of *all* of the injuries or damages.

Failure to avoid consequences: Pre–accident conduct by the victim that did not cause the accident but that was a cause of *some* (perhaps even all) of the injuries or damages.

Failure to mitigate damages: Post–accident conduct by the victim that was a cause of *some* of the injuries or damages.

2. *What should be the rule for failure to mitigate damages?* Most states have handled the mitigation of damages issue via jury instructions. See, *e.g.,* Michigan Standard Jury Instructions–Civil § 53.05 (2d ed. 1981):

> A person has a duty to use ordinary care to minimize his damages after he has been injured. It is for you to decide whether plaintiff failed to use such ordinary care and, if so, whether any damage resulted from such failure. You must not compensate the plaintiff for any portion of his damages which resulted from his failure to use such care.

Note that this has the effect of precluding recovery for all of the damages that resulted from the plaintiff's failure to mitigate, even though those damages also resulted from the defendant's negligence in causing the accident. Many courts continue to follow this approach. See, e.g., Adams v. Chenault, 836 So.2d 1193 (La.App. 2003), involving a traffic accident in which the plaintiff was an innocent passenger. The court held that the plaintiff's negligent failure to mitigate her damages—her conduct took the form of overusing prescription painkillers—necessitated reducing her damages award from $110,000 to $55,000. The Restatement (Third) of Torts: Apportionment of Liability § 3, cmt. *b,* illustration 4 (2000), calls for a different approach whereby a plaintiff's negligent failure to mitigate damages is penalized by a percentage–fault reduction rather than a total–bar rule.

3. *What should be the rule for failure to avoid consequences?* Here again the Restatement (Third) calls for a percentage–reduction approach. See Id., illustration 3. *Hutchins* took that general view. But as we saw in *Dare,* other courts want to forgive failures to avoid consequences. See also Miller v. Jeffrey, 213 W.Va. 41, 576 S.E.2d 520 (2002) (holding that a motorist's failure to wear his seat belt should have been kept entirely out of the case). Still others favor a total–bar approach (re the portion of the total damages that resulted from the plaintiff's culpable failure to avoid the consequences). See, e.g., Halvorson v. Voeller, 336 N.W.2d 118, 121 (N.D. 1983), setting forth the following jury instruction for cases involving injuries to motorcyclists:

> If you find (1) it was unreasonable for the plaintiff to not wear a helmet, and (2) the plaintiff would not have received some or all of his injuries had he worn a helmet, then (3) the amount of damages awarded the plaintiff for the injuries he sustained must be reduced in proportion to the amount of injury he would have avoided by the use of the helmet. The burden of proof on both (1) and (2) rests with the defendant.

The *Halvorson* court provided an example clarifying that it used the phrase "in proportion to the amount" to call for a cause–in–fact inquiry: What part of the plaintiff's total damages would the culpably–omitted helmet have prevented? Here is the example:

> Defendant's negligently–driven automobile collides with plaintiff's negligently–driven motorcycle, causing the plaintiff to sustain $100,000 in damages. The jury finds that the parties' accident–causing fault should be assessed 60% to defendant and 40% to plaintiff. The jury also finds that plaintiff should have been wearing a helmet and that, if he had been, he would have sustained only $40,000 in damages. The plaintiff should be awarded $24,000.

4. *A suggested exercise.* We have just seen three different treatments of a plaintiff's failure to avoid consequences: total forgiveness (*Dare* and *Miller*); percentage–fault–based reduction (*Hutchins* and Restatement); and total bar (of the relevant part of the damages) (*Halvorson*). The hypothetical case set forth below gives you the opportunity to see how each of the three approaches would affect the ultimate recovery of the plaintiff.

A motorist and a cyclist collide. The cyclist, who has sustained head injuries, a broken left arm, and a broken right leg, sues for personal injury damages. The complaint alleges that the motorist was negligent in running a red light. The motorist's answer denies her negligence and affirmatively pleads that the cyclist was negligent in failing to keep a proper lookout, traveling at an unsafe speed, and failing to wear a helmet.

The applicable comparative fault statute provides in pertinent part that "a claimant may recover damages only if his percentage of responsibility is less than or equal to 50%."

The case goes to the jury under instructions that permit the cyclist's failure to wear a helmet to be treated as part of his "percentage of responsibility." The jury finds that the motorist and the cyclist were each guilty of negligent conduct that was a cause in fact and a legal ("proximate") cause of the accident and the injuries, and that the cyclist's total damages were $100,000. In addition, the jury makes the following findings:

(1) Motorist's percentage of responsibility: 60%.

(2) Cyclist's percentage of responsibility: 40%.

(3) If you found that the cyclist sustained bodily injury damages as a proximate result of the motorist's negligence, what part, if any, of the damages so found do you find was proximately caused by the cyclist's failure to wear a protective helmet? (Answer in dollars.)

Answer: $76,000.

(4) If you assigned the cyclist a percentage of responsibility, what part, if any, of that percentage did you attribute to his failure to wear a protective helmet?

Answer: 25% [i.e., 10 of the 40 percentage points].

The trial judge who heard this case and submitted it to the jury has died before entering judgment, and you have been assigned to complete the case. Your research discloses that the state's law is unsettled as to the proper treatment of an injured cyclist's failure to wear a protective helmet. This means that you can treat it any way you think proper—provided the jury's findings are consistent with that treatment and with the basic law of cause in fact. Your research also convinces you that you are not free to grant JNOV or order a new trial; you *must* enter judgment on the jury verdict. What should the judgment provide?

5. *The "seat belt gag rule."* When the state legislatures started enacting statutes requiring seat belt use (by making nonuse a misdemeanor), many of them tacked on a provision that "the use or failure to use seat belts shall not be admissible in evidence in any litigation involving personal injuries or property damage resulting from the use or operation of any motor vehicle." The obvious purpose of these statutes was to protect plaintiffs from

being penalized for failure to wear seat belts. But read literally, they also effectively prevent plaintiff from suing auto manufacturers for faulty seat belts. Many courts have refused to read them literally. See, e.g., Bridgestone/Firestone, Inc. v. Glyn–Jones, 878 S.W.2d 132 (Tex. 1994) (with two justices vigorously dissenting); Fedele v. Tujague, 717 So.2d 244 (La.App. 1998). Other courts have disagreed. Olson v. Ford Motor Co., 558 N.W.2d 491 (Minn. 1997) held that the "seat belt gag rule" required summary judgment for the defendant in an action alleging that the car's seat belt failed in a collision, producing serious injuries.

Olson had a fascinating aftermath. The Minnesota legislature promptly amended the statute to except seat–belt–failure actions against car makers from the gag rule. Governor Jesse Ventura vetoed the amendment. The legislature then overrode the veto. Carlson v. Hyundai Motor Co., 164 F.3d 1160 (8th Cir. 1999), then held that the gag rule required the dismissal of a seat–belt–failure lawsuit that arose before the amendment.

D. ASSUMPTION OF THE RISK

In the pre–comparative fault era, the term "assumption of the risk" (or "assumed risk") undiscriminatingly covered a lot of territory. In modern thought, it covers three distinctly different defensive doctrines: express assumption of risk, implied primary assumption of risk, and implied secondary assumption of risk.

Only the last of these is an affirmative defense based on plaintiff's conduct. Express assumption of risk is concerned with contractual limitations on liability.[1] It is treated in Chapter X, Section C (p. 431.) Implied primary assumption of risk is a no–duty doctrine and thus doesn't belong in this chapter either; but in all of the cases, it is so intimately entwined with the affirmative defense–implied secondary–that we have no choice but to treat them together.

BENNETT v. HIDDEN VALLEY GOLF AND SKI, INC.

United States Court of Appeals, Eighth Circuit, 2003.
318 F.3d 868.

Murphy, Circuit Judge.

* * *

In the early morning of February 7, 1998, [Breanne] Bennett went with two older male friends to Hidden Valley for a midnight ski session. At the time Bennett was 16 years old and a high school student. She had limited experience as a skier, all of which had been at Hidden Valley where she had skied once before and had snowboarded twice.

While Bennett was skiing down a slope marked for intermediate difficulty, she fell at a spot which the parties have variously referred to as a bump, a ridge, a jump, a ramp, or a mogul. She was thrown about

---

1. See Restatement (Third) of Torts: Apportionment of Liability § 2 (2000).

five feet forward and hit the ground limp. * * * Both sides agree that the bump on the slope had not been intentionally created by Hidden Valley, but had formed as skiers and snow boarders cut across the slope and moved the snow. Bennett claims injuries as a result of the accident, including brain damage and a diminished future earning capacity.

[Bennett's action against Hidden Valley alleged that Hidden Valley was] negligent in the design, maintenance, and staffing of its skiing facilities; in the supervision of its customers "so as to prevent or cure dangers created by such business invitees"; in providing its customers with "unrestricted access to advanced and intermediate ski areas without assessing [their] ski aptitude, ability, or experience"; in permitting obstructions, including trees and jumps, to "exist in the path of skiers at a time when [it] ... should have known that such obstructions posed a hazard or risk of injury"; in failing to "warn of dangers and obstructions which it knew or reasonably should have known were present at its facilities and ski slopes"; and in failing "to guard against, barricade, protect, or cushion known or reasonably knowable obstructions in the path of skiers upon its ski slopes."

Hidden Valley denied negligence and raised assumption of risk as a defense. It waived a defense of comparative fault, however, and agreed that there was no issue as to whether Bennett had contractually released Hidden Valley from liability because she was a minor at the time of the accident.

The case proceeded to trial before a jury. Bennett * * * presented witnesses who described the accident, as well as expert evidence, to prove Hidden Valley's negligence and the extent of her injuries, including her diminished future earning capacity. After she rested, Hidden Valley put on evidence that it had exercised reasonable care and that the bump[s] * * * on the slope were risks inherent in the sport of skiing, in support of its assumption of risk defense. * * * At the close of all evidence, Bennett moved for a judgment as a matter of law, claiming that Hidden Valley had not established its affirmative defense of assumption of the risk. The district court denied the motion. * * * [T]he jury returned a verdict in favor of Hidden Valley.

[Bennett's most significant argument on appeal centers on the trial judge's Instruction 7, which directed the jury to find for Hidden Valley] if the conditions Bennett encountered "were a risk inherent in the sport of skiing." Bennett further argues that the district court should have granted her motion for judgment as a matter of law because Hidden Valley did not make out an assumption of risk defense. * * *

* * *

Instruction 7 was the verdict director for Hidden Valley's defense of implied primary assumption of risk. Under Missouri law, this defense "relates to the initial issue of whether the defendant had a duty to protect the plaintiff from the risk of harm."[3] The defense applies where

3. Missouri recognizes three forms of assumption of risk: express, implied primary, and implied secondary. Only implied primary assumption of risk is at issue in

"the parties have voluntarily entered a relationship in which the plaintiff assumes well–known incidental risks." A plaintiff's consent to assume the risk is "implied from the act of electing to participate in the activity" and "[a]s to those risks, the defendant has no duty to protect the plaintiff."[4]

Instruction 7 stated, "Your verdict must be for the defendant if you believe that the conditions that plaintiff encountered on defendant's ski slope on the day of the occurrence were a risk inherent in the sport of skiing." Bennett contends that the instruction misstated Missouri law because it did not require the jury to find that she had knowledge of, and appreciated, the specific dangers causing her injury. Hidden Valley argues on the other hand that under Missouri law, a plaintiff assumes any risk inherent in a sport regardless of her actual knowledge of the risk.

In a diversity case such as this we must follow state law as announced by the highest court in the state. The Supreme Court of Missouri has explained that a participant in sport "accept[s] ... those [hazards] that reasonably inhere in the sport so far as they are obvious and usually incident to the game." It has thus prevented a spectator injured by a foul ball at a baseball game from proceeding beyond the summary judgment stage, for

> [t]his risk [of being struck by a foul ball] is a necessary and inherent part of the game.... [It] is assumed by the spectators because it remains after due care has been exercised and is not the result of negligence on the part of the baseball club.

Anderson v. Kansas City Baseball Club, 231 S.W.2d 170, 173 (Mo.1950). Whether the plaintiff had subjective knowledge of the risk of being injured by a foul ball was immaterial. The risk assumed by a spectator was described in this way in [another Missouri Supreme Court case]:

> The patron ... subjects himself to the dangers necessarily and usually incident to and inherent in the game. This does not mean that he "assumes the risk" of being injured by the proprietor's negligence but that by voluntarily entering into the sport as a spectator he knowingly accepts the reasonable risks and hazards inherent in and incident to the game.

Hudson v. Kansas City Baseball Club, Inc., 349 Mo. 1215, 164 S.W.2d 318, 323 (1942). These cases show that the Missouri Supreme Court has

this case. Express assumption of risk "occurs when the plaintiff expressly agrees in advance that the defendant owes him no duty," and both parties agree that Bennett made no such agreement. Implied secondary assumption of risk "occurs when the defendant owes a duty of care to the plaintiff but the plaintiff knowingly proceeds to encounter a known risk imposed by the defendant's breach of duty." Hidden Valley did not claim that Bennett knowingly proceeded to encounter the particular risks; it thus did not raise a defense of implied assumption of risk in the secondary sense.

4. Because the doctrine of implied primary assumption of risk focuses on whether the defendant owed a duty to the plaintiff with respect to the risk in question, it is not strictly an affirmative defense. * * *

analyzed implied primary assumption of risk by focusing on whether the risk was incident to or inherent in the activity undertaken by the plaintiff, rather than on the plaintiff's subjective knowledge of the risk.

The lower courts in Missouri have generally taken the same approach. For example, injury to a professional hockey player was held not actionable because it was "part of the game of professional hockey." Similarly, a golf spectator injured by a rock hidden in the grass "assumed the risks ordinarily incident to watching such a match and to walking over the course." "Falling and colliding with other skaters is not an extraordinary occurrence for those indulging in that form of exercise. One who skates assumes those risks.... " "[P]ersons participating in sports may be held to have consented, by their participation, to those injuries which are reasonably foreseeable consequences of participating in the competition."

* * *

Bennett points to language in several Missouri cases to support her position that Hidden Valley had to show she knew that she might encounter conditions like those existing on the night she was injured. She cites Ross v. Clouser, a case in which a third basemen was injured by a sliding baserunner. 637 S.W.2d 11, 13 (Mo.1982) (en banc) (reversing a judgment notwithstanding the verdict which had been granted on the basis that the plaintiff had assumed the risk). Although the Missouri Supreme Court said in Ross that assumption of risk "bars recovery when plaintiff comprehended the actual danger and intelligently acquiesced in it," the court appeared to be speaking about implied secondary assumption of risk. * * *

* * *

We conclude that under Missouri law, a voluntary skier assumes the risks inherent in or incidental to skiing, regardless of her subjective knowledge of those risks. This principle can also be put in terms of duty: the proprietor of a ski area has no duty to protect a skier from those risks inherent in or incidental to skiing. Implied primary assumption of risk does not of course relieve a defendant of liability for negligence, because inherent risks "are not those created by a defendant's negligence but rather by the nature of the activity itself." By directing the jury to find for Hidden Valley if it determined that the conditions on the ski slope at the time Bennett was injured were inherent risks of skiing, Instruction 7 fairly and adequately submitted the issue to the jury. The district court therefore did not abuse its discretion by giving this charge.

* * *

[Affirmed.]

Notes

1. *The inherent risks of sports and recreational activities. Bennett* is one of a number of recent cases standing for the proposition that the organizers

of and participants in recreational and sports activities have no duty to guard against or warn of risks that are inherent in the activity. Other cases applying this rule include Knight v. Jewett, 3 Cal.4th 296, 11 Cal.Rptr.2d 2, 834 P.2d 696 (1992) (female player in impromptu touch football game injured by male coparticipant); Benejam v. Detroit Tigers, Inc., 246 Mich. App. 645, 635 N.W.2d 219 (2001) (baseball spectator struck by fragment of bat); Moser v. Ratinoff, 105 Cal.App.4th 1211, 130 Cal.Rptr.2d 198 (2003) (bicycle wreck during organized long–distance race).

A number of other recent cases achieve the same effect by holding that the duty owed by sports participants to one another is only to avoid intentional or reckless injury. See, e.g., Jaworski v. Kiernan, 241 Conn. 399, 696 A.2d 332 (1997) (female soccer player injured by male player); Crawn v. Campo, 136 N.J. 494, 643 A.2d 600 (1994) (base runner in softball game ran over catcher); Mark v. Moser, 746 N.E.2d 410 (Ind.App. 2001) (bicycle wreck during triathlon). For a good discussion of why the inherent–risk formulation is a better expression of the governing principle in this area than the avoidance–of–intentional–or–reckless–injury expression, see Phi Delta Theta Co. v. Moore, 10 S.W.3d 658 (Tex. 1999) (Enoch, J., dissenting from writ denial). (Recall that Overall v. Kadella, supra p. 51, expresses this same principle in treating the scope of the consent that a sports participant is deemed to confer on his fellow players.)

A few courts have laid down quite specific no–duty rules for particular recurrent types of sports injuries. See, e.g., *Benejam*, supra (specifying rules for designing baseball parks); Nemarnik v. Los Angeles Kings Hockey Club, L.P., 103 Cal.App.4th 631, 127 Cal.Rptr.2d 10 (2002) (similar essay re hockey arenas).

All of these cases manifest the basic inherent–risk principle. Almost all of them are in accord with *Bennett* in making it clear that the particular victim's extent of knowledge is irrelevant. This is true even though many, like *Bennett*, have chosen to name this rule implied primary assumption of risk. The term is potentially confusing, because its baggage includes a lot of victim–specific language about knowledge and consent.

The implied primary assumption of risk terminology is potentially confusing also because it may imply that the rule is an affirmative defense. The *Bennett* court is probably right in saying that it isn't. It may be too early to say for sure, but plaintiffs should be aware that they probably have the burden of proof on the issues of whether the particular activity is in the sports–and–recreation category so as to fall under the rule and on whether the injury in suit arose from an inherent risk of the activity.

The inherent risk concept is reasonably coherent: the inherent risks of an activity are those that are permitted by the rules, customs, and mores of the activity. Another way to say this is that a risk is inherent in a sport if its elimination would chill vigorous participation in the sport or alter the fundamental nature of the activity. Sanchez v. Hillerich & Bradsby Co., 104 Cal.App.4th 703, 128 Cal.Rptr.2d 529 (2002), applied this test in concluding that the manufacturer of a hollow aluminum baseball bat with a pressurized air bladder was not entitled to summary judgment in an action by a pitcher who was struck by a line drive traveling at more than 100 m.p.h. Noting that the bat's inventor had himself complained to the company that it was too dangerous, the court decided that this particular risk was not inherent to college baseball.

The coverage of the inherent–risk rule—the concept of sports and recreational activities—is less coherent at present. A number of older cases applied the inherent–risk rule (though without calling it that) to amusement park rides, fun houses, etc. See, e.g., Murphy v. Steeplechase Amusement Co., 250 N.Y. 479, 166 N.E. 173 (1929). Van Guilder v. Collier, 248 Mich. App. 633, 650 N.W.2d 340 (2001), held that driving together in off–road recreational vehicles did not come within the rule; each driver owed the other a duty of reasonable care. Perhaps the better label here is not sports and recreational activities but activities entailing elements of desirable danger.

2. *The primary/secondary distinction.* In the pre–comparative fault era, courts had no reason to draw a distinction between cases in which the plaintiff's recovery was defeated because the risk was inherent in the activity and those in which the plaintiff should lose because she (individually and subjectively) knew and voluntarily undertook the particular risk The *Bennett* court gleaned that distinction from a line of state–court decisions that had not expressed it. This was appropriate and necessary judicial activity in the ongoing development of tort law, but some might question whether a federal court—which has a constitutional obligation to follow the law as laid down by the state's legislature or highest court[2]—should be the first to "discover" such a distinction.[3]

3. *Implied secondary assumption of risk.* The affirmative defense of implied assumption of risk as an absolute bar to recovery was developed in the late nineteenth and early twentieth centuries. The doctrine was complex and controversial. See, *e.g.,* James, Assumption of Risk, 61 Yale L.J. 141 (1952); Keeton, Assumption of Risk and the Landowner, 20 Tex.L.Rev. 562, (1942). It was developed first in the context of employees impliedly assuming the risks inherent in their jobs,[4] but was then expanded to non–employment situations. The doctrine was sometimes called "implied assumption of risk" and sometimes called *volenti non fit injuria.*

Courts spent a great deal of time and energy determining whether a plaintiff was actually aware of a risk and whether a plaintiff voluntarily undertook it. See, e.g., Meese v. Brigham Young University, 639 P.2d 720

---

2. See Erie R. Co. v. Tompkins, 304 U.S. 64, 58 S.Ct. 817, 82 L.Ed. 1188 (1938).

3. Cf. Carlson v. Hyundai, supra p. 403, 164 F.3d at 1164 (Heaney, J., dissenting and criticizing the majority's interpretation of Minnesota law as "entirely inappropriate").

4. Tort actions by injured workers against their employers were bedeviled by what has been called the "unholy trinity" of a vigorous contributory negligence defense, the assumed risk defense, and the fellow servant rule. (Dobbs, The Law of Torts § 211, p. 538 (2000), conceptualizes the fellow servant rule as a subset of the assumed risk rule, but the more usual conceptualization treats "[t]he fellow servant doctrine [as] an exception to the common law rule of *respondeat superior*, which holds an employer liable for the torts of an employee committed within the scope of employment." Glass v. City of Chattanooga, 858 S.W.2d 312, 313 (Tenn. 1993) (abolishing the fellow servant rule).) These defenses were so effective in cutting injured workers out of the protections of negligence law that—in a movement that began in Germany and England in the late 19th century—legislatures began enacting workers' compensation statutes. See Epstein, The Historical Origin and Economic Structure of Workers' Compensation Law, 16 Ga.L.Rev. 775 (1982).

(Utah 1981) (knowledge of risk); Cincinnati, New Orleans & Texas Pacific Railway Co. v. Thompson, 236 Fed. 1 (6th Cir.1916) (knowledge of risk); Harrington v. Collins, 298 N.C. 535, 259 S.E.2d 275 (1979) (voluntarily assumed); Marshall v. Ranne, 511 S.W.2d 255 (1974) (voluntarily assumed).

After the advent of comparative negligence, many legislatures and courts abolished the affirmative defense of voluntary assumption of risk—we have now learned to call it implied secondary assumption of risk. See, *e.g.,* N.Y.Civ.Prac.Law. § 1411, supra p. 381; Ark.Stat. § 16–64–122(d), supra p. 382; Murray v. Ramada Inns, Inc., 521 So.2d 1123 (La.1988); Duncan v. Cessna Aircraft Co., 665 S.W.2d 414 (Tex.1984). The abolitions are expressed in various ways—the Restatement (Third) of Torts: Apportionment of Liability § 3, cmt. *c* (2000) would abolish both the defense and the term—but the basic idea is that a plaintiff's knowledge of the risk and voluntary conduct in encountering it are no longer a suitable basis for barring recovery but rather are appropriately factored into the questions of whether, and by how much, the plaintiff's conduct was substandard. The opinion in Perez v. McConkey, 872 S.W.2d 897, 903 (Tenn. 1994), is a thorough survey of the history and current jurisprudence of the assumed risk doctrine, concluding that only five states that have adopted comparative fault still retain the old total–bar assumed risk defense (listing Georgia, Nebraska, Mississippi, Rhode Island, and South Dakota).

In the states that retain the total–bar contributory negligence defense, retention of a largely duplicative total–bar assumed risk defense entails no internal dissonance and no confusion: those states just take a different view of victim fault than everybody else. But the law in the handful of states that have both a comparative fault rule and a total–bar affirmative defense of assumed risk is confusingly different from the law of the other comparative fault states in two respects. First, in those states a defendant who can prove that the plaintiff subjectively knew about and voluntarily encountered the exact risk that befell her will owe no damages, regardless of how reasonable it might have been for the plaintiff to run the risk (whereas in the other states, plaintiffs do not have their recoveries barred or even diminished unless their conduct is unreasonable). Probably this difference is mostly or wholly theoretical, because it is so easy for a court to shift the ostensible determination of whether the encounter was voluntary into an inquiry into whether it was reasonable. See, e.g., Pettry v. Rapid City Area School Dist., 630 N.W.2d 705, 709 (S.D.2001) (reversing summary judgment against a woman who fell while walking on a dark icy parking lot—she knew it was dark, and she knew it was icy, and she went there on purpose—because this might have been a "reasonable selection" of a route to her car).

The second unusual characteristic of the law of the assumed–risk states is that a plaintiff's knowing, voluntary, and unreasonable encounter with a risk can bar recovery whereas an otherwise identical encounter by a less discerning person will only diminish recovery (unless the victim in the second case is assessed with a fault percentage above the state's cut–off). Some analysts believe that such a distinction can sometimes make sense. See generally Simons, Reflections on Assumption of Risk, 50 U.C.L.A.L.Rev. 481 (2002). But the relative simplicity of the prevailing viewpoint seems preferable.

4. *Summarizing the prevailing viewpoint:* (a) A no–duty doctrine (of perhaps uncertain scope) protects the organizers of and participants in a sporting or recreational activity from liability for injuries resulting from risks that are inherent in the activity. Some courts think it is all right to call this doctrine implied primary assumption of risk, and some don't. (b) The fact that the plaintiff knowingly and voluntarily ran the risk that eventuated in harm does not itself justify barring recovery. If it was unreasonable to run the risk, the plaintiff's recovery should be diminished or barred under the applicable comparative–fault principles.

E. IMPUTED CONTRIBUTORY FAULT

Chapter VII addressed the issue of when a *defendant* will be charged with the legal effects of someone else's fault under the doctrine of vicarious liability. This section addresses the issue of when the *plaintiff* will be charged with the legal effects of someone else's fault. The question is this: In a tort action in which P seeks damages from D, under what circumstances will X's fault be attributed to P? The modern law answers this question affirmatively for only two types of cases: (a) cases in which the relationship between P and X is such that P would be vicariously liable for the damaging effects of X's fault; and (b) cases in which P's suit against D may be said to be somehow "derivative" of X's potential rights against D.

The Restatement (Third) of Torts: Apportionment of Liability (2000) treats the first group of cases in Section 5, providing:

The negligence of another person is imputed to a plaintiff whenever the negligence of the other person would have been imputed had the plaintiff been a defendant, except the negligence of another person is not imputed to a plaintiff solely because of the plaintiff's ownership of a motor vehicle or permission for its use by the other person.

Comment *b* then amplifies the basic rule:

This section adopts the so–called "both ways" rule. When a party would be responsible as a defendant for the negligence of a third person, the negligence of the third person is imputed to the party as a plaintiff. For example, when an employer would be vicariously liable for the negligence of an employee, the employee's negligence is imputed to the employer as a plaintiff. When a party would be vicariously liable for the negligence of an independent contractor, the independent contractor's negligence is imputed to the party as a plaintiff. When a member of a joint enterprise would be vicariously liable for the negligence of another member, the other member's negligence is imputed to the first member as a plaintiff.

Correlatively, when a party would not be responsible as a defendant for the negligence of a third person, the negligence of the third person is not imputed to the party as a plaintiff. Thus, the negligence of one spouse is not, on that basis alone, imputed to the other spouse. The negligence of a parent is not, on that basis alone, imputed to a child. The negligence of a child is not, on that basis alone, imputed to a parent.

Comment *c* then articulates the motor vehicle exception to the basic rule:

In some jurisdictions an owner of a motor vehicle is vicariously liable for the negligence of a person operating the vehicle. In such a jurisdiction, the negligence of the operator is not, for that reason alone, imputed to the owner as plaintiff.

CONTINENTAL AUTO LEASE CORPORATION v. CAMPBELL

Court of Appeals of New York, 1967.
19 N.Y.2d 350, 280 N.Y.S.2d 123, 227 N.E.2d 28.

KEATING, JUDGE.

Continental Auto Lease Corporation is engaged in the auto rental business. It sued Ralph B. Shepard for damage to its automobile as the result of an accident. Shepard died after the action was commenced and his administratrix, Doris B. Campbell, was substituted as defendant.

Continental leased the automobile to one Kamman for a four–day period for a fixed sum plus a charge for mileage. During the rental period, Kamman was involved in an accident with an automobile driven by Shepard. Upon the trial, the jury found both drivers negligent, but returned a verdict for Continental, as directed by the trial court. Judgment was entered accordingly, and affirmed, on appeal, by the Appellate Division, Fourth Department.

The question presented is whether the negligence of Kamman, the operator of Continental's automobile, is imputable to Continental so that it is barred by contributory negligence from recovery against Shepard.

At the outset, it should be noted that there is a distinction between imputed negligence and imputed contributory negligence. The effect of imputed negligence is to widen liability; the effect of imputed contributory negligence, to narrow it. Section 388 of the Vehicle and Traffic Law, Consol.Laws, c. 71 [provides in pertinent part:

Every owner of a vehicle used or operated in this state shall be liable and responsible for death or injuries to person or property resulting from negligence in the use or operation of such vehicle, in the business of such owner or otherwise, by any person using or operating the same with the permission, express or implied, of such owner.]

[This provision] imputes to the owner of a motor vehicle the negligence of one who uses or operates it with his permission for the purpose of imposing on the owner liability to an injured third party. This enactment expresses the policy that one injured by the negligent operation of a motor vehicle should have recourse to a financially responsible defendant. The owner of the automobile is the obvious candidate, for he can most easily carry insurance to cover the risk.

This policy—broadened liability for the protection of the injured plaintiff—gives no support to the doctrine of imputed contributory negligence, which narrows the liability of a negligent defendant to a plaintiff innocent of actual negligence. Mills v. Gabriel, 284 N.Y. 755, 31 N.E.2d 512 [1940], is the leading case refusing to impute contributory negligence to an absentee owner. In that case an action was brought to recover damages for injury to plaintiff's automobile sustained in a collision between such automobile, driven with [plaintiff's] permission but in her absence, and an automobile owned and driven by defendant. It was conceded that both operators were negligent, and that the operator of plaintiff's automobile was using it for his own private purpose and not for the benefit or on the business of the plaintiff. On those facts, we held that former section 59 of the Vehicle and Traffic Law [which was identical to section 388] was no bar to plaintiff's common–law right of recovery.

In contrast, in Gochee v. Wagner, 257 N.Y. 344, 178 N.E. 553 [1931], we held, on a different fact pattern, that the owner of the vehicle was barred by imputed contributory negligence. There, the accident occurred while the car was driven by plaintiff's wife, with his permission, while plaintiff was sitting in the rear seat. His wife was found negligent in her operation of plaintiff's car. We held for defendant, reasoning that: "When the respondent entered the car, he regained dominion over it * * *. It was respondent's car, he was present and had the legal right to control its operation, and the negligent conduct of the driver was imputable to him. The mere fact that he chose to sit on the rear seat and refrained from directing its operation did not change his rights or limit his liability."

Gochee v. Wagner (supra) makes it clear that the touchstone of imputed contributory negligence is the existence of a relationship between the owner of the vehicle and the operator such that the operator of the vehicle is subject to the owner's control. Such control need not be actually exercised—it can be inferred, as in *Gochee,* when the owner is physically present in the car. Likewise, the requisite degree of control might be found in the master–servant or principal–agent relationship when the physical operation of the vehicle is for the benefit of the owner.

Defendant urges that Continental should be barred from recovery because it was benefiting financially under the terms of the lease for each mile that the car was driven, and that this "benefit" distinguishes the present case from the gratuitous bailment involved in Mills v. Gabriel (supra). The mere fact that the bailment was commercial rather than gratuitous is not sufficient ground for denying to a plaintiff, guilty of no actual negligence, the right to recover his damages from a negligent defendant. If a car owner's relationship to the driver of his car is such that a degree of physical control over the driver can reasonably be deemed to exist, under Gochee v. Wagner (supra) the negligence of the driver can be imputed to the owner to bar the owner's recovery against a negligent third party. But Continental had no interest in where or when the vehicle was driven and no relationship to Kamman consistent with the inference that it had the right to control in any manner Kamman's conduct as a driver. Accordingly, Kamman's negligence should not be imputed to Continental to bar its recovery in this action.

The order of the Appellate Division should be affirmed, with costs.

Notes

1. *The "both ways" rule.* At one time the common law imputed contributory fault on the basis of relationships that would not have supported fault–attribution for purposes of vicarious liability. See, e.g., Thorogood v. Bryan, [1849] 8 C.B. 115, 137 Eng.Rep. 452 (imputing the negligence of a coach driver to the passengers so as to bar their recovery against the negligent operator of another vehicle). The "both ways" articulation arose in the modern cases repudiating the old broad imputation–to–plaintiff rule and insisting that relationships that cannot support vicarious liability cannot support imputation. See, *e.g.,* Rollins Leasing Corp. v. Barkley, 531 S.W.2d 603 (Tex.1975) (bailee's contributory fault will no longer affect bailor's property damage recovery).

2. *The motor vehicle exception to the both ways rule.* As the *Continental* case suggests, if the policy that supports vicarious liability in a particular relationship is wholly inapposite to the contributory fault issue, fault need not be imputed to the plaintiff even if it would have been imputed to that party as defendant. The *Continental* holding is consistent with decisions in other states. In McMartin v. Saemisch, 254 Iowa 45, 116 N.W.2d 491 (1962), the plaintiff sued another motorist for damage the plaintiff's automobile incurred while being driven by the plaintiff's wife. The defendant argued that the wife's negligent driving should bar recovery, invoking an old "family purpose" doctrine under which husbands had been held vicariously liable for and barred by wives' negligence in similar situations in previous cases. Rejecting the defendant's argument, the court held that the family purpose doctrine had been replaced by Iowa Code § 321.493, which provides in pertinent part that "in all cases where damage is done by any motor vehicle by reason of negligence of the driver, and driven with the consent of the owner, the owner of the motor vehicle shall be liable for such damage." The court further held that the statute did not provide for imputation of the driver's negligence to the owner as plaintiff.

The *Continental* result is also consistent with the Restatement (Third)'s Section 5, quoted in the introductory note to this section. But is it sustainable under the controlling New York statute (quoted in the fourth paragraph of the opinion)?

3. *The effect of imputation.* When the situation calls for charging someone else's fault to the plaintiff, the legal effect is the same as if the fault were plaintiff's own. Thus, in the contributory negligence era imputed contributory fault barred recovery. Today in comparative–fault jurisdictions it reduces recovery on a comparative fault basis and bars recovery only when the fault assigned to the plaintiff—which might consist of his own plus any

that is properly imputed to him—takes the plaintiff over the particular jurisdiction's limit. (In this connection, see the next case.)

4. Imputation in derivative–claim situations. The Restatement (Third) of Apportionment treats these cases in Section 6, which provides:

> (a) When a plaintiff asserts a claim that derives from the defendant's tort against a third person, negligence of the third person is imputed to the plaintiff with respect to that claim. The plaintiff's recovery is also reduced by the plaintiff's own negligence.

> (b) The negligence of an estate's decedent affects the estate's recovery under a survival statute to the same extent that it would have affected the decedent's recovery had the decedent survived. The negligence of a beneficiary of the decedent's estate is not imputed to the estate merely because of the beneficiary's status as a beneficiary.

The comments go on to explain that the principal categories of derivative–claim situations are wrongful death and survival actions, claims for consortium, and what we have called "uninjured bystander" or Dillon v. Legg claims (see Chapter VI, Section D, p. 243).[1]

WHITE v. LUNDER

Supreme Court of Wisconsin, 1975.
66 Wis.2d 563, 225 N.W.2d 442.

BEILFUSS, JUSTICE.

[Rosemary White was hurt in a boating mishap involving herself, her husband Lloyd, and defendant James Lunder. She sued Lunder for her personal injuries, and her husband sued for loss of consortium and medical expenses. The jury apportioned causal negligence among the parties thus: Rosemary White, 30%; Lloyd White, 33%; Lunder, 37%.

The Wisconsin comparative negligence statute provided:

Contributory negligence shall not bar recovery in an action by any person or his legal representative to recover damages for negligence resulting in death or in injury to person or property, if such negligence was not as great as the negligence of the person against whom recovery is sought, but any damages allowed shall be diminished in the proportion to the amount of negligence attributable to the person recovering.

The trial judge determined that the statute called for charging Lloyd White with 63% of the causal negligence and accordingly denied recovery to him. He appealed.]

The issues are:

1.   Where wife sustains bodily injury by reason of causal negligence of herself, her husband, and a third party, is the negligence of the spouses combined for purposes of comparing negligence with

---

1. As the Reporters' Note to § 6 acknowledges, putting Dillon v. Legg cases on the derivative–claim list is an educated guess. There are very few cases addressing the point, and they are divided.

that of the third party and thereby determining whether husband recovers for medical expenses and for loss of consortium?

2. Where wife sustains bodily injury, are her husband's causes of action for medical expenses and for loss of consortium both derivative actions?

The issues are discussed together here because they are closely related and involve basically the same principles. * * *

* * *

[T]he question of whether a spouse's cause of action for loss of consortium arising in personal injury actions is derivative is not clearly settled and the cases are confusing.

We deem it appropriate to declare, for the purpose of applying our comparative negligence statute, that both the causes of action for medical expenses and loss of consortium shall be deemed derivative; and that the causal negligence of the injured spouse shall bar or limit the recovery of the claiming spouse pursuant to the terms of the comparative negligence statute.

To declare both of these causes of action derivative might not be entirely logical but in our opinion does little violence to the prior expressions of this court and serves to simplify the rule in applying the comparative negligence statute.

To allow no recovery to the husband where, as here, the third party tortfeasor was more causally negligent than he, not only seems to be unjust but is not entirely consistent with our comparative negligence statute. It prohibits partial recovery only when the negligence of the claimant was equal to or greater than the person against whom the claim was made. ([It] was amended in 1971 to prohibit recovery only when causal negligence of the claimant is greater than the person against whom he seeks recovery. [The amendment was not applicable in this case, which arose in 1970.])

Likewise, it seems unjust for the husband to collect damages upon a formula that disregards either his causal negligence or that of his injured wife.

The comparative negligence statute does not by its terms specifically contemplate its effect in a situation like this where both spouses are causally negligent.

A workable construction, consistent with the statute, that will allow recovery in derivative actions where the causal negligence of the person against whom recovery is sought is greater than either the husband or wife can be accomplished by reducing the entire award for both medical expenses and loss of consortium by the percentage of negligence attributed to the injured spouse (here Rosemary White's 30 percent); and further reducing the entire award by the percentage of causal negligence attributable to the claiming spouse (here Lloyd White's 33 percent). By this method the person who was found to have been causally negligent in greatest degree cannot escape all liability but his liability is decreased by an amount proportionate to the two other tortfeasors.

By way of illustration, if the amount awarded for medical expenses and claimed by the husband was $5,000, the $5,000 would be reduced by 30 percent because it was a derivative claim and the injured spouse was 30 percent negligent. This reduction would be $1,500. The claimant husband's causal negligence also contributed 33 percent of the entire award. Therefore the entire award, namely, the $5,000 should be again reduced by 33 percent or $1,650. The total of these two deductions is $3,150; it is also 63 percent of the total causal negligence * * *. The husband's recovery in this hypothetical would be $1,850. Loss of consortium should be calculated upon the same basis.

If the causal negligence of the claiming spouse is greater than the person against whom the claim is made, he should be denied recovery because of the comparative negligence statute. Likewise, if the causal negligence of the injured spouse is greater than that of the person against whom recovery is sought, the claiming spouse should be denied recovery because his action is derivative.

Judgment reversed with directions to enter judgment consistent with this opinion on behalf of the plaintiff–appellant Lloyd White.

Notes

1. *A bias against using imputed negligence to bar recovery?* In the "both ways" context, the court in *Campbell* arguably took some liberties with a statute in order to avoid charging Continental with Kamman's negligence. In the derivative–claims context, cases from the contributory negligence era show courts similarly struggling to avoid imputation. See, e.g., Handeland v. Brown, 216 N.W.2d 574 (Iowa 1974) (refusing to impute minor child's negligence to father in father's action under a statute allowing parents to recover "for the expense and actual loss of services, companionship and society resulting from injury to or death of a minor child"). Plainly courts do not like the idea of barring a plaintiff entirely because of imputed fault. This disinclination probably explains the *White* court's creative reading of the Wisconsin comparative negligence statute. Did the court do any violence to the statutory language? Could the court's result have been achieved under a statute like the following (hypothetical) provision?

> Contributory negligence attributable to the plaintiff shall not bar recovery in an action by any person or his legal representative to recover damages for negligence resulting in death or in injury to person or property, if such contributory negligence attributable to the plaintiff was not as great as the negligence of the person against whom recovery is sought, but any damages allowed shall be diminished in proportion to the amount of contributory negligence attributable to the plaintiff.

2. *No imputation "inter se."* "The great weight of authority confines the doctrine of imputed negligence to claims against someone who is an outsider [to the relationship that gives rise to imputation.]" Webber v. Sobba, 322 F.3d 1032, 1036 (8th Cir. 2003) (holding that a joint enterprise doctrine would support imputing a host driver's negligence to a passenger in

the passenger's suit against another negligent motorist but not in the passenger's action against the host driver).

The rule quoted from *Webber* is very well settled. Thus, Yetsko v. Panure, 272 Kan. 741, 35 P.3d 904 (2001), seems hard to justify. In that case, Jonathan Panure, a licensed driver under the age of 16, was driving his mother's car with his mother as passenger. Jonathan's negligent driving, combined with that of another motorist, caused a collision that injured the mother. A Kansas statute provided:

> Every owner of a motor vehicle causing or knowingly permitting a minor under the age of sixteen years to drive such vehicle upon a highway, and any person who gives or furnishes a motor vehicle to such minor, shall be jointly and severally liable with such minor for any damages caused by the negligence of such minor in driving such vehicle.

Note that under the approach taken by the Restatement (Third), this statute would not support imputed contributing negligence at all; even in an action by the mother against the other motorist, Jonathan's negligence would not–at least not necessarily—have been charged against her. And certainly there is nothing in the statutory language suggesting that Jonathan's negligence would be attributed to the mother in an action brought by her against him.

But the *Yetsko* court saw the matter differently. The mother's injuries were fatal. Her other children brought a wrongful death action against Jonathan. The court reasoned as follows: (a) In a wrongful death action, the decedent's negligence is imputed to the plaintiff(s). This was in accordance with settled law. (b) Under the quoted statute, Jonathan's negligence is imputed to the decedent. This, as we have seen, is an exceedingly unusual ruling. (c) Therefore, there cannot possibly be any recovery; Jonathan is the only defendant; and any negligence proved against him will automatically be charged back against the plaintiffs, which necessarily "cancels any recovery."

Chapter X

OTHER AFFIRMATIVE DEFENSES

A. STATUTES OF LIMITATIONS

Statutes of limitations are not peculiar to tort law, of course; all causes of action are subject to them. This chapter treats only aspects of the subject that have special application to tort cases.

JOLLY v. ELI LILLY & CO.

Supreme Court of California, 1988.
44 Cal.3d 1103, 245 Cal.Rptr. 658, 751 P.2d 923.

PANELLI, JUSTICE.

* * *

Plaintiff Jolly was born in 1951. In 1972, she first learned that while she was *in utero* her mother had ingested the synthetic drug estrogen diethylstilbestrol (DES) for the prevention of miscarriage. Plaintiff was told in 1972 that DES daughters could suffer injuries. Therefore, she went to a DES clinic at the UCLA Medical Center for a check–up. She was diagnosed as having adenosis, a precancerous condition that required careful monitoring. In 1976, she had an abnormal pap smear and underwent a dilation and curettage, a surgical procedure to remove abnormal tissue. In 1978, plaintiff underwent a complete hysterectomy and a partial vaginectomy in order to remove malignancy. As of 1972, plaintiff was aware, or at least suspected, that her condition was a result of her mother's ingestion of DES during pregnancy.

Starting in 1972, plaintiff attempted to discover the manufacturer of the DES ingested by her mother. Efforts were increased in 1976 and 1978 when plaintiff's condition became acute. Unfortunately, the doctor who prescribed the drug had died, and plaintiff was unable to locate his records. Although the dispensing pharmacist did remember filling the DES prescription, he did not recall or have records pertaining to the specific brand used. * * *

In March 1980, we decided Sindell v. Abbott Laboratories, 26 Cal.3d 588, 163 Cal.Rptr. 132, 607 P.2d 924, and held that if a plaintiff could not identify the precise drug manufacturer of the ingested DES, she could state a cause of action against the DES manufacturers of a substantial percentage of the market share of the drug. Defendants would be liable, assuming the remaining material allegations in the complaint were proven, unless they could disprove their involvement. Almost one year after *Sindell,* plaintiff Jolly brought this action.

Defendants moved for summary judgment, asserting that the action [filed in 1981] was barred by Code of Civil Procedure section 340, subdivision (3), setting forth a one–year statute of limitations period for an action "for injury * * * caused by the wrongful act or neglect of another." Although conceding the applicability of the one–year statutory period, plaintiff denied that the suit was time–barred. She asserted that the statute did not commence until she learned of the *Sindell* decision, because only then did she realize that she would be able to successfully bring her claim.

* * *

[B]oth sides agree that the one–year limitations period of section 340, subdivision (3) applies to this case. Both sides also agree that the common law rule, that an action accrues on the date of injury applies only as modified by the "discovery rule." The discovery rule provides that the accrual date of a cause of action is delayed until the plaintiff is aware of her injury and its negligent cause.[4] A plaintiff is held to her actual knowledge as well as knowledge that could reasonably be discovered through investigation of sources open to her. The parties differ as to what constitutes sufficient knowledge to start the statute running.

The Court of Appeal applied Kensinger v. Abbott Laboratories, Inc., 171 Cal.App.3d 376, 217 Cal.Rptr. 313 (1985), a factually similar case, and found that it was a question of fact as to whether the statute of limitations began to run more than one year before plaintiff Jolly filed her complaint. The *Kensinger* court acknowledged the well established rule that ignorance of the legal significance of known facts or the identity of the defendant would not delay the running of the statute— only ignorance of one or more "critical facts" could have that effect.

However, the key point in *Kensinger* was its determination that one "critical fact" was knowledge of some wrongful conduct. Specifically, the court held that a plaintiff may have "no knowledge of facts indicating wrongdoing by a particular defendant. In such a situation, litigation might be premature for lack of knowledge of any *factual basis* for imputing fault to a manufacturer rather than ignorance of supportive legal theories. * * * Knowledge of the occurrence and origin of harm

---

4. Defendants argue that the statute should commence when the plaintiff knows of her injury and its *factual* cause. Although that position has been adopted in some jurisdictions (see e.g., United States v. Kubrick (1979) 444 U.S. 111, 100 S.Ct. 352, 62 L.Ed.2d 259 [concerning the Federal Tort Claims Act]; Anthony v. Koppers Co., Inc. (1980) 284 Pa.Super. 81, 425 A.2d 428, 436, revd. on other grounds, (1981) 496 Pa. 119, 436 A.2d 181), it is not the rule in California. (See, e.g., Sanchez v. South Hoover Hospital (1976) 18 Cal.3d 93, 99, 132 Cal. Rptr. 657, 553 P.2d 1129; Gutierrez v. Mofid (1985) 39 Cal.3d 892, 896, 218 Cal.Rptr. 313, 705 P.2d 886.)

cannot necessarily be equated with knowledge of the factual basis for a legal remedy * * *." Accordingly, the *Kensinger* court held that the statutory clock did not begin to tick until the plaintiff knew or reasonably should have known of the facts constituting wrongful conduct, as well as the fact of her injury and its relation to DES. The Court of Appeal, applying *Kensinger*, held that it could not be said that "as a matter of law" Jolly was or should have been aware of *facts* establishing wrongdoing, e.g., "either failure to test or failure to warn," until within one year of the date she filed suit.

The rule proposed in *Kensinger* goes too far.[6] Under the discovery rule, the statute of limitations begins to run when the plaintiff suspects or should suspect that her injury was caused by wrongdoing, that someone has done something wrong to her. * * * A plaintiff need not be aware of the specific "facts" necessary to establish the claim; that is a process contemplated by pretrial discovery. Once the plaintiff has a suspicion of wrongdoing, and therefore an incentive to sue, she must decide whether to file suit or sit on her rights. So long as a suspicion exists, it is clear that the plaintiff must go find the facts; she cannot wait for the facts to find her.

* * *

The foregoing is fully consistent with the policy of deciding cases on the merits as well as the policies underlying the statute of limitations. [T]he fundamental purpose of the statute is to give defendants reasonable repose, that is, to protect parties from defending stale claims. A second policy underlying the statute is to require plaintiffs to diligently pursue their claims. Because a plaintiff is under a duty to reasonably investigate and because a *suspicion* of wrongdoing, coupled with a knowledge of the harm and its cause, will commence the limitations period, suits are not likely to be unreasonably delayed, and those failing to act with reasonable dispatch will be barred. At the same time, plaintiffs who file suit as soon as they have reason to believe that they are entitled to recourse will not be precluded.

While resolution of the statute of limitations issue is normally a question of fact, where the uncontradicted facts established through discovery are susceptible of only one legitimate inference, summary judgment is proper. In this case it is clear that application of the discovery rule supports the trial court's judgment. Plaintiff stated that as early as 1978 she was interested in "obtaining more information" about DES because she wanted to "make a claim"; she felt that someone had done something wrong to her concerning DES, that it was a defective drug and that she should be compensated. She points to no evidence contradicting her candid statements. Thus, plaintiff is held to

---

6. We recognize that some jurisdictions have adopted rules similar to that set out in *Kensinger*. (See, e.g., Anthony v. Abbott Laboratories (R.I.1985) 490 A.2d 43 (relied on in *Kensinger*); Dawson v. Eli Lilly & Co. (D.D.C.1982) 543 F.Supp. 1330; Lopez v. Swyer (1973) 62 N.J. 267, 300 A.2d 563.) However, as will be shown, the rule in California is otherwise.

her admission; she suspected that defendants' conduct was wrongful during 1978—well over a year before she filed suit. This suspicion would not have been allayed by any investigation. To the contrary, a timely investigation would have disclosed numerous articles concerning DES and many DES suits filed throughout the country alleging wrongdoing.

* * *

In sum, the limitations period begins when the plaintiff suspects, or should suspect, that she has been wronged. Here, plaintiff suspected as much no later than 1978. Because she did not file suit until 1981, her suit, unless otherwise saved, is time–barred.

III.   THE EFFECT OF SINDELL

Plaintiff's major argument, which was summarily rejected by the trial court and the Court of Appeal, is that our landmark decision in *Sindell*, constituted the "fact" that activated the statute. Plaintiff does not dispute the general rule that ignorance of the identity of the defendant does not affect the statute of limitations. However, she asserts that the rule does not apply to the facts of her case.

* * *

* * * *Sindell* did not provide plaintiff with the critical "fact" that started the limitations period. Nor did it create a new tort with an independent starting date for purposes of the statute of limitations. Rather, *Sindell* demonstrated the legal significance of facts already known to plaintiff. The statute had started to run for plaintiff well before *Sindell* was decided.

At a less legalistic but more fundamental level, plaintiff argues, with some persuasive force, that prior to *Sindell* she could not have prevailed on her suit. She notes that during the time that defendants argue her action would have been timely, McCreery v. Eli Lilly & Co., 87 Cal. App.3d 77, 150 Cal.Rptr. 730 (1978) (overruled by *Sindell),* effectively barred her claim. In *McCreery,* the Court of Appeal held that a plaintiff who could not identify the precise manufacturer of the pills ingested by her mother did not allege a cause of action. Plaintiff undoubtedly fell into this group. The response to plaintiff's contention is that a change in the law, either by statute or by case law, does not revive claims otherwise barred by the statute of limitations.

* * *

[This] rule may work a harsh result. Nonetheless, it is justified in three ways. First, the rule encourages people to bring suit to change a rule of law with which they disagree, fostering growth and preventing legal stagnation. Second, the statute of limitations is not solely a punishment for slow plaintiffs. It serves the important function of repose by allowing defendants to be free from stale litigation, especially in cases where evidence might be hard to gather due to the passage of time. Third, to hold otherwise would allow virtually unlimited litigation every time precedent changed. For example, in Li v. Yellow Cab Co. (1975) 13 Cal.3d 804, 119 Cal.Rptr. 858, 532 P.2d 1226, this court held that contributory negligence was not a total bar to recovery. There were undoubtedly thousands of potential plaintiffs through the years who had been reasonably advised to the contrary by competent counsel and so failed to bring suit. Nevertheless, allowing them all to sue within a year after the *Li* decision would have been untenable. Courts simply are not equipped to handle cases dating back many years, eventually brought because the law has changed. This prohibition against revival of claims can obviously create a hardship on such unfortunate plaintiffs (and a windfall to fortunate defendants). However, the hardship is no greater than that incurred by plaintiffs who received an adverse final judgment based on the "old" law and are barred from relitigating their case by res judicata.

* * *

Moreover, in early 1978, plaintiff's legal situation was not as dismal as it initially appears. First, she was in no worse a position than Judith Sindell, who ultimately prevailed in changing the law. Second, there were other, more traditional theories available on which plaintiff could base her lawsuit, such as civil conspiracy or joint liability under Summers v. Tice. While it is true that these theories were not clearly meritorious (indeed they were ultimately rejected by us in *Sindell*), they did provide plaintiff with a nonfrivolous cause of action. Although in the latter part of 1978 *McCreery* appeared to foreclose such a suit, that case was an intermediate appellate court decision. In this regard, the last word on the subject had not been spoken, and other Courts of Appeal were free to disregard that case. Therefore, plaintiff was not entirely forestalled, even as a practical matter, from bringing a timely suit.

Finally, even without using any of the above theories, plaintiff could have filed a timely complaint under [Cal. Code of Civ. Pro. § 474], which allows suit to be filed against a Doe party. From the time such a complaint is filed, the plaintiff has three years to identify and serve the defendant. Hence, in the instant case, plaintiff could have brought a timely Doe action, effectively enlarging the statute of limitations period for three years. Had she done so, her complaint would have been pending when *Sindell* was decided.

In sum, plaintiff's argument that *Sindell* created or revived her cause of action must fail.

* * *

Notes

1. The discovery rule, though widespread, is not universal. Some states apply it only in certain types of cases, such as product liability cases or medical malpractice cases involving foreign objects left in the patient's body. In its absence, the limitations period begins to run whenever the statute says it does, regardless of the plaintiff's knowledge at that time. The California

statute, as interpreted by the courts, begins to run on the date of injury; the injury to DES daughters occurred before birth. The limitations period usually is "tolled", i.e., does not run, until the victim becomes an adult. If the age of majority in California at the time was 18, the statute would have run on Jolly in 1969, before she even learned that her mother had taken DES. That is the kind of injustice the discovery rule is designed to prevent.

2. With or without a discovery rule, there are many disagreements as to when the limitations period begins to run. Some statutes say it begins to run "when the tort occurs" and some say "when a cause of action accrues." Courts usually interpret both of these to mean "when injury occurs," on the ground that neither a tort nor a cause of action exists until there is both a tortious act and an injury. See, e.g., Lo v. Burke, 249 Va. 311, 455 S.E.2d 9 (1995) (limitations period began to run when plaintiff's cyst became cancerous, not when physician negligently interpreted CAT scan).

3. Under the discovery rule, the question is "discover what?" In the principal case the court says the discovery rule delays the running of the limitations period "until the plaintiff is aware of her injury and its negligent cause," but that this occurs when the plaintiff suspects negligence, even if she does not yet have proof. As the opinion acknowledges, some courts say discovery does not occur until plaintiffs knows or should know *facts* establishing wrongdoing (see footnote 6). On the other hand, some courts say discovery occurs when the plaintiff knows the factual cause, even if she does not yet suspect that it is a negligent cause (see footnote 4).

FELTMEIER v. FELTMEIER

Supreme Court of Illinois 2003.
207 Ill.2d 263, 798 N.E.2d 75, 278 Ill.Dec. 228.

JUSTICE RARICK.

[Plaintiff, Lynn Feltmeier, and defendant, Robert Feltmeier, were married in 1986 and divorced in 1997. In 1999, Lynn sued Robert for intentional infliction of emotional distress. She alleged that he engaged in a pattern of physical and mental abuse which began shortly after the marriage and did not cease even after its dissolution. Lynn alleged that Robert struck and kicked her, prevented her from leaving the house, threw things at her, abused her verbally, and, after the divorce, stalked her.

[Robert moved to dismiss on the ground that the complaint failed to state a cause of action and was barred by the statute of limitations and the terms of the divorce settlement. The trial court denied the motion to dismiss but certified all three issues for interlocutory appeal. The appellate court affirmed and Robert appealed. On the first issue, the supreme court held that the conduct alleged was sufficiently extreme, and the alleged distress sufficiently severe, to state a cause of action for intentional infliction.]

The second certified question we examine is whether Lynn's claim for intentional infliction of emotional distress based on conduct prior to August 25, 1997, is barred by the applicable statute of limitations.

Robert contends that each separate act of abuse triggered a new statute of limitations so that "all claims by Lynn based upon incidents occurring prior to August 25, 1997," or more than two years before the date on which Lynn filed her complaint, would be time–barred. Lynn responds that Robert's actions constitute a "continuing tort" for purposes of the statute of limitations and that her complaint, filed within two years of the occurrence of the last such tortious act, is therefore timely. The appellate court majority agreed with Lynn.

* * * Generally, a limitations period begins to run when facts exist that authorize one party to maintain an action against another. However, under the "continuing tort" or "continuing violation" rule, "where a tort involves a continuing or repeated injury, the limitations period does not begin to run until the date of the last injury or the date the tortious acts cease."

At this juncture, we believe it important to note what does *not* constitute a continuing tort. A continuing violation or tort is occasioned by continuing unlawful acts and conduct, not by continual ill effects from an initial violation. Thus, where there is a single overt act from which subsequent damages may flow, the statute begins to run on the date the defendant invaded the plaintiff's interest and inflicted injury, and this is so despite the continuing nature of the injury. For example, in [Bank of Ravenswood, 307 Ill.App.3d at 168, 240 Ill.Dec. 385, 717 N.E.2d 478 (1999)] the appellate court rejected the plaintiffs' contention that the defendant city's construction of a subway tunnel under the plaintiff's property constituted a continuing trespass violation. The plaintiffs' cause of action arose at the time its interest was invaded, *i.e.*, during the period of the subway's construction, and the fact that the subway was present below ground would be a continual effect from the initial violation, but not a continual violation.

A continuing tort, therefore, does not involve tolling the statute of limitations because of delayed or continuing injuries, but instead involves viewing the defendant's conduct as a continuous whole for prescriptive purposes. Thus, in [City of Rock Falls v. Chicago Title & Trust Co., 13 Ill.App.3d at 364, 300 N.E.2d 331 (1973)], where the defendant city and its mayor had continuously engaged in various acts of tortious interference with the utilization of the plaintiff's property over a period of three years, the appellate court held that the violation of the plaintiff's rights was a continuing tort that did not cease until the date of the last injury or when the tortious acts ceased.

This court recently examined the issue of whether a continuing violation existed in Belleville Toyota, Inc. v. Toyota Motor Sales, U.S.A., Inc., 199 Ill.2d 325, 264 Ill.Dec. 283, 770 N.E.2d 177 (2002). There it was held that the continuing violation rule did not apply where the defendants' misconduct in the allocation of vehicles to the plaintiff did not constitute "one, continuing, unbroken, decade–long violation" of the Motor Vehicle Franchise Act. Rather, each individual allocation, made two to four times per month, was a separate violation of the Franchise

Act supporting a separate cause of action, because each allocation was the result of a discrete decision by the defendants "regarding the numerous adjustable parameters that drove the computerized allocation system." * * *

In the instant case, Robert cites *Belleville Toyota* and maintains that "each of the alleged acts of abuse inflicted by Robert upon Lynn over a 12 year period are separate and distinct incidents which give rise to separate and distinct causes of action, rather than one single, continuous, unbroken, violation or wrong which continued over the entire period of 12 years." We must disagree. While it is true that the conduct set forth in Lynn's complaint could be considered separate acts constituting separate offenses of, *inter alia,* assault, defamation and battery, Lynn has alleged, and we have found, that Robert's conduct *as a whole* states a cause of action for intentional infliction of emotional distress. * * *

As did the appellate court below, we find the case of Pavlik v. Kornhaber, 326 Ill.App.3d 731, 260 Ill.Dec. 331, 761 N.E.2d 175 (2001), to be instructive. In *Pavlik,* the court first found that plaintiff's complaint stated a cause of action for intentional infliction of emotional distress, where the defendant's persistent notes, sexually explicit comments, insistence on meetings to discuss his desire for sexual contact and lewd behavior in their employer–employee relationship were such that a reasonable person would perceive them to be sufficiently offensive and sinister to rise to the level of extreme and outrageous behavior. The court in *Pavlik* then found that the trial court had erred in dismissing the plaintiff's claim as untimely. While the defendant argued that his sexual advances took place outside the two–year statute of limitations for personal injury, the plaintiff had alleged an ongoing campaign of offensive and outrageous sexual pursuit that established a continuing series of tortious behavior, by the same actor, and of a similar nature, such that the limitations period did not commence until the last act occurred or the conduct abated.

We find the following passage, wherein the *Pavlik* court explains its reasons for applying the continuing tort rule to the plaintiff's action for intentional infliction of emotional distress, to be particularly cogent:

> Illinois courts have said that in many contexts, including employment, repetition of the behavior may be a critical factor in raising offensive acts to actionably outrageous ones. It may be the pattern, course and accumulation of acts that make the conduct sufficiently extreme to be actionable, whereas one instance of such behavior might not be. It would be logically inconsistent to say that each act must be independently actionable while at the same time asserting that often it is the cumulative nature of the acts that give rise to the intentional infliction of emotional distress. Likewise, we cannot say that cumulative continuous acts may be required to constitute the tort but that prescription runs from the date of the first act. Because it is impossible to pinpoint the specific moment when enough conduct has occurred to become actionable, the termination of the

conduct provides the most sensible place to begin the running of the prescriptive period.

* * *

We believe the appellate court herein properly applied this reasoning to the facts of this case where:

> The alleged domestic violence and abuse endured by Lynn * * * spanned the entire 11–year marriage. No one disputes that the allegations set forth the existence of ongoing abusive behavior. Lynn's psychologist, Dr. Michael E. Althoff, found that Lynn suffered from the 'battered wife syndrome.' He described the psychological process as one that unfolds over time. The process by which a spouse exerts coercive control is based upon 'a systematic, repetitive infliction of psychological trauma' designed to 'instill terror and helplessness.' Dr. Althoff indicated that the posttraumatic stress disorder from which Lynn suffered was the result of the entire series of abusive acts, not just the result of one specific incident.

* * *

Therefore, based upon the foregoing reasons, we agree with the appellate court herein, the court in *Pavlik,* and with the growing number of jurisdictions that have found that the continuing tort rule should be extended to apply in cases of intentional infliction of emotional distress.

We note, however, that embracing the concept of a continuing tort in the area of intentional infliction of emotional distress "does not throw open the doors to permit filing these actions at any time." As with any continuing tort, the statute of limitations is only held in abeyance until the date of the last injury suffered or when the tortious acts cease. Thus, we find that the two–year statute of limitations for this action began to run in August 1999, because Lynn's complaint includes allegations of tortious behavior by Robert occurring as late as that month. Applying the continuing tort rule to the instant case, Lynn's complaint, filed August 25, 1999, was clearly timely and her claims based on conduct prior to August 25, 1997, are not barred by the applicable statute of limitations.

Robert contends that even if the acts of alleged abuse are considered to be a continuing tort, the discovery rule should apply to determine when the statute of limitations began to run. Contrary to Robert's contention, the discovery rule is inapplicable here. The discovery rule, like the continuing tort rule, is an equitable exception to the statute of limitations. However, under the discovery rule, a cause of action accrues, and the limitations period begins to run, when the party seeking relief knows or reasonably should know of an injury and that it was wrongfully caused.

By contrast, in the case of a continuing tort, such as the one at bar, a plaintiff's cause of action accrues, and the statute of limitations begins to run, at the time the last injurious act occurs or the conduct is abated.

* * * We therefore have no need to consider application of the discovery rule here, because we have found that Lynn's complaint was filed within two years of the accrual of her action for the continuing tort of intentional infliction of emotional distress. [ ]

[The court held that language in the divorce settlement releasing all claims did not bar future claims and under the continuing tort theory Lynn's cause of action did not accrue until after the settlement was signed.]

Notes

1. *Tort claims in divorce actions.* Some courts refuse to entertain claims for intentional infliction of emotional distress between divorced or estranged spouses, on grounds that the events leading to marital breakdown inevitably produce emotional distress, or that vindictive claims are too likely, or that tort law should leave such matters to the divorce courts. See Pickering v. Pickering, 434 N.W.2d 758 (S.D. 1989); Hakkila v. Hakkila, 112 N.M. 172, 812 P.2d 1320 (App. 1991). In an omitted portion of the principal opinion, the court rejected these arguments. It said the requirements that the conduct be extreme and outrageous and that the distress be severe will confine tort actions to the most egregious cases of spousal abuse. It noted that in Illinois, as in most states, divorce courts are not are not allowed to consider marital misconduct in the distribution of property when dissolving a marriage, so abuse will go uncompensated unless tort law intervenes. "After examining case law from courts around the country, we find the majority have recognized that public policy considerations should not bar actions for intentional infliction of emotional distress between spouses or former spouses based on conduct occurring during the marriage. See Henriksen [v. Cameron, 622 A.2d 1135 (Me. 1993)] and cases cited therein."

2. *Continuing tort in malpractice cases.* The continuing tort idea is frequently employed in medical malpractice cases to prevent the statute of limitations from beginning to run at least until the physician's negligence ceases, apparently on the theory that the defendant has a continuing duty to recognize the problem and try to remedy it. See, e.g., Farley v. Goode, 219 Va. 969, 252 S.E.2d 594 (1979). Some states hold that the statute does not begin to run until the course of treatment ends. See Borgia v. City of New York, 12 N.Y.2d 151, 237 N.Y.S.2d 319, 187 N.E.2d 777 (1962), aff'd, 15 N.Y.2d 665, 204 N.E.2d 207, 255 N.Y.S.2d 878. A similar rule sometimes delays the triggering of the statute in legal malpractice cases until the lawyer–client relationship terminates. See O'Neill v. Tichy, 19 Cal.App.4th 114, 25 Cal.Rptr.2d 162 (1993).

3. Under the continuing tort rule, the key determination is whether there is one continuing wrong or several separate ones. In the principal case, the court distinguished the *Belleville Toyota* case on the ground that the tortious conduct complained of there involved "separate and distinct incidents," while Robert's conduct "as a whole" was the basis of the complaint in *Feltmeier*. *Belleville Toyota* involved a claim that the defendant had violated a statute that forbade auto manufacturers from adopting or implementing an arbitrary or capricious system of allocating cars to dealers and from engaging in arbitrary, bad faith, or unconscionable actions toward

dealers. Is it clear that individual allocation decisions were not part of a continuing wrong under that statute–or that Robert's acts weren't separate and distinct?

B. STATUTES OF REPOSE

BRADWAY v. AMERICAN NATIONAL RED CROSS

United States Court of Appeals, Eleventh Circuit, 1993.
992 F.2d 298.

TJOFLAT, CHIEF JUDGE.

* * *

I.

In April 1983, when she was twenty years old, Carol Bradway underwent reconstructive surgery for facial birth defects at the Emory University Hospital in Atlanta, Georgia. Mrs. Bradway received two units of whole blood by transfusion after surgery. The hospital obtained the blood from an American National Red Cross blood bank. The Red Cross had no direct contact with Mrs. Bradway.

In July 1988, Mrs. Bradway was admitted into a hospital after a diagnosis of pneumocystis. On July 19, 1988, Mrs. Bradway's doctor informed her that she had AIDS. On April 19, 1989, Mrs. Bradway and her husband David filed a complaint * * * alleging that Mrs. Bradway contracted AIDS during her 1983 transfusion. The Bradways sought compensatory damages, contending that the Red Cross was negligent in screening blood donors and in testing blood samples for the presence of HIV. They specifically asserted that the Red Cross, by not asking potential blood donors whether they were homosexuals, negligently failed to identify individuals possessing a high risk of being infected with the AIDS virus.

* * * The Red Cross * * * moved the district court to dismiss the Bradways' action as barred by Georgia's statutes of limitation and ultimate repose for medical malpractice suits. See O.C.G.A. §§ 9–3–70–71 (1982 & Supp.1992).[1] The Bradways contended that the action was

---

1. O.C.G.A. § 9–3–70 states:

As used in this article, the term "action for medical malpractice" means any claim for damages resulting from the death of or injury to any person arising out of:

(1) Health, medical, dental, or surgical service, diagnosis, prescription, treatment, or care rendered by a person authorized by law to perform such service or by any person acting under the supervision and control of the lawfully authorized person; or

(2) Care or service rendered by any public or private hospital, nursing home,

clinic, hospital authority, facility, or institution, or by any officer, agent, or employee thereof acting within the scope of his employment.

O.C.G.A. § 9–3–71 states, in pertinent part:
(a) Except as otherwise provided in this article, an action for medical malpractice shall be brought within two years after the date on which an injury or death arising from a negligent or wrongful act or omission occurred.

(b) Notwithstanding subsection (a) of this Code section, in no event may an action for medical malpractice be brought

one for "ordinary" negligence, not medical malpractice. The district court concluded that under Georgia law "an action against a blood bank for the negligent collection and supply of human blood is an action for medical malpractice," and dismissed the case as barred by O.C.G.A. § 9–3–71.

The Bradways appealed this dismissal, arguing that the district court erred in classifying the case as a medical malpractice action rather than an "ordinary" negligence suit.* Since this Court determined that the case turned on an unanswered question of Georgia law, we certified the following question to the Georgia Supreme Court:

> Is a suit alleging that a not–for–profit blood bank was negligent in collecting and supplying human blood—including screening volunteer blood donors and testing blood for the presence of human immunodeficiency virus (HIV)—an action for medical malpractice and thus subject to Georgia's statutes of limitation and repose for medical malpractice actions, O.C.G.A. § 9–3–71?

The Georgia Supreme Court answered our certified question in the affirmative [on the ground that the collection, processing, and distribution of blood "are medical services involving medical judgment."] Bradway v. American Nat'l Red Cross, 426 S.E.2d 849, 850 (Ga.1993).

II.

In certifying the question above to the Georgia Supreme Court, we reasoned that "resolution of this issue of Georgia law will determine whether the Bradways' suit was dismissed properly by the district court." 965 F.2d at 993. The Bradways contend, however, that it remains to be determined "when a cause of action accrues in a medical malpractice action for injury from a hazardous substance such as the AIDS virus." They argue that the action did not accrue until the wrong was completed, i.e., when Mrs. Bradway became infected, and that "[i]t is a jury question as to when * * * Carol Bradway became infected with the AIDS virus." We cannot agree.

The plain language of the [repose] statute indicates that the period begins on "the date on which the negligent or wrongful act or omission occurred." The relevant acts or omissions of the Red Cross—the "screening" of the blood, the release of the blood to the hospital—each occurred more than five years before this suit was filed.

Notwithstanding the language of the statute, the Bradways contend that the statute of repose runs from the time the wrong was completed. This legal theory, however, is not open to us. One week after responding

more than five years after the date on which the negligent or wrongful act or omission occurred.

(c) Subsection (a) of this Code section is intended to create a two–year statute of limitations. Subsection (b) of this Code section is intended to create a five–year statute of ultimate repose and abrogation.

* As an "ordinary" negligence case, the suit would have been governed by O.C.G.A. § 9–3–33, which provides that "[a]ctions for injuries to the person shall be brought within two years after the cause of action accrues * * *." [Ed.]

to our certified question, the Georgia Supreme Court revisited the same statute of repose in *Wright v. Robinson,* 426 S.E.2d 870 (Ga.1993). * * * The court reasoned:

> There is a distinct difference between statutes of limitations and statutes of repose. "A statute of limitations normally governs the time within which legal proceedings must be commenced after the cause of action accrues * * *. A statute of repose, however, limits the time within which an action may be brought and is not related to the accrual of any cause of action. The injury need not have occurred, much less have been discovered."

> A statute of repose stands as an unyielding barrier to a plaintiff's right of action. The statute of repose is absolute; the bar of the statute of limitations is contingent. The statute of repose destroys the previously existing rights so that, on the expiration of the statutory period, the cause of action no longer exists.

The Georgia statute of repose for medical malpractice bars the Bradways' suit.[3] While we may regret the application of the statute of repose to the instant facts, we cannot honestly avoid it.

* * *

Notes

1. *Delayed claims.* Statutes of repose are a response to the possibility that despite statutes of limitations, actionable claims may arise many years after the tortious act occurs. This can happen under any statute of limitations that does not begin to run until injury occurs, and the problem is exacerbated by the discovery rule, which makes it possible for late–discovered claims to be brought many years after the injury. This creates problems not only for defendants but also for their insurers, who want to have a time certain when they can close their books on potential claims. Long–delayed claims occur with some regularity in medical malpractice and defective product cases, and it is these classes of potential defendants who have been most aggressive in persuading legislatures to protect them with statutes of repose. The statute in the principal case is typical. If repose is a good idea in these contexts, should it be extended to tort defendants generally?

2. *Tolling the statute of limitations.* The discovery rule is the most important deviation from the strict deadlines imposed by statutes of limitations. But there are other exceptions, often judicially created, that prevent the limitations period from running while the plaintiff is mentally or legally incapacitated or while the plaintiff is unable to sue because of the defendant's fraud or coercion. Do statutes of repose cut off claims even under these exceptional circumstances? As in the principal case, the statutes usually recognize no exceptions for incapacity or fraud, and their intent plainly is to provide an absolute deadline. There is no reason to think courts

---

3. All statutes of repose prevent plaintiffs with otherwise legitimate claims from having those claims addressed by a court of law. In passing a statute of repose, a legisla- ture decides that there must be a time when the resolution of even just claims must defer to the demands of expediency.

will be any more sympathetic to plaintiffs whose inability to file within the repose period was caused by incapacity than to those whose inability was due to ignorance of their injury. Does fraud or coercion by the defendant provide a stronger case for an exception? Cf. M.E.H. v. L.H., 177 Ill.2d 207, 226 Ill.Dec. 232, 685 N.E.2d 335 (1997) (plaintiffs' claim of child abuse by father barred by 12–year–statute of repose; plaintiffs did not explicitly argue fraud or coercion, but they did claim that trauma had caused them to repress memory of alleged abuse for 40 years).

3. *Constitutionality of statutes of repose.* Some state constitutions contain provisions guaranteeing "open courts" or "a remedy for every injury." Statutes of repose are sometimes found to violate these provisions when they deny the plaintiff any opportunity to bring a claim. See, e.g., Kenyon v. Hammer, 142 Ariz. 69, 688 P.2d 961 (1984). But see Mega v. Holy Cross Hospital, 111 Ill.2d 416, 95 Ill.Dec. 812, 490 N.E.2d 665 (1986), holding that the state constitutional promise that "[e]very person shall find a certain remedy in the laws for all injuries" must be "tempered" by the legislature's clear decision to impose an absolute deadline; the statute of repose was upheld even though it cut off plaintiff's claim before his injury was known.

C. EXPRESS ASSUMPTION OF RISK

HOLZER v. DAKOTA SPEEDWAY, INC.

Supreme Court of South Dakota, 2000.
610 N.W.2d 787.

GILBERTSON, JUSTICE.

This case arose from a personal injury accident at the Lake County Speedway, when a race car's wheel detached, struck and injured Vernon Holzer.[1] The circuit court granted both defendants, Dakota Speedway, Inc. (Speedway) and K & K Insurance Group, Inc. summary judgment based on a pre–accident release signed by Holzer. We affirm.

* * *

Before entering the pit area of the racetrack [to serve on the pit crew for one of the racers] on August 5, 1995, Holzer was requested by Speedway officials to sign a "Release and Waiver of Liability, Assumption of Risk and Indemnity Agreement." All individuals wishing to enter the pit area were required to pay an entry fee and sign the release form. This document provided that the signees covenant not to sue the track owners, their insurers and others and release, waive, discharge them from all liability "for any and all loss or damage, and any claim or demands herefore on account of injury to the person or property or resulting in death of the undersigned arising out of or related to the events, whether caused by the negligence of the releasees or otherwise." This release was a condition to being allowed into any "restricted area," such as the pit, and applied to anyone competing, officiating, observing,

---

1. This appeal is brought on behalf of Vernon Holzer by his co–guardians, Paul Holzer and Marjorie Walters (Holzer, collectively), as Vernon is in a coma.

working for, or participating in races at the speedway. The form defines restricted area as "any area requiring special authorization, credentials, or permission to enter or any area to which admission by the general public is restricted or prohibited." At the bottom of the form are lines allowing for eighteen signatures. Printed on each signature line in bold capitalized letters, is "I HAVE READ THIS RELEASE." Holzer signed this document literally on top of these capitalized words. He had previously signed the same agreement on June 14, 1995 and July 29, 1995.

Holzer argues the release violates public policy and therefore is ineffective and unenforceable. He also contends granting the motion for summary judgment was improper because whether he knowingly and voluntarily signed the release is a question of fact for the jury. We disagree with both arguments.

* * *

[R]eleases that are construed to cover willful negligence or intentional torts are not valid and are against public policy. "Willful and wanton misconduct is something more than ordinary negligence but less than deliberate or intentional conduct." Holzer alleged in his complaint that Speedway acted "negligently and with reckless disregard toward his life, safety, and health" by failing "to provide adequate protection from the racetrack for the individuals in the pits, they failed to warn individuals in the pits of the potential dangers, and they located the pits in an unsafe, unprotected and unsecured area."

Although Holzer raises this legal claim, the record does not contain any supporting facts showing Speedway recklessly or consciously disregarded any risk of harm to him. * * *

Holzer also argues the release violates public policy because it involves a public interest in recreation.

Some courts have found exculpatory releases violate public policy when they involve a matter of interest to the public at large or the state. * * *

The release Holzer signed in this case does not involve a matter of public interest, but rather, a private agreement between individuals. Such a release has very little, if any, negative impact on the general population. "We are dealing with a fairly narrow segment of the public participating in a relatively dangerous sporting activity. The general public as a whole is minimally affected." Nor does this case involve a utility or other quasi–public entity that supplies essential services.

Holzer participated in Speedway automobile races as a form of recreation—his livelihood did not depend on working as a member of a pit crew, as he served as a nonpaid volunteer for the Bortnem racing team. Thus, Holzer was not compelled in any way to enter the Speedway pit area. * * *

There is no public policy in this state against race promoters being afforded some contractual protection for sponsoring automobile racing, an inherently dangerous sport. "[F]ewer promoters would be willing to hold automobile races if courts refused to permit them to limit their exposure to liability for racetrack accidents, in what is undeniably a dangerous sport." We find the release in this case does not violate public policy.

Holzer also contends that whether he knowingly and voluntarily signed the release is a question of fact for the jury. "To be valid, a release must be fairly and knowingly made." However, we commence analysis of this claim mindful of our holding that "one who accepts a contract is conclusively presumed to know its contents and to assent to them, in the absence of fraud, misrepresentation or other wrongful act by another contracting party."

Holzer claims he was given no "meaningful opportunity to read the agreement before signing [it]." * * *

[Sanner, another pit crew worker, stated in an affidavit] that upon entrance to the pit area, pit workers were required to sign a waiver form and "that there are several people waiting to gain entrance to the pit area at the same time. The only thing on Affiant's mind at the time of entering the gate is racing and therefore no attempt is made to read the aforementioned waiver form." However, there is no evidence in the record that Holzer was denied the opportunity to step out of any line that may have existed and read the release had he so desired. There is no evidence in the record that he was forced to sign it. While "several people" may have been waiting at the same time to enter the pit area, there is no evidence pit workers were denied the opportunity to read the release or ask questions about it. * * *

Paul Holzer [Vernon's father] states in his affidavit that Holzer "was of lower intelligence and [Paul was] unsure whether [Holzer] could even read the release or underst[and] the implications of what he was signing." Paul Holzer further states in his affidavit:

> Vernon was a poor student. His reading comprehension was very low. The highest grade he attained in English or Literature was a D+ as a ninth grader. * * * Vernon was passed through school, although I do not believe he should have been. He graduated 105th in a class of 110. He had 14 days of absences as a senior * * * I always took care to read things to him and explain the writing to insure that he understood what he read, as his comprehension was poor.

* * *

[I]f Holzer's father typically had to explain writings to him to "insure that he understood what he read," then Holzer should have either requested someone to explain the release to him before signing it, or simply refused to sign. There are three unambiguous releases in the record, two from before the accident and the one in question, all with Holzer's signature.

* * *

AFFIRMED.

AMUNDSON and KONENKAMP, JUSTICES, concur.

SABERS, JUSTICE, concurring in result.

I would agree with Chief Justice Miller's writing if this were the first such * * * form that Vernon signed. Unfortunately for him, the fact is that this was the third release and waiver of liability form that Vernon signed.

MILLER, CHIEF JUSTICE, concurring in part and dissenting in part.

* * *

The waiver form and Sanner's affidavit, together with common knowledge, could well lead a factfinder to conclude that Holzer unknowingly or involuntarily signed the waiver form as part of the pressure–filled routine of gaining access to the pit area. These pieces of evidence show that Holzer was among a steady stream of people waiting to enter the pit area that night.

As Sanner's affidavit points out, the important ramifications of signing the waiver were not discussed or even mentioned to those participants waiting in line to enter. Instead, they were all handed the roster–like form, told to print and sign their name, and then required to pay a fee. In this situation, the last thing on the mind of these entrants was understanding their legal rights. Rather, they were focused on getting into the pit area to prepare for the race. Surely, when faced with the choice of blindly signing the roster–form and proceeding on into the pit area, or not signing and jeopardizing the qualification of his team to race, a participant would opt for the former.

* * *

That none of the participants appreciated the significance of what they were signing is evident from the waiver form itself. Where it directed participants to list their "duties," everyone, including Holzer, merely listed numbers, which presumably referred to the number of the car on whose team they worked. Such a vague response supports the contention that either the form was confusing or the signers were hurried into signing it, or both.

* * *

[T]here was no meaningful opportunity for Holzer to read the agreement before signing. "We cannot believe [Speedway] intended that entrants would hold up the progression of cars into the racetrack in order to read the release." In this situation, Holzer's signature would not have been entirely voluntary; at least a fact question for a jury is present.

Further compounding the hurried, pressure–filled situation facing Holzer was the fact that he might not have had the ability to read or comprehend the waiver form.* * * The form, which contains an abundance of legal terms, was seemingly a boilerplate document drafted by lawyers. To a person with limited reading function, the form could have just as well been one of Plato's dialogues, with legalese such as "indemnity," "in consideration of," "covenants not to sue," and "hold harmless" in bold capital letters. Holzer's poor reading ability, combined with the large crowd of participants waiting to gain access to the pit area behind him, surely could have created a situation where he signed the waiver form just to keep the flow of people going. At the very least, it creates a genuine issue of material fact.

* * *

Notes

1. *Exculpatory clauses disfavored?* Until recently it was generally agreed that contracts attempting to exculpate a party in advance for negligently causing personal injuries were disfavored. A widely followed decision held that an exculpatory provision could be held invalid if it exhibited some or all of the following characteristics: "It concerns a business of a type generally thought suitable for public regulation; the party seeking exculpation is engaged in performing a service of great importance to the public, which is often a matter of practical necessity for some members of the public; the party holds himself out as willing to perform this service for any member of the public who seeks it, or at least for any member coming within certain established standards; * * * the party invoking exculpation possesses a decisive advantage of bargaining strength against any member of the public who seeks his services; * * * the party confronts the public with a standardized adhesion contract of exculpation, and makes no provision whereby a purchaser may pay additional reasonable fees and obtain protection against negligence; the person or property of the purchaser is placed under the control of the seller, subject to the risk of carelessness by the seller or his agents." Tunkl v. Regents of University of California, 60 Cal.2d 92, 32 Cal.Rptr. 33, 383 P.2d 441 (1963).

2. In Berlangieri v. Running Elk Corp., 132 N.M. 332, 48 P.3d 70 (2002), the court held that the usual tort policies of compensating injuries and deterring negligent conduct in themselves constituted a sufficient public interest to support a per se rule invalidating releases: "Public policy imposes on commercial operators of recreational or sports facilities a *non–disclaimable* duty to exercise due care to avoid risks of physical injury to consumers."

3. At the other extreme, the majority in the principal case asserts that personal injury releases are subject to the principle that "one who accepts a contract is conclusively presumed to know its contents and to assent to them" unless the assent was obtained through misrepresentation. In fact, the majority does not appear to go quite as far as its rhetoric suggests: it does not treat the plaintiffs' public policy argument as foreclosed by the presumption. Nonetheless, the decision is illustrative of the trend of the last ten years, which is clearly in favor of enforcing exculpatory clauses. The dissent in the *Berlangieri* case, supra, characterized the decisions holding that such contracts should be disfavored as "a static minority" and cited numerous recent decisions enforcing them. The Restatement (Third) of Torts: Apportionment of Liability embraces the view that "the parties to a transaction should be able to agree which of them should bear the risk of injury, even when the injury is caused by a party's legally culpable conduct," and rejects the position that such clauses should be disfavored. Id. at. § 2 Comment b (1999).

4. Does it make sense to use standard contract principles to determine the enforceability of releases like the one Holzer signed?

Chapter XI

COMPARATIVE RESPONSIBILITY IN MULTIPARTY LITIGATION

A. INTRODUCTION

The shift to comparative fault has revolutionized tort law. At first, the shift appeared to be nothing more than a common sense abandonment of the harsh consequences of contributory negligence as a complete bar to recovery. As time went on, it became clear that the shift affected many other areas. In fact, the shift challenges the classical structure of tort law itself.

Comparative fault has a different underlying logic than the classical structure of tort law. Tort law traditionally has been structured along lines defined primarily by the type of injury the plaintiff suffers and the defendant's state of mind or culpability. The intellectual underpinning of this compartmentalized, tort–by–tort approach is that, when types of injuries change and states of mind or culpability changes, the policy concerns of tort law also change. Thus, in traditional thinking, when a defendant intentionally invades a plaintiff's rights, it makes sense to have different defenses, different rules about damages, and so on, than when a defendant is merely negligent, or, as in strict liability, is not even negligent. Historical reasons and pure fortuity also have influenced the structure of tort law and the available defenses, but the structure can be justified only by an argument that different torts—different types of injuries and different states of mind—evoke different policy concerns.

Comparative responsibility and comparative contribution raise a different set of concerns. When several actors cause a single injury, comparative responsibility asks a court to treat the injury as a unit and compare the contributions of the various actors. This creates tension with the compartmentalized structure of tort law. That structure divides the world according to causes of action; comparative responsibility focuses on the common contribution various actors make to a single injury. Comparative responsibility focuses on a single injury as an organizing event, calling for an evaluation of the conduct of the various actors that transcends the boundaries of the various torts. To the extent that courts compare all of the actors in a single set of percentages, they often have to forego having different apportionment rules apply to parties who commit different torts. Thus, some of the most complex and fundamental changes are occurring in cases involving multiple tortfeasors.

B. CONTRIBUTION AND INDEMNITY

BROCHNER v. WESTERN INSURANCE COMPANY

Supreme Court of Colorado, 1986.
724 P.2d 1293.

KIRSHBAUM, JUSTICE.

* * *

The Community Hospital Association (the hospital), which operates Boulder Community Hospital, granted staff privileges to Dr. Ruben Brochner in October 1964. Brochner performed numerous craniotomies at the hospital over the next few months. [A craniotomy is a type of brain surgery in which suspected abnormal or diseased brain tissue is removed.] In 1965, after reviews of those craniotomies indicated that tissue samples from many of the patients appeared normal, the hospital's executive committee orally required Brochner to obtain consultations before performing craniotomies if the relevant radiographic evidence did not clearly establish pathology. In 1966, the executive committee recommended to Brochner that he should obtain additional outside consultation on surgical pathological specimens.

In March 1968, the hospital's tissue committee received a report that fourteen of twenty–eight tissue samples taken from Brochner's neurosurgery patients were completely normal and that nine of the remaining fourteen samples indicated only low grade disease. An expert testified at trial that one normal tissue of 100 tissue samples was an acceptable ratio and that two normal tissues out of twenty–eight samples would require investigation.

On November 9, 1968, Brochner performed a craniotomy on Esther Cortez which resulted in injury to Cortez. Cortez later filed a civil action against Brochner and the hospital. She alleged that Brochner negligently diagnosed her need for a craniotomy, that the hospital negligently continued Brochner's staff privileges when it knew or should have known that he was incompetent, and that the hospital negligently allowed Brochner to perform unnecessary surgery. The claim against Brochner was severed, and trial of the claims against the hospital commenced April 3, 1978. Prior to the conclusion of that trial, Cortez and the hospital agreed to a settlement of $150,000. Some time later, Cortez reached a settlement of her suit against Brochner, who was uninsured, for an undisclosed sum.

In 1979, the hospital and its subrogee, Western Insurance Company (Western), filed this indemnity action against Brochner, alleging that Brochner's negligence was the active and primary cause of Cortez's injuries while the hospital's negligence was passive and secondary. On September 15, 1982, the trial court entered judgment for Western and the hospital against Brochner as follows: (1) $150,000 as the sum paid by Western on behalf of the hospital to Cortez in settlement of her claim against the hospital; and (2) $10,000 to the hospital for expenses incurred in connection with the Cortez lawsuit not reimbursed by insurance. The trial court found that Brochner had breached a pre–existing duty to the hospital to abide by its rules and regulations, that Brochner's negligence was the primary cause of Cortez's injuries, that the hospital was independently negligent toward the plaintiff, and that the hospital's negligence was only a secondary cause of those injuries. The trial court also awarded Western its attorney fees and costs incurred in defending the original lawsuit. The Court of Appeals affirmed the trial court's judgment.

* * *

[Under the Colorado version of the Uniform Contribution Among Tortfeasors Act, §§ 13–50.5–101 to–106, 6 C.R.S. (1985 Supp.)] [j]oint tortfeasors are now subject to contribution among themselves based upon their relative degrees of fault. That principle is at odds with the essential characteristic of our present rule of indemnity that, without regard to apportionment of fault, a single tortfeasor may ultimately pay the expense of all injuries sustained by a third party as the result of negligent conduct by two or more tortfeasors. There can be no mistake concerning the intent of the General Assembly to establish the policy of responsibility related to proportionate fault in the context of personal injury litigation. * * * More recently, the General Assembly has abolished the principle of joint and several liability. * * * This new provision extends the principle that liability for negligence should be based on proportionate fault.

In view of these legislative enactments, a tortfeasor no longer may unfairly be forced to pay all or a disproportionate share of damages suffered by an injured party as the result of negligent conduct by two or more joint tortfeasors. The principle of proportionate fault adopted by the General Assembly represents a rational and equitable approach to the problem of allocating ultimate responsibility between or among joint tortfeasors for the payment of damages to an injured party. Application of this principle will prove far more certain in varied factual contexts and will consequently promote more predictability than any continued effort to perpetuate ephemeral distinctions based on primary or secondary negligence concepts. For these reasons we conclude that the doctrine of indemnity insofar as it requires one of two joint tortfeasors to reimburse the other for the entire amount paid by the other as damages to a party injured as the result of the negligence of both joint tortfeasors, is no longer viable, and is hereby abolished.

* * * As a joint tortfeasor, the hospital has no right to seek indemnity from Brochner; its sole remedy lies in contribution pursuant to the terms of the Act. Section 13–50.5–105(1)(b) provides:

When a release or a covenant not to sue or not to enforce judgment is given in good faith to one or two or more persons liable in tort for the same injury or the same wrongful death:

* * *

It discharges the tortfeasor to whom it is given from all liability for contribution to any other tortfeasor.

* * * Because both Brochner and the hospital settled with Cortez * * *, neither is entitled to contribution from the other.*

* * *

Notes

1. *What is left of tort indemnity in the comparative fault era?* In an omitted footnote the court stated: "The question of whether our common law doctrine of indemnity should be preserved or abolished in situations where the party seeking indemnity is vicariously liable or is without fault is not presented by the circumstances of this case." Many comparative fault jurisdictions have concluded that indemnity should be retained when a defendant is liable purely vicariously, when an innocent retailer is liable for a manufacturer's defective product, and when there is a contract for indemnity, but otherwise should be jettisoned in favor of comparative–fault contribution. See, e.g., Bonniwell v. Beech Aircraft Corp., 663 S.W.2d 816 (Tex. 1984); see generally Prosser & Keeton on Torts § 51, p. 344 (5th ed. 1984).

2. *Abolishing joint and several liability eliminates the need for contribution.* The abolition of joint and several liability took effect in 1986, after the cause in action in *Brochner* arose, and therefore was inapplicable. Had it been, no tortfeasor would have been liable for more than its own percentage share, and there would have been no need for contribution.

C. JOINT AND SEVERAL LIABILITY

KAEO v. DAVIS

Supreme Court of Hawaii, 1986.
68 Haw. 447, 719 P.2d 387.

NAKAMURA, JUSTICE.

[Lurline Kido and Alfred Davis spent the afternoon in a tavern and then went for a drive. Davis, who had drunk several beers, was unable to keep the car on a winding road and hit a utility pole. Kido was severely injured. Her guardian sued Davis and the City of Honolulu. The City's alleged negligence was failure to maintain the road in a safe condition.]

At the close of evidence the case was submitted to the jury on interrogatories propounded by the trial judge. The special verdict re-

---

* Section D, infra, explores the effects of settlement on cotortfeasors' contribution rights and obligations. [Ed.]

turned by the jury found the negligence of Davis and the City caused the accident, 99% of the negligence was attributable to Davis and 1% to the City, and the plaintiff suffered damages amounting to $725,000. A judgment holding Davis and the City jointly and severally liable for the damages * * * was entered.

[The City appealed, asserting that the trial judge erred in: (a) excluding all evidence of Davis's beer consumption; and (b) refusing to give a jury instruction "that would have apprised the jury of the possible legal consequences of its verdict on the negligence attributable to each putative joint tortfeasor." The Supreme Court held that the trial judge was wrong to exclude the drinking evidence, and then turned to the matter of the instruction. The pertinent language of the instruction requested by the City was as follows:

> You are instructed that if you find Defendant Davis liable for any degree of liability and find the City liable for *any* degree of liability, under Hawaii law, the City is compelled to pay Defendant Davis' share of the entire judgment if he is unable to pay * * *.]

Wisconsin, an acknowledged pioneer in the area of comparative negligence, was also an early jurisdiction adopting a rule against "inform[ing] the jury expressly or by necessary implication of the effect of [a special verdict answer] upon the ultimate right of either party litigant to recover or upon the ultimate liability of either party litigant." Banderob v. Wisconsin Central Ry., 133 Wis. 249, 287, 113 N.W. 738, 751 (1907). The Supreme Court of Wisconsin in 1975 rationalized its continued adherence to the rule in these terms:

> Under our system of jurisprudence, the jury is the finder of fact and it has no function in determining how the law should be applied to the facts found. It is not the function of a jury in a case between private parties on the determination of comparative negligence to be influenced by sympathy for either party, nor should it attempt to manipulate the apportionment of negligence to achieve a result that may seem socially desirable to a single juror or to a group of jurors.

McGowan v. Story, [70 Wis.2d 189, 197, 234 N.W.2d 325, 329 (1975).] Few would dare take issue with these sentiments.

Yet other courts have eschewed Wisconsin's "blindfold" rule, concluding "that, ordinarily, a jury informed of the legal effect of its findings as to percentages of negligence in a comparative negligence trial is better able to fulfill its fact finding function." Roman v. Mitchell, 82 N.J. 336, 346, 413 A.2d 322, 327 (1980). And, "a growing trend is for courts and legislatures to require that the jury be informed of the results of apportioning negligence under a special verdict."

These courts do not deny " '[t]he [whole] thought behind the special verdict [was] to free the jury from [anything] which would inject the feeling of partisanship in their minds, and limit the deliberations to the specific questions submitted.' " Yet some courts and commentators are skeptical that "special verdicts really [have done] much to eliminate the effects of bias, sympathy and prejudice from jury deliberations and jury verdicts." Experience has taught them that "jurors are concerned about the effect of their verdicts on the ultimate outcome of the case and the use of a special verdict or special interrogatories does not magically eliminate that well known trait of American juries." * * *

We are convinced too that "in most cases the jury will in fact know which party is favored by a particular answer." A juror in all likelihood would deduce from what happens at trial "that it will be in the plaintiff's interest for him to answer 'No' to the question [on] contributory negligence" or that it may be in the plaintiff's interest to answer "yes" to the question on the negligence of a putative joint tortfeasor. "Thus an attempt to keep the jury in the dark as to the [legal] effect of its answers is likely to be unavailing. . . ."

Given these probabilities, we cannot discount "the danger that [jurors] will guess wrong about the law, and may shape [their] answers to the special verdicts, contrary to [their] actual beliefs, in a mistaken attempt to ensure the result [they] deem desirable." Nor can we dismiss the possibility that some jurors with incomplete knowledge of the law will exert undue influence in the deliberations. In either event, it would be " 'better for courts to be the vehicle by which the operation of the law is explained.' "

We believe the trial court, if requested and when appropriate, should inform the jury of the possible legal consequence of a verdict apportioning negligence among joint tortfeasors. An explanation of the operation of the doctrine of joint and several liability in that situation would be consistent with our directive in HRCP 49(a) that "[t]he court shall give to the jury such explanation and instruction concerning the matter * * * submitted as may be necessary to enable the jury to make its findings upon each issue."

The judgment is vacated, and the case is remanded for a new trial.

Notes

1. How does the city hope the new jury will react to the instruction on joint and several liability?

2. If *Kaeo* had been tried in the era before the adoption of comparative negligence principles and the jury had found that Davis and the city were each guilty of negligence, there would have been no basis or procedure for assigning percentages of fault to them. In that situation, joint and several liability would have been regarded as unremarkable. What has changed?

BROWN v. KEILL

Supreme Court of Kansas, 1978.
224 Kan. 195, 580 P.2d 867.

Fromme, Justice.

This appeal is from a judgment for damage to plaintiff's automobile resulting from a two car collision. The primary issues raised on appeal require a construction of the provisions of K.S.A. 60–258a, commonly referred to as the Kansas comparative negligence statute.

The plaintiff–appellant, Britt Brown, owned a Jaguar roadster. His son, Britt M. Brown, was the permissive driver of appellant's Jaguar at the time of the collision. * * * The defendant–appellee, Patricia L. Keill, was the driver of the other car involved in the collision. The collision occurred at a street intersection in Wichita. The reasonable cost of repair to the Jaguar amounted to $5,423.00. The circumstances surrounding the collision need not be detailed. Apparently the defendant–appellee settled her claim against the driver of the Jaguar out of court. The owner of the Jaguar then sued to recover his property loss. Defendant–appellee did not seek to have the son joined as an additional formal party to the action. She did not file a counterclaim or cross–claim.

* * *

At the close of a bench trial the court found: (1) The plaintiff–father, as bailor of the Jaguar, was guilty of no negligence; (2) the driver of the Jaguar was responsible for 90% of the causal negligence; (3) the defendant, Keill, was responsible for 10% of the causal negligence; (4) plaintiff sustained total damages in the amount of $5,423.00; and (5) pursuant to the comparative negligence statute of Kansas plaintiff was entitled to recover $542.30 or 10% of his total damage from the defendant, Keill. Judgment was entered for that amount and this appeal followed.

At the outset it should be noted that in the absence of evidence of a joint venture, agency or circumstances giving rise to vicarious liability the negligence of a bailee of a vehicle is not imputable to the bailor in an action by the bailor against a third party for damage to the bailed vehicle. The plaintiff in this case accordingly was guilty of no contributory negligence.

[T]he two ultimate questions to be decided on appeal are: (1) Has the rule of joint and several liability of joint tortfeasors been retained in actions now governed by the Kansas comparative negligence statute, K.S.A. 60–258a; and (2) is the causal negligence or fault of all parties to a collision or occurrence giving rise to plaintiff's claim in a comparative negligence action to be considered even though one of said parties is not served with process or joined as a formal party to the action?

We will consider first the question as to joint and several liability.

* * *

[U]nder the Kansas law as it existed prior to statutory comparative negligence a plaintiff could choose his tortfeasor and a defendant had no right to bring in another joint tortfeasor to plaintiff's action. [I]f plaintiff sued and recovered a judgment against two tortfeasors plaintiff could proceed to collect the judgment from either judgment debtor. When one judgment debtor had satisfied the entire judgment he could then recover one–half of the amount paid from the other judgment debtor. The effect of these prior holdings was to make each defendant jointly and severally liable for all of plaintiff's damage regardless of whether others contributed to cause such injuries. The right of contribution between judgment debtors in such case was on a fifty–fifty basis. Plaintiff controlled his own lawsuit and could collect a judgment from any judgment debtor he chose. The inability of any judgment debtor to pay his half of the judgment would concern only the judgment debtor who satisfied the judgment and then sought contribution.

* * *

In 1974 the Kansas legislature passed [K.S.A. 60–258a], which reads as follows:

> An Act concerning tort liability; abolishing contributory negligence as a bar to recovery; and providing for the awarding of damages on the basis of comparative negligence.

Be it enacted by the Legislature of the State of Kansas:

> Section 1. (a) The contributory negligence of any party in a civil action shall not bar such party or his legal representative from recovering damages for negligence resulting in death, personal injury or property damage, if such party's negligence was less than the causal negligence of the party or parties against whom claim for recovery is made, but the award of damages to any party in such action shall be diminished in proportion to the amount of negligence attributed to such party. If any such party is claiming damages for a decedent's wrongful death, the negligence of the decedent, if any, shall be imputed to such party.

> (b) Where the comparative negligence of the parties in any such action is an issue, the jury shall return special verdicts, or in the absence of a jury, the court shall make special findings, determining the percentage of negligence attributable to each of the parties, and determining the total amount of damages sustained by each of the claimants, and the entry of judgment shall be made by the court. No general verdict shall be returned by the jury.

> (c) On motion of any party against whom a claim is asserted for negligence resulting in death, personal injury or property damage, any other person whose causal negligence is claimed to have contributed to such death, personal injury or property damage shall be joined as an additional party to the action.

> (d) Where the comparative negligence of the parties in any action is an issue and recovery is allowed against more than one party, each such party shall be liable for that portion of the total dollar amount awarded as damages to any claimant in the proportion that the amount of his causal negligence bears to the amount of the causal negligence attributed to all parties against whom such recovery is allowed.

* * *

Both parties assert there are ambiguities in the comparative negligence statute, K.S.A. 60–258a, as passed by the Kansas legislature. We agree. Therefore, it becomes necessary to consider and apply rules of statutory construction. The fundamental rule of statutory construction, to which all others are subordinate, is that the purpose and intent of the legislature governs when that intent can be ascertained from the statute, even though words, phrases or clauses at some place in the statute must be omitted or inserted. In determining legislative intent, courts are not limited to a mere consideration of the language used, but look to the historical background of the enactment, the circumstances attending its passage, the purpose to be accomplished and the effect the statute may have under the various constructions suggested. In order to ascertain the legislative intent, courts are not permitted to consider only a certain isolated part or parts of an act but are required to consider and construe together all parts thereof in pari materia. When the interpretation of some one section of an act according to the exact and literal import of its words would contravene the manifest purpose of the legislature, the entire act should be construed according to its spirit and reason, disregarding so far as may be necessary the literal import of words or phrases which conflict with the manifest purpose of the legislature.

* * *

The appellant contends that the trial court erroneously ignored the principle of joint and several liability in entering judgment for only 10% of the total damages. He suggests that since K.S.A. 60–258a does not mention joint and several liability this court should construe the statute to retain joint and several liability, and adopt a rule of comparative contribution that would permit the joint judgment debtors to apportion damages on the basis of their relative fault. Under such a construction of the statute if plaintiff suffered damages in the amount of $5,423.00, as in this case, he could sue and recover said sum from either defendant regardless of such defendant's percentage of fault. In such case if the defendant against whom recovery was had was 10% at fault and the other defendant was 90% at fault, the plaintiff could collect the $5,423.00 from the defendant 10% at fault and such defendant would then have a right of contribution against the other joint tort–feasor for $90/100 \times \$5,423.00$ or $4,880.70, based on proportion of fault.

The substance of defendant–appellee's argument in support of the present judgment is that the legislature by adopting subsection (a) as well as subsection (d) of the statute meant to equate both the amount to be recovered by plaintiff and the liability of a defendant with the individual's degree of fault in all cases where the plaintiff's negligence was less than the fault of all other parties to the collision or occurrence. If this were the intention of the legislature it would of necessity require this court to hold our prior rules as to joint and several liability had been abolished by the legislature in comparative negligence cases.

* * *

The perceived purpose in adopting K.S.A. 60–258a is fairly clear. The legislature intended to equate recovery and duty to pay to degree of fault. Of necessity, this involved a change of both the doctrine of contributory negligence and of joint and several liability. There is nothing inherently fair about a defendant who is 10% at fault paying 100% of the loss, and there is no social policy that should compel defendants to pay more than their fair share of the loss. Plaintiffs now take the parties as they find them. If one of the parties at fault happens to be a spouse or a governmental agency and if by reason of some competing social policy the plaintiff cannot receive payment for his injuries from the spouse or agency, there is no compelling social policy which requires the codefendant to pay more than his fair share of the loss. The same is true if one of the defendants is wealthy and the other is not. Previously, when the plaintiff had to be totally without negligence to recover and the defendants had to be merely negligent to incur an obligation to pay, an argument could be made which justified putting the burden of seeking contribution on the defendants. Such an argument is no longer compelling because of the purpose and intent behind the adoption of the comparative negligence statute.

It appears more reasonable for the legislature to have intended to relate duty to pay to the degree of fault. Any other interpretation of K.S.A. 60–258a(d) destroys the fundamental conceptual basis for the abandonment of the contributory negligence rule and makes meaningless the enactment of subsection (d). If it were not the intention of the legislature to abolish joint and several liability by adopting subsection (d) that subsection would have little or no purpose, because the first two sections of the statute standing alone could have accomplished the legislative purpose urged by the appellant.

* * * Having considered the arguments in light of the statute, we hold under the provisions of K.S.A. 60–258a the concept of joint and several liability between joint tort–feasors previously existing in this state no longer applies in comparative negligence actions. The individual liability of each defendant for payment of damages will be based on proportionate fault, and contribution among joint judgment debtors is no longer required in such cases.

We turn now to the second question raised in this appeal. Is the causal negligence or fault of all parties to a collision or occurrence giving rise to plaintiff's claim in a comparative negligence action to be considered even though one or more of said parties is not served with process or joined as a formal party to the action?

The appellant points out that, while subsection (c) of the statute permits "any party against whom a claim is asserted" to bring in another person on motion, there is nothing in the statute which specifically requires the plaintiff to bring his action or file a claim against any particular person or group of persons. Appellant further notes that under subsection (d) the causal negligence or fault of all parties "against whom such recovery is allowed" is to be proportioned. Nowhere in the act does it state that persons who are not parties to the action are to have any impact on the ultimate judgment to be entered. Therefore, appellant asserts it is incumbent upon a defendant to join such additional parties as he may deem necessary or advisable to determine their fault.

Appellee, on the other hand, points to subsection (d) of the statute and says the comparative negligence of all parties whose fault contributed to the collision or occurrence must be determined if "each such party shall be liable for that portion of the total dollar amount awarded as damages to any claimant in the proportion that the amount of his causal negligence bears to the amount of the causal negligence attributed to all parties against whom such recovery is allowed." In addition appellee contends that subsection (c) of the statute must be construed as permissive for it is impossible and fruitless in many cases for a defendant to attempt to join and bring into the action those who have settled out under a covenant not to sue and whose liability for damages no longer exists. Other instances are cited where no recovery by plaintiff may be obtained against a party who is or may be at fault, such as cases of interspousal immunity and where there is an absence of information as to the name or whereabouts of a party to the occurrence.

In examining K.S.A. 60–258a we note that subsection (a) is concerned with changing our prior rule which denied recovery to a claimant whose negligence contributed to cause the collision or occurrence. It provides that a party's negligence shall not be a bar if such negligence was less than the causal negligence of the party or parties against whom claim for recovery is made. It further provides the award of damages to such party shall be diminished in proportion to the amount of negligence attributed to such party. This section, as well as other sections of the statute, speaks in terms of parties in or to the action rather than plaintiffs and defendants. We note, however, this wording in the statute can be construed as a means of accommodating cases in which both claims and counterclaims are filed as a result of one collision or occurrence rather than to imply it relates to parties to the occurrence. The position taken by plaintiff in this action has support because of the use of the phrases "party or parties against whom claim for recovery is made" in subsection (a), and "all parties against whom such recovery is allowed" in subsection (d).

Before answering the ultimate question being considered, several preliminary questions bearing on multiple party cases should be examined. * * *

* * * May the plaintiff avoid proportionate liability by suing and making a claim against only one of several tort–feasors? Presumably subsection (c) permits a defendant to file a motion and join other tort–feasors. However, plaintiff may have settled with that tort–feasor and no liability exists when the action is filed. The statute is silent as to what position the added party occupies once that party is joined. It is doubtful if the plaintiff in such a case can be forced to make a claim against the

added party. The legislative intent in including subsection (c) would appear to have been to * * * permit a defendant in a comparative negligence case to bring in other joint tort–feasors so their percentage of fault can be determined and their liability, if any, adjudged.

The next preliminary question that presents itself is will proportionate liability be defeated when a party joined under subsection (c) has a valid defense such as interspousal immunity, covenant not to sue and so forth? The added party in such case would not be a party "against whom such recovery is allowed" and if subsection (d) is taken literally such a party's percentage of fault should not be considered in determining the judgment to be rendered. It appears after considering the intent and purposes of the entire statute that such a party's fault should be considered in each case to determine the other defendant's percentage of fault and liability, if any. The proportionate liability of the other parties to the action under K.S.A. 60–258a(d) should not be increased merely because a party joined under subsection (c) has a valid defense to plaintiff's claim, other than lack of negligence.

Now we return to the ultimate question should the percentage of fault of one who is not or cannot be formally joined as a party under subsection (c) be considered under subsection (d) to arrive at the proportionate liability of the defendant or defendants?

After having answered the preliminary questions and having applied the rules of statutory construction previously set forth in this opinion, we conclude the intent and purpose of the legislature in adopting K.S.A. 60–258a was to impose individual liability for damages based on the proportionate fault of all parties to the occurrence which gave rise to the injuries and damages even though one or more parties cannot be joined formally as a litigant or be held legally responsible for his or her proportionate fault.

* * *

Judgment affirmed.

Notes

1. *Multiple positions on joint and several liability.* American states have taken a variety of positions on the impact of comparative fault on joint and several liability. Ten comparative fault states retain full joint and several liability (plus the five jurisdictions that retain contributory negligence as a complete bar). Thirteen states, like Kansas in *Brown*, have abolished or virtually abolished joint and several liability; each defendant is liable only for its own percentage share. The rest of the states have partially abolished joint and several liability. Some provide that an insolvent tortfeasor's share is reapportioned among the solvent defendants and the plaintiff proportionate to their respective percentages of fault. Others provide that any defendant below a specified percentage (ranging from 10% to 50%) is relieved of joint and several liability. Others provide that defendants are jointly and severally liable for pecuniary damages, such as lost wages and

medical bills, but not for nonpecuniary damages, such as pain and suffering. Several states have statutory schemes that combine these approaches. See Restatement (Third) of Torts: Apportionment of Liability § 17 (2000).

Can you think of arguments for and against the retention of joint and several liability?

2.   Some jurisdictions that abolish or partially abolish joint and several liability nevertheless provide that intentional tortfeasors are always jointly and severally liable. See, e.g., Fla.Stat.Ann. § 768.81(4)(b) (1995); Kansas State Bank & Trust Co. v. Specialized Transp. Services, Inc., 249 Kan. 348, 819 P.2d 587 (1991). See Restatement (Third) of Torts: Apportionment of Liability § 12 (2000).

3.   Vicarious liability is different from joint and several liability. Thus, an abolition of joint and several liability does not relieve a vicariously liable defendant from responsibility to the plaintiff for the entire share of the person for whom the defendant is vicariously liable. See, e.g., Restatement (Third) of Torts: Apportionment of Liability § 13 (2000); Rashtian v. BRAC–BH, Inc., 9 Cal.App.4th 1847, 12 Cal.Rptr.2d 411 (1992); Sieben v. Sieben, 231 Kan. 372, 646 P.2d 1036 (1982). Of course, an abolition of joint and several liability would relieve such a defendant of liability for the shares of other tortfeasors.

4.   *Who should be assigned a percentage?* A subsidiary, but crucial, issue is to whom should the jury assign a percentage of responsibility. Obviously, the jury must assign a percentage of responsibility to the plaintiff and the primary defendants. But what about third–party defendants? The jury must compare their fault to the fault of the primary defendants to determine contribution, but should the fault of a third–party defendant be included in the basic comparison between the plaintiff and the primary defendants? Do you see why it makes a difference, especially in a jurisdiction that has abolished joint and several liability? Do you see how it also affects the basic comparative fault calculation, especially in a jurisdiction that uses modified comparative negligence? Similar issues arise with respect to settling defendants, immune tortfeasors, and nonparty (or so–called "phantom") tortfeasors. Recall that the court in *Brown* held that the trier of fact should have assigned a percentage of responsibility to the driver of the Jaguar. The new Restatement gives different answers to these questions, depending on whether and to what extent a particular jurisdiction has abolished joint and several liability. See Restatement (Third) Torts: Apportionment of Liability §§ A19, B19, C19, C20, D19, E19 (2000). Can you see how these issues can affect a plaintiff's decision about whom to sue and/or settle with in a lawsuit?

A recurring problem in this area of the law is how the alleged fault of the plaintiff's employer (who normally is immune from tort liability) should be treated in a lawsuit against other tortfeasors. That issue is addressed in Varela v. American Petrofina, which follows.

VARELA v. AMERICAN PETROFINA COMPANY OF TEXAS, INC.

Supreme Court of Texas, 1983.
658 S.W.2d 561.

WALLACE, JUSTICE.

This is an appeal from a third–party negligence action brought by an employee covered by workers' compensation insurance. The trial court submitted an issue [a special verdict] inquiring as to the negligence of the employee, the employer and the * * * defendant. Judgment was rendered for the amount of damages found by the jury reduced by the proportion of negligence of both the employee and the employer. The court of appeals affirmed. [ ] We reverse the judgments of the courts below and render judgment for the employee for the total amount of damages found by the jury reduced only by the proportion of negligence of the employee.

Robert O. Varela was employed by Hydrocarbon Construction Company (Hydrocarbon), who was performing a "turnaround" on a fluid catalytic cracking unit owned and operated by American Petrofina Company of Texas (Petrofina). During the course of performing the "turnaround" Varela was injured as a result of a fall due to an alleged premises defect. After settling his workers compensation claim with Hydrocarbon's workers compensation carrier, Varela sued Petrofina for the damages resulting from his injuries. In response to a special issue, the jury apportioned the negligence of the parties as follows: Varela 15%, Hydrocarbon 42% and Petrofina 43%. The jury further found damages for Varela in the sum of $606,800. The trial court rendered judgment for * * * 43% of the total damages. The court of appeals affirmed.

The sole question before us is whether an employer's negligence may be considered in a third–party negligence action brought by an employee arising out of an accidental injury covered by workers' compensation insurance. We hold that under applicable statutes, the employer's negligence may not be considered.

Article 8306, Sec. 3. states in pertinent part:

The employees of a subscriber ... shall have no right of action against their employer or against any agent, servant or employee of said employer for damages for personal injuries ... but such employees ... shall look for compensation solely to the association.... If an action for damages on account of injury ... is brought by such employee ... against a person other than the subscriber ... and if such action results in a judgment against such other person, or results in a settlement by such other person, the subscriber, his agent, servant or employee, shall have no liability to reimburse or hold such other person harmless on such judgment or settlement.... No part of this Section is intended to lessen or alter the employee's existing rights or cause of action ... against ... any third party.

The above quoted statute abrogates the covered employee's right to recover common law damages from the employer for personal injury covered by the Workers' Compensation Act. However, the employee may seek recovery from a third party whose negligence contributed to the injury. In the event of recovery the negligent third party is barred from seeking contribution or indemnity from the employer, and the compensation carrier is entitled to reimbursement for all compensation and medical expenses paid.

Article 2212a generally governs the liability of joint tortfeasors. Section 1 provides that a plaintiff shall recover if his negligence is not greater than the negligence of the defendant and, " * * * any damages allowed shall be diminished in proportion to the amount of negligence attributed to the person or party recovering." Section 2(b) stipulates that " * * * contribution to the damages awarded to the claimant shall be in proportion to the percentage of negligence attributable to each defendant." Subsection 2(c) provides that "[e]ach defendant is jointly and severally liable for the entire amount of the judgment * * * except * * * a defendant whose negligence is less than that of the claimant * * *." Subsection 2(e) provides that in the event of a settlement with a defendant " * * * the settlement is a complete release of the portion of the judgment attributable to the percentage of negligence found on the part of the [settling] tortfeasor."

We hold that Article 8306, § 3 is an exception to Article 2212a, § 2(b). When read together those two Articles indicate the intent of the Legislature that where the * * * defendant's negligence is [equal to or] greater than that of the employee, the employee shall recover the total amount of damages as found by the jury diminished only in proportion to the amount of the negligence attributed to the employee.

Petrofina contends that upon settlement of the workers' compensation claim the employer became a settled tortfeasor and thus § 2(e) of Art. 2212a mandates that Petrofina be credited with a reduction of damages equal to that percentage of negligence attributable to Hydrocarbon. It simply stretches the concept of settlement too far to hold that by not rejecting coverage of workers' compensation insurance in writing within five days of commencing employment, an employee has settled any and all future claims against the employer. Further, a defendant's claim of contribution is derivative of the plaintiff's right to recover from the joint defendant against whom contribution is sought. The Workers' Compensation Act, Article 8306, § 3, precludes any right by Varela to a cause of action against Hydrocarbon for common law negligence. Since Varela had no cause of action against Hydrocarbon, Petrofina had no claim for contribution from Hydrocarbon. Since Petrofina had no claim for contribution, § 2(e) of Art. 2212a has no application to this case.

The judgments of the courts below are reversed and judgment is rendered for Varela in the amount of $515,780.00 plus interest from the date of judgment.

Notes

1. *Should the employer's fault be assessed and used to diminish the employee's tort recovery?* The central issue of *Varela*—whether the employee's tort recovery should be diminished to reflect the employer's percentage of fault—is a close one, and the law is unsettled. The United States Supreme Court has signaled its agreement with the *Varela* approach. See Edmonds v. Compagnie Generale Transatlantique, 443 U.S. 256, 99 S.Ct. 2753, 61 L.Ed.2d 521 (1979) (construing the Longshore and Harbor Workers' Compensation Act, 33 U.S.C. § 901 et seq.). But there has been considerable legislative movement in the other direction. See, e.g., La. Civ. Code arts. 2323 and 2324. The new Restatement provides that the employer's percentage of fault should be assessed and used to diminish the employee's tort recovery in, but only in, jurisdictions that have departed from full joint and several liability. See Restatement (Third) of Torts: Apportionment of Liability §§ A19, B19, C19, C20, D19, E19 (2000).

2. In jurisdictions where the employer's percentage of fault does not diminish the employee's recovery against the "third party tortfeasor," is there any reason for making the employer a party defendant or submitting the issue of the employer's percentage of fault to the jury? Most courts have answered no. See, e.g., Teakell v. Perma Stone Company, 658 S.W.2d 563 (Tex.1983), a companion case to *Varela*. See also *Edmonds,*supra note 1.

3. *Dealing with erroneous or unwanted percentage assignments.* Fairly often in multi–party comparative fault cases, an appellate court will conclude that a fault percentage the trial court has assessed against one of the parties should not be given effect. For example, the appellate court may decide that a party who was assigned a fault percentage by the trial court was immune, or was not guilty of negligence, or was not a proximate cause of the injuries. Or it may happen, as in *Varela,* that the appeals court disagrees with the trial judge as to the kinds of actors whose negligence should "count." (During the present era, when comparative fault systems are being enacted, developed, and tested in a variety of contexts, trial judges are bound to commit such "mistakes.") The appeals court must then decide what to do with the now–unwanted percentage finding.

In *Varela* the trial court found fault as follows:

Plaintiff: 15%

Defendant (Petrofina): 43%

Employer (Hydrocarbon): 42%

The supreme court held that the 42% finding did not "count" and should not have been made. At that point the supreme court had three options: (a) remand the case for a new trial; (b) award the plaintiff 85% of his full damages; (c) award the plaintiff $43/58$ths of his full damages. The court chose (b). Why?

The disadvantages of option (a) are obvious. As between (b) and (c), the pertinent question would seem to be, which more nearly reflects the jury's allocation of fault as between plaintiff and defendant. For decisions conclud-ing that (c) is the better approach, see Davis v. Commercial Union Ins. Co., 892 F.2d 378, 384–85 (5th Cir.1990); Cartel Capital Corp. v. Fireco of New Jersey, 81 N.J. 548, 410 A.2d 674, 685 (1980); Haney Elec. Co. v. Hurst, 624 S.W.2d 602, 612–13 (Tex.Civ.App.1981). The new Restatement provides for proportional reapportionment to avoid a new trial unless eliminating the nonliable person from the jury's determination would have substantially altered the jury's deliberations or reallocating the percentages would put a party on the other side of a discontinuity in the jurisdiction's rules about modified comparative negligence or joint and several liability. See Restate-ment (Third) of Torts: Apportionment of Liability § 7, cmt. *i* (2000).

4.   In connection with Petrofina's argument that the employer should have been treated as a settling tortfeasor, see generally section D, infra.

D. PARTIAL SETTLEMENTS

A person injured through the combined effects of the fault of several tortfeasors may well have good reason to settle with and release one of the tortfeasors while continuing to pursue the others. Until relatively recently, it was difficult to do that. Many states had rules providing that releasing one tortfeasor automatically released them all, no matter what the parties' intentions. Even in states that relaxed that rule somewhat, artificial rules for construing settlement agreements meant that a plain-tiff attempting to release one tortfeasor while reserving his rights against the others ran a high risk of inadvertently releasing everyone. See generally Prosser & Keeton on Torts § 49 (5th ed. 1984).

In most states nowadays, a plaintiff wishing to settle his claim against one tortfeasor while reserving his right to pursue the others can do so, provided the agreement effectuating the settlement and release is clear as to its intention and is in proper form. Plaintiff's counsel must study the particular state's laws with great care before entering into any release agreement. Inadvertently disposing of the entire case while attempting to settle with only one of several putative tortfeasors is always a possibility.

When the plaintiff *P*—injured through the combined negligence of tortfeasors *A, B, C,* and *D*—settles with and releases *A* and then gets a judgment against *B, C,* and *D,* what are the ultimate rights and obli-gations of the parties? There is much variation among the states. The first major question is whether *A* remains exposed to contribution liability to the other tortfeasors. Today there is a strong trend toward treating the settlement and release as insulating *A* from such liability. See, e.g., Restatement (Third) of Torts: Apportionment of Liability § 23, cmt. *i* (2000); Uniform Comparative Fault Act § 6; Brochner, supra section B. A related question is whether a settling tortfeasor can get contribution against non–settling tortfeasors. The new Restatement says yes, if the settling tortfeasor paid more than its share of the damages and obtained a release for the other tortfeasors. See Restatement (Third) of Torts: Apportionment of Liability § 23, cmt. *h* (2000).

The second major question is whether the judgment against *B*, *C*, and *D* for the full damages from the injury in question should be reduced in some fashion to reflect the fact that *P* has received partial payment for this injury from *A*. Most states hold yes. Depending upon a particular state's law, the judgment may be reduced by: (a) the dollar amount *A* paid in settlement (often called the "pro tanto" method); (b) *A's* "pro rata" share of the liability (here 1/4); or (c) an amount reflecting *A's* percentage of fault. The recent trend is toward method (c), for some of the reasons discussed in the next case.

McDERMOTT, INC. v. AmCLYDE

Supreme Court of the United States, 1994.
511 U.S. 202, 114 S.Ct. 1461, 128 L.Ed.2d 148.

JUSTICE STEVENS delivered the opinion of the Court.

A construction accident in the Gulf of Mexico gave rise to this admiralty case. In advance of trial, petitioner, the plaintiff, settled with three of the defendants for $1 million. Respondents, however, did not settle, and the case went to trial. A jury assessed petitioner's loss at $2.1 million and allocated 32% of the damages to respondent AmClyde and 38% to respondent River Don. The question presented is whether the liability of the nonsettling defendants should be calculated with reference to the jury's allocation of proportionate responsibility, or by giving the nonsettling defendants a credit for the dollar amount of the settlement. We hold that the proportionate approach is the correct one.

I

Petitioner McDermott, Inc., purchased a specially designed, 5,000–ton crane from AmClyde. When petitioner first used the crane in an attempt to move an oil and gas production platform—the "Snapper deck"—from a barge to a structural steel base affixed to the floor of the Gulf of Mexico, a prong of the crane's main hook broke, causing massive damage to the deck and to the crane itself. The malfunction may have been caused by petitioner's negligent operation of the crane, by Am-Clyde's faulty design or construction, by a defect in the hook supplied by River Don Castings, Ltd. (River Don), or by one or more of the three companies (the "sling defendants") that supplied the supporting steel slings.

Invoking the federal court's admiralty jurisdiction under 28 U.S.C. § 1333(1), petitioner brought suit against AmClyde and River Don and the three sling defendants. The complaint sought a recovery for both deck damages and crane damages. On the eve of trial, petitioner entered into a settlement with the sling defendants. In exchange for $1 million, petitioner agreed to dismiss with prejudice its claims against the sling defendants, to release them from all liability for either deck or crane damages, and to indemnify them against any contribution action. The trial judge later ruled that petitioner's claim for crane damages was barred by East River Steamship Corp. v. Transamerica Delaval Inc. 476 U.S. 858, 106 S.Ct. 2295 (1986).*

In its opening statement at trial, petitioner McDermott "accepted responsibility for any part the slings played in causing the damage."[4] The jury found that the total damages to the deck amounted to $2.1 million and, in answer to special interrogatories, allocated responsibility among the respective parties: 32% to AmClyde, 38% to River Don, and 30% jointly to McDermott and the sling defendants. The Court denied a motion by respondents to reduce the judgment pro tanto by the $1 million settlement, and entered judgment against AmClyde for $672,000 (32% of $2.1 million) and against River Don for $798,000 (38% of $2.1 million). Even though the sum of those judgments plus the settlement proceeds exceeded the total damages found by the jury, the District Court concluded that petitioner had not received a double recovery because the settlement had covered both crane damages and deck damages.

The Court of Appeals held that a contractual provision precluded any recovery against AmClyde and that the trial judge had improperly denied a pro tanto settlement credit. It reversed the judgment against AmClyde entirely and reduced the judgment against River Don to $470,000. It arrived at that figure by making two calculations. First, it determined that petitioner's "full damage award is $1.47 million ($2.1 million jury verdict less 30% attributed to McDermott/sling defendants)." Next, it deducted the "$1 million received in settlement to reach $470,000." It treated this figure as the maximum that could be recovered from the non–settling defendants. Because it was less than River Don's liability as found by the jury (38% of $2.1 million or $798,000), it directed the entry of judgment against River Don in that amount.

* * *

II

Although Congress has enacted significant legislation in the field of admiralty law, none of those statutes provides us with any "policy guidance" or imposes any limit on our authority to fashion the rule that will best answer the question presented by this case. We are, nevertheless, in familiar waters because "the Judiciary has traditionally taken the lead in formulating flexible and fair remedies in the law maritime."

In [United States v. Reliable Transfer Co., 421 U.S. 397, 95 S.Ct. 1708 (1975)] we decided to abandon a rule that had been followed for over a century in assessing damages when both parties to a collision are

---

* In *East River* the Supreme Court case held that pure economic loss, without personal injury or damage to property other than the product itself, is not recoverable under negligence or strict products liability.

4. McDermott's motive in taking upon itself responsibility for the sling defendant's

fault is obscure. Perhaps it thought doing so would prevent a contribution action against the sling defendants and thus relieve McDermott of its indemnity obligation.

at fault. We replaced the divided damages rule, which required an equal division of property damage whatever the relative degree of fault may have been, with a rule requiring that damages be assessed on the basis of proportionate fault when such an allocation can reasonably be made. Although the old rule avoided the difficulty of determining comparative degrees of negligence, we concluded that it was "unnecessarily crude and inequitable" and that "[p]otential problems of proof in some cases hardly require adherence to an archaic and unfair rule in all cases." Thus the interest in certainty and simplicity served by the old rule was outweighed by the interest in fairness promoted by the proportionate fault rule.

Our decision in *Reliable Transfer* was supported by a consensus among the world's maritime nations and the views of respected scholars and judges. No comparable consensus has developed with respect to the issue in the case before us today. It is generally agreed that when a plaintiff settles with one of several joint tortfeasors, the nonsettling defendants are entitled to a credit for that settlement. There is, however, a divergence among respected scholars and judges about how that credit should be determined. Indeed, the American Law Institute has identified three principal alternatives and, after noting that "[e]ach has its drawbacks and no one is satisfactory," decided not to take a position on the issue. Restatement (Second) of Torts § 886A, pp. 343–344 (1977). The ALI describes the three alternatives as follows:

> "(1) The money paid extinguishes any claim that the injured party has against the party released and the amount of his remaining claim against the other tortfeasor is reached by crediting the amount received; but the transaction does not affect a claim for contribution by another tortfeasor who has paid more than his equitable share of the obligation."

> "(2) The money paid extinguishes both any claims on the part of the injured party and any claim for contribution by another tortfeasor who has paid more than his equitable share of the obligation and seeks contribution." (As in Alternative (1), the amount of the injured party's claim against the other tortfeasors is calculated by subtracting the amount of the settlement from the plaintiff's damages.)

> "(3) The money paid extinguishes any claim that the injured party has against the released tortfeasor and also diminishes the claim that the injured party has against the other tortfeasors by the amount of the equitable share of the obligation of the released tortfeasor."

The first two alternatives involve the kind of "pro tanto" credit that respondents urge us to adopt. The difference between the two versions of the pro tanto approach is the recognition of a right of contribution against a settling defendant in the first but not the second. The third alternative, supported by petitioner, involves a credit for the settling defendants' "proportionate share" of responsibility for the total obligation. Under this approach, no suits for contribution from the settling defendants are permitted, nor are they necessary, because the nonsettling defendants pay no more than their share of the judgment.

The proportionate share approach[9] would make River Don responsible for precisely its share of the damages, $798,000 (38% of $2.1 million).[10] A simple application of the pro tanto approach would allocate River Don $1.1 million in damages ($2.1 million total damages minus the $1 million settlement). The Court of Appeals, however, made a different calculation. Because McDermott "accepted responsibility for any part the sling played in causing the damage," 979 F.2d at 1070, the Court of Appeals treated the 30% of liability apportioned to "McDermott/sling defendants" as if that 30% had been caused solely by McDermott's own negligence. Id., at 1081. The Court of Appeals, therefore, gave River Don a double credit, first reducing the total loss by the McDermott/sling defendants' proportionate share and then applying the full pro tanto reduction to that amount. This double credit resulted in an award of only $470,000 ($2.1 million minus 30% of $2.1 million minus $1 million).

III

In choosing among the ALI's three alternatives, three considerations are paramount: consistency with the proportionate fault approach of Reliable Transfer, promotion of settlement, and judicial economy. ALI Option 1, pro tanto setoff with right of contribution against the settling defendant, is clearly inferior to the other two, because it discourages settlement and leads to unnecessary ancillary litigation. It discourages settlement, because settlement can only disadvantage the settling defendant. If a defendant makes a favorable settlement, in which it pays less than the amount a court later determines is its share of liability, the other defendant (or defendants) can sue the settling defendant for contribution. The settling defendant thereby loses the benefit of its favorable settlement. In addition, the claim for contribution burdens the courts with additional litigation. The plaintiff can mitigate the adverse effect on settlement by promising to indemnify the settling defendant against contribution, as McDermott did here. This indemnity, while removing the disincentive to settlement, adds yet another potential burden on the courts, an indemnity action between the settling defendant and plaintiff.

9. In this opinion, we use the phrase "proportionate share approach" to denote ALI Option 3. We have deliberately avoided use of the term "pro rata," which is often used to describe this approach [ ] because that term is also used to describe an equal allocation among all defendants without regard to their relative responsibility for the loss. [ ]

10. * * * AmClyde is immune from damages because its contract with McDermott provided that free replacement of defective parts "shall constitute fulfillment of all liabilities ... whether based upon Contract, tort, strict liability or otherwise." 979 F.2d at 1075 (emphasis omitted). The best way of viewing this contractual provision is as a quasi-settlement in advance of any tort claims. Viewed as such, the proportionate credit in this case properly takes into account both the 30% of liability apportioned to the settling defendants (and McDermott) and the 32% allocated to AmClyde. This leaves River Don with $798,000 or 38% of the damages.

The choice between ALI Options 2 and 3, between the pro tanto rule without contribution against the settling tortfeasor and the proportionate share approach, is less clear. The proportionate share rule is more consistent with *Reliable Transfer*, because a litigating defendant ordinarily pays only its proportionate share of the judgment. Under the pro tanto approach, however, a litigating defendant's liability will frequently differ from its equitable share, because a settlement with one defendant for less than its equitable share requires the nonsettling defendant to pay more than its share.[14] Such deviations from the equitable apportionment of damages will be common, because settlements seldom reflect an entirely accurate prediction of the outcome of a trial. Moreover, the settlement figure is likely to be significantly less than the settling defendant's equitable share of the loss, because settlement reflects the uncertainty of trial and provides the plaintiff with a "war chest" with which to finance the litigation against the remaining defendants. Courts and legislatures have recognized this potential for unfairness and have required "good–faith hearings" as a remedy. When such hearings are required, the settling defendant is protected against contribution actions only if it shows that the settlement is a fair forecast of its equitable share of the judgment. Nevertheless, good–faith hearings cannot fully remove the potential for inequitable allocation of liability. First, to serve their protective function effectively, such hearings would have to be minitrials on the merits, but in practice they are often quite cursory. More fundamentally, even if the judge at a good–faith hearing were able to make a perfect forecast of the allocation of liability at trial, there might still be substantial unfairness when the plaintiff's success at trial is uncertain. In sum, the pro tanto approach, even when supplemented with good–faith hearings, is likely to lead to inequitable apportionments of liability, contrary to *Reliable Transfer*.

The effect of the two rules on settlements is more ambiguous. Sometimes the pro tanto approach will better promote settlement.[20] This

---

14. Suppose, for example, that a plaintiff sues two defendants, each equally responsible, and settles with one for $250,000. At trial, the non–settling defendant is found liable, and plaintiff's damages are assessed at $1 million. Under the pro tanto rule, the nonsettling defendant would be liable for 75% of the damages ($750,000, which is $1 million minus $250,000). The litigating defendant is thus responsible for far more than its proportionate share of the damages. It is also possible for the pro tanto rule to result in the nonsettlor paying less than its apportioned share, if, as in this case, the settlement is greater than the amount later determined by the court to be the settlors' equitable share. * * *

20. Illustration of the beneficial effects of the pro tanto rule requires substantial simplifying assumptions. Suppose, for example, that all parties are risk neutral, that litigation is costless, and that there are only

two defendants. In addition, suppose everyone agrees that the damages are $100, that if one defendant is found liable, the other one will also be found liable, and that if the defendants are liable, each will be apportioned 50% of the damages. And suppose, as frequently happens, that the plaintiff is more optimistic about his chances of prevailing than the defendants: plaintiff thinks his chances of winning are 60%, whereas the defendants think the plaintiff's chances are only 50%. In this case, under the proportionate setoff rule, settlement is unlikely, because the plaintiff would be reluctant to accept less than $30 (60% times 50% of $100) from each defendant, whereas neither defendant would be disposed to offer more than $25 (50% times 50% of $100). On the other hand, under the pro tanto rule, the plaintiff would be willing to accept a $25 settlement offer, because he would believe he had a 60% chance of recovering $75

beneficial effect, however, is a consequence of the inequity discussed above. The rule encourages settlements by giving the defendant that settles first an opportunity to pay less than its fair share of the damages, thereby threatening the non–settling defendant with the prospect of paying more than its fair share of the loss. By disadvantaging the party that spurns settlement offers, the pro tanto rule puts pressure on all defendants to settle. While public policy wisely encourages settlements, such additional pressure to settle is unnecessary. The parties' desire to avoid litigation costs, to reduce uncertainty, and to maintain ongoing commercial relationships is sufficient to ensure nontrial dispositions in the vast majority of cases. Under the proportionate share approach, such factors should ensure a similarly high settlement rate. The additional incentive to settlement provided by the pro tanto rule comes at too high a price in unfairness. Furthermore, any conclusion that the pro tanto rule generally encourages more settlements requires many simplifying assumptions, such as low litigation costs. Recognition of the reality that a host of practical considerations may be more significant than stark hypotheticals persuades us that the pro tanto rule has no clear advantage in promoting settlements.

The effect of the two rules on judicial economy is also ambiguous. The pro tanto rule, if adopted without the requirement of a good–faith hearing, would be easier to administer, because the relative fault of the settling defendant would not have to be adjudicated either at a preliminary hearing or at trial. Nevertheless, because of the large potential for unfairness, no party or amicus in this suit advocates the pro tanto rule untamed by good–faith hearings. Once the pro tanto rule is coupled with a good–faith hearing, however, it is difficult to determine whether the pro tanto or proportionate share approach best promotes judicial economy. Under either approach, the relative fault of the parties will have to be determined. Under the pro tanto approach, the settling defendant's share of responsibility will have to be ascertained at a separate, pretrial hearing. Under the proportionate share approach, the allocation will take place at trial. The pro tanto approach will, therefore, only save judicial time if the good–faith hearing is quicker than the allocation of fault at trial. Given the cursory nature of most good–faith hearings, this may well be true. On the other hand, there is reason to believe that reserving the apportionment of liability for trial may save more time. First, the remaining defendant (or defendants) may settle before trial, thus making any determination of relative culpability unnecessary. In addition, the apportionment of damages required by the proportionate share rule may require little or no additional trial time. The parties will often need to describe the settling defendant's role in order to provide context for the dispute. Furthermore, a defendant will often argue the "empty chair" in the hope of convincing the jury that the settling party

($100 minus the $25 settlement) at trial from the other defendant. Accepting the $25 settlement offer would give the plaintiff an expected recovery of $70 ($25 plus 60% of $75), which is more than the $60 (60% of $100) the plaintiff would expect if he went to trial against both defendants. * * *

was exclusively responsible for the damage. The pro tanto rule thus has no clear advantage with respect to judicial economy.

In sum, although the arguments for the two approaches are closely matched, we are persuaded that the proportionate share approach is superior, especially in its consistency with *Reliable Transfer*.

IV

Respondents advance [an additional argument] against the proportionate share approach: that it violates the "one satisfaction rule" * * *.

In the 19th and early 20th centuries, the "one satisfaction rule" barred a plaintiff from litigating against one joint tortfeasor, if he had settled with and released another. This version of the one satisfaction rule has been thoroughly repudiated. Respondents do not ask that the one satisfaction rule be applied with its original strictness, but rather in the milder form in which some courts still invoke it to reduce a plaintiff's recovery against a nonsettling defendant in order to ensure that the plaintiff does not secure more than necessary to compensate him for his loss. As a preliminary matter, it is far from clear that there was any danger of super–compensatory damages here. First, there is the question of the crane damages, which were not covered by the judgment against River Don. In addition, even limiting consideration to deck damages, the jury fixed plaintiff's losses at $2.1 million. Plaintiff received $1 million in settlement from the sling defendants. Under the proportionate share approach, plaintiff would receive an additional $798,000 from River Don. In total, plaintiff would recover only $1.798 million, over $300,000 less than its damages. The one satisfaction rule comes into play only if one assumes that the percent share of liability apportioned to McDermott and the sling defendants really represented McDermott's contributory fault, and that it would be overcompensatory for McDermott to receive more than the percentage of the total loss allocated to the defendants, here $1.47 million (70% of $2.1 million).

Even if the Court of Appeals were correct in finding that the proportionate share approach would overcompensate McDermott, we would not apply the one satisfaction rule. The law contains no rigid rule against overcompensation. Several doctrines, such as the collateral benefits rule, recognize that making tortfeasors pay for the damage they cause can be more important than preventing overcompensation. In this case, any excess recovery is entirely attributable to the fact that the sling defendants may have made an unwise settlement. It seems probable that in most cases in which there is a partial settlement, the plaintiff is more apt to accept less than the proportionate share that the jury might later assess against the settling defendant, because of the uncertainty of recovery at the time of settlement negotiations and because the first settlement normally improves the plaintiff's litigating posture against the nonsettlors. In such cases, the entire burden of applying a proportionate share rule would rest on the plaintiff, and the interest in avoiding overcompensation would be absent. More fundamentally, we must recognize that settlements frequently result in the plaintiff's getting more than he would have been entitled to at trial. Because settlement amounts are based on rough estimates of liability, anticipated savings in litigation costs, and a host of other factors, they will rarely match exactly the amounts a trier of fact would have set. It seems to us that a plaintiff's good fortune in striking a favorable bargain with one defendant gives other defendants no claim to pay less than their proportionate share of the total loss. In fact, one of the virtues of the proportionate share rule is that, unlike the pro tanto rule, it does not make a litigating defendant's liability dependent on the amount of a settlement negotiated by others without regard to its interests.

* * * In addition, * * * there is no tension between joint and several liability and a proportionate share approach to settlements. Joint and several liability applies when there has been a judgment against multiple defendants. It can result in one defendant's paying more than its apportioned share of liability when the plaintiff's recovery from other defendants is limited by factors beyond the plaintiff's control, such as a defendant's insolvency. When the limitations on the plaintiff's recovery arise from outside forces, joint and several liability makes the other defendants, rather than an innocent plaintiff, responsible for the shortfall. * * * [T]he proportionate share rule announced in this opinion applies when there has been a settlement. In such cases, the plaintiff's recovery against the settling defendant has been limited not by outside forces, but by its own agreement to settle. There is no reason to allocate any shortfall to the other defendants, who were not parties to the settlement. Just as the other defendants are not entitled to a reduction in liability when the plaintiff negotiates a generous settlement, so they are not required to shoulder disproportionate liability when the plaintiff negotiates a meager one.

V

The judgment of the Court of Appeals is reversed, and the case is remanded for further proceedings consistent with this opinion.

It is so ordered.

Notes

1. The new Restatement adopts the rule in McDermott, Inc. v. Am-Clyde. See Restatement (Third) of Torts: Apportionment of Liability § 16 (2000).

2. *Mary Carter agreements.* Sometimes settlements provide that, if the plaintiff recovers from a nonsettling defendant, the plaintiff will return some or all of the settlement to the settling defendant. These settlements are often called "Mary Carter" settlements, after Booth v. Mary Carter Paint Co., 202 So.2d 8 (Fla.Ct.App.1967). They come in a variety of forms. Can you see why they are attractive to the plaintiff *and* the settling defendant? If the settling defendant will be a witness at trial (or remains as a party), can you see any problems with such a settlement? Some courts have outlawed Mary Carter agreements. See, e.g., Elbaor v. Smith, 845 S.W.2d 240 (Tex. 1992); Lum v.

Stinnett, 87 Nev. 402, 488 P.2d 347 (1971); Trampe v. Wisconsin Telephone Co., 214 Wis. 210, 252 N.W. 675 (1934). Most courts that permit them require the plaintiff to reveal their terms to the jury.

3. In a jurisdiction that uses *pro tanto* reduction for settlors, how should a Mary Carter settlement be valued?

4. In a jurisdiction that uses percentage reduction for settlors, the jury obviously must assign a percentage of responsibility to settlors. In a jurisdiction that uses *pro tanto* reduction for settlors, the settlement scheme does not require the jury to assign a percentage of fault to settlors, but the rules about joint and several liability might require such a finding.

E. APPLICATION OF COMPARATIVE RESPONSIBILITY TO CAUSES OF ACTION OTHER THAN NEGLIGENCE

BONPUA v. FAGAN

Superior Court of New Jersey, Appellate Division, 1992.
253 N.J.Super. 475, 602 A.2d 287.

SKILLMAN, JUDGE.

This lawsuit arises out of a physical altercation between plaintiff and defendant in the parking lot behind Cammarano's Bar in Long Branch on March 26, 1987. Plaintiff's complaint and defendant's counterclaim each allege that they suffered personal injuries as a result of an assault and battery or, in the alternative, negligence of the other party. Each party's answer alleges that the other party's claim is barred or subject to reduction due to that party's contributory fault.

Defendant was convicted of aggravated assault * * * and sentenced to a seven year term of imprisonment, for his role in the altercation. * * *

Plaintiff moved for summary judgment on liability and the dismissal of defendant's counterclaim on the theory that defendant's conviction for aggravated assault conclusively established that he committed an intentional tort upon plaintiff, and that under the Comparative Negligence Act, N.J.S.A. 2A:15–5.1 to 5.8, any negligence or other fault of plaintiff would not bar or reduce his claim.*

The trial court granted plaintiff's motion in part, striking defendant's affirmative defense of comparative negligence and entering summary judgment on liability in favor of plaintiff, but refused to dismiss defendant's counterclaim. We granted defendant's motion for leave to

* N.J.S.A. 2A:15–5.1 sets out a 51%– modified rule of "comparative negligence" applicable to "action[s] . . . to recover damages for negligence." Section 2A:15–5.2 expands the coverage to include "strict liability actions" as well as "negligence actions" and sets forth definitions of each. The definition of "negligence actions" states that the term "includes, but is not limited to, civil actions for damages based upon theories of negligence," and goes on to provide that "[i]n determining whether a case falls within the term 'negligence actions,' the court shall look to the substance of the action and not the conclusory terms used by the parties." [Ed.]

appeal from the summary judgment on liability in favor of plaintiff and now reverse.[1]

Subsequent to the trial court's decision, the Supreme Court held in Blazovic v. Andrich, 124 N.J. 90, 590 A.2d 222 (1991), that the Comparative Negligence Act applies to intentional tortious conduct. Thus, the Act requires the trier of fact to apportion the fault of all culpable parties, regardless of whether their conduct was negligent or intentional. The Court stated:

> Refusal to compare the negligence of a plaintiff whose percentage of fault is no more than fifty percent with the fault of intentional tortfeasors is difficult to justify under a comparative–fault system in which that plaintiff's recovery can be only diminished, not barred. . . .
>
> Moreover, we reject the concept that intentional conduct is "different in kind" from both negligence and wanton and willful conduct, and consequently cannot be compared with them. Instead, we view intentional wrongdoing as "different in degree" from either negligence or wanton and willful conduct. * * * The different levels of culpability inherent in each type of conduct will merely be reflected in the jury's apportionment of fault. By viewing the various types of tortious conduct in that way, we adhere most closely to the guiding principle of comparative fault—to distribute the loss in proportion to the respective faults of the parties causing that loss. Thus, consistent with the evolution of comparative negligence and joint–tortfeasor liability in this state, we hold that responsibility for a plaintiff's claimed injury is to be apportioned according to each party's relative degree of fault, including the fault attributable to an intentional tortfeasor.

Plaintiff urges that the Comparative Negligence Act is inapplicable because defendant's intentional wrongdoing resulted in defendant's conviction of a criminal offense. However, we find nothing in *Blazovic* which suggests this limitation upon the application of the Act. Furthermore, whether a tortfeasor's conduct results in a criminal conviction is not an accurate barometer of the egregiousness of that conduct. Prosecuting authorities may decline to prosecute or be unable to obtain a conviction for serious wrongdoing while relatively minor misconduct may result in a conviction for a petty offense. We also note that conduct which is treated as negligence under the law of torts may result in a criminal conviction; for example, reckless driving which causes a death may result in a conviction for death by auto. Yet, a party convicted of death by auto would not be precluded in an automobile negligence case from urging that his liability should be reduced due to the decedent's contributory fault or shared with other culpable parties. The rationale of *Blazovic* does not provide any basis for concluding that a defendant alleged to have committed an intentional tort which has resulted in a criminal

---

1. Since plaintiff did not move for leave to appeal from the denial of his motion seeking dismissal of defendant's counterclaim, that denial is not before us.

conviction should be barred from relying upon the Comparative Negligence Act when an alleged negligent defendant would not be barred under the same circumstances.

Even if we assume that some intentional wrongdoing may be so offensive that the tortfeasor should not be allowed to assert the plaintiff's contributory fault, this determination should turn on the nature of the parties' conduct rather than the circumstance that the defendant has been convicted of a criminal offense. Therefore, defendant's criminal conviction does not preclude him from relying upon the Comparative Negligence Act as a defense to plaintiff's claim.

We are also satisfied that defendant's version of his altercation with plaintiff would support a jury finding that plaintiff was negligent or even guilty of intentional wrongdoing. Defendant testified that as he was talking to his girlfriend, plaintiff ridiculed him and called him a "faggot." Defendant then walked over to plaintiff's car, at which time plaintiff got out of the car and began hitting defendant. According to defendant, plaintiff's injuries resulted entirely from defendant's efforts to defend himself. If a jury believed even part of defendant's version of this incident, it could find that plaintiff committed an assault upon defendant or at least failed to exercise due care for his own safety.

Furthermore, such a finding would not be inconsistent with the criminal jury's finding that defendant was guilty of second degree aggravated assault. The criminal jury could have returned a guilty verdict even though it believed plaintiff initiated the altercation if it found that defendant responded to plaintiff's verbal abuse by assaulting him or used excessive force in repelling his aggression.

Accordingly, we reverse the summary judgment in favor of plaintiff and remand for further proceedings consistent with this opinion.

Notes

1. *Percentage–responsibility allocation in intentional tort situations.* Traditionally, the plaintiff's negligence was not a defense to intentional torts. See Restatement (Second) of Torts § 481. Thus, when most courts or legislatures adopted comparative responsibility schemes, the schemes did not apply to intentional torts. See, e.g., Tex.Civ.Prac. & Rem.Code, ch. 33, (1987). Applying comparative responsibility to intentional torts raises two issues. First, in a multi–party lawsuit in which one defendant is liable for an intentional tort, should the fact finder assign a percentage of responsibility to the intentional tortfeasor? Such a percentage could affect (1) the plaintiff's own percentage and thereby the corresponding reduction of the plaintiff's recovery against other defendants, including non–intentional tortfeasors, (2) whether to impose joint and several liability on certain defendants, (3) the allocation of responsibility to other defendants in the case, (4) the rules governing settlement, and (5) contribution and indemnity. Second, should a plaintiff's negligence affect (as a percentage reduction) the plaintiff's own recovery against the intentional tortfeasor?

These two issues are related. In a multi–party suit in which some defendants are negligent and some defendants are intentional tortfeasors, it would be cumbersome (1) to count an intentional tortfeasor's percentage of responsibility and (2) to count the plaintiff's negligence in claims against the negligent tortfeasors but (3) not to count the plaintiff's negligence in claims against the intentional tortfeasors. Consider the situation in which one tortfeasor shoots the plaintiff at a convenience store, the convenience store is negligent for not having proper security, and a doctor aggravates the injury through malpractice. All three tortfeasors jointly caused the aggravated portion of the injury. It would be difficult to allocate responsibility for either the initial injury or the aggravation without using the same comparative responsibility scheme for all the tortfeasors. Thus, a decision to include intentional tortfeasors in a comparative responsibility scheme supports a decision to count the plaintiff's negligence as a percentage reduction against an intentional tortfeasor.

Many people have an intuitive sense that a plaintiff's own failure to use reasonable care should not affect the plaintiff's recovery against an intentional tortfeasor. This intuition draws on the image of a mugger who claims that the victim was negligent for being out too late at night or wearing too much jewelry. In other situations, however, our intuition to reject a plaintiff's negligence as a percentage defense might not be as strong, such as when a defendant who batters a plaintiff honestly but unreasonably believes the conduct was privileged or was not harmful or offensive (such as when a defendant intentionally exposes a plaintiff to a pollutant that the defendant honestly but unreasonably believes is not harmful). Moreover, the fact finder can take the degree of intentionality or even deliberateness of the tortfeasor's conduct into account when assigning percentages to the various parties.

Courts could also develop "no duty" rules to cover certain types of plaintiff conduct, such as a claim that a victim of a sexual assault dressed provocatively, a claim involving domestic violence, or a claim by the mugging victim mentioned above. Courts have spent a great deal of time and energy developing "no duty" rules with respect to a defendant's conduct in negligence. Because most courts have not applied comparative responsibility to intentional torts, they have not had the opportunity to develop similar "no duty" rules for plaintiffs who encounter a defendant's intentional conduct.

2. *The new Restatement of Apportionment.* The new Restatement takes no position on the question of whether a plaintiff's negligence should reduce his or her recovery against an intentional tortfeasor. See Restatement (Third) of Torts: Apportionment of Liability § 1, cmt. *c* (2000). It provides that intentional tortfeasors are always jointly and severally liable, even if joint and several liability has otherwise been abolished or modified. See Id. It provides that, in multiparty litigation, the fact finder assigns a percentage of responsibility to intentional tortfeasors for the purpose of applying a jurisdiction's rules about joint and several liability to other tortfeasors. See Id. §§ A19, B19, C19, D19, E19. But it also provides that, regardless of a jurisdiction's other rules about joint and several liability, "[a] person who is liable to another based on a failure to protect the other from the specific risk on an intentional tort is jointly and severally liable for the share of comparative responsibility assigned to the intentional tortfeasor in addition to the share of comparative responsibility assigned to the person." Id. § 14. Under this provision, a hotel that negligently gave a criminal access to a guest's room would be liable for its own percentage share of responsibility

and jointly and severally liable with the criminal for the criminal's percentage share of responsibility. Whether the hotel would be jointly and severally liable for *other* tortfeasors' shares of liability would depend on the jurisdiction's general rules about joint and several liability.

3. Applying comparative responsibility to intentional torts is not the majority rule, but it commands significant support among courts that have addressed the question. Much of this growing support is in cases involving a comparison of *defendants'* responsibility, not a comparison of a *defendant* with a *plaintiff. Blazovic,* which the court quotes in *Bonpua,* was such a case.

Some of the support, however, is in cases that, like *Bonpua,* compare a *plaintiff's* responsibility with that of an intentional *defendant.* See, e.g., Comeau v. Lucas, 90 A.D.2d 674, 455 N.Y.S.2d 871 (1982). But see McLain v. Training and Development Corp., 572 A.2d 494 (Me.1990). There is also scholarly support for applying comparative responsibility to intentional torts. See McNichols, Should Comparative Responsibility Ever Apply to Intentional Torts, 37 Okla.L.Rev. 641 (1984).

4. *Comparative responsibility in strict products liability cases.* The application of comparative responsibility to strict products liability is addressed in Chapter XV. Before comparative fault, most courts did not apply contributory negligence as a defense in strict products liability. Comment *n* of Restatement (Second) of Torts § 402A provided that assumption of risk was a defense to strict products liability but that a plaintiff's mere negligent failure to discover or guard against the existence of a product defect was not a defense. Comment *n* was silent about a plaintiff's negligence that was more than a mere failure to discover or guard against a product defect but that did not rise to the level of assumption of risk. Some courts held that this type of negligence was not a defense to strict products liability. See, e.g., McCown v. International Harvester Co., 463 Pa. 13, 342 A.2d 381 (1975).

Most states apply their comparative responsibility scheme to strict products liability. See, e.g., N.J.S.A. 2A:15–5.2; Butaud v. Suburban Marine & Sporting Goods, Inc., 555 P.2d 42 (Alaska 1976). Many states hold at least that a plaintiff's negligence which constitutes more than a mere failure to discover or guard against a product defect justifies the fact finder in assigning a percentage of responsibility to the plaintiff. See, e.g., Daly v. General Motors Corp., 20 Cal.3d 725, 144 Cal.Rptr. 380, 575 P.2d 1162 (1978); Duncan v. Cessna Aircraft Co., 665 S.W.2d 414 (Tex.1984). Other jurisdictions have gone further to hold that all forms of plaintiff negligence are relevant for a fact finder's assigning a percentage of responsibility to the plaintiff. See, e.g., Pan–Alaska Fisheries, Inc. v. Marine Construction & Design Co., 565 F.2d 1129 (9th Cir.1977). This position is now the rule in Restatement (Third) of Torts: Products Liability § 13 (1998).

5. Comparative responsibility might also be used in other causes of action. This is especially true when a statutory cause of action calls for courts to develop common law principles to fill in unanswered questions about apportionment of loss among multiple parties. See, e.g., Comerica Bank–Detroit v. Allen Indus., Inc., 769 F.Supp. 1408, 1413–15 (E.D.Mich. 1991) (CERCLA); Franklin v. Kaypro Corp., 884 F.2d 1222, 1229–32 (9th Cir.1989), cert. denied, 493 U.S. 1024, 110 S.Ct. 729, 107 L.Ed.2d 748 (1990) (Securities Exchange Act); Dobson v. Camden, 705 F.2d 759, 768–71 (5th

Cir.1983) (Civil Rights Act), rev'd on other grounds, 725 F.2d 1003 (5th Cir.1984). See generally Kornhauser & Revesz, Settlements Under Joint and Several Liability, 68 N.Y.U.L.Rev. 427, 430–32 (1993).

On the other hand, the policies underlying certain statutory causes of action may be incompatible with applying plaintiff's negligence as a percentage defense. See, e.g., Boyles v. Hamilton, 235 Cal.App.2d 492, 45 Cal.Rptr. 399 (1965) (child labor statute); Zerby v. Warren, 297 Minn. 134, 210 N.W.2d 58 (1973) (sale of dangerous product to minors); Wells v. Coulter Sales, Inc., 105 Mich.App. 107, 306 N.W.2d 411 (1981) (workplace safety statute).

Suits under workers' compensation statutes to recover from an employer for workplace injuries are an example of a special cause of action that implicates distinct policies. Moreover, claims based on workers' compensation statutes do not often occur in hybrid cases in which some of the causes of action are governed by comparative responsibility. Claims based on workers' compensation statutes typically are governed by a special statute, are adjudicated in a separate lawsuit or administrative proceeding, and are governed by rules that do not consider the culpability or responsibility of the parties. Comparative responsibility would apply, of course, to the infrequent cases in which suits by employees against employers for workplace injuries are governed by common law causes of action or ordinary wrongful death statutes.

F. APPORTIONMENT BY CAUSATION AND FAULT IN THE SAME CASE

Current tort law provides two distinct ways of dividing damages among various parties. One body of law provides that any defendant is liable only for damages it caused. See Chapter IV. When two defendants cause separate harm, the court must sort out who caused what portion of the harm. A second body of law provides that damages are divided according to fault under a comparative scheme. Usually, this division is made when all of the parties being compared are joint causes of an indivisible injury. The law is unclear, however, about what happens when both issues arise in the same case, that is, when a court must divide damages according to causation *and* fault.

Consider a negligent motorist who is injured in a collision with another negligent motorist in which (1) the original impact causes injury to his back; (2) a defective steering wheel shatters, causing injury to his hand; and (3) a doctor treating him for the injured hand negligently administers a drug, causing a rash. (Similar problems could include plaintiff conduct—such as failure to wear a seat belt—that caused only a portion of the injuries.) The negligent motorist is a cause in fact of all the plaintiff's injuries under the "but for" test of causation. The steering wheel manufacturer is a cause in fact only of the cut hand and the rash. The doctor, in turn, is a cause in fact only of the rash. The plaintiff's negligent driving, of course, is a cause in fact of all three injuries.

Since the back injury was caused only by the other negligent motorist and the plaintiff, damages from the back injury should be shared by them under comparative fault. Since the hand injury was caused by the negligent motorist, the steering wheel manufacturer, and the plaintiff, the hand injury should be allocated among them under comparative fault. Since the rash was caused jointly by all three defendants and the plaintiff, it should be allocated among all four of them under comparative fault. The rash cannot be allocated by comparing cause in fact, because each defendant (and the plaintiff) was a cause in fact of the entire rash.

But how should all of this be submitted to the jury? Will the jury be asked to segregate the three separate injuries according to cause in fact (*i.e.,* the back, the hand, and the rash) and *then* apportion each injury among its causes according to fault? Doing so would require three separate strings of percentages, each totaling 100, because different sets of defendants caused each injury. This approach would be difficult to implement in some cases. Injuries are not always as easy to divide as are a back injury, a hand injury, and a rash. Maybe the doctor's malpractice aggravated the hand injury or caused more pain to the plaintiff's back. If so, the trial court could not simply ask the jury to ascertain comparative fault findings for each injury identified by the court in advance. The jury itself would have to resolve fact questions about how to divide the injuries on the basis of cause in fact. It would *then* somehow have to compare the fault of each defendant who caused each separate injury. This, to say the least, would be cumbersome. Moreover, the three strings of percentages are likely to be inconsistent with each other in the relative ratios of fault they assign to the various parties.

These difficulties could be avoided by asking the jury to perform both operations—division by cause in fact and allocation according to fault—in one step. The jury's percentage findings could reflect, under proper instruction, a determination of each party's responsibility for the plaintiff's injuries, taking into account *both* cause in fact and fault. Thus, in the example above, the jury could assign percentages to the motorist, the steering wheel manufacturer, the doctor, and the plaintiff by taking into account *both* the relative *fault* of the parties *and* the facts that the doctor had no *casual* connection with the back injury or the hand and that the steering wheel manufacturer had no *causal* connection with the back injury.

A difficulty arises, however, if a court takes this approach *and* retains joint and several liability. Again referring to the example, suppose the jury assigns 10% responsibility to the plaintiff, 50% responsibility to the other motorist, 25% responsibility to the steering wheel manufacturer, and 25% responsibility to the doctor. If the other motorist was insolvent, the steering wheel manufacturer and the doctor would be required to pay for the other motorist's 50% share. But this share includes liability for the back injury, which the steering wheel manufacturer and the doctor did not cause.

No court has addressed this problem expressly. A few courts have *implicitly* suggested approaches, but there has been no uniformity. See, e.g., Phelan v. Lopez, 701 S.W.2d 327 (Tex.App.1985); Moore v. Johns–Manville Sales Corp., 781 F.2d 1061 (5th Cir.1986).

In cases involving toxic exposures, it is common for parties to introduce evidence about the time and intensity of the plaintiff's exposure to (*i.e.,* "dosages" of) various sources of the toxin, such as exposure to asbestos at various worksites. It makes common sense to apportion liability according to these dosages. But this type of apportionment is not division according to fault; one source of the toxin may have a far more culpable state of mind than another. Nor, strictly speaking, is this type of apportionment necessarily division according to causation. The injury may be causally indivisible, such as death caused by cancer. In fact, in many toxic injuries, the precise nature of the causal link is not clear. The problem sometimes is that the scientific evidence does not fit neatly into any of the established legal categories of causation. Nevertheless, courts must apportion such injuries as a practical matter, and maybe apportionment by dosage is the best way to reach a fair result.

The new Restatement adopts the two–step process described above, unless this two–step process "is administratively unsuitable because the case is too complex for a jury to find the requisite facts." Restatement (Third) of Torts: Apportionment of Liability § 26 cmt. *j.* See also *id.,* cmts. *c, d.* But courts have made little progress solving (or even recognizing) these problems. With increased attention to multiparty litigation generally, and toxic tort litigation specifically, these problems will continue to arise. They are likely to present courts with challenges over the next several years.

Chapter XII

IMMUNITIES

Immunities protect certain types of defendants from all or some kinds of tort liability. They differ from the defenses addressed in Chapter IX in that they depend on the nature of the defendant, not on the nature of the plaintiff's conduct. Moreover, the subject of immunities goes beyond negligence liability; immunities often avail against intentional tort liability and strict liability as well as negligence. Claims of family or charitable immunity are usually treated as affirmative defenses, but governmental immunity may preclude subject matter jurisdiction. See, e.g., Mundy v. United States, 983 F.2d 950 (9th Cir. 1993).

At one time, federal and state governments were completely immune from suit and from liability for most forms of tortious conduct. The same was true of "charitable" corporations and institutions. Family members were sometimes immune from tort actions brought by fellow family members. Although the scope of all these immunities has been greatly restricted in the years since World War II, enough remains to make immunity an issue in many tort cases.

Charitable immunity has been abolished in most states as a general common-law doctrine, but aspects of it have reappeared in legislation immunizing or limiting liability of specific charitable organizations. See, e.g., Tex. Civ. Prac. & Rem. Code § 87.003, immunizing sponsors of livestock shows and rodeos from liability for injuries to participants; Md.Cts. & Jud. Pro.Code § 5–632, capping liability of charity hospitals at the amount of their insurance coverage provided that is at least $100,000. The remnants of charitable immunity are too scattered and idiosyncratic to be further explored here.

A. GOVERNMENT IMMUNITY

1. STATE AND LOCAL GOVERNMENTS

HICKS v. STATE

Supreme Court of New Mexico, 1975.
88 N.M. 588, 544 P.2d 1153.

MONTOYA, JUSTICE.

This appeal arises from an order of the Santa Fe County District Court granting the motion of defendant State of New Mexico to dismiss on the ground that the action of plaintiff Ron E. Hicks was barred by the doctrine of sovereign immunity.

Suit was originally brought in the District Court of Santa Fe County on August 6, 1973, to recover damages for the wrongful death of plaintiff's wife and minor daughter due allegedly to the negligence of the State Highway Department. These deaths were the result of an accident near Fort Summer, New Mexico, on December 26, 1972, when a school bus collided with a cattle truck on a narrow bridge constructed and maintained by the State Highway Department. Subsequently, defendant filed a motion to dismiss. After a hearing, the motion was granted by order of the trial court * * *.

In a memorandum decision, the district court stated that the doctrine of sovereign immunity was a long–standing common law principle which could now be changed only by legislative action. We do not agree that a change in this age–old doctrine can only be made by the legislature.

* * *

* * * The doctrine of sovereign immunity has always been a judicial creation without statutory codification and, therefore, can also be put to rest by the judiciary. * * * Merely because a court–made rule has been in effect for many years does not render it invulnerable to judicial attack once it reaches a point of obsolescence.

* * *

The original justification for the doctrine of sovereign immunity was the archaic view that "the sovereign can do no wrong." It is hardly necessary for this court to spend time to refute this feudalistic contention. This and all other rationalizations which have been advanced to justify continued adherence to this doctrine are no longer valid in New Mexico. The argument has been presented that the elimination of sovereign immunity will result in an intolerable financial burden upon the State. We believe it is safe to say that adequate insurance can be secured to eliminate that possible burden in a satisfactory manner. In addition, it would appear that placing the financial burden upon the

State, which is able to distribute its losses throughout the populace, is more just and equitable than forcing the individual who is injured to bear the entire burden alone. There are presently in New Mexico no conditions or circumstances which could rationally support the doctrine of sovereign immunity. We have long recognized that the doctrine is not applicable to municipalities when engaged in a proprietary function.

Several times in the recent past this court has cast aspersions upon sovereign immunity * * *. But unfortunately, in those cases, the issue was not squarely before us, as it is today. Thus, we take this opportunity to rid the State of this legal anachronism. Common law sovereign immunity may no longer be interposed as a defense by the State, or any of its political subdivisions, in tort actions. Sovereign immunity was born out of the judicial branch of government, and it is the same branch which may dispose of the doctrine. It can no longer be justified by existing circumstances and has long been devoid of any valid justification. In so doing, we join the growing number of States which have judicially abolished it.

We recognize that this is a far–reaching decision which, at first blush, does violence to the doctrine of "stare decisis." However, we do not feel that "stare decisis" should be used to perpetuate the harsh and unjust results which blind adherence to sovereign immunity rules mandated. We concede that there was ample authority which influenced our predecessors in adopting and upholding the doctrine of sovereign immunity. We also say that there is better reasoned authority to overturn it. We simply conclude that its continuance is causing a great degree of injustice.

In today's world, we cannot discount the extent of governmental intervention and actions which affect the conduct of human affairs. We agree with the reasoning of the Supreme Court of Pennsylvania in its discussion of the doctrine in Ayala v. Philadelphia Board of Public Education, 453 Pa. 584, 592, 305 A.2d 877, 881–82 (1973), when it stated:

> Today we conclude that no reasons whatsoever exist for continuing to adhere to the doctrine of governmental immunity. Whatever may have been the basis for the inception of the doctrine, it is clear that no public policy considerations presently justify its retention.

> Governmental immunity can no longer be justified on "an amorphous mass of cumbrous language about sovereignty * * * " As one court has stated:

>> " * * * it is almost incredible that in this modern age of comparative sociological enlightenment, and in a republic, the medieval absolutism supposed to be implicit in the maxim, 'the King can do no wrong,' should exempt the various branches of the government from liability for their torts, and that the entire burden of damage resulting from the wrongful acts of the government should be imposed upon the single individual who suffers the injury, rather than distributed among the entire

community constituting the government, where it could be borne without hardship upon any individual, and where it justly belongs." Likewise, we agree with the Supreme Court of Florida that in preserving the sovereign immunity theory, courts have overlooked the fact that the Revolutionary War was fought to abolish that "divine right of kings" on which the theory is based.

Moreover, we are unwilling to perpetuate the notion that "it is better that an individual should sustain an injury than that the public should suffer an inconvenience." Russell v. Men of Devon, * * * [2 T.R. 667, 673, 100 Eng.Rep. 359, 362 (1788)]. This social philosophy of nonliability is "an anachronism in the law of today." As has been noted:

> The social climate which fostered the growth of absolutism and the divine right of kings in England has long since been tempered with the warm winds of humanitarianism and individual freedom. The changes which have occurred in the last century with respect to the imposition of liability upon private corporate enterprises of any kind are well–known. Workmen's compensation laws have replaced the old theories which permitted the corporate organizations to escape liability under the fellow–servant rule or the doctrine of assumption of risk. Liability may now be predicated without fault merely on grounds that potential injuries to individuals must be calculated as a part of the cost of doing business, and must be paid for by the business enterprise. *There is widespread acceptance of a philosophy that those who enjoy the fruits of the enterprise must also accept its risks and attendant responsibilities.*

(emphasis added) (footnote omitted).

* * *

Though the foregoing case decided by the Pennsylvania Supreme Court related to liability of a local school board, we believe that the principles and reasoning enunciated therein apply equally to a State agency.

We, therefore, conclude that the ancient doctrine of sovereign immunity has lost its underpinnings by the social and governmental changes which have occurred. This view was expressed with great clarity by Justice Cardozo in the following words:

> A rule which in its origins was the creation of the courts themselves, and was supposed in the making to express the *mores* of the day, may be abrogated by the courts when the *mores* have so changed that perpetuation of the rule would do violence to the social conscience.

Cardozo, The Growth of the Law 136–37 (1924).

* * *

Accordingly all prior cases wherein governmental immunity from tort liability was recognized are expressly overruled and shall no longer be considered precedents in tort actions filed against governmental agencies.

Since this action involves a significant and major change in tort liability for governmental agencies, the question of its applicability to past, pending and future cases must be determined. * * * [I]t is our considered opinion that the rule of law announced herein shall have modified prospectivity. Consequently, the decision we announce herein applies to the case at bar, all similar pending actions and all cases which may arise in the future.

* * *

OPINION ON MOTION FOR REHEARING

McMANUS, JUSTICE.

[The issue on rehearing is limited to the issue of whether our] decision should apply: (1) only to cases arising in the future; (2) to cases arising in the future and to the case at bar; or (3) to cases arising in the future, to the case at bar and to all similar pending actions.

In the original *Hicks* decision we selected the third option. The briefs and arguments presented on rehearing developed this issue much more fully than had been done in the briefs and arguments on the appeal. We now conclude that the *Hicks* decision should apply only to cases arising in the future.

Many courts abolishing sovereign immunity have applied their decisions to cases arising in the future and to the case under consideration (the second option mentioned above).

At least two other courts have abolished sovereign immunity on a purely prospective basis, denying relief even to the plaintiffs who brought the action. Spanel v. Mounds View School District No. 621, 264 Minn. 279, 118 N.W.2d 795 (1962). In support of their decision the Minnesota Supreme Court in *Spanel* quoted Mr. Justice Cardozo from an article at 109 Pa.L.Rev. 13, as follows:

"The rule that we are asked to apply is out of tune with the life about us. It has been made discordant by the forces that generate a living law. We apply it to this case because the repeal might work hardship to those who have trusted to its existence. We give notice, however, that any one trusting to it hereafter will do so at his peril."

The Minnesota court went on to conclude:

"It may appear unfair to deprive the present claimant of his day in court. However, we are of the opinion it would work an even greater injustice to deny defendant and other units of government a defense on which they have had a right to rely. We believe that it is more equitable if they are permitted to plan in advance by securing liability insurance or by creating funds necessary for self–insurance.

In addition, provision must be made for routinely and promptly investigating personal injury and other tort claims at the time of their occurrence in order that defendants may marshal and preserve whatever evidence is available for the proper conduct of their defense."

We find this reasoning persuasive.

It is so ordered.

* * *

Sosa, Justice, dissenting.

I respectfully disagree with the majority's opinion that the ruling made in this case should not take effect until July 1, 1976. I feel that to deprive the parties who were responsible for the abolishment of the antiquated and anachronistic doctrine of sovereign immunity of having their day in court is like leaving a grieving widow at the grave of her deceased husband, killed through someone's negligence, without a cause of action or a remedy. I think this ruling is harsh and unjust. I would have made the ruling applicable to the case at bar and all those cases actually filed prior to our decision, which were undisposed. They were filed based on dicta that the doctrine's demise was near. I would not penalize those that took this court at its word.

The main reason for the abolishment of sovereign immunity was that it created an injustice in the law. I feel that the majority ruling making the ruling in the case effective beginning July 1, 1976, creates another injustice.

I respectfully dissent from the order on rehearing for the above stated reasons.

Notes

1. *Remnants of immunity.* Most states have at least partially abolished their sovereign immunity and that of their political subdivisions, either by judicial decision or by statute. Substantial amounts of immunity remain, however, despite arguments that it is archaic and unnecessary. For example, after the decision in the principal case, the New Mexico legislature restored that state's immunity, subject to broad exceptions. N.M.Stat. § 41–4–1 et seq. permits liability only for injuries arising out of specified activities, which include operation of motor vehicles, buildings, parks, machinery, airports, public utilities, hospitals, and highways, and intentional torts of law enforcement officers. Claims in these permitted categories are subject to a cap of $300,000 for medical expenses and $750,000 for all other claims. Despite the statutory exception for operation of streets and highways, claims like those in the principal case might still be barred because the legislature retained immunity for claims arising out of defective design of bridges. See N.M.Stat. § 41–4–11.

2. The state tort claims statutes vary widely. They often place dollar limits on the amount of recovery against a governmental entity. Some of them authorize suits against governments only in specified classes of cases, such as motor vehicle accidents. Some prescribe different rules for cities and

counties than for the state. Most contain an exception for discretionary functions similar to that of the Federal Tort Claims Act, which is excerpted below, but even where the language is the same, the federal cases do not control the interpretation of state statutes.

3. *Cities.* Municipal immunity was never as complete as that of the state and federal governments. The common law treated some municipal activities as "proprietary," rather than governmental, and held cities liable for torts arising from those activities. The proprietary–governmental distinction has often been criticized as inconsistent and arbitrary, but it survives in many states. For example, in states where the tort claims statute places a cap on damages, suits for torts arising from proprietary activities may not be subject to the cap on the ground that the liability in those cases derives from the common law, not the tort claims statute. It is impossible to know what activities will be treated as proprietary without a careful reading of the case law of the relevant jurisdiction. Some states have attempted to assimilate their case law into their tort claims act through long lists of municipal activities that are considered governmental or proprietary. See, e.g., Tex.Civ. Prac. & Rem.Code Sec. 101.0215 (containing a nonexclusive list of 36 types of activities considered governmental).

4. *Constitutional immunity of states.* Recent Supreme Court jurisprudence has added a federal constitutional dimension to the immunity of state governments. The Court has held that states are immune from private suits in federal courts under either federal or state law, see Kimel v. Florida Bd. of Regents, 528 U.S. 62, 120 S.Ct. 631, 145 L.Ed.2d 522 (2000), and cannot be sued by private parties under federal law even in their own courts, see Alden v. Maine, 527 U.S. 706, 119 S.Ct. 2240, 144 L.Ed.2d 636 (1999). Congress has no power to authorize such suits except pursuant to § 5 of the 14th amendment, which gives Congress power to enforce civil rights, see Seminole Tribe of Fla. v. Florida, 517 U.S. 44, 116 S.Ct. 1114, 134 L.Ed.2d 252 (1996). This jurisprudence, which the Court has ascribed to the Tenth and Eleventh Amendments and pre–Constitutional notions of sovereignty, means that state governments cannot be subjected to liability under federal statutes other than civil rights laws unless they waive their immunity.

This has little effect on ordinary tort claims based on state law because those are not cognizable anyway unless the state has abrogated its sovereign immunity. It has significant consequences, however, for maritime law and for federal statutory tort schemes such as the Federal Employers Liability Act, 45 U.S.C. 51 et seq., and the Jones Act, 46 U.S.C. app. 688(a). Those often create liability where state tort law would not, but they are now unavailable in suits against state governments. The federal constitutional immunity does not apply to municipal governments, however; see Alden v. Maine, supra.

2. FEDERAL GOVERNMENT

a. *Federal Tort Claims Act*

(Act of Aug. 2, 1946. 28 U.S.C.A. §§ 1346(b),
[2401(b)], 2402 & 2671 et seq.)

§ 1346. United States as Defendant

* * *

(b) Subject to the provisions of [sections 2671–80], the district courts * * * shall have exclusive jurisdiction of civil actions on claims against the United States, for money damages, accruing on and after January 1, 1945, for injury or loss of property, or personal injury or death caused by the negligent or wrongful act or omission of any employee of the Government while acting within the scope of his office or employment, under circumstances where the United States, if a private person, would be liable to the claimant in accordance with the law of the place where the act or omission occurred.

§ 2401. Time for commencing action against United States

* * *

(b) A tort claim against the United States shall be forever barred unless it is presented in writing to the appropriate Federal agency within two years after such claim accrues or unless action is begun within six months after the date of mailing, by certified or registered mail, of notice of final denial of the claim by the agency to which it was presented.

§ 2402. Jury Trial in Actions Against United States

* * * [A]ny action against the United States under section 1346 shall be tried by the court without a jury * * *.

§ 2671. Definitions

As used in this chapter and sections 1346(b) and 2401(b) of this title, the term—

"Federal agency" includes the executive departments, the judicial and legislative branches, the military departments, independent establishments of the United States, and corporations primarily acting as instrumentalities or agencies of the United States, but does not include any contractor with the United States.

"Employee of the government" includes officers or employees of any federal agency, members of the military or naval forces of the United States, members of the National Guard while engaged in training or duty under section 316, 502, 503, 504, or 505 of title 32, and persons acting on behalf of a federal agency in an official capacity, temporarily or permanently in the service of the United States, whether with or without compensation.

"Acting within the scope of his office or employment", in the case of a member of the military or naval forces of the United States or a member of the National Guard as defined in section 101(3) of title 32, means acting in line of duty.

§ 2674. Liability of United States

The United States shall be liable, respecting the provisions of this title relating to tort claims, in the same manner and to the same extent as a private individual under like circumstances, but shall not be liable for interest prior to judgment or for punitive damages.

If, however, in any case wherein death was caused, the law of the place where the act or omission complained of occurred provides, or has been construed to provide, for damages only punitive in nature, the United States shall be liable for actual or compensatory damages, measured by the pecuniary injuries resulting from such death to the persons respectively, for whose benefit the action was brought, in lieu thereof.

With respect to any claim under this chapter, the United States shall be entitled to assert any defense based upon judicial or legislative immunity which otherwise would have been available to the employee of the United States whose act or omission gave rise to the claim, as well as any other defenses to which the United States is entitled.

* * *

§ 2675.   Disposition by Federal Agency as Prerequisite; Evidence

(a) An action shall not be instituted upon a claim against the United States for money damages for injury or loss of property or personal injury or death caused by the negligent or wrongful act or omission of any employee of the Government while acting within the scope of his office or employment, unless the claimant shall have first presented the claim to the appropriate Federal agency and his claim shall have been finally denied by the agency in writing and sent by certified or registered mail. The failure of an agency to make final disposition of a claim within six months after it is filed shall, at the option of the claimant any time thereafter, be deemed a final denial of the claim for purposes of this section. The provisions of this subsection shall not apply to such claims as may be asserted under the Federal Rules of Civil Procedure by third party complaint, cross–claim, or counterclaim.

(b) Action under this section shall not be instituted for any sum in excess of the amount of the claim presented to the federal agency, except where the increased amount is based upon newly discovered evidence not reasonably discoverable at the time of presenting the claim to the federal agency, or upon allegation and proof of intervening facts, relating to the amount of the claim.

(c) Disposition of any claim by the Attorney General or other head of a federal agency shall not be competent evidence of liability or amount of damages.

§ 2680.   Exceptions

The provisions of this chapter and section 1346(b) of this title shall not apply to—

(a) Any claim based upon an act or omission of an employee of the Government, exercising due care, in the execution of a statute or regulation, whether or not such statute or regulation be valid, or based upon the exercise or performance or the failure to exercise or perform a discretionary function or duty on the part of a federal agency or an employee of the Government, whether or not the discretion involved be abused.

* * *

(h) Any claim arising out of assault, battery, false imprisonment, false arrest, malicious prosecution, abuse of process, libel, slander, misrepresentation, deceit, or interference with contract rights: Provided, That, with regard to acts or omissions of investigative or law enforcement officers of the United States Government, the provisions of this chapter and section 1346(b) of this title shall apply to any claim arising, on or after the date of the enactment of this proviso, out of assault, battery, false imprisonment, false arrest, abuse of process, or malicious prosecution. For the purpose of this subsection, "investigative or law enforcement officer" means any officer of the United States who is empowered by law to execute searches, to seize evidence, or to make arrests for violations of Federal law. * * *

(i) Any claim for damages caused by the fiscal operations of the Treasury or by the regulation of the monetary system.

(j) Any claim arising out of the combatant activities of the military or naval forces, or the Coast Guard, during time of war.

(k) Any claim arising in a foreign country.

* * *

UNITED STATES v. GAUBERT

Supreme Court of the United States, 1991.
499 U.S. 315, 111 S.Ct. 1267, 113 L.Ed.2d 335.

JUSTICE WHITE.

[A federal statute authorized the Federal Home Loan Bank Board (FHLBB) to prescribe rules and regulations governing federal savings and loan associations. During the savings and loan crisis of the 1980s the FHLBB and the Federal Home Loan Bank–Dallas (FHLB–D) undertook to advise about and oversee certain aspects of the operation of Independent American Savings Association (IASA), but instituted no formal action against the institution. At the FHLBB's request, respondent Gaubert, chairman of the board and IASA's largest stockholder, removed himself from IASA's management and posted $25 million as security for his personal guarantee that IASA's net worth would exceed regulatory minimums.

[Later the regulators threatened to close IASA unless all of its management and directors resigned. They did so and were replaced by new management and directors recommended by FHLB–D. Thereafter, FHLB–D became more involved in IASA's day–to–day business. Although IASA was thought to be financially sound while Gaubert managed it, after a few months the new directors announced that IASA had a substantial negative net worth, and the Federal Savings and Loan Insurance Corporation (FSLIC) assumed receivership of the institution.

[Gaubert filed an action in the District Court against the United States under the Federal Tort Claims Act (FTCA), seeking $100 million damages for the lost value of his shares and for the property forfeited under his personal guarantee on the ground that the FHLBB and FHLB–D had been negligent in carrying out their supervisory activities. The court granted the Government's motion to dismiss for lack of subject matter jurisdiction on the ground that the regulators' actions fell within the discretionary function exception to the FTCA. The Court of Appeals reversed in part. Relying on Indian Towing Co. v. United States, 350 U.S. 61, 76 S.Ct. 122, 100 L.Ed. 48 (1995), the Court of Appeals found that the claims concerning the regulators' activities after they assumed a supervisory role in IASA's day–to–day affairs were not "policy decisions," which fall within the exception, but were "operational actions," which it believed were not within the exception.]

* * *

The exception covers only acts that are discretionary in nature, acts that "involv[e] an element of judgment or choice," and "it is the nature of the conduct, rather than the status of the actor" that governs whether the exception applies. The requirement of judgment or choice is not satisfied if a "federal statute, regulation, or policy specifically prescribes a course of action for an employee to follow," because "the employee has no rightful option but to adhere to the directive."

Furthermore, even "assuming the challenged conduct involves an element of judgment," it remains to be decided "whether that judgment is of the kind that the discretionary function exception was designed to shield." Because the purpose of the exception is to "prevent judicial 'second–guessing' of legislative and administrative decisions grounded in social, economic, and political policy through the medium of an action in tort," when properly construed, the exception "protects only governmental actions and decisions based on considerations of public policy."

Where Congress has delegated the authority to an independent agency or to the Executive Branch to implement the general provisions of a regulatory statute and to issue regulations to that end, there is no doubt that planning–level decisions establishing programs are protected by the discretionary function exception, as is the promulgation of regulations by which the agencies are to carry out the programs. In addition, the actions of Government agents involving the necessary element of choice and grounded in the social, economic, or political goals of the statute and regulations are protected.

Thus, in [Dalehite v. United States, 346 U.S. 15 (1953)], the exception barred recovery for claims arising from a massive fertilizer explosion. The fertilizer had been manufactured, packaged, and prepared for export pursuant to detailed regulations as part of a comprehensive federal program aimed at increasing the food supply in occupied areas after World War II. Not only was the cabinet–level decision to institute the fertilizer program discretionary, but so were the decisions concerning the specific requirements for manufacturing the fertilizer. Nearly 30 years later, in [United States v. Varig Airlines, 467 U.S. 797 (1984)] the Federal Aviation Administration's actions in formulating and implementing a "spot–check" plan for airplane inspection were protected by the discretionary function exception because of the agency's authority to establish safety standards for airplanes. Actions taken in furtherance of the program were likewise protected, even if those particular actions were negligent. Most recently, in Berkovitz [v. United States, 486 U.S. 531 (1988)], we examined a comprehensive regulatory scheme governing the licensing of laboratories to produce polio vaccine and the release to the public of particular drugs. We found that some of the claims fell outside the exception, because the agency employees had failed to follow the specific directions contained in the applicable regulations, i.e., in those instances, there was no room for choice or judgment. We then remanded the case for an analysis of the remaining claims in light of the applicable regulations.

Under the applicable precedents, if a regulation mandates particular conduct, and the employee obeys the direction, the Government will be protected because the action will be deemed in furtherance of the policies which led to the promulgation of the regulation. If the employee violates the mandatory regulation, there will be no shelter from liability because there is no room for choice and the action will be contrary to policy. On the other hand, if a regulation allows the employee discretion, the very existence of the regulation creates a strong presumption that a discretionary act authorized by the regulation involves consideration of the same policies which led to the promulgation of the regulations.

* * *

When established governmental policy, as expressed or implied by statute, regulation, or agency guidelines, allows a Government agent to exercise discretion, it must be presumed that the agent's acts are grounded in policy when exercising that discretion. For a complaint to survive a motion to dismiss, it must allege facts which would support a finding that the challenged actions are not the kind of conduct that can be said to be grounded in the policy of the regulatory regime. The focus of the inquiry is not on the agent's subjective intent in exercising the discretion conferred by statute or regulation, but on the nature of the actions taken and on whether they are susceptible to policy analysis.[7]

---

7. There are obviously discretionary acts performed by a Government agent that are within the scope of his employment but not within the discretionary function exception because these acts cannot be said to be based on the purposes that the regulatory regime seeks to accomplish. If one of the officials involved in this case drove an automobile on a mission connected with his official duties and negligently collided with another car, the exception would not apply. Although driving requires the constant exercise of discretion, the official's decisions in exercising that discretion can hardly be said to be grounded in regulatory policy.

III

In light of our cases and their interpretation of § 2680(a), it is clear that the Court of Appeals erred in holding that the exception does not reach decisions made at the operational or management level of the bank involved in this case. A discretionary act is one that involves choice or judgment; there is nothing in that description that refers exclusively to policymaking or planning functions. Day–to–day management of banking affairs, like the management of other businesses, regularly requires judgment as to which of a range of permissible courses is the wisest. Discretionary conduct is not confined to the policy or planning level. "[I]t is the nature of the conduct, rather than the status of the actor, that governs whether the discretionary function exception applies in a given case."

* * *

IV

We now inquire whether the Court of Appeals was correct in holding that some of the acts alleged in Gaubert's amended complaint were not discretionary acts within the meaning of § 2680(a).

* * *

Specifically, the complaint enumerated seven instances or kinds of objectionable official involvement. First, the regulators "arranged for the hiring for IASA of * * * consultants on operational and financial matters and asset management." Second, the officials "urged or directed that IASA convert from a state–chartered savings and loan to a federally–chartered savings and loan in part so that it could become the exclusive government entity with power to control IASA." Third, the regulators "gave advice and made recommendations concerning whether, when, and how to place IASA subsidiaries into bankruptcy." Fourth, the officials "mediated salary disputes between IASA and its senior officers." Fifth, the regulators "reviewed a draft complaint in litigation" that IASA's board contemplated filing and were "so actively involved in giving advice, making recommendations, and directing matters related to IASA's litigation policy that they were able successfully to stall the Board of Directors' ultimate decision to file the complaint until the Bank Board in Washington had reviewed, advised on, and commented on the draft." Sixth, the regulators "actively intervened with the Texas Savings and Loan Department (IASA's principal regulator) when the State attempted to install a supervisory agent at IASA." Finally, the FHLB–D president wrote the IASA board of directors "affirming that his agency had placed that Board of Directors into office, and describing their mutual goal to protect the FSLIC insurance fund." According to Gaubert, the losses he suffered were caused by the regulators' "assumption of the duty to participate in, and to make, the day–to–day decisions at IASA and [the] negligent discharge of that assumed duty." Moreover, he alleged that "[t]he involvement of the FHLB–Dallas in the affairs of IASA went beyond its normal regulatory activity, and the agency actually substituted its decisions for those of the directors and officers of the association."

We first inquire whether the challenged actions were discretionary, or whether they were instead controlled by mandatory statutes or regulations.

* * *

The relevant statutory provisions were not mandatory, but left to the judgment of the agency the decision of when to institute proceedings against a financial institution and which mechanism to use. For example, the FSLIC had authority to terminate an institution's insured status, issue cease–and–desist orders, and suspend or remove an institution's officers, if "in the opinion of the Corporation" such action was warranted because the institution or its officers were engaging in an "unsafe or unsound practice" in connection with the business of the institution. The FHLBB had parallel authority to issue cease–and–desist orders and suspend or remove an institution's officers. Although the statute enumerated specific grounds warranting an appointment by the FHLBB of a conservator or receiver, the determination of whether any of these grounds existed depended upon "the opinion of the Board." The agencies here were not bound to act in a particular way; the exercise of their authority involved a great "element of judgment or choice."

We are unconvinced by Gaubert's assertion that because the agencies did not institute formal proceedings against IASA, they had no discretion to take informal actions as they did. Although the statutes provided only for formal proceedings, there is nothing in the language or structure of the statutes that prevented the regulators from invoking less formal means of supervision of financial institutions. Not only was there no statutory or regulatory mandate which compelled the regulators to act in a particular way, but there was no prohibition against the use of supervisory mechanisms not specifically set forth in statute or regulation.

* * *

Gaubert also argues that the challenged actions fall outside the discretionary function exception because they involved the mere application of technical skills and business expertise. But this is just another way of saying that the considerations involving the day–to–day management of a business concern such as IASA are so precisely formulated that decisions at the operational level never involve the exercise of discretion within the meaning of § 2680(a), a notion that we have already rejected in disapproving the rationale of the Court of Appeals' decision. It may be that certain decisions resting on mathematical calculations, for example, involve no choice or judgment in carrying out the calculations, but the regulatory acts alleged here are not of that genre. Rather, it is plain to us that each of the challenged actions involved the exercise of choice and judgment.

* * *

We find nothing in Gaubert's amended complaint effectively alleging that the discretionary acts performed by the regulators were not entitled to the exemption. By Gaubert's own admission, the regulators replaced IASA's management in order to protect the FSLIC's insurance fund; thus it cannot be disputed that this action was based on public policy considerations. The regulators' actions in urging IASA to convert to federal charter and in intervening with the state agency were directly related to public policy considerations regarding federal oversight of the thrift industry. So were advising the hiring of a financial consultant, advising when to place IASA subsidiaries into bankruptcy, intervening on IASA's behalf with Texas officials, advising on litigation policy, and mediating salary disputes. There are no allegations that the regulators gave anything other than the kind of advice that was within the purview of the policies behind the statutes.

* * *

V

Because from the face of the amended complaint, it is apparent that all of the challenged actions of the federal regulators involved the exercise of discretion in furtherance of public policy goals, the Court of Appeals erred in failing to find the claims barred by the discretionary function exception of the FTCA. We therefore reverse the decision of the Court of Appeals for the Fifth Circuit and remand for proceedings consistent with this opinion.

JUSTICE SCALIA, concurring in part and concurring in the judgment:

* * *

The Court of Appeals in this case concluded that a choice involves policy judgment (in the relevant sense) if it is made at a planning rather than an operational level within the agency. I agree with the Court that this is wrong. I think, however, that the level at which the decision is made is often relevant to the discretionary function inquiry, since the answer to that inquiry turns on both the subject matter and the office of the decisionmaker. In my view a choice is shielded from liability by the discretionary function exception if the choice is, under the particular circumstances, one that ought to be informed by considerations of social, economic, or political policy and is made by an officer whose official responsibilities include assessment of those considerations.

This test, by looking not only to the decision but also to the officer who made it, recognizes that there is something to the planning vs. operational dichotomy—though the "something" is not precisely what the Court of Appeals believed. Ordinarily, an employee working at the operational level is not responsible for policy decisions, even though policy considerations may be highly relevant to his actions. The dock foreman's decision to store bags of fertilizer in a highly compact fashion is not protected by this exception because, even if he carefully calculated considerations of cost to the Government vs. safety, it was not his responsibility to ponder such things; the Secretary of Agriculture's decision to the same effect is protected, because weighing those considerations is his task.

* * *

The present case comes to us on a motion to dismiss. Lacking any sort of factual record, we can do little more than speculate as to whether the officers here exercised policymaking responsibility with respect to the individual acts in question. Without more, the motion would have to be denied. I think, however, that the Court's conclusion to the contrary is properly reached under a slightly different approach. The alleged misdeeds complained of here were not actually committed by federal officers. Rather, federal officers "recommended" that such actions be taken, making it clear that if the recommendations were not followed the bank would be seized and operated directly by the regulators. In effect, the Federal Home Loan Bank Board (FHLBB) imposed the advice which Gaubert challenges as a condition of allowing the bank to remain independent. But surely the decision whether or not to take over a bank is a policy–based decision to which liability may not attach—a decision that ought to be influenced by considerations "social, economic, [or] political policy," and that in the nature of things can only be made by FHLBB officers responsible for weighing such considerations. I think a corollary is that setting the conditions under which the FHLBB will or will not take over a bank is an exercise of policymaking discretion. By establishing such a list of conditions, as was done here, the Board in effect announces guidelines pursuant to which it will exercise its discretionary function of taking over the bank. Establishing guidelines for the exercise of a discretionary function is unquestionably a discretionary function. Thus, without resort to item–by–item analysis, I would find each of Gaubert's challenges barred by the discretionary function exception.

Notes

1. The unstated assumption of the principal case is that the general rule of sovereign immunity is still in force. At the federal level that immunity is relaxed only to the extent that Congress has provided. Any suit that falls within one of the exceptions to the Tort Claims Act is therefore subject to the general principle of sovereign immunity and the court lacks subject-matter jurisdiction.

The Federal Tort Claims Act is the major, but not the only, abrogation of federal sovereign immunity in the tort area. For example, the claim in Ira S. Bushey & Sons, Inc. v. United States, supra p. 315, was permitted under the Suits in Admiralty Act, 46 U.S.C.app. § 742, which authorizes claims against the United States under admiralty law.

2. The discretionary function exception is the most heavily litigated of the FTCA's explicit limitations. Its interpretation has been permanently influenced (some might say warped) by the *Dalehite* case (cited in the principal case), the first Supreme Court decision interpreting the exception.

The case arose out of the Texas City disaster of 1947, an explosion that leveled the city and killed more than 560 people. Until September 11, 2001, it was the worst nonnatural disaster, in terms of lives lost, in American history. The government had agreed to accept the result in the case of Henry Dalehite as controlling on the liability issue in 300 other cases claiming damages of $200 million. The case thus involved potential federal liabilities that at the time may have seemed to be staggering.

3. *Operational vs. policy.* Until the decision in the principal case, most lower courts thought the controlling distinction was between operational decisions and planning or policy decisions. There was much dispute, however, as to how that distinction should be drawn. For example, compare Spillway Marina, Inc. v. United States, 330 F.Supp. 611 (D.Kan.1970), aff'd 445 F.2d 876 (10th Cir.1971) with Lindgren v. United States, 665 F.2d 978 (9th Cir.1982). In the *Spillway* case, failure to give notice each time the level of a government–run reservoir was lowered was held to be a planning decision and therefore immune. In *Lindgren* failure to post signs warning of hazards to water skiers when the lake level was low was held to be operational and therefore actionable; the court reasoned that giving this one–time warning would be less burdensome on the government than the periodic warnings that would have been required in *Spillway*. Does the statute authorize distinctions of this sort? Of the sort prescribed by the principal case? Does the statutory term "discretionary function" by itself provide a basis for decision?

4. Note that section 2680(a) contains two clauses. The first generates little litigation; *Dalehite* held that it "bars tests by tort actions of the legality of statutes and regulations."

5. *Procedural limitations.* The FTCA has three crucial procedural limitations. First, section 1346(b) gives the federal courts exclusive jurisdiction. Neither the government itself nor a federal employee charged with an employment–related tort can be sued in state court. Second, section 2402 precludes jury trial. Third, sections 2401(b) and 2675(a) require that the claim be presented to the governmental agency deemed responsible within two years after it arose. The claimant may file suit only if the agency denies the claim or fails to respond within six months.

b. Judicially Created Immunity

In addition to the pockets of immunity preserved by the exceptions in the FTCA, the Supreme Court has created doctrines that preserve two other important areas of immunity. One is the "government contractor defense," which holds that "[l]iability for design defects in military equipment cannot be imposed, pursuant to state law, when (1) the United States approved reasonably precise specifications; (2) the equipment conformed to those specifications, and (3) the supplier warned the United States about the dangers in the use of the equipment that were known to the supplier but not to the United States." Boyle v. United Technologies Corp., 487 U.S. 500, 108 S.Ct. 2510, 101 L.Ed.2d 442 (1988).

Strictly speaking this is not a rule of governmental immunity; it immunizes contractors. The Court described it as a federal common law rule justified by the federal interest in making sure the government gets the equipment it wants at prices that are not inflated by the contractor's risk of tort liability. Such liability would produce the same sort of second–guessing that the discretionary function exception aims to prevent when the decision in question is made by the government itself, the majority argued. Three dissenting justices argued that the decision ignored the basic tort law assumption that "the imposition of liability encourages actors to prevent any injury whose expected cost exceeds the cost of prevention." A state court applying the *Boyle* test said the decision gave defense contractors a result they had been unable to secure through 50 years of lobbying Congress. See Pietz v. Orthopedic Equipment Co., Inc., 562 So.2d 152, 156 (Ala. 1989).

Lower courts are in disagreement as to whether *Boyle* applies to all government procurement contracts or only to those for military equipment. Compare In re Hawaii Federal Asbestos Cases, 960 F.2d 806 (9th Cir. 1992) (military only) with Carley v. Wheeled Coach, 991 F.2d 1117 (3rd Cir. 1993) (nonmilitary contacts too).

The second judicially created exception to the FTCA is called the *Feres* doctrine. It is at issue in the following case.

UNITED STATES v. JOHNSON

Supreme Court of the United States, 1987.
481 U.S. 681, 107 S.Ct. 2063, 95 L.Ed.2d 648.

Justice Powell delivered the opinion of the Court.

This case presents the question whether the doctrine established in Feres v. United States, 340 U.S. 135, 71 S.Ct. 153, 95 L.Ed. 152 (1950), bars an action under the Federal Tort Claims Act on behalf of a service member killed during the course of an activity incident to service, where the complaint alleges negligence on the part of civilian employees of the Federal Government.

I

Lieutenant Commander Horton Winfield Johnson was a helicopter pilot for the United States Coast Guard, stationed in Hawaii. In the early morning of January 7, 1982, Johnson's Coast Guard station received a distress call from a boat lost in the area. Johnson and a crew of several other Coast Guard members were dispatched to search for the vessel. Inclement weather decreased the visibility, and so Johnson requested radar assistance from the Federal Aviation Administration (FAA), a civilian agency of the Federal Government. The FAA controllers assumed positive radar control over the helicopter. Shortly thereafter, the helicopter crashed into the side of a mountain on the island of Molokai. All the crew members, including Johnson, were killed in the crash.

Respondent, Johnson's wife, * * * sought damages from the United States on the ground that the FAA flight controllers negligently caused her husband's death. * * * The District Court * * * dismissed the complaint, relying exclusively on this Court's decision in *Feres.*

The Court of Appeals for the Eleventh Circuit reversed. 749 F.2d 1530 (C.A.11 1985). It noted the language of *Feres* that precludes suits by service members against the Government for injuries that "arise out of or are in the course of activity incident to service." The court found, however, that the evolution of the doctrine since the *Feres* decision warranted a qualification of the original holding according to the status of the alleged tortfeasor. The court identified what it termed "the typical *Feres* factual paradigm" that exists when a service member alleges negligence on the part of another member of the military. "[W]hen the *Feres* factual paradigm is present, the issue is whether the injury arose out of or during the course of an activity incident to service." But when negligence is alleged on the part of a Federal Government employee who is not a member of the military, the court found that the propriety of a suit should be determined by examining the rationales that underlie the *Feres* doctrine. Although it noted that this Court has articulated numerous rationales for the doctrine, it found the effect of a suit on military discipline to be the doctrine's primary justification.

Applying its new analysis to the facts of this case, the court found "absolutely no hint * * * that the conduct of any alleged tortfeasor even remotely connected to the military will be scrutinized if this case proceeds to trial." Accordingly, it found that *Feres* did not bar respondent's suit. * * *

II

In *Feres*, this Court held that service members cannot bring tort suits against the Government for injuries that "arise out of or are in the course of activity incident to service." This Court has never deviated from this characterization of the *Feres* bar. Nor has Congress changed this standard in the close to 40 years since it was articulated, even though, as the Court noted in *Feres*, Congress "possesses a ready remedy" to alter a misinterpretation of its intent. Although all of the cases decided by this Court under *Feres* have involved allegations of negligence on the part of members of the military, this Court has never suggested that the military status of the alleged tortfeasor is crucial to the application of the doctrine. Nor have the lower courts understood this fact to be relevant under *Feres.* Instead, the *Feres* doctrine has been applied consistently to bar all suits on behalf of service members against the Government based upon service–related injuries. We decline to modify the doctrine at this late date.[9]

9. Justice Scalia indicates that he would consider overruling *Feres* had this been requested by counsel, but in the absence of such a request he would "confine the unfairness and irrationality [of] that decision" to cases where the allegations of negligence are limited to other members of the military. In arguing "unfairness" in this case, Justice Scalia assumes that had respondent been "piloting a commercial helicopter" his family might recover substantially more in damages than it now may recover under the benefit programs available for a serviceman and his family. It hardly need be said that

A

This Court has emphasized three broad rationales underlying the *Feres* decision. An examination of these reasons for the doctrine demonstrates that the status of the alleged tortfeasor does not have the critical significance ascribed to it by the Court of Appeals in this case. First, "[t]he relationship between the Government and members of its armed forces is 'distinctively federal in character.'" This federal relationship is implicated to the greatest degree when a service member is performing activities incident to his federal service. Performance of the military function in diverse parts of the country and the world entails a "[s]ignificant risk of accidents and injuries." Where a service member is injured incident to service—that is, because of his military relationship with the Government—it "makes no sense to permit the fortuity of the situs of the alleged negligence to affect the liability of the Government to [the] serviceman." Instead, application of the underlying federal remedy that provides "simple, certain, and uniform compensation for injuries or death of those in armed services" is appropriate.*

Second, the existence of these generous statutory disability and death benefits is an independent reason why the *Feres* doctrine bars suit for service–related injuries.[10] In *Feres*, the Court observed that the primary purpose of the FTCA "was to extend a remedy to those who had been without; if it incidentally benefited those already well provided for, it appears to have been unintentional." Those injured during the course of activity incident to service not only receive benefits that "compare extremely favorably with those provided by most workmen's compensation statutes," but the recovery of benefits is "swift [and] efficient," "normally requir[ing] no litigation." The Court in *Feres* found it difficult to believe that Congress would have provided such a comprehensive system of benefits while at the same time contemplating recovery for service–related injuries under the FTCA. Particularly persuasive was the fact that Congress "omitted any provision to adjust these two types of remedy to each other." Congress still has not amended the Veterans' Benefits Act or the FTCA to make any such provision for injuries incurred during the course of activity incident to service. We thus find

predicting the outcome of any damages suit—both with respect to liability and the amount of damages—is hazardous, whereas veterans' benefits are guaranteed by law. If "fairness"—in terms of pecuniary benefits—were the issue, one could respond to the dissent's assumption by noting that had the negligent instructions that led to Johnson's death been given by another serviceman, the consequences—under the dissent's view—would be equally "unfair." "Fairness" provides no more justification for the line drawn by the dissent than it does for the line upon which application of the *Feres* doctrine has always depended: whether the injury was "incident to service?" In sum, the dissent's argument for changing the

interpretation of a congressional statute, when Congress has failed to do so for almost 40 years, is unconvincing.

* The Court was referring to the Veterans' Benefits Act, 33 U.S.C. § 301 et seq., which provides a workers'–compensation–like remedy for service–connected injuries. [Ed.]

10. Service members receive numerous other benefits unique to their service status. For example, members of the military and their dependents are eligible for educational benefits, extensive health benefits, home–buying loan benefits, and retirement benefits after a minimum of 20 years of service.

no reason to modify what the Court has previously found to be the law: the statutory veterans' benefits "provid[e] an upper limit of liability for the Government as to service–connected injuries."

Third, *Feres* and its progeny indicate that suits brought by service members against the Government for injuries incurred incident to service are barred by the *Feres* doctrine because they are the "type[s] of claims that, if generally permitted, would involve the judiciary in sensitive military affairs at the expense of military discipline and effectiveness." In every respect the military is, as this Court has recognized, "a specialized society." "[T]o accomplish its mission the military must foster instinctive obedience, unity, commitment, and esprit de corps." Even if military negligence is not specifically alleged in a tort action, a suit based upon service–related activity necessarily implicates the military judgments and decisions that are inextricably intertwined with the conduct of the military mission.[11] Moreover, military discipline involves not only obedience to orders, but more generally duty and loyalty to one's service and to one's country. Suits brought by service members against the Government for service–related injuries could undermine the commitment essential to effective service and thus have the potential to disrupt military discipline in the broadest sense of the word.

B

In this case, Lieutenant Commander Johnson was killed while performing a rescue mission on the high seas, a primary duty of the Coast Guard.[12] There is no dispute that Johnson's injury arose directly out of the rescue mission, or that the mission was an activity incident to his military service. Johnson went on the rescue mission specifically because of his military status. His wife received and is continuing to receive statutory benefits on account of his death. Because Johnson was acting pursuant to standard operating procedures of the Coast Guard, the potential that this suit could implicate military discipline is substantial. The circumstances of this case thus fall within the heart of the *Feres* doctrine as it consistently has been articulated.

III

We reaffirm the holding of *Feres* that "the Government is not liable under the Federal Tort Claims Act for injuries to servicemen where the injuries arise out of or are in the course of activity incident to service." Accordingly, we reverse the judgment of the Court of Appeals for the Eleventh Circuit and remand for proceedings consistent with this opinion.

11. Civilian employees of the Government also may play an integral role in military activities. In this circumstance, an inquiry into the civilian activities would have the same effect on military discipline as a direct inquiry into military judgments. For example, the FAA and the United States Armed Services have an established working relationship that provides for FAA participation in numerous military activities.

12. The Coast Guard, of course, is a military service, and an important branch of the Armed Services. 14 U.S.C. § 1.

It is so ordered.

JUSTICE SCALIA, with whom JUSTICE BRENNAN, JUSTICE MARSHALL, and JUSTICE STEVENS join, dissenting.

As it did almost four decades ago in Feres v. United States, the Court today provides several reasons why Congress might have been wise to exempt from the Federal Tort Claims Act (FTCA), 28 U.S.C. §§ 1346(b), 2671–2680, certain claims brought by servicemen. The problem now, as then, is that Congress not only failed to provide such an exemption, but quite plainly excluded it. We have not been asked by respondent here to overrule *Feres*; but I can perceive no reason to accept petitioner's invitation to extend it as the Court does today.

I

Much of the sovereign immunity of the United States was swept away in 1946 with passage of the FTCA, which renders the Government liable

"for money damages * * * for injury or loss of property, or personal injury or death caused by the negligent or wrongful act or omission of any employee of the Government while acting within the scope of his office or employment, under circumstances where the United States, if a private person, would be liable to the claimant in accordance with the law of the place where the act or omission occurred."

Read as it is written, this language renders the United States liable to all persons, including servicemen, injured by the negligence of Government employees. Other provisions of the Act set forth a number of exceptions, but none generally precludes FTCA suits brought by servicemen. One, in fact, excludes "[a]ny claim arising out of the combatant activities of the military or naval forces, or the Coast Guard, during time of war," demonstrating that Congress specifically considered, and provided what it thought needful for, the special requirements of the military. There was no proper basis for us to supplement—i.e., revise—that congressional disposition.

In our first encounter with an FTCA suit brought by a serviceman, we gave effect to the plain meaning of the statute. In Brooks v. United States, 337 U.S. 49, 69 S.Ct. 918, 93 L.Ed. 1200 (1949), military personnel had been injured in a collision with an Army truck while off duty. We rejected the Government's argument that those injured while enlisted in the military can never recover under the FTCA. We noted that the Act gives the District Courts "jurisdiction over any claim founded on negligence brought against the United States" and found the Act's exceptions "too lengthy, specific, and close to the present problem" to permit an inference that, notwithstanding the literal language of the statute, Congress intended to bar all suits brought by servicemen. Particularly in light of the exceptions for claims arising out of combatant activities, and in foreign countries, we said, "[i]t would be absurd to believe that Congress did not have the servicemen in mind" in passing the FTCA. We therefore concluded that the plaintiffs in *Brooks* could sue under the Act.

In dicta, however, we cautioned that an attempt by a serviceman to recover for injuries suffered "incident to * * * service" would present "a wholly different case," and that giving effect to the "literal language" of the FTCA in such a case might lead to results so "outlandish" that recovery could not be permitted.

That "wholly different case" reached us one year later in *Feres*. We held that servicemen could not recover under the FTCA for injuries that "arise out of or are in the course of activity incident to service," and gave three reasons for our holding. First, the parallel private liability required by the FTCA was absent. Second, Congress could not have intended that local tort law govern the "distinctively federal" relationship between the Government and enlisted personnel. Third, Congress could not have intended to make FTCA suits available to servicemen who have already received veterans' benefits to compensate for injuries suffered incident to service. Several years after *Feres* we thought of a fourth rationale: Congress could not have intended to permit suits for service–related injuries because they would unduly interfere with military discipline. United States v. Brown, 348 U.S. 110, 112, 75 S.Ct. 141, 143, 99 L.Ed. 139 (1954).

In my view, none of these rationales justifies the result. Only the first of them, the "parallel private liability" argument, purports to be textually based, as follows: The United States is liable under the FTCA "in the same manner and to the same extent as a private individual under like circumstances," 28 U.S.C. § 2674; since no "private individual" can raise an army, and since no State has consented to suits by members of its militia, § 2674 shields the Government from liability in the *Feres* situation. Under this reasoning, of course, many of the Act's exceptions are superfluous, since private individuals typically do not, for example, transmit postal matter, collect taxes or customs duties, impose quarantines, or regulate the monetary system. In any event, we subsequently recognized our error and rejected *Feres'* "parallel private liability" rationale. [Indian Towing Co. v. United States, 350 U.S. 61, 66–69, 76 S.Ct. 122, 100 L.Ed. 48 (1955).]

[T]he *Feres* rule is now sustained only by three disembodied estimations of what Congress must (despite what it enacted) have intended. They are bad estimations at that. The first of them, *Feres'* second rationale, has barely escaped the fate of the "parallel private liability" argument, for though we have not yet acknowledged that it is erroneous we have described it as "no longer controlling." The rationale runs as follows: Liability under the FTCA depends upon "the law of the place where the [negligent] act or omission occurred"; but Congress could not have intended local, and therefore geographically diverse, tort law to control important aspects of the "distinctively federal" relationship between the United States and enlisted personnel. *Feres* itself was concerned primarily with the unfairness to the soldier of making his recovery turn upon where he was injured, a matter outside of his control. Subsequent cases, however, have stressed the military's need for uniformity in its governing standards. Regardless of how it is understood, this second rationale is not even a good excuse in policy, much less in principle, for ignoring the plain terms of the FTCA.

The unfairness to servicemen of geographically varied recovery is, to speak bluntly, an absurd justification, given that, as we have pointed out in another context, nonuniform recovery cannot possibly be worse than (what *Feres* provides) uniform nonrecovery. We have abandoned this peculiar rule of solicitude in allowing federal prisoners (who have no more control over their geographical location than servicemen) to recover under the FTCA for injuries caused by the negligence of prison authorities. There seems to me nothing "unfair" about a rule which says that, just as a serviceman injured by a negligent civilian must resort to state tort law, so must a serviceman injured by a negligent Government employee.

To the extent that the rationale rests upon the military's need for uniformity, it is equally unpersuasive. To begin with, that supposition of congressional intent is positively contradicted by the text. Several of the FTCA's exemptions show that Congress considered the uniformity problem, yet it chose to retain sovereign immunity for only some claims affecting the military. § 2680(j). Moreover, we have effectively disavowed this "uniformity" justification—and rendered its benefits to military planning illusory—by permitting servicemen to recover under the FTCA for injuries suffered not incident to service, and permitting civilians to recover for injuries caused by military negligence. Finally, it is difficult to explain why uniformity (assuming our rule were achieving it) is indispensable for the military, but not for the many other federal departments and agencies that can be sued under the FTCA for the negligent performance of their "unique, nationwide function[s]," including, as we have noted, the federal prison system which may be sued under varying state laws by its inmates. In sum, the second *Feres* rationale, regardless of how it is understood, is not a plausible estimation of congressional intent, much less a justification for importing that estimation, unwritten, into the statute.

Feres's third basis has similarly been denominated "no longer controlling." Servicemen injured or killed in the line of duty are compensated under the Veterans' Benefits Act (VBA), and the *Feres* Court thought it unlikely that Congress meant to permit additional recovery under the FTCA. *Feres* described the absence of any provision to adjust dual recoveries under the FTCA and VBA as "persuasive [evidence] that there was no awareness that the Act might be interpreted to permit recovery for injuries incident to military service." * * *

The credibility of this rationale is undermined severely by the fact that both before and after *Feres* we permitted injured servicemen to bring FTCA suits, even though they had been compensated under the VBA. * * *

The foregoing three rationales—the only ones actually relied upon in *Feres*—are so frail that it is hardly surprising that we have repeatedly cited the later–conceived–of "military discipline" rationale as the "best" explanation for that decision. Applying the FTCA as written would lead, we have reasoned, to absurd results, because if suits could be brought on the basis of alleged negligence towards a serviceman by other servicemen, military discipline would be undermined and civilian courts would be required to second–guess military decisionmaking. (Today the Court goes further and suggests that permitting enlisted men and women to sue their Government on the basis of negligence towards them by any Government employee seriously undermines "duty and loyalty to one's service and to one's country.") I cannot deny the possibility that some suits brought by servicemen will adversely affect military discipline, and if we were interpreting an ambiguous statute perhaps we could take that into account. But I do not think the effect upon military discipline is so certain, or so certainly substantial, that we are justified in holding (if we can ever be justified in holding) that Congress did not mean what it plainly said in the statute before us.

* * *

In sum, neither the three original *Feres* reasons nor the post hoc rationalization of "military discipline" justifies our failure to apply the FTCA as written. *Feres* was wrongly decided and heartily deserves the "widespread, almost universal criticism" it has received. In re "Agent Orange" Product Liability Litigation, 580 F.Supp. 1242, 1246 (E.D.N.Y.), appeal dism'd, 745 F.2d 161 (C.A.2 1984).

* * *

I cannot take comfort, as the Court does, from Congress' failure to amend the FTCA to overturn *Feres*. The unlegislated desires of later Congresses with regard to one thread in the fabric of the FTCA could hardly have any bearing upon the proper interpretation of the entire fabric of compromises that their predecessors enacted into law in 1946. And even if they could, intuiting those desires from congressional failure to act is an uncertain enterprise which takes as its starting point disregard of the checks and balances in the constitutional scheme of legislation designed to assure that not all desires of a majority of the Legislature find their way into law.

We have not been asked by respondent to overrule *Feres*, and so need not resolve whether considerations of stare decisis should induce us, despite the plain error of the case, to leave bad enough alone. As the majority acknowledges, however, "all of the cases decided by this Court under *Feres* have involved allegations of negligence on the part of members of the military." I would not extend *Feres* any further. I confess that the line between FTCA suits alleging military negligence and those alleging civilian negligence has nothing to recommend it except that it would limit our clearly wrong decision in *Feres* and confine the unfairness and irrationality that decision has bred. But that, I think, is justification enough.

Had Lieutenant Commander Johnson been piloting a commercial helicopter when he crashed into the side of a mountain, his widow and children could have sued and recovered for their loss. But because Johnson devoted his life to serving in his country's Armed Forces, the Court today limits his family to a fraction of the recovery they might otherwise have received. If our imposition of that sacrifice bore the legitimacy of having been prescribed by the people's elected representatives, it would (insofar as we are permitted to inquire into such things) be just. But it has not been, and it is not. I respectfully dissent.

Note

Reconceptualizing Feres. While agreeing with Justice Scalia that *Feres* "flew directly in the face of a relatively recent statute's language and legislative history," the Second Circuit has suggested a test for applying the doctrine that it believes would respect the Court's concern for military discipline, its unwillingness to subject claims to the vagaries of local tort law, and its desire to make the federal system of military death and disability benefits the exclusive remedy. The key question in that test would be "was the plaintiff engaged in activities that fell within the scope of the plaintiff's military employment? Where the answer is 'yes,' so that the plaintiff would be entitled to receive standard workers' compensation payments [if he or she were in civilian employment], this will mean that the *Feres* doctrine applies, barring recovery under the FTCA. Conversely, if the answer is 'no,' * * * there should be no *Feres* bar" unless liability would directly threaten the military's disciplinary authority. See Taber v. Maine, 67 F.3d 1029 (2d Cir. 1995) (Calabresi, J.). Applying this test, the court said *Feres* did not bar suit by an off–duty enlisted man injured off–base in a collision with another off–duty serviceman, because there was nothing peculiarly military about the plaintiff's activity and imposing liability on the government would have no implications for military discipline.

Does this test make sense of the *Feres* doctrine? What result would it produce in the *Johnson* case?

3. IMMUNITY OF GOVERNMENTAL OFFICERS AND EM-PLOYEES

In addition to the government's immunity, governmental officers sometimes have immunity from claims against them individually. All federal officers and employees now enjoy virtually absolute immunity by virtue of the Federal Employees Liability Reform and Tort Compensation Act of 1988. Unless the tort involves violation of the Constitution or a federal statute, a federal employee sued personally is entitled to ask the attorney general to certify that the employee was acting within the scope of employment. If the attorney general so certifies, the United States becomes the defendant instead of the employee and the remedy against the government is exclusive. See 28 U.S.C. § 2679. Whether the government is liable for the employee's tort is determined by the Federal Tort Claims Act. See Williams v. United States, 71 F.3d 502 (5th Cir.1995).

At the state level, judges, prosecutors, legislators and high–ranking executives usually have absolute immunity as long as they are acting within the powers of their offices. Other officials and employees usually have qualified immunity from personal liability for torts committed within the scope of their government employment, meaning that they are protected if they act in a good faith (though possibly unreasonable) belief that their actions are lawful. In most jurisdictions, the state or local government pays at least part of any judgment against an employee acting within the scope of employment.

4. THE "PUBLIC DUTY" DOCTRINE

When governments are protected by sovereign immunity, it is unnecessary to decide what duties they owe to persons injured by their activities. Once immunity is abrogated, new duty issues emerge. In some areas, such as operation of motor vehicles, duties established in nongovernmental cases are easily adaptable to governmental defendants. But post–immunity claims often arise from activities that have no precise counterparts in the private sector, and as to which there are no established duty rules.

We saw this in Lacey v. United States, supra p. 223, where the question was whether the Coast Guard had a duty to rescue a pilot downed at sea, and in Galanti v. United States, supra p. 229, where the question was the FBI's duty to protect a third party put in danger by law enforcement activities. The courts resolved both of those cases by interpreting general duty principles to preclude liability. Sometimes, however, courts invoke a special duty rule to absolve governmental defendants from liability even when general duty principles would seem to make them potentially liable. In some states this rule, called the "public duty rule," is applied only to police protection, while in others it is applied widely to distinguish tort duties from broader governmental duties that the court believes are owed to the public at large but not to specific victims of governmental negligence.

RISS v. CITY OF NEW YORK

New York Court of Appeals, 1968.
22 N.Y.2d 579, 293 N.Y.S.2d 897, 240 N.E.2d 860.

BREITEL, JUDGE.

This appeal presents, in a very sympathetic framework, the issue of the liability of a municipality for failure to provide special protection to a member of the public who was repeatedly threatened with personal harm and eventually suffered dire personal injuries for lack of such protection. The facts are amply described in the dissenting opinion * * *. The issue arises upon the affirmance by a divided Appellate Division of a dismissal of the complaint, after both sides had rested but before submission to the jury.

[The dissenting opinion stated the facts as follows. Linda Riss, an attractive young woman, was for more than six months terrorized by a rejected suitor well known to the courts of this State, one Burton Pugach. This miscreant, masquerading as a respectable attorney, repeatedly threatened to have Linda killed or maimed if she did not yield to him: "If I can't have you, no one else will have you, and when I get through with you, no one else will want you". In fear for her life, she went to those charged by law with the duty of preserving and safeguarding the lives of the citizens and residents of this State. Linda's repeated and almost pathetic pleas for aid were received with little more than indifference. Whatever help she was given was not commensurate with the identifiable danger. On June 14, 1959 Linda became engaged to another man. At a party held to celebrate the event, she received a phone call warning her that it was her "last chance". Completely distraught, she called the police, begging for help, but was refused. The next day Pugach carried out his dire threats in the very manner he had foretold by having a hired thug throw lye in Linda's face. Linda was blinded in one eye, lost a good portion of her vision in the other, and her face was permanently scarred. After the assault the authorities concluded that there was some basis for Linda's fears, and for the next three and one–half years, she was given around–the–clock protection.]

It is necessary immediately to distinguish those liabilities attendant upon governmental activities which have displaced or supplemented traditionally private enterprises, such as are involved in the operation of rapid transit systems, hospitals, and places of public assembly. Once sovereign immunity was abolished by statute the extension of liability on ordinary principles of tort law logically followed. To be equally distinguished are certain activities of government which provide services and facilities for the use of the public, such as highways, public buildings and the like, in the performance of which the municipality or the State may be liable under ordinary principles of tort law. The ground for liability is the provision of the services or facilities for the direct use by members of the public.

In contrast, this case involves the provision of a governmental service to protect the public generally from external hazards and particularly to control the activities of criminal wrongdoers. The amount of protection that may be provided is limited by the resources of the community and by a considered legislative–executive decision as to how those resources may be deployed. For the courts to proclaim a new and general duty of protection in the law of tort, even to those who may be the particular seekers of protection based on specific hazards, could and would inevitably determine how the limited police resources of the community should be allocated and without predictable limits. This is quite different from the predictable allocation of resources and liabilities when public hospitals, rapid transit systems, or even highways are provided.

Before such extension of responsibilities should be dictated by the indirect imposition of tort liabilities, there should be a legislative determination that that should be the scope of public responsibility.

It is notable that the removal of sovereign immunity for tort liability was accomplished after legislative enactment and not by any judicial arrogation of power. * * *

When one considers the greatly increased amount of crime committed throughout the cities, but especially in certain portions of them, with a repetitive and predictable pattern, it is easy to see the consequences of fixing municipal liability upon a showing of probable need for and request for protection. To be sure these are grave problems at the present time, exciting high priority activity on the part of the national, State and local governments, to which the answers are neither simple, known, or presently within reasonable controls. To foist a presumed cure for these problems by judicial innovation of a new kind of liability in tort would be foolhardy indeed and an assumption of judicial wisdom and power not possessed by the courts.

* * *

For all of these reasons, there is no warrant in judicial tradition or in the proper allocation of the powers of government for the courts, in the absence of legislation, to carve out an area of tort liability for police protection to members of the public. Quite distinguishable, of course, is the situation where the police authorities undertake responsibilities to particular members of the public and expose them, without adequate protection, to the risks which then materialize into actual losses (Schuster v. City of New York, 5 N.Y.2d 75, 180 N.Y.S.2d 265, 154 N.E.2d 534 [1958]).

Accordingly, the order of the Appellate Division affirming the judgment of dismissal should be affirmed.

KEATING, JUDGE, dissenting.

* * *

No one questions the proposition that the first duty of government is to assure its citizens the opportunity to live in personal security. And no one who reads the record of Linda's ordeal can reach a conclusion other than that the City of New York, acting through its agents, completely and negligently failed to fulfill this obligation to Linda.

Linda has turned to the courts of this State for redress, asking that the city be held liable in damages for its negligent failure to protect her from harm. With compelling logic, she can point out that, if a stranger, who had absolutely no obligation to aid her, had offered her assistance, and thereafter Burton Pugach was able to injure her as a result of the negligence of the volunteer, the courts would certainly require him to pay damages. (Restatement 2d, Torts, § 323.) Why then should the city, whose duties are imposed by law and include the prevention of crime and, consequently, extend far beyond that of the Good Samaritan, not be responsible? If a private detective acts carelessly, no one would deny that a jury could find such conduct unacceptable. Why then is the city not required to live up to at least the same minimal standards of professional competence which would be demanded of a private detective?

* * *

It is not a distortion to summarize the essence of the city's case here in the following language: "Because we owe a duty to everybody, we owe it to nobody." Were it not for the fact that this position has been hallowed by much ancient and revered precedent, we would surely dismiss it as preposterous. To say that there is no duty is, of course, to start with the conclusion. The question is whether or not there should be liability for the negligent failure to provide adequate police protection.

* * *

The fear of financial disaster is a myth. The same argument was made a generation ago in opposition to proposals that the State waive its defense of "sovereign immunity". The prophecy proved false then, and it would now. The supposed astronomical financial burden does not and would not exist. No municipality has gone bankrupt because it has had to respond in damages when a policeman causes injury through carelessly driving a police car or in the thousands of other situations where, by judicial fiat or legislative enactment, the State and its subdivisions have been held liable for the tortious conduct of their employees. Thus, in the past four or five years, New York City has been presented with an average of some 10,000 claims each year. The figure would sound ominous except for the fact the city has been paying out less than $8,000,000 on tort claims each year and this amount includes all those sidewalk defect and snow and ice cases about which the courts fret so often. * * * Certainly this is a slight burden in a budget of more than six billion dollars (less than two tenths of 1%) and of no importance as compared to the injustice of permitting unredressed wrongs to continue to go unrepaired. * * *

* * *

* * * Bernardine v. City of New York, 294 N.Y. 361, 62 N.E.2d 604 [1945] * * * is cited generally for the proposition that the State's waiver of "sovereign immunity" is applicable to its subdivisions. What is of greater interest about the case is that it premised liability on pure common–law negligence. But although "sovereign immunity", by that name, supposedly died in Bernardine v. City of New York, it has been revived in a new form. It now goes by the name "public duty". The [public duty] rule is judge made and can be judicially modified. By statute, the judicially created doctrine of "sovereign immunity" was destroyed. It was an unrighteous doctrine, carrying as it did the connotation that the government is above the law. Likewise, the law should be purged of all new evasions, which seek to avoid the full implications of the repeal of sovereign immunity.

No doubt in the future we shall have to draw limitations just as we have done in the area of private litigation, and no doubt some of these limitations will be unique to municipal liability because the problems will not have any counterpart in private tort law. But if the lines are to be drawn, let them be delineated on candid considerations of policy and fairness and not on the fictions or relics of the doctrine of "sovereign immunity."

The Appellate Division did not adopt the "no duty" theory, but said there was no negligence here because the danger was not imminent. * * * This finding does not stand examination and to its credit the city does not argue that this record would not support a finding of negligence. The danger to Linda was indeed imminent, and this fact could easily have been confirmed had there been competent police work.

* * *

Notes

1. *Subsequent history.* Burton Pugach was convicted and served fourteen years in prison. Eight months after he was released, he and Linda Riss were married. After 23 years of marriage to Linda, Pugach was charged with threatening to kill another woman after she broke off her five–year extramarital affair with him. Linda testified as a character witness for Pugach. To a reporter, Pugach sang his version of a Frank Sinatra song: "The end is near. This is chapter three, the final chapter in a stupid life. But I did it my way. And boy, did I foul up." See A Tangle of Affairs of the Heart, N.Y.Times April 21, 1997, at B8. Pugach was ordered to undergo counseling and stay away from the woman he had threatened. See Wife Defends Man Ordered by Court to Avoid Mistress, Buffalo News, May 8, 1997 at A9.

2. In *Schuster,* cited near the end of the majority opinion, a police informant was killed. The police had publicized the informant's part in capturing a fugitive, and the informant told the police he had been threatened. His estate alleged that the police were negligent for exposing him to risk and for failing to supply him with a bodyguard. The court held that the allegation stated a cause of action.

3. *Voluntarily assuming a duty.* In Florence v. Goldberg, 44 N.Y.2d 189, 404 N.Y.S.2d 583, 375 N.E.2d 763 (1978), a first–grade student was hit by a taxicab at a busy intersection near his school. For the first two weeks of class, the police department had furnished a crossing guard at the intersection, and the victim's mother, having observed the presence of the guard, ceased accompanying her child to school. On the day the child was injured, the regular guard was ill and the police department failed to provide a substitute. The court held that "a municipality whose police department voluntarily assumes a duty to supervise school crossings—the assumption of that duty having been relied upon by parents of school children—may be held liable for its negligent omission to provide a guard. * * * The department's failure to perform this duty placed the infant plaintiff in greater danger than he would have been had the duty not been assumed * * *."

4. One reason for the "public duty rule" may be to avoid judicial interference with executive and legislative decisions as to the allocation of public services. In Florence v. Goldberg, supra note 3, the court said "[d]eployment of these resources remains, as it must, a legislative–executive decision which must be made without the benefit of hindsight. Had the city established that a shortage of personnel precluded assignment of a patrolman to cover the intersection * * * notification of this contingency to the

school principal or other appropriate action would have been sufficient to relieve the police department and New York City from liability * * *." Does this suggest that the interference–with–resource–allocation problem can be solved by something short of a no–duty rule?

5. The "public duty rule" sometimes seems to reflect a belief that compensating all the injuries and property losses that could be attributed to police negligence would create too much liability. The dissent in *Riss* argues that this is simply untrue—that liability for these injuries would impose only a slight burden on the city. Another argument might be that even if the potential liabilities are large, the legislature in abolishing sovereign immunity decided that the amount of potential liability is not "too much." But in other areas of tort law, such as pure economic loss and emotional distress, courts have created no–duty rules for the apparent purpose of preventing "too much" liability. Is it possible that the legislature expected the courts to use similar techniques to prevent "too much" liability once sovereign immunity was abolished?

6. The New York Court of Appeals later extrapolated from *Riss*, *Florence*, and other cases the proposition that "where there is no special relationship, a municipality does not owe a duty to its citizens in the performance of governmental functions, and thus courts will not examine the 'reasonableness' of the municipality's actions." Sorichetti v. City of New York, 65 N.Y.2d 461, 467, 482 N.E.2d 70, 74, 492 N.Y.S.2d 591, 595 (1985). Is that consistent with the legislature's decision to abrogate sovereign immunity?

B. FAMILY IMMUNITIES

PRICE v. PRICE

Supreme Court of Texas, 1987.
732 S.W.2d 316.

KILGARLIN, JUSTICE.

This case presents us with the opportunity to re–examine the validity of the doctrine of interspousal immunity. The case originated as a civil action of negligence for personal injuries brought by Kimberly Parmenter Price against her husband, Duane Price. Duane Price's motion for summary judgment was granted. The court of appeals affirmed that judgment. We reverse the judgment of the court of appeals and remand this cause to the trial court.

In July of 1983, Kimberly Parmenter * * * was injured when a motorcycle on which she was riding collided with a truck. The motorcycle was driven by Duane Price. Six months after the accident, Duane and Kimberly were married. After marriage, Kimberly brought this action seeking recovery from her husband, Duane, and from the driver of the truck, claiming that the negligence of these drivers had caused her injuries. The driver of the truck and his employer settled. The trial court, in granting summary judgment for Duane, relied on the doctrine that one spouse could not sue another for negligent conduct.

The doctrine of interspousal immunity is a part of the common law, having been judicially created. Its origins are shrouded in antiquity, but the basis of the doctrine is *"that a husband and wife are one person."*

A woman's disability during coverture was an essential ingredient in fostering the doctrine. As was stated in Thompson v. Thompson, 218 U.S. 611, 614–15, 31 S.Ct. 111, 54 L.Ed. 1180 (1910):

> At common law the husband and wife were regarded as one,—the legal existence of the wife during coverture being merged in that of the husband; and, generally speaking, the wife was incapable of making contracts, of acquiring property or disposing of the same without her husband's consent. They could not enter into contracts with each other, *nor were they liable for torts committed by one against the other* (emphasis added).

An earlier thesis on American law expanded the concept of superiority of the husband over the wife even to the extent of restraining her liberty or disciplining her. While in this, the last quarter of the twentieth century, such views seem preposterous, recognition that those views were prevalent in the law makes easily understandable why suits by wives against husbands were not permitted.

However, the husband/wife unity argument as grounds for the doctrine was severely impeded by the adoption of what were known as Married Women Acts. These legislative acts occurred principally in the latter half of the nineteenth century and early twentieth century. These acts, while varying from state to state, generally gave wives the rights to own, acquire and dispose of property; to contract; and, to sue in respect to their property and contracts. Most importantly, many of the statutes specifically abolished the doctrine of the oneness of husband and wife. [One important consequence of these acts was permitting a wife to sue her husband for tortious damage to her separate property. Another was permitting binding contracts between husbands and wives. Thus, spousal immunity in modern times has been confined to personal injury suits.]

With the demise of the legal fiction of the merger of husband and wife into a single entity, the doctrine of interspousal immunity found support in considerations of marital harmony, as well as the potential for collusive lawsuits.

American jurisdictions, in upholding the doctrine, early on espoused the premise that a civil suit by one spouse against another would destroy the harmony of the home. One court, in a fire and brimstone opinion upholding the prohibition against suits between spouses, foresaw all manner of evil should the immunity doctrine be terminated. In Ritter v. Ritter, 31 Pa. 396 (1858), that court, while observing that a favorite maxim at common law was that marriage makes a man and woman one person at law, also said:

> Nothing could so complete that severance [of the marriage relationship] and degradation, as to throw open litigation to the parties. The maddest advocate for woman's rights, and for the abolition on earth

of all divine institutions, could wish for no more decisive blow from the courts than this. The flames which litigation would kindle on the domestic hearth would consume in an instant the conjugal bond, and bring on a new era indeed—an era of universal discord, of unchastity, of bastardy, of dissoluteness, of violence, cruelty, and murders.

The second argument for barring interspousal suits, the possibility of collusive lawsuits, is entirely inconsistent with the subjugation of wife to husband and preservation of happy homes theses. Nevertheless, such inconsistency did not seem to trouble the courts. The possibility of collusion was alluded to in Abbott v. Abbott, 67 Me. 304 (1877), where it was suggested that a widow could raid her deceased husband's estate by claiming all sorts of wrongs by him during his lifetime. The fraud theory expanded into vogue with the advent of insurance to cover vehicular accidents. In Newton v. Weber, 119 Misc.Rep. 240, 196 N.Y.S. 113, 114 (1922), the court said of allowing a tort action by a wife against her husband, "[t]he maintenance of an action of this character, unless the sole purpose be a raid upon an insurance company, would not add to conjugal happiness and unison."

Without ascribing any reasons for doing so, Texas adopted the doctrine of interspousal immunity one hundred years ago in Nickerson and Matson v. Nickerson, 65 Tex. 281 (1886) * * *.

* * *

The doctrine remained firmly established as Texas law until Bounds v. Caudle, 560 S.W.2d 925 (Tex.1977). *Bounds* abrogated the rule as to intentional torts. In *Bounds,* this court concluded that suits for willful or intentional torts would not disrupt domestic tranquility since "the peace and harmony of a home" which had "been strained to the point where an intentional physical attack could take place" could not be further impaired by allowing a suit to recover damages.

Is there today any policy justification for retaining this feudal concept of the rights of parties to a marriage? Apparently, our colleagues on the Court of Criminal Appeals have decided "no" in respect to the marital discord argument. With their September 1, 1986 promulgation of Tex.R.Crim.Ev. 504, that court abolished the long–standing rule that one spouse could prevent the other from voluntarily giving testimony in a criminal prosecution. * * *

* * *

* * * It is difficult to fathom how denying a forum for the redress of any wrong could be said to encourage domestic tranquility. It is equally difficult to see how suits based in tort would destroy domestic tranquility while property and contract actions do not.

As to the potential for fraud and collusion, we are unable to distinguish interspousal suits from other actions for personal injury. In Whitworth v. Bynum, 699 S.W.2d 194, 197 (Tex.1985) [which held unconstitutional a statute limiting actions against automobile drivers by passengers who were close relatives of the driver], this court "refuse[d] to indulge in the assumption that close relatives will prevaricate so as to promote a spurious lawsuit." Our system of justice is capable of ascertaining the existence of fraud and collusion. * * *

* * *

The doctrine of interspousal immunity has previously been abrogated as to some causes of action in this jurisdiction. We now abolish that doctrine completely as to any cause of action. We do not limit our holding to suits involving vehicular accidents only, as has been done by some jurisdictions and as has been urged upon us in this case. To do so would be to negate meritorious claims such as was presented in Stafford v. Stafford, 726 S.W.2d 14 (Tex.1987). In that case a husband had transmitted a venereal disease to his wife, resulting in an infection that ultimately caused Mrs. Stafford the loss of her ovaries and fallopian tubes, ending for all time her ability to bear children. While we ruled for her, the issue of interspousal immunity had not been preserved for our review. To leave in place a bar to suits like that of Mrs. Stafford or other suits involving non–vehicular torts would amount to a repudiation of the constitutional guarantee of equal protection of the laws. This we will not do.

* * *

BROADBENT v. BROADBENT

Supreme Court of Arizona, 1995.
184 Ariz. 74, 907 P.2d 43.

CORCORAN, JUSTICE.

We must determine whether the doctrine of parental immunity bars Christopher Broadbent's action against his mother for negligence. We also discuss the viability of the line of Arizona cases creating and refining the parental immunity doctrine. * * *

FACTS AND PROCEDURAL HISTORY

I. Facts

Christopher and his mother, Laura J. Broadbent, went swimming at the family residence on April 13, 1984, their first day of swimming that year. Christopher was wearing "floaties," which are inflatable rings worn on the arms to assist a child in staying afloat. Laura understood that a child could still drown while wearing floaties and should be supervised. At the time of the accident, Christopher was two–and–a–half years old and did not know how to swim.

Laura and Christopher were by the side of the pool when the telephone rang. Laura left Christopher alone by the pool to answer the phone. Laura saw Christopher remove his floaties before she answered the phone. Laura talked on the phone 5 to 10 minutes and could not see Christopher from where she was talking. She also did not have on her contact lenses. Laura said that if she stretched the phone cord and her body, she could see the pool area, but when she did this, she could not see Christopher. She dropped the phone, ran toward the pool, and found Christopher floating in the deep end of the pool.

Laura administered cardio–pulmonary resuscitation and telephoned for the paramedics. Neither Laura nor the paramedics were able to revive Christopher. The paramedics took Christopher to the hospital where he was finally revived. As a result of this near drowning, Christopher suffered severe brain damage because of lack of oxygen. He has lost his motor skills and has no voluntary movement.

* * *

A complaint was filed on behalf of Christopher, as plaintiff, against his mother, alleging that she was negligent and caused his injuries. This action was brought to involve the Broadbents' umbrella insurance carrier in the issue of coverage. * * * The trial court granted Laura's motion for summary judgment and ruled that the parental immunity doctrine applied to the facts of this case.

* * *

Discussion

I. *History and Purpose of the Parental Immunity Doctrine*

A. *The Origins of Parental Immunity*

We begin by stating a few basic facts about the treatment of children under the law and family immunities. Under common law, a child has traditionally been considered a separate legal entity from his or her parent. Children have generally been allowed to sue their parents in property and contract actions.

The doctrine of parental immunity is an American phenomenon unknown in the English common law. See Gibson v. Gibson, 3 Cal.3d 914, 92 Cal.Rptr. 288, 289, 479 P.2d 648, 649 (1971). Courts in Canada and Scotland have held that children may sue their parents in tort.

* * *

In Hewlett v. George, 68 Miss. 703, 711, 9 So. 885, 887 (1891), the Supreme Court of Mississippi held, without citation to legal authority, that a child could not sue her parent for being falsely imprisoned in an insane asylum because of parental immunity, a doctrine which that court created from whole cloth. As its rationale, the court stated:

> [S]o long as the parent is under obligation to care for, guide and control, and the child is under reciprocal obligation to aid and comfort and obey, no such action as this can be maintained. The peace of society, and of the families composing society, and a sound public policy, designed to subserve the repose of families and the best interests of society, forbid to the minor child a right to appear

in court in the assertion of a claim to civil redress for personal injuries suffered at the hands of the parent.

Hewlett, 68 Miss. at 711, 9 So. at 887.

Hewlett was followed by two cases that were also decided on parental immunity grounds, and these came to be known as the "great trilogy" of cases establishing the parental immunity doctrine. In McKelvey v. McKelvey, the Tennessee Supreme Court held that a minor child could not sue her father for "cruel and inhuman treatment" allegedly inflicted by her stepmother with the consent of her father. 111 Tenn. 388, 77 S.W. 664, 664–65 (1903). *McKelvey* cited *Hewlett* as the only authority for the doctrine of parental immunity and analogized the parent–child relationship to that of the husband–wife relationship, noting that the basis for the spousal immunity was, in part, the fact that husband and wife are a legal entity.

In Roller v. Roller, the Supreme Court of Washington cited *Hewlett* and held that a minor child could not sue her father for rape, even though he had been convicted of the criminal violation, because of the doctrine of parental immunity. *Roller,* 37 Wash. 242, 79 P. 788, 788–89 (1905). The *Roller* court argued that if the child recovered a money judgment from the parent and then died, the parent would then become heir to the property that had been taken from him. In addition, *Roller* argued that "the public has an interest in the financial welfare of other minor members of the family, and it would not be the policy of the law to allow the estate, which is to be looked to for the support of all the minor children, to be appropriated by any particular one."

This "great trilogy" was the inauspicious beginning of the doctrine of parental immunity, which was soon embraced by almost every state. * * * However, the courts soon began fashioning several exceptions to the doctrine, and in several states the doctrine has been abolished. * * * In several situations, parental immunity does not apply: if the parent is acting outside his parental role and within the scope of his employment; if the parent acts willfully, wantonly, or recklessly; if the child is emancipated; if the child or parent dies; if a third party is liable for the tort, then the immunity of the parent does not protect that third party; and if the tortfeasor is standing *in loco parentis,* such as a grandparent, foster parent, or teacher, then the immunity does not apply.

B. Parental Immunity in Arizona

In 1967 the doctrine of parental immunity was first recognized in Arizona in Purcell v. Frazer, 7 Ariz.App. 5, 8–9, 435 P.2d 736, 739–40 (1967). In *Purcell,* the Arizona Court of Appeals held that the doctrine of parental immunity prohibited children from suing their parents for injuries resulting from a car accident allegedly caused by the parents' negligence. *Purcell,* however, was soon overruled in 1970 by Streenz v. Streenz, which held that an unemancipated minor could sue her parents for injuries resulting from a car accident. *Streenz,* 106 Ariz. 86, 88–89, 471 P.2d 282, 284–85 (1970). In *Streenz,* this court adopted the standard from the Wisconsin Supreme Court set forth in Goller v. White, 20 Wis.2d 402, 122 N.W.2d 193, 198 (1963). Under the *Goller* standard, parental immunity is abrogated except:

> (1) where the alleged negligent act involves an exercise of parental authority over the child; and

> (2) where the alleged negligent act involves an exercise of ordinary parental discretion with respect to the provision of food, clothing, housing, medical and dental services, and other care.

The cases following *Streenz* show the difficulty in applying this ambiguous standard.

In Sandoval v. Sandoval, a child sued his parents alleging that his father had negligently left the gate open, which allowed the 4–year–old child to ride his tricycle from the front yard into the street where he was run over by a car. 128 Ariz. 11, 11, 623 P.2d 800, 800 (1981). In *Sandoval,* this court devised a new test for applying the standard set forth in *Streenz:* the parent would not be immune if the parent had a duty to the world at large. If the parent's duty was "owed to the child alone and a part of the parental 'care and control' or 'other care' to be provided by the parents," then the parent was immune from liability. The court held that "the act of leaving a gate open should not subject the plaintiff's parents to suit." Further, the court noted that it did not limit the abrogation of the parental immunity doctrine to negligence in car accident cases and would, instead, "continue to consider, on a case by case basis, the actual cause of the injury and whether the act of the parent breached a duty owed to the world at large, as opposed to a duty owed to a child within the family sphere." The court reasoned that when a parent was driving a car, he had a duty to the world to drive carefully, whereas the duty to close the gate was a duty owed only to the child, and that the direct cause of the child's injuries in *Sandoval* was the car that struck him in the street, not the gate being open.

Applying *Sandoval,* the court in Schleier v. Alter held that the parents had a duty to the world at large and therefore were not immune from liability. *Schleier,* 159 Ariz. 397, 399–400, 767 P.2d 1187, 1189–90 (App.1989). In that case, the family dog, which had a history of attacking children, bit the Alters' 11–month–old child. The court of appeals characterized the duty that the parents owed as a general duty to the world to supervise their dog, which the court found to be the equivalent of a "dangerous instrumentality" to children.

The most recent Arizona case on parental immunity found the doctrine to be applicable. In Sandbak v. Sandbak, the Sandbaks' child wandered onto the next door neighbors' property where the neighbors' pit bull terrier severely mauled her. 166 Ariz. 21, 22, 800 P.2d 8, 9 (App.1990). The parents knew that the next door neighbors owned pit bull terriers and that their daughter had a habit of wandering onto the neighbors' property. The court held that the child's claim of negligent supervision was barred, rejecting the child's argument that immunity only applied to parents' negligence with regard to legal obligations. The court rejected the Wisconsin Supreme Court's limiting interpretation of the *Goller* test in Thoreson v. Milwaukee & Suburban Transport Co., 56 Wis.2d 231, 201 N.W.2d 745, 753 (1972), which held that acts involving an "exercise of discretion with 'respect to the provision of food, clothing, housing, medical and dental services, and other care'" meant that parents were allowed "discretion in performing their legal duties." (Emphasis added.) In *Thoreson,* the Wisconsin court concluded that the parent was not immune from liability for negligently supervising her child who wandered out of the house and into the street where he was injured.

Further, in *Sandbak,* the Arizona Court of Appeals rejected the argument that allowing the child to trespass on the neighbors' property was a violation of the parents' duty to the world at large, finding that violation of that duty, if it even existed, was not the proximate cause of the injury.

C. *Analysis of the Policy Reasons Advanced in Support of Parental Immunity*

Courts and commentators have postulated many policy reasons for the parental immunity doctrine. The primary justifications for this immunity are:

(1) Suing one's parents would disturb domestic tranquility;

(2) Suing one's parents would create a danger of fraud and collusion;

(3) Awarding damages to the child would deplete family resources;

(4) Awarding damages to the child could benefit the parent if the child predeceases the parent and the parent inherits the child's damages; and

(5) Suing one's parents would interfere with parental care, discipline, and control.

We believe that all of these justifications provide weak support for the parental immunity doctrine.

The injury to the child, more than the lawsuit, disrupts the family tranquility. In fact, if the child is not compensated for the tortious injury, then peace in the family is even less likely. In the seminal Arizona case on parental immunity, the court recognized that family tranquility would not be disturbed if the parents had liability insurance.

This fear of upsetting the family tranquility also seems unrealistic when we consider how such a lawsuit is initiated. The parent most often makes the decision to sue himself, and the parent is in effect prepared to say that he was negligent.

The danger of fraud and collusion is present in all lawsuits. We should not deny recovery to an entire class of litigants because some litigants might try to deceive the judicial system. The system can ferret out fraudulent and collusive behavior in suits brought by children against their parents just as the system detects such behavior in other contexts.

We note, too, that both of these arguments—disturbing domestic tranquility and danger of fraud and collusion—were also justifications for spousal immunity, which has been abrogated in Arizona. These same concerns could justify an immunity from suits brought by one sibling against another; however, this is an immunity that the courts have not felt the need to create. Furthermore, one of the justifications for spousal immunity was that husband and wife were considered a single legal entity, yet this legal fiction was not applied to the parent–child relationship. As noted earlier, children have always been able to maintain actions against their parents in contexts other than negligence actions, such as contract actions or for willful conduct by the parent. Therefore, the reliance on spousal immunity as a justification for parental immunity is not sound.

A damage award for the child will not deplete, or unfairly redistribute, the family's financial resources. These cases will generally not be brought if no insurance coverage is available, and therefore the worry that the family's resources will be depleted for the benefit of one child is illusory. The opposite is true. If a child has been seriously injured and needs expensive medical care, then a successful lawsuit against the parent and subsequent recovery from the insurance company could ease the financial burden on the family. It would not be a viable rule to say that liability only exists where insurance exists, but we recognize that lawsuits generally will be brought when there is potential insurance coverage.

The possibility that the parent might inherit money recovered by the child is remote. This becomes a concern only if the parent inherits as a beneficiary under intestate succession laws. This is a concern for the probate courts and the laws of intestate succession, not tort law. The remedy would be to prohibit inheritance by the parent—not to deny recovery to the injured child.

The Arizona courts have embraced the rationale that allowing a child to sue a parent would interfere with parental care, discipline, and control. See *Streenz,* 106 Ariz. at 89, 471 P.2d at 285. We have cited with approval the Wisconsin Supreme Court's statement that:

> [a] new and heavy burden would be added to the responsibility and privilege of parenthood, if within the wide scope of daily experiences common to the upbringing of children a parent could be subjected to a suit for damages for each failure to exercise care and judgment commensurate with the risk.

Sandoval, 128 Ariz. at 13, 623 P.2d at 802, quoting Lemmen v. Servais, 39 Wis.2d 75, 158 N.W.2d 341, 344 (1968).

The justification that allowing children to sue their parents would undercut parental authority and discretion has more appeal than the other rationales. However, if a child were seriously injured as a result of the exercise of parental authority, such as by a beating, then it would constitute an injury willfully inflicted, and parents are generally not immune for willful, wanton, or malicious conduct. Furthermore, such a willful beating would probably constitute child abuse and could be criminally prosecuted. See A.R.S. § 8–546 (Supp.1994).

We want to protect the right of parents to raise their children by their own methods and in accordance with their own attitudes and beliefs. The New York Court of Appeals aptly stated this concern:

> Considering the different economic, educational, cultural, ethnic and religious backgrounds which must prevail, there are so many combinations and permutations of parent–child relationships that may result that the search for a standard would necessarily be in vain. * * * For this reason parents have always had the right to determine how much independence, supervision and control a child should have, and to best judge the character and extent of development of their child.

Holodook v. Spencer, 36 N.Y.2d 35, 364 N.Y.S.2d 859, 867, 324 N.E.2d 338, 346 (1974) * * *. Though we recognize the importance of allowing parental discretion, we disagree that our searching for a standard would be "in vain." Parents do not possess unfettered discretion in raising their children.

II. *The Abolishment of Parental Immunity and Adoption of the "Reasonable Parent" Standard for Parent–Child Suits*

Although the above concerns make it difficult to draft a proper standard for the type of action a child may maintain against a parent, we will attempt to do so. We need to "fashion an objective standard that does not result in second–guessing parents in the management of their family affairs." First, we should make clear what the standard is *not*. We reject and hereby overrule *Sandoval,* which created the "duty to the world at large versus duty to the child alone" distinction. This distinction is not capable of uniform application and has no connection with the rationale for parental immunity. This is especially evident when we compare the facts of *Schleier* and *Sandbak.*

In *Schleier,* the negligent act was failure to restrain a dog, and the court found that this was a duty to the world; therefore, parental immunity did not apply. In *Sandbak,* the negligent act was failure to supervise a child who was bitten by a neighbor's dog, and the court found this was a duty to the child alone; therefore, parental immunity applied. The children in *Schleier* and *Sandbak* suffered similar injuries; neither case involved parental discipline, and neither case involved the "provision of food, clothing, housing, medical and dental services, and other care," unless "other care" is broadly defined. Both cases involved the negligent supervision of children. If we were to hold that parents are immune for negligent supervision of children, then the issue of liability would revolve around whether an activity could be described as "supervision" and whether lack of supervision was the cause of the injury. This would not involve a consideration of whether the activity infringed on the parents' discretionary decisions regarding care, custody, and control. Almost everything a parent does in relation to his child involves "care, custody, and control."

We add that parents always owe a parental duty to their minor child. The issue of liability should revolve around whether the parents have breached this duty and, if so, whether the breach of duty caused the injury.

In accord with the California Supreme Court, "we reject the implication of *Goller* [which this court approved in *Streenz*] that within certain aspects of the parent–child relationship, the parent has carte blanche to act negligently toward his child. * * * [A]lthough a parent has the prerogative and the duty to exercise authority over his minor child, this prerogative must be exercised within reasonable limits." *Gibson*, 479 P.2d at 652–53. We hereby reject the *Goller* test as set forth in *Streenz*, and we approve of the "reasonable parent test," in which a parent's conduct is judged by whether that parent's conduct comported with that of a reasonable and prudent parent in a similar situation.

A parent is not immune from liability for tortious conduct directed toward his child solely by reason of that relationship. And, a parent is not liable for an act or omission that injured his child if the parent acted as a reasonable and prudent parent in the situation would.

III. Application to the Present Case

In this case, the trier of fact may find that the mother, Laura Broadbent, did not act as a reasonable and prudent parent would have in this situation. The finder of fact must determine whether leaving a two–and–a–half year old child unattended next to a swimming pool is reasonable or prudent. We fail to see why parents should not be held liable for negligence in failing to supervise their own children near the pool, when their liability would be clear had the children not been their own. We think that in most cases, if not all, the standard of care owed to a parent's own child is the same as that owed to any other child.

The paradox of parental immunity can be seen if we assume that a neighbor child from across the street was a guest and was injured at the same time and under the same circumstances as Christopher. Should the neighbor child be permitted to sue and recover damages from Laura but Christopher be denied the same opportunity?

A parent may avoid liability because there is no negligence, but not merely because of the status as parent. Children are certainly accident prone, and oftentimes those accidents are not due to the negligence of any party. The same rules of summary judgment apply to these cases as to others, and trial courts should feel free to dismiss frivolous cases on the ground that the parent has acted as a reasonable and prudent parent in a similar situation would.

CONCLUSION

We vacate the court of appeals' decision in this case, reverse the trial court's rulings on summary judgment, and remand to the trial court for proceedings consistent with this opinion. Laura Broadbent is not immune from liability in this case because of the doctrine of parental immunity, which we hereby abolish. We overrule *Sandoval* on the issue of parental immunity and no longer follow the *Goller* test as adopted in *Streenz.*

MOELLER, V.C.J., and ZLAKET and MARTONE, JJ., concur.

FELDMAN, CHIEF JUSTICE, specially concurring.

I join in the abrogation of parental immunity and the court's adoption of the reasonable and prudent parent test but write separately to sound a note of caution. Although we abolish a rule of tort immunity, we must bear in mind that "difficult problems" remain in "determining when a physical harm should be regarded as actionable." Restatement (Second) of Torts § 895G cmt. k. If the alleged tortious conduct does not grow out of the family relationship, the question of negligence "may be determined as if the parties were not related." Id. However, there are areas of broad discretion in which only parents have authority to make decisions. In these areas, I agree with the Restatement's view that "the standard of a reasonable prudent parent * * * recognize[s] the existence of that discretion and thus * * * require[s] that the [parent's] conduct be palpably unreasonable in order to impose liability." Id. If, however, the charged breach of duty falls outside the area of a parent's discretionary authority and is, instead, within the obligation of due care owed by anyone who has supervisory or other responsibility for another's safety, then the test should be much more flexible.

Thus, the parent who decides to enroll a two–year–old child in swimming lessons at a neighborhood pool operates within the realm of parent–child decision–making. Although the child might be hurt during the course of such lessons, the decision to put the child in that position is peculiarly a matter of parental authority rather than a question of supervisory care or performance. Under the proper application of the reasonable and prudent parent test, as a matter of law there should be no liability unless one could say the decision was palpably unreasonable under given circumstances.

The facts of this case illustrate the other side of the coin. The act of leaving an unsupervised two–year–old child, who was unable to swim, at the side of a swimming pool was not an exercise of parental decision–making but an inadvertent act in the performance of duties owed by a caretaker. As the Restatement indicates, the reasonable and prudent parent test extends a great deal of flexibility to the first example but much less, if any, to the second.

Chapter XIII

MEDICAL MALPRACTICE

Medical malpractice is a species of negligence. As with any cause of action for negligence, the plaintiff must prove that the defendant failed to exercise reasonable care and that this substandard conduct was a factual and legal cause of the plaintiff's injuries. Proving negligence and causation in a lawsuit against medical defendants presents special problems and issues. Consequently, we have presented these medical negligence cases in a separate chapter.

A. PROFESSIONAL STANDARD OF CARE

MELVILLE v. SOUTHWARD

Supreme Court of Colorado, 1990.
791 P.2d 383.

CHIEF JUSTICE QUINN.

[Plaintiff won a $56,000 judgment against a podiatrist for malpractice resulting in a permanent foot injury that interfered with plaintiff's ability to walk and balance herself. She had consulted the defendant in 1980 about an ingrown toenail. Defendant removed the ingrown toenail but also suggested the plaintiff should have a metatarsal osteotomy (cutting and shortening the metatarsal bone of a toe) to relieve discomfort. The podiatrist performed the surgery a month later in his office. He made a small incision in the top of the plaintiff's foot, used a drill to fracture the metatarsal bone and a dental burr to remove bone fragments, wrapped the foot in a bandage soaked in antibiotic, placed the foot in a half–shoe, and told the plaintiff to soak the foot in vinegar and water.

One week later plaintiff returned for a check up. The defendant commented "I don't like the looks of this," rewrapped the foot and provided plaintiff with an antibiotic. After another week, the plaintiff complained that her foot was red, swollen, and painful. Defendant advised her to increase the amount of vinegar and soak the foot more frequently. Two days later, he told her the foot was healing and rewrapped it with clean bandages. The next day the plaintiff noticed fluid exuding from a sore near the incision and called her family physician, Dr. McGarry, who recognized that the surgical site was badly infected, admitted plaintiff to a hospital for X–rays and intravenous administration of antibiotics, and referred her to Dr. Barnard, an orthopedic surgeon.]

Plaintiff's counsel asked Doctor Barnard whether he had an opinion to a reasonable medical probability on whether the osteotomy was performed below the standard of care for such a surgical procedure. The defendant objected to this line of questioning on the basis that no foundation had been laid regarding Barnard's knowledge of the standard of care applicable to podiatry. The trial court overruled the objection and permitted Barnard to testify. Barnard testified that the osteotomy performed by the defendant was below the standard of care for two reasons: first, the surgery was unnecessary because none of the pre–surgical X–rays indicated a deformity in the metatarsal; and second, even assuming the surgery was necessary, the osteotomy was performed in an unsterile office environment and thereby subjected the bone to a high risk of infection. Barnard acknowledged in his testimony that he was unfamiliar with the standards applicable to podiatric foot surgery, was not familiar with podiatric literature, had never received any instruction on podiatry, and had never performed the surgical procedure involved in this case.

Doctor Barnard also testified, again over the defendant's objection, that the defendant's post–operative treatment of the plaintiff fell below the proper standard of care for treating an osteotomy. Barnard testified that there is a uniform physiological bone healing process for all types of bone surgeries and that proper post–operative treatment of foot surgery requires that the foot be elevated for 24 to 48 hours without weight–bearing as a means of reducing inflammation. Inflammation, according to Barnard, can cause infection. Barnard further testified that a review of the plaintiff's medical history and the defendant's notes, as well as an examination of the plaintiff's foot, revealed that the plaintiff had received inadequate post–operative treatment. Barnard based his opinion on the fact that the plaintiff's right foot had not been adequately immobilized and on the further fact that the soaking treatment provided only semi–antibiotic surface treatment of the wound and not the type of internal treatment necessary for the healing of a post–operative infection.

* * *

II.

In a medical malpractice case, * * * the plaintiff must establish that the defendant failed to conform to the standard of care ordinarily possessed and exercised by members of the same school of medicine practiced by the defendant. The standard of care in a medical malpractice action is measured by whether a reasonably careful physician of the same school of medicine as the defendant would have acted in the same manner as did the defendant in treating and caring for the plaintiff.

Unless the subject matter of a medical malpractice action lies within the ambit of common knowledge or experience of ordinary persons, the plaintiff must establish the controlling standard of care, as well as the defendant's failure to adhere to that standard, by expert opinion testimony. The reason for the requirement of expert opinion testimony in most medical malpractice cases is obvious: matters relating to medical diagnosis and treatment ordinarily involve a level of technical knowledge and skill beyond the realm of lay knowledge and experience. Without expert opinion testimony in such cases, the trier of fact would be left with no standard at all against which to evaluate the defendant's conduct.

* * *

As a prerequisite to admitting expert testimony, a trial court must make the following two preliminary determinations: first, the court must decide if the expert testimony will assist the trier of fact in understanding the evidence or in determining a fact in issue; and second, the court must determine whether the witness is properly qualified by knowledge, skill, experience, training, or education, to offer an opinion on the issue in question. * * *

The evidentiary standard for determining whether a member of one school of medicine may offer an opinion concerning the standard of care applicable to another school has been articulated by several appellate courts in various ways. One line of cases places emphasis on whether the expert witness is sufficiently knowledgeable of and familiar with the standard of care governing the defendant's specialty to offer an informed opinion on that issue. Another line of cases focuses primarily on whether the standard of diagnosis or treatment applicable to the expert witness' specialty is substantially identical to the standard for the defendant's practice.

There is merit in both of the above approaches. * * * In our view, therefore, the dispositive consideration in ruling on the admissibility of expert opinion testimony by a medical witness regarding whether the defendant, who practices in another school of medicine, has adhered to or deviated from the requisite standard of care in diagnosing or treating the plaintiff should be the following: (1) whether the testifying expert, although practicing a specialty different from that of the defendant, nonetheless is, by reason of knowledge, skill, experience, training, or education, so substantially familiar with the standard of care applicable to the defendant's specialty as to render the witness' opinion testimony as well–informed as would be the opinion of an expert witness practicing the same specialty as the defendant; or (2) whether the standard of care for the condition in question is substantially identical for both specialties.[1] If a proper foundation establishes either of these evidentiary

---

1. In 1988, the General Assembly enacted a statutory provision that purports to establish criteria for permitting an expert witness to testify in a medical malpractice

predicates for admissibility, the witness should be permitted to offer an expert opinion on the standard of care applicable to the defendant's specialty and on whether the defendant breached that standard of care. * * *

III.

The practice of podiatry is defined by statute as "the diagnosis and the medical, surgical, mechanical, manipulative, and electrical treatment of disorders of the human toe and foot, including the ankle and tendons that insert into the foot." § 12–32–101(3), 5 C.R.S. (1985).[2] The practice of medicine, in contrast, includes the diagnosis, treatment, or prevention of "any human disease, ailment, pain, injury, deformity, or physical or mental condition, whether by the use of drugs, surgery, manipulation, electricity, or any physical, mechanical, or other means whatsoever." Section 12–36–106(1)(a), 5 C.R.S. (1985). Orthopedic surgery is a medical subspecialty that involves the utilization of medical, surgical, and physical methods in treating the extremities, spine, and associated structures, and, as such, includes not only foot surgery encompassed by the practice of podiatry but also other treatments and medical practices not within podiatric practices.

The fact that practicing podiatrists and orthopedic surgeons are authorized to perform surgical procedures on a patient's foot is not to say that the standard of care applicable to each discipline is necessarily the same. A patient seeking podiatric treatment is entitled to receive treatment in accordance with the principles and practices of podiatry, rather than some other school of medicine, and a podiatrist rendering

action. The statutory provision in question, which was enacted as part of the Health Care Availability Act, applies to acts or omissions occurring on or after July 1, 1988. [It states that] "No person shall be qualified to testify as an expert witness concerning issues of negligence in any medical malpractice action or proceeding against a physician unless he not only is a licensed physician but can demonstrate by competent evidence that, as a result of training, education, knowledge, and experience in the evaluation, diagnosis, and treatment of the disease or injury which is the subject matter of the action or proceeding against the physician defendant, he was substantially familiar with applicable standards of care and practice as they relate to the act or omission which is the subject of the claim on the date of the incident. The court shall not permit an expert in one medical subspecialty to testify against a physician in another medical subspecialty unless, in addition to such a showing of substantial familiarity, there is a showing that the standards of care and practice in the two fields are similar. The limitations in this section shall not apply to expert wit-

nesses testifying as to the degree or permanency of medical or physical impairment."

We express no opinion on the validity of this legislation or on what effect, if any, the statute would have on facts similar to those present here.

2. The statutory definition of podiatry in section 12–32–101(3) also states:

* * * except that "podiatry" does not include the amputation of the foot and the administration of an anesthetic other than a local anesthetic. Surgical procedures of the ankle below the level of the dermis may be performed only in a licensed or certified hospital by a podiatrist licensed in this state who is: (a) Certified by the American board of podiatric surgery; or

(b) Performing surgery under the direct supervision of a licensed podiatrist certified by the American board of podiatric surgery; or

(c) Performing surgery under the direct supervision of a person licensed to practice medicine and certified by the American board of orthopedic surgery.

treatment to a patient is entitled to be judged by the standard of reasonably careful podiatric practice exercised by members of that specialty, and not by some other school of medicine.

In this case Doctor Barnard, an orthopedic surgeon, testified that in his opinion the metatarsal osteotomy performed by the defendant did not conform to the standard of care applicable to such a surgical procedure and that the defendant did not adhere to the standard of care applicable to post–operative care and treatment of the plaintiff. We consider separately each aspect of the doctor's opinion testimony.

A.

The trial court ruled that, because an orthopedic surgeon receives more training and education than a podiatrist, Doctor Barnard was qualified to render an opinion on the standard of care exercised by the defendant in performing the metatarsal osteotomy on the plaintiff's foot. The court of appeals disagreed with the trial court's ruling and held that Barnard's opinion testimony was nothing more than an expression of opinion that the general practice of podiatry did not meet the standard of care observed by an orthopedic surgeon in performing foot surgery. We agree with the court of appeals that the trial court erred in its evidentiary ruling.

The plaintiff failed to establish an evidentiary foundation that Doctor Barnard, by reason of his knowledge, skill, experience, training, or education, was so substantially familiar with the standard of care for podiatric surgery as to render his opinion testimony as well informed as that of a podiatrist. On the contrary, Barnard expressly acknowledged that he was not familiar either with podiatric foot care or with the standard of care applicable to a podiatrist. Under this state of the record, there was no evidentiary basis to accept Barnard, an orthopedic surgeon, as an expert witness on the standard of care applicable to the surgical procedure performed by the defendant and to permit the doctor to express the opinion that the defendant failed to exercise reasonable care in operating on the plaintiff. Nor did the plaintiff establish by way of an evidentiary predicate that the standard of care for a metatarsal osteotomy was substantially identical for both the practice of orthopedic surgery and podiatry. The court of appeals, therefore, correctly concluded that the opinion testimony of Doctor Barnard should not have been admitted on the issue of the defendant's alleged negligence in performing the metatarsal osteotomy in question.

B.

The plaintiff's malpractice claim was based not only on the defendant's alleged negligence in performing the metatarsal osteotomy but also in the defendant's post–operative care and treatment of the plaintiff. Again, a review of the record reveals that the plaintiff did not establish the necessary foundation for the admission of Doctor Barnard's expert opinion testimony on this aspect of the defendant's conduct.

The primary basis for the plaintiff's claim of negligent post–operative care and treatment was the presence of an infection that the defendant failed to adequately treat. The mere presence of an infection following surgery, however, does not establish a prima facie case of negligence. More importantly, although Doctor Barnard testified that there exists a uniform physiological bone healing process and that the diagnosis of an existing bone infection includes a consideration of such symptoms as localized swelling, redness, or drainage, and an analysis of X–rays in the case of suspected osteomyelitis, there was no foundation evidence in this case linking the particulars of Barnard's opinion testimony to the standard applicable to post–operative podiatric care and treatment. The plaintiff, for example, did not establish that Barnard, by reason of knowledge, skill, experience, training, or education, was familiar with the standard of care applicable to podiatric post–operative care and treatment of a metatarsal osteotomy. Nor did the plaintiff establish that the standard of care for treating such a condition is substantially identical for practitioners of orthopedic surgery and podiatric surgery.[3]

IV.

Although the trial court erred in permitting Doctor Barnard to offer opinion testimony on the defendant's failure to use reasonable care in the performance of the metatarsal osteotomy and in his post–operative care and treatment of the plaintiff, we believe the proper disposition of this case is not a dismissal of the plaintiff's complaint with prejudice, as ordered by the court of appeals, but a remand of the case for a new trial. In ordering the dismissal of the plaintiff's complaint, the court of appeals reasoned that when Doctor Barnard's opinion testimony was excluded from consideration, the other evidence offered by the plaintiff failed to establish a prima facie case of negligence. The plaintiff, however, never had reason to establish an adequate foundation for Barnard's opinion testimony because the trial court simply overruled the defendant's objection and thus admitted the opinion testimony without requiring any further foundation.

If the trial court had sustained the defendant's objections to Doctor Barnard's opinion testimony, as it should have done, the plaintiff might have been able to lay an adequate foundation for at least some of the doctor's opinion testimony. Although Barnard acknowledged that he was not familiar with the standard of care applicable to a podiatric metatarsal osteotomy, he might have been sufficiently familiar with the podiatric standard of care applicable to post–operative care and treatment or might have been of the view that the post–operative standard of care for

---

3. Later in the trial, after Doctor Barnard had completed his testimony, the defendant testified that podiatrists diagnose an infection in the same manner as orthopedic surgeons. The defendant also acknowledged that the X–rays relied on by Doctor Barnard for his diagnosis revealed the presence of a lytic area which, according to the defendant, could be symptomatic of osteomyelitis. This testimony of the defendant, however, occurred long after Doctor Barnard had offered his opinions on the defendant's surgical and post–surgical care and treatment of the plaintiff and cannot serve to remedy the foundational defect in Doctor Barnard's opinion testimony.

a metatarsal osteotomy was identical for both orthopedic surgery and podiatry. Moreover, in the event the defendant's objection had been sustained, the plaintiff might have been able to present an adequate foundation through Doctor McGarry or some other expert witness for eliciting opinion testimony on the issue of the defendant's alleged post–operative negligence. In light of the particular circumstances of this case, we believe the appropriate disposition is to remand the case to the court of appeals with directions to return the case to the district court for a new trial. * * *

Notes

1. *The professional standard.* In most negligence cases, the jury decides what reasonable care requires. In Chapter III we saw that industry custom, though relevant, is not controlling. The standard of the profession is controlling only in malpractice cases—not only in medical malpractice, but also in cases alleging malpractice by lawyers, accountants, engineers, and other professionals. Only rarely do courts allow recovery without proof of a violation of the professional standard. In one case, the Washington Supreme Court decided that glaucoma tests were so clearly desirable that it should be negligence as a matter of law not to give them to all ophthalmologic patients, even though the ophthalmology profession believed they were unnecessary for most patients under 40. See Helling v. Carey, 83 Wash.2d 514, 519 P.2d 981 (1974). The state legislature effectively reversed that decision, however. See Harris v. Robert C. Groth, M.D., Inc., 99 Wash.2d 438, 663 P.2d 113 (1983).

2. *Expert testimony.* As the principal case indicates, a corollary of the special standard for malpractice cases is that what the standard requires must be established by expert testimony. Usually this means the plaintiff must find a physician who is willing to testify against a professional colleague. Sometimes, however, the standard of care can be established through the defendant's own testimony. The defendant may agree as to what the standard is and deny only that he or she breached it. Or one defendant may establish the standard of care for a co–defendant to whom he or she seeks to shift responsibility. See, e.g., Clark v. Gibbons, 66 Cal.2d 399, 58 Cal.Rptr. 125, 426 P.2d 525 (1967) (defendant anesthesiologist's testimony established defendant surgeon's obligation to advise of duration of anesthesia needed).

3. *Expert testimony sometimes unnecessary.* Occasionally courts hold that the negligence is so obvious that the jury may infer lack of reasonable care without expert testimony. Sometimes they explain by saying: "The law is well established that expert testimony is not required where the common knowledge or experience of laymen is capable of inferring lack of care and also the required causal link." King v. Williams, 276 S.C. 478, 279 S.E.2d 618, 620 (1981) (defendant failed to order X–rays of plaintiff's injured foot despite pain and swelling that continued for nine months). Sometimes they explain by saying "res ipsa loquitur." See, e.g., Gold v. Ishak, 720 N.E.2d 1175 (Ind.App. 1999) (spark from surgical instrument used near an oxygen source caused fire); Funk v. Bonham, 204 Ind. 170, 183 N.E. 312 (1932) (sponge left inside patient's abdomen after surgery).

4. *The locality rule.* At one time doctors got the benefit not only of a standard of care determined by their own profession, but one determined by the doctors in their own locality, and a few states still follow this rule, at least with respect to general practitioners. In most states this rule has given way either to a "modified" locality rule holding doctors to the level of skill and knowledge of physicians and surgeons of ordinary ability and skill in the same or similar communities, or (especially in cases involving medical specialists) to a rule that abandons any reference to locality. Even in states that recognize a statewide or nationwide standard, the standard usually allows the jury to take into account the facilities available to the physician in the locality. See generally Annotation, modern status of "locality rule" in malpractice actions against physician who is not a specialist, 99 A.L.R.3d 1133 (1980).

The "strict" locality rule greatly exacerbated plaintiffs' difficulties in obtaining expert testimony, since only a physician from the defendant's community was qualified to testify. The "modified" locality rule does not eliminate this problem entirely, and this consideration has been cited by several courts as a reason for abandoning the locality rule altogether. See, e.g., Vergara v. Doan, 593 N.E.2d 185 (Ind.1992).

5. *Alternative medicine.* Suppose the defendant is a holistic healer who treats a breast cancer with an herbal ointment, a midwife who attempts a breech delivery, or a person who treats a case of acute appendicitis by acupuncture. Would the court exclude a physician's testimony unless the physician claims knowledge of the standards of holistic healing, midwifery, or acupuncture?

Some courts hold that practitioners other than medical doctors must refer the patient to a medical doctor when the practitioner should realize that the problem is not amenable to treatment by his or her methods. See, e.g., Rosenberg v. Cahill, 99 N.J. 318, 492 A.2d 371 (1985). Other courts require the practitioner only to explain to the patient the limitations of the proposed treatment. See, e.g., Kerkman v. Hintz, 142 Wis.2d 404, 418 N.W.2d 795 (1988).

B. INFORMED CONSENT

In some circumstances (for example, when immediate action is necessary to save a patient's life or prevent serious injury), a physician may proceed without obtaining the patient's consent (although generally not over the patient's objections). Normally, however, any medical procedure that would be an offensive (or harmful) touching if done by a stranger is actionable as battery if done by a physician without consent. See, e.g., Gragg v. Calandra, 297 Ill.App.3d 639, 231 Ill.Dec. 711, 696 N.E.2d 1282 (1998)(maintaining patient on life support despite contrary instructions in living will held to be actionable battery). As we have already seen in Chapter II, supra, consent obtained by misrepresentation is ineffective, so in those cases also liability can be based on battery. But what of the far more common scenario, in which there was no misrepresentation but the plaintiff would not have consented if the physician had fully disclosed the risks? Such cases have generated their own special malpractice theory, grounded in negligence rather than battery.

HARNISH v. CHILDREN'S HOSPITAL MEDICAL CENTER

Supreme Judicial Court of Massachusetts, 1982.
387 Mass. 152, 439 N.E.2d 240

O'CONNOR, JUSTICE.

The plaintiff underwent an operation to remove a tumor in her neck. During the procedure, her hypoglossal nerve was severed, allegedly resulting in a permanent and almost total loss of tongue function.

The plaintiff's complaint charges the defendant physicians and hospital with * * * negligence in failing to inform her before surgery of the risk of loss of tongue function. The complaint alleges that the purpose of the operation was cosmetic, that the loss of tongue function was a material and foreseeable risk of the operation, and that, had the plaintiff been informed of this risk, she would not have consented to the operation. There is no claim that the operation was negligently performed.

A medical malpractice tribunal, convened pursuant to G.L. c. 231, § 60B,* concluded that the plaintiff's offer of proof was insufficient to raise a question appropriate for judicial inquiry. The action was dismissed after the plaintiff failed to post a bond in accordance with G.L. c. 231, § 60B. The plaintiff appeals from the judgment of dismissal, claiming that her offer of proof * * * was sufficient to raise a question of liability under the doctrine of lack of informed consent. We reverse so much of the judgment of dismissal as applies to Drs. Holmes and Mulliken, and affirm the dismissal of the complaint against Dr. Gilman and Children's Hospital Medical Center.

1. *The rule of liability.* * * * The performance of a surgical procedure by a physician without the patient's consent constitutes profession-

---

* *§ 60B. Malpractice actions against providers of health care; tribunal*

Every action for malpractice, error or mistake against a provider of health care shall be heard by a tribunal consisting of a single justice of the superior court, a physician licensed to practice medicine in the commonwealth * * * and an attorney authorized to practice law in the commonwealth, at which hearing the plaintiff shall present an offer of proof and said tribunal shall determine if the evidence presented if properly substantiated is sufficient to raise a legitimate question of liability appropriate for judicial inquiry or whether the plaintiff's case is merely an unfortunate medical result.

* * *

If a finding is made for the defendant or defendants in the case the plaintiff may pursue the claim through the usual judicial process only upon filing bond in the amount of six thousand dollars in the aggregate secured by cash or its equivalent with the clerk of the court in which the case is pending, payable to the defendant or defendants in the case for costs assessed, including witness and experts fees and attorneys fees if the plaintiff does not prevail in the final judgment. * * * [Ed.]

al misconduct, is malpractice within G.L. c. 231, § 60B, and is subject to the procedures established by this statute.

"There is implicit recognition in the law of the Commonwealth, as elsewhere, that a person has a strong interest in being free from nonconsensual invasion of his bodily integrity. * * * In short, the law recognizes the individual interest in preserving 'the inviolability of his person.' One means by which the law has developed in a manner consistent with the protection of this interest is through the development of the doctrine of informed consent." "[I]t is the prerogative of the patient, not the physician, to determine * * * the direction in which * * * his interests lie." Cobbs v. Grant, 8 Cal. 3d 229, 104 Cal.Rptr. 505, 502 P.2d 1 (1972); Canterbury v. Spence, 464 F.2d 772, 781 (D.C.Cir.), cert. denied, 409 U.S. 1064, 93 S.Ct. 560, 34 L.Ed.2d 518 (1972). Every competent adult has a right "to forego treatment, or even cure, if it entails what for him are intolerable consequences or risks however unwise his sense of values may be in the eyes of the medical profession." Knowing exercise of this right requires knowledge of the available options and the risks attendant on each. We hold, therefore, that a physician's failure to divulge in a reasonable manner to a competent adult patient sufficient information to enable the patient to make an informed judgment whether to give or withhold consent to a medical or surgical procedure constitutes professional misconduct and comes within the ambit of G.L. c. 231, § 60B.

While we recognize that a patient ordinarily cannot make an intelligent decision whether to undergo a medical or surgical procedure without receiving from the physician information significant to the decision, we also recognize that there are limits to what society or an individual can reasonably expect of a physician in this regard. Medical matters are often complex. Recommendations of treatment frequently require the application of considerable medical knowledge gained through extensive training and experience. Communication of scientific information by the trained physician to the untrained patient may be difficult. The remotely possible risks of a proposed treatment may be almost without limit. The patient's right to know must be harmonized with the recognition that an undue burden should not be placed on the physician. These interests are accommodated by the rule that we adopt today, that a physician owes to his patient the duty to disclose in a reasonable manner all significant medical information that the physician possesses or reasonably should possess that is material to an intelligent decision by the patient whether to undergo a proposed procedure. The information a physician reasonably should possess is that information possessed by the average qualified physician or, in the case of a specialty, by the average qualified physician practicing that specialty. What the physician should know involves professional expertise and can ordinarily be proved only through the testimony of experts. However, the extent to which he must share that information with his patient depends upon what information he should reasonably recognize is material to the plaintiff's decision. "Materiality may be said to be the significance a reasonable person, in what the physician knows or should know is his patient's position, would attach to the disclosed risk or risks in deciding whether to submit or not to submit to surgery or treatment." The materiality determination is one that laypersons are qualified to make without the aid of an expert. Appropriate information may include the nature of the patient's condition, the nature and probability of risks involved, the benefits to be reasonably expected, the inability of the physician to predict results, if that is the situation, the irreversibility of the procedure, if that be the case, the likely result of no treatment, and the available alternatives, including their risks and benefits. The obligation to give adequate information does not require the disclosure of all risks of a proposed therapy, or of information the physician reasonably believes the patient already has, such as the risks, like infection, inherent in any operation.

Many jurisdictions have adopted the rule that a physician must disclose to his patient only such information as is customarily disclosed by physicians in similar circumstances. We think that the better rule is the one we adopt today. The customary practice standard overlooks the purpose of requiring disclosure, which is protection of the patient's right to decide for himself.

We recognize that despite the importance of the patient's right to know, there may be situations that call for a privilege of nondisclosure. For instance, sound medical judgment might indicate that disclosure would complicate the patient's medical condition or render him unfit for treatment. "Where that is so, the cases have generally held that the physician is armed with a privilege to keep the information from the patient * * *. The physician's privilege to withhold information for therapeutic reasons must be carefully circumscribed, however, for otherwise it might devour the disclosure rule itself. The privilege does not accept the paternalistic notion that the physician may remain silent simply because divulgence might prompt the patient to forego therapy the physician feels the patient really needs." A full discussion of the privilege is neither required nor attempted here, because the burden of proving it must rest with the physician, and thus the question of privilege is inappropriate to the directed verdict standard to be applied to the plaintiff's offer of proof before the medical malpractice tribunal.

2. *Causation*. We turn to the question of causation. "An unrevealed risk that should have been made known must materialize, for otherwise the omission, however unpardonable, is legally without consequence." Canterbury v. Spence, supra, at 790. Whether the alleged undisclosed risk materialized is a medical question appropriate to the tribunal's inquiry. At trial, the plaintiff must also show that had the proper information been provided neither he nor a reasonable person in similar circumstances would have undergone the procedure. Such proof, not relating to medical questions, is not appropriate to the tribunal's inquiry.

3. *The offer of proof*. The plaintiff's offer of proof [alleges that the surgery] resulted in severance of the hypoglossal nerve with resulting

severe dysfunctions in speech, mastication, saliva management, and swallowing. The severance of the nerve, with the ensuing consequences, was foreseeable as a probability despite proper performance of the surgery. Standard and acceptable medical practice required that the plaintiff be informed before the operation of the risk of nerve severance and the consequences of severance. The plaintiff was not given that information. If she had been, she would have declined the operation.

According to the offer of proof, Dr. Mulliken was the admitting physician and surgeon in charge of the operation. Dr. Holmes and Dr. Gilman assisted at the operation. In addition, before the operation Dr. Holmes discussed with the plaintiff the potential consequences, risks and side effects of the surgery, but he never informed her of the risk of loss of tongue function and its consequences. He told the plaintiff that he would perform the operation successfully.

It is apparent that the offer of proof was sufficient to raise a question appropriate for judicial inquiry with respect to the defendants, Mulliken and Holmes. [The court held that Dr. Gilman merely assisted in the surgery and therefore had no duty to obtain informed consent, and that the hospital was not vicariously liable for the alleged negligence of Mulliken and Holmes.]

Notes

1. The allegation in plaintiff's offer of proof that "standard and acceptable medical practice required that the plaintiff be informed * * * " turned out to be unnecessary, in light of the court's adoption of the rule requiring disclosure of risks that would be material to a reasonable patient. The "customary practice standard," which the court purports to reject, merely applies conventional malpractice principles to the question of informing the patient, however, and presumably continues to be available to supplement the reasonable patient standard. There seems to be no logical reason why a plaintiff could not pursue both theories.

2. *Causation in informed consent cases.* Note that on the causation issue, the court says the plaintiff must prove that if properly informed, "neither he nor a reasonable person in similar circumstances would have undergone the procedure." But if proper disclosure would have dissuaded the patient from consenting, however unreasonably, the failure to disclose would seem to be a but–for cause of the harm without regard to what a reasonable person would have done. See Arena v. Gingrich, 305 Or. 1, 748 P.2d 547 (Or. 1988) (holding that "What the patient in fact would have done after a full explanation is a question about that patient's behavior, not about some other 'reasonable' patient's * * *."). Nevertheless, most courts employ the double test of "causation," apparently because they distrust the plaintiff's testimony as to what he or she would have done. It has been said that "The real effect of the rule is to limit the defendant's duty of disclosure for the protection of patients who have the same feelings about the risks and advantages of the operation that the mainstream of reasonable people would have." Dan B. Dobbs, The Law of Torts 657 (2000).

3. *Statutory restrictions.* The tribunal referred to in the principal case was created by one of many statutory "reforms" that have been passed to restrict liability for medical malpractice. The objective of this statute is to weed out weak claims before they get to court. Other statutes forbid the use of res ipsa loquitur in malpractice cases, e.g., N.H.Rev.Stat. § 507–C:2; reinstitute the locality rule for determining the standard of care, e.g., Idaho Code § 6–1012; or impose caps on damages, e.g., Cal.Civ.Code § 3333.2. Some forbid courts from using the informed consent theory, e.g., N.C.Gen. Stat. § 90–21.13, or restrict it to a list of specified risks developed by a panel, e.g., Tex.Rev.Civ.Stat. art. 4590i, §§ 6.06–6.08.

4. *Malpractice crisis?* The impetus for such legislation has been the perception that a proliferation of unfounded malpractice claims was driving up the cost of malpractice insurance, in some cases so much that physicians were forced out of practice. Whether this perception is grounded in fact is much disputed. One study indicated that physicians' incomes had increased more than the cost of insurance. See 1 Barry R. Furrow, et al., Health Law 517 (1997). Some authorities believe the incidence of medical mistakes is far higher than the number of malpractice claims suggests. See, e.g., Paul C. Weiler et al, A Measure of Malpractice (1993) (reporting that 27,179 instances of negligent medical injuries produced only 3,682 claims). The Institute of Medicine, a branch of the National Academy of Science, estimated that medical errors caused between 44,000 and 98,000 deaths in hospitals each year—more than die from auto accidents or cancer. See Linda T. Kohn et al., To Err is Human: Building a Safer Health System (2000). The American Medical Association said those figures included patients who would have died anyway, and estimated that no more than 5,000 to 15,000 deaths a year are clearly caused by medical mistakes. See Rodney A. Hayward and Timothy P. Hofer, Estimating hospital deaths due to medical errors: Preventability is in the eye of the reviewer, J. of Am. Med. Ass'n, July 25, 2001.

Chapter XIV

COMMON LAW STRICT LIABILITY

In the cases you have studied so far, the plaintiff has been required to prove that the defendant acted with "fault," that is, that the defendant either intentionally or negligently caused injury to the plaintiff. Certain types of cases, however, are governed by doctrines under which the plaintiff need not prove negligence or intent. Courts usually refer to these doctrines as "strict liability." This chapter addresses two traditional strict liability contexts: trespassing animals and wild animals, and abnormally dangerous activities. A newer body of law, strict liability for product injuries, is addressed in Chapter XV.

The term "strict liability" means that the plaintiff need not prove negligence or intent. It does not mean that a defendant who causes injury is automatically liable, without any means of escape. Making a defendant liable on the basis of factual causation alone would be "absolute liability" or "insurer's liability." Courts often emphasize that strict liability is not the equivalent of absolute liability. (Occasionally, however, "absolute liability" is used to *mean* strict liability.)

Strict liability means different things in different contexts. For example, the doctrine of strict liability for defective products is vastly different from strict liability for abnormally dangerous activities. The common thread is that both eschew the requirement that the plaintiff prove negligence or intent.

A. ANIMALS

The early common law rule was that the owner of animals was liable, without proof of fault, for damage caused by the animals' trespassing onto a neighbour's land. (Exceptions were made for livestock that wandered off the highway on their way to market and for wandering dogs and cats.)

The early English rule was not uniformly accepted in the United States. In several western states, where livestock needed to be left free to graze, the English rule was rejected. The cattle–oriented states passed "fencing out" statutes that permitted courts to impose liability only if cattle broke through the complaining landowner's fence. Farm–oriented states passed statutes imposing liability unless ranchers fenced in their cattle. The current patchwork of laws on the subject of trespassing animals reflects conflict between ranching and farming interests in particular localities. These fencing statutes can also affect the respective rights of animal owners and highway users. A motorist whose vehicle collides with a cow in an open range area is in a different legal position from one who hits an animal that has escaped a statutorily required fence.

English and American courts also impose strict liability for injuries caused by wild animals. Under this rule a person who keeps a lion or tiger is liable without proof of negligence if the animal mauls or bites someone. This version of strict liability has been extended to domestic animals in the limited situation in which the owner has reason to know that the particular animal had vicious propensities. Otherwise, domestic animal owners are liable only if negligence or intent is shown. (This is the source of the common but somewhat misleading view that "every dog is entitled to one bite."). Negligence may be based upon the violation of a statute such as a leash law.

Although liability for injuries caused by wild animals is "strict," it is not "absolute." It extends only to the types of injuries that are foreseeable, given the nature of the animal. It also extends only to classes of persons to whom injury is reasonably foreseeable. The defendant may also be able to raise comparative negligence of the plaintiff as a defense.

B. ABNORMALLY DANGEROUS ACTIVITIES

RYLANDS v. FLETCHER

House of Lords, 1868.
L.R. 3 H.L. 330.

THE LORD CHANCELLOR (LORD CAIRNS).

My Lords, in this case the Plaintiff [Fletcher] is the occupier of a mine and [mine] works under a close of land. The Defendants [Rylands, et al.] are the owners of a mill in his neighbourhood, and they proposed to make a reservoir for the purpose of keeping and storing water to be used about their mill * * *. Underneath the close of land of the Defendants on which they proposed to construct their reservoir there were certain old and disused mining passages and works. There were five vertical shafts, and some horizontal shafts communicating with them. The vertical shafts had been filled up with soil and rubbish, and it does not appear that any person was aware of the existence either of the vertical shafts or of the horizontal works communicating with them. In the course of the working by the Plaintiff of his mine, he had gradually worked through the seams of coal underneath the close, and had come into contact with the old and disused works underneath the close of the Defendants.

In that state of things the reservoir of the Defendants was constructed. It was constructed by them through the agency and inspection of an engineer and contractor. Personally, the Defendants appear to have taken no part in the works, or to have been aware of any want of security connected with them. As regards the engineer and the contractor, we must take it from the case that they did not exercise, as far as they were concerned, that reasonable care and caution which they might have exercised, taking notice, as they appear to have taken notice, of the vertical shafts filled up in the manner which I have mentioned. [W]hen the reservoir was constructed, and filled, or partly filled, with water, the weight of the water bearing upon the disused and imperfectly filled–up vertical shafts [ ] broke through those shafts. The water passed down them and into the horizontal workings, and from the horizontal workings under the close of the Defendants it passed on into the workings under the close of the Plaintiff, and flooded his mine, causing considerable damage, for which this action was brought.

The Court of Exchequer * * * was of opinion that the Plaintiff had established no cause of action. The Court of Exchequer Chamber, before which an appeal from this judgment was argued, was of a contrary opinion, and the Judges there unanimously arrived at the conclusion that there was a cause of action, and that the Plaintiff was entitled to damages.

My Lords, the principles on which this case must be determined appear to me to be extremely simple. The Defendants, treating them as the owners or occupiers of the close on which the reservoir was constructed, might lawfully have used that close for any purpose for which it might in the ordinary course of the enjoyment of land be used; and if, in what I may term the natural use [ ] of that land, there had been any accumulation of water, either on the surface or underground, and if, by the operation of the laws of nature, that accumulation of water had passed off into the close occupied by the Plaintiff, the Plaintiff could not have complained that that result had taken place. If he had desired to guard himself against it, it would have lain upon him to have done so, by leaving, or by interposing, some barrier between his close and the close of the Defendants in order to have prevented that operation of the laws of nature.

* * *

On the other hand if the Defendants, not stopping at the natural use of their close, had desired to use it for any purpose which I may term a non–natural use, for the purpose of introducing into the close that which in its natural condition was not in or upon it, for the purpose of introducing water either above or below ground in quantities and in a manner not the result of any work or operation on or under the land,— and if in consequence of their doing so, or in consequence of any imperfection in the mode of their doing so, the water came to escape and to pass off into the close of the Plaintiff, then it appears to me that that which the Defendants were doing they were doing at their own peril;

and, if in the course of their doing it, the evil arose to which I have referred, the evil, namely, of the escape of the water and its passing away to the close of the Plaintiff and injuring the Plaintiff, then for the consequence of that, in my opinion, the Defendants would be liable.
* * *

My Lord, these simple principles, if they are well founded, as it appears to me they are, really dispose of this case.

The same result is arrived at on the principles, referred to by Lord *Blackburn* in his judgment, in the Court of Exchequer Chamber, where he states the opinion of that Court as to the law in these words:

"We think that the true rule of law is, that the person who, for his own purposes, brings on his land and collects and keeps there anything likely to do mischief if it escapes, must keep it in at his peril; and if he does not do so, is *prima facie* answerable for all the damage which is the natural consequence of its escape. He can excuse himself by showing that the escape was owing to the Plaintiff's default; or, perhaps, that the escape was the consequence of *vis major,* or the act of God; but as nothing of this sort exists here, it is unnecessary to inquire what excuse would be sufficient. The general rule, as above stated, seems on principle just. The person whose grass or corn is eaten down by the escaping cattle of his neighbour, or whose mine is flooded by the water from his neighbour's reservoir, or whose cellar is invaded by the filth of his neighbour's privy, or whose habitation is made unhealthy by the fumes and noisome vapours of his neighbour's alkali works, is damnified without any fault of his own; and it seems but reasonable and just that the neighbour who has brought something on his own property (which was not naturally there), harmless to others so long as it is confined to his own property, but which he knows will be mischievous if it gets on his neighbour's, should be obliged to make good the damage which ensues if he does not succeed in confining it to his own property. But for his act in bringing it there no mischief could have accrued, and it seems but just that he should at his peril keep it there, so that no mischief may accrue, or answer for the natural and anticipated consequence. And upon authority this we think is established to be the law, whether the things so brought be beasts, or water, or filth, or stenches."

My Lords, in that opinion, I must say I entirely concur. Therefore, I have to move your Lordships that the judgment of the Court of Exchequer Chamber be affirmed, and that the present appeal be dismissed with costs.

Judgment of the Court of Exchequer Chamber affirmed.

Note

The basis of liability in *Rylands* is not clear. The case was decided at a time when English courts were starting to apply negligence rather than strict liability to certain types of cases. For example, in 1856 the Court of

Exchequer had decided Blyth v. Birmingham Waterworks Co., 11 Ex. 781, 156 Eng.Rep. 1047 (1856). The case was similar to Grace v. City of Los Angeles, Chapter III, section B, supra p. 77. The defendant's pipes burst in "[o]ne of the severest frosts on record." A plug had been installed to relieve pressure, but it failed because it was encrusted with snow and ice. The escaping water damaged the plaintiff's house. The court held that the defendant was not negligent and, therefore, was not liable. Baron Bramwell, who dissented in Fletcher v. Rylands in the Court of Exchequer by voting in favor of liability, had stated in *Blyth* that "the plaintiff was under quite as much obligation to remove the ice and snow which had accumulated as the defendants."

At the time of *Rylands* trespass to land cases were governed by strict liability. But Fletcher did not sue for trespass, perhaps because Rylands acted through an agent rather than directly.

Lord Blackburn's opinion in the Exchequer Chamber seemed to portray a background system of liability that generally applied strict liability, with certain exceptions where negligence was required. He argued that the common thread of the cases in which negligence was required was that, in all of them, the plaintiff could be viewed as having assumed the risk, such as by venturing out on the public highway. On that view, the *Rylands* plaintiff had an uncomplicated strict liability case. (Lord Blackburn did not cite *Blyth,* but he might have distinguished it on the ground that it involved a defendant acting in accordance with a municipal charter.)

Lord Cairns' opinion in the House of Lords had a different flavor. Unlike Lord Blackburn, Lord Cairns did not distinguish the growing number of cases requiring proof of negligence. He believed that strict liability governed any case in which a person brings something onto his land that later escapes to injure someone else's land.

Note that Lord Cairns distinguished the defendant's reservoir from water (or some other substance) that occurs naturally on the defendant's land. We saw a similar distinction in Chapter V in connection with the duties of owners and occupiers of land. There is no overt reliance in Lord Cairns' opinion on the unusual or abnormal nature of a reservoir in a coal–mining region of England. Instead, his point seems to have been that owners and occupiers of land were strictly liable for artificial (non–natural) conditions on their land that caused injury to their neighbour's land.

Notwithstanding the ambiguity of the original basis of liability in *Rylands,* the case was later interpreted by American courts and scholars to embody a special island of strict liability in a sea of negligence. Ultimately, courts and scholars came to interpret *Rylands* as embodying strict liability for abnormally dangerous (that is, abnormal *and* dangerous) activities. These courts and scholars pointed to the fact that a reservoir was unusual or abnormal in a coal–mining region. They then relied on this fact to interpret Lord Cairns' reference to "non–natural" uses as meaning "abnormal" or "unusual" uses.

This interpretation is both broader and narrower than *Rylands* might have been interpreted. It is broader because it applies to situations other than injury to land. It is narrower because it does not apply to all non–natural uses of land; it applies only to abnormally dangerous activities.

A famous American case adopting strict liability for abnormally dangerous activities is Exner v. Sherman Power Construction Co., 54 F.2d 510 (2d Cir.1931). The defendant stored dynamite for use on a construction project. The dynamite exploded, and the concussion injured the plaintiff and his real property. The court held that blasting cases are governed by strict liability. The opinion, written by Augustus Hand, did not make absolutely clear why this was so. At times Judge Hand relied on the fact that trespasses to land had historically been governed by strict liability. But at other times he suggested that the distinction between trespassory and non–trespassory causes of action was not controlling. (*Exner* itself did not involve an action for trespass in the traditional sense; the plaintiff and his land were injured by the concussion, not by any debris.) Thus, as with *Rylands,* the basis of liability in *Exner* is somewhat obscure. Nevertheless, *Exner* too came to be interpreted as an example of strict liability for abnormally dangerous activities, irrespective of whether the case involved an injury to land.

Not all American courts have adopted the "doctrine of Rylands v. Fletcher." For example, in Turner v. Big Lake Oil Co., 128 Tex. 155, 96 S.W.2d 221 (1936), the defendant used artificial ponds to collect salt water residue from its oil well operations. When the salt water escaped and polluted a neighbour's ponds, the neighbour sued. The Court rejected strict liability under the "doctrine of Rylands v. Fletcher." It instead required the plaintiff to prove negligence. The Court reasoned that a reservoir might have been an abnormal use of land in a coal–mining region of England, but artificial ponds are normal and essential in semi–arid portions of Texas. Moreover, salt water ponds are normal and essential in oil–producing portions of Texas. Under this reasoning, the Court could have approved the concept of strict tort liability for abnormally dangerous activities and then declined to apply it to the facts of *Turner.* The Court's language, however, clearly rejected the doctrine of strict liability itself.

A significant group of courts, backed by the Restatements of Torts, have relied on *Rylands* and applied strict liability to abnormally dangerous activities. Siegler v. Kuhlman is an example.

SIEGLER v. KUHLMAN
Supreme Court of Washington, 1972.
81 Wash.2d 448, 502 P.2d 1181.

HALE, ASSOCIATE JUSTICE.

Seventeen–year–old Carol J. House died in the flames of a gasoline explosion when her car encountered a pool of thousands of gallons of spilled gasoline. She was driving home from her after–school job in the early evening of November 22, 1967, along Capitol Lake Drive in Olympia; it was dark but dry; her car's headlamps were burning. There was a slight impact with some object, a muffled explosion, and then searing flames from gasoline pouring out of an overturned trailer tank engulfed her car. The result of the explosion is clear, but the real causes of what happened will remain something of an eternal mystery.

Aaron L. Kuhlman had * * * been driving for Pacific Intermountain Express for about 4 months, usually the night shift out of the Texaco bulk plant in Tumwater. * * * Before leaving the Texaco plant, he inspected the trailer, checking the lights, hitch, air hoses and tires. Finding nothing wrong, he then set out, driving the fully loaded truck tank and trailer tank * * *. Running downgrade on [a freeway] offramp, he felt a jerk, looked into his left–hand mirror and then his right–hand mirror to see that the trailer lights were not in place. The trailer was still moving but leaning over hard, he observed, onto its right side. The trailer then came loose. Realizing that the tank trailer had disengaged from his tank truck, he stopped the truck without skidding its tires. He got out and ran back to see that the tank trailer had crashed through a chain–link highway fence and had come to rest upside down on Capitol Lake Drive below. He heard a sound, he said, "like somebody kicking an empty fifty–gallon drum and that is when the fire started." The fire spread, he thought, about 100 feet down the road.

* * * When the trailer landed upside down on Capitol Lake Drive, its lights were out, and it was unilluminated when Carol House's car in one way or another ignited the spilled gasoline.

Carol House was burned to death in the flames. There was no evidence of impact on the vehicle she had driven, Kuhlman said, except that the left front headlight was broken.

Why the tank trailer disengaged and catapulted off the freeway down through a chain–link fence to land upside down on Capitol Lake Drive below remains a mystery. * * *

* * *

* * * From a judgment entered upon a verdict for defendants, plaintiff appealed to the Court of Appeals which affirmed. We granted review and reverse.

In the Court of Appeals, the principal claim of error was directed to the trial court's refusal to give an instruction on res ipsa loquitur, and we think that claim of error well taken. * * *

But there exists here an even more impelling basis for liability in this case * * * and that is the proposition of strict liability arising as a matter of law from all of the circumstances of the event.

Strict liability is not a novel concept; it is at least as old as Fletcher v. Rylands, L.R. 1 Ex. 265, 278 (1866), affirmed, House of Lords, 3 H.L. 330 (1868). In that famous case, where water impounded in a reservoir on defendant's property escaped and damaged neighbouring coal mines, the landowner who had impounded the water was held liable without proof of fault or negligence. Acknowledging a distinction between the natural and non–natural use of land, and holding the maintenance of a reservoir to be a non–natural use, the Court of Exchequer Chamber imposed a rule of strict liability on the landowner. The ratio decidendi included adoption of what is now called *strict liability,* and * * * announced, we think, principles which should be applied in the instant case:

[T]he person who for his own purposes brings on his lands and collects and keeps there anything likely to do mischief if it escapes, must keep it in at his peril, and, if he does not do so, is prima facie answerable for all the damage which is the natural consequence of its escape.

[Not all] of the Justices in Fletcher v. Rylands, [drew] a distinction between the natural and non–natural use of land, but such a distinction would, we think, be irrelevant to the transportation of gasoline. The basic principles supporting the *Fletcher* doctrine, we think, control the transportation of gasoline as freight along the public highways the same as it does the impounding of waters and for largely the same reasons.

In many respects, hauling gasoline as freight is no more unusual, but more dangerous, than collecting water. When gasoline is carried as cargo—as distinguished from fuel for the carrier vehicle—it takes on uniquely hazardous characteristics, as does water impounded in large quantities. Dangerous in itself, gasoline develops even greater potential for harm when carried as freight—extraordinary dangers deriving from sheer quantity, bulk and weight, which enormously multiply its hazardous properties. And the very hazards inhering from the size of the load, its bulk or quantity and its movement along the highways presents another reason for application of the Fletcher v. Rylands rule not present in the impounding of large quantities of water—the likely destruction of cogent evidence from which negligence or want of it may be proved or disproved. It is quite probable that the most important ingredients of proof will be lost in a gasoline explosion and fire. Gasoline is always dangerous whether kept in large or small quantities because of its volatility, inflammability and explosiveness. But when several thousand gallons of it are allowed to spill across a public highway—that is, if, while in transit as freight, it is not kept impounded—the hazards to third persons are so great as to be almost beyond calculation. As a consequence of its escape from impoundment and subsequent explosion and ignition, the evidence in a very high percentage of instances will be destroyed, and the reasons for and causes contributing to its escape will quite likely be lost in the searing flames and explosions.

* * *

Recently this court, while declining to apply strict liability in a particular case, did acknowledge the suitability of the rule in a proper case. In Pacific Northwest Bell Tel. Co. v. Port of Seattle, 80 Wash.2d 59, 491 P.2d 1037 (1971), we observed that strict liability had its beginning in Fletcher v. Rylands, but said that it ought not be applied in a situation where a bursting water main, installed and maintained by the defendant Port of Seattle, damaged plaintiff telephone company's underground wires. There the court divided—not on the basic justice of a rule of strict liability in some cases—but in its application in a particular case to what on its face was a situation of comparatively minor hazards. Both majority and dissenting justices held, however, that the strict liability principles of Fletcher v. Rylands, should be given effect in some cases;

but the court divided on the question of whether underground water mains there constituted such a case.

The rule of strict liability, when applied to an abnormally dangerous activity, as stated in the Restatement (Second) of Torts § 519 (Tent. Draft No. 10, 1964), was adopted as the rule of decision in this state in Pacific Northwest Bell Tel. Co. v. Port of Seattle, as follows:

(1) One who carries on an abnormally dangerous activity is subject to liability for harm to the person, land or chattels of another resulting from the activity, although he has exercised the utmost care to prevent such harm.

(2) Such strict liability is limited to the kind of harm, the risk of which makes the activity abnormally dangerous.

As to what constitutes an abnormal activity, § 520 states:

In determining whether an activity is abnormally dangerous, the following factors are to be considered:

(a) Whether the activity involves a high degree of risk of some harm to the person, land or chattels of others;

(b) Whether the gravity of the harm which may result from it is likely to be great;

(c) Whether the risk cannot be eliminated by the exercise of reasonable care;

(d) Whether the activity is not a matter of common usage;

(e) Whether the activity is inappropriate to the place where it is carried on; and

(f) The value of the activity to the community.

Applying these factors to this system, we do not find the activity to be abnormally dangerous. There has never been a break in the system before, absent an earthquake, and the pipe could have been expected to last many more years. It is a system commonly used for fire protection, and its placement under ground is, of course, appropriate. We do not find § 519 of the Restatement, (Tent. Draft No. 10, 1964), or Rylands v. Fletcher, applicable.

* * *

Transporting gasoline as freight by truck along the public highways and streets is obviously an activity involving a high degree of risk; it is a risk of great harm and injury; it creates dangers that cannot be eliminated by the exercise of reasonable care. That gasoline cannot be practicably transported except upon the public highways does not decrease the abnormally high risk arising from its transportation. Nor will the exercise of due and reasonable care assure protection to the public from the disastrous consequences of concealed or latent mechanical or metallurgical defects in the carrier's equipment, from the negligence of third parties, from latent defects in the highways and streets, and from all of the other hazards not generally disclosed or guarded against by reasonable care, prudence and foresight. Hauling gasoline in great quantities as freight, we think, is an activity that calls for the application of principles of strict liability.

The case is therefore reversed and remanded to the trial court for trial to the jury on the sole issue of damages.

ROSELLINI, ASSOCIATE JUSTICE, concurring:

I agree with the majority that the transporting of highly volatile and flammable substances upon the public highways in commercial quantities and for commercial purposes is an activity which carries with it such a great risk of harm to defenseless users of the highway, if it is not kept contained, that the common–law principles of strict liability should apply. In my opinion, a good reason to apply these principles, which is not mentioned in the majority opinion, is that the commercial transporter can spread the loss among his customers—who benefit from this extrahazardous use of the highways. Also, if the defect which caused the substance to escape was one of manufacture, the owner is in the best position to hold the manufacturer to account.

I think the opinion should make clear, however, that the owner of the vehicle will be held strictly liable only for damages caused when the flammable or explosive substance is allowed to escape without the apparent intervention of any outside force beyond the control of the manufacturer, the owner, or the operator of the vehicle hauling it. I do not think the majority means to suggest that if another vehicle, negligently driven, collided with the truck in question, the truck owner would be held liable for the damage. But where, as here, there was no outside force which caused the trailer to become detached from the truck, the rule of strict liability should apply.

* * *

Notes

1. What the court quoted was a tentative version of Restatement (Second) of Torts sections 519 and 520. The ALI ultimately adopted a version that was virtually identical to the version quoted in *Siegler*. In the Third Restatement, the corresponding provision is simpler. An activity is abnormally dangerous and therefore subject to strict liability if it "creates a foreseeable and highly significant risk of physical harm even when reasonable care is exercised" and it is "not a matter of common usage." Restatement (Third) of Torts § 20 (2001).

2. Most American jurisdictions now apply some form of strict tort liability to abnormally dangerous activities. As the court's discussion of *Pacific Northwest Bell* suggests, the recurrent litigation point is whether a specific activity is "abnormally dangerous."

3. What policies support the application of strict liability to abnormally dangerous activities even though proof of negligence is required in other cases? Do they support the application of strict liability to the facts of *Siegler?*

4. Justice Rosellini states that strict liability would not obtain if the explosion had been caused by a negligent motorist's colliding with the tanker truck. Do you think the majority agreed?

In Klein v. Pyrodyne Corp., 117 Wash.2d 1, 810 P.2d 917 (1991), the court held that a pyrotechnic company conducting a public fireworks display was subject to strict liability under Second Restatement sections 519 and 520. The defendant, citing Justice Rosellini's concurring opinion in *Siegler* and dicta in a subsequent Washington Supreme Court case, argued that the manufacturer's improper construction of the shell that caused the accident was an intervening or outside force that cut off its liability. The court noted that section 522 of the Second Restatement took an opposite position: even the "unexpectable" negligent or reckless conduct of a third person did not affect liability. The *Klien* court adopted a middle ground, holding that because improper manufacture was not unforeseeable, the defendant remained liable, but rejecting the Restatement's view that an unforeseeable intervening force would not affect liability. The Third Restatement adheres to the position of the Second on this issue. See Restatement (Third) of Torts § 24 & comment *b* (2001).

5. Note that subsection 519(b) limited liability to "the kind of harm, the possibility of which makes the activity abnormally dangerous." This is analogous to the "risk rule" of legal causation in negligence. The Third Restatements concurs. See Restatement (Third) of Torts § 20 (2001).

Chapter XV

PRODUCTS LIABILITY

A. INTRODUCTION

"Products liability" refers to civil liability for injuries caused by defective products. It generally covers several different theories of liability, including negligence, breach of warranty, strict tort liability, and misrepresentation. These theories are not mutually exclusive, but can be combined in the same lawsuit. The Restatement (Third) of Torts: Products Liability, adopted by the American Law Institute in 1998, suggests that courts should combine these traditional theories into a single theory of liability for selling a "defective product." Restatement (Third) of Torts: Products Liability § 1 cmt. *a*; § 2, cmt. *n* (1998). Nevertheless, most courts still speak the language of the traditional categories.

Negligence, misrepresentation, and breach of warranty were developed primarily outside of the context of product injuries. You have already studied negligence. Warranty law was developed primarily in the context of commercial dealings. Its roots are in contract law, and most of its aspects are addressed in the contracts course. The law of misrepresentation was also developed primarily in the context of commercial dealings. Its roots are in tort law. It is addressed in courses on commercial torts.

Unlike the other three theories, so-called strict tort liability was developed as a special theory to deal with injuries caused by defective products. After a brief discussion of the other three theories in the context of product cases, this chapter focuses on strict tort liability. A more detailed examination of the other three theories in the context of product injuries is made in an upper level course on products liability.

Negligence

Today, courts apply negligence principles to products cases much as they apply negligence principles to any other case involving personal injury. The plaintiff must prove that the defendant failed to use reasonable care in manufacturing, designing, or marketing the product and that this failure was a cause-in-fact and a legal cause of the plaintiff's injuries. The question of reasonable care turns in large part on whether the defendant created a foreseeable, unreasonable risk of injury, judged from the perspective of the defendant's expertise concerning the product. The defendant can escape or reduce its liability by proving that the plaintiff was also negligent.

The full applicability of negligence law to product injury cases was a relatively recent development. At the turn of the twentieth century, courts did not apply normal negligence principles to product cases. Instead, they applied a limited duty rule that protected manufacturers from liability for their negligence except to the immediate purchaser, that is, except to persons who were in privity of contract with the manufacturer. Because manufacturers seldom sell directly to the public, and because a plaintiff usually cannot prove a retailer was negligent, the privity rule virtually eliminated recovery for injuries caused by negligently manufactured products.

The origin of the privity rule was Winterbottom v. Wright, 10 M. & W. 109, 152 Eng.Rep. 402 (1842). The court there held that a person who negligently repaired a stagecoach could not be held liable to a coach driver who was injured in an accident caused by the negligence. The court based its decision on the fact that the driver did not have a contract with the repairer. In the last half of the nineteenth century, courts began to recognize an exception to the privity rule for "imminently" or "inherently" dangerous products. A leading case was Thomas v. Winchester, 6 N.Y. 397, 57 Am.Dec. 455 (1852). The defendant's negligence caused a poison (belladonna) to be placed in a bottle labeled extract of dandelion. The defendant sold the bottle to a druggist, who in turn sold it to a customer. The court held that the customer could recover from the defendant, notwithstanding the absence of privity, because poison is inherently dangerous.

Then, in 1916, in a famous opinion by Justice Cardozo, the New York Court of Appeals decided MacPherson v. Buick Motor Co., 217 N.Y. 382, 111 N.E. 1050 (1916). Buick sold a car with a defective wheel to a retailer, who in turn sold it to the plaintiff. The court held that the "inherently dangerous" exception to the privity requirement applies to products that are "dangerous if defective," not just to products, like poisons, that "in their normal operation are implements of destruction."

Although *MacPherson* purported to address an exception to the privity requirement, it came to stand for the proposition that privity is never required in a negligence case involving a defective product. Courts in virtually all states have followed *MacPherson*. This does not mean, however, that liability extends to anyone injured by a negligently manufactured product; liability extends only to reasonably foreseeable plaintiffs.

Even after abolition of the privity rule, some courts applied a "no duty" rule that protected a product seller from liability for negligence if the product danger was "open and obvious." Most courts have now abandoned the special rule, holding that the obviousness of the danger is only a factor in evaluating the defendant's conduct. See, e.g., Micallef v. Miehle Co., 39 N.Y.2d 376, 384 N.Y.S.2d 115, 348 N.E.2d 571 (1976). Some courts, however, continue to apply a categorical "no duty" rule. See, e.g., Pressley v. Sears–Roebuck and Co., 738 F.2d 1222 (11th Cir.1984) (applying Georgia law). The rule is similar to the "no duty" rule for open and obvious dangers for owners and occupiers of land.

MacPherson and *Micallef* eliminated special *doctrinal* obstacles to recovery for negligence in products cases, but practical problems remained. In most early product cases, the plaintiff's theory of negligence was that an employee in the manufacturer's factory engaged in a specific act of negligence, such as not tightening a nut on a bolt. Such conduct occurred before the plaintiff bought the product and outside the view of persons other than the defendant's employees. Discovery practices did not offer plaintiffs the same access to manufacturers' records that plaintiffs have today. Under those circumstances, plaintiffs had a difficult time producing direct proof of acts of negligence. Courts commonly granted directed verdicts for defendants, refusing to let juries infer negligence from the mere existence of a defect. In time some courts applied *res ipsa loquitur* to help plaintiffs overcome the problem of direct proof. See, e.g., Escola v. Coca Cola Bottling Co. of Fresno, 24 Cal.2d 453, 150 P.2d 436 (1944). Other courts and scholars began to suggest applying other theories of recovery that did not require proof of negligence, specifically breach of warranty and strict tort liability.

Warranty

Warranties have a dual significance for products liability law. First, although strict tort liability has shed most of its warranty heritage, warranty law spawned strict tort liability and influenced its early development. Second, warranty law still provides an effective remedy for injured consumers. Plaintiffs can join claims of strict tort liability and breach of warranty, and an action for breach of warranty can provide a victim with certain remedies that are not available under strict tort liability, such as recovery of pure economic damages and a variety of remedies available under some states' consumer protection and deceptive trade practices statutes.

Because warranty law developed primarily to regulate commercial dealings, it covers a variety of issues that are not relevant to products liability litigation. The basic source of warranty law is Article 2 of the Uniform Commercial Code, which was adopted in most states in the 1960's and early 1970's. Some warranties are also governed by the federal Magnuson–Moss Act (15 U.S.C. §§ 2301–12) or by state consumer protection or deceptive trade practice legislation. Most states also have common law warranties for certain transactions that are not covered by the various statutes.

Before the U.C.C., most states had developed a fairly extensive body of warranty law either as a body of common law or as an interpretation of their version of the old Uniform Sales Act. A landmark case in applying warranty law to a product injury was Henningsen v. Bloomfield Motors, Inc., 32 N.J. 358, 161 A.2d 69 (1960). Mr. Henningsen purchased a Plymouth from Bloomfield Motors and gave it to his wife as a gift. Ten days after delivery of the car, Mrs. Henningsen was injured in an accident caused by the steering's failing suddenly and without warning. She sued Bloomfield Motors and Chrysler for breach of express and implied warranties and for negligence. The court held that Mrs. Henningsen could recover for breach of implied warranty even though she was not in privity of contract with either defendant and even though the sales contract, in fine print, contained a disclaimer of the warranty. *Henningsen* is important historically because it influenced the codification of warranty law in Article 2 of the U.C.C.

Warranties respecting the sale of goods are now governed principally by Article 2 of the U.C.C. Section 2–313 governs express warranties, section 2–314 governs implied warranties of merchantability, and section 2–315 governs implied warranties of fitness for a particular purpose.

Section 2–318 governs the privity requirement. The drafters gave states three options. Under alternative A, purchasers, family members, and household guests can recover for breach of warranty. Under alternative B, any foreseeable plaintiff who suffers personal injury or property damage can recover. Under alternative C, any foreseeable plaintiff can recover, irrespective of the type of injury.

Sellers of goods can do much to avoid liability for breach of warranty by disclaiming warranties (section 2–316) and by limiting the buyers remedies (section 2–719). The ability of sellers to disclaim warranties and limit remedies is not absolute, however, and much warranty litigation involves questions about the validity of specific disclaimer and remedy limitations. Nevertheless, disclaimers and remedy limitations have turned out to be significant obstacles to recovery. So too has the requirement of section 2–607 that an injured buyer give timely notice of injury to the seller.

The details of the law governing the Article 2 warranties can be complex. They are addressed in the first–year contracts course and in an upper–level course on products liability.

Misrepresentation

Most states apply the misrepresentation principles summarized in section 9 of the Restatement (Third) of Torts: Products Liability (formerly section 402B of the Restatement (Second) of Torts. It provides:

> One engaged in the business of selling or otherwise distributing products who, in connection with the sale of a product, makes a fraudulent, negligent, or innocent representation of material fact concerning the product is subject to liability for harm to persons or property caused by the misrepresentation.

Section 9 is an outgrowth of the law of intentional misrepresentation (fraud) and negligent misrepresentation, both of which were developed primarily in non–product cases. The law of fraud and negligent misrepresentation is important in products cases for two reasons. First, by relying directly on fraud and negligent misrepresentation, a plaintiff can recover for pure economic loss. (In many states, negligence, strict tort liability, and innocent misrepresentation under Section 9 do not allow a plaintiff to recover for pure economic loss.) Second, other than the issues specifically addressed by section 9—such as the defendant's state of mind—many of the general rules governing fraud and negligent misrepresentation are applicable to innocent misrepresentation under section 9.

B. EMERGENCE OF STRICT TORT LIABILITY

GREENMAN v. YUBA POWER PRODUCTS, INC.

Supreme Court of California, 1963.
59 Cal.2d 57, 27 Cal.Rptr. 697, 377 P.2d 897.

TRAYNOR, JUSTICE.

Plaintiff brought this action for damages against the retailer and the manufacturer of a Shopsmith, a combination power tool that could be used as a saw, drill, and wood lathe. He saw a Shopsmith demonstrated by the retailer and studied a brochure prepared by the manufacturer. He decided he wanted a Shopsmith for his home workshop, and his wife bought and gave him one for Christmas in 1955. In 1957 he bought the necessary attachments to use the Shopsmith as a lathe for turning a large piece of wood he wished to make into a chalice. After he had worked on the piece of wood several times without difficulty, it suddenly flew out of the machine and struck him on the forehead, inflicting serious injuries. About ten and a half months later, he gave the retailer and the manufacturer written notice of claimed breaches of warranties and filed a complaint against them alleging such breaches and negligence.

After a trial before a jury, the court ruled that there was no evidence that the retailer was negligent or had breached any express warranty and that the manufacturer was not liable for the breach of any implied warranty. Accordingly, it submitted to the jury only the cause of action alleging breach of implied warranties against the retailer and the causes of action alleging negligence and breach of express warranties against the manufacturer. The jury returned a verdict for the retailer against plaintiff and for plaintiff against the manufacturer in the amount of $65,000. The trial court denied the manufacturer's motion for a new trial and entered judgment on the verdict. The manufacturer and plaintiff appeal. Plaintiff seeks a reversal of the part of the judgment in favor of the retailer, however, only in the event that the part of the judgment against the manufacturer is reversed.

Plaintiff introduced substantial evidence that his injuries were caused by defective design and construction of the Shopsmith. His expert witnesses testified that inadequate set screws were used to hold parts of the machine together so that normal vibration caused the tailstock of the lathe to move away from the piece of wood being turned permitting it to fly out of the lathe. They also testified that there were other more positive ways of fastening the parts of the machine together, the use of which would have prevented the accident. The jury could therefore reasonably have concluded that the manufacturer negligently constructed the Shopsmith. The jury could also reasonably have concluded that statements in the manufacturer's brochure were untrue, that they constituted express warranties, and that plaintiff's injuries were caused by their breach.

The manufacturer contends, however, that plaintiff did not give it notice of breach of warranty within a reasonable time and that therefore his cause of action for breach of warranty is barred by section 1769 of the Civil Code. Since it cannot be determined whether the verdict against it was based on the negligence or warranty cause of action or both, the manufacturer concludes that the error in presenting the warranty cause of action to the jury was prejudicial.

Section 1769 of the Civil Code provides: "In the absence of express or implied agreement of the parties, acceptance of the goods by the buyer shall not discharge the seller from liability in damages or other legal remedy for breach of any promise or warranty in the contract to sell or the sale. But, if, after acceptance of the goods, the buyer fails to give notice to the seller of the breach of any promise or warranty within a reasonable time after the buyer knows, or ought to know of such breach, the seller shall not be liable therefore."

Like other provisions of the uniform sales act (Civ.Code, §§ 1721–1800), section 1769 deals with the rights of the parties to a contract of sale or a sale. It does not provide that notice must be given of the breach of a warranty that arises independently of a contract of sale between the parties. Such warranties are not imposed by the sales act, but are the product of common–law decisions that have recognized them in a variety of situations. It is true that in many of these situations the court has invoked the sales act definitions of warranties (Civ.Code, §§ 1732, 1735) in defining the defendant's liability, but it has done so, not because the statutes so required, but because they provided appropriate standards for the court to adopt under the circumstances presented.

The notice requirement of section 1769, however, is not an appropriate one for the court to adopt in actions by injured consumers against manufacturers with whom they have not dealt. "As between the immediate parties to the sale [the notice requirement] is a sound commercial rule, designed to protect the seller against unduly delayed claims for damages. As applied to personal injuries, and notice to a remote seller, it becomes a booby–trap for the unwary. The injured consumer is seldom 'steeped in the business practice which justifies the rule,' [James, Product Liability, 34 Texas L.Rev. 44, 192, 197] and at least until he has had legal advice it will not occur to him to give notice to one with whom he has had no dealings." (Prosser, Strict Liability to the Consumer, 69 Yale

L.J. 1099, 1130, footnotes omitted.) * * * We conclude, therefore, that even if plaintiff did not give timely notice of breach of warranty to the manufacturer, his cause of action based on the representations contained in the brochure was not barred.

Moreover, to impose strict liability on the manufacturer under the circumstances of this case, it was not necessary for plaintiff to establish an express warranty as defined in section 1732 of the Civil Code. A manufacturer is strictly liable in tort when an article he places on the market, knowing that it is to be used without inspection for defects, proves to have a defect that causes injury to a human being. Recognized first in the case of unwholesome food products, such liability has now been extended to a variety of other products that create as great or greater hazards if defective.

Although in these cases strict liability has usually been based on the theory of an express or implied warranty running from the manufacturer to the plaintiff, the abandonment of the requirement of a contract between them, the recognition that the liability is not assumed by agreement but imposed by law, and the refusal to permit the manufacturer to define the scope of its own responsibility for defective products make clear that the liability is not one governed by the law of contract warranties but by the law of strict liability in tort. Accordingly, rules defining and governing warranties that were developed to meet the needs of commercial transactions cannot properly be invoked to govern the manufacturer's liability to those injured by their defective products unless those rules also serve the purposes for which such liability is imposed.

We need not recanvass the reasons for imposing strict liability on the manufacturer. They have been fully articulated in the cases cited above. The purpose of such liability is to insure that the costs of injuries resulting from defective products are borne by the manufacturers that put such products on the market rather than by the injured persons who are powerless to protect themselves. Sales warranties serve this purpose fitfully at best. In the present case, for example, plaintiff was able to plead and prove an express warranty only because he read and relied on the representations of the Shopsmith's ruggedness contained in the manufacturer's brochure. Implicit in the machine's presence on the market, however, was a representation that it would safely do the jobs for which it was built. Under these circumstances, it should not be controlling whether plaintiff selected the machine because of the statements in the brochure, or because of the machine's own appearance of excellence that belied the defect lurking beneath the surface, or because he merely assumed that it would safely do the jobs it was built to do. It should not be controlling whether the details of the sales from manufacturer to retailer and from retailer to plaintiff's wife were such that one or more of the implied warranties of the sales act arose. "The remedies of injured consumers ought not to be made to depend upon the intricacies of the law of sales." (Ketterer v. Armour & Co., D.C., 200 F. 322, 323 [S.D.N.Y. 1912].) To establish the manufacturer's liability it was sufficient that plaintiff proved that he was injured while using the Shopsmith in a way it was intended to be used as a result of a defect in design and manufacture of which plaintiff was not aware that made the Shopsmith unsafe for its intended use.

* * *

The judgment is affirmed.

Notes

1. *The Restatement.* The Restatement of Torts (Second) § 402A (1965) adopted the rule embodied in *Greenman*. It provided:

> § 402A. Special Liability of Seller of Product for Physical Harm to User or Consumer
>
> (1) One who sells any product in a defective condition unreasonably dangerous to the user or consumer or to his property is subject to liability for physical harm thereby caused to the ultimate user or consumer, or to his property, if
>
> > (a) the seller is engaged in the business of selling such a product, and
> >
> > (b) it is expected to and does reach the user or consumer without substantial change in the condition in which it is sold.
>
> (2) The rule stated in Subsection (1) applies although
>
> > (a) the seller has exercised all possible care in the preparation and sale of his product, and
> >
> > (b) the user or consumer has not bought the product from or entered into any contractual relation with the seller.

Section 402A was replaced in 1998 with the Restatement (Third) of Torts: Products Liability. The new Restatement reflects an extensive body of caselaw that followed the basic rule in section 402A. Section 1 contains the basic rule of liability. It provides:

> One engaged in the business of selling or otherwise distributing products who sells or distributes a defective product is subject to liability for harm to persons or property caused by the defect.

2. *Do the policy justifications that have been proposed for strict tort liability support it?* Courts and scholars have advanced a variety of policy justifications for strict tort liability. Five of them are set forth below. As you study strict liability consider whether these policies are valid and whether the courts are effectively implementing them. Consider also whether these policies provide an adequate justification for applying strict liability to product injuries, even though proof of negligence is generally required for all other types of injuries. See generally Powers, A Modest Proposal to Abandon Strict Products Liability, 1991 Ill.L.Rev. 639.

a. Compensation (or loss spreading). Losses inevitably result from the use of products. These losses can have a disastrous effect on the individual who experiences them. It is humane and fair to shift these losses to all consumers of the product. This can be accomplished by imposing liability on manufacturers, forcing them to raise prices enough to pay for the losses or insure against them.

b. Cost internalization. Forcing manufacturers to raise prices in order to pay for harm caused by their products will lead to a more efficient allocation of resources. The prices of products will then more nearly include all of their true costs, including accident costs. Being aware of the true costs of products, consumers will make more intelligent decisions about which products to purchase.

c. Deterrence. Tort liability increases costs to manufacturers, but competition induces manufacturers to minimize these costs. Imposing liability provides manufacturers with an incentive to market safer products. In theory, strict liability may create more deterrence than negligence–based liability, since negligence imposes liability only if the defendant fails to take measures that a plaintiff can prove a reasonable person would have taken. Strict liability induces manufacturers to do more if the cost of the added safety measures is less than the potential cost of liability.

Nevertheless, courts also want to encourage useful products. Although compensation and deterrence are most commonly cited as the bases for strict tort liability, they are clearly not the only considerations because they almost always point in the direction of imposing liability. No court has imposed the liability of an insurer on manufacturers by requiring them to pay for all harm caused by their products. This is because of the fear that such absolute liability would place unreasonable burdens on manufacturers and discourage them from producing useful products. The policy of avoiding over–deterrence by balancing the needs of defendants against the needs of plaintiffs is clearly at work, although it is seldom articulated.

d. Proof problems. Quite often the manufacturer of a defective product is negligent. Modern industrial and technological complexities, however, frequently make it very difficult for the plaintiff to establish this. This is particularly so because any negligent conduct usually occurred before the plaintiff purchased the product and at a place controlled by the defendant. Imposing strict liability relieves the plaintiff of the burden of proving specific acts of negligence.

e. Protection of consumer expectations. Consumers should be protected from unknown dangers in products. This is particularly true when advertising and marketing techniques induce consumers to rely on manufacturers to provide them with safe, high–quality products.

C. DEFECT

GRAY v. MANITOWOC CO., INC.

United States Court of Appeals, Fifth Circuit, 1985.
771 F.2d 866.

DAVIS, CIRCUIT JUDGE.

Earnest M. Gray brought this action for injuries which he sustained when he was struck by the boom of a construction crane manufactured by defendant, The Manitowoc Company, Inc. (Manitowoc). Gray's wife,

Hughlene Gray, joined in this action seeking damages for loss of consortium and companionship. The Grays sought recovery under Mississippi law on theories of strict liability, implied warranty and negligence asserting that Gray's injuries were caused by a defect in the design of the crane and that Manitowoc had provided inadequate warnings of this defect. After the jury returned a verdict for the Grays, Manitowoc moved for judgment notwithstanding the verdict and for a new trial, asserting that the Grays failed to establish either the existence of a defect or a breach of a duty to warn. The district court denied Manitowoc's motion and entered judgment for the Grays. We conclude that the evidence was insufficient to establish that the crane possessed a latent hazard, as required by Mississippi law, for recovery on any of the theories of liability presented by the Grays and, therefore, reverse.

* * *

Gray was struck in two separate incidents by the butt end of the boom of a Manitowoc 4100W crane while working as an ironworker foreman on a construction project near Port Gibson, Mississippi. These incidents occurred while Gray's crew was changing sections of the crane's boom and had placed the boom in a plane roughly parallel to the ground (the "boom down" position). Gray was standing on the left side of the crane, supervising this operation, as the crane operator swung the lowered boom in Gray's direction, striking Gray in the back.

Testimony at trial established that the operator's vision to the left side of the Manitowoc crane is obscured by the boom when the crane is operated in the "boom down" position. To compensate for the operator's incomplete field of vision, users of cranes such as the 4100W place a signalman at various locations on the ground to guide the operator. This procedure was followed by Gray's employer during both incidents in which Gray alleged that he was struck. Gray contends, however, that Manitowoc should have provided mirrors, closed circuit television cameras or other devices to enable the operator to see to the left side of the crane when the crane is operated in the "boom down" position. Gray asserts that had these safety devices been placed on the crane, the crane operator would have seen Gray standing on the left side of the boom and would have avoided hitting him with the boom.

Manitowoc responds that even if mirrors or other devices would have permitted the operator to observe the area on the left side of the crane, the omission of these devices did not render the crane defective. Manitowoc argues that the hazards of operating the crane in the boom down position were open and obvious to ordinary users of the crane and that Mississippi law does not permit recovery under any theory of products liability for a manufacturer's failure to correct such patent dangers.

* * *

Under Mississippi's version of strict liability for hazardous products, manufacturers are not insurers of the products they produce; the existence of a product defect must be established before recovery may be obtained for a resulting injury. Mississippi has adopted the following formulation of the doctrine of strict liability for product defects (as it applies to manufacturers) from The Restatement (Second) of the Law of Torts, § 402A(1) (1965): "One who sells any product in a defective condition unreasonably dangerous to the consumer or to his property is subject to liability for physical harm thereby caused to the ultimate user or consumer, or to his property * * *."]

Comment (g) to the Restatement § 402A defines the term "defective condition": "The rule stated in this Section applies only where the product is, at the time it leaves the seller's hands, in a condition not contemplated by the ultimate consumer, which will be unreasonably dangerous to him." Comment (i), in turn, gives substance to the phrase "unreasonably dangerous":

> The rule stated in this Section applies only where the defective condition of the product makes it unreasonably dangerous to the user or consumer.... The article sold must be dangerous to an extent beyond that which would be contemplated by the ordinary consumer who purchases it, with the ordinary knowledge common to the community as to its characteristics.

As these comments illustrate, the consumer expectation test of section 402A is rooted in the warranty remedies of contract law, and requires that harm and liability flow from a product characteristic that frustrates consumer expectations.

In the seminal Mississippi case for strict liability for defective products, [State Stove Manufacturing Co. v. Hodges, 189 So.2d 113, 118 (Miss.1966)], the Mississippi Supreme Court indicated that the patent danger bar adopted by the Restatement was incorporated into Mississippi's doctrine of strict liability. The court quoted the consumer expectation definition of defectiveness set forth in comment (g) to section 402A of the Restatement. In [Ford Motor Co. v. Matthews, 291 So.2d 169 (Miss.1974)], the Mississippi Supreme Court expounded on the concept of a product defect. The court quoted the relevant portions of comments (g) and (i) to the Restatement § 402A and also quoted the following passage from W. Prosser, Handbook of the Law of Torts § 99, at 659–60 (4th Ed.1971): "The prevailing interpretation of 'defective' is that the product does not meet the reasonable expectations of the ordinary consumer as to its safety." Id. The *State Stove* and *Ford* courts' commitment to the consumer contemplation test for product defects has not been undermined by any subsequent decision of the Mississippi Supreme Court, nor have we discovered any reported decisions in which Mississippi courts or we have permitted recovery in strict liability for a patently dangerous product design.

We recognize that excluding patent hazards from the definition of a product design defect has been subject to much scholarly criticism, and has been rejected in a number of jurisdictions. Nonetheless, the patent danger bar was, until recent years, generally thought to be the prevailing rule in the various states and, in the face of scholarly criticism, has been reaffirmed in a number of jurisdictions. In the absence of any sign that this rule has been, or would be, rejected by the Mississippi Supreme Court, we are bound to apply it in this case. Hence, we conclude that the Grays' right to recover under the theory of strict liability depends upon whether the evidence was sufficient to permit the jury to find that the 4100W crane was "dangerous to an extent not contemplated by the ordinary consumer who purchased it, with the ordinary knowledge common to the community as to its characteristics."

* * *

We are persuaded that the record does not support a finding that the blind spot in the 4100W was a latent hazard. The evidence was overwhelming that the existence of this blind spot was common knowledge in the construction industry. Gray's supervisor, testifying as Gray's witness, stated that the existence of a blind spot in the crane operator's field of vision had been widely discussed at the Grand Gulf job site. The business manager of Gray's union local, again testifying as Gray's witness, indicated that the left side of the 4100W crane was referred to as the "blind side". * * *

Balanced against this evidence favorable to Manitowoc was Gray's testimony that he did not learn of the blind spot until after his second accident and the testimony of one inexperienced co-worker of Gray's that he also was unaware of the blindspot. [W]e must, of course, credit this testimony. Nonetheless, both the Restatement's theory of strict liability and Mississippi's theories of negligence and implied warranty require an objective appraisal of the obviousness of a product hazard. Gray and his inexperienced co-worker's testimony concerning their subjective ignorance has little significance to this objective inquiry. In light of the overwhelming evidence indicating that the existence of a blind spot in the 4100W was common knowledge in the construction trade, we must conclude that the testimony of Gray and his inexperienced co-worker did not create a jury question as to the knowledge or expectations of the ordinary observer or consumer. We conclude that no reasonable jury could have found that the blind spot of the Manitowoc 4100W was not open and obvious, nor could any reasonable jury have concluded that the 4100W was dangerous to a degree not anticipated by the ordinary consumer of that product.

Since the Grays failed to establish that the Manitowoc 4100W crane was defectively designed under any proper theory of Mississippi law, the district court erred in refusing to grant defendant's motion for judgment notwithstanding the verdict. We therefore

Reverse and Render the judgment.

PHILLIPS v. KIMWOOD MACHINE COMPANY

Supreme Court of Oregon, 1974.
269 Or. 485, 525 P.2d 1033.

HOLMAN, JUSTICE.

Plaintiff was injured while feeding fiberboard into a sanding machine during his employment with Pope and Talbot, a wood products manufacturer. The sanding machine had been purchased by Pope and Talbot from defendant. Plaintiff brought this action on a products liability theory, contending the sanding machine was unreasonably dangerous by virtue of defective design. At the completion of the testimony, defendant's motion for a directed verdict was granted and plaintiff appealed.

As is required in such a situation, the evidence is recounted in a manner most favorable to the plaintiff. The machine in question was a six–headed sander. Each sanding head was a rapidly moving belt which revolved in the direction opposite to that which the pieces of fiberboard moved through the machine. Three of the heads sanded the top of the fiberboard sheet and three sanded the bottom. The top half of the machine could be raised or lowered depending upon the thickness of the fiberboard to be sanded. The bottom half of the machine had powered rollers which moved the fiberboard through the machine as the fiberboard was being sanded. The top half of the machine had pinch rolls, not powered, which, when pressed down on the fiberboard by use of springs, kept the sanding heads from forcefully rejecting it from the machine.

On the day of the accident plaintiff was engaged in feeding the sheets of fiberboard into the sander. * * * During the sanding of * * * thick sheets, a thin sheet of fiberboard, which had become mixed with the lot, was inserted into the machine. The pressure exerted by the pinch rolls in the top half of the machine was insufficient to counteract the pressure which the sanding belts were exerting upon the thin sheet of fiberboard and, as a result, the machine regurgitated the piece of fiberboard back at plaintiff, hitting him [in] the abdomen and causing him the injuries for which he now seeks compensation.

Plaintiff asserts in his complaint that the machine was defective in its design * * * because there were no safety devices to protect the person feeding the machine from the regurgitation of sheets of fiberboard.

While we do not here attempt to recount all of the testimony presented by plaintiff concerning the defective design of the machine, there was evidence from which the jury could find that at a relatively small expense there could have been built into, or subsequently installed on, the machine a line of metal teeth which would point in the direction that the fiberboard progresses through the machine and which would press lightly against the sheet but which, in case of attempted regurgitation, would be jammed into it, thus stopping its backward motion. The evidence also showed that after the accident such teeth were installed upon the machine for that purpose by Pope and Talbot, whereupon subsequent regurgitations of thin fiberboard sheets were prevented while the efficiency of the machine was maintained. There was also evidence that defendant makes smaller sanders which usually are manually fed and on which there is such a safety device.

It was shown that the machine in question was built for use with an automatic feeder and that the one installed at Pope and Talbot is the only six–headed sander manufactured by defendant which is manually fed. There also was testimony that at the time of the purchase by Pope and Talbot, defendant had automatic feeders for sale but that Pope and Talbot did not purchase or show any interest in such a feeder. Pope and Talbot furnished a feeding device of their own manufacture for the machine which was partially automatic and partially manual but which, the jury could find, at times placed an employee in the way of regurgitated sheets.

* * *

In defense of its judgment based upon a directed verdict, defendant contends there was no proof of a defect in the product, and therefore strict liability should not apply. This court and other courts continue to flounder while attempting to determine how one decides whether a product is "in a defective condition unreasonably dangerous to the user." It has been recognized that unreasonably dangerous defects in products come from two principal sources: (1) mismanufacture and (2) faulty design. Mismanufacture is relatively simple to identify because the item in question is capable of being compared with similar articles made by the same manufacturer. However, whether the mismanufactured article is dangerously defective because of the flaw is sometimes difficult to ascertain because not every such flaw which causes injury makes the article dangerously defective.

The problem with strict liability of products has been one of limitation. No one wants absolute liability where all the article has to do is to cause injury. To impose liability there has to be something about the article which makes it dangerously defective without regard to whether the manufacturer was or was not at fault for such condition. A test for unreasonable danger is therefore vital. A dangerously defective article would be one which a reasonable person would not put into the stream of commerce if he had knowledge of its harmful character. The test, therefore, is whether the seller would be negligent if he sold the article knowing of the risk involved. Strict liability imposed what amounts to constructive knowledge of the condition of the product.

On the surface such a test would seem to be different than the test of 2 Restatement (Second) of Torts § 402A, Comment i., of "dangerous to an extent beyond that which would be contemplated by the ordinary consumer who purchases it." This court has used this test in the past. These are not necessarily different standards, however. As stated in

Welch v. Outboard Marine Corp., [481 F.2d 252 (5th Cir.1973),] where the court affirmed an instruction containing both standards:

> "We see no necessary inconsistency between a seller–oriented standard and a user–oriented standard when, as here, each turns on foreseeable risks. They are two sides of the same standard. A product is defective and unreasonably dangerous when a reasonable seller would not sell the product if he knew of the risk involved or if the risks are greater than a reasonable buyer would expect."

To elucidate this point further, we feel that the two standards are the same because a seller acting reasonably would be selling the same product which a reasonable consumer believes he is purchasing. That is to say, a manufacturer who would be negligent in marketing a given product, considering its risks, would necessarily be marketing a product which fell below the reasonable expectations of consumers who purchase it. The foreseeable uses to which a product could be put would be the same in the minds of both the seller and the buyer unless one of the parties was not acting reasonably. The advantage of describing a dangerous defect in the manner [we now use] is that it preserves the use of familiar terms and thought processes with which courts, lawyers, and jurors customarily deal.

While apparently judging the seller's conduct, the test set out above would actually be a characterization of the product by a jury. If the manufacturer was not acting reasonably in selling the product, knowing of the risks involved, then the product would be dangerously defective when sold and the manufacturer would be subject to liability.

In the case of a product which is claimed to be dangerously defective because of misdesign, the process is not so easy as in the case of mismanufacture. All the products made to that design are the same. The question of whether the design is unreasonably dangerous can be determined only by taking into consideration the surrounding circumstances and knowledge at the time the article was sold, and determining therefrom whether a reasonably prudent manufacturer would have so designed and sold the article in question had he known of the risk involved which injured plaintiff. The issue has been raised in some courts concerning whether, in this context, there is any distinction between strict liability and negligence. The evidence which proves the one will almost always, if not always, prove the other. We discussed this matter recently in the case of Roach v. Kononen, 525 P.2d 125 (Or.1974), and pointed out that there is a difference between strict liability for misdesign and negligence. We said:

> "However, be all this as it may, it is generally recognized that the basic difference between negligence on the one hand and strict liability for a design defect on the other is that in strict liability we are talking about the condition (dangerousness) of an article which is designed in a particular way, while in negligence we are talking about the reasonableness of the manufacturer's actions in designing and selling the article as he did. The article can have a degree of

dangerousness which the law of strict liability will not tolerate even though the actions of the designer were entirely reasonable in view of what he knew at the time he planned and sold the manufactured article. As Professor Wade points out, a way of determining whether the condition of the article is of the requisite degree of dangerousness to be defective (unreasonably dangerous; greater degree of danger than a consumer has a right to expect; not duly safe) is to assume that the manufacturer knew of the product's propensity to injure as it did, and then to ask whether, with such knowledge, something should have been done about the danger before it was sold. In other words, a greater burden is placed on the manufacturer than is the case in negligence because the law assumes he has knowledge of the article's dangerous propensity which he may not reasonably be expected to have, had he been charged with negligence."

525 P.2d at 129.

To some it may seem that absolute liability has been imposed upon the manufacturer since it might be argued that no manufacturer could reasonably put into the stream of commerce an article which he realized might result in injury to a user. This is not the case, however. The manner of injury may be so fortuitous and the chances of injury occurring so remote that it is reasonable to sell the product despite the danger. In design cases the utility of the article may be so great, and the change of design necessary to alleviate the danger in question may so impair such utility, that it is reasonable to market the product as it is, even though the possibility of injury exists and was realized at the time of the sale. Again, the cost of the change necessary to alleviate the danger in design may be so great that the article would be priced out of the market and no one would buy it even though it was of high utility. Such an article is not dangerously defective despite its having inflicted injury.

In this case defendant contends it was Pope and Talbot's choice to purchase and use the sander without an automatic feeder, even though it was manufactured to be used with one, and, therefore, it was Pope and Talbot's business choice which resulted in plaintiff's injury and not any misdesign by defendant. However, it is recognized that a failure to warn may make a product unreasonably dangerous. Comment j, Section 402A, Restatement (Second) of Torts, has the following to say:

> In order to prevent the product from being unreasonably dangerous, the seller may be required to give directions or warning, on the container, as to its use. The seller may reasonably assume that those with common allergies, as for example to eggs or strawberries, will be aware of them, and he is not required to warn against them. Where, however, the product contains an ingredient to which a substantial number of the population are allergic, and the ingredient is one whose danger is not generally known, or if known is one which the consumer would reasonably not expect to find in the

product, the seller is required to give warning against it, if he had knowledge, or by the application of reasonable, developed human skill and foresight should have knowledge, of the presence of the ingredient and the danger. Likewise in the case of poisonous drugs, or those unduly dangerous for other reasons, warning as to use may be required.

It is our opinion that the evidence was sufficient for the jury to find that a reasonably prudent manufacturer, knowing that the machine would be fed manually and having the constructive knowledge of its propensity to regurgitate thin sheets when it was set for thick ones, which the courts via strict liability have imposed upon it, would have warned plaintiff's employer either to feed it automatically or to use some safety device, and that, in the absence of such a warning, the machine was dangerously defective. It is therefore unnecessary for us to decide the questions that would arise had adequate warnings been given.

In Anderson v. Klix Chemical, 256 Or. 199, 472 P.2d 806 (1970), we came to the conclusion that there was no difference between negligence and strict liability for a product that was unreasonably dangerous because of failure to warn of certain characteristics. We have now come to the conclusion that we were in error. The reason we believe we were in error parallels the rationale that was expressed in the previously quoted material from Roach v. Kononen, supra, where we discussed the difference between strict liability for misdesign and negligence. In a strict liability case we are talking about the condition (dangerousness) of an article which is sold without any warning, while in negligence we are talking about the reasonableness of the manufacturer's actions in selling the article without a warning. The article can have a degree of dangerousness because of a lack of warning which the law of strict liability will not tolerate even though the actions of the seller were entirely reasonable in selling the article without a warning considering what he knew or should have known at the time he sold it. A way to determine the dangerousness of the article, as distinguished from the seller's culpability, is to assume the seller knew of the product's propensity to injure as it did, and then to ask whether, with such knowledge, he would have been negligent in selling it without a warning.

It is apparent that the language being used in the discussion of the above problems is largely that which is also used in negligence cases, i.e., "unreasonably dangerous," "have reasonably anticipated," "reasonably prudent manufacturer," etc. It is necessary to remember that whether the doctrine of negligence, ultrahazardousness, or strict liability is being used to impose liability, the same process is going on in each instance, i.e., weighing the utility of the article against the risk of its use. Therefore, the same language and concepts of reasonableness are used by courts for the determination of unreasonable danger in products liability cases. * * *

* * *

The case is reversed and remanded for a new trial.

Notes

1. *Three categories of defective products.* As the opinion in *Phillips* suggests, courts have identified three categories of product defect. A "manufacturing defect" or "flaw" involves a product that does not conform to the manufacturer's specifications or intentions, such as a bottled soft drink with a piece of glass in it. A "design defect" involves a product that is like every other product in the line, but the entire line has a feature that is unreasonably dangerous. A "warning defect" involves a product that is made unreasonably dangerous because of the warning or instructions for use, or lack thereof, such as a drug that does not have a warning that it has adverse side effects for fetuses. See Restatement (Third) of Torts: Products Liability § 2 (1998).

2. Most early products liability cases involved flaws. In these cases, the consumer expectation test (used in comments g and i of section 402A and in *Gray*) was intuitively easy to apply. In design defect cases and in more complex cases generally, however, it is often difficult to determine what ordinary consumers expect, even assuming they have any specific expectations about the details of the product. As cases became more complex, more courts began using the risk–utility test that was used in *Phillips*. The Restatement (Third) of Torts: Products Liability § 2 (1998) adopts the risk-utility test for design defects and warnings. Consumer expectations about a product may affect risk and utility, but consumer expectations do not constitute an independent test. *Id.,* comment g. The new Restatement provides that a product has a manufacturing defect when it "departs from its intended design, even though all possible care was exercised in the preparation and marketing of the product."

Some courts use a different test for different types of defect, and some courts use a test that combines risk–utility and consumer expectations. The leading case applying a combined test is Barker v. Lull Engineering Co., 20 Cal.3d 413, 143 Cal.Rptr. 225, 573 P.2d 443 (1978). The court held that the jury should be instructed that a product is defective if it either fails to meet ordinary consumer expectations or has risks that outweigh utility.

3. In applying the risk–utility test, courts consider a variety of factors, including product cost and product performance. The analysis properly focuses on the particular product feature, not on the product as a whole. For example, in *Phillips* the appropriate focus was on the risks and benefits of not having teeth on the sander, not on the overall risks and benefits of the sander.

4. The plaintiff must prove that the defect existed when the product left the defendant's control. This burden is not difficult to meet in most cases involving design defects and warnings. In cases involving flaws, however, defendants commonly claim that the product became flawed after it left the defendant's control.

A common situation is a product sold in a sealed container. As the court said in McKisson v. Sales Affiliates, Inc., 416 S.W.2d 787 (Tex.1967), "[w]hen it is shown that the product involved comes in a sealed container, it is inferrable that the product reached the consumer without substantial changes in the conditions in which it was sold." If other evidence proves that the sealed container was invaded or that the product became flawed after it left the defendant's control, however, the inference breaks down. See, e.g., Klein v. Continental–Emsco, 445 F.2d 629 (5th Cir.1971); Carroll v. Ford Motor Co., 462 S.W.2d 57 (Tex.Civ.App.–Houston [14th Dist.] 1970, no writ).

A product's failure caused merely by normal wear is not sufficient to establish that it was defective when it was sold. The plaintiff need not, however, prove that the product failed immediately upon delivery. If the product is designed or manufactured to have a propensity to deteriorate more quickly than normal, it might be defective when it is delivered, even though the danger is not manifested until later. In such cases, the defect is the propensity to deteriorate too quickly, which was present when the product was delivered.

5. The court in *Phillips* used a hindsight test to evaluate both the design defect and the failure to warn. The court evaluated the product with current ("time–of–trial") knowledge rather than the state of knowledge when the product was sold. Even so, the inquiry still focused on the risks and benefits (as the court knew them) that the product actually had when it was sold. For cases involving alleged design defects or failure to warn, most courts today take into account only risks that were *reasonably* foreseeable when the product was sold. See Restatement (Third) of Torts: Products Liability § 2 comment m (1998). Even courts that use a hindsight test for design defects nevertheless use a foresight test to cases involving a failure to warn. The risk–utility test from a foresight perspective is very close, if not identical, to negligence. The appropriate standard in warnings cases is addressed in Feldman v. Lederle Laboratories, which follows.

FELDMAN v. LEDERLE LABORATORIES

Supreme Court of New Jersey, 1984.
97 N.J. 429, 479 A.2d 374.

SCHREIBER, J.

In this case defendants and *amici* drug manufacturers argued that the doctrine of strict products liability should not apply to prescription drugs. We hold otherwise and conclude that drug manufacturers have a duty to warn of dangers of which they know or should have known on the basis of reasonably obtainable or available knowledge.

Plaintiff, Carol Ann Feldman, has gray teeth as a result of taking a tetracycline drug, Declomycin. Plaintiff's father, a pharmacist and a medical doctor, prescribed and administered the drug to her when she was an infant to control upper respiratory and other secondary types of infections. Since Dr. Feldman claimed that he had administered Declomycin, suit was instituted against defendant, Lederle Laboratories, which manufactured and marketed Declomycin. The action was presented to the jury on the theory that the defendant was strictly liable, not because the drug was ineffective as an antibiotic, but because defendant had failed to warn physicians of the drug's side effect, tooth discoloration.

[Declomycin was first marketed in 1959. The plaintiff took it from 1960 to 1963. The evidence was sharply divided as to whether the defendant could have known that it caused tooth discoloration in children in 1960. By 1962 the defendant did know about this risk. It amended its labeling to warn about the risk in 1963.]

* * * [D]efendant argued that it had complied with the state of the art in its warning literature. It had not warned of possible tooth discoloration because, the defendant claimed, the possibility of that side effect was not known at the time its literature was disseminated.

The jury found for the defendant. The Appellate Division affirmed in an unreported opinion. Plaintiff petitioned for certification and we summarily remanded the cause to the Appellate Division to reconsider in light of Beshada v. Johns–Manville Prods. Corp., 90 N.J. 191, 447 A.2d 539 (1982),* which was decided after the Appellate Division decision. [ ] The Appellate Division reaffirmed the judgment for the defendant, holding that prescription drugs are a special category of products and that drug manufacturers would not be strictly liable for failing to warn of a side effect that was unknown when the drug was sold. [ ] We granted plaintiff's petition for certification. * * *

* * *

* * * The defendant and the drug manufacturing *amici curiae* urge [ ] that public policy as explicated in comment k to section 402A of the *Restatement (Second) of Torts* (1965) * * * should immunize drug manufacturers from liability for side effects of prescription drugs. Comment k suggests that strict liability should not apply to certain unavoidably unsafe products. We do not agree that the protective shield of comment k immunizes all prescription drugs. Moreover, we are of the opinion that generally the principle of strict liability is applicable to manufacturers of prescription drugs.

* * *

Defendant and drug manufacturing *amici* also contend that all prescription drugs are unavoidably unsafe and therefore that drug manufacturers of these products fall within the protective aegis of comment k of the *Restatement,* supra. Comment k reads as follows:

> *Unavoidably unsafe products.* There are some products which, in the present state of human knowledge, are quite incapable of being made safe for their intended and ordinary use. These are especially common in the field of drugs. An outstanding example is the vaccine for the Pasteur treatment of rabies, which not uncommonly leads to very serious and damaging consequences when it is injected. Since the disease itself invariably leads to a dreadful death, both the marketing and the use of the vaccine are fully justified, notwithstanding the unavoidable high degree of risk which they involve.

* In *Beshada* asbestos manufacturers were sued in strict liability for failure to warn about the risks of exposure to asbestos. Some of the plaintiffs were exposed as early as the 1930's. The court rejected the defendants' argument that they had no duty to warn about risks of which they were not aware at the time the asbestos was sold. [Ed.]

Such a product, properly prepared, *and accompanied by proper directions and warning,* is not defective, nor is it *unreasonably* [emphasis in original] dangerous. The same is true of many other drugs, vaccines, and the like, many of which for this very reason cannot legally be sold except to physicians, or under the prescription of a physician. It is also true in particular of many new or experimental drugs as to which, because of lack of time and opportunity for sufficient medical experience, there can be no assurance of safety, or perhaps even of purity of ingredients, but such experience as there is justifies the marketing and use of the drug notwithstanding a medically recognizable risk. The seller of such products, *again with the qualification that they are properly prepared and marketed, and proper warning is given,* where the situation calls for it, is not to be held to strict liability for unfortunate consequences attending their use, merely because he has undertaken to supply the public with an apparently useful and desirable product, attended with a known but apparently reasonable risk. [Emphasis added.]

Comment k immunizes from strict liability the manufacturers of some products, including certain drugs, that are unavoidably unsafe. However, we see no reason to hold as a matter of law and policy that all prescription drugs that are unsafe are unavoidably so. Drugs, like any other products, may contain defects that could have been avoided by better manufacturing or design. Whether a drug is unavoidably unsafe should be decided on a case–by–case basis; we perceive no justification for giving all prescription drug manufacturers a blanket immunity from strict liability manufacturing and design defect claims under comment k.

Moreover, even if a prescription drug were unavoidably unsafe, the comment k immunity would not eliminate strict liability for failure to provide a proper warning. As Justice Pollock stated in [O'Brien v. Muskin Corp., 94 N.J. 169, 183, 463 A.2d 298, 305 (1983)], "[w]ith those products, the determination of liability may be achieved more appropriately through an evaluation of the adequacy of the warnings." Thus, a manufacturer who knows or should know of the danger or side effects of a product is not relieved of its duty to warn. Rather, as the comment expressly states, it is only the unavoidably unsafe product "*accompanied by proper * * * warning*" that is not defective. [Emphasis added.] Contrary to *amici*'s claim, we find nothing in the proceedings of the American Law Institute that justifies a different conclusion. Irrespective of whether a court or a jury decides that the drug falls within the special category of comment k, that finding may not absolve the manufacturer of its failure to warn the physician or consumer of the condition within the manufacturer's actual or constructive knowledge affecting the safety, fitness, or suitability of the drug. See Wade, "On the Effect in Product Liability of Knowledge Unavailable Prior to Marketing," 58 N.Y.U.L.Rev. 734, 745 (1983) [hereinafter cited as Wade (1983)].

* * *

This is a strict–liability–warning case. The product has been made as the manufacturer intended. The plaintiff does not contend that it contained a manufacturing defect. Declomycin's purpose was to act as did other tetracyclines—as an antibiotic. However, it had several advantages over other antimicrobial therapeutics. The plaintiff does not dispute this. Indeed, there is no evidence that plaintiff's usage of Declomycin was not adequate in this respect. Nor was there any proof that it was improperly designed. The crux of the plaintiff's complaint is that her doctor should have been warned of a possible side effect of the drug in infants, discoloration of teeth.

* * *

The emphasis of the strict liability doctrine is upon the safety of the product, rather than the reasonableness of the manufacturer's conduct. It is a product–oriented approach to responsibility. Generally speaking, the doctrine of strict liability assumes that enterprises should be responsible for damages to consumers resulting from defective products regardless of fault. The doctrine differs from a negligence theory, which centers on the defendant's conduct and seeks to determine whether the defendant acted as a reasonably prudent person. This difference between strict liability and negligence is commonly expressed by stating that in a strict liability analysis, the defendant is assumed to know of the dangerous propensity of the product, whereas in a negligence case, the plaintiff must prove that the defendant knew or should have known of the danger. This distinction is particularly pertinent in a manufacturing defect context.

When the strict liability defect consists of an improper design or warning, reasonableness of the defendant's conduct is a factor in determining liability. The question in strict liability design–defect and warning cases is whether, assuming that the manufacturer knew of the defect in the product, he acted in a reasonably prudent manner in marketing the product or in providing the warnings given. Thus, once the defendant's knowledge of the defect is imputed, strict liability analysis becomes almost identical to negligence analysis in its focus on the reasonableness of the defendant's conduct. * * *

Generally, the state of the art in design defect cases and available knowledge in defect warning situations are relevant factors in measuring reasonableness of conduct. Thus in [Suter v. San Angelo Foundry & Machine Co., 81 N.J. 150, 406 A.2d 140 (1979)], we explained that other than assuming that the manufacturer knew of the harmful propensity of the product, the jury could consider "the technological feasibility of manufacturing a product whose design would have prevented or avoided the accident, given the known state of the art." Id. at 172, 406 A.2d 140. We observed that "the state of the art refers not only to the common practice and standards in the industry but also to the other design alternatives within practical and technological limits at the time of distribution." Id. Moreover, in *O'Brien*, supra, we again referred to the state of the art as an appropriate factor to be considered by the jury to determine whether feasible alternatives existed when the product was marketed.

Similarly, as to warnings, generally conduct should be measured by knowledge at the time the manufacturer distributed the product. Did the defendant know, or should he have known, of the danger, given the scientific, technological, and other information available when the product was distributed; or, in other words, did he have actual or constructive knowledge of the danger? The *Restatement,* supra, has adopted this test in comment j to section 402A, which reads in pertinent part as follows:

> *Directions or warning.* In order to prevent the product from being unreasonably dangerous, the seller may be required to give directions or warning, on the container, as to its use. * * * Where the product contains an ingredient * * * whose danger is not generally known, or if known is one which the consumer would reasonably not expect to find in the product, the seller is required to give warning against it, *if he has knowledge, or by the application of reasonable, developed human skill and foresight should have knowledge,* of the presence of the ingredient and the danger. [Emphasis added.]

Under this standard negligence and strict liability in warning cases may be deemed to be functional equivalents. Constructive knowledge embraces knowledge that should have been known based on information that was reasonably available or obtainable and should have alerted a reasonably prudent person to act. Put another way, would a person of reasonable intelligence or of the superior expertise of the defendant charged with such knowledge conclude that defendant should have alerted the consuming public?

* * *

This test does not conflict with the assumption made in strict liability design defect and warning cases that the defendant knew of the dangerous propensity of the product, if the knowledge that is assumed is reasonably knowable in the sense of actual or constructive knowledge. A warning that a product may have an unknowable danger warns one of nothing. Neither [Cepeda v. Cumberland Eng'g Co., 76 N.J. 152, 386 A.2d 816 (1978)] nor *Suter*, supra, stated that the manufacturer would be deemed to know of the dangerous propensity of the chattel when the danger was unknowable. In our opinion *Beshada*, supra, would not demand a contrary conclusion in the typical design defect or warning case. If *Beshada* were deemed to hold generally or in all cases, particularly with respect to a situation like the present one involving drugs vital to health, that in a warning context knowledge of the unknowable is irrelevant in determining the applicability of strict liability, we would not agree. Many commentators have criticized this aspect of the *Beshada* reasoning and the public policies on which it is based. *But see* Hayes v. Ariens Co., 391 Mass. 407, 413, 462 N.E.2d 273, 277–78 (1984) (citing *Beshada* with approval for the proposition that in Strict Liability the seller "is presumed to have been informed at the time of the sale of all risks whether or not he actually knew or reasonably should have known of them"). The rationale of *Beshada* is not applicable to this case. We do not overrule *Beshada,* but restrict *Beshada* to the circumstances giving rise to its holding. * * * We note, in passing, that, although not argued and determined in *Beshada,* there were or may have been data and other information generally available, aside from scientific knowledge, that arguably could have alerted the manufacturer at an early stage in the distribution of its product to the dangers associated with its use.

In strict liability warning cases, unlike negligence cases, however, the defendant should properly bear the burden of proving that the information was not reasonably available or obtainable and that it therefore lacked actual or constructive knowledge of the defect. * * *

One other aspect with respect to warnings based on subsequently obtained knowledge should be considered. Communication of the new warning should unquestionably be given to prescribing physicians as soon as reasonably feasible. Although a manufacturer may not have actual or constructive knowledge of a danger so as to impose upon it a duty to warn, subsequently acquired knowledge, both actual and constructive, also may obligate the manufacturer to take reasonable steps to notify purchasers and consumers of the newly–discovered danger.

The timeliness of the warning issue is obliquely present in this case. It is possible that Dr. Feldman already had Declomycin on hand when defendant became aware of Declomycin's side effect. If that state of affairs existed, defendant would have had an obligation to warn doctors and others promptly. This most assuredly would include those to whom defendant had already furnished the product. The extent and nature of post–distribution warnings may vary depending on the circumstances, but in the context of this case, the defendant at a minimum would have had a duty of advising physicians, including plaintiff's father, whom it had directly solicited to use Declomycin.

The trial court charged the jury that the manufacturer of a drug has the obligation to warn if he knew or should have known of the need to issue such a warning. In determining whether defendant should have known of the danger, it referred the jury to the circumstances, relating particularly to the state of knowledge, as evidenced by the literature, in the scientific community. However, upon the retrial the charge should also include the principle expressed herein that a reasonably prudent drug manufacturer should be deemed to know of reasonably obtainable and available reliable information. In addition, we now place the burden of proving the lack of knowledge on the defendant.

* * *

The jury was given two basic issues: (1) did plaintiff take Declomycin, and (2) did defendant know (actually or constructively) of its side effect. The jury returned a general verdict for the defendant and we do not know the basis of its decision. [ ] We must assume, therefore, that the jury's determination hinged on the absence of proof of knowledge.

* * *

Apart from plaintiff's evidence to the effect that defendant should have known of the side effect as early as 1960, the record overwhelmingly demonstrates that defendant actually knew of the danger by the end of 1962. Defendant nonetheless continued to market the drug in 1963 and plaintiff continued to ingest the drug that year. Insofar as that period of time is concerned, a jury determination based on defendant's lack of knowledge would be "a miscarriage of justice under the law." [ ] In that event defendant would be responsible at least for the enhancement of the condition.

We reverse and remand for a new trial.

Notes

1. In *Feldman* the court rejected the defendant's argument that strict tort liability should not apply to drugs. Most courts have done the same. But in Brown v. Superior Court, 44 Cal.3d 1049, 245 Cal.Rptr. 412, 751 P.2d 470 (1988), the California Supreme Court accepted the argument. Do any of the policies underlying strict tort liability support exempting drugs?

2. *Two meanings of "state of the art."* Courts use the term "state of the art" to describe two different concepts. In *Feldman* the court sometimes used the term to refer to the defendant's claim that, given the state of technology when the drug was sold, the defendant had no way of *knowing* about its risks. Using the term "state–of–the–art" to refer to the defendant's knowledge is just another way of using a foresight test. Most courts use the term to refer to a different claim: that, even if a product's risks were known when it was sold, the state of technology was such that nothing could be done to eliminate or reduce the risks. For example, an airplane sold in 1935 could not have been equipped with radar, because radar had not yet been invented.

Recall from *Phillips* that some courts use, and many courts used to use, a hindsight test of defectiveness in cases involving design defects. It would be impossible in a design case for a court to apply the state–of–the–art defense to the defendant's *knowledge* without destroying the hindsight nature of the test. But it is possible to permit defendants in design cases to argue that, under the state–of–the–art at the time of sale, an alternative design was not technologically feasible, and several courts have done so. See, e.g., Boatland of Houston, Inc. v. Bailey, 609 S.W.2d 743 (Tex.1980). Notwithstanding this practice, however, it is difficult to understand why a court should preclude a defendant from arguing that it had no way of *knowing* the problem, but should permit a defendant to argue that it had no way of *correcting* the problem, even if it had known. Of course, this is not a problem in most states and under the new Restatement, because they use a foresight test for design defects as well as for warnings.

3. As applied to technical infeasibility, the state–of–the–art doctrine is often called a "defense." In fact, it is often unclear whether the defense

precludes a finding of defect or is just a factor the jury can take into account. The latter position probably is a better description of practice; the cases are usually submitted to the jury. But this may be because fact questions typically exist concerning the actual level of technology at the time the product was sold.

4. In *Boatland*, supra note 2, the plaintiff's decedent was killed when he fell out of a ski–boat and the boat turned and ran over him. His estate argued that the boat was defective because it did not have a "kill switch" that would shut off the engine when the driver fell out. The defendant argued that, when the boat was sold, kill switches were not available, though the plaintiff disputed this point. The court held that the defendant should have been permitted to introduce state–of–the–art evidence.

5. For more on alternative designs, and for evidence that debate over the proper test of defect is not over, consider the following case.

POTTER v. CHICAGO PNEUMATIC TOOL CO.

Connecticut Supreme Court, 1997.
241 Conn. 199, 694 A.2d 1319.

KATZ, J.

[Shipyard workers claim they were injured as a result of using defectively designed pneumatic hand tools manufactured by defendants].

Product liability law has * * * evolved to hold manufacturers strictly liable for unreasonably dangerous products that cause injury to ultimate users. * * *

Section 402A [of the *Restatement (Second) of Torts*] imposes liability only for those defective products that are "unreasonably dangerous" to "the ordinary consumer who purchases it, with the ordinary knowledge common to the community as to its characteristics." [Section 402A, comment (i).] Under this formulation, known as the "consumer expectation" test, a manufacturer is strictly liable for any condition not contemplated by the ultimate consumer that will be unreasonably dangerous to the consumer. [ ]

* * *

In Barker v. Lull Engineering Co. the California Supreme Court established two alternative tests for determining design defect liability: (1) the consumer expectation analysis, and (2) a balancing test that inquires whether a product's risks outweigh its benefits. Under the latter "risk–utility" test, the manufacturer bears the burden of proving that the product's utility is not outweighed by its risks in light of various factors. * * * Other jurisdictions apply only a risk–utility test in determining whether a manufacturer is liable for a design defect. * * *

* * *

* * * In Garthwait v. Burgio [ ] this court became one of the first jurisdictions to adopt the rule provided in § 402A. This court has long held that in order to prevail in a design defect claim, the plaintiff must

prove the product is unreasonably dangerous. * * * We have derived our definition of "unreasonably dangerous" from comment (i) to § 402A, which provides that "the article sold must be dangerous to an extent beyond that which would be contemplated by the ordinary consumer who purchases it, with the ordinary knowledge common to the community as to its characteristics." [§ 402A, comment (i).] * * *

The defendants propose that it is time for this court to abandon the consumer expectation standard and adopt the requirement that the plaintiff must prove the existence of a reasonable alternative design in order to prevail on a design defect claim. We decline to accept this invitation.

* * *

To support their position, the defendants point to the second tentative draft of the Restatement (Third) of Torts: Products Liability (1995), which provides that, as part of a prima facie case, the plaintiff must establish the availability of a reasonable alternative design. Specifically, § 2(b) of the Draft Restatement [Third] provides: "[A] product is defective in design when the foreseeable risks of harm posed by the product could have been reduced or avoided by the adoption of a reasonable alternative design by the seller or other distributor, or a predecessor in the commercial chain of distribution, and the omission of the alternative design renders the product not reasonably safe." The reports to the Draft Restatement [Third] state that "[v]ery substantial authority supports the proposition that [the] plaintiff must establish a reasonable alternative design in order for a product to be adjudged defective in design."

* * * [O]ur independent review of the prevailing common law reveals that the majority of jurisdictions to not impose upon plaintiffs an absolute requirement to provide a feasible alternative design.*

In our view, the feasible alternative design requirement imposes an undue burden on plaintiffs that might preclude otherwise valid claims from jury consideration. Such a rule would require plaintiffs to retain an expert witness even in cases that infer a design defect from circumstantial evidence. Connecticut courts, however, have consistently stated that a jury may, under appropriate circumstances, infer a defect from the evidence without the necessity of expert testimony. * * * Moreover, in some instances, a product may be in a defective condition unreasonably dangerous to the user even though no feasible alternative design is available. In such instances, the manufacturer may be strictly liable for a design defect notwithstanding the fact that there are no safer alternative designs in existence. Accordingly, we decline to adopt the requirement

---

* Our research shows that six jurisdictions affirmatively state that a plaintiff need not show a feasible alternative design to establish a manufacturer's liability for a design defect [ ]; sixteen jurisdictions hold that a feasible alternative design is merely one of several factors the jury may consider in determining whether a product design is defective [ ]; three jurisdictions require the defendant, not the plaintiff, to prove the product was not defective [ ]; and eight jurisdictions require that the plaintiff prove a feasible alternative design to establish a prima facie case of design defect. [ ]

that a plaintiff must prove a feasible alternative design as a sine qua non to establishing a prima facie case of design defect.

* * * [W]e nevertheless recognize that there may be instances involving complex product designs in which an ordinary consumer may not be able to form expectations of safety. In such cases, a consumer's expectations may be viewed in light of various factors that balance the utility of the product's design with the magnitude of its risks.* * * [U]nder this modified formulation, the consumer expectation test would establish the product's risks and utility, and the inquiry would then be whether a reasonable consumer would consider the product design unreasonably dangerous.

In our view, the relevant factors a jury may consider include the usefulness of the product, the likelihood and severity of the danger posed by the design, the feasibility of an alternative design, the financial cost of an improved design, the ability to reduce the product's danger without impairing its usefulness or making it too expensive, and the feasibility of spreading the loss by increasing the product's price. The availability of a feasible alternative design is a factor the plaintiff may, rather than must, prove in order to establish that a product's risks outweigh its utility.

* * * [O]ur adoption of a risk–utility balancing component to our consumer expectation test does not signal a retreat from strict tort liability. In weighing a product's risks against its utility, the focus of the jury should be on the product itself, and not on the conduct of the manufacturer.

* * * [W]e emphasize that we do not require a plaintiff to present evidence relating to the product's risks and utility in every case. * * * [T]he ordinary consumer expectation test is appropriate when the everyday experience of the particular product's users permits the inference that the product did not meet minimum safety expectations.

* * *

* * * It is the function of the trial court to determine whether an instruction based on the ordinary consumer expectation test or the modified consumer expectation test, or both, is appropriate in light of the evidence presented. * * *

Note

The use of strict products liability to condemn an entire product has been controversial, particularly under the risk–utility test. See, e.g., Powers, Is There a Doctrinal Answer to the Question of Generic Liability?, 72 Chi.–Kent L.Rev. 169 (1996). After much heated debate, the new Restatement waffled on the issue. See Restatement (Third) of Torts: Products Liability § 2 & comment e (1998).

D. CAUSATION

Cause–in–fact applies to strict tort liability cases in the same way it applies to negligence cases. See generally Chapter IV, supra. The plaintiff must prove that the defect existed when the defendant sold the product and that the defect was a factual cause (usually a "but for" cause) of the plaintiff's injuries.

Three types of factual causation problems occur frequently in product cases. Each of them is addressed in Chapter IV, dealing with causation.

First, plaintiffs often have a difficult time proving that a defendant's failure to warn was a cause–in–fact of their injuries. Defendants can argue that consumers often fail even to read product labels, much less follow instructions on the labels. Most courts have created a rebuttable presumption in these cases that a proper warning, if it had been given, would have been read and heeded by the consumer.

Second, a commonly alleged defect in automobiles is that they are not "crashworthy," that is, that they are designed in a way that aggravates injuries during an accident. In these cases, the seller of the defective product is liable only for the aggravated injuries caused by the defect. It is often difficult to separate the injuries that would have occurred anyway from those caused by the car's lack of crashworthiness. When the facts do not permit the injuries to be separated, some courts treat them as though they were indivisible, thereby making each of the multiple causes jointly and severally liable unless they can show which portion of the injuries each of them caused.

Third, plaintiffs in drug cases often have a difficult time proving which manufacturer of a drug actually produced the particular lot that injured the plaintiff. This problem is especially acute when a long time elapses between the plaintiff's taking the drug and the manifestation of the injury. A few courts have adopted the "market share" theory of causation, whereby the plaintiff can recover from the manufacturers in proportion to their share of the relevant market.

Recall from Chapter V that foreseeability is the backbone of legal cause in negligence. It is also the backbone of legal cause in jurisdictions that use a foresight test for defectiveness. But the foreseeability approach to legal cause does not work well in jurisdictions that use a hindsight test for defectiveness. It would be inconsistent for a court to conclude that a product was defective, even though its risks were not known or reasonably foreseeable, but then to conclude that there was no legal cause because the result was unforeseeable.

Nevertheless these courts cannot merely apply cause–in–fact, with no additional limiting notion of "legal" or "proximate" cause, because doing so would open defendants up to liability for very attenuated injuries. Lacking a better alternative, several courts have turned to the familiar concept of foreseeability, notwithstanding their use of hindsight to define a defect.

On one issue—whether the plaintiff is an appropriate person to recover—all courts rely on foreseeability. They do not require the plaintiff to have purchased the product, but they require more than that the plaintiff was in fact injured by the product. The case that follows is the leading case.

ELMORE v. AMERICAN MOTORS CORP.

Supreme Court of California, 1969.
70 Cal.2d 578, 75 Cal.Rptr. 652, 451 P.2d 84.

PETERS, JUSTICE.

[Anna Waters was injured and her husband was killed when the car her husband was driving and in which she was riding was struck by a car driven by Sandra Elmore. The accident was caused by Elmore's car's drive shaft suddenly falling out of the car. Waters sued American Motors under strict tort liability, claiming that the accident was caused by a defect in Elmore's car. After holding that the plaintiffs could rely on circumstantial evidence to support a finding that Elmore's car was defective, the court addressed the question of whether Mrs. Waters could recover against American Motors.]

* * *

The authors of the restatement have refrained from expressing a view as to whether the doctrine of strict liability of the manufacturer and retailer for defects is applicable to third parties who are bystanders and who are not purchasers or users of the defective chattel. The authors pointed out that as yet (1965) no case had applied strict liability to a person who was not a user or consumer. Two recent cases, however, have held manufacturers of defective goods strictly liable in tort for injuries caused to persons who were mere bystanders and were not users or consumers. There are also several cases which have permitted recovery in strict liability by persons who were not purchasers or users, although possibly they should not be categorized as bystanders. Several cases, most of them earlier, have refused to extend the doctrine in favor of the bystander. * * *

In Greenman v. Yuba Power Products, Inc., [supra page 540] we pointed out that the purpose of strict liability upon the manufacturer in tort is to insure that "the costs of injuries resulting from defective products are borne by the manufacturers that put such products on the market rather than by the injured persons who are powerless to protect themselves." We further pointed out that the rejection of the view that such liability was governed by contract warranties rather than tort rules was shown by cases which had recognized that the liability is not assumed by agreement but imposed by law and which had refused to permit the manufacturer to define its own responsibility for defective products. Similarly, in Vandermark v. Ford Motor Co., [391 P.2d 168

(Cal.1964)] we held that, since the retailer is strictly liable in tort, the fact that it restricted its contractual liability was immaterial.

These cases make it clear that the doctrine of strict liability may not be restricted on a theory of privity of contract. Since the doctrine applies even where the manufacturer has attempted to limit liability, they further make it clear that the doctrine may not be limited on the theory that no representation of safety is made to the bystander.

The liability has been based upon the existence of a defective product which caused injury to a human being, and in both *Greenman* and *Vandermark* we did not limit the rules stated to consumers and users but instead used language applicable to human beings generally.

It has been pointed out that an injury to a bystander "is often a perfectly foreseeable risk of the maker's enterprise, and the considerations for imposing such risks on the maker without regard to his fault do not stop with those who undertake to use the chattel. [A restriction on recovery by bystanders] is only the distorted shadow of a vanishing privity which is itself a reflection of the habit of viewing the problem as a commercial one between traders, rather than as part of the accident problem." (2 Harper and James, The Law of Torts (1956) p. 1572, fn. 6.)

If anything, bystanders should be entitled to greater protection than the consumer or user where injury to bystanders from the defect is reasonably foreseeable. Consumers and users, at least, have the opportunity to inspect for defects and to limit their purchases to articles manufactured by reputable manufacturers and sold by reputable retailers, whereas the bystander ordinarily has no such opportunities. In short, the bystander is in greater need of protection from defective products which are dangerous, and if any distinction should be made between bystanders and users, it should be made, contrary to the position of defendants, to extend greater liability in favor of the bystanders.

* * *

The judgments are reversed.

Notes

1. After *Elmore*, other courts followed suit to permit bystanders to recover under strict tort liability. See, e.g., Haumersen v. Ford Motor Co., 257 N.W.2d 7 (Iowa 1977); Giberson v. Ford Motor Co., 504 S.W.2d 8 (Mo.1974); Howes v. Hansen, 56 Wis.2d 247, 201 N.W.2d 825 (1972); Passwaters v. General Motors Corp., 454 F.2d 1270 (8th Cir.1972); Darryl v. Ford Motor Co., 440 S.W.2d 630 (Tex.1969).

2. The fact that bystanders can recover under strict tort liability does not mean that anyone whose injury is caused by a defective product, no matter how attenuated the causal connection, can recover from the manufacturer. For example, if Mr. Waters' children were injured on a trip to visit their father's grave, the causal connection between the defect in Ms. El-

more's car and the injury would undoubtedly have been too attenuated to support recovery against American Motors.

3. In most states, strict tort liability applies to any seller of a defective product, as long as the seller is in the business of selling the product. This includes manufacturers, wholesalers, and retailers. A few states apply strict tort liability only to manufacturers.

E. PURE ECONOMIC LOSS

SARATOGA FISHING CO. v. J.M. MARTINAC & CO.

Supreme Court of the United States, 1997.
520 U.S. 875, 117 S.Ct. 1783, 138 L.Ed.2d 76.

JUSTICE BREYER.

The issue before us concerns limits upon the damages that a tort plaintiff in admiralty can recover for physical damage to property caused by a defective product. In East River S.S. Corp. v. Transamerica Delaval Inc. [476 U.S. 858 (1986)], the Court held that an admiralty tort plaintiff cannot recover for the physical damage the defective product causes to the "product itself"; but the plaintiff can recover for physical damage the product causes to "other property." In this case all agree that the "product itself" consists at least of a ship as built and outfitted by its original manufacturer and sold to an initial user. This case asks how this corner of tort law treats the physical destruction of extra equipment (a skiff, a fishing net, spare parts) added by the initial user after the first sale and then resold as part of the ship when the ship itself is later resold to a subsequent user. Is that added equipment part of the "product itself," in which case the plaintiff cannot recover in tort for its physical loss? Or is it "other property," in which case the plaintiff can recover? We conclude that it is "other property." Hence (assuming other tort law requirements are satisfied) admiralty's tort rules permit recovery.

I

This case arises out of an engine room fire and flood that led to the sinking of the fishing vessel M/V Saratoga in January 1986. We must assume that a hydraulic system defectively designed by respondent Marco Seattle Inc. was one significant cause of the accident. About 15 years before the accident, respondent J.M. Martinac & Co. had built the ship, installed the hydraulic system, and sold the ship new to Joseph Madruga. Madruga then added extra equipment—a skiff, a seine net, and various spare parts—and used the ship for tuna fishing. In 1974, Madruga resold the ship to the petitioner, Saratoga Fishing Co., which continued to use the ship for fishing. In 1987, after the ship caught fire and sank, Saratoga Fishing brought this tort suit in admiralty against Marco Seattle and J.M. Martinac.

The District Court found that the hydraulic system had been defectively designed, and it awarded Saratoga Fishing damages (adjusted to reflect Saratoga Fishing's own partial fault). Those damages included damages for the loss of the equipment that Madruga had added after the initial purchase of the ship.

The Ninth Circuit held that the District Court should not have awarded damages for the added equipment. A majority noted that the equipment, though added by Madruga, was part of the ship when Madruga resold the ship to Saratoga Fishing, and, for that reason, the majority held, the added equipment was part of the defective product that itself caused the harm. Applying *East River's* distinction between the product that itself caused the injury and "other property," the majority concluded that Saratoga Fishing could not recover in tort for the loss. A dissenting judge believed that the "product itself" was the ship when launched into the stream of commerce by Martinac, its original builder. Consequently, the added equipment was "other property." We granted certiorari to resolve this uncertainty about the proper application of *East River*. We now agree with the dissenting judge.

II

The facts before us show: (1) a Component Supplier who (2) provided a defective component (the hydraulic system) to a Manufacturer, who incorporated it into a manufactured product (the ship), which (3) the Manufacturer sold to an Initial User, who (4) after adding equipment and using the ship, resold it to a Subsequent User (Saratoga Fishing). The applicable law is general maritime law, "an amalgam of traditional common–law rules, modifications of those rules, and newly created rules," drawn from both state and federal sources. The context is purely commercial. The particular question before us requires us to interpret the Court's decision in *East River*: does the term "other property," as used in that case, include the equipment added by the Initial User before he sold the ship to the Subsequent User? We conclude that it does: When a Manufacturer places an item in the stream of commerce by selling it to an Initial User, that item is the "product itself" under *East River*. Items added to the product by the Initial User are therefore "other property," and the Initial User's sale of the product to a Subsequent User does not change these characterizations.

East River arose at the intersection of two principles that govern recovery in many commercial cases involving defective products. The first principle is that tort law in this area ordinarily (but with exceptions) permits recovery from a manufacturer and others in the initial chain of distribution for foreseeable physical harm to property caused by product defects. The second principle is that tort law in this area ordinarily (but with exceptions) does not permit recovery for purely economic losses, say, lost profits. See Restatement (Third) of Torts: Products Liability § 6, Comment d (Proposed Final Draft, Preliminary Version, Oct. 18, 1996). The Court in *East River* favored the second principle, for it held that an injury to the defective product itself, even though physical, was a kind of "economic loss," for which tort law did not provide compensation.

The Court reasoned that the loss of the value of a product that suffers physical harm—say, a product that destroys itself by exploding—is very much like the loss of the value of a product that does not work properly or does not work at all. In all such cases, the Court held, "[c]ontract law, and the law of warranty in particular, is well suited" to setting the responsibilities of a seller of a product that fails to perform the function for which it was intended. The commercial buyer and commercial seller can negotiate a contract—a warranty—that will set the terms of compensation for product failure. If the buyer obtains a warranty, he will receive compensation for the product's loss, whether the product explodes or just refuses to start. If the buyer does not obtain a warranty, he will likely receive a lower price in return. Given the availability of warranties, the courts should not ask tort law to perform a job that contract law might perform better.]

The Ninth Circuit reasoned that *East River* required it to define the defective "product itself" by looking to that which the plaintiff had purchased, for that is the product that, in principle, the plaintiff could have asked the seller to warrant. Since Saratoga Fishing, the Subsequent User, might have asked Madruga, the Initial User, to warrant the M/V Saratoga, skiff, nets, and all, that product, skiff, nets, and all, is the "product itself" that stands outside the reach of tort recovery. In our view, however, this holding pushes *East River's* principle beyond the boundary set by the principle's rationale.

For one thing, the Ninth Circuit's holding creates a tort damage immunity beyond that set by any relevant tort precedent that we have found. State law often distinguishes between items added to or used in conjunction with a defective item purchased from a Manufacturer (or its distributors) and (following *East River*) permits recovery for the former when physically harmed by a dangerously defective product. Thus the owner of a chicken farm, for example, recovered for chickens killed when the chicken house ventilation system failed, suffocating the 140,000 chickens inside. A warehouse owner recovered for damage to a building caused by a defective roof. And a prior case in admiralty (not unlike the one before us) held that a ship charterer, who adds expensive seismic equipment to the ship, may recover for its loss in a fire caused by a defective engine. Indeed, respondents here conceded that, had the ship remained in the hands of the Initial User, the loss of the added equipment could have been recovered in tort. We have found no suggestion in state (or in federal) law that these results would change with a subsequent sale—that is, we have found no case, other than the Ninth Circuit case before us, that suggests that the courts would deny recovery to a subsequent chicken farmer, who had later purchased the farm, chickens, coop, ventilation system, and all.

Indeed, the denial of recovery for added equipment simply because of a subsequent sale makes the scope of a manufacturer's liability turn on what seems, in one important respect, a fortuity, namely whether a defective product causes foreseeable physical harm to the added equipment before or after an Initial User (who added the equipment) resells the product to a Subsequent User. One important purpose of defective–product tort law is to encourage the manufacturer of safer products. The various tort rules that determine which foreseeable losses are recoverable aim, in part, to provide appropriate safe–product incentives. And a liability rule that diminishes liability simply because of some such resale is a rule that, other things being equal, diminishes that basic incentive. That circumstance requires a justification. That is to say, why should a series of resales, after replacement and additions of ever more physical items, progressively immunize a manufacturer to an ever greater extent from the liability for foreseeable physical damage that would otherwise fall upon it?

The *East River* answer to this question—because the parties can contract for appropriate sharing of the risks of harm—is not as satisfactory in the context of resale after an initial use. That is because, as other courts have suggested, the Subsequent User does not contract directly with the Manufacturer (or distributor.) Moreover, it is likely more difficult for a consumer—a commercial user and reseller—to offer an appropriate warranty on the used product he sells akin to a manufacturer's (or distributor's) warranty of the initial product. The user/reseller did not make (or initially distribute) the product and, to that extent, he normally would know less about the risks that such a warranty would involve. That is to say, it would seem more difficult for a reseller to warrant, say, a ship's engine; as time passes, the ship ages, the ship undergoes modification, and it passes through the hands of users and resellers.

Of course, nothing prevents a user/reseller from offering a warranty. But neither does anything prevent a Manufacturer and an Initial User from apportioning through their contract potential loss of any other items—say, added equipment or totally separate physical property—that a defective manufactured product, say an exploding engine, might cause. No court has thought that the mere possibility of such a contract term precluded tort recovery for damage to an Initial User's other property. Similarly, in the absence of a showing that it is ordinary business practice for user/resellers to offer a warranty comparable to those typically provided by sellers of new products, the argument for extending *East River*, replacing tort law with contract law, is correspondingly weak. That is to say, respondents have not explained why the ordinary rules governing the manufacturer's tort liability should be supplanted merely because the user/reseller may in theory incur an overlapping liability in contract.

Respondents make two other important arguments. First, they say that our reasoning proves too much. They argue that, if a Subsequent User can recover for damage a defective manufactured product causes to property added by the Initial User, then a user might recover for damage a defective component causes the manufactured product, other than the component itself. Saratoga Fishing, for example, could recover the damage the defective hydraulic system caused to any other part of the ship. But the lower courts, following *East River*, have held that it is not a component part, but the vessel—as placed in the stream of commerce by the manufacturer and its distributors—that is the "product" that itself caused the harm. As the Court said in *East River*,

> Since all but the very simplest of machines have component parts, [a contrary] holding would require a finding of 'property damage' in virtually every case where a product damages itself. Such a holding would eliminate the distinction between warranty and strict products liability.

Our holding here, however, does not affect this rule, for the relevant relations among initial users, manufacturers, and component suppliers are typically different from those at issue here. Initial users when they buy typically depend upon, and likely seek warranties that depend upon, a manufacturer's primary business skill, namely the assembly of workable product components into a marketable whole. Moreover, manufacturers and component suppliers can allocate through contract potential liability for a manufactured product that does not work, thereby ensuring that component suppliers have appropriate incentives to prevent component defects that might destroy the product. There is no reason to think that initial users systematically control the manufactured product's quality or, as we have said, systematically allocate responsibility for user–added equipment, in similar ways. Regardless, the case law does suggest a distinction between the components added to a product by a manufacturer before the product's sale to a user and those items added by a user to the manufactured product; and we would maintain that distinction.

Second, respondents argue that our holding would impose too great a potential tort liability upon a manufacturer or a distributor. But we do not see how that is so. For one thing, a host of other tort principles, such as foreseeability, proximate cause, and the "economic loss" doctrine already do, and would continue to, limit liability in important ways. For another thing, where such principles are satisfied, liability would exist anyway had the manufactured product simply remained in the hands of the Initial User. Our holding merely maintains liability, for equipment added after the initial sale, despite the presence of a resale by the Initial User.

We conclude that equipment added to a product after the Manufacturer (or distributor selling in the initial distribution chain) has sold the product to an initial User is not part of the product that itself caused physical harm. Rather, in *East River's* language, it is "other property." (We are speaking, of course, of added equipment that itself played no causal role in the accident that caused the physical harm.) Thus the extra skiff, nets, spare parts, and miscellaneous equipment at issue here, added to the ship by a user after an initial sale to that Initial User, are not part of the product (the original ship with the defective hydraulic system) that itself caused the harm.

The decision of the Ninth Circuit is reversed.

JUSTICE SCALIA, with whom JUSTICE THOMAS joins, dissenting.*

* * *

The Court's opinion suggests that this is a rather straightforward case. The relevant facts—according to the Court—are quite simple, showing: "(1) a Component Supplier who (2) provided a defective component ... to a Manufacturer, who incorporated it into the manufactured product (the ship), which (3) the Manufacturer sold to an Initial User, who (4) after adding equipment and using the ship, resold it to a Subsequent User." What the Court's opinion does not disclose is that Madruga—the Court's "Initial User"—was perhaps not only a user of the boat but also an entrepreneur in the business of designing, assembling and distributing what might be described as "fully equipped tuna–fishing machines." The M/V Saratoga was not an isolated purchase by tuna–fisherman Madruga from Martinac, but was the third of seven steel–hull tuna seiners Madruga commissioned. She was designed, in part by Madruga, specifically for use as a tuna seiner, and her construction at Martinac's shipyard was supervised personally by Madruga and by an engineer in Madruga's employ. Madruga negotiated over the specifications and equipment for the vessel and ordered numerous changes to it during the course of construction. When delivered by Martinac, the M/V Saratoga was certainly functional as a boat, but it was not yet capable of performing the task for which it was specially designed. It was arguably still just a component of a larger tuna–fishing machine that would not be complete until Madruga installed the seine, skiff, and electronic equipment; and arguably a component of a tuna–fishing machine that Madruga was in the business of marketing.

As respondent points out, there is no finding in the record as to whether Madruga was engaged in the business of selling such products and the issue was never raised or considered. I assume that the Court disregards this issue (neither resolving it nor remanding for its consideration) because the Court deems the question irrelevant. Under the Court's test, as I understand it, the "product" is fixed when it is sold to an "Initial User," even if that user is also in the business of modifying and reselling the product. In my view, there is little to recommend such a rule.

The Court is driven to take the position it does by the concern that liability would otherwise turn on "a fortuity, namely whether a defective product causes ... harm to the added equipment before or after an Initial User (who added the equipment) resells the product to a Subsequent User." But the initial–user rule the Court embraces simply makes liability turn on a different fortuity, namely whether the person who adds additional equipment to the product uses that product before selling it. If Madruga was engaged in the business of assembling and distributing tuna seiners, why should the fact that he briefly used the

---

vessel before selling it enable petitioner to obtain tort damages that would plainly not be recoverable if Madruga had simply installed the components and sold the vessel? Or put in more commonplace terms: Why should the buyer of a car whose engine catches fire and destroys the entire vehicle be able to recover in a tort action against the manufacturer for the value of the dealer–added hi–fi stereo system if the car was a "demo," but not if the car was brand new?

One rule that generally avoids making liability turn on either of the above described "fortuities" is what might be called the "last–402A–seller rule." Under this rule, the "product" would be fixed when it is sold by the last person in the chain of distribution who is, in the words of § 402A of the Restatement (Second) of Torts (1964), "engaged in the business of selling such a product." This would offer at least as much predictability as can be expected from the Court's approach, would ensure that the availability of tort remedies will be uniform with regard to all end–users, and would avoid making liability turn on the seemingly irrelevant question of whether the distributor of the product used it before sale. The last–402A–seller rule is also more consistent with one of the principal considerations underlying our decision in *East River*: the desirability of invoking tort protection only where contract–warranty protection is infeasible. Defining the product as what was sold by the last person engaged in the business of selling such products denies tort recovery for those additions to the originally manufactured product which the purchaser could have covered by warranty protection (persons in the business will generally offer warranties covering the entire product; user–sellers will generally not).

The last–402A–seller rule appears to me superior to the initial–user rule adopted by the Court today, but the two are in reality quite similar and will in most cases produce the same result. Each essentially attempts to differentiate between additions made before and after the product has left the market chain of distribution. I doubt, however, whether leaving the market chain of distribution ought to be so momentous an event for the purpose at hand. So long as the plaintiff is a commercial entity (and I understand the rule under consideration to be one applicable only to commercial, as opposed to consumer, transactions,) it seems to me to make no difference whether the purchase was made from a "402A seller" or not. Commercial entities do not typically suffer, at the time they make their purchase, a disparity in bargaining power that makes it impossible for them to obtain warranty protection on the entire product; nor are they unable to insure the product they have purchased, including those portions of it added by upstream owners. Our decision in *East River* suggests that in such circumstances there is inadequate reason to interfere with private ordering by importing tort liability—that is, inadequate reason to permit the purchaser to recover any tort damages for loss of the product he purchased.]

In recognition of that reality, an impressive line of lower court decisions, applying both federal and state law, has held that the purchaser of a product damaged by a defective component cannot recover in tort against the manufacturer of the component on the theory that the remainder of the product is "other property." Although the holdings of these cases are not precisely on point (since the plaintiff was the initial purchaser–user of the defective product), the rationale of those decisions is in tension with the Court's holding today, and supports what might be called an "object–of–the–bargain" rule. They rest on the premise that one must look to the product purchased or bargained for by the plaintiff in determining whether additions constitute "other property." * * *

As I have confessed above, I have little confidence in my ability to make the correct policy choice in an area where courts more experienced than we have not yet come to rest. I would have been inclined to let the lower federal courts struggle with this issue somewhat longer, in the hope that there would develop a common–law consensus to which we could refer for our admiralty rule, as we did in *East River*. Put to a choice, however, I would not select the rule adopted by the Court today. I would adopt the rule proposed by respondents and define the "product" for purposes of *East River's* economic–loss rule as the object of the purchaser's bargain. That was essentially the approach followed by the Court of Appeals below, and I would accordingly affirm its judgment.

I respectfully, and indeed diffidently, dissent.

Notes

1. In Seely v. White Motor Co., 63 Cal.2d 9, 45 Cal.Rptr. 17, 403 P.2d 145 (1965), the plaintiff purchased a truck manufactured by the defendant. When the brakes failed and the truck crashed, the plaintiff sued for the cost of repairing the truck and lost profits. The court upheld an award based on breach of warranty, but it stated that strict tort liability does not provide for damages for pure economic loss, including damage to the product itself.

Santor v. A & M Karagheusian, Inc., 44 N.J. 52, 207 A.2d 305 (1965), is the leading case allowing recovery for pure economic loss. The plaintiff purchased carpeting that developed unsightly lines as the pile wore down. The court held that the plaintiff could recover for the lost value of the carpeting under either breach of warranty or strict tort liability.

Seely and *East River* represent the majority view.

2. Damage to property other than the defective product itself is recoverable under strict tort liability. So is economic injury caused by such property damage or by personal injury.

3. Pure economic damages are recoverable in an action for breach of warranty under the U.C.C. Suit under the U.C.C. has its own obstacles, however, not the least of which is that a seller can disclaim its warranties.

4. In cases involving injury only to the defective product itself, some courts have distinguished between a slowly developing defect and a "sudden and violent" occurrence, permitting recovery for the latter.

5. Recall that, in non–product negligence cases, pure economic loss is not recoverable in many jurisdictions. See Chapter VI, Section E.

F. CONSUMER CONDUCT DEFENSES

DALY v. GENERAL MOTORS CORP.

Supreme Court of California, 1978.
20 Cal.3d 725, 144 Cal.Rptr. 380, 575 P.2d 1162.

RICHARDSON, JUSTICE.

The most important of several problems which we consider is whether the principles of comparative negligence expressed by us in Li v. Yellow Cab Co. (1975) 13 Cal.3d 804, 119 Cal.Rptr. 858, 532 P.2d 1226, apply to actions founded on strict products liability. We will conclude that they do. * * *

* * * In the early hours of October 31, 1970, decedent Kirk Daly, a 36–year–old attorney, was driving his Opel southbound on the Harbor Freeway in Los Angeles. The vehicle, while travelling at a speed of 50–70 miles per hour, collided with and damaged 50 feet of metal divider fence. After the initial impact between the left side of the vehicle and the fence the Opel spun counterclockwise, the driver's door was thrown open, and Daly was forcibly ejected from the car and sustained fatal head injuries. It was equally undisputed that had the deceased remained in the Opel his injuries, in all probability, would have been relatively minor.

* * * The sole theory of plaintiffs' complaint was strict liability for damages allegedly caused by a defective product, namely, an improperly designed door latch claimed to have been activated by the impact. It was further asserted that, but for the faulty latch, decedent would have been restrained in the vehicle and, although perhaps injured, would not have been killed. Thus, the case involves a so–called "second collision" in which the "defect" did not contribute to the original impact, but only to the "enhancement" of injury.

* * *

Over plaintiffs' objections, defendants were permitted to introduce evidence indicating that: (1) the Opel was equipped with a seat belt–shoulder harness system, and a door lock, either of which if used, it was contended, would have prevented Daly's ejection from the vehicle; (2) Daly used neither the harness system nor the lock; (3) the 1970 Opel owner's manual contained warnings that seat belts should be worn and doors locked when the car was in motion for "accident security"; and (4) Daly was intoxicated at the time of collision, which evidence the jury was advised was admitted for the limited purpose of determining whether decedent had used the vehicle's safety equipment. After relatively brief deliberations the jury returned a verdict favoring all defendants, and plaintiffs appeal from the ensuing adverse judgment.

* * *

In response to plaintiffs' assertion that the "intoxication–nonuse" evidence was improperly admitted, defendants contend that the deceased's own conduct contributed to his death. Because plaintiffs' case rests upon strict products liability based on improper design of the door latch and because defendants assert a failure in decedent's conduct, namely, his alleged intoxication and nonuse of safety equipment, without which the accident and ensuing death would not have occurred, there is thereby posed the overriding issue in the case, should comparative principles apply in strict products liability actions?

* * *

[In Li v. Yellow Cab Co. we adopted] a "pure" form of comparative negligence which, when present, reduced but did not prevent plaintiff's recovery. We held that the defense of assumption of risk, insofar as it is no more than a variant of contributory negligence, was merged into the assessment of liability in proportion to fault. Within the broad guidelines therein announced, we left to trial courts discretion in the particular implementation of the new doctrine.

* * *

Those counseling against the recognition of comparative fault principles in strict products liability cases vigorously stress, perhaps equally, not only the conceptual, but also the semantic difficulties incident to such a course. The task of merging the two concepts is said to be impossible, that "apples and oranges" cannot be compared, that "oil and water" do not mix, and that strict liability, which is not founded on negligence or fault, is inhospitable to comparative principles. The syllogism runs, contributory negligence was only a defense to negligence, comparative negligence only affects contributory negligence, therefore comparative negligence cannot be a defense to strict liability. While fully recognizing the theoretical and semantic distinctions between the twin principles of strict products liability and traditional negligence, we think they can be blended or accommodated.

The inherent difficulty in the "apples and oranges" argument is its insistence on fixed and precise definitional treatment of legal concepts. In the evolving areas of both products liability and tort defenses, however, there has developed much conceptual overlapping and interweaving in order to attain substantial justice. The concept of strict liability itself, as we have noted, arose from dissatisfaction with the wooden formalisms of traditional tort and contract principles in order to protect the consumer of manufactured goods. Similarly, increasing social awareness of its harsh "all or nothing" consequences led us in *Li* to moderate the impact of traditional contributory negligence in order to accomplish a fairer and more balanced result. We acknowledged an intermixing of defenses of contributory negligence and assumption of risk and formally effected a type of merger. * * *

Furthermore, the "apples and oranges" argument may be conceptually suspect. It has been suggested that the term "contributory negligence," one of the vital building blocks upon which much of the argument is based, may indeed itself be a misnomer since it lacks the first element of the classical negligence formula, namely, a duty of care owing to another. A highly respected torts authority, Dean William Prosser, has noted this fact by observing, "It is perhaps unfortunate that contributory negligence is called negligence at all. 'Contributory fault' would be a more descriptive term. Negligence as it is commonly understood is conduct which creates an undue risk of harm to others. Contributory negligence is conduct which involves an undue risk of harm to the actor himself. Negligence requires a duty, an obligation of conduct to another person. Contributory negligence involves no duty, unless we are to be so ingenious as to say that the plaintiff is under an obligation to protect the defendant against liability for the consequences of his own negligence." (Prosser, Law of Torts, § 65, p. 418 [4th ed. 1971].)

We think, accordingly, the conclusion may fairly be drawn that the terms "comparative negligence," "contributory negligence" and "assumption of risk" do not, standing alone, lend themselves to the exact measurements of a micrometer–caliper, or to such precise definition as to divert us from otherwise strong and consistent countervailing policy considerations. Fixed semantic consistency at this point is less important than the attainment of a just and equitable result. The interweaving of concept and terminology in this area suggests a judicial posture that is flexible rather than doctrinaire.

We pause at this point to observe that where, as here, a consumer or user sues the manufacturer or designer alone, technically neither fault nor conduct is really compared functionally. The conduct of one party in combination with the product of another, or perhaps the placing of a defective article in the stream of projected and anticipated use, may produce the ultimate injury. In such a case, as in the situation before us, we think the term "equitable apportionment or allocation of loss" may be more descriptive than "comparative fault."

Given all of the foregoing, we are, in the wake of *Li,* disinclined to resolve the important issue before us by the simple expedient of matching linguistic labels which have evolved either for convenience or by custom. Rather, we consider it more useful to examine the foundational reasons underlying the creation of strict products liability in California to ascertain whether the purposes of the doctrine would be defeated or diluted by adoption of comparative principles. We imposed strict liability against the manufacturer and in favor of the user or consumer in order to relieve injured consumers "from *problems of proof* inherent in pursuing negligence * * * and warranty * * * remedies * * *." [ ] As we have noted, we sought to place the burden of loss on manufacturers rather than " * * * injured persons *who are powerless to protect themselves* * * *."

The foregoing goals, we think, will not be frustrated by the adoption of comparative principles. Plaintiffs will continue to be relieved of proving that the manufacturer or distributor was negligent in the production, design, or dissemination of the article in question. Defendant's liability for injuries caused by a defective product remains strict.

The principle of protecting the defenseless is likewise preserved, for plaintiff's recovery will be reduced *only* to the extent that his own lack of reasonable care contributed to his injury. The cost of compensating the victim of a defective product, albeit proportionately reduced, remains on defendant manufacturer, and will, through him, be "spread among society." However, we do not permit plaintiff's own conduct relative to the product to escape unexamined, and as to that share of plaintiff's damages which flows from his own fault we discern no reason of policy why it should, following *Li,* be borne by others. Such a result would directly contravene the principle announced in *Li,* that loss should be assessed equitably in proportion to fault.

* * *

A second objection to the application of comparative principles in strict products liability cases is that a manufacturer's incentive to produce safe products will thereby be reduced or removed. While we fully recognize this concern we think, for several reasons, that the problem is more shadow than substance. First, of course, the manufacturer cannot avoid its continuing liability for a defective product even when the plaintiff's own conduct has contributed to his injury. The manufacturer's liability, and therefore its incentive to avoid and correct product defects, remains; its exposure will be lessened only to the extent that the trier finds that the victim's conduct contributed to his injury. Second, as a practical matter a manufacturer, in a particular case, cannot assume that the user of a defective product upon whom an injury is visited will be blameworthy. Doubtless, many users are free of fault, and a defect is at least as likely as not to be exposed by an entirely innocent plaintiff who will obtain full recovery. In such cases the manufacturer's incentive toward safety both in design and production is wholly unaffected. Finally, we must observe that under the present law, which recognizes assumption of risk as a complete defense to products liability, the curious and cynical message is that it profits the manufacturer to make his product so defective that in the event of injury he can argue that the user had to be aware of its patent defects. To that extent the incentives are inverted. We conclude, accordingly, that no substantial or significant impairment of the safety incentives of defendants will occur by the adoption of comparative principles.

In passing, we note one important and felicitous result if we apply comparative principles to strict products liability. This arises from the fact that under present law when plaintiff sues in negligence his own contributory negligence, however denominated, may diminish but cannot wholly defeat his recovery. When he sues in strict products liability, however, his "assumption of risk" *completely bars* his recovery. Under *Li,* as we have noted, "assumption of risk" is merged into comparative principles. The consequence is that after *Li* in a negligence action, plaintiff's conduct which amounts to "negligent" assumption of risk no longer defeats plaintiff's recovery. Identical conduct, however, in a strict liability case acts as a complete bar under rules heretofore applicable.

Thus, strict products liability, which was developed to free injured consumers from the constraints imposed by traditional negligence and warranty theories, places a consumer plaintiff in a worse position than would be the case were his claim founded on simple negligence. This, in turn, rewards adroit pleading and selection of theories. The application of comparative principles to strict liability obviates this bizarre anomaly by treating alike the defenses to both negligence and strict products liability actions. In each instance the defense, if established, will reduce but not bar plaintiff's claim.

A third objection to the merger of strict liability and comparative fault focuses on the claim that, as a practical matter, triers of fact, particularly jurors, cannot assess, measure, or compare plaintiff's negligence with defendant's strict liability. We are unpersuaded by the argument and are convinced that jurors are able to undertake a fair apportionment of liability.

* * *

We note that the majority of our sister states which have addressed the problem, either by statute or judicial decree, have extended comparative principles to strict products liability.

* * *

Moreover, we are further encouraged in our decision herein by noting that the apparent majority of scholarly commentators has urged adoption of the rule which we announce herein.

* * *

Having examined the principal objections and finding them not insurmountable, and persuaded by logic, justice, and fundamental fairness, we conclude that a system of comparative fault should be and it is hereby extended to actions founded on strict products liability. In such cases the separate defense of "assumption of risk," to the extent that it is a form of contributory negligence, is abolished. While, as we have suggested, on the particular facts before us, the term "equitable apportionment of loss" is more accurately descriptive of the process, nonetheless, the term "comparative fault" has gained such wide acceptance by courts and in the literature that we adopt its use herein.

[The court then held that its decision would not be applied retroactively, not even to the case before it. Under the law existing at the time of trial, evidence of the plaintiff's intoxication and failure to use a seat belt should have been excluded.]

The judgment is reversed.

Jefferson, Justice, concurring and dissenting.

* * *

The majority * * * does not consider it significant that it is unable to determine what labels should be given to the new comparative principles—whether the new doctrine should be known as comparative fault, equitable apportionment of loss, or equitable allocation of loss. This inability to give the new doctrine an appropriate label is some indication of the shaky ground upon which the majority has decided to tread.

The majority rejects what I consider to be a sound criticism of its holding—that it is illogical and illusory to compare elements or factors that are not reasonably subject to comparison. The majority states that it is convinced that jurors will be able to compare the noncomparables— plaintiff's negligence with defendant's strict liability for a defective product—and still reach a fair apportionment of liability.

I consider the majority conclusion a case of wishful thinking and an application of an impractical, ivory–tower approach. * * *

* * *

What the majority envisions as a fair apportionment of liability to be undertaken by the jury will constitute nothing more than an *unfair reduction* in the plaintiff's total damages suffered, resulting from a jury process that necessarily is predicated on speculation, conjecture and guesswork. Because the legal concept of negligence is so utterly different from the legal concept of a product defective by reason of manufacture or design, a plaintiff's negligence is [not] capable of being rationally compared with a defendant's defective product * * *.

* * *

The guessing game that will be imposed on juries by the application of comparative negligence principles to defective product liability cases will be further enhanced in those cases in which several defendants are joined in an action—some being sued on a negligence theory and others on the defective product theory and where there are several plaintiffs whose conduct may range from no negligence at all to varying degrees of negligence. The jury will be required to determine percentages of fault with respect to all the parties (and perhaps some nonparties) by seeking to compare and evaluate the *conduct* of certain parties with the *product* of other parties to produce 100 percent of fault as the necessary starting point in order to calculate a reduction in the damages suffered by each plaintiff found to be negligent. I cannot agree with the majority that such a process is reasonably workable or that it will produce an equitable result to injured plaintiffs. If a just or fair result is reached by a jury under the majority's holding, it will be strictly accidental and accomplished by pure happenstance.

* * *

MOSK, JUSTICE, dissenting.

* * *

This will be remembered as the dark day when this court, which heroically took the lead in originating the doctrine of products liability and steadfastly resisted efforts to inject concepts of negligence into the newly designed tort, inexplicably turned 180 degrees and beat a hasty retreat almost back to square one. The pure concept of products liability so pridefully fashioned and nurtured by this court for the past decade and a half is reduced to a shambles.

The majority inject a foreign object—the tort of negligence—into the tort of products liability by the simple expedient of calling negligence something else: on some pages their opinion speaks of "comparative fault," on others reference is to "comparative principles," and elsewhere the term "equitable apportionment" is employed, although this is clearly not a proceeding in equity. * * *

* * *

The defective product is comparable to a time bomb ready to explode; it maims its victims indiscriminately, the righteous and the evil, the careful and the careless. Thus when a faulty design or otherwise defective product is involved, the litigation should not be diverted to consideration of the negligence of the plaintiff. The liability issues are simple: was the product or its design faulty, did the defendant inject the defective product into the stream of commerce, and did the defect cause the injury? The conduct of the ultimate consumer–victim who used the product in the contemplated or foreseeable manner is wholly irrelevant to those issues.

* * *

The majority deny their opinion diminishes the therapeutic effect of products liability upon producers of defective products. It seems self–evident that procedures which evaluate the injured consumer's conduct in each instance, and thus eliminate or reduce the award against the producer or distributor of a defective product, are not designed as an effective incentive to maximum responsibility to consumers. The converse is more accurate: the motivation to avoid polluting the stream of commerce with defective products increases in direct relation to the size of potential damage awards.

In sum, I am convinced that since the negligence of the defendant is irrelevant in products liability cases, the negligence—call it contributory or comparative—of the plaintiff is also irrelevant. * * *

* * *

Notes

1. As the opinion in *Daly* indicates, most states that have comparative negligence schemes apply some type of comparative scheme to strict tort liability.

2. Justice Mosk's opinion in *Daly* reflects a common objection to applying comparative negligence principles to strict tort liability. Why is it that Justice Mosk thinks an analysis of the plaintiff's negligence is intrinsically incompatible with the theory of strict tort liability?

3. Once a court adopts a comparative scheme for strict tort liability, it must decide what the contours of that scheme will be. For example, will it be a pure comparative scheme—in which a plaintiff assigned more than 50% "fault" can still recover—or a modified comparative scheme—in which such a plaintiff is completely barred from recovery?

4. Restatement (Second) of Torts, § 402A, comment *n*, provided that negligence that was merely a failure to discover or guard against the possibility of a product defect was not a defense against strict tort liability. The idea seems to be that a consumer should not be denied recovery altogether merely because he or she failed to inspect the product for defects. After the advent of comparative responsibility, comment *n* created difficulties. In a case involving claims of negligence and strict tort liability, possibly against different types of defendants, a jury might have to consider the plaintiff's negligent failure to discover or guard against the possibilities of a defect with respect to recovery against some defendants, but not others. Moreover, the advent of comparative responsibility lowered the stakes with respect to plaintiff negligence by reducing the plaintiff's recovery, rather than barring it altogether. Consequently, most courts now count all forms of plaintiff negligence, including a plaintiff's negligently failing to discover or guard against a product defect. See Restatement (Third) of Torts: Products Liability § 17 & comment *b* (1998).

G. PARTIES AND TRANSACTIONS GOVERNED BY STRICT TORT LIABILITY

At its core, strict tort liability applies to "product sales." The favorable treatment plaintiffs receive under strict tort liability has caused plaintiffs to allege strict tort liability claims in a variety of analogous transactions. This has forced courts to determine the applicability of strict tort liability to transactions involving leases, bailments, used products, real estate, and services. Full treatment of these issues is beyond the scope of these materials. The two cases that follow focus on one important area of litigation: the applicability of strict tort liability to services. *Hoffman* addresses the question of whether pure service transactions should be governed by strict liability. *Hoover* addresses the question of whether, in a jurisdiction that does not apply strict liability to pure services, strict liability should be applied to hybrid transactions involving both products and services. As you read these cases, you should consider whether the original purposes underlying the adoption of strict tort liability suggest limits to the theory's scope of application.

HOFFMAN v. SIMPLOT AVIATION, INC.

Supreme Court of Idaho, 1975.
97 Idaho 32, 539 P.2d 584.

SHEPARD, JUSTICE.

This is an appeal from a judgment in favor of plaintiffs–respondents following trial and jury verdict in an action resulting from an airplane accident. The principal questions presented are: 1) whether the rule of strict liability in tort in the field of products liability * * * should be extended beyond sales and into the area of personal services, and, 2) the application of the doctrine of implied warranty to personal services and availability of the defenses of [the victim's] fault or negligence. We decline to so extend the rule of strict liability and hold that the jury was erroneously instructed as to the doctrine of implied warranty. We reverse and remand for a new trial.

* * *

[Hoffman took his vintage airplane to Simplot for repairs. Hoffman was later injured when the plane crashed. He alleged that the crash was caused by a rusted bolt and that, although the bolt was not part of Simplot's repairs, Simplot should have discovered the bolt and replaced it.]

It is apparently conceded by all that none of the repair work performed by the Simplot employees was a causative factor in the crash of the aircraft. Similarly no part or product placed upon the aircraft by the Simplot employees was a causative factor. While the Simplot employees were repairing the damage to the left landing gear which was occasioned by the first accident, they were working in close proximity to the clevis bolt which attached the left wing strut to the fuselage.

The principal factual dispute relates to the condition of the clevis bolt at the time that the Simplot employees had completed the repairs and made the visual inspection of the aircraft. There was testimony to the effect that the bolt showed signs of rust and therefore failure could have been anticipated. However, the Simplot employees denied that the rust was visible to them as they worked on and inspected the aircraft and that because of the age and condition of the aircraft rust had no significance.

* * * Plaintiffs alleged liability on four theories: 1) negligence, 2) breach of express warranty, 3) breach of implied warranty, and 4) strict liability. At the conclusion of trial, lengthy jury instructions were given by the trial judge, including instructions on all four of the theories of liability.

The jury returned two forms of special verdict. On the first, the jury found both parties equally negligent, thus holding against Hoffman in accordance with Idaho's comparative negligence statute. I.C. § 6–801. On the second special verdict the jury found against Hoffman on the theory of strict liability and also against Hoffman on the theory of express warranty. However, on the theory of breach of implied warranty and only on that theory the jury returned a verdict in favor of Hoffman. Damages were assessed at $11,600 and judgment entered for that amount.

Appellants argue that the trial court erred in accepting special verdicts from the jury which were inherently contradictory in themselves and also in giving jury instructions setting forth plaintiffs' theories of strict liability and implied warranty.

In Shields v. Morton Chemical Company, 95 Idaho 674, 518 P.2d 857 (1974) this court adopted the rule of strict liability in tort as set forth in the Restatement of the Law, Torts 2nd, § 402(A) (1965). The Restatement deals specifically and only with the sale of a product. Neither this court nor, with one exception, any other court has adopted strict liability in tort absent fault in the context of personal services. We decline to extend the rule of *Shields* to cases involving personal services. We find no consideration of such extension of the rule of strict liability in either the Uniform Commercial Code or the Restatement of Torts, 2nd. Almost uniformly, any such extension of the rule has been consistently and expressly rejected.

It would serve no purpose herein to extensively review the policy considerations which militate against the extension of the strict liability rule to cases involving personal service. The rationale has been thoroughly explored [by other] authorities and commentators * * * and reiteration herein would serve no purpose. It is sufficient to say that as contrasted with the sales of products, personal services do not involve mass production with the difficulty, if not inability, of the obtention of proof of negligence. The consumer in the personal service context usually comes into direct contact with the one offering service and is aware or can determine what work was performed and who performed it.

We therefore hold the instructions of the trial court dealing with the theory of strict liability in the case at bar constituted error. The jury held against the plaintiff on the theory of strict liability and therefore defendants–appellants would not ordinarily be heard to complain. Our reversal and remand for a new trial for reasons stated infra has required the foregoing discussion.*

It is undisputed here that none of the materials or services of the defendants in the actual repair of the aircraft caused the accident. Any liability for breach of implied warranty must be based on defendants' inspection of the aircraft following the performance of the repairs and their failure during that inspection to discover the defect in the clevis bolt. The jury could have found that the defect in the bolt should have been discovered by defendants since they were working in close proximity thereto when they were performing the repairs on the landing gear. It is conceded by appellants that the issue of appellants' negligence posed a jury question. In effect, it is also conceded by appellants that there was a question of express warranty correctly submitted to the jury * * *.

Appellants assign error to the trial court's instruction on the doctrine of implied warranty. The only theory upon which the jury found against the defendants–appellants in this case was in its special verdict

* Ultimately, the court offers no explanation of the relationship between its disapproval of the strict liability instructions and its holding on the implied warranty theory. Presumably, though, it believed the strict liability instructions may have improperly influenced the jury's consideration of the implied warranty claim. [Ed.]

relating to implied warranty. Appellants assert that the special verdict on implied warranty could only have resulted from the instruction setting forth that theory. We agree. We also agree that such instruction was erroneous in that it permitted the jury to find liability absent any proof of fault or negligence by the defendants. Unfortunately our holding is not yet dispositive since the case will be tried again and we must determine if the theory of implied warranty was correctly before the court and, if so, the correct theory of implied warranty must be supplied.

It is clear that in a sales transaction an implied warranty may be imposed upon the seller to the effect that the goods are merchantable or are fit for the particular purpose for which purchased. I.C. §§ 28–2–314, 315. In circumstances involving personal services, however, the warranty is implied that the services will be performed in a workmanlike manner. The standard imposed may vary depending upon the expertise of the actor, either possessed or represented to be possessed, the nature of the services and the known resultant danger to others from the actor's negligence or failure to perform.

However, as stated in the landmark case of Gagne v. Bertran, 43 Cal.2d 481, 275 P.2d 15 (1954):

> The services of experts are sought because of their special skill. They have a duty to exercise the ordinary skill and competence of members of their profession, and a failure to discharge that duty will subject them to liability for negligence. Those who hire such persons are not justified in expecting infallibility, but can expect only reasonable care and competence. They purchase service, not insurance.

The more vexing problem of theory is the distinction, if any, between the doctrines of implied warranty and negligence in circumstances involving the rendering of personal services. Although such causes of action are generally thought to be independent of each other, in the instant circumstances they merge into one cause of action. A fundamental component in a negligence action is the existence of a duty (most often to refrain) toward another and a breach thereof. In circumstances involving the rendition of personal services the duty upon the actor is to perform the services in a workmanlike manner. Pepsi Cola Bottling Co. v. Superior Burner Service, 427 P.2d 833 (Alaska 1967) is remarkably similar in its problems of theory and doctrine to the case at bar. Justice Rabinowitz there concluded that in the area of personal services there is a duty upon the actor to perform in a workmanlike manner and there is an implied warranty that the services will so be provided. However, it was there stated:

> Whether the tort standard of care is considered, or the duty of care imposed by an implied warranty of workmanlike performance is taken as the applicable standard, in our view the resultant standard of care required of appellee's employees in the circumstances of this case is identical. In both instances the standard of care is imposed by law and under either theory there is no difference in the standard of care required of the party rendering the personal services.

Characterization of the gist, or gravamen, of appellant's cause of action in the factual context of this case is not free of difficulties. Whether an action is one in contract or tort may have significant procedural and substantive ramifications. In the case at bar appellant's central argument in support of its contention that it was entitled to go to the jury on both a tort cause of action and breach-of-an-implied-warranty-of-workmanlike-quality cause of action is that contributory negligence would not be a bar to recovery under the latter.

* * * We hold that under the circumstances of the case at bar the implied warranty theory of plaintiffs should have been submitted to the jury with proper instructions. The jury should have been instructed that plaintiffs were entitled to have defendants' services rendered in a workmanlike manner. The standard of care so imposed on the defendants should be determined in light of relevant factors such as: The inherent danger posed by an aircraft; the expertise possessed, or represented as possessed, by the defendants; the knowledge of the defendants' intended use of the aircraft, and the contributory negligence of or assumption of the risk by the plaintiffs, if any, in consideration of factors such as the age of the aircraft, its previous status and record of repair and maintenance and the previous accident.

Plaintiffs–respondents argue that the recent case of S.H. Kress & Co. v. Godman, 95 Idaho 614, 515 P.2d 561 (1973) militates against our result here. We do not agree. In *Kress* personal services were involved and there as here defendants were called to make repairs and it was alleged that such were made negligently. There also, it was argued that following the repairs an inspection in the immediate repair area would have revealed defects in parts which later caused an accident. *Kress* was reversed on the sole basis that the existence of a duty on the repairman and a breach thereof were questions which should have been submitted to the jury. There it is implicit that the cause of action was brought in negligence and that the contributory negligence of the owner was a defense. So in the case at bar we hold that contributory negligence or assumption of the risk are defenses to plaintiffs' theory of implied warranty.

In summary we hold that plaintiffs–respondents were entitled to have their theory of implied warranty submitted to the jury. Since the case involved the rendition of personal service, a cause of action does not exist for breach of implied warranty in the absence of fault on the part of the actor. The jury should be instructed also that the defenses of contributory negligence or assumption of the risk are available to defendants–appellants.

* * *

Reversed and remanded for a new trial consistent with this opinion. Costs to appellants.

Notes

1. The opinion does not indicate why Hoffman was contributorily negligent. It is possible that he should have discovered the bolt or should have responded better to the emergency when the bolt broke.

2. The passage from Gagne v. Bertran is quoted in nearly every opinion rejecting the application of strict liability—either in the form of strict tort liability or in the form of breach of warranty—to pure service transactions. The quote does not further the analysis, however. We could just as easily say:

> Those who hire persons to build their products are not justified in expecting infallibility, but can expect only reasonable care and competence. They purchase a product, not insurance.

3. The opinion in *Hoffman* stated that strict tort liability should not be applied to services because "as contrasted with the sale of products, personal services do not involve mass production with the difficulty, if not inability, of the obtention of proof of negligence. The consumer in the personal service context usually comes into direct contact with the one offering service and is aware or can determine what work was performed and who performed it." For an argument that no other rationales underlying strict tort liability support a distinction between products and services, see Powers, Distinguishing Between Products and Services in Strict Liability, 62 N.C.L.Rev. 415 (1984).

HOOVER v. MONTGOMERY WARD & CO., INC.

Supreme Court of Oregon, 1974.
270 Or. 498, 528 P.2d 76.

HOWELL, JUSTICE.

[Hoover purchased tires from Montgomery Ward, who installed them. She was then injured in a one–car accident and alleged that the tires were improperly installed.]

The trial court refused to submit the issue of strict liability to the jury, and the jury returned a verdict for the defendants on the issue of negligence. The plaintiff appeals.

* * *

In Newmark v. Gimbel's Incorporated, 54 N.J. 585, 258 A.2d 697 (1969), the New Jersey Supreme Court held a beauty shop strictly liable under an implied warranty of fitness when defective permanent wave lotion was applied to a patron's hair. The court reasoned that if the lotion had been sold over the counter there would have been strict liability. There was no logical reason to hold otherwise merely because the defective lotion was applied in a service context, especially when the cost of the service included the price of the lotion.

In *Newmark* it is clear that the product, as opposed to the service, was defective. In the case at hand, as stated above, there was no allegation that the tire was defective.

As one author notes:

> When the contract between plaintiff and defendant is commercial in character, the courts are willing to extend liability without fault to the hybrid sale–service transaction, provided that a defective product is supplied to the plaintiff or used by the defendant in the course of performing the service. * * *

Note, Products and the Professional: Strict Liability in the Sale–Service Hybrid Transaction, 24 Hastings J. 111, 116 (1972).

[C]ourts have also been reluctant to extend the definition of "product" beyond the article actually manufactured or supplied.

In the instant case it is obvious that the product sold to plaintiff was not dangerously defective. Even if we accepted plaintiff's version of the cause of the accident, it was not a dangerously defective tire which caused plaintiff's injuries, but rather the installation of the wheel on the hub and axle of the auto. In such case it might be said that plaintiff's auto became dangerously defective, but certainly not the tire. Plaintiff herself must have recognized this feature, because in her complaint she does not allege that the tire was an unreasonably dangerous product but that "the automobile was unreasonably dangerous for its intended use * * *."

It is clear that this was not a proper case for strict liability in tort and the trial court correctly refused to submit that issue to the jury.

* * *

Affirmed.

Notes

1. The court in *Hoover* distinguished between the installation of a defective tire and the defective installation of a tire. What policies underlying strict tort liability support this distinction? Consider the reasoning used by the court in *Hoffman* to conclude that pure services are not governed by strict tort liability. Does this reasoning support the distinction suggested in *Hoover*?

2. Suppose the plaintiff claimed that the defendant defectively installed a defective tire. Would the claim about defective installation be governed by negligence and the claim about the defective tire be governed by strict tort liability?

3. In Magrine v. Krasnica, 94 N.J.Super. 228, 227 A.2d 539 (1967), affirmed sub nom. Magrine v. Spector, 100 N.J.Super. 223, 241 A.2d 637 (1968), affirmed 53 N.J. 259, 250 A.2d 129 (1969), the plaintiff was injured when a defective needle being used by her dentist broke off in her gum. The court held that the dentist's services were not governed by strict tort liability. *Magrine* is often compared to Newmark v. Gimbel's, Inc., which is discussed in *Hoover*. In *Newmark* the court applied strict tort liability to a beauty parlor that applied a permanent wave solution to the injured plaintiff. In addition to the fact that *Magrine* involved a professional—a factor that seems to have influenced courts on the propriety of applying strict

liability to services—*Magrine* is an example of a common class of cases in which a service provider uses a defective product in rendering the service. *Newmark* may be distinguishable from *Magrine* because in *Newmark* the defective wave solution was "sold" to the plaintiff in the sense that it was used up. But would the result in *Magrine* have been different if the needle had been disposable? Maybe the distinction is that the plaintiff in *Newmark* was intended to take some of the wave solution away with her (on her hair). But would the result have been different if the case had involved shampoo, which was intended to be totally washed from the hair?

Cases involving the *use* of defective products by service providers—as distinguished from cases like *Hoover* in which the service provider also *sells* a product—have caused courts a great deal of difficulty. *Newmark* demonstrates the difficulty courts face in categorizing a transaction as one type or the other. Do the policies underlying strict tort liability or underlying the decision not to apply strict tort liability to pure services help sort out these cases?

Remember that, in a case like *Magrine,* the plaintiff can sue the needle manufacturer under strict tort liability. The manufacturer clearly sold a product, and the plaintiff's status as a "bystander" does not defeat liability.

4. *Hoover, Magrine*, and *Newmark* involve transactions that are truly "hybrid," that is, the transactions have a component that is clearly a service. Other cases do not involve a complex transaction of this sort but nevertheless are difficult to classify as a product or a service. For example, is the delivery of a utility—such as electricity, natural gas, or water—a product or a service?

Several courts have considered cases involving the sale of electricity. One recurrent type of case involves a plaintiff who touches an overhead line with a ladder or antenna. Nearly all courts have held that in such a case the plaintiff must prove negligence and cannot rely on strict liability, either because electricity in an overhead line is not a product or because it has not yet entered the stream of commerce. See, e.g., United Pacific Insurance Co. v. Southern California Edison Co., 163 Cal.App.3d 700, 209 Cal.Rptr. 819 (1985).

A second frequently litigated situation involves a power surge through the plaintiff's meter that causes a fire or other damage. Several courts have permitted plaintiffs to recover under strict tort liability in this type of case. See, e.g., Pierce v. Pacific Gas & Electric Co., 166 Cal.App.3d 68, 212 Cal.Rptr. 283 (1985). How would you analyze the difference between these two types of cases?

5. Should strict tort liability apply to a map, navigational chart, cookbook, financial newsletter, or legal brief?

Chapter XVI

NUISANCE

A private nuisance is a substantial and unreasonable interference with quiet use and enjoyment of real property. A public nuisance is an unwarranted interference with public safety, health, convenience, or morals. This chapter deals primarily with private nuisance.

The law of private nuisance is relatively amorphous in that it lacks much theory and structure. Courts sit almost as though they were zoning commissions charged with the task of resolving disputes over competing uses of land. Their decisions are usually fact specific. They sometimes incorporate bits of doctrine from other torts, such as negligence, and they sometimes develop "rules" for resolving disputes. But these rules tend to be fluid, and adjudication tends to be ad hoc.

A plaintiff who proves a private nuisance has available several remedies. If the nuisance is temporary, the plaintiff can recover lost rental value and consequential damages, such as lost profit, damage to the real property, damage to crops and livestock, and personal injury. If the nuisance is continuous or permanent, the plaintiff can recover lost market value of the land and consequential damages. In some cases, a plaintiff can get an injunction.

AMPHITHEATERS, INC. v. PORTLAND MEADOWS

Supreme Court of Oregon, 1948.
184 Or. 336, 198 P.2d 847.

BRAND, JUSTICE.

[Plaintiff owned an outdoor drive–in movie theater. Defendant owned a horse race track on adjacent property. The race track was equipped with lights for night racing. The plaintiff sued for trespass to land and nuisance, claiming that the lights from the race track interfered with the movie screen. The trial court directed a verdict for the defendant on both theories. The portion of the Supreme Court's opinion dealing with trespass to land is reproduced in Chapter II, section F, supra, p. 37. In that portion of the opinion, the Court held that the trial court did not err by directing a verdict in favor of the defendant on the trespass theory.]

In installing outdoor moving picture theaters, it is necessary to protect the premises from outside light interference. For that purpose the plaintiff constructed wing fences for a considerable distance on each side of the screen and along the westerly line of Union Avenue for the purpose of shutting off the light from the cars traveling on that arterial highway. It was also necessary to construct a shadow box extending on both sides and above the screen for the purpose of excluding the light from the moon and stars. The testimony indicates that the construction of the shadow box was necessary if a good picture was to be presented on the screen. The extreme delicacy of plaintiff's operation and the susceptibility of outdoor moving pictures to light in any form was conclusively established by the evidence.

* * *

As its second assignment, the plaintiff asserts that the trial court erred in failing to submit the case to the jury on the theory of nuisance.

This is a case of first impression. It differs in essential particulars from any case which has received consideration by this court. The nuisance cases appearing in our reports fall into four easily recognizable classes: (1) Cases involving harm to human comfort, safety or health by reason of the maintenance by a defendant upon his land of noxious or dangerous instrumentalities causing damage to the plaintiff in respect to legally protected interests of the plaintiff in his land. (2) Cases involving illegal or immoral practices, most of them being public as distinct from private nuisances. They relate to bawdy houses, gambling, abortions, lotteries, illegal possession of liquor, and acts outraging public decency. (3) Cases involving obstructions to streets, public ways, common rights, access to property and the like. (4) Cases involving damage to the land itself, as by flooding. The cases, with the exception of those falling in the first class, bear no resemblance to the one at bar, and require no further comment.

* * *

The cases listed in the first class are the only ones which bear any faint resemblance to the case at bar. Examination of those cases will disclose that no Oregon decision has ever held that the casting of light in any quantity or form upon the land of another gives rise to a cause of action upon any legal theory. If the cases involving smoke, noxious odors, flies and disease germs are claimed to be analogous to the case at bar, it must be answered that in every case the activity or thing which has been held to be a nuisance has been something which was, 1, inherently harmful, and 2, an unreasonable and substantial interference with the ordinary use or enjoyment of property. No one can contend that light is inherently harmful to persons in the ordinary enjoyment of property.

Since there is no Oregon precedent to support plaintiff's contention we must go back to fundamental principles. Plaintiff relies upon the general definition of a nuisance * * *. A private nuisance is defined as "anything done to the hurt, annoyance, or detriment of the lands or hereditaments of another, and not amounting to a trespass". Definitions in such general terms are of no practical assistance to the court. * * *

The statement of Addison, Torts, 8th Ed. 66 [(1906)], that "The due regulation and subordination of conflicting rights constitute the chief part of the science of law" is peculiarly applicable in the field of private nuisance, for the rights of neither party in the use and enjoyment of their respective properties are absolute. "What is a reasonable use and whether a particular use is a nuisance cannot be determined by any fixed general rules, but depend upon the facts of each particular case, such as location, character of the neighborhood, nature of the use, extent and frequency of the injury, the effect upon the enjoyment of life, health, and property, and the like."

Notwithstanding the fact that the existence vel non of a nuisance is generally a question of fact, there have arisen several rules of law which guide and sometimes control decision. It is established law that an intentional interference with the use and enjoyment of land is not actionable unless that interference be both substantial and unreasonable.

Again it is held that whether a particular annoyance or inconvenience is sufficient to constitute a nuisance depends upon its effect upon an ordinarily reasonable man, that is, a normal person of ordinary habits and sensibilities. * * * This doctrine has been applied in many cases involving smoke, dust, noxious odors, vibration and the like, in which the injury was not to the land itself but to the personal comfort of dwellers on the land.

* * *

[T]he plaintiff's only basis of complaint is the fact that it is attempting to show upon the screen moving pictures, and * * * the operation is such a delicate one that it has been necessary for the plaintiff to build high fences to prevent the light of automobiles upon the public highway from invading the property and to build a shadow box over the screen to protect it from the ordinary light of moon and stars, and * * * it now claims damage because the lights from the defendant's property, which it has not excluded by high fences, shine with the approximate intensity of full moonlight upon the screen and interfere thereby with the showing of the pictures. We think that this is a clear case coming within the doctrine of the English and American cases * * * that a man cannot increase the liabilities of his neighbor by applying his own property to special and delicate uses, whether for business or pleasure.

* * *

By way of summary, we have found no case in which it has been held that light alone constitutes a nuisance merely because it damaged one who was abnormally sensitive or whose use of his land was of a peculiarly delicate and sensitive character.

It is not our intention to decide the case upon authority alone, divorced from reason or public policy. The photographic evidence discloses that the properties of the respective parties are not in a residential district, and in fact are outside the city limits of Portland, and lie adjacent to a considerable amount of unimproved land. Neither party can claim any greater social utility than the other. Both were in process of construction at the same time, and the case should not be decided upon the basis of the priority of occupation. The case differs fundamentally from other cases, all typical cases of nuisance, in that light is not a noxious, but is, in general, a highly beneficial element. The development of parks and playgrounds equipped for the enjoyment of the working public, whose recreation is necessarily taken after working hours, and frequently after dark, is a significant phenomenon in thousands of urban communities. The court takes judicial knowledge that many lighted parks and fields are located adjacent to residential property and must to some extent interfere with the full enjoyment of darkness (if desired), by the residents.

We do not say that the shedding of light upon another's property may never under any conditions become a nuisance, but we do say that extreme caution must be employed in applying any such legal theory. The conditions of modern city life impose upon the city dweller and his property many burdens more severe than that of light reflected upon him or it.

In this case, the court directed a verdict for the defendant. We recognize the general rule to be that the existence or nonexistence of a private nuisance is ordinarily a question of fact for the jury, but the rule is subject to exceptions. * * *

* * * We limit our decision to the specific facts of this case and hold as a matter of law that the loss sustained by the plaintiff by the spilled light which has been reflected onto the highly sensitized moving picture screen from the defendant's property 832 feet distant, and which light in intensity is approximately that of a full moon, is *damnum injuria.*

The trial court did not err in directing a verdict. The judgment is affirmed.

Notes

1. *Public vs. private nuisance.* The court in *Amphitheaters* referred to "four easily recognizable classes" of nuisance. Categories (2) ("[c]ases involving illegal or immoral practices") and (3) ("[c]ases involving obstructions to streets * * * and the like") are examples of public nuisance. Public nuisance is a different tort than private nuisance. Generally speaking, it involves an unwarranted interference with public safety, convenience, health, or morals. Usually, only a public entity such as the state can sue for public nuisance. An exception exists when a private individual suffers special harm, not merely the kind of harm suffered generally by the public. Private

nuisance, on the other hand, involves an interference with a private person's interest in quiet use and enjoyment of land.

2. *Private nuisance factors.* Courts have referred to a variety of factors in determining whether a specific interference constitutes a nuisance. One important factor is the propriety of the defendant's activity to the time and place. Church bells ringing for ten minutes at eleven o'clock in the morning are not a nuisance, but they probably are in a residential neighborhood at three o'clock in the morning. Similarly, a court might distinguish between factory smoke in an industrial area and in a residential neighborhood.

It is not conclusive which competing use was first. A plaintiff can sometimes "move to a nuisance" and recover, if the defendant's activity is inappropriate to the area as it has evolved. However, the timing of the competing uses can be significant. (Note that the parties in *Amphitheaters* "were in process of construction at the same time.")

3. Courts often say that the defendant's state of mind is not a crucial element of nuisance. In fact, however, most nuisances are intentional, at least in the sense that the defendant continued the activity, knowing with a substantial certainty that the interference was taking place.

4. When considering the law of nuisance, it is useful to compare its features to those of trespass to land.

BOOMER v. ATLANTIC CEMENT CO.

Court of Appeals of New York, 1970.
26 N.Y.2d 219, 309 N.Y.S.2d 312, 257 N.E.2d 870.

BERGAN, JUDGE.

Defendant operates a large cement plant near Albany. These are actions for injunction and damages by neighboring land owners alleging injury to property from dirt, smoke and vibration emanating from the plant. A nuisance has been found after trial, temporary damages have been allowed; but an injunction has been denied. [The plaintiffs appealed, urging that the injunction should have been granted.]

The public concern with air pollution arising from many sources in industry and in transportation is currently accorded ever wider recognition accompanied by a growing sense of responsibility in State and Federal Governments to control it. Cement plants are obvious sources of air pollution in the neighborhoods where they operate.

But there is now before the court private litigation in which individual property owners have sought specific relief from a single plant operation. The threshold question raised by the division of view on this appeal is whether the court should resolve the litigation between the parties now before it as equitably as seems possible; or whether, seeking promotion of the general public welfare, it should channel private litigation into broad public objectives.

A court performs its essential function when it decides the rights of parties before it. Its decision of private controversies may sometimes greatly affect public issues. Large questions of law are often resolved by the manner in which private litigation is decided. But this is normally an incident to the court's main function to settle controversy. It is a rare exercise of judicial power to use a decision in private litigation as a purposeful mechanism to achieve direct public objectives greatly beyond the rights and interests before the court.

Effective control of air pollution is a problem presently far from solution even with the full public and financial powers of government. In large measure adequate technical procedures are yet to be developed and some that appear possible may be economically impracticable.

It seems apparent that the amelioration of air pollution will depend on technical research in great depth; on a carefully balanced consideration of the economic impact of close regulation; and of the actual effect on public health. It is likely to require massive public expenditure and to demand more than any local community can accomplish and to depend on regional and interstate controls.

A court should not try to do this on its own as a by–product of private litigation and it seems manifest that the judicial establishment is neither equipped in the limited nature of any judgment it can pronounce nor prepared to lay down and implement an effective policy for the elimination of air pollution. This is an area beyond the circumference of one private lawsuit. It is a direct responsibility for government and should not thus be undertaken as an incident to solving a dispute between property owners and a single cement plant—one of many—in the Hudson River Valley.

The cement making operations of defendant have been found by the court of Special Term to have damaged the nearby properties of plaintiffs in these two actions. That court, as it has been noted, accordingly found defendant maintained a nuisance and this has been affirmed at the Appellate Division. The total damage to plaintiffs' properties is, however, relatively small in comparison with the value of defendant's operation and with the consequences of the injunction which plaintiffs seek.

The ground for the denial of injunction, notwithstanding the finding both that there is a nuisance and that plaintiffs have been damaged substantially, is the large disparity in economic consequences of the nuisance and of the injunction. This theory cannot, however, be sustained without overruling a doctrine which has been consistently reaffirmed in several leading cases in this court and which has never been disavowed here, namely that where a nuisance has been found and where there has been any substantial damage shown by the party complaining an injunction will be granted.

* * *

Although the court at Special Term and the Appellate Division held that injunction should be denied, it was found that plaintiffs had been damaged in various specific amounts up to the time of the trial and damages to the respective plaintiffs were awarded for those amounts.

The effect of this was, injunction having been denied, plaintiffs could maintain successive actions at law for damages thereafter as further damage was incurred.

The court at Special Term also found the amount of permanent damage attributable to each plaintiff, for the guidance of the parties in the event both sides stipulated to the payment and acceptance of such permanent damage as a settlement of all the controversies among the parties. The total of permanent damages to all plaintiffs thus found was $185,000. This basis of adjustment has not resulted in any stipulation by the parties.

This result at Special Term and at the Appellate Division is a departure from a rule that has become settled; but to follow the rule literally in these cases would be to close down the plant at once. This court is fully agreed to avoid that immediately drastic remedy; the difference in view is how best to avoid it.*

One alternative is to grant the injunction but postpone its effect to a specified future date to give opportunity for technical advances to permit defendant to eliminate the nuisance; another is to grant the injunction conditioned on the payment of permanent damages to plaintiffs which would compensate them for the total economic loss to their property present and future caused by defendant's operations. For reasons which will be developed the court chooses the latter alternative.

* * *

[T]o grant the injunction unless defendant pays plaintiffs such permanent damages as may be fixed by the court seems to do justice between the contending parties. All of the attributions of economic loss to the properties on which plaintiffs' complaints are based will have been redressed.

The nuisance complained of by these plaintiffs may have other public or private consequences, but these particular parties are the only ones who have sought remedies and the judgment proposed will fully redress them. The limitation of relief granted is a limitation only within the four corners of these actions and does not foreclose public health or other public agencies from seeking proper relief in a proper court.

It seems reasonable to think that the risk of being required to pay permanent damages to injured property owners by cement plant owners would itself be a reasonable effective spur to research for improved techniques to minimize nuisance.

* * *

The judgment, by allowance of permanent damages imposing a servitude on land, which is the basis of the actions, would preclude future recovery by plaintiffs or their grantees.

---

* Respondent's investment in the plant is in excess of $45,000,000. There are over 300 people employed there.

This should be placed beyond debate by a provision of the judgment that the payment by defendant and the acceptance by plaintiffs of permanent damages found by the court shall be in compensation for a servitude on the land.

Although the Trial Term has found permanent damages as a possible basis of settlement of the litigation, on remission the court should be entirely free to re–examine this subject. It may again find the permanent damage already found; or make new findings.

The orders should be reversed, without costs, and the cases remitted to Supreme Court, Albany County to grant an injunction which shall be vacated upon payment by defendant of such amounts of permanent damage to the respective plaintiffs as shall for this purpose be determined by the court.

JASEN, JUDGE, dissenting.

* * *

It has long been the rule in this State, as the majority acknowledges, that a nuisance which results in substantial continuing damage to neighbors must be enjoined. To now change the rule to permit the cement company to continue polluting the air indefinitely upon the payment of permanent damages is, in my opinion, compounding the magnitude of a very serious problem in our State and Nation today.

* * *

I see grave dangers in overruling our long–established rule of granting an injunction where a nuisance results in substantial continuing damage. In permitting the injunction to become inoperative upon the payment of permanent damages, the majority is, in effect, licensing a continuing wrong. It is the same as saying to the cement company, you may continue to do harm to your neighbors so long as you pay a fee for it. Furthermore, once such permanent damages are assessed and paid, the incentive to alleviate the wrong would be eliminated, thereby continuing air pollution of an area without abatement.

It is true that some courts have sanctioned the remedy here proposed by the majority in a number of cases, but none of the authorities relied upon by the majority are analogous to the situation before us. In those cases, the courts, in denying an injunction and awarding money damages, grounded their decision on a showing that the use to which the property was intended to be put was primarily for the public benefit. Here, on the other hand, it is clearly established that the cement company is creating a continuing air pollution nuisance primarily for its own private interest with no public benefit.

This kind of inverse condemnation may not be invoked by a private person or corporation for private gain or advantage. Inverse condemnation should only be permitted when the public is primarily served in the taking or impairment of property. The promotion of the interests of the polluting cement company has, in my opinion, no public use or benefit.

* * *

I would enjoin the defendant cement company from continuing the discharge of dust particles upon its neighbors' properties unless, within 18 months, the cement company abated this nuisance.

It is not my intention to cause the removal of the cement plant from the Albany area, but to recognize the urgency of the problem stemming from this stationary source of air pollution, and to allow the company a specified period of time to develop a means to alleviate this nuisance.

I am aware that the trial court found that the most modern dust control devices available have been installed in defendant's plant, but, I submit, this does not mean that better and more effective dust control devices could not be developed within the time allowed to abate the pollution.

* * *

Notes

1. At the conclusion of the trial, the plaintiffs had achieved an aggregate award of damages to the time of trial of $44,835, an implicit recognition that they could return to court and sue for similar damages in the future, and a determination that their permanent damages came to $185,000. They obviously preferred not to stipulate that payment of the latter sum would forever resolve their controversy with Atlantic Cement. Instead, they appealed, contending that they were entitled to an injunction in addition to the $44,835 damages award. From the plaintiffs' perspective, did appealing turn out to be a good idea?

2. In real property law, "condemnation" (sometimes also called "eminent domain" and occasionally called "expropriation") refers to a governmental entity's or public utility's legally authorized taking of private property for public use on payment of just compensation. The dissenter's term "inverse condemnation" was a way of characterizing the majority's decision as having authorized Atlantic Cement to force the plaintiffs to sell it their clean-air rights.

3. Note that the court had no difficulty concluding that the cement factory constituted a nuisance, notwithstanding its social value. The only difficult issue was whether to issue an injunction.

On the question of whether a nuisance exists, courts often say that the interference must be unreasonable, but "unreasonable" apparently means something different in nuisance than in negligence. *Prosser and Keeton* states that "if it appears to be fairer and more feasible, technologically and economically, to internalize [the harm] as a cost of carrying on the defendant's industrial or business enterprise, the interference will be regarded as unreasonable." Prosser and Keeton on Torts, § 88, p. 627 (5th ed. 1984). Similarly, § 826 of the Restatement (Second) of Torts states:

An intentional invasion of another's interest in the use and enjoyment of land is unreasonable if

(a) the gravity of the harm outweighs the utility of the actor's conduct, or

(b) the harm caused by the conduct is serious and the financial burden of compensating for this and similar harm to others would not make the continuation of the conduct not feasible.

Comment f to section 826 states that "[i]t may sometimes be reasonable to operate an important activity if payment is made for the harm it is causing, but unreasonable to continue it without paying."

4. Historically, English courts of law could not grant injunctions; by and large they could only award money damages. The chancellor, who was an officer of the king, could grant various forms of "equitable" relief, including injunctions, if the "legal" remedy was inadequate. Over time, formal courts of equity were established with a complex set of substantive and procedural rules of their own. A party seeking relief from a court of equity was required to show more than the violation of a legal right. He was also required to show, among other things, that he would suffer irreparable harm that could not be remedied by money damages and that equitable relief would not disserve the public interest.

During the last hundred years, American jurisdictions have "merged" courts of law and courts of equity. Today in most states, only one courthouse exists with one set of judges. Nevertheless, a plaintiff must still make a special showing to obtain equitable relief.

5. Refusing an injunction for "equitable" reasons is not unique to the law of nuisance. In Crescent Mining Co. v. Silver King Mining Co., 17 Utah 444, 54 P. 244 (1898), the defendant laid a pipe across plaintiff's "barren, valueless land." Even though the defendant's conduct was clearly a trespass to land, the court refused to enjoin it. The court balanced the harm to the plaintiff, which was minimal, with the harm an injunction would cause the defendant, which was great.

*

Index

References are to Pages

601

608 INDEX

References are to Pages

INTENT—Cont'd
Willful and Wanton Conduct, this index

INTENTIONAL INFLICTION OF EMOTION-AL DISTRESS
Generally, 28 et seq.
Direct and parasitic claims, 235
Divorce torts, 427
Intent to inflict, 32, 36
Prima facie case, 31, 34
Recklessness, 37
Severity of injury, 37

INTENTIONAL TORTS
Generally, 8 et seq.
See also Intent, this index
Actual damages as element of case, 325
Assumption of risk, 407
Cause in fact, 163
Children's actions, 16, 17
Comparative responsibility, 461
Consent as defense
Generally, 49
Medical treatment, 519
Contributory and comparative negligence, 384, 392
Defenses, 49 et seq.
Duty to protect against, see Duty, this index
Elements of tort, 8
Express assumption of risk, 432
Felony merger rule, 350
Immunities, this index
Legal cause standard of liability, 183
Mental and emotional harm, 235
Necessity, 68
Negligence distinguished, 74
Prima facie case, 8
Releases, 432
Self-defense, 58
Strict Liability, this index
Vicarious liability, 318

INTERFERENCE
Economic loss without physical injury, 253

INTOXICATION
Consent, 58
Standard of care, 88

INVASION OF PRIVACY
Generally, 48

JOINT AND SEVERAL LIABILITY
Generally, 439 et seq.
See also Apportionment of Damages; Comparative Responsibility, this index
Definition, 133
One satisfaction rule, 156

JUDGMENTS
JAML, 4
JNOV, 6

JURY INSTRUCTIONS
Generally, 6
Joint and several liability rules, 439
Personal injury damages, 327
Special verdicts, 439
Special verdicts and comparative negligence, 383

JURY QUESTIONS
See Law and Fact Questions, this index

JURY SELECTION
Generally, 3

LAW AND FACT QUESTIONS
Duty vs. legal cause analyses, significance of, 170, 200, 302
Legal cause, 169
Prima facie case, 76

LEARNED HAND FORMULA
Generally, 81, 170

LEGAL CAUSE
Generally, 169 et seq.
See also Cause in Fact; Foreseeability, this index
Ad hoc no-duty rules
Generally, 214
See also Duty, this index
Apportionment of damages, see Comparative Responsibility, this index
Cause in fact distinguished
Generally, 117, 119, 170
Intentional torts, 183
Comparative fault and, 213
Criminal acts, intervening
Generally, 208, 214
See also Duty, this index
Directness test, 174
Duty questions, distinguishing, 170, 199, 214, 302
Economic Loss Rule, this index
Eggshell skull victim, 179
Extent rule, 179
Foreseeable risks analysis, 171, 175
Harmless negligence, 186
Improbable consequences, 192
Intentional acts, intervening, 214
Intentional torts, 183
Intervening acts
Generally, 191
Intentional, 214
Law and fact questions, 169
Mechanism rule, 180
Natural and probable rule, 205
Negligence per se liability compared, 171
Prima facie elements of negligence generally, 76
Products liability, 564
Proximate cause, 117, 119, 169
Reckless behavior, 183
Rescuers' claims against original tortfeasors, 182
Suicide of injured person, 182, 192

WRITS
Common law forms of action, 44, 74

WRONGFUL DEATH ACTIONS
Generally, 350 et seq.
Co-habitants, 352
Damages, 353
Felony-merger rule, 350
History, 350

WRONGFUL DEATH ACTIONS—Cont'd
Pain and suffering, 358
Statutory basis, 351, 354
Survival actions distinguished, 357

ZONE OF DANGER RULE
See Negligent Infliction of Emotional Distress, this index

†

0–314–14615–6

90000

9 780314 146151